The Long Argument

The Long Argument
English Puritanism and the Shaping of New England Culture, 1570–1700

STEPHEN FOSTER

Published for the Institute of
Early American History and Culture,
Williamsburg, Virginia,
by The University of North Carolina Press
Chapel Hill and London

The Institute of Early American History and Culture is sponsored jointly by The College of William and Mary and the Colonial Williamsburg Foundation.

Library of Congress Cataloging-in-Publication Data

Foster, Stephen, 1942–
    The long argument : English Puritanism and the shaping of New England culture, 1570–1700 / by Stephen Foster.
        p.   cm.
    Includes bibliographical references and index.
    ISBN 0-8078-1951-4 (cloth : alk. paper)
    1. Puritans—New England.
    2. Puritans—England.   3. New England—Civilization—17th century.
    I. Institute of Early American History and Culture (Williamsburg, Va.)   II. Title.
    F7.F758   1991
    974'.02—dc20   90-41564
                CIP

Portions of Chapters 1, 2, and 3 appeared in somewhat different form in David D. Hall and David Grayson Allen, eds., *Seventeenth-Century New England,* © 1984 by the Colonial Society of Massachusetts, *Publications* 63. Used with permission.

A portion of Chapter 4 appeared in somewhat different form in David D. Hall et al., eds., *Saints and Revolutionaries: Essays on Early American History,* © 1984 by W. W. Norton & Co. Used with permission.

Manufactured in the United States of America

95 94 93 92 91   5 4 3 2 1

For EDMUND S. MORGAN

Contents

Preface   ix

Acknowledgments   xvi

A Note on Dating, Transcription, Citation, and Bibliography   xviii

Introduction: The Puritan Movement   1

1. The Elizabethan Contribution: The Celebration
of Order, 1570–1610   33

2. Continuity and Ambiguity: "The Gospel
Doing," 1590–1630   65

3. From Engagement to Flight: The Failure of
Politics, 1610–1630   108

4. From Exodus to Revelation: The Move toward Sectarianism
in England and America, 1630–1650   138

5. Reconstruction and Conflict: The Halfway Covenant
and Declension Controversies, 1650–1680   175

6. Israel's Fate: The Definition of Establishment in
Puritan America, 1681–1700   231

Envoi: The Long Argument and Its Ending   286

Appendix: Editions and Pressruns
before the Civil War   315

Notes   319

Index   377

Preface

An unwelcomed but necessary invitation to address the Newberry Library fellows seminar on "your work" finally forced me to think coherently about what I was doing and, especially, about how it related to the considerable body of historiography to which I was adding still another title. Up until that seminar I had managed to stifle the inevitable inquiry with the simple reply, "Puritans." Occasionally a particularly stubborn interrogator would get past the first hurdle to ask *which* Puritans, English or American, generally to be stopped by the equally laconic "both." The Newberry obliged me (as part of the terms of my keep) to fill in an hour on who I was and how I fit in and so at last to be compelled to realize the obvious: that I had worked my way back over a very long period of time to the tradition in which I was trained more than twenty years earlier.

The distinctive feature of the study that follows is its transatlantic approach. Of and in itself, this statement is only marginally more informative than my one-word evasions. In a sense, all American colonial history ought by definition to be transatlantic, but some historians working in the period have always managed to get around this apparently unwaivable requirement, and so transatlantic historiography most frequently implies either comparative studies of some specific aspect of seventeenth- and eighteenth-century life common to both sides of the Atlantic or, alternatively, elaborations of the ways in which the New World remained linked to and, to a degree, under the hegemony of the Old. Comparative studies were once mainly institutional and political (how the legislatures of England and the colonies did or did not resemble each other in their respective workings, for example); now, they are mainly social and cultural (what percentage of each population was dependent poor, how English was American law, and so on). Connective studies have followed a similar but less complete evolution because interest in such obvious points of contact as the mechanisms of royal government has remained strong and has even intensified, but these first lines of inquiry have been supplemented more recently by accounts of the enormous intellectual debts colonial Americans owed to their British correspondents and mentors and by studies of the most direct and powerful of connections, commerce, finance, and immigration.

Generally, comparativists discover America diverging from "Europe" and especially England so that there is something natural and appropriate about the Revolution when it comes to pass. Connectivists mostly take the opposite tack, finding so much still working, or indeed, in the course of strengthening, in the ligaments of the "Atlantic world" that, as a very recent study puts it, "American Separatism was not an unfolding of the inevitable but a revolutionary achievement." Sometimes, however, the thrust of the arguments can be interchanged. Comparative studies, for example, will discover that the vaunted lack of a dependent wage-earning class in America before the nineteenth century is illusory and that English and American social structures do not appear so very different when viewed in gross over a sufficient time span. Or students of transatlantic intellectual networks will puzzle out lines of communication and migration that selectively, almost perversely, channeled variant and dissident British enthusiasm into the colonies, where they became orthodoxy and endowed Americans with an unearned sense of grievance. In every case, however, the looked-for conclusion is the American Revolution and the attainment of an American identity, whether reprocessed European or New World indigenous.

There has always been something a little suspect, or at least underscrutinized, in this preoccupation with Americanness, but at this late date little point remains in faulting the origins of an inquiry that has yielded such respectable dividends in the historical literature of early America. Still, there is value in contrasting these two forms of transatlantic history with a third, quite as well worked but fundamentally different in the way its own central question has been posed. Both of the approaches sketched out so far ponder the relationship between the Old World and the New in the period between early exploration and the coming of the Revolution. This present study, by contrast, is the latest manifestation of a project to annex the relevant period of American history whole to the long flow of English history before the Atlantic migration and by doing so to turn that event into merely an important incident set somewhere in the middle of an extended story. However feebly they may be deployed here, the concerns and insights that inform this work belong to a distinguished tradition in American historiography primarily associated in recent decades with Yale University but dating back a good fifty years and more to the Harvard American Civilization program and especially to the work of the late Perry Miller.

A quarter-century after his death and almost four decades after the publication of the last volume in his New England Mind trilogy, Miller is in danger of becoming a historical artifact in his own right. His scholarship is beginning to be reduced to evidence about the past (*his* past, that is, the milieu of American intellectuals from the interwar years to the Cold War decades), and his sins are already often generally forgiven as the faults of someone who practiced the historian's craft so long ago that to judge him by contemporary standards amounts to anachronistic "Whiggery." But any attempt to rehabilitate Miller as an active participant (and as a valid target) in the ongoing scholarly conversation must confront the awkward fact that there are many Millers capable of being assembled, depending on which sections of his corpus are placed in conjunction with one another. (The same complaint can be made to a degree against any major intellectual figure who writes at length over a long period, but Miller must have been inordinately fond of a Whitman-like largeness that cheerfully contains unreconciled multitudes.) Invoking Perry Miller's name, therefore, does not carry the discussion much further until one specifies the convention of Millerites being declared for.

Among the multiple time schemes at work in the New England Mind series, the most popular has been the one in which *Orthodoxy in Massachusetts* is mostly ignored and *From Colony to Province* is, according to Miller's own directions, "imagined as taking place, so to speak, inside *The Seventeenth Century*." The architectonic structure of Puritanism in *The Seventeenth Century*, revealed there as a perilous synthesis of contradictory impulses, comes apart slowly and almost invisibly over the considerable length of *From Colony to Province*, until "a hundred years after the landings," New Englanders "were forced to look upon themselves with amazement, hardly capable of understanding how they came to be what they were." This particular narrative line does have the advantage of tragic dignity, and in the telling Miller is little short of stunning in his analysis of the complex response of intellectual discourse to the reality it seeks to delineate, disguise, or domesticate. For all that, the periodization of American history laid out, although formulated with exemplary sophistication, is at bottom that Turnerian transition from European to American, or in Miller's own words, the story "of the accommodation to the American landscape of an imported and highly articulated system of ideas." Putting more emphasis on a psychic conflict in which internal tensions count for as much as external pressures adds a dramatic element, but the ultimate shock of recognition is so appealing because the organizing motif is discovered to be safely familiar after all.

Miller himself, however, comes up with another way to read the New England Mind series, potentially more fruitful because less predictable in its outcome, when he complains of having written his trilogy "in the wrong order." *The Seventeenth Century* should be read first, followed by the two chronologically arranged books so that "*Orthodoxy in Massachusetts* constitutes the first chapters of a tale which *The New England Mind: From Colony to Province* resumes." But that tale is not, as Miller elsewhere would have it, an account of a process "which began the moment the ships dropped anchor in Boston harbor." *Orthodoxy in Massachusetts* begins with the Elizabethan Reformation, and the ships in question do not get around to so much as weighing anchor until halfway through the book. American history begins before America, and the process that most interested Miller was already in full swing at the time of settlement. Admit as much, and the later chapters of Puritan history in America can cease to be either the traditional declension or Miller's version of "adaptation" (meaning a dilution of the force of the original synthesis and a progressive incoherence until the Great Awakening blows away the shell that the once mighty structure has become). Change in New England can be seen as a continuation of Puritanism—further shifts in the viable contradictions that Miller took so much delight in when writing *The Seventeenth Century*. More broadly, here is an entire past world opened up in which England and America are no longer treated as separate entities, whether contrasted or interconnected, but are placed together on a continuum, English past continuing to unfold in an American present along lines laid down before colonization but necessarily subject to the accidents of history in the New World.

The clearest and most compelling demonstrations of the potential inherent in the New England Mind's approach have generally come in relatively short works, directly or indirectly descended from the trilogy, that concentrate on some single central set of ideas coupling England and its colonies. Of these works, in turn, the greatest influence on the present study is Edmund S. Morgan's *Visible Saints* and its case for an American invention of one of the most distinctive aspects of New England Congregationalism, the requirement of a conversion narrative as a prerequisite for church membership. I suppose at first I took the argument in as a sort of ingenious refinement of the progression implied in the familiar yoking of *From Colony to Province* with *The Seventeenth Century*: the American realization of English aspirations had to be perforce a new and original creation because Puritan polity had existed only in the imagination until its realization after the Great Migration gave it complexity and variegation. That conception echoes up and down my opening engagement with the Puritans, a study of their social thought. Twenty years later I know better—or, anyway, I know differently.

My sense of the tradition in which I work has been altered by something quite outside it, the development of the historical literature about the English Puritans and my own brief experience of participating in it (in a couple of spearbearer roles). When *Orthodoxy in Massachusetts* was published in 1933 there had been no major contribution to the history of Puritanism in England since S. R. Gardiner, Roland G. Usher, and Champlin Burrage. (Even M. M. Knappen's *Tudor Puritanism* appeared six years later, the same year as *The Seventeenth Century*; William Haller's *The Rise of Puritanism* antedates both works by less than a year and can hardly have influenced either.) Since that time there have been a score or more of significant titles, of which the most influential have been first Haller's two titles, then the massive corpus of Christopher Hill, and finally the four book-length studies, along with a raft of articles, by Patrick Collinson.

Two notions fundamental to this study are directly indebted to Collinson, especially as I came to understand his work in writing my own little account of the Puritan "underground" of the Caroline period. The first is the sense of Puritanism as a "movement"—a congruence (more than an alliance) of progressive Protestants, lay and clerical, gentle and ordinary, thrown up by the fortuitous circumstance that England's official Reformation took root unevenly. The second follows directly from the first: a commitment to establishment was native to English Puritanism and in a paradoxical but perfectly intelligible way was responsible for the movement's equally strong sectarian impulse. In the extended moment of the inception of the English Reformation, at dead lift, those who made the most willing response to the new orthodoxy often got well out in front of both its official sponsors and the larger part of a population initially hostile to religious change.

This understanding of the English Puritan movement endows the New Englanders, even in 1630, with a vital, evolving culture, one based on long practice and developed institutions, such as the conventicle and the combination lectureship, no less than on hitherto untested ecclesiastical theories. Accordingly, further change in America in the later seventeenth century merely continues a long story, and the claims for "declension" can be exposed for what they were, partisan documents in an internal controversy as old as the Puritan movement. *Visible Saints* now gets a different reading, while the most compelling trajectory for the New England Mind series becomes the one that runs from *Orthodoxy in Massachusetts* to *From Colony to Province*.

I am hardly the first person to have the epiphany in question. A great deal of what is written about colonial noetic culture (political and legal no less than religious) now works on the premise that a lengthy and dynamic European past undergirds the history of the same subject in America, which is also seen as "constantly diverted or stimulated by the influx of ideas from Europe" (Miller's words). My own essay is a little different mainly in attempting a more self-conscious and sustained juxtaposition of the respective concerns of English and American historiography on the matter of Puritans. Collinson's duality between the necessarily interlocked sectarian and establishmentarian drives in the English Puritan movement undoubtedly derives from British scholarship alone, but it looks as if it were conceived of especially to fit in with the anxious intellectual structure described in *The Seventeenth Century* or with the narrow path between mutually fructifying extremes that John Winthrop must walk in *The Puritan Dilemma*. Taken together, the two distinct sets of scholarship can be arranged to their mutual benefit.

This *mutuality*, I think, needs a little extra emphasis. As colonial history is made to center on the Revolution and its role in American identity, so the Civil War and the issue of its fundamentality in creating a "modern" England still preoccupy English historiography, and if anything, the origins and nature of the English crisis is the more controverted question at the moment. The advent of revisionism, the case that the causes of the Civil War were mostly adventitious and to be located in purely political and religious tensions generated mainly in the era of the Personal Rule of Charles I, has set off something that looks like the scholarly equivalent of house-to-house fighting. Puritanism figures prominently as a prize position in the disputed territory because the dating and extent of Puritan disaffection are powerful explanatory devices for all sides. Revisionists are quite as willing as many of their adversaries (and more willing than some) to let Puritans start the Civil War, provided they can confine their period of prior alienation to the 1630s and define Puritan grievances as a particularly angry formulation of the complaint of the Protestant governing classes generally. For this reason (and because the revisionist case has real substantive validity if not overstated for polemical purposes), English Puritanism, in British historiography, has lost its capital "P," and with the uppercase letter much of its distinctive agenda, except for brief periods of militance before 1603 and after 1633.

Here there is a certain use for an Americanist willing to poach at intervals in an English preserve. Critics of revisionism often argue that the apparently confused constitutional conflict of the 1620–42 period will become more purposive if the subject is viewed in a longer perspective. The same may be said for a similarly extensive view of religious tensions in which the Great Migration of the 1630s, rather than the Civil War, serves as the climactic episode. The strength of the revisionist case against a stolidly deterministic irrepressible conflict between Puritans and the Church of England can be acknowledged in full, and yet in the long view the distinctiveness of the Puritan movement will still stand out and its potential for friction with authority can be reasserted. Admittedly, there were more Puritans in England than ever thought of coming to America, but the American Puritans were a substantial portion of the English movement (certainly a much larger fraction than they were of the English nation), and their undertakings after arrival in the colonies can be shown to be genuine variations on the same agenda agitating the English movement at the same time. The history of the Puritans who emigrated may not tell everything about England on the eve of the Civil War, but at least it is a well-defined and trackable segment of what has otherwise become an historiographic tangle of exemplary proportions.

A tale that claims to have two morals and to speak to two distinct scholarly literatures, American and English, constitutes a double burden of presumption for the author to bear as he prepares to turn his work over to his readers for their disposal. Every author becomes shy at the point at which he finally takes in the whole of what he has done, of what he is asking of those whom he addresses. Such sudden delicacy must seem conventional, the ordinary stuff of prefaces, but it is more than that at this moment—probably it *always* is more than that for every author when the same moment is reached. Confidence for the final commitment can be found only in remembering my teachers and the formidable achievement in general of the fields of historiography in which I have pursued my own work for what has become a longish time. There follows all that I can do, however little that may be, to make some return for what has been given me.

SF

The Newberry Library, Chicago
Summer 1989

Acknowledgments

Most of this book was written during two periods of leave from Northern Illinois University, in 1979–80 and again in 1986–87. In both cases I had the good fortune to enjoy a sabbatical salary from Northern, supplemented in the first instance by a fellowship for independent research from the National Endowment for the Humanities and in the second by a Newberry Library/NEH fellowship. James Norris, the dean of the College of Liberal Arts and Sciences at Northern, and Otto Olsen, chair of the history department, also arranged for additional funding in 1986–87, making possible a full year's leave. Thanks should also be extended here to the John Solomon Guggenheim Memorial Foundation, which was acknowledged in the book I wrote as a result of my spell as a Guggenheim fellow but may yet be interested in seeing at last the book I said I was going to write. If it is any consolation, that earlier effort was a source for the present one.

Once I put together something that looked a little like a finished typescript, copies were read by Timothy H. Breen, Richard L. Greaves, Philip Gura, David D. Hall, Michael McGiffert, and Edmund S. Morgan. My thanks to all six for their time and comments, as well as to W. Brown Patterson for going over a strange agglomeration subsequently to evolve into chapters 3 and 4, and to Edward M. Cook, Jr., for the amount of his time I took up reciting my current enthusiasms in the course of lunch, coffee, and walking down stairwells and for his helpful replies to my outpourings.

A number of libraries and archival depositories were important in the research for this study, and I am grateful to the staffs of all of these various institutions for their assistance. The composition of the book and the final stages of research, however, took place entirely in the Newberry Library and, given my habits, could not have been accomplished anywhere else. There is no more indulgent or helpful group of people than the staff of the Newberry. Most of them can be acknowledged only in general, but particular mention must be made of John Aubrey, Richard H. Brown, Paul F. Gehl, Karen Klutho, John Long, and Karen Skubish.

Help also came in the form of advice, encouragement, and practical knowledge provided at increasingly regular intervals by successive editors of publications at the Institute of Early American History and Culture: Norman

Fiering, Philip Morgan, A. Roger Ekirch, Tom Purvis, and Fredrika Teute, as well as by the managing editor, Gilbert B. Kelly. At the University of North Carolina Press the manuscript was taken in hand and shepherded along by Lewis Bateman and Sandy Eisdorfer, while the copyediting that (among other things) endowed capitalization, hyphenation, and the names of various personages with a degree of consistency can be credited to Trudie Calvert. At Northern the first drafts of the book were typed by Elaine Kittleson and the final version put on hard disk by Cheryl Fuller, who has the distinction of being the only person in the Midwest able to distinguish between my own eccentric orthography and that of my sources.

Finally, Arthur Weinberg, who was my lunchtime companion at the Newberry on irregular but not infrequent occasions for over twenty years, died early in 1989. By a fortunate combination of circumstances we were thrown together almost daily during the final stages of composition of this work. Arthur's own field (early twentieth-century America) was centuries later than my own and his particular interests light years away, but he patiently endured the chatter of a younger man absorbed in esoteric pursuits, when asked lent me the use of his typewriter (even more of a dinosaur than my own), and now and again got in the odd word about *his* work. Such services never get acknowledged until they cease to be rendered. Anyway, thank you, Arthur, very much.

A Note on Dating, Transcription, Citation, and Bibliography

All the events described in this book occurred while England and its colonies retained the Julian calendar. For the sake of convenience all dates are given Old Style, just as contemporaries recorded them. (That is, no attempt had been made to add days to synchronize Julian dates with the Gregorian calendar.) The new year, however, is counted as beginning on 1 January, not 25 March, and I have not double dated for the two months and twenty-five days between these two dates.

Transcription is a more difficult problem. Sixteenth-, seventeenth-, and to a degree eighteenth-century people lacked generally fixed conventions for spelling, capitalization, and punctuation, although, as everyone who has ever worked with primary sources from this period has reason to be grateful for, printed materials are always much more standardized in all three areas than sources that originally existed only in manuscript form. Accordingly, because they rarely present much difficulty apart from the capricious use of typographic forms of emphasis, material actually printed in the period under study is reproduced exactly as it appeared in the original except that catchwords have been dropped, the odd instances where "i" has been exchanged for "j" or "u" for "v" have been normalized, and obvious typographical errors have been silently corrected, although where there is any possible controversy over the meaning, the correction has been noted in the appropriate citation. Manuscript materials have been transcribed by a version of the expanded method popularized by Samuel Eliot Morison and associated with the grand tradition of American historical editing begun by Julian Boyd and Lyman Butterfield. A decade ago such a declaration would have needed no amplification or apology, but now it is necessary to explain this choice.

Since 1978 the expanded method has been under attack for taking too many liberties with the text, and as technological change has made much more literal forms of transcription both practical and affordable, documentary editors working on American materials have increasingly employed them. Ironically, in recent years most of the sources for English history (and most of the editions of canonical British authors) for this period have appeared in completely normalized texts. The transcription controversy has begun to resemble the parallel one in music over the use of authentic instruments, but it is no more necessary for me to take sides on the one as the other, since what is at issue here is the best method of rendering quotations in a secondary source. The quoted material is merely meant to substantiate the argument, not to serve as a primary text for someone else's historiography, and for this purpose the expanded method is in my opinion still the preferred form of transcription: it provides the minimum amount of editorial intervention necessary to secure facility of interpretation, thereby easing the reader's task while limiting the risk of inadvertent alteration of the evidence.

My own version of the expanded method differs in a very few particulars from the classic formulation, to be found in the section by Morison in Frank Friedel, ed., *Harvard Guide to American History*, rev. ed. (Cambridge, Mass., 1974), 1:30–31. All original punctuation, capitalization, and spelling have been retained, but superscripts have been lowered, all abbreviations now conventionally spelled out are expanded, ampersands have been transcribed as "and," and the "y" that came to stand in for the Old English thorn has been rendered as "th." In any instance in which the expansion could be disputed brackets have been put around the letters that have been supplied.

Both practices of transcription conform pretty well to the dictum "Consistency first, last, and always." The rub comes in dealing with material originally in manuscript but quoted from a printed edition. Quotations derived from editions in which the editor employs a more literal method of transcription than my own (for example, *Records of the Governor and Company of the Massachusetts Bay in New England*) have been modernized just enough to conform to it; quotations from editions that use more normalized forms than the expanded method warrants (for example, *Commons Debates, 1628*) have been rendered exactly as they are printed. This solution introduces the kinds of inconsistencies interdicted by Morison, but I can see no alternative in dealing with the variety of editorial practice encompassed in editions produced between 1798 and 1988.

In an effort to keep down the number and length of the notes, secondary sources have been cited only for the same purpose as primary—to substantiate assertions made in the text. There are no notes intended primarily to demonstrate familiarity with the literature, to provide extended bibliographic references, or to intervene in some current historiographic debate. When my disagreement with other authors is of a reasonably specific nature and confined to matters of fact, however, I have explained the crux in the apposite note out of respect for those authors and my readers alike. Equally, I have cited very recent secondary titles a little more fully than older ones to indicate where in the ongoing scholarly discussion I happened to be when I put pencil to paper.

Readers who are interested in more detail about the scholarly literature of English and American Puritanism in the last three decades will find comprehensive treatments in Michael McGiffert, "American Puritan Studies in the 1960s," *William and Mary Quarterly*, 3d ser., 27 (1970): 36–67; Patrick Collinson, *English Puritanism*, Historical Association General Series, 106 (London, 1983); Richard L. Greaves, "The Puritan-Nonconformist Tradition in England, 1560–1700: Historiographical Reflections," *Albion* 17 (1984–85): 449–86; David D. Hall, "On Common Ground: The Coherence of American Puritan Studies," *William and Mary Quarterly*, 3d ser., 44 (1987): 193–229. There is also a very complete listing (with spirited commentary) of the postwar historiography of Great Britain in the Stuart period, J. S. Morrill, *Seventeenth-Century Britain, 1603–1714* (Hamden, Conn., 1980), and a review of still more recent material can be found in Derek Hirst, *Authority and Conflict: England, 1603–1658* (London, 1985), 364–72. Alas, the relevant period of American history has nothing comparable to Morrill and Hirst. The first two volumes in the Goldentree series are good but out-of-date: Alden Vaughan, comp., *The American Colonies in the Seventeenth Century* (New York, 1971); Jack P. Greene, comp., *The American Colonies in the Eighteenth Century, 1689–1763* (New York, 1969). An updated edition of each bibliography would be welcome, but in the meantime a good sampling of the more recent secondary literature can be found in the extensive annotation to Jack P. Greene and J. R. Pole, eds., *Colonial British America: Essays in the New History of the Early Modern Era* (Baltimore, 1984), and in Jack P. Greene, *Pursuits of Happiness: The Social Development of Early Modern British Colonies and the Formation of American Culture* (Chapel Hill, 1988). The most recent bibliography, David L. Ammerman and Philip D. Morgan, comps., *Books about Early America: 2001 Titles* (Williamsburg, Va., 1989), is more selective than either of the Goldentree titles and does not deal with journal articles at all but is comprehensive in coverage and could hardly be more current.

Introduction
The Puritan Movement

In earlier eras time itself was a shorter, more bounded commodity. The "Apostle" of Elizabethan Norwich, John More, undertook *A Table from the Beginning of the World to This Day* and promised his readers to include "what yeere of the World every thing was done, both in the Scriptures mentioned, and also in prophane matters." That job accomplished in just under 230 pages, he finished off the work with a brief appendix on the fall of the Roman Empire. More's chronology (slightly garbled) was probably the one employed some seventy years after its publication by a local notable in colonial Connecticut to place an obscure life spent in an insignificant town within a cosmic but very exact scheme. Sixteen Sixty-Three, Thomas Minor told his diary on the New Year's Day, was "from the Creation the yeare .5612." A further two hundred years had to pass before, sometime well into the nineteenth century, the earth became very old and the precisely delineated and divided narrative of human history spread out into a prolonged incident of undefined and undefinable boundaries. The fall of Genesis took with it the authority of every other temporal landmark, be it 323 B.C. or A.D. 1066, that had commemorated some decisive transition. In back of every date could now be found another date no less valid as a point of entry to the continuing story so that an eminent Victorian's much-quoted injunction to begin at the beginning was appropriately assigned by him to an arbitrary monarch reigning in a place called Wonderland.

The presentation of American history has had its wondrous aspects, not the least of them the claims to an exemption from the curse of indefinite origin. This happy fiction, however, is maintained by the use of word play so transparent it would scarcely have amused Alice. The population native to the North American continents for millennia prior to the settlement of Old World peoples ends up a portion of the colonial environment, reduced to the status of an especially important item in the introductory survey of climate, soils, and indigenous flora and fauna. The Spanish settlements, though as old as or older than their English counterparts, are classified as "borderlands," peripheral by definition. And the Old World culture of the migrants is described in probate metaphors as an "inheritance" or "legacy"—significant but isolable and discrete items, readily inventoriable and quite external to the lives of the main characters in the unfolding drama. In the end, the initial chapters that open many efforts in early American history look like nothing so much as the expository amnesia of the first scene dialogue that is a frequent feature of the drama written in the period so cavalierly disposed of.

These desperate shifts collapse entirely when the English settlement of New England is the subject of the inquiry. Allowing for the inherent awkwardness of all beginnings, an era of American history of sorts is inaugurated by the publication of *An Admonition to the Parliament* in 1572 quite as definitively as by the signing of the Mayflower Compact or the Declaration of Independence. John Field and Thomas Wilcox, the admonitionists, rightfully earned the title of Founding Fathers by enunciating a full-dress, unqualified statement of the Puritan conviction that the accession of Elizabeth and the official return of the nation to the Protestant religion had turned out to be promises without fulfillment: "We in England are so fare of[f], from having a church rightly reformed, accordyng to the prescript of Gods worde, that as yet we are not come to the outwarde face of the same."[1] The document itself is implicitly and explicitly radical, in what it says, in the timing of its issue, and in the implications of the reforms it demands. Field and Wilcox produced a detailed and comprehensive indictment of the Church of England, ranging over everything from liturgy to the quality of the clergy to the inadequacy of discipline, and they carried on with such vehemence at (what to their critics) was the most ill-chosen of moments that they scared off most of the older leadership of English Protestantism: coming when the new religious settlement was still thin on the ground and Catholic missionaries trained abroad were just returning to England to launch their counterattack, the *Admonition* seemed premature, imprudent, and downright impractical to almost any committed Protestant reformer who did not accept the whole of the Puritan case.[2]

What distinguishes the Puritan movement from English Protestantism as a whole, in those rare moments before the Civil War when it did stand apart in a distinctive position, is this very conviction that there *is* a case to be accepted in its totality. The religious establishment that was the object of the admonitionists' attention did not exist simply to save souls; the Church of

England was charged no less with providing the nation with moral direction and with serving as the custodian of its high culture, and it had the further duty of bearing the standard around which the international forces of Protestantism were supposed to rally. There was no question of ranking these four functions in any order of priority: anyone who thought they could be so much as conceived of separately was no Puritan. The promulgation of the *Admonition* under the circumstances was a very deliberate and broad-ranging challenge. In the subsequent controversy a self-conscious opposition movement coalesced around a set of demands that would inevitably have required fundamental changes in English society if they had ever been satisfied and that put a severe strain on English politics in every period in which they were pressed.

Some six decades separate the first assertion of militant Puritanism from the departure of the Winthrop fleet for America in 1630, but in broad outline the goals of the New England Way were still the agenda articulated by the Elizabethan radicals, and the reason for creating a New England at all was yet another setback in the continuing campaign to reshape English life on English soil. Puritanism would subsequently be further defined and transformed in New England over the course of the seventeenth century in a lineal continuation of the fluctuations that had repeatedly restructured the English movement from its Elizabethan genesis onward. And in a magnificent irony, the sole remaining bearers after 1660 of ideals deriving from the very special circumstances of England's Reformation would be those Puritans left in America. It is almost as if the subplot of some intriguingly complicated Renaissance or Restoration drama were suddenly, roughly at act three, to take on the sole burden of bringing the action to a conclusion, or, better still, as if the characters in a particularly tricky modern vehicle, their natures and destinies partly unfolded in the first part of one play, should suddenly have to finish their performance in another. A second Victorian comic genius, appropriately a dramatist, saw the joke exactly when he had his Lord Illingworth remark that claims for the youth of America were the country's oldest tradition—"It has been going on now for three hundred years."

In the century or so allotted them before their own demise, New England Congregationalists did finally fulfill the imperatives first laid down by their Elizabethan forebears. Out of the peculiar civilization so created in New England would come, in time, when the formation of the United States opened up an arena for their talents, corps of clergymen, bureaucrats, technicians, educators, and literary personages, major and minor, who provided the disparate regions of nineteenth-century America with a large share of their limited stock of national institutions. Yet the enduring reach of the Puritan movement is more easily asserted in general than specified in any detail. Americans like their new order of the ages to begin, reasonably enough, at the water's edge, and if not then, as soon thereafter as possible. The English have their reasons for thinking that their history goes nowhere in particular and, therefore, for rejecting the possibility of historical movements that are either purposive or long term. Caught between these curiously complementary national moods, recent historiography has come up with a plethora of terminus ad quems for an anomalous phenomenon that obstinately links age to age and continent to continent in a common cause. Puritanism is said to have ceased to be a meaningful ecclesiastical option after the Hampton Court Conference of 1604, to have collapsed as a political force in the divided parliaments of the 1620s, to have lost its spiritual power to the seductive lure of commercialism in the urbanized centers of New England by 1660, to have vanished as a force for community in all but the most isolated country towns by the early 1700s, and to have come to a grand smashup in the Old Light–New Light schisms of the 1740s. None of these claims for Puritan morbidity is without significance, but taken together the multiple demises do suggest that in a number of instances a simple shift in direction has been transformed into the final climacteric. This confusion derives in turn from the elusive character of the Puritan movement itself, which altered its tactics and emphases as its fortunes varied over time and which was never homogeneous at any single period in its eventful history. Without some longer view that fuses the American and English histories of the Puritans and thereby locates enduring commitments and points of accord in decade after decade of reverses, internal divisions, and lamentations of decline, the inevitable temptation has been to single out as definitive some one characteristic or another of a much broader movement and to tie the fate of a protean phenomenon to purely temporary arrangements.

Puritans may seem pretty definite characters in their writings, armed with five distinctions and another four disjunctions. But the precision of the treatises was usually aimed at developing some applied point within the shared Reformation theology of European Protestantism. They were never very good at spelling out what they were in toto. When they were foolish enough to try, they either botched the job and split their ranks or they made a great show out of solemnly dodging the divisive issues. The Elizabethan militants spent several years over their Book of Discipline in the 1580s only to produce a thin and inconsistent pamphlet still unacceptable to much of the membership of their organizations. The next attempt at a common statement, the work of the Westminster Assembly during the 1640s, brought to a head the growing division in the ranks of the godly party and indirectly led to a rival statement of polity, the Independents' Savoy Platform; even the more enduring Westminster Confession, the classic theological statement of English-speaking Calvinism, appeared at just the moment when the predestinarian consensus in England was finally dissolving. In America the Cambridge Platform of 1648 had a happier history but only because its authors did little more than frame existing ambiguities in writing while failing to mention those points not suitable for verbal compromise. Connecticut's Saybrook Result of 1708 was a more definite affair that did actually change the colony's polity, but the platform's specifics were still so general that two simultaneous "clarifications" produced entirely opposite interpretations; in any case, its adoption owed more to an ecclesiastical coup than to the drafting of a widely acceptable statement.[3]

Credal formulations provoked such difficulties because Puritanism was above all else a *movement*: a loose and incomplete alliance of progressive Protestants, lay and clerical, aristocratic and humble, who were never quite sure whether they were the vanguard or the remnant. This uneasy and under-defined collaboration resists denominational taxonomy and can be described only in historical terms, by reference to various successive challenges Puritans faced and the particular cultural resources they drew on to meet them. There is, however, a real and continuing historical entity out there, and we have played blind men to the elephant over it for so long in large part because the subject of our study has been indefensibly bifurcated. Reassemble the English and American halves, examine the result over time and with a proper regard to its settings, and the rough outline of the beast becomes visible enough.

Strictly speaking, the Puritan movement owed its ambivalent stance and its very existence to the distinctive ecclesiastical conditions in England in the latter half of the sixteenth century and the first half of the seventeenth. Puritans, that is, were not Huguenots, a Protestant minority in a Catholic state, nor were they simply the most zealous members of an officially sponsored reformed church on the Dutch or Swiss model. Unlike either instance, the Puritans were at once a self-conscious minority and full-fledged members of the class of the well endowed and well connected.[4] Their England was, in their eyes, "but halfly reformed," yet most Puritans were thoroughly committed to that half, and, if anything, their xenophobic pride in their nation's special attainments increased over time: where the Elizabethans faulted their church for its failure to advance further along Continental lines, the generation of the New England migration made invidious comparisons between the effectiveness of English "heart religion" and the mere formalism of other reformed churches.[5] Up to a point the Puritans even embraced the unreformed half (or, more likely, nine-tenths) of their nation as weak Christians betrayed by a church and state that had failed to fulfill their promise. But with their other voice, they exalted the saints, that very select group who had heeded the preacher's message, and, however diffidently, they separated themselves from the carnal majority so as to pursue the discipline a rigorously predestinarian theology imposed on its adherents. In the end the Puritans found themselves both the saving remnant preserving the spark of the gospel in an unregenerate society and, simultaneously, participants in a gigantic national experiment employing the combined resources of a godly state and a Protestant religious establishment to raise the state of civility and Christianity of the English people beyond the merely nominal.

As often as not, such distinctive Puritan traits as did emerge were the product of the movement's continuing existence rather than a contributing cause of its separate identity. For example, the Puritan discovery that the Bible required a strict, "Judaic" observation of the Sabbath (the origin of our "blue laws") was actually a Continental import that did not arrive until the 1580s and that met a divided response within the movement at its first assertion. The subsequent adoption of a Jewish-style Sabbath as a semiofficial Puritan position was largely the result of a process of opposition. When the movement came under attack from the Elizabethan state after 1588, non-Puritans prudently dissociated themselves from Sabbatarianism as the property of a seditious faction, and the Puritans united behind their notion of Sunday as a relatively safe way to exert an influence on English religious life when other forms of activity were being closed to them. Collective fasting is a similar case in point. We may not be able to think of anything more Puritan than bemoaning a public calamity by a day's worth of sermons and abstinence, but fasts were originally a shared rite of the entire English church until the Puritans' special penchant for the activity drove the episcopal authorities in the 1630s into an attempt to restrict the practice. Both Sabbatarian observances and collective fasts were devised as evangelical techniques to bring the gospel home to the multitudes in a particularly tangible form. Both ended up in the serpentine course of the Puritan movement in England as the occasion of conventicles, extralegal gatherings of the chosen few in defiance of the ordained forms of public worship.[6]

The adherents of the Puritan movement perceived no inherent contradiction in their goals because to them their situation was as apparently inevitable as the English landscape, partly the work of man over a long time, partly the work of nature over a longer one, and entirely a "given." Their double-edged response to the political Reformation was grounded in the fundamental facts of English culture. Contemporary observers from abroad always marveled at the way ordinary Englishmen (really *some* ordinary Englishmen) could explain and argue about their religion. This much-remarked-on skill was in part the effect of the spread of Protestantism, but its origins are to be found much deeper and earlier. Before Elizabeth, before Luther and Calvin for that matter, segments of the English population were already unusually well schooled and, to a degree that made the higher clergy acutely uncomfortable, knowledgeable participants in and critics of the state-sponsored religion.[7] Our first response is usually to identify such lay activity before the Reformation with Lollardry, that small but widespread and irrepressible demand for a simple, deritualized vernacular religion that seems to anticipate Protestantism by a good two centuries. The Lollards do merit a place in the prehistory of Puritanism because they persisted as an exclusively popular heresy for several generations after the authorities had frightened off the movement's original university-based leadership and its knightly supporters and because in some undetermined and perhaps indeterminable way they contributed to the Reformation itself. In particular, in the populous southeast of England onetime Lollard centers uncannily became Puritan strongholds at a later date.[8] But in fact the Lollards were never very numerous and most of lay religion on the eve of the Reformation was perfectly orthodox, which is to say that worship was overwhelmingly intercessory. An assortment of professional services were rendered for the benefit of the laity, often at their behest, but rarely with their active participation except for footing the bill and, in some instances, joining in the ceremony performed by the professionals.[9] In the diocese of York (in its pre-Reformation extent the largest see in England and one of the most populous, embracing 10 percent of the national population) by 1530, after two hundred years of educational expansion, male literacy stood at 20 to 25 percent, formidable by medieval standards, respectable even by the lights of the next century. Yet the spiritual priorities of this relatively literate laity are perhaps best indicated by the extraordinary statistic that at about the same date five out of seven secular priests in the county of York were engaged in saying masses for the souls of the dead rather than in holding cures of souls of the living, and the incidence of chantry foundations elsewhere suggests that those proportions held through the diocese. Nor can the cult of purgatory be assigned exclusively to the unlearned three-quarters of the male population. For one thing, they could not have afforded it, for another, the increase in schooling had been based in the first instance on the need to meet the growing demand for mass priests, and although the schools became increasingly lay in enrollment and control, much of the teaching was always done by chantry priests and stipendiary chaplains simply because there were so many of them that they could keep their prayers for the dead going in perpetuity and still find time to supplement their income by teaching the laity. Without the pervasive conviction that the real drama of salvation took place in the *next* life, there never would have been so many well-schooled laymen in York diocese in this one.[10]

The English, then, were not natural Protestants, despite the persistence of Lollardry. But enough of them were sufficiently well educated and sufficiently drawn to participating in religious concerns to embrace a dogmatic brand of Protestantism willingly and knowledgeably when it was finally propagated and so to make England unique in Europe in the extent to which the official Reformation developed a popular momentum. The religion of the prince was also the voluntary faith of a share of the people. The Puritan movement took shape at just this juncture, in the tension between the demonstrable potential for creating a meaningful Protestant culture, self-evident to the substantial minority who had indeed embraced it, and an actual situation in which, unredeemed "papists" aside, the bulk of the population still had not entered into the official religion with anything more than quiet acquiescence to what authority in its wisdom had chosen to ordain. We have no right to regard this "carnal multitude," as the Puritans termed them, in Puritan terms, as superstitious and insincere, but we have to understand that the Puritans defined themselves according to their fundamental (and accurate) assumption that their knowing and voluntary endorsement of the common orthodoxy made them visibly a minority.[11]

The Puritans' attitude toward the majority cut two distinct ways, of which "hands off" was the more obvious, if not the more idealistic. The Lollards, as a fugitive movement, had been obliged to embrace this choice alone: as late as 1551, in the midst of the Edwardian Reformation, a conventicle of them arrested in Bocking in Essex (a parish that was later to contribute a sizable contingent to the Great Migration) had been charged with holding that it was sinful to extend greetings to a sinner "or a man whome they knowe not."[12] Puritans just as fastidious are not hard to find, either in England or America, but they were never in the same position as the Lollards for all their own screams of "persecution." They were less concerned with survival and bearing witness than with consolidation and expansion. Along with the exclusivist Lollard response they were also willing, in England at least, to lay the blame for the gospel not taking more root on the imperfections of church and society as much as on the obduracy of the many. Out of their own personal experiences and of the experience of England since the late Middle Ages, the Puritans formed a vision of some combination of order imposed from above and enthusiasm elicited from below that would redeem vast classes of the nation from their ignorant slavery to immediate contingencies. If it were possible to identify a single quintessential Puritan assertion, it surely would be the doctrine of a New England sermon that read, "If you are heedless of your works, if you will live at randome according to your hearts desire you may be sure you are no believer."[13] Minister or layman, patron and magistrate or humble professor, what made people into Puritans was, first, their own attainment of a sense of purpose, their forsaking of a life "at randome," and second their perception of how little church and state were doing to give that same sense to England as a whole. The self-assertion of the godly was inevitably both an affirmation of their own unique privileges and a campaign to fashion a pervasive Christian society for the many.

This fundamental ambivalence accounts for the sheer variety of types who became Puritans. The differences in their respective roles and social situations, in turn, ensured that the movement could not afford too definitive a program. In the most general terms, the magistracy stood for order, for creating the material circumstances under which the gospel could take root; the bulk of the laity for purity, for an ecclesiology that recognized the special attainments of the elect; and the ministry straddled the gap between establishment and sect, evangelists to the many and shepherds to the few. The respective aims of the components of the movement usually overlapped, but they were never identical and often came into conflict with one another. Yet the ramshackle nature of the whole arrangement was also a source of its vitality as long as diverse temperaments could be accommodated through concentrating on intellectual structures (discipline, devotional techniques, the *ordo salutis* generally) around which very different experiences could be organized.[14] If the Puritan movement was forever falling apart, it was also regularly being put back together again; its strength, in the times of its health, lay in the comprehensiveness that its anomalous composition allowed.

For us, at a distance of three or four centuries, the official side of the Puritan duality is the more accessible—the painful preacher and the godly magistrate. The attraction in wielding the weapons of intellect requires little explanation, even at a distance of three centuries. We are at a loss, rather, to understand why anyone would willingly choose to be on the receiving end of high Calvinism. Because we can see a little too clearly the minister's exhortation and the magistrate's wholesome severity, the best place to lay hold of the Puritan movement is with its other and less obvious side, the substantial following of relatively humble adherents who lived under the godly ministry and sheltered behind the magistrate's sword. For them Puritanism could offer all the emotional power of a faith that looked backward to the struggling Apostolic church before the triumph of Constantine: it drew a good part of its strength from those who understood very well the imagery of the church under the cross.

It may seem a little incongruous that the poor and persecuted people of God should include so many masters of arts and armigerous gentlemen, that the clerical leadership should enjoy vicarages and rectories and the laity of influence include magistrates and members of Parliament. But in the age of the Reformation Protestantism carried a price, actual and potential. For the first Puritans, especially, the Marian persecutions were a recent experience that they had endured personally, and the memory of the exiles and martyrs of those five years was kept alive long after by Foxe's Book of Martyrs. A return of Catholicism seemed a real enough possibility throughout the reign of Elizabeth, and the menace loomed up once again in the 1630s and early 1640s in the fear of the "moderate popery" of the Laudian bishops and of a Spanish or Irish invasion. Even in more confident times, Puritanism often attracted a following in the areas, particularly in the north of England, where the Catholics continued to hold their own, open recusancy encouraging the most forward form of Protestantism in response by "antiperistasis," as Thomas Fuller called it. For example, the Lancashire of Richard Mather, founder of the American clerical dynasty, was the Northern Ireland of the early seventeenth century, "the cock-pit of conscience" for "constant combats betwixt religion and superstition." Lancashire was by any count the most Catholic county in England, but it also held one of the most fully developed and popularly based Puritan movements. In sections of the county where both groups were strong they jockeyed for control of the pulpits and the schools, alternating lawsuits with other forms of harassment and occasionally resorting to outright violence. Mather himself recalled that the Protestant schoolmaster of his native Winwick Parish successfully intervened to prevent his parents from apprenticing him to Catholic merchants on the grounds "that he should be undone by Popish Education."[15] After Mather left the parish to minister to "the Holy Land" of Toxteth Park, a Protestant citadel in the recusant haven of west Lancashire, the nomination of a leading Puritan to the Winwick rectory in 1624 set off a riot between the nominee's supporter and partisans of the candidate of the local recusant gentry. Winwick, however, turns out to have been a prize worth fighting over: the schools of the parish were a center for preparing would-be ministers, like Mather, for entering the universities and for training teachers for the whole of Lancashire. There had been a similar duel for control of the nearby Prescot grammar school in the 1590s, and in neighboring Yorkshire the educational foundations also divided into warring establishments that owed their existence to the Catholic-Puritan rivalry.[16] Further south the domestic "old church" was mostly a paper tiger, at least by the accession of James in 1603, but anywhere in England at any time to wear one's Protestantism on one's sleeve, Puritan fashion, was to run certain risks in the event of a Catholic revival and also to enroll in the same cause as the Lollards and the Smithfield martyrs.

More often, however, the Christian warfare was a diffuse sort of guerrilla skirmishing between the "godly" and the "vulgar." The use of these terms for their non-Puritan neighbors reveals well enough how the chosen few felt themselves alone in a hostile sea of indifferent formalists and practical atheists, who lacked the conviction even to be papists but who could attack the godly with enthusiasm all the same. Visible religious differences always provided a marvelous means in both England and America for representing and prolonging local conflicts whose social and economic bases were as varied as the locales in which they took place but whose course was monotonously unvaried.[17] Puritan preachers routinely encouraged their hearers to turn from the wicked, and the saints, in their turn, were often drawn together for mutual comfort and edification. Puritan "singularity," therefore, meaning an affected clubbing together of pious hypocrites too proud to fraternize with any but their own kind, became a favorite theme in the manifold forms of harassment and defamation by which feuds at close proximity were generally carried on. One Sussex man had to bring suit in the Star Chamber in 1632 because in a rhymed ballad (to the tune of "Tom O'Bedlam") circulating the Rye alehouses he was described as a member of the "holie Brotherhood" who used the pretext of private religious conferences for sexual affairs, while "soe holie he is, that he will speake to noe bodie he meets." Another of the brethren, a Surrey man this time, who migrated to Massachusetts in 1638, reported that at home in England upon his being "much affected" with a sermon against drunkenness and forsaking his tippling companions for "private societies of saints," he "found communion with God and His people so sweet that I resolved against ill company and hence [was] hated."[18]

Such bitter relations were only to be expected. Explaining "this great fray in the world betwixt God's children and world[ly] ones," Paul Baynes in his popular commentary on Ephesians attributed the root cause to guilty consciences: "They nickname these [saints], persecute them so far as they dare. Why? Because that the lives of the godly do control [reprove] them, this is it that breedeth the hatred, great estrangement."[19] And providing the conflict stayed at the level of an occasional nuisance, there was a comfort of sorts in persecution. An ordinary individual was given importance by his neighbors' hostility, and a weak Christian had his faith affirmed by opposition. Edward Shephard, a Yorkshire sailor come to New England, described himself as happiest at sea, isolated among the reprobates, because "the Lord kept me with a heart desiring to follow Him in the use of means. But when I came here and not seeing the need and necessity of the Lord I thought myself miserable."[20]

Before expending too much sympathy on these suffering brethren, one should recur to the example of another North Country man, the nonconformist minister Adam Martindale, who took a special pride late in life in recounting his youthful skill at "club law."[21] As individuals the saints probably gave as good as they got. But they also needed powerful official protection to shore up their legal vulnerabilities. In an age when most prosecutions originated with informers, the vulgar were perfectly capable of carrying the infighting into the church courts or occasionally before ordinary criminal tribunals. The godly magistrate in England was a particular prize not just because of what he could do for the cause but because of the protection his influence and considerable discretionary powers could afford to the saints when their enemies took advantage of their variance from the prescribed standards of uniformity. Leaving one's parish to hear a powerful preacher in a neighboring church might be a necessary duty, for example, but it could also be construed as a breach of canon law and of an Elizabethan statute against recusants. "Many bad minded people," a Jacobean Puritan petition from Suffolk complained, "doe take occasion by Justices and ecclesiasticall courtes to ponish" honest subjects merely seeking a sermon abroad when there was none to be had at home. Or, as an emigrant from that county who had determined "to hear them that were most suitable to my condition" put it, after traveling up to twenty miles to hear powerful preachers, "being persecuted and courted for going from the place where we lived . . . I used means to come hither [to New England] where we might enjoy more freedom."[22]

Sermon gadding was, from the standpoint of authority, a disorderly nuisance in the misdemeanor category. The godly were likely to get into a lot more trouble when their exercises in parish busting became collective in nature because of the putatively sinister intent of any unofficial organized gathering. (Alehouses, mystery plays, and eventually the London theaters came in for the same suspicious treatment on parallel grounds.) From at least 1585 onward the characteristic Puritan meetings for "repitition" of sermons, scriptural conferences, or fasting and prayer all fell under the definition of "conventicles."[23] It has been said that the basic unit of Puritan religious life was the household, but the episcopal authorities would never have fretted so much about the movement if the household exercises had not had the habit of widening into neighborhood extraparochial assemblies. The church courts attempted to intervene at precisely the point at which more than the usual household residents began to attend a meeting, provoking the Puritan response that such interference meant that "these tymes may also be justly called tymes of persecution."[24] One gets something of the excitement of the primitive church gathered in the catacombs from Oliver Heywood's reminiscences of Lancashire in the 1630s, when "in the heat and height of the Bishop's tyranny over godly ministers" the campaign against lay conventicling was also relatively vigorous: "I can remember something of the warm spirit of prayer in those days . . . that when at my father's house they had a private fast when I was a child, they set me a singing, about doores, that when the [ap]paratour . . . came he might not hear them pray."[25]

As in so many other areas, the Laudian assault on conventicling mainly heightened existing tensions, setting the godly off still more distinctly as besieged knots of the faithful in the wilderness of antichristian England. When the Civil War finally took the lid off, long-standing enmities, brought to a head in the decade of the 1630s, could finally be paid off with interest. The bishops took their share of knocks from the London mobs, but in the countryside it was liable to be the saints, a self-confessed remnant, who were at the mercy of those of the multitude with old scores to settle. Joseph Lister recording the rise in secret prayer meetings in his native Bradford in the 1630s, also recorded the aftermath: "At that time all profaness came swelling in upon us, swearing and sabbath-breaking, profane sports, and those even authorized by law; and the people of God not knowing what the end of these things would be, they being almost at their wit's end, parliaments were broken up, and all things going to wreck both in the church and state. Horse and foot were now brought into the town and quartered in it, who rode round about it swearing what they would do, like so many blood-hounds."[26]

Under other circumstances the withdrawal of the godly might have become complete long before the creation of Dissent by act of Parliament in

1662. Before that date only a few Puritans, more consistent than most, or just more beaten about, did take the insistence on separation to its logical, sectarian conclusion and repudiate both the Church of England and any hope of a comprehensive godly society. William Bradford of the *Mayflower* and New Plymouth colony attributed his Yorkshire company's initial turn to outright Separatism to their having been "both scoffed and scorned by the prophane multitude" and hauled through the church courts; his pastor during the Pilgrim's Leiden exile, John Robinson, credited his own decision to forsake his English ministry to an uncompromising interpretation of the duty of separation he had heard Paul Baynes preach at Cambridge.[27] Yet theirs was never the typical nor even a particularly common path, except perhaps during seasons of unusual frustration for the Puritan movement as a whole, such as the period of disappointment after the Hampton Court Conference (when both Robinson and Bradford made their decisive break) or the high tide of the Laudian repression. Most of the time, without ever becoming so alienated from their society as the expatriate Separatists of the Netherlands, the bulk of the godly managed to weave together a coherent sense of membership in a common cause and yet still to fit snugly within the interstices of the official institutions of church and state. Richard Baxter would one day complain of the "narrow minds" of the "people," which "do looke allmost only to those little societies where they are present."[28] But in the England of Elizabeth and the early Stuarts the popular sense of separateness was actually the basis for a larger loyalty often unavailable to ordinary people in the culture of their day on any other terms.

Take the case of John Trumbull, a mariner who eventually found his way to Massachusetts. Living originally in some unnamed English place without a preaching minister or a local group of saints, he lived "in sin without contradiction," a man who regarded "nothing but back and belly and fulfilling my own lusts." His initial breakthrough came only after he put to sea, when having accepted a copy of Arthur Dent's *Plaine Mans Path-way to Heaven*, solely to practice his reading, he was accidentally taken with its substance and, like Eve, he knew shame—"so saw my misery," as he laconically put it. Accordingly, he moved "to a place where the means were twice," that is, where he could hear a Sunday sermon and a weekday lecture, and the usual internal struggle ensued. He was frustrated by his own weaknesses and tempted by former friends and other carnal men who ridiculed the saints, but he eventually did manage to fall into godly company and profit by the experience. It was another voyage however, that sealed his conversion: putting into London he was brought over by hearing Obadiah Sedgwick, the lecturer at

St. Mildred's Bread Street, explain the difference between hypocrites and true believers and though further doubts and difficulties inevitably ensued, his fate was effectively secured. Welcomed into the ranks of God's people, he traveled with them to New England to a respectable position in Cambridge and Charlestown society and a place at the base of an American family tree.[29]

Trumbull may seem a little unusual in having been saved by going to sea, but it was seaborne commerce and the contacts it brought that represented for him a peculiarly literal link with a wider world than the anonymous place without means of his early life. What he glimpsed in the Puritan message conveyed by tract and preacher was a vision that made his previous experience seem ignorant and aimless, a vision that represented his only real contact with any form of high culture. Less dramatically than Trumbull, perhaps, yet for much the same reasons, thousands of others made the same choice. In an age of primitive communications and an official policy that considered the circulation of any news, good or bad, seditious libel, the saints were able to become joint participants in a conflict that merged their personal psycomachia, the salvation history of the Christian church, and the politics of the leading Protestant power in Christendom. Inward-looking and self-concerned as they may have been, the little societies of the godly flourished best in those locations most closely tied to the national culture.

This assertion may seem at odds with much of the recent historiography concerning the social sources of Puritanism in England and America. It has been suggested, with some plausibility, that in England Puritanism took hold particularly in sparsely populated wood-pasture areas, where, among scattered farmsteads, manorial and communal controls were insignificant and the family was the center of all social existence. In such suitably bleak surroundings, runs the thesis, the autonomous family patriarch, Bible in hand, laying down the law to his household, would make a perfect type of the angry God who could be appeased only by unconditional obedience. It has, however, also been suggested that Puritanism was particularly the creed of those who were bereft of the traditional stability of the patriarchal household and who sought for meaning in chaos by pledging themselves to an omnipotent God and a common bond less transient than the fragile ties of blood and marriage. And it has still more recently been argued that Puritanism was the perfect religious fit for the prosperous yeoman class in densely populated semi-industrial parishes because it provided the ideal analogy (a narrowly defined body of the elect amid the dissolute multitude) for growing social polarization between the parochial elites and the mass of the laboring poor.[30]

On the American side, the tragedy of the decline of rural Puritanism is usually enacted through the collapse of the movement's alleged inner mechanism, a compact, autonomous village settlement employing open-field farming under strict communal control—that is, in a 180-degree variance from its English equivalent, the argument is that New England Puritanism was a bastion of traditional values rather than a substitute for them and, consequently, was unable to hold its own against family-centered acquisitiveness created by an *increase* in scattered farmsteads and an expansion of the pastoral economy.[31] All these explanations of the social basis of Puritanism contain some truth: in the single English county of Yorkshire, an area slightly larger than Connecticut, concentrations of Puritans were to be found in the scattered farms of the Pennine uplands, the squire-dominated open-field regions of the East Riding, the industrial towns such as Halifax and Leeds, and commercial centers like Hull and Beverley.[32] One can find the saints under a great variety of conditions, but rarely, let it be stressed, in isolation, though that element seems the one thing common to much of the diverging speculations on what soils produced the greatest harvest of the godly.[33]

Ironically, the Puritan concept of the ideal town would *never* have been a self-contained country village with few connections to the larger economy, such as Birdsall, "an obscure Towne in Yorkshire," where Henry Burton was born, "and the more obscure, as having never had a preaching minister time out of minde," or Fossecut in Northamptonshire, "a most blind town and corner," where Thomas Shepard spent a part of his youth. Both men thanked God for delivering them from these pristine, bucolic scenes of their boyhood, Burton to a career as a London lecturer, Shepard "to the best country in England, *viz.*, to Essex," and to a place in its dense clerical network.[34] In any projected Puritan utopia there would be a plenitude of means available. A painful learned minister on an adequate stipend would reside on the site, a grammar school would be nearby, the closest member of the gentry would be a well-affected justice who suppressed enormities and patronized promising young candidates for the ministry. Not far away would be found a flourishing market town, preferably on some major trade route, supplied with an endowed weekly lecture, a stationer, and, in general, a continuous sampling of what was going on out there, however much filtered through Puritan lenses.

As a habit of mind Puritanism required a special kind of cosmopolitanism transcending the intensely local and regional loyalties by which most Englishmen gained their identity. The real ligaments of the movement before the Civil War are to be found in the half-accidental, always loosely connected network by which the godly associated themselves with each other and with the great events of their day. By way of his enemies, for example, we learn of Calvin Bruen, the Puritan sheriff of the city of Chester, who owned a copy of Alexander Leighton's inflammatory *Sions Plea against the Prelacy* only a short time after it came off the presses at Amsterdam in 1630. The tract was apparently obtained through the city's only stationer, who made sure that "no Puritanical books [appear] but our citizens get them as soon as any." In the case of the radical Canterbury politician Thomas Scott, his own memoranda indicate how he kept himself informed by a steady diet of newsletters and tracts, distilling the information throughout the 1620s in circular letters to his constituents in which he spiced his tart political commentary with apt quotations from Chaucer. For Colchester in Essex we have the word of an informant that Thomas Cotton, who kept a "privat church" in the town, also maintained a "pevish intelligencer" in London, whose dispatches he read publicly at the town market, while about him, "the zealants thronge as people use where Ballads are sunge."[35] In the course of the Great Migration to America in the 1630s we can very occasionally observe these scattered knots of the faithful serving as recruiting agents or cheering off their New England–bound brethren and publicizing the good news from the Puritan colonies as it filtered back across the Atlantic.[36]

America was a challenge to these requirements, especially in the earliest decades of settlement, but in the course of the seventeenth century the obvious logistical limitations of the new environment were very largely overcome. We retain, absurdly, an irresistible compulsion to think of the New England town as a hermetically sealed unit throughout its prerevolutionary history. Even some of the most recent historiography tells its tale as if the unfolding dynamic of the Puritan movement in America could be explained solely in terms of events so locally bounded the entire setting would have served Bertrand Russell well for his paradox of the Spanish barber—located (for the purposes of philosophical rigor) in an imaginary village where nobody comes and nobody goes. Perhaps the best single charm for breaking the spell of this picture-postcard mental image (snow-covered village snuggled in a small clearing in the fastness of an impenetrable forest) is a simple repetition of a sentence in a letter written one Wednesday in 1681 by the minister of New London, Connecticut. The author begs his correspondent, a fellow clergyman in Boston, to give him the latest reports about Bay Colony and English politics but prefaces his request with the caution that the information had better be really current: "For newes, we have the same you have, and as late as last Friday by one that came then from Boston."[37]

Now, New London enjoyed the best harbor in Connecticut, to be sure, but it was located a fair way from Boston by sea and it was only one of twelve towns in the colony (out of twenty-six) that possessed some sort of shipping at the time when the news available there was, by seventeenth-century standards, up-to-date. Throughout New England most of the inland towns were situated at some manageable distance from the coastal ports or near navigable rivers or an overland transportation center. Two of the seven ships registered at New London could have gone upriver to Norwich (only twelve miles away), and in most years all seven could have sailed the Connecticut River up to Hartford to bring the fresh advices from Boston. And they would bring more than advices: Connecticut still had no printing press in the 1680s, but the majority of its households possessed books.[38]

Isolation was scarcely an option in locating a town, if it was to be founded in the first place or to survive once it was. As in contemporary England, much of a locality's economic exchanges took place over only a small neighboring area, but some necessaries (as well as all luxuries) were carried in regularly over networks covering long distances. Rural town clerks and country ministers, not to mention every rustic somebody or other whose diary or letters is held up as evidence of the "real" New England, all relied on white paper manufactured in France or, less frequently, in Italy or the Netherlands and imported into London from Rouen, or Caen, or Bordeaux, or Amsterdam. From London it was reexported to Boston, from whence it was distributed to the smaller ports and directly or indirectly to the interior of New England so that in what we persist in imagining as so many self-contained, inward-looking towns this basic staple of the written record could be covered with the ink marks that three hundred years later would be read, strange to say it, as the authentic documentation of colonial lives lived out in an isolated village culture sheltered for a generation or two from the storms of modernity racking their European counterparts.[39] We consign the Puritans to Arcadia; they themselves would no doubt have preferred urban centers and bustling market towns.[40]

The most genuinely paradoxical aspect of the Puritan movement during its English career is located just here: in the ways in which unabashed engagement with national causes and unashamed enthusiasm for cultural progress (as we usually conceive it) could somehow lead to a growing sense of alienation from the nation and its state and culture. Public commitment, Puritan style, could be exercised only in a manner that necessarily set the committed apart from the body of their countrymen. Excluded from the kinds of connections around which the Puritan movement cohered, the great mass of the English population too ordinary to possess extensive family ties or university affiliations lacked any real alternative foci for involvement in the official concerns of their country. They could at best snap up such snippets of gossip as happened to spill over from the tables of the local representatives of the professionally well-informed classes, generally tales of court intrigue and political controversy reduced to personnel conflicts—the sort of disconnected babble that leads to a generalized cynicism and often enough a reflexive royalism.[41] The godly had more sustained sources of information and a more systematic context into which to fit what they heard: they were enjoined to fit their own spiritual strivings into a set of other grand struggles, national and international.

Some indication of the way these activities fused political and religious concerns can be gleaned from the instance of the man who eventually led the migration to Connecticut, Thomas Hooker, while he was still serving as a lecturer at Chelmsford in Essex in the late 1620s. By the admission of his admirers, Hooker was "a great inquirer after News," although not, we are assured, "out of *Athenian* curiosity, but christian conscientiousness, to sympathise with the church of God." It takes no great imagination to guess in what direction these sympathies might lead at a time when the Puritans were increasingly concerned about England's failure to play its part in the battle against the power of Rome. Preaching a funeral sermon in 1626, Hooker, in the course of calling for national moral regeneration, explicitly compared the spiritual state of the individual believer to the imperiled condition of England, menaced from without and still more formidably from within: "It is not the weakness of our land, nor the power of the enemy, that can so much hurt us as our treacherous hearts at home." Then, in a piece entitled *Spiritual Munitions*, he gave in to temptation entirely. Alluding to a cause célèbre of some five years earlier, he made an analogy (a strained one) between those who would "oppose and secretly undermine any that is a true faithful minister of Jesus Christ" and the unnamed courtiers who arranged the widely reprobated sale of one hundred ordinance in the Tower to the Spanish for use against the Protestants in the war in Germany.[42] Nor was Hooker's influence limited to his immediate public auditory. He had ample opportunity to broadcast his opinions by way of "divers young ministers" who "spent thire time in private meetings and conferences with him or with such as are of his society and returne home in the end of the week and broch on the Sundaies what he hath brewed, and trade upon his stocke." At least one of those ministers, Thomas Weld of Terling, encouraged private meetings of the godly of his parish, as did Hooker himself at Chelmsford, where he gathered an exclusive, covenanted "company of Christians" to compliment his work as a preacher to the multitude.[43]

There was an ironic resemblance between these activities and the other great bugbear of authority, though the godly would have hardly enjoyed the comparison. The nearest rival to Puritan institutions as a source of mutuality and information alike was probably the ever more ubiquitous alehouse, regarded as a center of the same kind of rumor mongering and unrest as the sedition-spouting preacher and the schismatic conventicle.[44] From the standpoint of enlightened statecraft in a dangerous age, informed people who took the slogans of the last war a little too seriously were troublemakers. But Puritans were bound to make trouble sooner or later because a perfectly lawful form of spiritual conversion led to the rejection of a reactive, purposeless existence for several forms of commitment, none separable from the others. Effectively, long before the two became temporarily identified by the laws of Massachusetts and New Haven, sainthood for the Puritans had already become the entrée to citizenship.

At the other end of the Puritan movement the leadership, clerical and lay, found its allegiances similarly double-edged, drawn at once into the running of their society and into a distanced, often bitter criticism of it. Gentlemen— and gentle ladies—were known to choose exile in the Netherlands or New England out of love to the brethren, yet they also saw themselves charged with a duty to serve in the station to which God had called them. Mostly, however, the Puritan grandees could live with their contradictions if they were not pressed too hard: whatever the central government was up to, it was usually possible to hollow out islands of godliness in aristocratic households, parishes under lay patronage, and semiautonomous urban centers. The Puritan ministry, by contrast, felt the dilemma of its dual role almost daily as the ordinary result of professional commitments. The ministers' solution to the competing demands of the faithful and the unconverted constitutes much of the formal intellectual record of Puritanism both in England and in its continuation in America.

One may wonder why so much of the ministry remained a part of the establishment for so long. The Elizabethans could afford a degree of inconsistency in the freshness of their reformation, assuming that one upheaval or so more in the series they had already experienced would bring them into their Presbyterian zion.[45] After the abrupt reverses of the 1590s the initial momentum of the movement obviously faltered; yet it was the 1630s before overtly Separatist tendencies really began to gain ground among the Puritans and 1662 before nearly eighteen hundred ministers and their lay followers finally brought the Puritan drama to an end in England by forming Dissent.

Thomas Hooker shrewdly remarked in 1633 that men able to undergo "half an hour's hanging" would never bear to remain all their lives "in the ditch and to be cast into a blind corner like broken vessels." College graduates exercising a socially approved vocation on a narrow but guaranteed income were not especially eager to lay down their ministry in exchange for poverty, uselessness, and liability to abusive treatment. Amid all the Puritan martyrologies stands the refreshing confession of Harvard's Henry Dunster that, rather than "bid adieu all wordly treasures," he deliberately put off reading the books that would have convinced him of the corruptions of the Church of England and continued his Lancashire ministry for ten years in self-inflicted ignorance. Still, as Dunster said, "the Lord helped me against all," and he landed in New England in 1640. Fourteen years later the Lord helped him again, for he laid down his Harvard presidency in 1654 and subsequently risked the penalties of his own Puritan law out of newly acquired Baptist convictions. His example, writ large at the Restoration by almost 1,800 deprived ministers, only 171 of whom afterward conformed, argues strongly against too much cynicism in explaining the Puritan ministers' allegiance to their rickety church and wayward society.[46]

A fairer interpretation would explain the Puritan clergy less as prisoners of their stipends than as creatures of their upbringing and their vocation. However varied their backgrounds, they mostly bore the common stamp of training in one of two universities and often in one of the colleges famous for its zeal. Many of them fitted into that web of marriage relationships and mentor-protégé friendships William Haller has made famous as the "spiritual brotherhood." Most, when they could, kept up their common identity by one form or another of clerical exercise, most commonly the regular meetings attendant on the combination lectureships. They could hardly help conceiving of themselves as a distinct order of society with unique prerogatives and special responsibilities: such a definition was the very sum of the experiences that made their lives purposeful in the same way as the message they preached brought order out of aimlessness for all the John Trumbulls of England. Through the very process of preaching that created a sectlike band of believers they affirmed the importance of a state-supported priestly caste, and it is no wonder if, at any given time, most of them were disposed to suffer evils under the establishment while evils were sufferable, at least sufferable enough for them to get on with their great work without too frequent twinges of conscience.[47]

Preaching, above all else, was the flashpoint for these tensions. Characteristically, the Puritans insisted that the minister was first and foremost a man who opened and applied the Bible for his audience. According to their spokesman William Bradshaw in his classic statement of the Jacobean phase of the movement, the "rigid" Puritans, the uncompromising kind, "hould that the highest and supreame office and authoritie of the Pastor, is to preach the gospell solemnly and publickly to the Congregation, by interpreting the written word of God, and applying the same by exhortation and reproofe unto them."[48] We are liable to stumble over this assertion, seeing it pointing inevitably in a sectarian direction to the tub preacher and the hedgepriest and, ultimately, to the nineteenth-century revivalist. In this overneat scheme the Puritan preachers are a link between the mendicant friars and the hot-gospelers, itinerants come to gather a self-sustaining nucleus of believers and then move on to a fresh challenge. Puritan clergymen were given, most un-reasonably, to sticking in one place for a long time. To turn them into simple evangelists is to strip the sermon of its surrounding context. The practice of piety, to use a Puritan term, was always a difficult, complex business requir-ing communal supervision. The preacher's role could not be separated from the overall work of the ministry, the ministry from the instituted churches, or the churches from the society they served, at least they could not if obdurate, perversely clever human nature was to be brought, all unwillingly, to follow a unifying divine purpose rather than its own spasmodic inclinations.

Certainly, there were a few Puritan hedgepriests before 1660, especially in border areas along the Celtic fringes, but by the standards of most of their clerical brethren such a ministry was too hopelessly incomplete to deserve the name. We have from Thomas Shepard, for instance, a full account of why an itinerant's lot was neither a happy nor a holy one. Kicked out of the diocese of London by William Laud in 1632, Shepard traveled north in search of a cure of souls, eventually arriving in Northumberland, in a parish near New-castle called Heddon, which he described as "that rude place of the north where was nothing but barbarous wickedness generally." Heddon, though, provided an education for Shepard; it was where he came to "know more of the ceremonies, church government and estate, and the unlawful standing of bishops than in any other place." What he found was a parish where the lack of a capable resident minister was repaired from time to time by Cornelius Glover, an itinerant out of Lancashire and Yorkshire, described by the Dur-ham High Commission in 1634 as "of noe certaine abode, nor likelie to be apprehended." When Glover came through Heddon, the "schismaticall sect" flocked in from all over the area, including Newcastle, and the parish curate, an individual distinguished largely for his drinking bouts, was persuaded "to make short praiers and to be gone" to allow more time for the visitor's sermon. ("I had not been here to day els," one prominent member of the godly remarked.) When the High Commission went after Glover for "preachinge sediccious doctrine," his mantle was offered to Shepard, and for once a Puritan cleric had no hesitation about a call: he turned it down flat. Heddon had taught Shepard that it was time to go to New England if he wanted to fulfill the Puritan ideal of the ministry as a public office with a full range of distinct functions rather than simply serve in the manner of Glover as yet another prophet in the wilderness. "I saw it [was] my duty to desire the fruition of all God's ordinances[,] which I could not enjoy in Old England," and "I saw no reason to spend my time privately when I might possibly exercise my talent publicly." As far as Shepard was concerned, the only way the Heddon people were going to get a genuine minister was to emigrate with him.[49]

The New England migration resolved (for a time) many of the clergy's long-standing paradoxes. In the English situation their championing of the sermon did, up to a point, undercut their equally intense insistence on the church as the institution through which believers came to grace and were disciplined into a godly life, encouraging instead what the Separatist minister John Robinson called "spiritual vagabandry."[50] As Robinson's acid label suggests, the impulse was lay, not clerical, and the activity left the clergy of very divided minds. Laymen could legitimately defend their shopping about from minister to minister by citing their particular and individual spiritual needs. Having been in London attending "private christian meetings" that threw him into a state of spiritual anxiety, Edward Collins, later a leading citizen of Cambridge, Massachusetts, "came to my own place," Bromford in Suffolk, "where though [there was] an orthodox minister," he preferred "going to Dedham and Mr. Greenhill" at Oakley "and others and there God carried on His work by Himself and wrought peace."[51] The laity also were far less vulnerable to prosecution than the clergy when they indulged in liturgical cutting and pasting. The technique employed at Heddon—abridging the service on occasions when a real preacher came by—would do in some of the wilder regions of the North, but in the better-served parts of England the more common practice was to come in to the service late or to leave early, stopping long enough to savor the sermon but shunning the ritual. The anti-Puritan satire from Rye of 1632 takes note of this kind of activity in recounting that after its holier-than-thou male protagonist has "instructed" his female companion in secret, "the bell ringing away they hast[e] to sermon." The allusion is to the popular belief that Puritans rang the church bells a second time to summon the godly once the obnoxious parts of common prayer were completed and the preaching was about to start. There is no

convincing evidence that the English Puritans practiced anything like so formal a secession from the prescribed ceremonial, but the Laudian bishop of
Norwich, Mathew Wren, took the notion seriously enough to forbid more
than one round of bell ringing in his diocese.[52] Actually, most churches were
so tightly packed and so broken up by various temporary structures thrown
up over the years that the worshipers could pretty much come and go and do
as they pleased, regardless of what was supposed to be happening according
to the Book of Common Prayer. Anti-Puritan tactics in the 1630s, therefore,
included enlarging church seating and tearing out box pews and other obstructions to permit churchwardens to keep an eye on would-be defectors
from uniformity, but the net effect of these efforts was probably merely to
increase the separation between the extraparochial worship of the godly and
the authorized public services.[53]

As advocates of a comprehensive religious life under the guidance of a
settled ministry, the English Puritan clergy regarded these exercises in lay
autonomy with at most carefully qualified indulgence—if that. There was
little they could do, however, besides enjoin and exhort, while their version of
the minister's function was necessarily interfered with at a dozen points by
episcopal visitors, church courts, and lay patrons and by the general tendency
of the laity to make up their spiritual itineraries on a day-to-day basis. The
conversion narratives of some particularly unattached members of the godly
read a little like a hypochondriac's account of a round of visits to various
unnamed "doctors" and "specialists," hearing here "a minister," and there
"a preacher," until some particularly effective physician of the soul finally
completes the cure. These scattered experiences could be brought together,
however, by supplementing the imperfect parish assemblies with private exercises centering on the public preaching. The sermon when provided with
such a context integrated the Puritan clergy into their culture as no other
aspect of their calling could.[54]

Before and after conversion, the godly life was lived under conditions
determined collectively. Wherever possible a learned ministry spoke to a
knowledgeable and disciplined audience actively involved in searching the
meaning and application of the Scriptures. One did not just wander in to
hear a sermon one morning, see the light, and wander out again a new
creature. The Elizabethan Puritans were fond of pointing out that it was just
short of a literal miracle when anyone was converted on the canonical minimum of four sermons a year. Salvation was a hard, long, and always reflective business, more often than not pursued in company. The trouble with
enthusiasts, from the Puritan point of view, was that their conversion was

always too quick and easy—and too mindless. The pretended converts who inclined to Antinomianism could not say *why* they believed, they could only recount some particularly rapturous fits of alleged intimacy with the Holy Ghost. But as John Cotton warned, "it behoves every christian man to know well, what he believes, and practise[s] . . . and that not because men say so, but because you see light for it from the word of the Son of God."[55] Saul of Tarsus aside, one was not knocked over by God; with great difficulty and much hesitation, by the grace of God, one found the basis over time to make a knowing choice.

Of course, the choice was a guided one, but it was still to be an informed decision acted upon from an understanding systematically acquired. After the sermon the laity would meet, using their notes to go over its lesson: "We must conferre and speake, and reason of the word of god; those that doe thus, they show they regard; they that doe not, its manifest, they heed it not."[56] Heads of households similarly could mirror the pastor's role for their families and servants (and to the bishops' grief, for their neighbors) by opening passages of Scripture at regular exercises. Further, because saving knowledge had no meaning apart from practice, these same meetings could exercise the functions of government by punishing disorders among those over whom the householder had jurisdiction, turning a private exercise into a more complete replica of the model Puritan church than could be obtained in the public parishes.

To assist the laity with these paraministerial duties, the Elizabethan radical Dudley Fenner prepared the second translation of the logic of Petrus Ramus, as well as the first English rendering of the companion treatise on rhetoric by Talaeus, and brought the two out as one volume "togeather with examples for the practice of the same, for Methode in the government of the familie." Putting a Latin treatise on rhetoric into English may not seem a particularly revolutionary act, but Fenner intended it as the basis of a change comparable to rendering the Bible in the vernacular. In addition to providing the godly householder with the tight fist of logic, to facilitate his following the preacher's exegeses and to enable him to cut some scriptural knots himself, Fenner offered as well the open hand of rhetoric, by which the learned communicated their mystery to the public.[57] He and his successors were assuming, indeed encouraging, wholesale lay participation in the work of grace through the same tools as those available to the ministry. The preachers' words would stick because they were both prepared for in advance and reinforced afterward through the collective religious life of the godly: "improving, and blowing up grace by spirituall exercises of reading, singing, medication, conference, private communication of gifts," as Samuel Wales put it in a tract with the significant title *Totum Hominis, or the Whole Duty of a Christian.*[58] The godly found a purpose in the Puritan message because they heard it in the course of participating in a purposeful coordinated world; each individual search was merged in a common, orderly effort.

To suggest, as has sometimes been the case, that the sermon was an oral bridge between a literate elite and the nonliterate multitude is to ignore the totality of the Puritan scheme. Conceivably, some of the participants in the exercises of the godly, younger, simpler, or more humble than the rest, may have lacked sufficient learning. Watching the educated at work was always a favorite Puritan form of education, but for any of the exercises to have worked, a high proportion of the members would have needed to be literate and the leading actors would have needed a degree of proficiency in excess of that of the despised "reading ministry" (ministers so poorly trained they could not compose a sermon but were forced to read from the Homilies and the Book of Common Prayer). The Puritans' only concession to illiterates was an effort to teach them to read; in their proposed society the painful and learned preacher was essentially the main shaft in a well-organized machine that assumed a high degree of education and discipline in most of its parts.[59]

Perhaps we are now in a position to understand the mystery of the Puritans' ambivalence toward their culture and to look forward a little to the consequences for the shaping of New England. Ministers and laity alike were so deeply embedded in the society of their day, so taken up with its concerns, that most of the time they seemed to fault their fellow Englishmen primarily for failing to fulfill the nation's potential. As Thomas Hooker said when he finally despaired of "this wicked land" in 1631, "the poor native Turks and Infidels shall have a more cool summer-parlor in hell than England shall have; for we stand upon high rates." But as individuals, by hard experience, the godly and their ministers and patrons knew themselves to be the party of the saving remnant, God's "Noahs and his Lots," as Hooker called them in the same sermon.[60] All the constituent groups in the Puritan movement shared this double life in some measure, but they had differing first priorities: the godly were most concerned with the special and exclusive communion of those who had shared in the work of grace, the ministry with their professional supervision of the means of salvation, the grandees with their own responsibilities and perquisites as patrons and with the need for lay direction of any further reformation. At any time in the history of the Puritan movement the component elements were in danger of coming unglued, if, for example, the godly carried conventicling totally beyond clerical control or the clergy went gunning for the impropriated tithes and rights of presentation that added to the wealth and power of their gentry allies. The movement cohered most effectively when a sense of progress and momentum could be invoked to put off spelling out potentially divisive issues. Conversely, the movement faltered and suffered defections when official opposition and political frustrations brought out the radical propensities of some of the members and thereby frightened off a portion of the rest.

By the time Thomas Hooker took to anathematizing his native country the Laudian repression was beginning to reopen deep (and, as it turned out, permanent) fissures in the Puritan movement. Granted a new opportunity after 1640, the English Puritans found that they no longer had the capacity to effect a coherent goal. The task of realizing the original vision was reserved instead for the Noahs and the Lots whom God had begun "to ship away" to New England, "a rock and a shelter for his righteous ones to run unto." Hooker's recourse to Old Testament imagery marked a significant redefinition: without abandoning either the chosen few or the Christian nation, the Puritans were replacing the suffering saints of Apostolic times with the New Israel. Reformation and purity would no longer be kept in tandem with difficulty in a polity where the voting majority were saints to begin with. New England, however, was not just a fulfillment of unrealized English Puritan aspirations; it was also a continuation of the duality between the insular and the comprehensive that had always been at the heart of the movement. Without the exclusive societies of saints looking out toward a wider world, there would have been no New England in the first place, except perhaps on the same terms as Virginia or South Carolina. Instead, in the Puritan colonies we are dealing with a much yeastier blend of the unreflectively traditional and the deliberately innovative.

Perhaps the best way to descend from these abstractions to actual colonists is to come down on an unusually vivid instance from the East Riding of Yorkshire. Rowley parish and the nearby areas of Cottingham and Holme upon Spalding Moor supplied most of the immigrants who founded Rowley, Massachusetts, in 1638. The Yorkshire emigrants were so conservative that in most respects they behaved in America as if they were still in the North Wold, the chalky uplands on which Rowley parish lies.[61] The largest contingent had come from the extremely damp marshlands of Holme, at the western side of the wold, and that village, rather than its lightly populated English namesake, gave the New England town its farming methods, its system of land distribution, and its preference in village officeholders, all with minimal adaptations to new circumstances. Even the choice of the New England site, by the Merrimac River, probably reflected the skills acquired by the farmers of Holme in the course of working the wettest single village of the Vale of York.[62] The only curiosity is why these thoroughly unlikely pioneers ever went to Massachusetts, and the answer is not to be sought in anything peculiar to the chalk of the wold or the marsh of the vale but in the influence of two English Puritans, one of whom came to America and one of whom only contemplated migration.

Ezekiel Rogers, M.A. (Cantab.) and rector of Rowley parish, was a forceful member of a distinguished Essex clerical family. Upon leaving Cambridge he hesitated to seek a cure because of his distaste for the ceremonies and "therfor Chose Rather to lye hide" as chaplain to the Essex Puritan grandee Sir Francis Barrington. Clergymen in aristocratic households were supposed to practice the insinuating manner appropriate to their position, but the pugnacious and unremittingly frank Rogers did not fit the mold. Sir Francis was a bluff fellow himself, however, and he and Rogers got on very well. The clergyman spent twelve years in the service of the head of a leading family connection in probably the most organized gentry community of any English county. Hatfield Broad Oak, the Barrington seat, was the center for a great deal of politicking, county and national, in which Rogers participated in his way. "He there," according to Cotton Mather, "had opportunity not only to *do good* by his profitable preaching, but also to *get good* by his conversation with persons of honour, who continually resorted thither, and he *knew* and *used* his opportunity to the utmost."[63]

Like other Essex gentry families, the Barringtons' influence extended beyond Essex, in their case to marital and business alliances with the Puritan members of the Yorkshire gentry. In the course of these arrangements an ancestor of Sir Francis had incidentally acquired the fat living of Rowley, to which Rogers was presented as rector in 1621 for the purpose of "*awakening* these drowsy corners of the north." Here by "the Gentlenesse" of Archbishop Tobie Matthew he was "favored both for subscription and Cerimonies." His "lively ministry" (and his organizational talents) cracked the isolation of the parish quickly enough: his own preaching lured in hearers from the surrounding area, and he invited "strange" (nonresident) preachers into his pulpit and founded a regular meeting of the East Riding Puritan clergy after the model of the more famous West Riding "exercise" at Halifax.[64] Rogers had indeed learned a good deal at Hatfield Broad Oak about how things can be run.

When the reforming regime of the new archbishop, Richard Neile, caught up with Rogers in 1634 he was treated with a certain deference as the leading member of the riding clergy. He tried to finesse the Chancery Court on secondary issues, but "for Refusing to Reade that accursed Booke that allowed sports on Gods holy Sabbath" he was suspended from his ministry, "and by it and other sad signes of the times," including his failure to get Sir Thomas Barrington, patron of the living in succession to his deceased father, to reimburse him for his expenses in repairing the Rowley parsonage, he was "Driven with many of my hearars into New England" to found their village by the shore of the Merrimac. By the time of his emigration in 1638 Rogers had been finished with his mother church for some period: he had already told Sir Thomas Barrington that it was a burdensome thing to be "clogged" with the right of appointing the pastor, "which ought to be the priviledge of the flocke," and on arriving in Boston he announced that he and "his company" had "of a good time, withdrawn themselves from the church communion of England, and that for many corruptions which were among them."[65]

Rogers's forcefulness showed up even in the naming of the New England town after the depopulated parish that had been the focal point of the settlers' English life, though most of them had actually resided in other East Riding villages. His influence is obvious too in the unusually large percentage of the town inhabitants who quickly joined his newly formed church, and a touch of his personality lingered on long after his death in 1662 in the Rowley church's sustained resistance to liberalized admission procedures, for which the members still saw little need. Even Rogers's considerable entrepreneurial skills are apparent in the efforts to set up a clothmaking industry in Rowley and in his negotiations to break the Boston monopoly on imports by establishing a separate trading arrangement between his town and merchants in Yorkshire. It is easy enough to see how the course of his energetic English ministry had thrust national concerns on a provincial region of the East Riding and converted otherwise unremarkable farmers into founders of a Puritan state. But there was another power in that part of south Holderness besides the expatriate Essex minister, a Yorkshire man whose impact is harder to gauge but palpable all the same.

Sir William Constable, Bart., lord of the manor of both Flamborough and Holme upon Spalding Moor, was an unlikely Puritan. He was the head of a gentry clan scattered all over Yorkshire but overwhelmingly Catholic in its sympathies, and he was also the last of a very long line of the crème de la crème of border ruffians. His great-great-great-grandfather at an advanced age had commanded the English left wing at Flodden, his great-great-grandfather had been hanged in chains at York for his leading part in the Pilgrimage of Grace, and the grandfather who recovered the family estates as a reward for his military services under Elizabeth had been a bigamist.[66] For all their gaudy history, the Constables were always great promoters of education, maintaining a school at Holme from the 1470s onward. The victor of Flodden Field also left money for four scholarships at St. John's College, Oxford, and a son of the rebel leader in the Pilgrimage of Grace was arrested in 1536 while on an educational tour in the company of a schoolmaster.[67] This union of opposites continued in Sir William. Like his ancestors, he was a soldier and administrator and did well at both callings. He had a lifelong penchant for opposition to the crown, but he was as fierce a Puritan as Sir Robert Constable, the hero of the Pilgrimage of Grace, had been a Catholic. He began his career fighting under the Earl of Essex in Ireland and took an active part in Essex's Rising: he was at the performance of *Richard II* on the eve of the Rising, and on the day itself, target in hand and halberd at the ready, he barred the gate to Essex House to keep Sir John Popham, the Lord Chief Justice, from leaving, before accompanying his master on his abortive sally into the City. Somehow Constable managed to secure a pardon through Sir Robert Cecil's intervention and shortly thereafter, in 1605, gained some minor patronage from the crown, either because of James I's desire to reconcile the surviving Essexites or because his skill at foils took the king's fancy.[68] On his father's death he settled down to a busy role in East Riding local and parliamentary politics, resisting the fiscal and religious policies of Charles I. In 1627 he was bounced from his office of custos rotulorum of the East Riding justices of the peace and jailed for refusing the forced loan. In the Parliament of 1628 he spoke in favor of impeaching the duke of Buckingham, and on the tumultuous last day of the session of 1629, he can be found chiming in, right after Denizel Holles, "That the Sp[eaker] wold signify the desire of the house to the Clerk to have that read," when "that" referred to Sir John Eliot's three resolutions against arbitrary taxation and Arminianism.[69] By 1635 Constable had apparently had enough and, along with several other Yorkshire militants, he embarked on a plan to settle a colony at Saybrook in Connecticut. When that effort fell through, he and the other "Gentlemen of the North" migrated to Arnhem in 1637 to form a congregational church under Thomas Goodwin and Philip Nye, who later returned to England to become the leaders of the Independents in the Westminster Assembly.[70] Constable was back in Yorkshire by 1642, served in the Long Parliament as an extreme war party man and in the parliamentary army as a successful field commander, and then, with unfailing consistency, climaxed his career by signing the death warrant of Charles I. In the last years of his life (he died in 1655) he was a frequent member of the Commonwealth's Council of State and its president twice.

The Constables had held the lordship of Holme since at least the late thirteenth century. Partly because of the cost of opposition politics, partly because of his notorious and rather un-Puritan extravagance, Sir William sold the manor in 1634 but immediately reentered it as principal tenant; Holme, indeed, was the only family property he managed to retain. His effect there on the Puritanism of the inhabitants and on their decision to migrate to New England can only be surmised. We have the word of Philip Nye that the gathering of servants and supplies for Saybrook by Constable and a fellow East Riding baronet left their "Countrie full of the reports of their going," and the Rowley migration occurred within twelve months of Sir William's own exodus to the Netherlands. Members of the East Riding squirearchy were well known for persuading their tenants to join them in their religious and political preferences by all the considerable means available to manor lords, and the later history of Holme proves it no exception. Constable had sold the manor to the Langdales, but they were leading royalists and unable to take effective control from him at any time during the Civil War. At the Restoration, however, Sir Marmaduke Langdale was at last able to assume his lordship. He had been a lukewarm Anglican, but, with his family, he was eventually reconciled to Rome. There had always been a few recusants at Holme, but from the moment one of the Langdales first showed up among them, in 1644, the number shot up, and after the family took up the lordship at the Restoration the onetime stronghold of Puritans gradually became what it remains today, a historic center of North Country Catholicism.[71]

Neither Rogers nor Constable was a purely local phenomenon. Together they brought a more cosmopolitan set of loyalties to the Rowley area, and as a result some Yorkshire farming folk ended up as New England Puritans. But the pair represented something more for the life of the East Riding and for the Puritan movement. Their Puritanism is a reminder of just how thoroughly saving grace, like everything else in seventeenth-century England, ran along the familiar channels of kinship and clientage networks. (Fierce Puritan that he was, as head of a great North Country clan Constable could not resist the temptation to let his numerous Catholic relatives out of the recusancy fines when he presided over the East Riding bench.) Yet the rector and the baronet, like most of the emigrants from the Rowley area, were also visible saints; they were in their world, very much of it, and also disaffected from it, so much so that they eventually chose exile over the retention of lifelong privilege. Their rejection of the things of this world was just as incomplete as their commitment: Rogers took time off to advise a nephew to emigrate from an England clearly in its last days ("a fine dying time in regard of the *termi-*

nus a quo and *ad quem*") while on a visit back to Hatfield to try once again to get back some of the money he had sunk in the Rowley parsonage. Constable, in London to arrange for his own departure, still helped in the extended negotiations for the marriage of his nephew, the future commander in chief of the New Model Army, Sir Thomas Fairfax. And Rogers once he arrived in Massachusetts, Constable back in England after his exile in the Netherlands, found worldly matters as absorbing as ever.[72]

The sometime pilgrims who doubled as public administrators were a very English phenomenon, the product of the distinctive course of the Reformation in that country, which encouraged the faithful to separate themselves at the same time as it lured them into the task of civilizing and Christianizing their recalcitrant countrymen. Just at the point when it was disintegrating in England this tangled and shifting pattern of Puritan imperatives would reappear in America, transported relatively intact in the Great Migration. In New England, Puritanism had another hundred or so years of life left, but that century to come would draw heavily on the mechanisms for the great task that had been worked out over the first sixty years of the movement's history.

I

The Elizabethan Contribution
The Celebration of Order, 1570–1610

At a time when doctrinal dispute within the Church of England was at a low ebb, the Puritan movement was at its most visible as measured by programmatic statements, recognized leadership, and, in the 1580s, formal organization. This overt distinctiveness elicited a reaction from the government and the hierarchy that seems unjustified by the substantive differences over liturgy and polity. What the Elizabethan Puritans had to say, particularly what they chose to demand, becomes of peculiar interest precisely because of these two circumstances. In its Elizabethan phase, as in no other subsequent formulation, the Puritan movement's defining imperatives are most easily disentangled from a broader Protestant consensus dominating so much in English religious life. The immediate progenitors of the American colonists often muted and modulated the distinguishing features of the Puritan movement in their commitment to working within the recognized limitations of church and state. But at full cry, unrestrained by temperamental or tactical moderation, the Elizabethans eerily anticipated their radical descendants on both sides of the Atlantic a full half-century later. John Udall in 1588 laid down the method for the congregation's choice of its minister with an exactitude that could have been incorporated into the Cambridge Platform. The authors of the Marprelate tracts of 1589, the most uncompromising of Puritan manifestos before 1640, required resistance to antichristian bishops on a scale merely echoed by Alexander Leighton and William Prynne in a later generation. And, perhaps most significantly, the Dedham "orders" of 1585 might have served as a blueprint for a large fraction of the Puritan edifice gradually erected in New England over the course of the latter part of the seventeenth century. Often cited for one part or another, this classic Puritan text is rarely examined in its totality, though the comprehensiveness and common purpose of the various articles is the most revealing aspect of the

33

document. Carefully read, the Dedham orders reveal in an unusually stark formulation the recurrent, even obsessive, themes that preoccupied the Puritan movement from the admonitionists of 1572 to the heyday of Increase and Cotton Mather.

The document is recorded in the minute book of the secret classis of clergymen who met in the Essex town of Dedham and takes the form of a proposed agreement between the two ministers of the town and the "Auncients of the Congregation," very evidently at the instance of the former. The orders were drawn up on 9 August 1585 and accepted on 20 October in "a profession freely made and approved by the voyces and handes" of the town's nine leading inhabitants, who undertook to "joigne together" for that favorite Elizabethan goal, "the observation and mayntenance of all christian order as well in our owne persons and families as also on the whole body of the towne, and for the banishing of the contrary disorder." Christian order in Dedham was defined by a set of fifteen articles requiring the cooperation of church and town governors at every stage, and so much of this program spells out just what the Puritans were up to that all fifteen are worth dwelling on briefly before considering them as a whole.[1]

Several of the articles merely make an attempt—not a very successful one, in the end—to bring some semblance of decorum to the chaos of Elizabethan parochial worship. One can gain some slight sense of the problem from the work of a Puritan minister belonging to the Bury classis, the northern neighbor of the Dedham meeting, who composed an authoritative treatise on the Sabbath at about the same time the orders were being drawn up. Nicholas Bownd devoted pages to persuading the worshipers not to bring their hunting hawks into church during the service, and he repeatedly criticized the casual manner in which the members of a household would straggle in during public worship and then straggle out again: "First comes the man, then a quarter of an houre after his wife, and after her, I cannot tell how long, especially the maidservants, who must needes bee as long after her, as the menservants are after him."[2] The Dedham ancients did not address the question of the hawks, but they did agree to get "all governors of household[s]" to come to worship in a body with their servants before the service began, as well as to sit through the entire proceeding, and they proposed to keep the Sabbath strictly "in holie exercises publikely and at home." To give direction to the newly methodized religious life of the community the sacrament would henceforth be offered once a month (an increase in frequency), and this new communion Sunday would become the focus for disciplining the townspeople in systematic Christianity. On the Wednesday, Thursday, and Saturday before communion "maryed persons or householders" would repair to church at six in the morning to be examined in their Christian knowledge, and the Dedham youth came in for the same treatment on Saturday afternoon. (These educational arrangements were fleshed out in further articles dealing with compulsory catechizing of the youth and with the householders' obligation to attend the two weekly lecture sermons, bringing as many of their servants as could be spared from their trades.) On Sunday, at the communion itself, the churchwardens were to take a collection for the poor, "after the cuppe be delyvered," while making sure that the communicants "sytte orderly and comly in their places," presumably to prevent them from walking away from their charitable duties. And on the Tuesday following, the two ministers and the "ancients" would meet "to conferre of matters concerninge the good government of the towne."

No less than seven of the fifteen articles explain the meaning of good government in the Puritan sense. Two dealing exclusively with the poor are as concerned with reformation as with relief. In proportion to their abilities, the townspeople were to invite into their houses "such of their poore neighbors as have submitted themselves to the good orders of the Churche, and walke christianly and honestlie in their callinges." Additionally, the two ministers and a few of the ancients, "alwaies accompanied with one of the Constables," were to make quarterly inspections of the poor, "and chiefly the suspected places, that understandinge the miserable estate of those that wante and the naughtie disposition of disordered persons, they may provide for them accordinglie." Another two articles envision a fully literate Dedham: all the young were to be taught to read (the poor at public expense), and any new illiterates kept from settling in town by an agreement among the ministers and the "governors" of families to employ only apprentices already able to read. Still other disorders were to be remedied by providing a special ceremony of public humiliation for married couples known to have been guilty of prenuptial fornication and by an agreement to force out of town unattached individuals who were neither responsible for themselves by virtue of possessing a household or honest calling nor "retayned of any" who might undertake their edification and discipline.

The one remaining article, the eighth in order, will look familiar to students of the New England town. On top of knowledge and virtue, admission to communion would require a pledge of love and harmony: "8. Item. that so many as shalbe admitted to the Communion promise and professe to live charitablie with all their neighbors, and if any occasion of displeasure arise, that they refraiginge from all discord or revenging by wordes, actions or suites will firste make the mynister and two other godlie and indifferent neighbors acquaynted with the state of their causes before they proceed further by lawe or compleint out of the towne." With only a slight change in wording and none whatever in substance, this item might be the third term of the town covenant of Dedham, Massachusetts, in 1639.[3] A direct connection between the two documents, separated by over fifty years, is conjectural at best, and it is not necessary to find an unbroken line of descent. Some local mechanism for mediation is not unique—Kilby in Northamptonshire and the town of Northampton had similar devices—and, when taken by itself, not especially significant for the Puritan movement. Certainly, the elusive hope of living in charity with one's neighbors should not be seen either as the swelling up of some sort of peasant communalism or as an assertion of a peculiar attachment to local control, though both interpretations have been aired.[4]

Like the other fourteen articles, item eight was ministerially inspired and intended to be imposed from above as part of an attempt to cure old and, by Puritan lights, bad habits. English villagers playing their time-honored game of deadly malice against their neighbors were not fit members of the body of Christ by anyone's standards and should be kept from communion until reconciled. In any case, they often refused to share the sacrament with their enemies while the recurring cycle of feuding was going on. A few months before the Dedham orders were drawn up, another member of the classis, Henry Sands of Boxford, later to have a decisive influence on the Winthrop family, asked his fellow ministers what to do about members of his congregation who "wold come to the worde diligently but tooke every light occasions of brawles to hinder their comming to the Communion." Three years later the vicar of Wenham was asking the same body if he could bar from the sacrament "a couple of persons that were in hatred one against thother for wordes defamatory, viz. saying that he had killed a sheepe." And so it went during the brief life of the Dedham classis, just as it had always gone whenever English countrymen lived near enough to one another to alternate defamation with battery (and the attendant lawsuits on both counts) in about equal measures. The proposed compulsory mediation in the village of Dedham was an abortive attempt to short-circuit these quarrels before they had hardened into a way of life through tedious prosecutions in the church and common law courts.[5] The minister and the ancients were expected to function as an informal and decidedly extralegal congregational consistory, but the classis as a whole had no special love for local government per se. With an indifference as to means they referred cases of "disorder" requiring outside help variously to the household governors, the leaders of the towns, the county justices of the peace, and, at least once, the bishop of London, not to mention calling in a great magnate such as Robert, Lord Rich when the occasion warranted.[6] In strictly spiritual affairs discipline at the local, congregational level always had a fascination for the Puritans, but the demands of their overall program and the personal and institutional ties of their clerical element routinely generated crosscurrents pulling in the direction of centralization.

No one article in the Dedham orders matters as much as the concept of order affirmed by all of them jointly. For this Essex town to achieve godliness by Puritan standards every available institution, civil and ecclesiastical, would have been pressed into service, and in a coordinated manner. At the root of this enduring Puritan obsession was a severely guarded optimism about human nature. "Great and diligent teaching" would be necessary "because men are made of a dull metal, and hard to conteine spirituall and heavenly things."[7] Nevertheless, the perverse human heart could be reached, bringing salvation for the elect and at least a degree of external decency for the rest, but only by a systematic and continuous assault on all fronts. Most of the elements of the projected Puritan machine were in place in the Dedham orders: literacy, charity, voluntary regimentation, drill, and discipline, as well as the exclusion of the uncontrollable and an extra dose of the universal supervision for servants, youth, and the poor, suspect classes presumed disorderly by nature. Even the insistence on "humbling" erring couples when they presented for baptism the proof of their sin, a baby born less than nine months after their marriage, is a perfect instance of Puritan "reproof." The minister was to "publikely note and declare out the fault to all the congregation," but the couple was not required to do some form of penance, the punishment the same offense would have merited in the ecclesiastical courts. Rather, though punishing the transgressors and serving as a deterrent to potential sinners, reproof was mainly a didactic public rite that inculcated and overtly affirmed the collective commitment. In New England the county courts would deal with prenuptial fornication, but the method of treatment would be nearly identical. Whether administered by magistrate, consistory, or body of the congregation, the Puritan exercise of justice was supposed to be in its way a kind of public worship and a means of mass edification, part of that larger edifice needed to bring people to godly courses despite themselves.

Later generations of Puritans would have found the Dedham orders and the various schema of the Elizabethan Puritans in general to have struck a relatively one-sided balance between order and love and between participation and regimentation. As the size, autonomy, and reputation of the godly grew—that is, as the sectarian thrust in Puritanism became more overt—a more equal emphasis would fall on these competing motifs. All of the towns-people would sign the Dedham, Massachusetts, covenant, and they would do their godly walking in the name of love as well as of obedience. But the most fundamental of Puritan assumptions remained as it had been when first enunciated by the Elizabethans: that the fate of individual believers was inseparable from their cultural and social circumstances. The Elizabethans proposed to address those circumstances and to order them for their own purposes, and this fact accounts both for their passing peculiarities and for their often remarkable prescience in anticipating the arrangements their suc-cessors would make at a much later date and on another continent.

The nature of their challenge, as the Elizabethans conceived it, is best illus-trated by one of their more engaging literary devices. Puritan propagandists liked to put speeches in the mouths of fictional honest countrymen, simple rustic souls going straight to hell because of their untutored reliance on earthy commonplaces and a vaguely defined bonhomie. Typifying the "com-mon professors," they were the products of a Catholic heritage and of the paper Protestantism of the present, convenient religious settlement. George Gifford's "Atheos," for example, declines to look too deeply into theology on the grounds that "it was never merry since men unlearned have medled with the scriptures" and declares his allegiance to the ignorant ways of "our forefathers" because "then they lived in friendshippe, and made merrie to-gether, now there is no good neighbourhoode: now every man for himselfe and are readie to pull one another by the throate." Not really an atheist, Atheos sums up the "country divinity" when he declares that "I meane well: I hurt no man nor I thinke no man any hurte: I love God above all: and put my whole trust in him: what would yee have more?" His notion of worship is equally ingenuous. "Is it not inough," he tells Gifford's persona Zelotes, "for plaine country men, plow men, Tailours, and such other, for to have their ten commaundementes, the Lords prayer, and the Beleefe [Creed]: I thinke these may suffice us, what shoulde wee meddle further?"[8]

These reprobate Sancho Panzas, and not some latter-day equivalent of Aristides the Just, form the original of the "Civil Man," one of a triptych of stock villains in the sermon literature along with the dissembling hypocrite and the superstitious formalist. Ignorant of doctrine, resistant to any but the most resolute teaching, the typical common professors are presented as nice enough sorts who have no idea of the meaning of the ritual confession of sin they make every Sunday and who hope to get by through occasional good works and their comparative insignificance. After all, their neighbors are no better than they are; many, indeed, are worse. But they have heard "some better learned" speak of the general promises of mercy in the Scripture, and that will suffice them. Except as a blurred jumble of familiar-sounding passages, they have no sense of the Bible and when examined in the official predestinarian dogma of their church by a knowledgeable interrogator, they become confused or angry and end the conversation with a shrug: "But al this time while you reason with us of these matters, we thinke our selves in a wildernes, or as a fish out of the water, and so glad as may be to be rid of your company. And some of us will not answere you at all, but shake you off as busie bodies in great anger, willing you to see to your owne soules, and let ours alone."[9]

Our own sympathies are probably with the honest countrymen, not with the university-educated missionaries who would forcibly intrude total depravity and unalterable decrees into their simple and good-natured universe. Before we rush to side with the rustics, however, it might be well to recall that the motives of the Puritan preacher included a respect for the capacities of ordinary and obscure individuals uncommon in an age that usually saw in the population at large only the many-headed monster. A later and more romantic generation would find sermons in stone instead of in the pulpits and thus idealize the natural wisdom of country folk. The Puritans were unaware that there was any wisdom there to idealize, but they did insist that all but the intellectually impaired had the right and duty to confront complex doctrine. It would be an uphill fight, to be sure, when "even of nature all men seeke lets unto themselves in hearing the word," and many of the country people who were given access to the means of grace were foredoomed to reject them, justifying their reprobation. But before the few could be chosen, the many must be called—"hardly men do well with teaching, never without."[10]

Teaching, unfortunately, was hard to find in the England of Elizabeth if the ideal envisioned was a learned minister systematically expounding Scripture to a comprehending audience. The coming of Protestantism made an educated clergy all but mandatory, but the politics of the Reformation had seriously weakened the nation's clerical establishment. A gradual increase in the number of the trained minority among the sixteenth-century ministers was seriously interrupted by the successive purges of the Marian reaction and the Elizabethan reform, and it had become necessary to ordain unqualified replacements simply to have enough clergy to staff rural parishes. The Reformation also further weakened the already shaky funding of the parish clergy by the wholesale scramble for parochial "impropriations" that resulted from the crown's acquisition and resale of monastic and episcopal lands. But through outright expropriation of the tithes and "simonical bargains" forced on a minister as the price of his presentation, the new "cormorant patrons" of the parish livings left them with insufficient revenues to attract qualified candidates.[11] In some areas the Puritan gentry were among the chief of sinners in their treatment of impropriations, but they were no worse than the Oxford and Cambridge colleges that funded their fellowships out of the same sources or than those bishops who repaired the ravaged finances of their dioceses by imitating the lay piracy of parochial resources. In Yorkshire, where the Puritan patrons had a relatively good record on this score and the archbishops a deplorable one, Robert Moore, a longtime Puritan minister fortunate enough to obtain title to a rectory with restored revenues, summed up the effect of impropriation in his will of 1642:

> But most wofull and lamentable above all other abuses are those
> dangerous and sacrilegious robberyes and spoyles of our Churches both
> in the South and in the North parts whereby our Rectories and Parson-
> ages are impropriated and wrongfully turned into the possession of Cov-
> etous worldlings and soe into Vicarages and miserable Curateshipps of 5
> li x li or 20 Markes pensions per annum or the like. . . . Satan hath too
> violently and necessarily drawne in a nother mischiefe worse (if possible)
> then the former which is our blind Guides or ignorant reading Ministers
> the very Poison and plague of our Churches the disgrace and shame of
> the gospell and distruct[i]on of our people from [in]sufficient mainte-
> nance hath bred insufficient Ministers and these Two are the most wofull
> and dangerous in our English Church and most necessarye to bee
> reformed.[12]

As Moore wrote, one evil bred the other. Inadequate livings made it difficult to attract talented preachers and encouraged clerical pluralism, by which one man pieced together a living from several benefices and hired a curate at desperately low pay for the parishes in which he did not reside. The undereducated, "subprofessional" clergy willing to serve under such conditions accounted for the major portion of the jolly "Sir Johns" who had nothing to share with the Atheoses except a common ignorance and a taste for a careless, thoughtless, all-too-amiable style of life. Throughout the reign of Elizabeth, Puritan polemicists, especially the Presbyterian radicals, took a scandalmonger's delight in circulating long lists of "unpreaching" and vicious clergy, broken down region by region with complete particulars on the various individuals' failings. With an anachronistic love of statistics they reckoned up that "scarce in the tenth parysh of this realme ... there is resydent a vygalant and watchefull shephard or pastor," or, in another version of the calculation, that "throughout the land where these blind guides be" there were "not past two or three of an hundred" parishioners who could give a meaningful account of their faith as Protestants. A more pessimistic bit of arithmetic put the proportion at four or five in a thousand, but either way the prospect of a Catholic restoration was held to be near enough, should there be another shift in political fortunes, when "three parts at least of the people of this lands [are] so ignorant and wedded to theyr olde superstytion styll."[13]

Begin with this conception of the task to be undertaken and of the limitations of the established means for undertaking it, and the vexed and obscure controversies over both conformity and church government become a little more comprehensible in all their ambiguity. Though argued out in absolute terms, the Elizabethan polemics were conditioned by the preachers' perception of their own mission and of their audience. For this reason, conformity in time became an increasingly tractable issue, but government remained a sticking point between Puritan and bishop and, as it turned out, between Puritan and Puritan.

The opponents of conformity made their most telling arguments on pragmatic grounds, in their complaints about the subversive effects of the ceremonies, rather than through the exchanges of competing scriptural exegeses. Even at its best, ran their critique, the Book of Common Prayer, in prescribing an elaborate ceremonial as part of required worship, indirectly legitimated the standing of a minister so ignorant that he needed directions as to "where to stande, to sit, to kneele, to move, to lift up or let downe his voyce." Such a creature would suit very well the tastes of the honest countrymen, disinclined to think through the unpleasant truths of original sin and not likely to be troubled by them when a reading minister was all they had for a pastor. Instead, they would be reassured by the uncritical droning out of portions of the Bible, "which wee heare as a storie that concerned the people of olde time, without any further application thereof unto our selves." After a little further memorizing of the Lord's Prayer, the Creed, the Decalogue, "and peradventure some part of the Catechisme: (which we know full little what they meane)," they would think themselves "to be in as good case, and as farre forward in the way of salvation" as the most determined sermon goer.[14]

At the worst, the "popish dregs" left intact in the ceremonies could confirm an obdurately ignorant populace in the old superstition. One young nonconformist minister, growing eloquent on the "superstitious speaches of the people," announced that "a thousand in Shropshire" believed the sign of the cross in baptism was necessary to the salvation of their children and lectured the bishop of Coventry and Lichfield that "by your practise" the people of the area would fall "into a seconde poperye that wilbe worse then the first."[15] The repatriated Marian exile Anthony Gilby, who had good reason to call himself the pope's "sworn enemy," seconded the point in 1581 in a bitter condemnation addressed to conformist ministers by a longtime sufferer for the cause: "My harte ariseth in my body, when I see thee and thy fellows cloathed like his Chaplaines, that burned the blessed Bible, and our faythfull fathers, and deare Brethren in our eyes."[16]

Nonconformist and *Puritan* rapidly became interchangeable terms, and conformity was made the standard test of loyalty to the establishment from the vestments controversy of 1565 to the act of uniformity almost a century later. In the 1580s the radical wing of the Puritan movement, despite its admission that its aims extended to church government, was able to put together a precarious Presbyterian coalition largely on the basis of pervasive hostility to ritualism, especially after Archbishop John Whitgift imposed a test oath in 1583 requiring an unqualified endorsement of the ceremonies.[17] Yet the subject remained curiously negotiable, belying the elaborate critiques of conformity that make up such a large part of the literature of Puritan dissent. In 1588, for example, Robert Lewis, in trouble with the church courts, inquired plaintively of his fellow members of the Dedham classis "whether he might weare the surplice, rather than forsake his mynistery." He was neither the first nor the last nonconformist clergyman under pressure to ask that question. Had he only known it, he could have claimed a good precedent in the archspokesman of Elizabethan Puritanism, Thomas Cartwright, who was sorely beset by much the same temptation about 1577.[18] Under Whitgift, Richard Bancroft, and even Laud, when the campaign for conformity was pressed vigorously enough, the relatively small numbers of intransigents who gave up their ministry were dwarfed by the majority of ministers blowing with the episcopal wind, at least until the bishops' visitors were looking into the affairs of some other parish.

The ceremonies were unpalatable but not unendurable, except in certain contexts. The vivid memory of the recent Catholic past, when the surplice was the "livery" of Antichrist, died out with the Anthony Gilbys—and it was Gilby who had the moral authority to recall the wavering Thomas Cartwright in 1577. Similarly, the ceremonies that seemed so objectionable when read out by an ignorant minister to an easygoing band of rural solipsists in a manner that made "all the English service, like the old Mattins and Masse," became far more palatable when part of a routine including several powerful sermons a week attended by an earnest, mostly literate audience.[19] If anything, it could seem more than a little perverse to lay down one's ministry over the ceremonies when good preachers were hard to find, thereby exalting a delicate conscience over the obligation to bring the message of salvation to hungry souls. "Many of our Ministers are content to yeald to some things which they judge not so counvenient (if it did otherwise some good to the State) to the end they may utter the truth," William Bradshaw wrote in 1614, early in the eminently endurable regime of Archbishop Abbot. Bradshaw was not one of this pliable many, but he had no special difficulty in understanding the logic of the compromise.[20]

One could use the same circumstances to make the counterargument that to deprive scrupulous ministers for omitting ceremonies of no great value in themselves was to squander the church's limited preaching resources when they were most needed. More moderate Puritans used this line as their standard apology and found some sympathy for it among equally moderate members of the episcopal bench, who kept their demands for conformity to a satisfactory symbolic minimum. But there was a hard core of radicals in the Puritan movement for whom no such pleasant accommodation was possible because their differences with the establishment went much deeper. For them preaching was just one-half of the minister's office in guiding his reluctant sheep. The other half was the "discipline" or "government" of the church, in the words of the architects of the Presbyterian organization, John Field and Thomas Wilcox, a matter "of far greater waight and importaunce, then ceremonies, and therefore more earnestly to be sought for, and quickly pursued after."[21] From the Elizabethan Presbyterians to the Civil War Independents, polity was the rock on which radical Puritanism was built and on which the movement as a whole repeatedly foundered.

Thomas Cartwright is usually thought of as initiating a specifically Presbyterian phase of Puritanism when he announced in 1570 that the Scriptures permitted and required only one form of church government, but the Congregationalists in both England and America also claimed him as their progenitor. At issue for the Elizabethan militants, as well as for their radical successors until the confused period of the 1640s, was less the various details of congregational liberty and ministerial authority than the simple and prior assertion of the centrality of government to an effective reformation. Moderate Puritans of the stripe of the famous and irenic soul doctors William

Perkins and Richard Greenham flirted with the classical movement briefly and then quickly abandoned it in the face of government disapproval because they did not find the necessity of discipline great enough to justify either disobedience to the prince or a possible schism in a church still able to work much good through its imperfect constitution.[22] The radicals of the Elizabethan phase of the movement were of a fierier temperament to begin with, but they also could not envision that a wrongly constituted church could accomplish very much in the way of reformation, whatever the power of its preachers or the truth of its doctrine. John Udall, who went to prison over the point, wrote in the climactic year of 1588 that the bishops might "think that government not so needfull, and your fault but small (if it be any) in continuing your course begon." They were wrong—willfully wrong if truth were told as Udall chose to tell it. The clear word of Scripture dictated only one form of church government by *jus divinum*, and "the gospell can take no roote, nor have any free passage, for want of it." Failure to provide this government for the church was "the cause, of all the ignorance, Atheisme, schismes, treasons, poperie and ungodlines, that is to be founde in this land."[23]

What, then, was the true government of the church? Anthony Gilby was lapidary enough in defining it in 1577, when he argued Cartwright out of conformity—"ministers electede by the Congregation, and grave Elders that will be carefull for the flocke." Instead, good or bad, the ministers of the Church of England were thrust on the flock by "the hands of the byshop alone" (the words of Field and Wilcox), and the disciplining of the people was carried on under unreformed canon law in church courts, "which make a riche gayne of sinne" (Gilby again).[24] If the patrons had always made a wise choice and the church courts had routinely exercised a judicious and effective severity (both propositions necessarily contrary-to-fact conditionals in the eyes of the radicals), the whole exercise would still have been accounted miserably disordered. Without the self-conscious participation of the people, religion would remain an affair of my lord and his cleric. The honest countryman would probably pay his betters their due by sweating through the appointed incumbent's sermons, at least on some Sundays. He would do his best to avoid trouble with the church courts, and when he did come foul of them he would hire a proctor to represent him and, if convicted, he would try to get his penance commuted to a money fine. Otherwise, he would spend the rest of his life unaffected by the gospel, imagining that the only real sin a poor man was capable of was bad fellowship. Government for the radicals was the weapon needed to break into this happy-go-lucky mind-set and bring its victims to active, intelligent membership in the ordered universe of meaningful Christian faith.

The people would hear and understand their minister not just when he preached well but when he was genuinely *their* pastor. As John Udall wrote, "but for the people to consent in the election of their governors procureth greatest reverence, in their hearts towards them: Therefore election by the people is the best, and all others bee unlawfull." Having made trial of a candidate's gifts, the congregation in calling him to his clerical office would comprehend with full force the joint commitment of people to pastor and pastor to people, and they would learn the real meaning of their common pursuit of their faith when they saw and participated in the ceremony that ordained him to minister over them in particular. For a bishop to lay his hands on a man and then call him a priest was only a pointless carryover from the Catholic past; for the elders of the congregation to do the same in the name of the flock that had chosen him their shepherd "affecteth the ordeyners, when they feele him for whom they pray; and the ordeyned when he feeleth a calling and charge from God (as it were) sensiblie comming upon him, and the congregation, when they see him seperated from the rest, by whome they shall reape muche comfort or griefe."[25]

To the objection that "our people be ignorante" and therefore incapable of a wise choice of minister came the reply that if only there were enough competent preaching they would not remain so long. "We should also finde our people to have knowledge, if they had teaching," as John Udall put it, adding for good measure that even a benighted flock could hardly come up with a worse minister than the man they generally ended up stuck with by the patron's appointment and the bishop's approbation. Further, there were precautions that could be taken because, as ever, the particular exercise of calling a minister could not be separated from the reform of the church as a whole. "If Gods order had hir place" in England, the popular choice would be drawn from an ample pool of qualified candidates sent from "the schooles of the prophets," and "some grave and good minister" would direct the congregation "which should be the manner in the elections."[26] Popular consent was not primarily an end in itself for Udall or for most of the other radicals, some of whom proposed even sharper limitations on the democratic element in their ideal polity.[27] Consent of some sort there must be, but above all as a means of allowing the gospel to take root. Knowledge, assuming that precious commodity could be obtained through preaching, would broaden into faith, a sense of the personal application of abstract dogma, through the believer's tangible participation in the fabric and ongoing struggle of the instituted church.

Discipline, in the narrow sense of the reformation of sinful offenses, was the counterpoint to the same theme, if that metaphor is not an understatement for what hostile observers took to be the radicals' idée fixe. The nick-name *disciplinarian* faction indicates its significance, as does the label *presby-terian*, which refers to the congregational presbytery or eldership ("the verie senew of Christs Church") intended to replace the church courts as the source of judgment. A parish ideally would have two ministers, a teacher to expound the Scriptures and a pastor (the senior order, let it be noted) to bring them home by instruction, application, and general admonition. The two, together with elected lay elders, would constitute the seigniory or pres-bytery, the congregation's executive and its judicial tribunal, exercising sanc-tions that extended from mild personal admonitions to full-scale excom-munication. Whether, and to what degree, appeals might be carried beyond the individual congregation was an unresolved and mostly undebated prob-lem for the Elizabethans; it becomes significant only in light of the Presbyte-rian-Independent divisions of the Civil War, a very different phenomenon than the Elizabethan search for an effective ecclesiastical order. Appeals or not, the congregational seigniory was to be fully competent and the principal court of judicature. Only when discipline was local would it perform its God-ordained didactic function, "whereby men learne to frame their wylles and doyngs accordyng to the law of God, by instructing and admonishing one another, yea and by correcting and punishing all wylfull persones, and contemners of the same."[28]

In discipline the Presbyterians had come up with another form of guided choice to indoctrinate a parish conceived of, as always, as a core of believing Christians leavening a lump of civil men. The congregation would learn what the word really meant by participating in the ceremony of correcting sin. The sinner would be tried and punished in front of them, in their name, possibly even with their consent in some indirect way. (Udall implies as much, but the question was a tricky one and never fully opened.) The remote and mechani-cal operations of the church courts, the Puritans held, even when they were not ineffective or corrupt, effectively taught the gospel's irrelevance and un-did whatever good a painful preacher might have done. "Diligent care," according to a Puritan statement drawn up for the Parliament of 1586, needed to "be had that the word be not despised and troden under foote, and therfore, according as it is preched, so it be executed."[29] The effect of disci-pline in punishing and reforming the sinner was important but secondary to its collective exercise by and for all who would be believers. Discipline, that is, was the cutting edge of the gospel. Preaching alone would not turn Atheos into Zelotes—he was much too shrewd for that. But preaching by an elected minister to an informed congregation, coupled with the collective exercise of discipline and, as opportunities permitted, the cooperation of the local authorities on the order of the Dedham agreement, might, taken together, each element reinforcing the other, slowly inculcate vital religion in selected areas and create oases of godliness in the semipagan desert. It was by definition a tightly focused rather than a broad-spectrum approach, but given the realities of Elizabethan England, for the Presbyterians it was what they had.

Perhaps the most startling aspect of the various Elizabethan radical programs is the degree to which they anticipate the Congregationalism of the 1630s and 1640s rather than the rival Presbyterianism of the Westminster Assembly. As early as 1611 George Downame noticed that the "new disciplinarians," who claimed Cartwright as their prophet, were far more sympathetic to the autonomy of "Parishionall Presbyteries" than the "elder" school of Calvin and Théodore Beza.[30] At their most extreme (not necessarily their most typical) archradicals like Field and Wilcox look decidedly out of place in a formal Presbyterian movement, as when they define a church in 1572 as "a company or congregatione of the faythfull called and gathered out of the worlde" and hold that "it is not lawfull for any church to challendge, usurpe, or exercise any sovereigntie or rule over another." These assertions may betray the influence, later seriously diluted, of early Separatist contacts before it became apparent that Separatism implicitly required the repudiation of a pervasive religious establishment.[31] Even at their most corporate, however, the Elizabethan radicals usually thought of England as a collection of congregations, in the plural, supervised by ministerially dominated regional associations of highly uncertain authority. On two questions, the representative status of the congregational presbytery and the extent of classical authority over individual congregations, the Elizabethan Presbyterians were divided and rather fuzzy compared to their seventeenth-century Congregational successors. Had they been pressed on the subject, as they never were, they probably would have been forced to champion the authority of the elders over the people and the classical eldership at the expense of any individual congregation. This balance would shift after 1603, at least on paper, but in practice the enduring hallmark of all the Puritan radicals of all periods remained their absorption with the individual congregation and the significance of its members' active involvement in the life of the churches. If practice alone is to be consulted, the Dedham classis functioned very much like a late seventeenth-century Massachusetts ministerial association.[32] The Westminster Assembly would be the first body to assume that to spell out a "Presbyterian" platform required concentrating on a detailed description of the rights, powers, and duties of a reformed hierarchy of presbyters. Before 1642 or so, as the Independent minority in the assembly pointed out with a certain relish, the literature of the English Puritans contained almost nothing advocating "a combined classical Presbyteriall government as it is *authoritatively* practiced in the most reformed Churches." Rather, "the full strength and streame of our Non-conformists writyings" was devoted to an attack on episcopal government "and in maintayning those severall officers in [individual] churches which Christ hath instituted in stead thereof."[33]

The contrast between Presbyterian and Congregational goes fatally amiss in seeing the issue in terms of the positions of the 1640s, when English Presbyterianism was a very different creature than its sixteenth-century namesake. In the Elizabethan period it would have been hard to find rigorous philosophical commitment to the distinguishing shibboleths of a later era— "no church larger than a congregation," for example. Nor are such meticulously absolute definitions important in tracing the genealogy of radical Puritanism. The seventeenth-century Congregationalists, and especially the New Englanders, end up in a direct line of descent from the Elizabethans mainly because of their common conviction about the centrality of polity as a means for stirring up and disciplining the faith that brought people to obedience and love. In the seventeenth century the Congregationalists turned out to be the champions of the grave seigniory in each church, complete with its two distinct kinds of ministers and its elected lay specialists in government, the ruling elders. The platform of discipline that came out of the Westminster Assembly had only a few words to devote to the office of ruling elder, but the subject received extended discussion in New England. And in the conflicts over polity in the assembly, "the Independent men . . . were for the divine institution of a Doctor in every congregation as well as a Pastor," but the majority was "extremlie opposite," insisting "somewhat bitterlie" on the two offices' "simple identitie."[34] To those who did not share in the assumptions behind them, the mechanisms of the radical program always seemed impossibly overelaborate, whether the reign was that of Elizabeth or Charles I.

Most members of the Puritan movement, including those who enlisted under the Presbyterian banner when it was displayed from time to time, really did not care much about what the Yorkshire veteran Robert Moore in 1642 called "things of small matter not touching matter but manner . . . not piety but pollity."[35] The case for Presbyterianism as a scripturally dictated necessity did get a revival of sorts in the 1640s, partly because of an injection of Scottish blood into the debate, but for most English Puritans most of the time, including the Interregnum, it seemed incredible that the subject was worth fighting over unless one were a sectary, a fanatic, or a Scot. The repeated preference of the majority for "Presbyterian" solutions represented nothing more for most of them than a practical response to the hard realities of taking over the national church intact. If the hated hierarchy was to be replaced and a reformed liturgy and ministry imposed, then the easiest single way of carrying on the remodeled and Puritanized Church of England was simply to substitute mixed commissions of clergy and laity at the diocesan level to continue all of the old episcopal functions, including ordination, visitation, licensing of preachers, and discipline. In this respect the 1580s were not very much different from the 1640s. The proposed reform legislation put before the Elizabethan sessions of Parliament by Puritan MPs bears only an oblique relationship to the literature on polity put out by the movement's clerical theoreticians and concentrates instead on the area where the latter said least, supraparochial administration, leaving little space and less responsibility to the individual congregations except as the lowest unit in a hierarchical organization now sans bishops.[36] Had the Elizabethan movement been granted a modicum of the temporary success enjoyed by the Puritans of the Civil War, the same conflicts that appeared during the Interregnum might have been played out fifty years ahead of schedule, with the genuine Presbyterians cast as the defenders of the congregations against the Erastian compromises spun out by a majority among clergy and Parliament that was willing to settle for a suitably purged version of the existing establishment.

The differences between radicals and pragmatists within the movement came down in the end to a reflection of the enduring Puritan double vision. The moderates saw only the mass of the unconverted—to be reached by powerful preaching, however secured, and even at the cost of some minimal concessions to ceremonialism. Otherwise, the Catholic "wolves" would quickly regain control of ignorant and shepherdless flocks. Consequently, although Presbyterian government might be generally preferable to episcopal, even the latter was acceptable if the bishops did not push conformity too energetically and showed themselves reasonably enthusiastic in the good cause.[37] Patronage, similarly, was the source of frequent abuses, but in the hands of well-affected gentry it was a weapon as well and, therefore, not an issue of the first magnitude in any campaign for reform. The radicals, by contrast, made government an absolute, even in the work of conversion, because they had witnessed a primitive foreshadowing of their new order in the lively, semiautonomous religious life of their most enthusiastic converts. They had lived with the godly, had encouraged their sense of separateness, and had become sensitive enough to their volatility to insist on the rights of the congregation in the choice of its minister and the correction of its members and also to be frightened of the consequences if the ideal government were not effected. "We can not see," 175 Northampton petitioners informed the queen in 1583, "how the Lord should holde his revenging hand from punishing this slackenes in the rulers and most horrible and grievous sinne in the subjects, which aboundeth infinite waies more then it should doe, if we had this discipline."[38]

On the whole, moderates and radicals often spoke from very different kinds of experiences. A moderate such as Richard Greenham doubted he had made one convert during a particularly strenuous and systematic ministry at Dry Dayton, Cambridge, but John Udall as a lecturer at Kingston-upon-Thames in Surrey had little difficulty in attracting a select band of the "children of God," who engaged in private exercises on a regular basis and developed an exclusive form of communion. The difference was institutional as well as personal: Greenham was a rector charged with responsibility for the entire parish; Udall, like the overwhelming majority of the radical leadership, enjoyed the status of lecturer. The latter position was that of an unbeneficed stipendiary preacher who had no formal pastoral duties and was free to gather an informal cure (sometimes at the expense of the parochial incumbent) solely out of such zealous souls as responded to his sermons.[39]

Though the lecturer's unofficial position was peculiarly suited to serving as a nucleus for sectarian activity, the problem went deeper, to the root of the Puritan clergy's fundamental tactical dilemma. If the full quota of Puritan reforms had somehow been implemented early in the reign of Elizabeth, the radical wing of the movement would never have developed such a distinct sectarian impulse. But the radicals were never able to resort to their preferred means of persuasion and coercion and so found themselves in their alternative schemes calling out the godly from the mass of the population even as they attempted to do their duty to the unconverted. In the absence of a universal preaching ministry, for example, a supplementary exercise merely intended for "stirring up and increasing of the ministers gifts" among the people might end up as what Archbishop Whitgift would call a conventicle because it competed effectively with all of the regularly ordained services throughout the entire neighborhood, bringing together the self-selected godly without regard to the parish of their residence.[40] Circulation of Puritan controversial tracts had the same effect: addressed to all open-minded individuals, they were actually passed around for safety's sake only among true believers, reinforcing their common sense of belonging to a chosen people. Bancroft, who made this underground literature his special study, complained that "there be no precisians in England, though by a great distance of place they be severed, but they know by reports one another."[41] Even the lack of effective congregational discipline tended in the same direction because the conscientious Puritan minister found himself encouraging one or another form of social ostracism as a replacement for the sacramental excommunication reserved to the episcopal courts. Rendering its advice in 1589, just as it was about to expire, the Dedham classis endorsed "discountenancing" as a way of correcting spiritual offenders in "thenglishe Churche (where the right discipline is not in use)." The exercise required the offending individual's neighbors to withdraw "from him the common tokens of love and cheerful salutations," while nearby ministers and magistrates harassed both "the private offendors and negligent backwarde professors of the congregation to their Christian duities in this behalfe."[42]

As early as the late Elizabethan period the Puritan ministry was already feeling the tug between its loyalty to the ideal of a comprehensive church and the reality that it was often leading only one of two spiritual nations. Another generation of Puritans would patch over the distinction, and still another would have to face up to it—more or less successfully in America, with disastrous consequences at home in Interregnum England. But the Elizabethans never had to deal with the challenge of partial success. Their precarious coalition of moderates and radicals came apart as soon as the cost of opposition to authority became evident.

John Udall accused Elizabeth's bishops of a multitude of sins, but never more succinctly than when he pretended to address them directly in a clandestine pamphlet of 1588: "You care for nothinge but the maintenaunce of your dignities, be it to the damnation of your owne soules, and infinit millions mo[re]."[43] Though hardly a charitable judgment, it was not as sweeping an indictment as the vehemence of Udall's tone suggests, and therein lay much of the weakness of the radical position. Udall did not assume any irreconcilable ideological differences between himself and the remaining limbs of Antichrist in the English church. Though wedded to the perquisites of their offices, the bishops were still presumably sound on doctrine and were not given to making suspiciously neopopish claims about the *jure divino* basis of their office or the special sacerdotal value of the allegedly "indifferent" ceremonies they enforced. Richard Hooker, Lancelot Andrewes, and George Downame were yet to be heard from in 1588, let alone John Cosin, Richard Montagu, and William Laud. Elizabeth's bishops had nothing to fall back upon but the argument that their order was decreed by authority. In 1588, however, that form of appeal was irresistible.

Woven into the fabric of the radical critique of the Church of England was a sustained criticism of institutionalized privilege, and such criticism was presumed to have just one consequence at any point in the sixteenth century: disrespect leading to riot leading to insurrection and assassination. John Aylmer, bishop of London, was being professionally humorless because it was the safest thing for an officer of state to be when he made this traditional equation for the benefit of Lord Treasurer Burghley in 1586. Reporting on "the sower fruites of these newe reformes and especially of such as be mercenarye [i.e., salaried lecturers]," Aylmer described an incident at Maldon in Essex during the course of his episcopal visitation: "One was by certaine younge heades in the towne (men of occupacon there) to be hired to come into the Church besurered [sic; besmeared?] like a foole and to take my Cappe of my heade and to twirle it about his finger, and then to have cast it, and tossed it to and fro amonge them in the middest of the people, whereupon it is not to be doubted but a daungerous tumulte would have risen."[44] Make fun of the miter in the presence of the multitude and the result would be chaos of a sort the more dreadful for being left unspecified. It was nervous logic but plausible enough to those who thought their station made them vulnerable.

The Presbyterians would have denied any such disruptive intentions, and there were plenty of well-to-do laymen who certainly enjoyed a laugh at the expense of the upstart bishops. But criticism long continued and directed at well-established institutions did have an unpleasant way of spilling over beyond its announced targets. It had in the 1540s, it would again in the era of the Great Migration and the Civil War, and it surely did in the 1570s and 1580s. Nominally, the radicals required only the abolition of episcopacy, along with the training of qualified ministers and their placement in the parishes by popular consent and with proper financial support. But where were the personnel and the funding for such a major reform to come from, and what became of the universities, tithes, and rights of patronage while it was in progress? Further, just what verdict did these so-called reformers implicitly render on a ruling class that systematically squeezed the poor for the purpose of misappropriating the funds meant for the care of their souls and took advantage of every known legal trick to foist upon the inhabitants of the parishes "seeley" ministers willing to bargain away three-quarters of their maintenance to grub along on the remainder? The answer to these questions was not especially reassuring, even when coupled with a certain reverence toward the sanctity of private property.

If there was a shortage of educated preachers, more than one Puritan apologist came up with one or another variant on the same proposed solution. Smaller parishes could be united without much regard to the perquisites of their patrons, noblemen could forgo their private chaplains and join the nearest congregation, and the universities could restrict themselves to training ministers, forbidding their students to waste "so much time in other vaine and unprofitable studies, as commonlie thei do." Impropriated tithes were to be "redeemed" in some unspecified way, and the congregation received the right to approve the patron's nominee (in those schemes that bothered to recognize the rights of patronage at all).[45] Quite apart from the loss of income that would be involved, all of these plans casually waived the largesse and personal distinction that were the hallmarks of aristocracy and calmly contemplated reversing the gentry's newly acquired dominance of higher education if the needs of the church required it.

Reform bills put before the parliaments of the 1580s, with their preponderance of gentry MPs in the Commons, naturally displayed considerably more tenderness for the holders of impropriations, who were to have their patronage expropriated gradually and to be awarded compensation. Apologists for episcopacy, however, had little difficulty in focusing attention on the intensity and scope of the Puritan criticism of "these cormorant patrons, & *Jeroboom* his Priests" and the attendant threatening of spoliators of the church with the fate of Achan and Ananias. *The Lamentable Complaint of the Commonalite* of 1586, for example, rejects any legal reform as impractical in the face of the patrons' notorious cunning and calls instead for the complete abolition of patronage. The tract then concludes with a full-scale blast against the prevailing social and economic sins (all somehow traced to the lack of a learned ministry). Deviating into "civill matters, though it be beside our purpose, yet constrained by necessitie," an appendix denounces the nobility and gentry for engaging in direct farming, "to the great decay of yomanrie," and goes after the "greedie Farmers" guilty of depopulation and enclosure and the avaricious landlords who deprive "poore Cotingers" of their plots for dairy animals and vegetable gardens. Usury and bravery in apparel also receive a fair share of vitriol, all in the course of a petition for ecclesiastical reform.[46]

Anti-Puritan satire sometimes portrayed its targets as the creatures of the gentry, who had volumes to say against the surplice but who meekly looked the other way when it came to their principals' rack renting and enclosure. Paid propagandists that they were, the proestablishment satirists knew better. Pointed in the right direction—and there were plenty to do the pointing—the gentleman of property, perhaps including an impropriation, was less likely to be impressed with the appended paper schemes for reform that accompanied

Puritan polemic than with the probable effects of the invective on a potentially excitable commons. Henry Sands had suggested to the Dedham classis that every member "acquainted with any gentlemen of worth and of godlines should stirre them up to be zealous for reformation."[47] But the gentlemen had some cause to wonder just who would be stirred up in the course of Presbyterian agitation and what the consequences of the proposed reformation might be for the preservation of their gentility.

As a class the clergy did not do much better than the gentry in the New England of the Presbyterian vision, at least when it came to their emoluments and social position. The more cautious ministers wondered how far invoking the consent of the people could be carried, no matter how much clerical supervision was also proposed, before the flock began to think themselves their own shepherds. There is a hint that even the radicals were uneasy over the possibility: they went as far as to defend their conventicling on the grounds that a private exercise directed by a clergyman and held in a gentleman's house was the best possible way to prevent the same company of enthusiasts from meeting on their own initiative with an agenda of their own devising.[48] Equally, the campaign against impropriations brought up indirectly the subject of tithes, always a favorite focus for anticlericalism. Throughout the years of vigorous Presbyterian campaigning, the younger zealots in the movement sometimes seemed to be advocating voluntary maintenance and implying as well that the clergyman who made full use of his rights to tithes was a very near kin to the rack renter and the depopulator. In his frequently quoted colloquy with the chancellor of the diocese of Coventry and Lichfield, the young militant William Axton disclaimed the titles "vicar" and "parson" for that of "pastor" because he held the living by election and (as he saw it) received its income simply as part of an equitable contractual arrangement. "I do receave these temporall thinges of the people because I, beinge their pastor, do mynister unto them spirituall thinges." A few years earlier, in 1575, a dispute between the son of the incumbent of Cranbrook in Kent and a partisan of the famous radical lecturer of the parish mushroomed into an unqualified demand for country justice in the matter of clerical support. Thomas Good told John Fletcher (a future bishop of London) that his father looted the poor for his tithes while flattering the rich, compared the senior Fletcher's holding plural benefices to putting two "hey ricks into one," and by way of contrast extolled his hero, John Strowd, for living off the free gift of his hearers.[49]

Bishop Aylmer was not very far off the mark in complaining of stipendiary lecturers "reteined to preach in divers places besides the ordinary ministers." No matter what the lesson that was preached, there was another obvious one to be learned simply by comparing the two clergymen's respective forms of maintenance. Aylmer had once asked another young radical, Francis Marbury (the father of Anne Hutchinson), where he proposed to get the livings to support a ministry of educated preachers and had been told in response, "A man might cut a good large thong out of your hyde and the rest, and it would not be missed."[50] The bishop could have shot back that if the program of the radicals continued to receive wide publicity, more than episcopal hides were likely to be skinned by a gentry ever jealous of clerical revenues and a populace looking for an opportunity to resist ecclesiastical taxation.

The essential problem was that opposition well short of outright sedition became increasingly suspect the longer it was carried on without obtaining its object. Proposed reforms gradually came to seem less significant, even in the estimation of their moderate supporters, than the likely consequences of continued criticism of arrangements upheld by lawful authority. Strains in the Presbyterian movement were becoming apparent well before the Martin Marprelate episode exposed the underground classes in late 1589. At the same meeting of the Dedham classis in 1588 Robert Lewis made his plaintive request for an endorsement of his conformity to save his ministry and the ever-militant Henry Sands moved that "the course of the Bishops were such and of such moment, that they were not to be thought of as brethren." Lewis's question was "deferred till we [have] heard from our brethren"; Sands's motion "was debated of but not concluded."[51] The next year moderates such as John Stubbs petitioned the short parliament of 1589 for "a Christian and peaceable toleration, not contrary to the law," and the people behind Martin Marprelate went about proving that any Puritan denials of schismatic or seditious intentions were very much subject to interpretation.[52]

The Martin Marprelate tracts were eight viciously effective antiepiscopal satires printed between October 1588 and July 1589 under one or another variant of that pseudonym. Their invective was incendiary enough that the author or authors had to be sure that their identity remained absolutely secret, no mean trick in the gossipy Puritan movement, and it continues a matter of controversy to this day.[53] But the series was clearly the work of Presbyterian extremists, the organizing geniuses of the classical movement, and they relied heavily on their existing connections for its peripatetic printing and distribution. As a consequence, the unusually vigorous government crackdown precipitated by the Martinists inevitably uncovered the whole of the classical organization. In 1590 and 1591 all of its surviving major figures ended up in prison and on trial before the Star Chamber while Richard Bancroft sifted through their confiscated papers for choice examples of Puritan schism and rebelliousness to publish in his exposé of 1593, *Dangerous Positions and Proceedings*.[54]

The damage done to the Presbyterian movement went well beyond the fact of its discovery. Frustrated by the repeated failure of reform in the 1580s and the growing conservatism of the episcopacy, Martin became something akin to the dangerous firebrand of anti-Puritan propaganda. Other Puritan tracts had generally appeared in conjunction with sessions of Parliament and at least pretended to be calls for reformation of grievances by the ordinary course of statute and proclamation. But at a time when the people seemed so many barrels of gunpowder on a short fuse, Martin brazenly adopted a railing, popular style to get "the most part of men" to resist antichristian episcopal government by whatever means proved necessary.[55] At his most extreme, in one of the last tracts, Martin's position is indistinguishable from that of the Separatists, and it was not to be seen again in respectable Puritan circles until the 1630s. He considers the moderate defense of episcopacy, that bishops are officers of state created at the queen's discretion for the better ordering of her church, and quickly overrules it in a neat bit of revolutionary logic: there is only one divinely ordained form of church government, therefore "no magistrate may lawfully maim or deform the body of Christ, which is the church," and "no lawful church government is changeable at the pleasure of the magistrate." Just in case the practical implications of this point should be missed, prelacy is declared unlawful "notwithstanding it be maintained and in force by human laws and ordinances," and any concessions to episcopal government, however indirect, become communion with Antichrist. In the future, "godly ministers" will have to ordain their own candidates without the least notice of episcopal approbation, "the very mark of the Beast, Antichrist." Equally, "the citations, processes, excommunications, & c. of the prelates are neither to be obeyed nor regarded." It would be a sin "to appear in their courts" or to "seek any absolution at their hands," and "every minister is bound to preach the Gospel notwithstanding the inhibition of the bishops." Having both authorized and required civil disobedience, Martin then takes his case a step further and warns the magistrates that to "maintain two contrary factions under their government" will inevitably prove "very dangerous unto our State." One or the other, the true doctrine or the prelacy, must be suppressed "even for the quieting of our outward State."[56] Had Martin been identified and apprehended, he might have claimed on examination that he was only warning of civil combustions and not encouraging them, but the context of his prophecy vitiates such a claim. In any case, this style of apology was a routine defense in many of the treason and sedition trials of the period—and one the judges always found notably unconvincing.

So staunch a lay pillar of the Puritan clergy as Sir Francis Hastings recoiled at this incitement to direct action. "I fynd," he wrote his brother Sir Edward Hastings in 1590, "that hearby he [Martin] hathe geven greate offence and advantage, and done no good at all. . . . It is a commendable thing to longe affter reformation, but it deservith no commendation to seek it unorderly." Martin's colleagues in the Presbyterian movement offered similar testimony of the extent to which the Marprelate tracts played into the hands of the Bancrofts. Edmund Chapman, the leading moderate in the Dedham classis, complained bitterly to Thomas Cartwright of "that marre matter marten," and Josias Nichols, one of the chief classical organizers for Kent, recalled a few years later "that it plainly appeared, to the wiser and discreter sorte, that the Devill was the author of this disgrace."[57] With Martin as semiofficial prophet, the Puritan movement, already divided and demoralized, remained largely inert throughout the stormy 1590s, when economic dislocation and social unrest severely limited the hearing afforded certified disturbers of the peace.

Such initiative as was left passed into the hands of moderate figures centered in Cambridge University, who in the end fared little better than their more radical brethren. Putting polity aside, they attempted to gain explicit recognition for an unqualified Calvinist orthodoxy as the defining credal formulation of the Church of England. The campaign did secure the Lambeth Articles of 1595, which more or less answered the bill, but the victory turned out to be ambiguous if not downright pyrrhic when the queen emphatically rejected any official recognition for the document. Although the Lambeth Articles would be much invoked in subsequent debate as evidencing a broad predestinarian consensus, a later generation of Arminians was left free to dismiss them (as they did) as no more authoritative an interpretation of the Thirty-Nine Articles than their own redaction.[58]

The unrepentant Presbyterians were not finished. Their history is very hazy for the remainder of Elizabeth's reign, but in less formal ways the brethren did keep in touch, especially in their regional strongholds, and their hopes and organizing activities revived with the prospect of the accession of James I. In the last grand effort, radicals such as Henry Jacob and Arthur Hildersham played an important part in putting together the Millenary Petition, but at the ensuing Hampton Court Conference of 1604 moderates of the Nichols stamp assumed full control of the official representation of Puri-

tan grievances. Anxious to undo the legacy of Martin Marprelate, they hopelessly understated the extent of the movement's differences with the episcopal
establishment. In the restricted format of the Hampton Court Conference the
full Puritan case never really surfaced, and in the unhappy sequel—the failure
of the accommodations agreed on at the conference and the drive for conformity under the new canons of 1604—the moderates ended up as discredited
as the radicals before them.[59] After Hampton Court the Puritan movement
was seriously in need of reformulation if its two diverging streams were not
to issue in, respectively, lukewarm conformity and outright Separatism. A
kind of modus vivendi did emerge early in the reign of James I, however, and
the ultimate denouement of English Puritanism was put off for another few
decades.

Slightly restated, the radical position that originated with the Elizabethan
Presbyterians was carried on in the Jacobean period by the group of men
somewhat misleadingly called nonseparating Congregationalists: William
Bradshaw and Henry Jacob, especially, and also Robert Parker, Paul Baynes,
and William Ames. In their personal association and the rough congruity of
their thought, the five form a school of sorts, and they would be claimed by
the Congregationalists of the 1640s as their legitimate ancestors in place of
the embarrassing Separatist pedigree foisted on them by "Presbyterians" of
the Westminster Assembly variety. Yet, though not quite inaccurate, the line
of descent from these five men to the Dissenting Brethren is little more than a
polemical convenience. The Jacobean radicals were creatures of their immediate Presbyterian past, not prophets of a new Congregational order to come.
Particularly in their early efforts, they were trying to get a fresh hearing for
the radical position by ridding the Presbyterian movement of its post-Martin
reputation for disloyalty while preserving the long-standing commitment to a
reformed polity at the congregational level. If they went beyond the Fields
and Cartwrights on some points, it was largely because in the reign of James I
it was necessary to guard against Separatists no less than bishops.

The continuity with the Presbyterian movement appears most obviously
in the careers of Bradshaw and Jacob. Bradshaw had come under the influence of Anthony Gilby and was intimately associated with Thomas Cartwright during the latter's exile in Guernsey (where a Presbyterian polity had
actually been erected), and Jacob was a prime mover in the petition drive that
culminated in the Hampton Court Conference. The early works of both men,
from 1604 through 1606, are primarily taken up with presenting a more
fundamental alternative to the overly modest list of Puritan demands put

forth in anticipation of Hampton Court by such efforts as Josias Nichols's *Plea of the Innocent* and with rejecting the validity of the conference itself.[60] In his *Christian and Modest Offer* of a new and more meaningful Puritan-episcopal debate Jacob repudiated Hampton Court on the grounds that "most of the persons, appoynted to speake for the Ministers, were not of their chosing, nor nomination, nor of their judgment in the matters then and now in question, but of a cleane contrary." As for "the Discipline which is desired," desired by real Puritans, it was still that enjoyed by "all other Reformed Churches."[61] Bradshaw similarly brought out his *English Puritanisme* in 1605 to broadcast "the maine Opinions of the rigidest sort of those that are called Puritanes," that is, as a summary of the views of those least willing to compromise. Bradshaw never intended the tract for what it was later taken to be, a platform for a new, post-Presbyterian polity. His aim was more immediate, to refute the convenient implication in the moderate Puritan apologies that there was only Brownist schism to the left of their position and to demonstrate that his Puritans, the undiluted kind, were no real menace to the peace and safety of the realm. In a passage whose heavy irony is somehow frequently missed, he teased his readers with a mock declaration of his intention to reveal the horrible secrets of *his own party*: "But thou maist herein observe, what a terrible Popedome & Primacie these rigid Presbyterians desire. And with what painted bug beares and Scare Crowes, the Prelates goe about to fright the States of this Kingdome withall. Who will no doubt one day see, how their wisdomes are abused."[62]

Bradshaw and Jacob, with assistance from a few others, including Ames, Parker, and Arthur Hildersham, were the heart of the group Mark Curtis has called the "London Propagandists." They alone carried on the radical tradition of clandestine pamphleteering between 1605 and the discovery of their printer, the senior William Jones, in 1609.[63] Bradshaw and Jacob wrote most of the material, but they also brought out at least one tract by Parker. The contribution of Ames and Baynes to the campaign is less easy to pinpoint but clear enough in general. Ames had met Jacob in 1609 while still at Christ College, Cambridge, when the latter, although an outsider, had "carried a great hand" among the fellows in their unsuccessful attempt to block the election of an anti-Puritan master.[64] The next year, 1610, Ames, now expelled from his fellowship, went into exile in the Netherlands with the avowed purpose of publishing Puritan books (presumably the titles William Jones was no longer in a position to print). His first effort was a Latin translation of Bradshaw's *English Puritanisme* preceded by a long preface of his own. Later, in 1620, he arranged for the posthumous publication of

Baynes's *Diocesan's Trial*, a work written much earlier as a continuation of the London group's assault on the newfangled claims of *jure divino* status for episcopal polity. Ames survived longest of the London group, keeping up a barrage of antiepiscopal material, sandwiched between the works on casuistry and divinity that made him the radicals' first systematic theologian. In his last year he became, as well, a living link with several of the leading divines who forged the New England Way and who ever after recurred to his name and corpus for proof that their Congregationalism was no sudden novelty.[65]

For the most part, the form of polity advanced by the London Propagandists involved little more than altering the mantle of Field and Wilcox to accommodate new political circumstances. They remained obsessed, as had their predecessors, with the congregational presbytery and the congregation, but after the suppression of the classical associations they had to find some practical substitute for the broad supervisory authority originally given in one form or another to ministerial synods. Their most significant innovation, therefore, became the discovery of the civil magistrate. If "a wholl Churche or Congregation shall erre," according to Bradshaw, the other churches have power "onely to counsell and advise the same, and so to leave their Soules to the immediate Judgment of Christ, and their bodies to the sword and power of the civil Magistrat, who alone upon Earth hath power to punish a whol Church or Congregation."[66] Like his Elizabethan forebears, Bradshaw did little more than adopt a pragmatic view toward the problem of providing the watchdog for wayward flocks, though the solution hit upon was doubly convenient for crying up authority at a time when the Puritan movement was widely suspected of the opposite notions. In the reign of James I even the minimal formality of the Dedham classis appeared seditious, and it fell to Bradshaw and his associates to reassure their critics by abandoning entirely the underdeveloped subject of the coercive power of synods and exalting instead the sword of the magistrate. When enumerating the rights of government left inherent in the congregation after the election of the eldership, Bradshaw, Baynes, and, more surprisingly, Jacob, guarded themselves against charges of advocating a popular anarchy by being more Presbyterian than many of the Elizabethans. After assigning the right of intervention in congregational affairs to "the meanest next dwelling officer of justice," Jacob argued that such exercises of magisterial authority would be infrequent because of the strictness with which the elders would keep the people in line: "This government is to be informed, directed, and guided by the Pastor chiefly, and also by the grave assistant Elders. And therefore indeed this government is not simply and plainly Democraticall, but partly Aristocraticall, and partly Monarchicall. And so it is that mixt government which the learned do judge to be the best government of all."[67]

In many respects this group was merely redesignating the ecclesiastical status quo under a new set of labels that gave the Puritans a chance to regain their distinctive stance without becoming involved in the sinister-seeming classes that caused them so much embarrassment in the previous reign. One could call a parish a "true visible church of christ" if it was, however, imprecisely, a "companie, congregation or Assemblie of men, ordinarilie joyneing together in the true worship of God." Such "churches" were declared sufficient unto themselves, subject only to the moral suasion of other churches and the sword of the magistrate, again a celebration of the actual state of affairs after the suppression of the classes. In theory, the magistrate could not deprive a church of its minister and should limit himself to "Civill mulcts" on the congregation to force them "to make better choyse." But if in practice the magistrate went beyond his right and by his "permission" some "other Ecclesiastical officers" (read "bishops") suspended or deprived a minister rightly chosen by his people, the answer, in direct refutation of the embarrassing Martinist extremism, was not to deny the power as antichristian. Rather, a humble suit should be made "unto Civil authoritie" for the minister's reinstatement. Should these measures fail, the stricken flocks must still "acknowledge" their ministers "to the death, their spirituall Guides and Governours, though they bee rigorously deprived of their Ministrie and service." Acknowledgment, however, was a purely moral act and a long way from resistance.[68] By these new glosses on the existing religious situation the Puritan vision of a congregation as the voluntary gathering of the godly was once more readjusted to fit in with the anomalous structure of a national church.

There was more to the exercise, however, than a nice leavening of radical ecclesiology with prudential affirmations of the rights of authority. Bradshaw, Jacob, Ames, and Hildersham all had to undertake a sustained series of replies to the Separatists, who sought to prove that the Puritans on their own terms were compromising fatally with an antichristian church. The Elizabethan Presbyterians had rarely given the matter much thought. Field and Wilcox had dismissed the Separatists as "rather brute beasts then Christians" because they saw them as living outside all church discipline. Cartwright had similarly hooted down his Separatist sister-in-law on the grounds that, lacking a learned minister to expound Scripture, her little separated group could not possibly be a church.[69] Both claims, unfortunately, no longer held up very well after the organization of the Ancient Church in London and Amsterdam and the defection of a series of indisputably learned ministers to the other side between 1595 and 1605, including Francis Johnson, Henry Ainsworth, John Robinson, and John Smyth. At the same time, the saving assumption that radical action was unnecessary because reform in the English church was an imminent possibility was clearly becoming a transparent fiction. Anyone who knew the temper of the godly was now obliged to take the Separatists seriously and to come to terms with their vision of a pure church.

The effect of the prolonged duel with the Separatists was to crystallize some of the standing ambiguities of the radical position in a more explicitly Congregational formulation. At the outset, the nonseparating case was woefully underdeveloped. In 1595 both Jacob and Hildersham replied to the claim that the English ministry received its standing by the ordination of the antichristian bishops with the counterassertion that many ministers also enjoyed a popular call from the inhabitants of the parishes they served. Francis Johnson promptly shot back that the reply was irrelevant because the people of a parish, unseparated and uncovenanted, were just a civil division of the population and not a voluntarily gathered church enjoying the privilege of calling a minister. Hildersham failed to put in a rejoinder; Jacob, later the organizer of a covenanted church, initially had no better response than to argue that at least some of the people of some of the parishes had originally professed Protestantism freely, and not by compulsion, either in Mary Tudor's reign or in the first six months of Elizabeth's before the new order became legally established.[70] It took quite some time to come up with a revised radical ecclesiology that satisfied the sectarian temper by showing that it could be indulged within the existing establishment. Eventually the standard nonseparating apology would run: everything the Separatists demanded was more or less legitimate by Scripture and right reason, but there was enough of the true church by their own definition in the structure of many English parishes to make separation unnecessary and unlawful. Even the Separatist insistence on separating out the more obvious goats from the sheep was conceded after a fashion: the "people" who made a parish a church were, Henry Jacob knew enough to say by 1613, "only such people as are not ignorant in religion, nor scandalous in their life. For only of such Christes Visible Church ought to consist."[71] Early in the reign of James the demand for knowledge and virtue already excluded a formidable part of the population; only in later decades would a more exacting generation in New England and Holland insist on more than these "common" graces as the basis for church membership.

Significantly, Jacob, Parker, and Ames, the three apologists who lived abroad and had personal contact with the most plausible of the Separatist champions, John Robinson, found, like him, that the powers of discipline were committed to the whole congregation and that churches were gathered by covenant ("implicit" rather than "explicit" in the case of the English parishes). They were preempting the Separatist appeal and also learning what it was they needed to preempt, thereby indirectly appropriating the experience of Congregationalism in practice gained by the Separatists in order to clarify and refine their own theoretical efforts. Henry Jacob, in turn, took their concessions one step further and translated reformulated theory back again into practice. After threatening for more than a decade that continued failure to achieve reform would force conscientious Puritan ministers to leave their "ordinary standing" in their church, he returned to England in 1616 to found an illegal covenanted Congregational church in the London suburb of Southwark. Often called "semiseparatist" by contemporaries, the Southwark church acknowledged no episcopal authority but did not require its members to repudiate the Church of England as a term of acceptance. (Indeed, Jacob and his followers occasionally took the sacrament at one of London's parochial churches.)[72] Jacob was, nonetheless, an embarrassment to other Puritans, and the Congregationalists of the 1640s usually left him off their honor roll when they were reciting the list of respectable forebears that ran from Bradshaw to Ames. But his Southwark church endured to become a window on the left for the Puritan movement, bringing its radical wing in contact with the various sectarian groups that clustered in London and the Netherlands. It would over time send some of its members to New England and import from there various particulars of Congregational practice, as well as exercise an influence on Welsh Congregationalism and father several of the Baptist churches that played an important part in the Civil War.[73] Jacob bequeathed a legacy to Independents and New Englanders through his living Congregationalism just as emphatically as the irreproachable Ames did by his systematics.

It would be extravagant to suggest that either Jacob or Ames, or Bradshaw and Parker, "saved" a faltering Puritan radicalism. The recuperative power of the radicals lay in their ability to attract a lay following and to discipline its energies within the bounds of the established church. The nonseparating Congregationalists performed their indispensable service by finding a theory to justify and direct practice, and, in Jacob's case, by organizing a more self-conscious form of practice around the reconsidered theory. Collectively their work amounted to the only fully worked-out statement of polity of native origin available to the Puritan movement in the early seventeenth century. Not every Puritan may have been very interested in what they had to say, but some people must have thought highly of their work, which was printed clandestinely in single editions in England or smuggled into the country in very small batches from the Netherlands, or this fugitive literature would not have survived for a quarter-century and more, to reemerge in the 1640s as ammunition for apologists of English Independency and the New England Way.[74] As the sectarian thrust within Puritanism gained strength, the chief clerical practitioners of the movement's always breathtaking balancing act were perforce increasingly drawn to the writings of these Jacobean bridge figures as the only obvious way of directing and legitimating Congregationalism when it became possible to attempt a reformed establishment in England and America.

One may wonder why anyone wanted to walk this tightrope, why the final solution anticipated by the Separatists and made general for the movement in 1660 did not come sooner. But in the first two or three decades of the seventeenth century there were good and sufficient reasons for radical and moderate Puritans alike to remain attached to a church they characterized as "halfly reformed." The dissolution of the classical movement had been a blessing to the Puritans in a way, for it allowed a release of energy into new areas for the creation of the Christian order. Gradually, a discovery was being made: quite apart from polity, the culture of the age offered a multitude of means to draw people voluntarily into a disciplined life and a purposive society.

2

Continuity and Ambiguity
"The Gospel Doing," 1590–1630

As Elizabethan Puritans go, Robert Cawdry, sometime rector of South Luffenham in Rutlandshire, is a radical of the radicals, a standout for unremitting and uncompromising zeal in a diocese notorious for its zealots. In the
course of a single lecture sermon at an exercise in a neighboring town in
1586 he proclaimed both the equality of the ministry (thus disposing of the
hierarchy) and the sinfulness of nonresidence (with particular and pointed
application to the hapless vicar from whose borrowed pulpit he spoke).
Then, turning to the Book of Common Prayer, "of earnest zeale, some-what
forgetting himselfe," he proceeded to "brake out in termes" by declaring "it
was a vile booke, and, fie upon it." Called to account for these words,
Cawdry lost his living and his ministry, though not without a spirited legal
battle, but he continued to occupy his parsonage for several years after his
deprivation and to hold private meetings at which, it was alleged, the godly of
South Luffenham were treated to readings of the Marprelate tracts.[1] Eventually, however, he gave over the battle and left for Coventry to resume his old
trade of schoolteaching—one would like to imagine the young John Davenport, later the dour patriarch of New Haven, boyishly lisping his first Latin
under Cawdry. During this last, least visible segment of an otherwise flam-
boyant life, Cawdry, the cashiered radical, brought out two closely related
works not unimportant to the history of English culture and not unrepresen-
tative of the reaffirmation of English Puritanism in the first third of the
seventeenth century.

The earlier and less well-known title, *A Treasurie or Storehouse of
Similies*, was published in 1600 and consists of 860 quarto pages of alpha-
betized edification in the form of multiple analogies to words and concepts
commonly employed in sermons. As far back as 1580, while still at South
Luffenham, Cawdry had complained that the labor of the most painful

preachers was "for the moste part utterly lost" because of their audiences' incapacity to understand their meaning. He had sought at the time to lay "a good foundation" for receiving the word through preparatory catechizing, and now in 1600 with *A Treasurie* he offered a new didactic tool for use at the other end of the sermon: the "industrious and careful Reader" on returning home from hearing the Sabbath service or from a lecture sermon by some godly preacher was immediately to turn to the book's index and locate "any principle of God his religion, handled and spoken off: Or else any vertue commended, or vice condemned" in order to expand and reinforce the knowledge newly gained from the pulpit by studying the apposite set of similitudes. Cawdry had also meant to include as part of *A Treasurie* a "Treatise of Diffinitions" of the most important terms likely to be used in preaching or catechizing, "which I am assured will give some goodlight, and helpe to the better understanding and effectual profiting hereby," but, fortunately for his posthumous fame, this second effort grew so long he had to publish it separately. *A Table Alphabeticall Conteyning and Teaching the Understanding of Hard Usuall English Words* first appeared in 1604 and reached its fourth edition in 1617. It is the first monolingual English dictionary.[2]

Cawdry in his later career almost too perfectly suggests a Puritan in transition from militance to something very like rapprochement with the existing order. In these two books the Presbyterian begins to subside in the Elizabethan, or so it would seem. There is all the quintessential fascination with his own language, all the naive enthusiasm for that newly rediscovered weapon, system, and all the endearing confidence in improving manuals and, more generally, in the battery of cultural tools by which men of good hope sought to broadcast knowledge wholesale, if not to democratize it totally. We seem, that is, with the later Cawdry to be on the threshold of the age of the preachers and practical divines, post-Cartwright but pre-Laud, when Puritanism at its most attractive is alleged to have abandoned the external reshaping of church and state for the disciplining of each individual heart.

This familiar claim for the triumph of a second, supposedly more enduring Puritanism rising on the ruins of the Presbyterian movement has always had a degree of merit. At the height of the "first" Puritanism of the classical organizations, in the 1580s, many Puritans were little more than sympathetic onlookers, and even some of the participants were not convinced of the urgency of their cause: along with the committed came any number of recruits who joined the Fields and Wilcoxes primarily out of a combination of frustration, unwarranted optimism over eventual sanction from officialdom, and reactive solidarity against Archbishop Whitgift's heavy-handedness in enforcing conformity. A certain amount of pressure from above and a little rumbling from below were all it took to dishearten this nervous constituency, bringing the Presbyterian experiment to an end and ushering in a more de-centralized phase in the history of English Puritanism. But the suppression and collapse of the classes marks the end of a chapter and not an ultimate terminus ad quem. One can forget the Fields and present the William Perkin-ses and Richard Sibbeses as merely the more unqualified exponents of a broadly accepted Protestant consensus only by ignoring both the irreconcil-able elements within the Puritan movement and the growth of a distinctive anti-Puritan group among the church hierarchy. In this less troubled age of Puritanism, the fiercely hostile Richard Bancroft was nonetheless primate of all England for seven years, claims for *jure divino* episcopacy were broached with unprecedented confidence and publicity, and Richard Neile built the "Arminian" machine he would hand on to William Laud. Not coincidentally, such leading practical divines as William Bradshaw, Ezekiel Culverwell, Paul Baynes, and Arthur Hildersham found themselves without gainful employ-ment for large parts of their lives. Insisting on two Puritanisms, one of polity, the other of piety, overstates the discontinuities in the Puritan movement and, more important, deprives it after the suppression of the classes of any real, distinctive identity within English Protestantism until its apparently inexpli-cable reemergence under the Laudian hammer in the 1630s.

Certainly, our exemplar Robert Cawdry would not have thought of him-self as rejecting his past endeavors when he turned to lexicography and schoolteaching. If he had merely consented to make a few moderate noises, there would have been plenty of fresh preferment available for an individual of his powers and connections. (His patrons had included Queen Elizabeth's godson, Sir James Harrington, to whom the *Treasurie* is dedicated, and Lord Treasurer Burghley, who repeatedly intervened with the hierarchy on his behalf.)[3] Instead, Cawdry's similes for "Minister" and for the catchword "Disscipline" mark a thoroughly unrepentant radical. A church without proper discipline was like an orchard without a fence or a city without a government, unguarded and ineffectual: "In the Church where Discipline wanteth, although there be never so sound & good preaching with Catechis-ing, against sin and wickednes, yet the edge therof is so dulled, that it is fruitlesse and of little force."[4]

For all that, Cawdry and others like him were actually settling for second best by the beginning of the reign of James I. They could hardly do otherwise in the aftermath of Hampton Court, and, in any case, like their critics, they too could wonder a little anxiously whether a reformation without official structed at the end of the journey by the spectacle of the "very brisk Lad" Ignorance being ferried across the river of Death in dumb equanimity by Vain-hope, only to be refused entrance to the City and then tied hand and foot and cast into hell. He had, indeed, been forewarned at his very first appearance on the progress that "God saith, Those that no understanding have, / (Although he made them) them he will not save."[11] Puritans as a group had little use for pious simpletons and were not much given to contrasting an untutored but intuitive understanding of the fundamentals of religion with the snares of learned sophistries. By Bunyan's time it could possibly be assumed that lack of understanding was to a degree self-inflicted when so many forms of learning were so widely available (Ignorance's home is Conceit, not Darkness), but three-quarters of a century earlier no less a champion of predestinarian theology than William Perkins invoked the very existence of persons physically incapable of learning or unreachable by the limited educational resources of his own day as a commonsense refutation of the Arminian claim that God in the first instance wills that all people may have the benefit of Christ's sacrifice. The scriptural verses in dispute allegedly favoring a universal offer of salvation that the reprobate supposedly knowingly and willingly reject could not possibly be understood by any rational individual as comprehending those "borne leprose, blinde, foolish, very poore, unmeete for this temporary felicity," not to mention the many who were "foolish and madde all their life long, upon whom we cannot say that this universall grace is bestowed."[12] Growth in the number of knowledgeable sheep had incidentally highlighted the intractable obduracy of large portions of the remaining goats, in effect making the case for predestination, among other things, a matter of simple logic.

Historical faith, however, was only the first step toward knowledge in its fullest sense. This sort of learning in itself was incomplete because still lacking the essence of saving faith, "affiance," meaning trust or confidence not simply in the verity of the doctrine taught but especially in its personal application. Just about everyone, it was assumed, who took in a decent course of sermons did more than get a sense of Christian fundamentals; they also gave a limited assent to what they heard, a general acknowledgment of its truth that would not have occurred had they merely attended, say, a particularly lucid set of lectures on the tenets of Islam. But this combination of learning and a hazy conviction was not yet saving faith because the knowledge so far attained was still verbal and facile. Some people able to make a competent profession did so merely out of respect for the magistrate who compelled a particular religion. Other dissemblers, more subtle, made an excellent job of manipulating intellectual counters through a profession wholly temporary. Their show of understanding, however outwardly convincing, failed in the end because they acted not out of the genuine conviction of the saints but from an egotistical desire for worldly credit or a faithless fear of punishment in this world and the next.[13]

Such hypocrites have come to have a fascination for our own times that they lacked for all but of a few of the Puritans who dealt with the phenomenon. Influenced perhaps by developments in fiction over the last century or so, our hypocrites are individuals so much a prisoner of their own playacting that they cannot tell unpalatable truth from self-serving falsehood and so either persevere undisturbed in their Babbitry to the end or, better still, spin out their wretched lives in a continuous agony of unresolvable doubt. The latter type, in particular, we assume must have peopled many a Puritan meeting. Some compound of nineteenth-century optimism and twentieth-century anxiety makes us prone to imagine the victims of predestinarian theology indulging in orgies of self-indictment in the mostly futile hope of an eventual assurance that all but the most spiritually hardy could never have quite attained. In the Puritan scheme of things, however, the hypocrites were nothing but "very common" sorts (the phrase is Perkins's), easy enough to detect because they never accused themselves of hypocrisy. Those strings of self-accusation that make up many spiritual autobiographies constitute the record of so many moments of reassurance and deepening perception as saving knowledge became increasingly "operative." "Temptations and doubtings" were both an inevitable concomitant and a desirable reinforcement of true faith, weak or strong, because sincere converts needed to come to terms through experience with that single irreducible fact it was easiest to affirm notionally or verbally and hardest of all to grasp vitally, as a fundamental axiom of a God-created universe—their own inability. "God will not have men perfect in this life, [but leaves them prey to doubts] that they may alwaies goe out of themselves, and depend wholly on the merit of Christ."[14] Accordingly, self-accusation could be used as its own refutation. Richard Greenham, a specialist if ever there was one in this lugubrious activity, is said to have responded "to a godly Christian, much inveighing against her [own] unbeleefe" with a comfortable message that could have stood as the routine therapy for all such cases: "I doe not now suspect your estate, when you seeme to me rather to have faith, than when you seeme to your selfe to have it. For faith being the gift of God, is then most obtained and increased of God, when you thirsting after the increase of present feeling, thinke the smallest measure obtained to be no faith. . . . And surely experience proveth, understand the communion with Christ that came as a part of faith, except as a dead metaphor. Even the sexual coupling of husband and wife was instanced as the most palpable analogy there was to this otherwise inconceivable "conjunction" between believer and Christ.[18] William Ames, as abstract a thinker as anyone could wish, was celebrating this unity of theory and practice when he wrote, a bit cryptically, that "every theologian truly lives well. The theologian who lives best is the best theologian. The person who is only an observer and teacher of theology is no theologian." The latter individual literally did not know what he was talking about.[19]

Calls for an internal and individual revolution come easily enough to those who perceive their inability to effect the material and collective kind, and we may wonder if we are reading in Ames, a permanent exile in the Netherlands, a wistful attempt to go on fighting old battles on a front where no High Commission or Star Chamber could ever intervene. Ames, however, had plenty left to say on the subjects of polity and liturgy, and he continued to say it, none too discreetly.[20] Equally, the devotional techniques that were the hallmark of much of Jacobean Puritan practical divinity had their origin in the work of an earlier generation still also committed to the importance of a Presbyterian remodeling of the Church of England. Moreover, as we shall see, the Jacobeans did not lack a political program with intimate links, personal and substantive, to the causes championed under Elizabeth.[21] Operative knowledge was in reality a concept that provided a common rationale for the Puritan movement over a very long period. The Presbyterian phase of the movement, to be sure, had centered on a single all-purpose device, discipline, to set the gospel "doing"—to give it a lively meaning by practice and participation. The congregation that elected its preaching minister and joined with its eldership in church sanctions would come to an understanding of the word not obtainable in the unadorned act of hearing, no matter how pure the doctrine and how powerful the preacher. Practical divinity gave expression to the same imperatives in a more diffuse manner but with a greater sensitivity to political realities and to the exploitation of cultural achievements largely ignored at the height of the Presbyterian enthusiasm. In his similes and his dictionary Robert Cawdry had bemoaned the failure of discipline, but the Puritans were nonetheless forging a substitute with his books and with others of the same sort as the Ramism for householders of Dudley Fenner or the Sabbatarian directories of Nicholas Bownd and Richard Greenham. All in their various ways continued and elaborated the continuing Puritan fascination with the totality of godliness.

Puritanism was shaped by an intelligent if partisan engagement with the world of its own day, and never more so than in the case of practical divinity. The dominant features of that world were its material and cultural attainments and their palpable incompleteness and fragility. Agricultural advance was imperiled by increases in population. Regional economic specialization and the growth of extraregional contacts with London and the Continent brought the means of enlightenment to many a backwater but also a heightened and widened vulnerability to disruptions of European markets. The great increase in the university-trained ministry accompanied the despoliation of church revenues that might have supported them (some of the ministers were children or grandchildren of the despoilers), and the growth of literacy was so checkered that regress was as likely as progress and dramatic contrasts could be observed within single regions.[22] Modern scholarship has a curious penchant for locating the motor force of Puritanism rather indirectly in the anxieties attributable to this situation, more or less equating "Puritan" with "stress," "transition," or "discontinuity." Puritans, it seems, were a nervous lot, even if they did not always know what they were nervous about. Yet every other major intellectual movement of the same period is explained as an informed response to the potentialities of change and not simply as an attempt to reject the new world of the sixteenth and seventeenth centuries or to accommodate it only by disguising the unacceptable through complex mythologizing. Unless we are to proceed on the dogmatic assumption that the function of religion is always anodynic or manipulative, then, on the face of the most obvious evidence, the Puritans should probably be reinstated in the company of the Henrician and Edwardian reformers who preceded them in their hopes and disappointments alike. When the most disappointed Puritans of all, the migrant generation of the 1630s, called down the fate of Sodom upon their native land, it was not modernity they cursed but the failure of the English to respond to the unique opportunities and insights that modern times alone had brought (the "high rates" of Thomas Hooker's farewell sermon). Such imprecations were uttered, in any event, at the end of the miserable decade of the 1620s or in the midst of the 1630s, which were, if anything, worse.

Earlier, for most of the reign of James I, it was still possible to celebrate the achievements of the age and respond to its failings with a well-tempered optimism. How, asked John Dod and Robert Cleaver, can men neglect the Christian education of their children, "now, when youth was never so apt to good learning, as it is at this day: and learning and all good meanes never so plenteously flourishing; being restored and reduced into such a facilitie, and a compendious breifenesse: yea, never so good, learned and skilfull schoole-masters: never such plentie of so good and plaine books printed, never so good cheape: the holy Ghost mercifully offering his gifts, as it were, into the mouthes of all men." Dod and Cleaver no less than Winthrop after them possessed the Puritan sense of wasted opportunities. Along with their rhap-sody to the flourishing state of learning they added the prophecy that in one form or another would work so great an effect in the decade of the Great Migration. If the English persisted in "this our great unthankfulnesse" and neglected the means God had provided, "these so manifold heavenly bless-ings shall be taken from us, and given to some other nation, that will both be more thankful for them, and also shew forth better fruits of Christianitie, than we hitherto have done."[23]

Keenly aware at once of his society's capacities and its limitations, the practical divine developed a strategy not very different from that of the re-forming administrator or the improving projector: a relatively low-cost re-organization of existing resources in a more thoughtful, systematic form, allowing for more sustained application of as many means as possible si-multaneously.[24] The corresponding vices in this scheme accordingly were impulsivity and shortsightedness so that the traditional sin of covetousness, for example, was conceived of primarily as feverish moneygrubbing (the "busiebody" pieceworker spoiling the Sabbath by scrabbling together an extra pittance) or as a lust for gain so obsessive it led to outright acts of cruelty (the rack renter, the engrosser, the brutal taskmaster). Careful, calcu-lated aggrandizement was another matter, neither right nor wrong of and in itself: harnessed to the right motives, manifested by the right deeds, system-atic acquisitiveness could be a virtue in a pillar of Israel.[25]

Because practical divinity was so deeply rooted in its own time and place, many of its means for a "lively" education in godliness were endorsed by a great variety of Englishmen who can in no sense be termed Puritan. Frequent points of contact, however, never added up to wholesale congruence, and it has become too easy to dissolve the Puritan movement in the larger culture of which it was a subspecies. In a recent study of English higher education one can find Archbishop James Ussher of Armagh classified as a "moderate" Puritan and George Downame, bishop of Derry and early apologist for *jure divino* episcopacy, awarded the title "radical" in the same cause, both appar-ently because of their respective attainments as covenant theologians and Ramist logicians. With equal lack of caution, an influential account of Eliza-bethan popular culture discusses, as a compendium of Puritan ideas, the twin treatises of Christopher Sutton on the arts of living and dying simply because they are important instances of the genre of devotional literature at which the Puritans also excelled.[26] Sutton, however, was a massive pluralist, and his work, in addition to championing the observance of Christmas, the Feast of the Circumcision, Epiphany, and Easter Day, observes of "the superstitious manner of the Jewes in keeping their Sabbath," that "these men are gone, but yet their fancies in some part remaine." The first treatise opens with a blast against "our adversaries" for their "unpriestly" reviling of the national church "in many spitefull Pamphlets," the second with a condemnation of "publike controllers of all others, by plausible pretenses of reformation."[27] These pointed prefaces did not stop John Trumbull, the pilgrim mariner en route to assurance, from turning to the manuals at a crucial point in his spiritual travail, but for a purpose their author explicitly rejected as pharisaical: to prove to himself that his inner struggles over the Sabbath demonstrated that he was one of the elect, set apart from his untroubled shipmates, who were placidly content with regular, ritualized public observance.[28] Attribution of the term *Puritan* to so unlikely a character as Sutton, as to Downame and Ussher, is a measure of our failure to look more deeply at the peculiar twists that Jacobean Puritans, lay and clerical alike, could give to the common cultural property of their generation. They were in their world right enough and with a greater zest than their Elizabethan forebears, but they were not always entirely of it.

So, for example, Ramist logic survived unadulterated in the Harvard curriculum long after it had been superseded in England, but at its first reception into the mother country Ramism had received an enthusiastic endorsement from a whole spectrum of intellectuals, Puritan and otherwise. The earliest English Ramists saw in this new logic, in contrast to prevalent versions of Aristotelianism, a genuine weapon for the progressive discovery of the truth (rather than just the stuff of monkish disputations) and a basis of communication by which unbigoted members of all religious groups could come to agree on fundamentals.[29] Puritans *as Puritans*, however, were attracted to Ramus (if and when they were) more because of his pioneering theories of instruction, which offered an adaptable methodology designed to engage students in active collaboration with their teachers. Ramism perceived from this angle was the ideal pedagogy of "divinity practiced," just as Ramist logic and rhetoric seemed to offer an unprecedented means for the minister to "open" Scripture in a way that lifted the listeners out of the role of passive bystanders. Equipped with the same dialectical tool as the clergy, the laity too would become masters of exegesis and participate meaningfully in the common saving truths.[30] But Ramism so Puritanized lost its original cosmopolitan and irenic character. Fenner's translation of Ramus for householders' religious exercises, as well as Anthony and Samuel Wotton's version intended for "any one of indifferent capacitie," were taken as subversive documents, and the neo-Aristotelian counterattack, when it emerged, was justified on the anti-Puritan grounds that it was necessary to provide untutored but loyal clergy with an appropriate, un-Ramist tool "to deale with subtill sophisters and caveling schismatics (whereof in these dayes, the more is the pitty, there are too many)."[31]

Household religion offers another, perhaps less rarefied instance of a common English enthusiasm set to special Puritan uses. The household as spiritual training ground has no special affinity with Puritanism: the right of discovery can be variously assigned to the humanists of the early sixteenth century or to the scholastics of the fifteenth who favored lay participation in religion, and the glories of the godly family were subsequently elaborated by Protestants of all shades as well as by Catholics.[32] Puritans made their distinctive contribution, here as elsewhere, in the particular context they provided for a device so routinely praised by all parties that the subject was becoming stereotypical. Puritan households were to be "the lowest place of the Church," that is, integral units in a large-scale scheme of mutually reinforcing means designed to train the weak Christians and provide the strong Christians with arenas to test and display their training.[33] As the characteristic Puritan sin was mindless, impulsive behavior, so the characteristic cure, in place of the Discipline, became many disciplines in as many different environments as could conveniently be harnessed to a single end. But all of the different forms of godliness needed somehow to be connected, and most often the binding ligament was the preaching of the word.

The interrelatedness of the "means" appears clearly in the most distinctive of the causes of middle-period Puritanism, an insistence on a strict, Hebraicized observation of the Sabbath. The Elizabethan Puritans had not been of one mind about the Sabbath, nor, initially, greatly fascinated by the subject, but after some hesitancy and a good deal of internal argument, the Puritan movement as a whole had by early in the reign of James I adopted the Fourth Commandment in toto as a perpetual moral obligation still binding on Christians in the new dispensation.[34] In purely intellectual terms, this development was not especially anomalous: the Puritan preference in disputed questions generally came down on the side of seeking scriptural prescriptions rather than expanding the indifferent areas open to human convenience, and Sabbatarianism also fit in nicely with covenant theology. What is surprising is the

Puritans' rapid and growing passion for their belated discovery. By the mid-1630s ordinarily discreet clergymen willing to do a bit of business over the ceremonies were sacrificing their pulpits rather than endorse the Book of Sports. In America at the same time an émigré, Thomas Shepard, could tell a group of Harvard students that this uniquely English institution (he ignored its Continental ancestry) had been more than equal compensation for the failings of the English nation in polity and liturgy: "If there hath beene more of the power of godlinesse appearing in that small inclosure of the British Nation then in those vast continents elsewhere, where Reformation and more exact Church-Discipline have taken place, it cannot well be imputed to any outward meanes more, then their excelling care and conscience of honouring the Sabbath."[35]

In the quest for operative knowledge the Sabbath became an unparalleled weapon for proclaiming and organizing the believer's participation in a Christian universe. After a generation of Puritans had learned to use the observance over and over as the most reliable bulwark in their long-disputed passage from weakness to strength, the Sabbath, no longer an incidental and slightly controversial tenet, had assumed a central position in Puritan devotion. The impact of Sabbatarian opinion on the Winthrop family in late 1616 and early 1617 gives as good an example as any of the catalytic power of the ordinance. Henry Sands, who had first brought the Sabbatarian question before the Dedham and Braintree classes some thirty years earlier, was in attendance throughout much of December 1616 on the dying Thomasine Winthrop, the young wife of the future governor. She repaid his solicitousness in a round of pious farewells, including the parting injunctions to her maidservants to "bringe up thy children well, you poore folks commonly spoyle your children, in suffering [them] to breake Gods Sabaothes, etc." (Sands uncharitably remarked of the deathbed scene that he had previously taken Thomasine "for a harmelesse younge woman, and well affected, but did not thinke she had been so well grounded.") Whatever the effect of her final monition on her maids, the point took with her bereaved husband. A few weeks later Sands solemnly delivered his opinion to the spiritually restless John Winthrop "as upon his best Judgment and experience, that a Christian is bounde to make use of his Sabaothe businesse all the weeke after, and that so to doe would keepe away much uncomfortable discontent from a Christian minde." Winthrop, his longtime spiritual travail and immediate sense of loss coming together, seized on the advice avidly, embracing the Sabbath as "the markett of our soules," the place to vend the fruits of the previous week's exercises and to store up the provisions needed to survive the tests of the coming week. He had suffered for years from an inability to fashion his religious life into a coherent, continuous whole, but now under Sands's Sabbatarian tutelage his disparate impulses fused at last, and within a relatively short period he was able to begin the transition from weak to strong Christian.[36]

The commonly used metaphor of the Sabbath as a "market" or "fairday" should surprise those who have always assumed that the dominant feature of Sabbatarianism was a joyless schedule of prohibited activities. That list is certainly a long one, taking in every form of work and recreation, as well as travel over three miles in distance. The Puritans, however, whatever their other faults, were rarely given to confusing religious duties with self-inflicted wounds. Observing the Sabbath in its Puritan fashion was first and foremost a didactic exercise, a weekly "instruction" and "evidence" of God's promises to the elect and their obligations of obedience, "so that the sabbath is a document and pledge of Gods will, whereby we should know what he is unto us, and wherein we should learne what we should do to him."[37] In a two-part lesson the believer would be abruptly called to attention when worldly activity came grinding to a halt, and the time liberated could be redeemed by the undistracted pursuit of scriptural meaning. The sermons delivered on the Sabbath, important as they were, were still only the centerpieces of a day's worth of observance in varying forms. Sunday was the day to take instruction but also to meditate, to apply, and to deepen personal application of Scripture through action. Nicholas Bownd, Richard Greenham's stepson and a major theoretician of the Sabbatarian movement, devised a set of complementary exercises for the householder and his family under the headings of preparing for the work of the public ministry and of finishing the job "afterwards [to] make it most profitable to himselfe or them." One should begin with private prayer and Scripture reading and follow through, after the day's sermon or sermons, with private conferences with others on pertinent topics, all to be accompanied by careful introspective analysis "wisely to examine howe the case standes betweene the Lord and ourselves." The theme is just another formulation of the recurring Puritan insight: knowledge passively received is not really knowing until the hearers in company with other hearers make their own personal contributions. Mere hearers who neglect conference and other collective activities are "benumed" without "sense or feeling" of the word they have just heard, but "the meetings of the godlie is like a great many of firebrands layde together, in which though there be some heate when they are apart by themselves, yet being laid together, it is doubled, and otherwise every one would dye of itselfe."[38]

Bownd's metaphor suggested the warmth and even passion of Sabbath exercises, but it was a little too apt: the firebrands also suggested the "beautefeau," the incendiary raiser of faction in church and state. The issue of the Sabbath had first emerged in the meetings of the Essex classes and was mostly promoted by men formerly active in the classical movement at the very time when the details of that failed experiment were being publicized in the most lurid terms. Such parentage ensured that the Sabbath was ridiculed at an early date as a newfangled substitute for the suppressed disciplinarianism. One can still find the young Joseph Hall in 1606 writing verses in praise of "Greenham's sabbath," but on the whole, outside the ranks of the Puritans the proponents of putting the whole of Sunday to the Lord's use, such as James Ussher, went out of their way to insist that it was no Hebraicized Sabbath that they envisioned. Sabbatarianism was always in danger of having a party label attached to it, and the actual practice of the exercise was calculated to make it a Puritan peculiarity. Devout Sabbatarians were likely to end up as members of a chosen band set apart from hostile neighbors by the timing of their Sunday observances, by the unusual and obvious limitations they placed on their own activities, and, to the extent that they fulfilled the injunction to seek conferences, by their conventicling. Renewed attack on Sabbatarianism in the Laudian years only made this weekly schism in the Church of England acute, turning the inadvertent into the self-conscious. As one New Englander recalled, "When the book of liberty [of sports] came forth and being afraid I should not stand in trials, hence I looked this way." His pastor Thomas Shepard, who had looked and come the same way, would make the identical point with less economy of style, when he demanded of his Harvard students, "how hath that little flock of slaughter, which hath wept for it [the Sabbath], and preacht and printed, and done, and suffered for it, been hated and persecuted?"[39] A more homely "document" of the way in which the new Israel stood heir to the old could not be imagined than to be one of the band of Hebrews among the Canaanites for one day out of every seven. Here was operative knowledge with a vengeance: the endless neighborhood sniping and parish factionalism of seventeenth-century England clothed in Scripture.

In mood our own time is probably more in sympathy with the Canaanites. Sabbatarianism seems the ideal form for a sour-minded assault on the appealing earthy pastimes of the ordinary rustics, if not a weapon to replace an integrated, spontaneous world at one with the rhythm of nature by the machine age of lockstep and fragmentation. A more sophisticated version of this romantic critique of modernity would have the newly emergent capitalist of the early modern era embracing the Puritan version of Sunday in order to secure the labor discipline impossible under the old regime of frequent holy days and unpredictable bouts of recreation. The Sabbath certainly was designed to inculcate method and meaning, and one could if one wished find in the observances another source of the habits of order and regularity so dear to Max Weber's "spirit of capitalism." (The point is at least arguable, if not entirely resolvable.) But one should not confuse Puritan Sabbatarianism with a more generalized hostility to popular recreations and to what was seen as pervasive indolence and viciousness in the work force.[40] Employers in search of disciplined labor would have found the Puritan Sabbath per se a dubious blessing, assuming that in the overspecialized, vulnerable, and poorly organized economy of the day they really could have found a use for a work force drilled into keeping at it eight hours a day six days a week. To the extent that they followed Sabbatarian restrictions the Puritan merchants would have found themselves every Sunday unable to move their goods, no matter how perishable, and Puritan farmers would have been obliged to interrupt their harvest time without regard to the perils of the weather. Correspondence would similarly go unopened, however urgent, business transactions would be left uncompleted, however contingent; indeed, the least thought of business was held to violate the Fourth Commandment.[41] Nor would the other six days of the week be much compensation if the aim was to squeeze the most out of one's employees on the occasions when it became lawful to do a little squeezing. To begin with, the due and meet recreations prohibited on Sunday were supposed to be made up during the workweek, and the laborers themselves were explicitly warned against overwork on the grounds that drudgery and compensatory intemperance would equally render them unfit to concentrate on the word when the Lord's day came back around.[42] There was not even much comfort to be found in the elimination of holy days, which were at least predictable, when the Sabbath was to be supplemented by frequent days of fasting and humiliation, to be held as occasions warranted and on private initiative if the public authorities neglected their duty.

Whatever contributions the Puritans made to the culture of the assembly line, their Sabbath institutions are a very unlikely choice for a share of the honors. The importance of the Sabbath, rather, is as the central boss around which the Puritan didactic structure came to be erected. Reading, meditation, and conference would all take place at other times as well, and especially on lecture days, but on the Sabbath alone word and world be briefly conjoined. It was, as Greenham wrote, "an holy schoole to teach us the worship of God."[43]

In contrast to the Sabbath, the observances connected with household religion seem mere auxiliary tools for providing a supervised context in which to comprehend the fullness of doctrine. Dudley Fenner in his Ramist manual for householders was already saying in 1584 what was to become a commonplace used to justify almost any device from the catechism to the conventicle. "Men both themselves and their families," he complained, "go to the publike ministery, as to a common matter, let it fall after to the ground, without any looking into the certainetie of doctrine, the power and practise of it." There must, therefore, be preparation, review, and application or the most powerful of sermons would be wasted.[44] Josias Nichols, William Perkins, John Dod, and Robert Cleaver, among others, all carried on in the same strain subsequently, so that, though it remained the custom to begin these manuals with a lament for the lack of interest in godly domestic government, by early in the reign of James I the sincere Puritan householder can hardly have wanted for detailed advice.[45] At a reasonable price a variety of tracts provided drills and exercises for supplementing the work of the ministry at home, as well as more general injunctions of an unoriginal nature on the upbringing of children (gently but firmly and always without anger), the governing of servants (attentively, with proper care for their morals and education), and the appropriate relationship between man and wife (loving and forbearing, allowing the husband his proper place as the dominant partner but assigning both spouses the duty of creating a godly household). Many of these works enjoyed only restricted circulation, but *A Godly Forme of Houshold Government* by Dod and Cleaver proved quite popular, in part because most of it was a shameless cut-and-paste job compiled from the competing manuals, in part because it was genuinely "practical" in descending to such minutiae as the question of which spouse should beat which erring servant.[46]

Recent interest in the Puritan family has focused on placing it somewhere in a continuum between traditional/patriarchal/repressive and modern/romantic/affective. Opinions have differed, and by way of a compromise "transitional" seems to have become the majority verdict on whether godly parents had much emotional investment in their children and on the degree to which Puritan husbands looked on their wives as loving companions. These concerns, however, were at best of secondary interest to men intent on creating a mechanism for instruction and edification. Inevitably when we put our questions to their records, formal and informal, the response is incomplete and contradictory. Still, we keep on asking, and in the process slight some striking aspects of the godly household integrally related to the Puritanness of its proponents and, particularly, the ways in which they meant the family to continue the drive for discipline and to provide the literate environment essential to salvation. Dod and Cleaver, for example, saw godly house-holders who would "joyne their helping hands to Magistrates and Ministers" as a substitute of sorts for the classical eldership originally charged with giving the gospel point by disciplining offenders in view of the congregation. They were perfectly frank in directing their popular guide to those house-holders who "may long enough talke of Discipline, and still complaine of the want of Church-government." It was "all in vaine, and to no purpose," it turned out, "unless they will begin in this most necessary discipline, in reforming their owne houses according to the directions in this Treatise."[47] Within his four walls the householder was a governor no less than a bishop—or, rather, they might have said, a ruling no less than a teaching elder, if those politically embarrassing terms had not been studiously avoided. The house-holder possessed a real rod, not just a spiritual one, and he was expected to use it on errant children and servants, but he was assigned as well the dis-tinctly more spiritual duty of "rebuke or reproof." This latter was conceived of as a formal exercise performed solemnly and publicly before the entire household, a ceremony that resembled in form and intent the lively discipline unobtainable from congregational eldership or diocesan court: "a pronounc-ing of some misbehaviour, or knowne wickednesse of any, with condemning of the same (by the word of God) whereby they may have shame, that others might feare."[48]

Along with the function of ersatz consistory, the household was also assigned the role of substitute or supplementary schoolhouse, for a multiplic-ity of teachers was as central to the Puritan scheme as a multiplicity of governors. Without the Bible studiously and systematically digested, without catechisms, exegetical works, and devotional literature, without a reasonably comprehensive plan to coordinate reading and hearing, the sermon would most likely fall on fallow ground. "For let the best know this, that if they use not reading," wrote Richard Rogers in a book widely circulated in various forms, "they shall finde much more incumbrance in their life, unsavourinesse also, unquietnesse, unfruitfulnessne, and uncheerefulnesse, with such like, yea though they use other helpes."[49] In an age when so many could not read, literacy was held essential to salvation, and any chance encounters with il-literates were deemed suitable occasions for readers to turn to the praise of God for bestowing on them, at least, this precious gift. The well-governed, well-read household, in turn, was one of the few devices the Puritans ever seriously proposed for bringing their brand of faith to those who could not read.

There are times when Puritan authors seem singularly uninterested in addressing the problem of illiteracy, or even remembering it, as when William Perkins makes two of the seven cavils of the *common* people against hearing sermons the claim that they can do better at home just reading the Bible.[50] When the illiterate did receive attention, a single thread of hope was offered them, customarily in a very few words. Nicholas Bownd can speak for all his brethren in his advice to any whose inability to read prevented them from observing the duty of private scriptural study on the Sabbath: "Let them see the want of it to be so great in themselves, that they bring up their children unto it, and in the meane season repayre to those places where they may have the Scriptures read unto them."[51] Ordinarily, the place in question was the godly household engaged in the routines prescribed in the manuals. There the believing illiterates, whether visitors or permanent residents, surrounded by a literate majority, could learn their saving lessons incidentally and at second hand. Limited as such a formula might be, it was all the English Puritans could think of, and ministerial author after ministerial author repeated it when confronted with the needs of those unequipped for the rigorous course of spiritual education they required. Josias Nichols may have the distinction of being almost the only writer to address the problem who offered any additional advice: he enjoined the rich to pay for the education of the poor and "householders of all sortes, poore and rich" to teach reading to every member of their household, to which end he closed his *An Order of Household Instruction* with an appendix offering a short course in literacy.[52] The rest was up to schoolmasters, ministers, authors, and magistrates because, for all the enthusiasm of any given preface for any given reform, the Puritans rarely indulged in single-solution programs. The godly household was an obvious and "natural" occasion for collective religious life, but, like everything else Puritan, it functioned at all times as part of a larger society whose overall spiritual health and cultural vitality ultimately determined the efficacy of the whole Puritan undertaking. When that society began to falter, as it did in the 1620s, the Jacobean rapprochement would prove more contingent and less complete than it had originally seemed.

For a time the rest of the English nation did its part, or at least enough of it to justify the Dod-Cleaver style of sober cheerfulness. The education of the ministry clearly improved as the heterogeneous cadre recruited early in the reign of Elizabeth died off and successive generations of graduate clergy filled their places. The literacy of the congregations is more difficult to measure, but the broad trend was probably upward and the availability of education was visibly on the increase between the accession of James I and the coming of the Civil War. And when it came to material to read, the situation was indisputably encouraging. As Nichols, another classical veteran turned practical divine, put it, "God hath given a marveilous blessing of printing to further his Gospell." Quite apart from the widespread circulation of Bibles, the printing presses after 1590 or so brought forth a flood of religious material that dwarfed in volume and availability alike every other form of "popular" literature except the ubiquitous almanacs. When they rejoiced that there was "never such plentie of so good and plaine books printed, never so good cheape," Dod and Cleaver knew whereof they spoke.[53]

A particularly gaudy mayor of New York City once remarked that no girl was ever ruined by a book. Equally, no soul was ever saved by one, or rather only by a book, except perhaps in very rare instances the Bible. Reading was another part of the network of means revolving around Scripture and the sermon—it added informed reflection to the lively teachings of the pulpit and the pious life, as they in turn breathed meaning into the abstractions of print. There is an unusually full account of one set of these mutually reinforcing activities in John Winthrop's religious "experiencia" for his crisis year of 1617 that combines, in almost textbook fashion, print, pulpit, household, and Sabbath. In the final throes of his conversion, Winthrop followed Henry Sands's injunctions on the Sabbath by arising early one Sunday morning to "read over the covenant of certaine Christians" in Richard Rogers's *Seven Treatises*. "Therewith my heart beganne to breake" and those ever plaguing worldly distractions to recede so that he concluded with "prayer in tears" before proceeding to family religious exercises and then to hear the sermon at the Groton church, his mood "somewhat humbled." After the service he returned home for the noon meal and another round of family exercises before rereading Perkins's *Treatise tending unto a Declaration*, the work that had first shocked him into thinking of his own possible hypocrisy, and "thereby as my heart grewe more humbled, so my affections were more reclaimed." Thus prepared, he went on to Boxford church—the pulpit of his mentor Sands—for the afternoon lecture sermon, "where I heard with some affection and found sometymes a comfortable consent in prayer." And so it went with Winthrop, rout alternating with rally, all the rest of the day, concluding with a modest victory by nightfall that gave him the strength "to walke uprightly with my God, and dilligently in my callinge, and haveinge an heart willinge to denye myselfe, I founde the Godly life to be the only sweet life, and my peace with my God to be a true heaven upon earthe." Worldly distractions managed to gain the upper hand later in the week on this occasion, but there would be other Sabbaths with their interconnected rounds of hearing, reading, and family exercises, and by 1617 Winthrop was basically past the acute stage of his spiritual struggles and on his way, somewhat hesitantly, toward assurance.[54]

Winthrop had used these treatises by Rogers and Perkins almost as reference works. Rogers himself had counseled repetitious but thorough engagement with a few good books in preference to a smattering knowledge of a variety of titles, and he had also described the pattern into which the different kinds of good reading needed to fit. The literature of "instruction" simplified and schematized predestinarian theology, while the second main division of the godly literature helped "more specially to practise knowledge, by confirming faith, and endevouring to keepe a good conscience." Rogers not too modestly, if deservedly, gave his own *Seven Treatises* as a prime instance of this second, practical genre, and the book does seem archetypal in its form, at least: an ostentatiously advertised organizing structure is superimposed on a jumble of devotional and casuistical excursions. William Perkins enjoyed his peculiarly high standing (as to a lesser extent John Preston did after him) because he alone, as Rogers pointed out, managed to combine fire and system, practical and doctrinal modes, "containing the summe of many learned Authors, in a plainer manner about the matter of christianity."[55] Perhaps this was the reason that Winthrop, whose very soul called out for coherence, was so drawn to Perkins. In the case of Puritan works of practical divinity, however, if they were not of some length and bound together between hard covers, one would be tempted to deny to them the very name of book—until one remembers Rogers's advice and Winthrop's practice. These saving titles were not intended mainly for uninterrupted cover-to-cover reading but for recurrent use on appropriate occasions in the course of the reader's particular pilgrimage. Many of the most frequently reprinted works of the seventeenth century were probably employed in this manner, as vade mecums, spiritually and literally. Their octavo, duodecimo, or sixteenmo form—they resemble short, tubby bricks—made them ideal as pocket books for ready recourse, and the low survival rate of the most popular titles, despite the tens of thousands of copies produced, indicates how regularly and fervently they were hauled out for consultation. Indeed, the later reprintings of the most dearly loved of the omnium-gatherums, such as Lewis Bayly's encyclopedic *Practice of Piety* or Arthur Dent's *The Plaine Mans Path-way to Heaven*, may have been intended less for new readers than as replacement copies for the original owners, who wore out the earlier editions carrying them about with them.[56]

Puritans, however, would not have been Puritans if they had not put their favorite devices to more than one purpose. "Good and holie books" also contributed to the suspense and excitement of the drama of salvation for veteran professor and recent convert alike. Even the popular devotional manuals were initially more than familiar textbooks for one class of believers, the first-generation saints. Richard Eccles, a New England migrant "brought up in popery a good many years," recorded his initial shock on encountering the predestinarian universe for the first time through two well-known titles. "In *Practice of Piety* I read torments of hell which affected my heart with my estate by Adam's fall," he recalled, and in Perkins's *Exposition of the Creed* "I saw my condition bad." Eccles decided to go "to Yorkshire, where there were good means," that is, "a powerful ministry," and the preaching, not reading, secured his conversion. But to Bayly and Perkins goes the credit for setting him on his adventure while he was still searching for the light preceding the saving power of the word.[57]

Veteran sermon hearers, brought up on a plenitude of means, would hardly have been thrilled by Eccles's reading. Their excitement came in the succession of new titles regularly appearing to teach some familiar point in a different way. Like practiced theatergoers witnessing their tenth performance of, say, *King Lear*, they would lack the naive enthusiasm of a virgin audience, but they could still be surprised and moved by a fresh and powerful interpretation. This was the audience William Greenhill had in mind when he prefaced a fellow Congregational divine's latest work with the observations that "many would reade little, if new bookes were not set forth dayly" and that "new bookes are like new fashions, taken up at first with affection."[58] The curious publication history of most of the titles by prolific and avowedly popular preachers amply bears out Greenhill's good-natured strictures on the vagaries of this seasoned readership. In a large number of instances the sermons of ministers of great repute went through one edition only or achieved a fair number of editions in a short period and then sank from sight, occasionally lingering on in the form of extracts in some anthology such as the long-lived *A Garden of Spiritual Flowers*. As part of these compendia they were put to routine use in some semiregular devotional round, but taken at their first blush before they were interred in abridgments or neglected for the next entry from the same pen they served a more exciting purpose. *The Wedding Garment* of a Henry Smith (nine authorized editions between 1590 and 1592 plus some pirated versions), the Richard Sibbes collection published as *The Bruised Reed* (five editions, 1630–37), and hundreds of similar titles gave a knowing, godly readership a source of continuing stimulation that really does challenge comparison with the experience of a similarly initiated theater audience.

The same double appeal accounts for the popularity of the casuistical treatise. Weak Christians pressed on in their duties because the experience ultimately added to the operative knowledge that strengthened their affiance; strong Christians attempted to fulfill the law, while acknowledging their own personal incapacity, out of obligation and thankfulness to the God who honored the intent and forgave the inevitable failure. Both needed guides, general and specific, if they were not to make too much of a shipwreck of good consciences, and they turned avidly to these most practical of all the pieces of Puritan divinity. Characteristically, the most "popular" sins, judging from the circulation of the antidotes, were the hot ones, the crimes of passion rather than calculation. Thus in the combat against the typically impetuous vice of loose words, Perkins's *A Direction for the Government of the Tongue* achieved thirteen editions between 1593 and 1634, and Jeremy Dyke's *The Mischiefe and Miserie of Scandall* eight editions between 1630 to 1635. The Dyke piece was such a success in the era of the Great Migration that John Harvard left it to the college that bears his name, and John Humphries, one of the founders of the Massachusetts Bay Company, made a special point of sending over a first edition to his friend Isaac Johnson in New England during the terrible first winter after the arrival of the Winthrop fleet. (Humphries lacked a sense of the appropriate: Johnson was already dead of exposure by the time this tract against talebearing was dispatched; the fate of the copy is unknown.)[59]

Even in the case of this genre, it would be a mistake to make too much of its "bourgeois" character, parallel as these conduct manuals may seem to the simultaneously proliferating books of instruction on horsemanship, husbandry, housekeeping, and other practical subjects. Among religious "how-to" books, the single most popular category offered advice on how to die. At eleven editions between 1595 and 1638 *A Salve for a Sicke Man, or the Right Manner of Dying Well* was among the best-selling of William Perkins's titles, but it in no way exhausted the market for essays on the *ars moriendi*: the reading public that had already absorbed eighteen editions of Thomas Becon's similarly titled *The Sicke Mannes Salve* at the time when Perkins's entry first appeared, still managed to find room for another ten editions of the earlier work by 1632.[60] If the example of *A Salve for a Sicke Man* is in any way typical—and it could easily be multiplied—then one effect of the advent of printing was less to shunt aside a medieval outlook than to broadcast certain well-known medieval motifs: thanks to the printing press, far more Englishmen were introduced to the ars moriendi in the sixteenth and seventeenth centuries than ever could have come in contact with the fifteenth-century manuscript original that gives the genre its name. No wonder the

Puritans blessed God for the wonderful mercy of printing. However indispensable the preacher and his sermon, the tracts could and did go cheaply where no preaching minister was or could even be contemplated, and, for established professors like John Winthrop, they could fill in the lonely intervals between sermons, deepening the resonance and clarifying the implication of the Word in between those high moments of the week when it was actually received. Not everyone in England took the bait—that much was predestined—but the figures on the circulation and price of Puritan literature indicate just how widely available it became.[61]

To give full meaning to this information, it may first be helpful to consider the competition. Moralists regularly bemoaned the tastes of a reading public with a yen, they alleged, more for ballads and plays than for the gospel and sermons. Although it is fun to quote these lamentations to redeem English people of the period from the charge of an excess of sobriety, they are not really to be believed. Plays did *not* constitute any more than a tiny fraction of the output of the printing press, despite our propensity to equate the cultural life of Elizabethan and Jacobean England with the miracle of its dramatic literature. There is no meaningful way to compare topical ephemera of the broadside variety with long-lived sermons or treatises, but one can apply similar standards of measurement to religious literature and to the editions of romantic adventures and comic or grotesque tales credited by contemporaries with seducing unfortunate souls from godly reading. As it turns out, most of these distractions from the "heart-qua[l]mes" of conscience (Arthur Dent's term) appeared in only a handful of editions, if that. Among the more popular, tales of Sir Bevis of Hampton (the most widely condemned of this literature) did tolerably well by running to eight editions between 1560 and 1640, for perhaps twelve thousand total copies; the story of the seven champions of Christendom in one version or another reached seven or so editions between 1596 and 1639, about eleven thousand copies; and some form or another of the adventures of Adam Bell was printed eleven times between 1536 and 1632, for a maximum of seventeen thousand copies. Robert Greene's *Pandosto* (the source of *The Winter's Tale*), although neglected by Puritan moralists, actually sold better than their bêtes noires, reaching twelve editions (perhaps nineteen thousand copies) by 1640, and there were also, then as now, regular reprints of the immortals—Aesop, Reynard the Fox, the Faust book in one or another version. None of these figures, however, came near the circulation routinely achieved in much shorter periods by works from the godly side of the fence. Dent's *Plaine Mans Path-way to Heaven* has twenty-five known editions between 1601 and 1640 for thirty-eight thousand copies at a conservative estimate; the commentary of Dod and Cleaver on the Ten Commandments ran to twenty editions in just thirty-two years (thirty-five thousand copies using the same cautious method of estimation); and the best-selling manual of all, Bayly's *Practice of Piety*, reached at a bare minimum fifty-four editions (eighty-seven thousand copies at least) before 1640. Or, to make the same point another way, editions of the sermons of widely read preachers appeared with greater regularity than the news books. There were few years between 1590 and 1630 that did not see a new edition of the compositions, for example, of either Henry Smith or Arthur Dent or both, and even the exceptional years are very likely illusory: gaps in the numbering of the editions suggest that a year without Smith or Dent was just a year when all the copies of an impression were used up by enthusiastic readers, leaving no survivors to be entered in the *Short Title Catalogue*.

Data on prices point in the same direction, to a wide and growing accessibility for Puritan literature. Between 1550 and 1650, despite a dramatic increase in wages and prices, the costs of books generally remained relatively stable, making them one item that in real terms became steadily more affordable.[62] At about 9d. to 1s.6d. per copy, *The Practice of Piety* or *The Plaine Mans Path-way* or *The Bruised Reed* was available to almost anyone able to read and not forced to subsist on charity. The "footstools" of the commonwealth, the agricultural day laborers, could have purchased them in the 1630s with about one to two days' ordinary work, not insubstantial but not insuperable.[63] John Bunyan, indeed, priding himself on his wife's poverty at the time of their marriage ("not having so much household-stuff as a Dish or Spoon betwixt us both"), could still boast, "yet this she had for her part, *The Plain Man's Pathway to Heaven*, and *The Practice of Piety*, which her father had left her when he died."[64] For individuals only a little higher up the social scale the shilling cost represented a much smaller proportional outlay: Dent has sent the Warwickshire rustics who inhabit his *Plaine Mans Path-way* abroad in search of a good cow for which they were willing to pay £3.0.0 (double the going price, but in May "we shall finde deare ware of her") when they fall into religious company and engage in the dialogue on heavenly matters that sold for one-sixtieth of that sum.[65] Nor was one shilling the rock-bottom minimum price for godliness. Our sometime heathen mariner John Trumbull reports that he was saved in part by another popular Dent title, *A Sermon on Repentance*, which ran to thirty-eight editions and cost at the outside 3d. a copy. In 1620 (about when Trumbull encountered the sermon) that figure would have purchased only three-quarters of a peck of barley (the poor man's grain), one pound of Suffolk cheese, or one egg—though the hen that laid it cost in the same year 1s.4d. or just over five 3d. sermons.[66]

There is, nonetheless, a distinction to be made among Puritan titles. Duodecimos and octavos are one thing, folios and (most of the time) quartos quite another. In folio Sibbes's *The Saint's Cordials* sold for 8s. in 1629, barely affordable for a poor believer, and the three volumes of William Perkins's *Workes* went at 33s. (unbound) as of 1633, a price that must have been beyond a £30 a year middling vicar unless he bought the set on credit, paid in irregular installments, and hoped the bookseller died well before the full sum came due.[67] The prize for contriving to have the most limited appeal of all, however, can probably be awarded to John Downame, who brought out his devotional works as the seventeenth-century equivalents of coffee-table books: large in format, long in pages, and formidable in price. Of interest today as much for the elaborate symbolism of their title pages as for their substance, *The Christian Warfare* enjoyed at best a modest circulation and *A Guide to Godlynesse*, a fat folio of a thousand pages, was such a disaster that the copyright and unsold copies had to be unloaded on a new set of stationers, who reissued it a full seven years after its initial publication in 1622 in an attempt to sell out its single print run.[68] Other works, such as Richard Rogers's *Seven Treatises*, fell into a middle case between the squat pocket manuals and the luxury folios. In its folio and quarto forms the work reached a respectable six editions over a twenty-seven-year period, but a cheaper duodecimo abridgment was able to add another five editions in just seventeen years, and most readers probably came across the work through the extensive extract in *A Garden of Spiritual Flowers*, which, appearing variously as an octavo or a duodecimo, ran to thirty editions in just over twenty years. When the Puritan ministry rejoiced from time to time over the great variety of good books suitable in their diversity to the great differences in the situations of the godly, they were probably referring as much to distinctions of purse as of person. But in whatever form, godly literature of some sort, cheap and plentiful, was there as part of the great achievement of the age, the loosely textured fabric of means with which the Puritan ministry hoped to blanket its converts. "And so I went [on] in use of means," explained a Kentish layman who had, indeed, used most of them. "And I hearing—seek the Lord—I sought."[69]

In the 1580s and 1590s Puritan ministers found themselves obliged to evaluate several decades of official Protestantism by addressing the recurring question, Why has the gospel not taken more root? Richard Greenham and Robert Cawdry, among others, answered in ways typical of their respective careers, Greenham by glumly observing that a sure sign of the true word was the multitudes who refused to heed it, Cawdry by declaring with his usual enthusiasm that the word needed better preparation, simpler explanation, and more systematic enforcement.[70] Morose or undaunted, in their responses both men admitted that the dismal state of English religion needed explanation, lest irreligious or popish scoffers claim "the word now preached not to be the right word." Forty years later, in the early years of the Great Migration, Thomas Hooker and John Cotton were defending the English ministry from Separatist attack by invoking its unparalleled *success*.[71] A few years further on still, Ezekiel Rogers and his Yorkshire congregation newly come to New England prefaced their withdrawal from communion with their mother church by a congratulatory paean to "the work of conversion" and "the power of religion," which had been greater "in England than in all the known world besides."[72]

Something had happened between Greenham and Ezekiel Rogers, and that was the increasing effectiveness of "practical divinity." It had worked wonderfully in the estimation of its later practitioners, who were increasingly proud of the special qualities of the church capable of such miracles. Our attention has already been drawn to a growing aggressiveness in official Anglican apologetics after 1603, as the by then time-honored liturgy and hierarchy came to be regarded less as pardonable deviations from Continental reforms and more as parts of a distinctive national heritage. The same chauvinism, however, is increasingly evident in the Puritan wing of the English ministry, ever more sure that their incompletely reformed church was more than compensated for its formal deficiencies in the distinctive evangelical and didactic efficacy of its clergy. Mutual enthusiasm for the national achievements in practical divinity encouraged a degree of collaborative, or at least parallel, enterprise within the various groups comprising the Church of England.[73] Joseph Hall, Thomas Morton, James Ussher, and George Downame, all loyal members of the episcopal bench, shared in theological endeavors with leading Puritan ministers, and the omnipresent *Practice of Piety* that brought so many of the laity to their first sense of sin was the work of the bishop of Bangor. (Lewis Bayly, however, unlike the others, was a bishop with a difference, in whom John Cotton could claim an "interest" when he needed a graduate of his informal divinity seminary at Boston ordained without embarrassing interrogatories.)[74] One can see in these circumstances if one wishes, and many church historians of irenic bent have so wished, the basis for detente, if not reconciliation, within the Church of England, until the rise of the Laudians in the late 1620s and 1630s set the ecclesiastical clock back half a century to the days of Thomas Cartwright and the irreconcilables of the Elizabethan classes.

One does need to remember the relative harmony of the middle period of Puritan history and its sense of achievement to appreciate in full the subsequent conviction of betrayal that spread among the Puritan ranks in the 1630s and the simultaneous contamination of moderate opinion by its continuing willingness to look for some basis of cooperation with authority. But Laud did not somehow raise the shades of Field and Udall to walk again in their old militancy. He simply worsened enormously tensions within the Puritan movement already extant and growing. No matter how ensconced in the national establishment some Puritan divines may have been, by the death of James I in 1625 the sectarian thrust in their movement was waxing strong because of two parallel phenomena: developments inherent within the techniques of practical divinity itself and the effective detachment of a substantial segment of the Puritan ministry from a comprehensive parochial charge. The reign of James I was no more a golden age for the Puritan movement than any other period in its long and usually roiled history; rather, embedded deep within the logic of this particular resolution of the ongoing Puritan tensions were the seeds of its own subsequent instability.

Practical divinity scored its successes because of its uniquely effective capture of the convert's imagination. To take one of the more obscure instances, Thomasine Clopton Winthrop may have been a young woman of simple gifts—and one suspects, given that characterization, of limited opportunities within the Winthrop household—but she had a chance on her deathbed to give a last performance that her attendant and grieving husband, John Winthrop, could then write up in terms heroic enough to have been reserved for Sir Richard Grenville and the *Revenge*. Nor was her final conflict in any sense singular: holy lives and deaths of various individuals were a common literary genre. (Women in particular seem to have been assigned affecting last days.)[75] What Thomasine Winthrop achieved in dying was a narrative plot: a coherence, struggle, and climax that gave a meaning to the life she was then leaving. There were, of course, less ultimate means to the same end, through ordered routines, constant reiteration of purpose, the excitement of progressive mastery of a difficult art, the comfort of regular repetition, and the stimulation of fresh challenges. All the exercises in personal history—conversion narratives, spiritual autobiographies, diaries—bear eloquent witness to the power of practical divinity to transform what was in most instances unpromising biographical material into the stuff of epics. The Puritan ministry was thus correct to claim in its most egregious moments of self-congratu-lation that the demonstrative power of some godly neighbor's ordered regi-men could bowl over a "carnal" man or woman who had finally gotten around to asking of life, Isn't there something more than *this*?[76] Therein, however, lay a curse no less than a blessing. Still another recruit would be added to the Puritan cause, peopling it, however, more and more with indi-viduals rejecting past life and past associates as so much living "at random," and whose means to salvation was the exclusive company of each other.

A good instance is Anne Etherington, another one of Thomas Shepard's redeemed Northerners. She was conquered (as she was meant to be) by her abrupt injection, as a servant, into the routine of a Puritan household. "She living in ignorance till she came to Newcastle to a godly family and it was harsh to her spirit being bound seven years. And I resolved if [I were] ever loose I would be vile." But she never was loose again. A godly husband ("who thought me so, but I was not") succeeded the godly family, and then, seeking a more enveloping net of godliness, she left Newcastle for New England: "and feeling not the means work[,] hence I desired hither to come[,] thinking one sermon might do me more good than a hundred there."[77] She had learned the first two lessons of practical divinity, that divinity was best "practiced" in a matrix of means and that there was danger in wandering too far from it. Anne Etherington's discovery that life among the godly was the surest means to get and keep godliness eventually led her, and others like her, to flee the mixed multitudes at home for New England in search of an environment where the impact of grace could be multiplied by the prepon-derance of the gracious in the population. In England the same impulse, derived ironically from an attempt to broaden the Puritan mission, went a long way toward creating a separated people well before an immigrant ship crossed the Atlantic. As one of the chief executors of this tangled legacy, John Winthrop would find himself complaining in the 1630s of the failure to succor weak and faltering Christians because of "that spirituall pride, that Sathan rooted into the hearts of their brethren, who when they are Con-verted, doe not, nor will not strengthen them, but doe Censure them, to be none of Gods people, nor any visible Christians," even as he shepherded those he criticized into an exodus more final in its denial of the weak and faltering than any cold shouldering back in England.[78]

By the time of the Migration the long apprenticeship in the means had begun to work a little too well, nourishing a sense of self-assurance and mutuality not anticipated by the original authors of devotional manuals and the early proponents of the neo-Hebraic Sabbath. In 1644 John Cotton was able to enlarge on the traditional justification of lay participation in discipline, which had stressed the didactic qualities of congregational assent, and to appeal to the saint's duty "to watch over his neighbor's soul, as his own, and to admonish him of his sin, unless he be a scorner."[79] He could go further than his sixteenth-century predecessors and speak of individual rights and of the obligations of love as integral parts of "church order" because his saints had gone further than *their* Elizabethan forebears. Cotton had come around to defending openly what had been going on quietly for years in meetings in which the godly had passed well beyond simple scriptural exegesis to probe into one another's spiritual affairs under the guise of personal application of the doctrine. Practical divinity earnestly practiced over a period of decades had provided the experiential legitimation for much of mature congregational polity. The confidence, for example, with which the members of gathered churches came to weigh the genuineness of new candidates' conversions and to exclude the reprobate originated in exercises developed by practical divines whose intentions had been anything but sectarian. They had written so much on the "morphology of conversion" and enjoined so much soul-searching that their following inevitably developed a certain sophistication in these matters.[80] And the same divines had thrust personal spiritual experience out of the privacy of individual meditation into the public arena of the extraparochial gatherings. Part of the learning by participation came through the example and conversation of the godly, with whom one compared experiences at those much praised fruitful Sabbath conferences. "Neither must wee blush or be abashed to acknowledge our wants unto our brethren," Richard Greenham had cautioned saints he assumed would be overshy at such meetings, "but with all humilitie earnestly deale with them, and enquire of them . . . how they can gather of the creatures and works of God some fruitfull matter of thanksgiving, that by their godly participation wee may have either our ignorance helped, or our infirmities relieved."[81] Cautious and discreet fellow that he was, Greenham would surely have winced, had he lived to see it, at the later stages of the process he helped set in motion. By the 1620s these meetings had become semiformal in Cotton's own Boston, as well as in Thomas Hooker's Chelmsford, where there was "a company of Christians who held frequent communion together, used the censure of admonition, yea and of excommunication, with much presence of Christ, only they had not officers nor the sacraments."[82] In time—and not a long time—the godly would take the next logical step and demand the exclusion of the unworthy from their church fellowship. Hints of the trouble to come can be found as early as the mid-1620s, but the movement for purity did not reach full flower until the years of Laudian domination, when the English faithful would come to seem less a vanguard than a saving remnant. For the middle period of Puritanism the dominant movement was merely the growth in the sense of solidarity and autonomy among the godly and a broadening of the agenda they chose to address. In the domain of the conventicle, questions of practice had an unhappy genius for turning into issues of politics.

Greenham in his treatise on the Sabbath had complained that conferences among "equals" (that is, unsupervised lay meetings) were likely to wander from the ministerially defined curriculum "to talke of other matters above their capacitie and knowledge."[83] His proposed solution (echoed elsewhere), placing an able minister in charge of every such exercise, was neither universally practical nor necessarily efficacious. Much of the problem was again of the clergy's own making. The ministers who warned against private individuals meddling in affairs reserved to the governors of church and state also exhorted the godly to use the exercises to weigh seriously the works of God as manifested in his latest providences—to undertake "the consideration of his creatures" in Nicholas Bownd's phrase. Bownd meant the weather, neither an inconsequential nor a nonpolitical topic in Elizabethan or Jacobean times. Drought and flood, good and bad harvests, were God's doing, and disasters especially could be understood as judgments for the failings of an unworthy people. Bownd himself attributed the poor harvests of the 1590s to the magistrates' failure to enforce a strict Sabbath, and in the next run of dearth years, the 1620s, Thomas Hooker would locate the cause in the marriage of Charles I to the Catholic Henrietta Maria.[84]

Fasts, above all, invited topical exposition because by definition they were called in response to some public calamity and because they were often held in defiance of authority. Prohibitions, as in the new canons of 1604, which banned unauthorized fasts, merely made the exercise more distinctive and more urgent because private individuals would now have to atone for the sin of magisterial negligence along with the provoking evil of the particular moment. If the authorities failed to require a public repentance, then the prayers and tears of the godly in secret were all the more likely to appease an angry God for the benefit of the whole nation; at the least, such clandestine activities would preserve the participants themselves in the midst of the deserved general punishment. Bownd, the theoretician of fasting as he was of the Sabbath, prudently hedged on the question of whether the praying, fasting individuals might meet together when the magistrate forbade such a gathering, but Arthur Hildersham, who more than equaled him in prestige, had no such hesitations. "These tymes," he pronounced, "may also be justly called tymes of persecution," when Christians could lawfully practice their religious duties secretly in defiance of the magistrate, because "this Christian duty of publick fasting (which god hath also streightly commanded to be taught and practiced when such occasions is given) is not only not allowed but opposed and persecuted."[85] (Hildersham, as we shall see, practiced what he preached.) Private fasts can be found taking on an unashamedly partisan form by, once again, the mid- to late 1620s. Hugh Peter graced an unauthorized fast arranged by the Earl of Warwick by praying for the conversion of the queen, and Henry Burton, between shots at the Duke of Buckingham, explicated "*Joshua* his removall of the *excommunicate thing*" by telling his audience "in plain tearmes, that the main thing was *that damnable Hierarchie*."[86] The origins of what was by this late date a growing schism, however, can be found in apparently uncontroversial and wholesome activity. Weak Christians, in company with proven saints, were to work out the meaning of Scripture, and, through the complete sense of the word understood in terms of their own personal experience and their observation of the world around them, their salvation. When that world and their experience of it came to seem peculiarly menacing, the same individuals who attributed bad harvests to unsanctified royal marriages were just as likely to possess hearts first pierced to the quick by their discovery of official misconduct. A good instance is Richard Conder, a Cambridge yeoman of modest acres who founded a Nonconformist clerical dynasty and who frequented a conventicle held regularly in the 1630s on market day at Royston. Meeting in a private room, the participants discussed "how they had heard on the Sabbath-day, and how they had gone on the week past." When the talk turned to "*what means God first visited their souls and began a work of grace upon them*," Conder's saving instrument turned out to be the reissued Book of Sports:

> When our minister was reading it, I was seized with a chill and horror
> not to be described. Now, thought I, iniquity is established by a law, and
> sinners are hardened in their sinful ways! What sore judgments are to be
> expected upon so wicked and guilty a nation! . . . And God set in so with
> it, that I thought it was high time to be earnest about salvation. . . . So
> that I date my conversion from that time; and adore the grace of God in
> making that to be an ordinance to my salvation, which the devil and
> wicked governors laid as a trap for my destruction.[87]

In 1645 a Gloucestershire Puritan minister named John Corbet (who was no Independent) would make the same observation another way when he boasted of the ability of "a practicall ministry" to "inable vulgar capacities more fitly to apply themselves to such things as concerne the life of a morall man." (He meant by "such things" the transgressions of Charles I and by a "morall man" the kind willing to fight for Parliament.) Such awakened souls might not be fit to be governors, but through their religious training they had learned enough to participate in government, for they had learned to know truth from falsehood when it was put to them by those claiming authority in church and state.[88]

Ordinarily the clergy were less appreciative of lay assertiveness. Corbet was writing in the Civil War, and composing a front-line dispatch at that, issued from a city that stood out alone for Parliament in the midst of the royalist countryside because of the enthusiasm of its citizens for the godly cause. He was obliged to think highly of the capacities of these shopkeeper and artisan students of practical divinity because they, unlike the Gloucester-shire gentry and their tenants, were on the right side. Before this enforced upward valuing of their abilities, the godly appeared to most of the Puritan ministry as volatile allies at best, and many of the clergy rejected the alliance altogether. Nonetheless, at any time after 1585 a significant, if relatively small, portion of the Puritan ministry found themselves moving in tandem with the most restive members of the godly, obliged to embrace the sectarian implications of practical divinity openly and explicitly. These were clergymen deprived of their ministry in one or another crackdown who were unwilling either to accept Separatism or to throw away their talents in premature retire-ment. They chose instead to hang on to their calling in disguised form, occasionally surfacing subsequently to resume ministerial office.

Although the number of such anomic clergy can easily be inflated, at the moment we are in danger of underestimating their impact in the pre-Laudian period because of the dominance of a single potentially misleading statistic. After detailed and careful research into the impact of the new canons of 1604, S. B. Babbage concluded that between 1604 and 1610 only about eighty to ninety Puritan ministers lost their benefices to the most systematic purge of the clergy before 1662, Archbishop Bancroft's campaign for confor-mity and especially for subscription (an oath of assent to the proposition that the Book of Common Prayer and the Thirty-Nine Articles contained nothing contrary to the word of God). Since about one-fifth of an already small body of martyrs later conformed, we are apparently left with only a very small force of out-of-work clerics to roil the waters during the otherwise halcyon days of James I by separating out the Puritan laity, no matter how restless the latter's growing proficiency in things of the spirit may have left them.[89]

Babbage's estimates—or, rather, the uses to which others have put his estimates—can be faulted in several ways. To begin with, they cover only those beneficed ministers who officiated in one of the fifteen dioceses that possess surviving records of the Bancroft deprivations. A minister without a benefice to lose is never considered, and so the casualty list does not include (among others) four of the five men who laid down the basis for nonseparating Congregationalism because they had been lecturers, like the leading Elizabethan Presbyterians before them. After brief careers they were effectively barred from exercising further public clerical functions by their loss or failure to obtain the episcopal license to preach, a disability that did not necessarily put an end to their activities. William Ames did leave England to live out his life in exile in Holland, but William Bradshaw certainly, and Paul Baynes very probably, merely carried on their ministry to select congregations without either preferment or episcopal supervision, and Henry Jacob founded his Southwark church.[90] Bradshaw, Baynes, and Jacob are exceptions for the publicity they received in their lifetimes and consequently in our knowledge of what they did after "silencing," but there is nothing unique about their situation: in the archdeaconry of Essex alone ten curates and lecturers lost their posts under the new canons of 1604, none of them by definition included in Babbage's count, and all of them (for the moment) are too obscure to be traced subsequently.[91] Yet, if anything, Bancroft's hand came down hardest on the unbeneficed clergy, who, as the archbishop well knew, could be dealt with summarily, unlike the holders of livings, who could be deprived only after a lengthy legal procedure.[92]

Babbage's figures also suffer from systematic gaps in the attempt to identify deprivations among the beneficed ministry. The entire province of York is omitted from the study, though the 1604 canons were enforced there too. The clerical casualties were certainly much fewer in the northern archdiocese—Matthew Hutton and his successor Tobie Matthew were much more easygoing prelates than Bancroft—but they were not insignificant: the activities of Richard Clifton, Robert Southworth, and John Robinson (deprived in Norfolk but active in the North) among the disaffected laity of the archdeaconry of Nottingham indirectly issued in the mother church of New England at Plymouth and in virtually all of the General Baptist congregations of Interregnum England.[93] In the province of Canterbury, where enforcement of the canons was more vigorous, deprived Nonconformists fail to show up in the Babbage figures if they happen to have held their livings in dioceses with missing or faulty records or even if the history of their suspension and deprivation happens to show up in some less obvious source. Babbage could identify only three deprived ministers in the markedly Puritan diocese of Peterborough; the institution books turn up the names of another fifteen. In

Warwickshire (divided between two dioceses, neither well documented) the lone incontrovertible clerical casualty probably had plenty of company, since, as Babbage notes, twenty-seven threatened ministers from the county petitioned the Privy Council in 1604, describing themselves as "allreadie for the most part suspended from the former use of our ministerie and [we] doe all expect presentlie to be full deprived." Some may have escaped or been reinstated but surely not all of them.[94]

When some clergymen managed to attain the minimal significance or notoriety to make their life stories capable of reconstruction, the individual biographies can be similarly suggestive, both about the degree of underrecording of deprivations and about the consequences for the peace of church and state in the reign of James I. In the diocese of Salisbury, for example, Robert Parker (the only one of the Jacobean Congregationalist theorists to have a benefice) was deprived of his Wiltshire living in 1607 and left free to develop his ideas of polity while in exile in the Netherlands.[95] And in Ely, a diocese where Bishop Martin Heaton boasted that his moderate courses had produced universal conformity, Josiah Horne nevertheless lost the rectory of Orwell in Cambridgeshire in 1605 and embarked on a career as interesting in its way for the subsequent development of the Puritan movement as Parker's. He immediately went to London to join forces with Jacob and Bradshaw in their campaign against Bancroft, then disappeared from sight until he gained a new living in 1616 as rector in Winwick in Lancashire, where his status as a beleaguered Protestant missionary in recusant territory earned his Puritanism a measure of official toleration.[96] In between Orwell and Winwick lie ten years or more when it is very difficult to believe solely on the basis of lack of information that so consistently pugnacious and well connected an individual somehow lapsed into loyal passivity.

To complete the picture of the body of Puritan ministers liberated from parochial obligations, one must also recall those cashiered Elizabethan Presbyterians who survived into the seventeenth century. The indomitable Robert Cawdry at Coventry, for example, was joined by the equally formidable and long-lived Humphrey Fenn, who lost his benefice in 1590 but carried on in his native city as a lecturer, unlicensed, unrepentant, and until the 1620s officially unrecognized, and who died in 1634 leaving a last will and testament condemning the want of discipline in his nation's churches.[97] Another of the leading Elizabethans, Josias Nichols, stayed on in his Kentish parish of Eastwell for almost four decades after his deprivation in 1602, and we might be tempted to imagine for him too a long untroubled retirement were it not for the notice that he was implicated in the propaganda campaign against Bancroft in 1606 and then took the lead in opposition to the forced loan of

1614.[98] Once again, it is hard to believe that a man of such zeal and proven activism would give up his clerical activities for the last thirty-seven years of his life.

There are a few other prominent individuals who are like William Bradshaw and Humphrey Fenn in that their late and less official clerical careers can be definitely established, and a few others like Nichols for whom there is enough evidence to establish the presumption that they too belonged to this shadow ministry. For the rest little can be said, except to note that a suspiciously large number of unrepentant Nonconformists suddenly surfaced in 1625 or immediately thereafter, resuming their vocations when Charles I at the beginning of his reign instructed his bishops to grant an amnesty to the surviving members of the deprived clergy.[99] Ezekiel Culverwell, for example, returned to his native London in 1609 after losing Great Stanbridge, Essex, and the man under whose preaching John Winthrop as well as many others first experienced the power of the gospel did not again officially hold another pulpit, apparently contenting himself with the composition of the frequently reprinted *Treatise of Faith*. Yet suddenly in 1626 there is an indication that he served as lecturer to the London parish of St. Boltolph, Aldgate, and that the vestry of the same parish tried to get him formally appointed to that post in 1627.[100] How he filled in the other years between 1609 and his death in 1631 we can only conjecture. Other deprived Puritan clergy have not left even these hints of a postdeprivation ministry carried on in "private" at least intermittently between periods of legally recognized clerical activity. But in the light of what we do know from the chance survival of scraps of information about some of their more famous colleagues in the same predicament, there are no good grounds for taking the silence of the records as straightforward proof that the bulk of the deprived simply lapsed into inactivity. Apart from some details about a few otherwise obscure individuals that suggest quite the opposite, we also have the testimony of John Sprint, a renegade Nonconformist who subsequently made his submission to the bishops. In the course of his apology he tells us that his former brethren who suffered deprivation then practiced "privat meanes of privat reading, catechising, instruction, reproofe, comfort, exhortation, and invocation, in the absence of the publike." And Sprint went on to claim that the consequences of the deprivations under the new canons had been the growth of a schismatic spirit among the clerical casualties and their followings:

> Verily in sundry others, especially the younger and more unstaied sort, especially of them which draw neere the brincke of Brownisme, it hath falne out, that after the losse and leaving their Ministrie, small other

fruite had happened in them, then to make the Churches rent the wider, to speake evill, and scoffe at persons in authoritie . . . to breede distraction in the hearts of the people, to villifie their Godly breathren, which have submitted themselves to conformitie . . . and to prepare the mindes of unstable persons, of tender consciences, and shallow knowledge to schisme and seperation.[101]

If only in some bit of marginalia Sprint had spelled out just which of the sundry others had drawn "neere the brincke of Brownisme" and especially just which of the younger sort, we might know something more of the tiny cracks in the Puritan movement that would widen into visible fissures after 1630. As ever, a few (and only a very few) of these individuals are visible in their particularity—the former London lecturer John Trundle, for example, inhibited from preaching in 1606 but still at it in 1607 anyway and then, after his suspension, discovered in 1608 preaching at a Separatist conventicle in his old parish of Christ Church, Newgate. Similarly, among the Nottinghamshire Separatist leaders, Robinson and Clifton are known to have gone into exile in the Netherlands, but no one can say what subsequently happened to Southworth, who served as unlicensed curate of Scrooby in 1607 when Robinson was organizing the likes of William Bradford and William Brewster into a Separatist church.[102]

In many ways those of the deprived who only drew near Separatism's brink are more interesting for the subsequent progress of the Puritan movement than that handful known to have actually crossed over. They remained a respectable part of the Puritan ministry, harassed but not fugitives, and therefore still able to edge a portion of their own camp ever closer to the practices of their avowed enemies. We can get a glimpse of the process at work in tracing in greater than usual detail the careers of two leading figures of the middle period, Arthur Hildersham and John Dod. Neither man indulged in any form of Separatism; both, indeed, repudiated doctrinal sectarianism when they saw it. Yet because both men were bridge figures between the days of the Elizabethan Presbyterians and the period of Laudian repression, the ambiguities of Jacobean Puritanism are embodied in their lengthy careers. They were the joint literary executors of Thomas Cartwright's manuscripts, they had been active members of their respective classes, and both subsequently made great names for themselves through their writings as practical divines. And both were appropriately hardy, Hildersham surviving until 1632, Dod until 1645.

Hildersham was the more radical of the two, and had he chosen to write more on polity, he would probably have earned a place as a "nonseparating Congregationalist" alongside his longtime close associate William Brad-shaw.[103] (With or without Hildersham, it would be no more unwieldy and rather more accurate to term the position associated with these men postclassical disciplinarianism.) Originally ordained vicar of the Earl of Hunting-don's seat of Ashby-de-la-Zouche in Leicestershire in 1593, Hildersham became prominent in Puritan politicking just before and just after Hampton Court. His zeal for national reform was matched on the local level by the zest with which he built up a distinct party among his parishioners: when one of his Ashby opponents, a certain Richard Spencer, suffered losses by fire in 1605, he lost no time in improving the misfortune from the pulpit by announcing that "there was three dwelling houses burned and 2. of them were Chrestians and the third meaning the said Spencer, he could not tell what to make of him." The new canons cost Hildersham his benefice in the same year, but he was immediately licensed as a lecturer in the neighboring diocese of Coventry and Lichfield, where he carried on a twice weekly lecture at two separate sites in conjunction with his old friend Bradshaw and also reentered Ashby, as a lecturer this time, in 1609. Richard Neile, however, suppressed the joint lectureships in 1611, and two years later, in 1613, the Ashby pulpit went the same way when the High Commission suspended Hildersham. During the next three years, Hildersham's disgruntled followers made life miserable for the new, conformist vicar, holding "sundry conventicles or exercises of religion in privat houses," as well as public disputations criticizing the ceremonies, and taking their families "to other parishes to hear unconformable ministers, and carried many of the parish of Ashby after them." (Hildersham's defense of conventicling may date from this period.)[104] Two of the ringleaders and Hildersham again were prosecuted by the High Commission in 1616 at the instance of the embattled vicar, and on this occasion the Puritan champion was obliged to go into hiding for a period of years to escape a severe sentence. He was finally restored to his Ashby lectureship in 1625, the year of Charles I's amnesty, and held it with only a single, brief suspension during the remaining seven years of his life. As a practical divine Hildersham, though in no sense a "liberal," usually goes down as an inclusionist who stressed the necessity to prepare all men to receive intelligently the grace the elect alone were ultimately predestined to enjoy; as a practicing cleric he was, out of necessity and inclination alike, the pastor of the faithful few, consistently partisan and, for years at a time, clandestine in the conduct of his ministry. All in all, his is not a life history of much value in illustrating the spirit of comprehension allegedly pervading the Church of England in the years between Whitgift and Laud.

John Dod was less overtly sectarian after his deprivation under the new canons, possibly because of his temperament, possibly because by removal from his old parish he avoided the temptations to factionalism inherent in staying on.[105] Rather, he typified the deprived minister launched on an unattached missionary career after his cure was lost. He and his frequent collaborator Robert Cleaver were deprived of their Oxfordshire pulpits for nonsubscription in 1607 and, like Hildersham and Bradshaw, at once engaged in a joint lecturing mission at several different sites in a neighboring diocese, Peterborough. In 1611 Archbishop Abbot, apparently provoked by the irrepressible Neile, ordered the bishop of Peterborough to suppress these lectures, as well as several others, but Thomas Dove was no Richard Neile, and Abbot found himself repeating the same instructions (with unknown success) three years later in 1614. At some point not too long after that Cleaver died, but Dod stayed on in the diocese, at Canons Ashby, Northamptonshire, under the protection of the influential Knightley family, who had performed the same service for Martin Marprelate. Finally, he too resumed his public ministry in 1625, when his patrons resorted to a legal fiction to appoint him curate of a depopulated parish, their family seat of Fawsley, Northamptonshire. "At *Fausley*," Samuel Clarke remarks with unconscious humor, "he had quietnesse from the Courts, as also at [Canons] *Ashby*; for in neither of those places was there any Church-wardens."[106] In total, this exemplar of respectable Puritanism spent eighteen years, the most vigorous of his long life, in private capacities, which extended even to running a graduate seminary at Canons Ashby for Puritan aspirants to the ministry. Thomas Fuller, the premier irenicist of the seventeenth century, said more than he meant, or meant what he said and deliberately said it a little obliquely, in observing that Dod when he was silenced "instructed almost as much as before, by his holy demeanor and pious discourse."[107]

Other, less well-known men with roughly analogous histories can also be adduced. Of the sixteen individuals in Peterborough diocese, for example, who were deprived of their benefices under the new canons, four at the least are known to have continued their ministry in private, and of the rest we have no record. Similarly, of eight ministers deprived for the same cause in the diocese of Norwich, there is evidence to suggest that one eventually conformed and another five disappeared without a trace, but James Harrison continued on in a string of informal lectureships across the diocesan border in Essex before becoming chaplain to the Barrington family in his last years, and George Hulkes surfaced again a few years after his deprivation "preachinge once in a moneth" at the church of Wickham Market, Suffolk, "not knowne to be licensed."[108] The prevalence of clergy whose postdeprivation careers fall into the unknown category obscures the shape and exact size of the nicodemite Puritan ministry, not its existence. In close proximity to the bright noon of the Jacobean settlement, in which moderate Calvinist bishops persuaded nonconformists of a peaceable disposition into minimal concessions, lay a tenebrous domain of uncertain boundaries in which lecturers on the run or tucked away in quiet corners ministered intermittently to a floating collection of self-certified saints.

The reign of James I and the primacy of Archbishop Abbot left the Puritan movement as inherently paradoxical as in the heyday of the Elizabethan classes, though the enduring dilemma was differently posed. In the Elizabethan period the intimate link between participation and separation was tangible enough: the ordinary English laity who took up the cause of the international Reformation were by definition members of a distinct minority in their own country, where the official religion of the statute books made only the most gradual headway in the parishes against outright resistance and the forces of inertia. After the collapse of the Presbyterian movement, however, the central duality of Puritanism continued in a more muted form. Alongside a genuine rapprochement with the Jacobean church in the triumphal process of achieving a comprehensive Protestant national culture, a portion of the most committed of the Puritan ministry and the larger share of the godly laity were slowly accreting into a "church within a church" more durable and less detectable, because less self-conscious, than the ephemeral classical organizations.

It was a delicate moment in the history of the English movement, though not totally lacking in possibilities for adjustment and redirection; the Puritans had recovered from worse after the suppression of the classes. But in 1590 repression had preceded a long run of natural and military disasters that punctuated a decade's worth of ever more violent political conflict. The Puritan movement had already been driven so far underground by the time the crisis of the 1590s exploded that it could in no way profit from the widespread discontent and instability of the times. Instead, its leadership did little more than try to keep together what few traces of organization were left in order to concentrate their hopes and energies on persuading a new monarch to come to their aid when advancing age finally carried the old one off. In the 1620s the disasters and the new reign came first and then, only after the alienation from a faltering, unattractive political system was all but complete, would William Laud and his associates come into the fullness of their power. The result of this peculiar sequence of events was at first a growing frustration and increasing militancy in a segment of the English Puritan ranks and a reactive, conservative panic among the rest, followed in 1640 by an excess of success that exposed the chasm and made it unbridgeable. In America, as well, the effects of these disruptions were of great and formative significance, sharply altering the character of the Puritan faith as it was in the process of translation to New England.

3

From Engagement to Flight
The Failure of Politics, 1610–1630

John Winthrop had been very much the political animal from the age of twenty-five, when just five months after resolving that "I will faithfully endeavour to discharge that callinge which he shall appoint me unto," he had enrolled at Gray's Inn. In 1613 Nicholas Fuller, the leading Puritan oppositionist in the early parliaments of James I, was still a prominent member of the Inn's society, and the student admitted just after Winthrop was a Cope, the student just before a Knightley. (The Fleetwoods and the Mildmays, among other prominent families both Puritan and political, were also represented at the Inn that year.)[1] In the intervening years before the Migration, Winthrop had drafted bills for submission to Parliament, initiated the successful campaign to get Sir Robert Naunton, master of the Court of Wards, elected knight of the shire for Suffolk, and, in 1626, connived at smuggling news of public affairs to Sir Francis Barrington, imprisoned in the Marshalsea for refusing to assist in the forced loan.[2] A record five parliamentary elections were held between 1621 and 1628, and unless Winthrop or the others most deeply involved in the founding of New England were exceptionally private men—he and they were, in fact, just the opposite—it would have been impossible not to have been caught up in the great political drama of the decade. It would have been equally impossible to have remained indifferent to that drama's outcome, the abrupt collapse of parliamentary politics in 1629.

When Winthrop broached the idea of emigration for the very first time, on 15 May 1629 in a letter to his wife, Margaret, that she later told him "did make a very good supply in stead of a sarmon," he had been in London (with one interruption) since the previous October. His stay had placed him in position to take in the details of the disastrous final session of what had begun as a hopeful parliament dedicated to solving the outstanding religious and constitutional conflicts that had embittered three reigns. Winthrop had already learned from his brother-in-law Emmanuel Downing, who had minor court connections, how on the final day in the Commons, 2 March, the MPs had forcibly prevented a dissolution and voted by acclamation their three resolutions against arbitrary taxation and Arminianism. Subsequently he would express an interest in the fate of the imprisoned leaders of the parliamentary protest, and though he made no recorded comment on it, he must also have known as of 15 May of the royal proclamation of 27 March 1629, only seven weeks before, squelching all hope of any further parliaments for the foreseeable future. Winthrop chose this moment, when the one remaining engine of national reformation had been silenced, to give up on politics at last and on an England that had been repeatedly warned to change its ways, to be worthy of the religion bestowed upon it, and that had rejected opportunity after opportunity until the Lord was now abandoning the nation to his wrath: "The Lord hath admonished, threatened, corrected, and astonished us, yet we growe worse and worse, so as his spirit will not allwayes strive with us, he must needs give waye to his furye at last. . . . My deare wife I am veryly perswaded, God will bringe some heavye Affliction upon this lande, and that speedyle."[3]

Hope was now confined to the English godly, not their benighted land. Their prayers and tears might preserve them in the general overthrow, and, better still, "if the Lord seeth it wilbe good for us, he will provide a shelter and a hidinge place for us and ours as Zoar for Lott, Sarephtah for his prophet etc."[4] We have learned to think of the Puritan migration to New England as a trek to Zarephath rather than Zoar, that is, as a search for a temporary refuge like that of Elijah during the eight years' drought in Israel before his return to overthrow idolatry and reestablish the faith with the help of the hundred prophets saved from the slaughter by Obadiah. (Carried to its logical conclusion, this biblical analogy also has the intriguing effect of turning Charles and Henrietta Maria into Ahab and Jezebel respectively, though not even one of Winthrop's "etc.'s" is likely to have hidden that radical an analogy.) Winthrop's mind in 1629, however, was not on strategic retreats but headlong flight from the justly doomed city. England was Sodom, too corrupt to be saved, or at best Jerusalem in her last moments before the destruction of the Temple: "Shall not the iniquity of the prophett and Priestes and the crye of innocent blood make all her confidence vain?"[5] The period of exile was going to be a long one.

There was nothing particularly cranky about this chilling verdict. On "this dismall day of breach of parliament," Thomas Bourchier wrote his aunt, the Puritan matriarch Lady Joanna Barrington, to "take notice" in her prayers "of the horrible sinns which crye aloude in the eares of the almighty for a spedye powringe his vengeance upon this lukewarme nation."[6] Winthrop himself was the more convinced of impending destruction because he was so sure that his opinions were shared by those likely to join him in the new Zoar. He liked to ask skeptical correspondents in 1629 what the state of England was and then cite "the grones and fears of Godes people" as "a silent answer." Equally, God's "Embassadours," the ministry, he noted with satisfaction, "constantly denounce wrathe and judgment against us," and their "soules wepe in secret" because of the deadly certainty that there was no longer "hope that our hurt may be healed."[7] Two ministers at least among the scores destined for New England, and surely others, did their best to validate Winthrop's generalization. In early January of 1630 Charles Chauncy caused "a great distraccion and feare amongst the people" at Ware, Hertfordshire, by linking the planned migration with a warning that a French invasion was imminent and that "the preaching of the Gospell would be suppressed." And just over a year later, in March of 1631, Thomas Hooker, who had been foretelling doom for at least five years, took the exodus to New England, now well under way, as proof that the Lord had finally narrowed the object of his temporal mercies to the handful of the righteous: "God begins to ship away his Noahs, which prophesied and foretold that destruction was near; and God makes account that New England shall be a refuge for his Noahs and his Lots, a rock and a shelter for his righteous ones to run unto; and those that were vexed to see the ungodly lives of the people in this wicked land, shall there be safe."[8]

There is an extraordinary state of mind to be found in these particular years, one that seems more appropriate to 1649 or 1666, or just possibly to 1914. Two aspects of this increasingly exhilarating despair, however, stand out: the extent to which the indictment extends to the whole of English society and is not focused intensively on the national church and the lack, apart from the suspension of Parliament, of some dramatic precipitating event for so urgent and acute a sense of crisis. Admittedly, there was valid cause for alarm by the end of the 1620s wherever committed Puritans might turn their attention. In the midst of a desperate conflict between Protestant and Catholic on the Continent, England, the leading Protestant military power, was dilatory and inconsistent in aiding endangered coreligionists and hopelessly incompetent on the three successive occasions between 1624 and 1628 when some effort was made. At home the situation was no better: the troubled economy throughout the decade could be seen as both a justly merited admonition to a corrupt society and a further period of probation when the English were once more searched for the Christian virtues of charity and moderation, only to be found wanting. Repeated reverses for the Protestants in Germany and France provided a grim example of what was to come for an unrepentant England the more culpable in failing its own greater and more special responsibilities. "We sawe this," Winthrop wrote Margaret in 1629, "and humbled not ourselves, to turne from our evill wayes, but have provoked him more then all the nations rounde about us: therefore he is turninge the cuppe [of tribulation] towards us also, and because we are the last, our portion must be, to drinke the verye dreggs which remaine." In Winthrop's own East Anglia at the time and in adjoining Essex the harvests were bad and the state of the clothworking industry very bad. (Rioting broke out in one depressed parish, Maldon, in March and May of the same year.) Winthrop must have had these conditions in mind when in listing his reasons for emigrating he made his famous remark that "this Land growes weary of her Inhabitantes," as well as his less well-known warning of a social war in England as bitter and as violent as the Peasants' War had been in Germany.[9]

Nonetheless, neither set of misfortunes, foreign or domestic, effectively explains why Winthrop chose to give up on England exactly when he did or why others should share with him well into 1630 this sense of an immediate and acute peril. Even out in Chauncy's Ware they must have known that at the time their vicar conjured up his enemy fleet peace with France had been in force for months. And anyone born in 1588, as Winthrop was, knew after four decades of experience that the cycle of prosperity came and went and would come again. The years 1629 and 1630 were certainly bleak: a pervasive crisis in employment in the textile industries was followed hard by a particularly poor harvest. In neither case, however, did the experience of the recent past suggest anything that contemporaries would have interpreted as a structural collapse in the economy.[10] Winthrop, though undoubtedly writing in good faith, was still decidedly calculating about his use of the argument for overpopulation, relying on it especially as an unobjectionable rejoinder to critics of the New England venture. The copy of "the grounds of settling a plantation in New England" that went to Sir John Eliot in the Tower, where hostile eyes might see it and its recipient bridle at too Puritan a logic, consists exclusively of these innocuous arguments for migration, never mentioning any national moral failings or impending judgment. Versions of the same paper in more general circulation contain warnings of dangers to come but never as a deserved punishment for a lax and apostate people. Winthrop's public statements never descend to particularizing the sins of the land except for two complaints that might be the typical cri de coeur of many a Suffolk squire: it was hard for an honest man to maintain his standing with his neighbors unless he spent as extravagantly as they did, and one could barely afford to send children to the universities anymore, nor was their education worth the exorbitant cost considering the luxurious and vicious habits they picked up. Relying only on the collection of truisms and minor failings itemized in the "General Considerations," there would be no reason in 1629 to urge on the migration in the manner of the cheerfully enthusiastic anathema of Robert Ryce, the Suffolk antiquary, who concluded a favorable gloss on one of Winthrop's tracts with the injunction "to make haste owte of Babylon, and to seek to dye rather in the wyldernes then styll to dwelle in Sodome Mesheck and in the tentes of Kedar."[11]

In his letters to his friends and to Margaret, Winthrop was a good deal more pointed on the nature of the country's crisis, and these statements go a lot further in explaining his (and the general Puritan) now-or-never mood than the semipublic pronouncements (which were so widely circulated in manuscript that one of them eventually turned up in the state papers sporting the endorsement of a government clerk).[12] The problem was not poor harvests and depression per se, any more than it was Catholic military successes. Rather, the real provoking evil could be found in the national reaction to these challenges: the intertwined vices of hard-heartedness, self-indulgence, and outright cruelty and dishonesty, in turn the inevitable results of an overall moral climate that allowed and encouraged purposeless, unreflective egotism. Winthrop attributed the danger of social conflict on a large scale in 1629 as much or more to the shortsighted selfishness of the rich as to the desperation of the poor, and when in the next year he told an audience on board the *Arbella* in midpassage that inequality existed primarily "that every man might have need of other, and from hence they might be all knitt more nearly together in the Bond of brotherly affeccion" he was offering a sharp indictment of the nation so recently left behind.[13] England's failure to play its proper part in defense of the international Protestant cause could be attributed to the same source, not in the main a shortage of resources but their maldistribution and misemployment. As early as 1621, when Sir James Perrot, the leading Welsh Puritan MP, advocated a "diversory war" against Spain, he admitted that the country's economy was in a slump but argued that in the past more had been done with less. Limited as it was, the wealth of the kingdom could have been effectively employed in a just war were it not for the pervasive manic obsession with self-display and immediate gratification and the debilitating concentration of wealth in a few hands that was both cause and effect of the general demoralization:

The Kingdom of England is poore, tis trew though not so poore as it is made. 2 parts of 4 [of the national wealth] is in the Cyty. We want 200,000*li.* per annum that Tobacco caryes away, which would mainetain 15,000 men in the Field. All expend in the Cyty and the 4th part retournes not. The E[a]st India [Company] have 14,000*li.* in bancke, which we must needs want, and theay bring us nothing but druggs. The userers in the Cyty hoording allso. *Lex sumptuaria* is necessary now. Braceletts, eareings, etc., have ben given [to the war effort], though women opposed it; but laws may rule them then though ther husbands cannot.[14]

Puritans would not have been Puritans if they had gone no further than a blanket denunciation of personal sins or simple exhortations to the sinful to bethink themselves. Simple and indiscriminate moralizing recommended itself particularly to the likes of William Laud. Under attack from the Commons, he proposed to fob off demands for political and ecclesiastical reforms as a preventive to further chastisement by attributing the run of disasters to individual moral failings alone—"we shall prevent them [punishments] best by a true and religious remonstrance of the ammendment of our lives."[15] His Puritan adversaries sought public and institutional causes for the general declension and singled out church and state for their failure to fulfill their sacred trusts. It was not sin that called down judgment, it was sin unreproved, sin ignored and ultimately fostered by unjust judges, corrupt courtiers, scandalous and ignorant clergymen, and (it would come to seem by 1629) worldly, pompous prelates ever more enamored of the decadent splendors of their Roman counterparts. We think of ecclesiastical failings as somehow more central to the Puritan indictment, but throughout the 1620s, even as late as 1629, for Winthrop, as for the Old Testament prophets he cited, the blatant sins, the ones that most cried for vengeance, were immorality, oppression, and injustice. Winthrop dismissed the Church of England in brief, almost lapidary terms—"Let not us trust to the Temple of the Lord." The "many faithfull ministers and good people" traditionally invoked as the justification for tolerating the imperfections of a fundamentally sound structure no longer sufficed when the overall character of the established church could be compared to Sodom in "pride and intemperance," Laodicea in lukewarm temporizing, the other churches of Asia "in the sins for which their Candlesticke was removed," the Turks and "other heathens" in "abominations," and, in a reference to ceremonialism and Arminianism at the climax of his antilitany, to "the Sinagogue of Antichrist in her superstition." But the transgressions of the "civil state" defied even biblical analogies, despite the wealth of possibilities in Amos or Jeremiah: "What means then the bleating of so many oppressed with wronge, that drink wormwood, for righteousnesse? why doe so many seely [defenseless] sheep that seeke shelter at the judgment seates returne without their fleeces? why meet we so many wandering ghostes in shape of men, so many spectacles of misery in all our streetes, our houses full of victuals, and our entryes of hunger-starved Christians? our shoppes full of rich wares, and under our stalles lye our own fleshe in nakednesse."[16]

Amos to Jeremiah, admonition to imprecation and lamentation, sums up the progress of English Puritanism in the decade of the 1620s. This progressive dismay and anger, culminating in unalloyed despair upon the collapse of parliamentary politics, distinguishes the specifically Puritan perspective from all the other kinds of glum moralism prevalent in the decade. One did not have to be a Puritan merely to think that desperate radical disorders in the commonwealth mirrored the destruction of religion abroad.[17] But only in the case of Puritans was this widely shared rage and frustration, which so enlivened politics at the beginning and end of the 1620s, organized into an ominous pattern of warnings given and unheeded, remedies proposed and rejected, and, therefore, judgment justly apprehended. The history of the rather rapid Puritan disillusion with England is of necessity a public one—of the immediate anxieties over royal policy, foreign and domestic, with which the 1620s opened, of risky gambles taken in consequence and hopes raised and dashed repeatedly in the middle years of the decade (when a preacher could offer cautions instead of unmixed maledictions), and finally at the very end, as part of a wide and disorganized coalition, a last-ditch, head-on assault on the knot of lay and clerical politicians, "the Achan faction," who were seen as preventing Israel's reformation in time to stave off the full force of the Lord's wrath. The discomfiture of English Puritanism is, in fact, very much a matter of the history of parliaments, the one place where wholesome regulations might be made, the defects of the established church corrected, and the troublers of Israel impeached. When after 2 March 1629 parliaments appeared to be in permanent suspension, it was naturally enough the moment to inquire if the Lord had not appointed some place other than England as a refuge for those whom he meant to save from the general destruction.

Puritan politics from the accession of James I until the era of the Great Migration fundamentally paralleled Puritan divinity of the same period: pragmatic and partially reconciled, collaborative in tactics, distinctive mainly in the overall scheme into which individual measures were fitted. Political action of this sort is ambiguous by definition, so many choices made faute de mieux, but the legislative record is nonetheless a good place to seek for an identifiable Puritan position in the period 1604 to 1629 precisely because the

Puritan movement in these years was more thoroughly integrated into official culture than at any other time, and its current demands seemed attainable enough, despite successive setbacks, to be voiced in an official forum. Until 1629 politics was still the art of the possible, rather than a suitably theatrical arena for symbolic acts of defiance, and the Puritan movement was capable, because of its very looseness, of attracting allies on the right measures and at the right moments. A very rough measure of the fluctuating fortunes of Puritans in English politics, from the irresolute confrontation at Hampton Court to the unambiguous statement of the Winthrop fleet, can be recovered from the record of the fate of the movement's parliamentary program and in particular from what was asked for and what was held in abeyance at various times and even from what could almost never be mentioned at any time.

Three main areas occupied Puritan politicians: moral legislation, reform of the clergy and protection of the nonconformists among them, and (very occasionally) measures to give force to the rights claimed by the godly laity. This last set, proposals that would recognize that the laity had a religious life of their own outside of that ordained by authority and that would provide a degree of participation for them in the discipline and polity of the established church, can be dealt with most succinctly because the relevant measures rarely saw the light of day until the Long Parliament and its republican successors tried and failed to face up to the issues involved. Three intriguing bills are proposed in a document in the Winthrop papers composed sometime between 1610 and 1625, but only one of them ever surfaced in Parliament before the Civil War, in 1626 as a proposed "Act Concerning Hearing or Preaching." Even this bill was not an unqualified license to go where the preaching was best but only a genuinely modest proposal to authorize individuals burdened with nonpreaching ministers in their home parishes to frequent religious services elsewhere without incurring penalties in secular or church courts. A similar bill actually passed the Commons in 1628, and when it died in the prorogation, it was deemed important enough to be reintroduced early in the wild and desperate final session of 1629. The instance, however, is a freak, a testimony to the extent to which the general fear of what Charles I's appointees in church and state might do with existing statutes and canons overcame the usual horror of initiatives from the vulgar.[18] Bills to protect "the liberty of hearing," like the draft bills in the Winthrop papers to protect conventicling and reserve a share in discipline to the minister and congregation, are certainly a sign that the godly were there, actors within the Puritan movement well in advance of the era of the sects, and that magistrates no less than ministers were obliged now and again to take this awkward situation into account in their political strategy. Such minimal legislative notice of the godly laity is a harbinger—an oblique indicator of the forces of popular religion that would have to be tamed or accommodated in America and that would one day be let loose in Interregnum England. But the eventful political history that brought Winthrop and his company to Cowes in the spring of 1630 was always, parliamentary session of 1604 or of 1629, centered on a program of reformation *de haut en bas*.

Puritans in the Jacobean parliaments proposed to attack the natural self-indulgence of the English people by empowering the state to take effective action against prevailing vices and by improving the discipline of the church and the quality of its ministry. Of the two causes, moral legislation had by far the brighter prospects because, though generally Puritan in origin and sponsorship, measures against blasphemy, excess in apparel, drunkenness, and especially the profanation of the Sabbath were still attractive to a wide spectrum of MPs. These bills always stood a fair chance of making their way through both houses and receiving the royal assent.[19] The sole prominent exception, Sabbatarian legislation, reveals immediately the nub of the Puritan problem: royal hostility. Virtually every parliament in the reign of James I, Lords no less than Commons, passed a Sabbath bill, and the king just as regularly refused his assent to the "Puritan Bill," as he (inaccurately) called the 1621 version.[20] However stringent the limitations on Sunday activities envisioned in the bills at their first readings, by the time they received the assent of both houses none would have enacted an unqualified prohibition on all work, commerce, and travel. They gained their very broad consensus, extending to Archbishop Abbot, by banning merely popular recreations, such as sports, dances and plays, that were considered unseemly on the Lord's Day.[21] James I, however, strenuously resisted these relatively mild proposals as a way of reminding Parliament that his hostility to anything resembling Puritanism, however many times diluted, remained unabated, even if he was flexible about when and where to give his antipathy expression. His decision to issue the proclamation of 1618 requiring the clergy to read a declaration in favor of the lawfulness of most of the activities forbidden by the Sabbatarian bills, when this legislation had a demonstrated appeal to the governing classes generally, is surely a measure of a curious and unexpected recklessness that afflicted him intermittently in the last third of his reign. And though, more characteristically, he backed off from confrontation when Abbot resisted this burden on the consciences of his clergy, James had begun a final anti-Puritan campaign that would color the course of parliamentary politics for the remainder of his reign and for the first four years of his son's.

Fluctuations in James's attitudes, or rather in the rigidity with which he maintained them, account for the peculiar fate of the other main form of Puritan political activity, proposals to reform the ecclesiastical establishment and secure a measure of protection for nonconformist ministers. James's earliest parliaments addressed the subject with far more courage than any of their successors before 1640. Remarkably enough, until the members of the Long Parliament most reluctantly turned their attention to the issue of episcopacy, they had not passed or debated a single item of legislation affecting the clergy or discipline of the Church of England that had not already been passed, in its entirety or in greater part, and mostly more than once, by the Commons of the first Parliament of James I in its four sessions between 1604 and 1610. If the successful measures of the 1610 session alone, most of them authored by the veteran Puritan radical Nicholas Fuller, had somehow also made their way through the Lords and received the royal assent, there would have been very little left for the Long Parliament to take up in ecclesiastical matters: clerical nonresidency would have been prohibited on pain of deprivation, pluralists would have been forced to choose between benefices, and scandalous ministers would have summarily lost their cures on their second conviction before a justice of the peace for a minor offense or the first for a major one. Nor would it have been necessary for the Long Parliament to impeach the thirteen bishops or Archbishop Laud because none of them would have been able to do most of the things of which they stood accused. If the Long Parliament abolished the High Commission in 1641, the Commons in 1610 contented themselves with passing a bill severely limiting its jurisdiction and hobbling the use of the ex officio oath (compelling the accused to testify against themselves), and although they did not, as in 1641, require parliamentary approval for *all* canons of the Church of England, the Commons in 1610 passed a bill with the same proviso for any canon touching "any person in his or their life, liberty, lands or goods." Relief for the nonconforming clergy would have come in 1610 not by impeaching obnoxious bishops and their minions but by an act narrowly limiting the subscription oath to doctrinal sections of the Thirty-Nine Articles, along with a second measure allowing ex post facto appeals; the two bills together (if they could have cleared the Lords and gotten by James I) would have effectively reinstated the victims of Bancroft's purge. Taken together, the entire package amounted to little short of a legalized toleration of clerical nonconformity, which would have remained cognizable only in ordinary diocesan courts obliged to operate under considerable procedural restrictions.[22]

So precocious are these early attempts at reform, so long is the list of them, and so frequently do they recur in the first parliaments of James I that the simplest way to explain this aggressive Puritan campaign in a period generally taken to be more harmonious than not would seem to be by suggesting that these measures are not Puritan at all but the common sense of earnest Protestants of all persuasions. Unfortunately this convenient line of argument cannot account for the fate of the bills in the Lords, where they hardly attracted so much as a single supporter no matter how earnestly pressed by committees of the Commons, and, more interestingly, cannot explain the lack of success of the very same measures in the Commons in the later parliaments of James I in the face of the king's undisguised and reiterated hostility to anything remotely Puritan in association. Once James was dead, the familiar campaign for church reform would revive, but the peculiarly ambiguous nature of Puritan political influence is clearly revealed in the last sessions of his reign. At no time in the seventeenth century was there a Puritan-dominated House of Commons—there were never enough genuinely Puritan MPs, unless as in 1642 and at successive intervals thereafter somebody first conducted one or another purge among the majority of the members. The amount of support Puritan measures could attract depended very much on which political winds were blowing from what corner, and Puritan politics was for much of the period a tale of reduced expectations, lesser goods traded for greater, and alliances built on lowest common denominators.

To be sure, MPs sufficiently committed to offer and chivy along bills for church reform could be found in virtually every session of Parliament; indeed, as a group they constitute an overlapping set of generations uniting the Elizabethan Presbyterians with the leadership of the Long Parliament. Sir Anthony Cope and Nicholas Fuller were heroes of the classical movement who were active in the Commons as late as the "addled" parliament of 1614.[23] Sir James Perrot, who had made up a committee of three with Cope and Fuller for one of the bills to establish a learned ministry in 1606, continued after their deaths to speak with their voice on church reform throughout the parliaments of the 1620s. In 1614 Perrot began his routine practice of moving the requirement that MPs take the sacrament in an effort to eliminate Catholics from participation in the House, and on this first occasion Fuller was appropriately joined with him to monitor the administration of communion and identify the abstainers. In 1621 Perrot would move the resolution that became the declaration announcing the Commons's willingness to support a war of religion, and in his last parliament in 1628 he was particularly violent in his attacks on Laud.[24] The major draftsman of the church reform legislation of the 1620s, however, was Sir Walter Earle, who would play a similar role in keeping religious grievances at the fore in the Short Parliament of 1640 and in the composition of the Grand Remonstrance of 1641 as well as distinguish himself as an early opponent of Arminianism. Earle had been a silent member of the Parliament of 1614, but from 1621 on he was very much Elisha to Fuller's Elijah, his inheritance of the prophetic mantle evident in his sponsorship of the very same bills for church reform and Sabbath regulation that were for so long identified with his deceased predecessor. John Pym made his maiden speech in Earle's defense in 1621, when the latter was attacked for introducing the Sabbatarian bill James I so disliked, and Pym and Earle were closely associated ever after as Earle (like Fuller before him) attained an oppositionist political record quite as perfect as his Puritan pedigree.[25]

All in all it was an impressive collection and one that belies the repeated claims for discontinuity within the Puritan movement. But at the best these MPs were merely the general staff of an army whose resolve was ever more uncertain. Whoever introduced and spoke for the bills, most of the votes had to come from that broad mass of MPs who considered themselves both good Protestants and men of moderation, who might not be unsympathetic to the plight of the suspended minister and who were not totally disinclined toward the reform of the clergy, who might in the right circumstances enjoy lowering the pretensions of the episcopal bench a peg or two, but who really could not see the urgency of the whole matter and who had little desire to fly directly in the face of the express wishes of his gracious majesty. The litmus paper of Puritanism on the floor of the Commons was the depth and urgency of the conviction that church reform was central to every other major issue before Parliament. If the price of this proposition was too high for an MP to pay because of the evident royal displeasure over it, if church reform, however desirable in theory, was held to be merely ancillary to other matters considered more pressing and in danger of being compromised by Puritan associations, then Sabbatarian bills might still sail through both houses, but the panoply of reform bills fathered first by Fuller and then by Earle would be quietly sidetracked should their hard-core supporters be indiscreet enough to press them.

Even in the days when James's frowns were not quite so much in evidence, there was all the difference in the world between the support most MPs politely extended to Puritan measures and the enthusiasm with which the small band of genuine partisans brought them forward. In his last parliament, the "addled" session of 1614, Nicholas Fuller reintroduced virtually every one of his bills for church reform, and all received a respectful hearing, though few progressed very far in a house caught up in the issues of extraparliamentary taxation and the liberties of the Commons.[26] On the second reading of the clerical nonresidency bill, virtually every MP who spoke to this perennial commended it, including the privy councillors in the Commons, perhaps trying to improve their battered standing by adding to the chorus endorsing a popular cause.[27] It took Sir Anthony Cope, however, to declare a resident ministry "a knot of God's own knitting" that "never pope nor any other" (including, presumably, a king or his agents) could untie and then to conclude his long speech with the proposal that the members should "petition the King that the souls of his subjects might be precious with him and that parliament might not be dissolved till some course taken about this." An anonymous verdict on this remarkable final performance, with which Cope concluded nearly forty years of continuous service in Parliament, was that he "made a long and good speech but out of season, that made the House not have patience to hear him."[28]

So neat a division over the centrality of church reform was uncommon in the earlier half of James I's reign. While the king was unsure of his position and the church was under the primacy of the unpopular Bancroft, the tenacity with which an MP adhered to Puritan logic was rarely put to the test. A moderate and judicious country grandee such as Sir Edward Montagu, whose family were longtime patrons of the godly ministers of Northamptonshire, could be found (in a considered and sober way, of course) ranked on the same side as Nicholas Fuller and even offering a bill of his own in 1610 against pluralism and nonresidency that was sent to the Lords "specially commended." In 1614 he was active again on behalf of Fuller's bills. But in 1621, awaiting a peerage and well aware that a newly intransigent James I thought he "smelt a little of puritanism," Montagu said little, even about Earle's version of the nonresidency bill. He restricted his activities to chairing the committee appointed to water down Earle's Sabbath legislation and otherwise contented himself with the grandiloquent but empty declaration that "I am not ashamed for any nick[name] to further the observance of any of God's commandments."[29] The Sabbatarian bill went to the Lords, as did Montagu; the nonresidency bill never reached a second reading. The grandson of a chief justice and the head of a county family who numbered a bishop and the lord treasurer among his brothers, Montagu was merely running true to type. He did not in any sense sell his religion for a barony; rather, he was merely a typical member of the group of earnest Protestant aristocrats who could not be counted on to support Puritan measures once the royal displeasure was explicitly made known (if not flaunted). His job and that of his family was to govern, and that task in the end came down to carrying on the king's government, adapting and moderating the royal injunctions when possible to fit the sense and needs of his native Northamptonshire. There was a point in sticking with church reform in the 1620s only if one believed with Perrot that the proper order of procedure, even on the great question of aid to European Protestants, was "that first our religion be secured at home and then to provide for others abroad."

Favor was not to be found throughout most of the 1620s even with those MPs who were willing to bait the king. Their priorities, too, were elsewhere. Most Puritan MPs, it is true, were, with varying degrees of flexibility, active in the ranks of the parliamentary opposition to royal policy. Their moral stance and their need for reformation by statute lead them to hostility to extraparliamentary taxes on constitutional and political grounds—a too well-endowed monarch might not need parliaments—and anxious to extend the areas of policy suitable for parliamentary discussion. On the monarch's requests for money, the principal reason for indulging in the unpleasant business of a session, most Puritan MPs were in no hurry to proceed to supply while there were grievances to discuss. Though the need for extra revenue might be considered legitimate in general, it was also taken to be a sign of the court's extravagance and corruption, and there were similar reasons to be skeptical of the discretionary and patronage powers of the crown, which were held to be lavished on popish favorites, grasping monopolists, and all manner of immoral sycophants. But in the ordinary course of things the Puritanism of Puritan MPs produced nothing more than a natural drift toward oppositionist positions. There were also Puritan officeholders, lots of them, as long as support of the religious policies of the crown was not considered a sine qua non of holding office, and there were a few Puritan courtiers, however difficult their balancing act was at times.[30] Nor was the equation between Puritan and opposition, limited as it was, inherently reversible. At best, Puritans were useful allies, at worst downright liabilities. Forced to make choices, as they were from 1621 on, few opposition figures had any desire to contaminate their campaigns for a Protestant foreign policy and limitations on the prerogative with a minority enthusiasm over the particulars of the generally accepted religion. When Ignatius Jordan, the archetypal Puritan magistrate, revived Earle's scandalous ministers bill late in the session of 1621, after it had been prudently allowed to languish for months following its first reading, such leading parliamentarians as Sir Dudley Digges, Sir Thomas Wentworth, and Sir Edward Coke, none of them likely to be accused of Puritanism, were, respectively, hostile, indifferent, and lukewarm. Only the indomitable Perrot and a handful of MPs who often followed his lead spoke strongly in the bill's favor, and then it was kicked along through a second reading before disappearing without further trace.[31]

The reasons behind James I's pronounced anti-Puritanism after 1617 require a separate discussion. The important point in understanding the apparent subsidence of parliamentary Puritanism in the early and mid-1620s is to realize that the king's hostility was both unmistakable and apparently immutable and that it was manifest well before the Arminian controversy disturbed the last three years of his reign. The Sunday bill of 1621 was scarcely any different from its many predecessors, but James went out of his way, in reply to a petition against recusants, to tell the Commons that he wanted them to kill it because he "had upon mature diliberacion writt an edict against Puritanes," the Book of Sports of four years earlier, and he ordered Secretary of State Sir George Calvert (an undisguised Catholic) to add that as the Commons "had stricken with the right hand against Papists *Soe* [he desired] *we would strike with the left against Puritans.*" (The emphasis was added by John Pym.)[32] In a further bit of gratuitous nastiness James intervened to stop the proceedings against Dr. John Lambe, chancellor of the diocese of Peterborough, who had been complained of to the Commons for extortion, arbitrary conduct, abuse of the ex officio oath, and harassment of individuals who left a parish that lacked a preaching minister to hear a sermon at a neighboring church. Lambe's defense was worth a knighthood: he told James that his accusers were "troupes" of Puritans and agents of "greater persons," who "through me, ayme att your Majesty's Ecclesiasticall Jurisdiction." There was once again from 1621 on an obvious profit to be made from Puritan baiting, for the incident turned out to be a decisive turning point in a long and belligerent but hitherto undistinguished career.[33]

However unsavory such details, their meaning was obvious. From the very start of the decade of the 1620s, in the midst of a successful Catholic onslaught against the Protestants on the Continent, the English Puritans were obliged to confront their own political weakness and isolation. The words with which John Pym complained of an anti-Puritan MP in 1621 were to be repeated with minimal variations in successive parliaments: "As he would devide the Kinge from us soe would he devide us amongst our selves, exasperatinge one partie by that odious and factious name of Puritans."[34] Accordingly, Puritan political activity in the parliaments of 1624 and 1625, and even, to a degree, in the more contentious session of 1626, was controlled by a lesson well learned. It was essential in times scarcely less perilous than those of the 1590s to mute characteristic Puritan demands and to establish common ground with leading MPs who were Puritan neither in their convictions nor their followings. Puritan politicians with court connections or a yen for the sweets of office also sought to establish good relations out of Parliament with what was essentially a sort of early reversionary interest built around the duke of Buckingham, whose intermittent support for military aid to the endangered European Protestants, along with his unbridled adventurism generally, went a long way to muddle the politics of the 1620s.[35] These two forms of coalition were, as it turned out, contradictory: it would eventually become necessary to choose between Buckingham and alliances made in the Commons.[36] But in the middle years of the decade, carefully considered, relatively inconspicuous roles in both court and parliamentary coalitions seemed deceptively integrated in the single popular theme of anti-Catholicism. A Protestant foreign policy (a largely naval, "diversionary" war against Spain and in aid of the Netherlands) combined nicely with an assault on the increasingly vocal faction within the church establishment, which through "these degrees of plausible *Arminianisme*" was attempting "even to put in these little theeves (they seeme little to naturall men) into the window of a church, and then they may unlocke the dores of a *Church*, and let in all *Popery*."[37]

Up to a point this self-enforced symbiosis, in which specifically Puritan demands were subordinated to more popular causes, was a reasonable strategy. The repression of Arminianism and the relief of the Protestant churches on the Continent were urgent objectives, and time would prove that as a result of the credit and influence gained in these cooperative ventures the Puritan leadership would also be able to resume its own special initiatives when opportunities allowed. There is as a result a certain cautious optimism in Puritan ranks in the middle years of the 1620s that distinguishes the mood of this period from the black despair that opened the decade and the zestful pronouncements of imminent doom that would close it. Thomas Hooker, who was threatening destruction in 1629 and practically ordering the Lord to deliver it in 1631 (he was emigrating himself), was in 1626 not without hope for the English if they would show that they had taken stock of their corruptions. The "liberty and safety of a nation" could be upheld "when men begin to be sensible of misery, when they have eyes to see the plague, and hearts affected with the sins committed and with the judgments deserved, when they observe what will befall, they will use some means that it may not befall."[38]

Because the tactics were so moderate and seemed so realistic, their repeated failures were all the more infuriating. "All our counsels," wrote William Prynne in that year of crashing disappointments, 1629, "have beene infatuated, our designes frustrated, our hopes dashed, our prayers unanswered, our Parliaments broaken up in discontent: the curse and vengeance of God hath clinged close unto us to our great destruction." He attributed the disaster solely to "the Tares of Popery and Arminianisme [that] have sprung up within our Church," and in a way he was right.[39] The Arminian issue came from 1625 on to have the force of a lodestone within the crosscurrents of parliamentary politics, drawing irresistibly to itself a tangled mass of accusations and arguments from which could be extracted almost every theme of current controversy: toleration of papists, foreign policy, reform of the clergy, resistance to nonparliamentary taxation and absolutist pretensions. "It is the nature of contrary opinions to join all [together] against the truth," Pym told the Commons when reporting in the articles of impeachment against the leading Arminian publicist, Richard Montagu, in 1628. Failure to punish Montagu and John Cosin and to neutralize the influence of Richard Neile and William Laud necessarily had to bring on dire consequences because of the entire collection of policies that group of men had come to stand for.[40] The Arminians were attacked in the main not for what they had done—with the exception of Neile, most of them were not yet before 1629 in much of a position to do anything—but for what it was assumed, by no means idly, they must do once they came to dominate the hierarchy. And for the most part they did come eventually to be guilty as prospectively charged—not, of course, of being crypto-Catholics, but of advancing a vision of English religious life opposed at almost every point to all that the Puritans had achieved since the collapse of the classical movement and that they had vainly sought to protect and further in the stormy politics of the 1620s.

Sooner or later there had to be Arminians while the Church of England contained Puritans but was in no real sense Puritanized. Whether the clash between the two camps had to be so sustained or fought for such high stakes is less clear, but that question by no means turns solely on the quirks of royal temperament. Arminianism surfaced as a major issue in 1624 and 1625 for reasons rooted in the dynamics of the politics of the decade. The subsequent patronage of the movement by James in his last years and Charles throughout his reign, however imprudent, was based on the very real advantages the two monarchs saw in a national church in which tendentious doctrine was denatured and potential opposition identified, isolated, and crushed.

The key person in the inception of the Arminian controversy was no Arminian but James I. Despite his vacillations and devious tactics, James held a consistent and plausible notion of Puritanism from (at the latest) the mid-point of his English reign.[41] He applied the term to the ministry of Scotland, no less than to that of England, and developments in his northern kingdom always had a considerable influence on his actions in England, especially in the last eight years of his life. Scottish or English, Puritans in James's view suffered fatally from the sin of pride. If he had formally offered in answer to a petition of the Commons in 1610 to review the cases of unusually worthy suspended ministers, he was more candid in private: "I had rather have a conformable man with but ordinary parts than the rarest man in the world that will not be obedient, for that leaven of pride sours the whole loaf."[42] Sure of his special ability to ascertain and apply the divine will, a Puritan was always laying down unalterable fundamental principles that licensed disobedience to governors and, through cobwebs of ingenious interpretation, ended up giving law to princes: God forbade the use of the surplice, God set limits on the use of the prerogative, God required war with Spain, God ordained what any conclave of ministers chose to derive from their inspired generalities by deduction or analogy. James held that in areas in which the nature of his office and the course of a nation's history gave the king authority, he alone was the proper judge of its lawful use, and resistance or interference could come only from those presumptuous enough to challenge prerogative by argument from abstract first principles: "No christians but papists and puritans were ever of that opinion."[43]

James became more aggressive in his hostility to the Puritans of both kingdoms as a result of his trip to Scotland in 1617. The four articles of Perth he forced through a rigged assembly of the Church of Scotland were designed for exactly the same purpose as the Book of Sports, which he first issued on his way back south, as he passed through Lancashire, and then made general for the entire kingdom in 1618: to force his clerical opponents either to submit to a humiliating and unpopular ceremony that would break their pride and deprive them of any further claims to legitimate disobedience or to come out in an open and unequivocal defiance of royal authority, for which they could be punished. He subsequently told the Scottish episcopacy that "hereafter that rebelious and disobedient crew must eyther obey or resist" and reminded them likewise that with the Perth articles "the sword is now putte in your hands; go on therefor to use it."[44] The Book of Sports would similarly take its toll by the requirement first announced in 1617 that "the principall ministers that be preachers within anie Diocess" expound its text. Conformable men might not like the order, but they would obey it; the retailers of unalterable law would be hoist with their own petard, either obeying and openly contradicting their principles or resisting and suffering the consequences. Thomas Shepherd, the MP who unexpectedly denounced the Sabbatarian bill in 1621, obviously had this aspect of the book in mind when in the course of his maiden (and last) speech he accused the framers of the Sunday legislation of violating the 1617 proclamation and then asked rhetorically, "Shall we make all thes engines and Barracado's against Papists and not a Mouse-trappe to catch a Puritan?"[45] Had it been enforced in 1618, the Book of Sports would have been far more than a trap for mice, as many a new immigrant to New England could subsequently testify when Laud in 1633 finally undertook to finish what James had started.

In general, from 1617 on James was laying down the ecclesiastical policy that would be more energetically pursued by his son. The two measures that ruined Charles I's credit in England and Scotland, the reissued Book of Sports and the Anglican liturgy, were little more than repetitions with some extension of moves initiated by James under nearly identical circumstances. Charles too made a trip to Scotland, in 1633, and, with Laud's encouragement, he also inaugurated a drive for ceremonial conformity that ended in 1637 with the St. Giles's riot. Again like his father, immediately on his return to England he issued on 18 October 1633 the original Book of Sports (with a section tacked on in favor of church ales to make it even more obnoxious to Puritan sensibilities).

Even the prominence of William Laud under Charles was an indirect legacy of the earlier Scottish trip of James. Richard Neile, then bishop of Lincoln, had been taken along by James, probably as a further snub to critics of his policies. (Neile had been bitterly attacked in the Parliament of 1614 as a Romanizing Hispanophile with absolutist pretensions.)[46] On his return, Neile was translated to the lucrative see of Durham, just as his younger protégé Laud would gain Canterbury on his own return with Charles sixteen years later. The revenues of his new diocese and its magnificent London residence enabled Neile, in the manner of his great medieval predecessors, to organize "Durham College," the collection of like-minded younger men of ability he patronized at Durham House in London and whose careers at court and within the church establishment his new standing and influence enabled him to promote. (His bright young men included Montagu and Cosin, who would share with him and Laud the brunt of the attack in the parliamentary sessions of 1628 and 1629, as well as a number of less well-known but important figures in the development of Arminian theology.)[47] With "Durham College" there was ready at hand for the first time a distinctive and coherent Arminian party and policy, well endowed and well connected, at just the moment when James found their position, properly put, more and more suited to his deteriorating political situation.

James had backed off from requiring the clergy to read the Book of Sports in the face of opposition from Archbishop Abbot, but his animosity toward what he called Puritanism was, if anything, strengthened and broadened in its application by the rapid succession of events that followed the Defenestration of Prague in 1618. The Thirty Years' War and the renewal of conflict between the Netherlands and Spain required the most delicate and clear-headed handling by the monarch, who still aspired to be the peacemaker of Europe, and James's own dynastic interests were immediately bound up in the fate of the Palatinate and its exiled rulers. Under such circumstances, adherence to a confessional foreign policy, never a firm principle in any case, became for James pure anathema, and those who would urge it on him in or out of Parliament were in time to be duly anathematized.[48] Whether it was popular preachers meddling in concerns far beyond their calling, or clandestine literature printed abroad and circulated in England by sympathizers and agents of the Dutch Republic and the Elector Palatine, or forward MPs in 1621 and 1624 invading the royal prerogative in foreign policy, the same "Puritan" arguments seemed to be trotted out on all sides in opposition to James's pursuit of an understanding with Spain and in advocacy of an ill-considered war on the side of the Protestants of the Continent. Samuel Ward, Richard Everard, Thomas Scott, John Reynolds, Alexander Leighton, all began to look alike to the king—all professed loyalty and courted popularity, all quoted Scripture while inciting to faction, all were therefore Puritans. When in July of 1624 James refused to sign a rather ordinary proclamation against "popish and seditious" publications without the addition of a parallel condemnation of "seditious Puritanicall" tracts, the current cause célèbre (in which he took a very personal interest) was two short works by Reynolds that advocated a Protestant foreign policy without even vaguely coming near the subject of the Church of England.[49] But nice distinctions no longer mattered. James's lifelong hostility to what he conceived of as Puritanism had reached its logical conclusion: popular and meddlesome politics was assumed to be the inevitable issue, directly or indirectly, of preachers who preached too much. Nobody but a Puritan would see a common profession of faith as an imperative basis for an alliance among sovereigns; no one but a Puritan would have the temerity to invade a prince's mystery by offering him unwanted advice in the popular (and, therefore, seditious) mediums of pamphlet and sermon.

James responded by trying to choke off opposition at its theological source, and here the Arminians stood ready to help him. They alone (ironically enough in the event) could claim to possess a soteriology largely free of divisive polemic, dangerous speculation, and unwanted political implications.

But it was James who took the lead, Montagu and Laud who courted a royal favor he was already prepared to extend for reasons of his own. On 12 August 1622 the king issued his *Directions* to preachers with the intention of removing political agitation from the pulpit. Only one of the six articles, however, straightforwardly prohibited the preacher "to declare, limit, or bound out" the prerogative or the sovereign's duty "or otherwise meddle with these matters of state and the differences betwixt princes and the people." The real innovations lay in the first three articles, limiting even the subjects of sermons on strictly religious themes and recommending the simplistic homilies "not only for a help of the nonpreaching, but withal for a pattern and boundary, as it were, for the preaching ministers." Most significant of all, the third article forbade any preacher under the rank of bishop or dean to "presume to preach in any popular auditory the deep points of predestination, election, reprobation, or of the universality, efficacy, resistibility or irresistibility, of God's grace." The basic staple of predestinarian preaching since the Reformation had suddenly become "fitter for the schools and universities, than for simple auditories."[50]

Peter Heylyn, Laud's biographer, claimed that the *Directions* originated in an Oxford controversy that his hero reported to James, and that document itself was "so done as *Laud* appears to have a hand in the doing of it." Neither claim is well supported by other testimony or very likely, though James did take notice of the Oxford incident and it may have influenced his timing. The gist of the *Directions*, linking "pragmatical" preaching with too definite a notion of God's intentions and associating predestinarianism with opposition to the Spanish Match, fitted very neatly James's notion of Puritanism without any help from Laud. The future archbishop, rather, was the king's pupil: he incorporated the 1622 *Directions* or comparable inhibitions in all his own attempts to limit preaching from 1629 onward. Even his notorious prohibition of Sunday afternoon sermons was anticipated by James in 1617 and in 1622.[51] When Richard Montagu nominally inaugurated the Arminian controversy in 1624, he was doing no more than filling a space James I had deliberately created for anyone with the proper views, talent, and courage.

By his own account, Montagu hurried to write *A New Gagg for an Old Goose* between October and December 1623, the months when the negotiations for the marriage of Prince Charles to the Spanish Infanta seemed about to be concluded. A man who wrote his preface from Windsor and was already able to obtain considerable preferment no doubt could sense the right moment to bring to the attention of his majesty a systematic theology free of the political liabilities of its predestinarian rival.[52] Certainly, Montagu's chosen target can have been little more than a pretext for his having decided to come into print at that precise time: *A New Gagg* purports to be an answer to *The Gagge of the New Gospel*, a slender, much reprinted work of Catholic apologetics designed exclusively for the use of ordinary laymen of (judging by the preface's schoolmarmish tone) modest education. Carefully numbering each item in the arsenal, John Heigham, the author, supplied would-be parish controversialists on the side of Rome with a set of instances, fifty-three in all, when they might use the King James Version to trip up their Protestant neighbors by demonstrating that their notion of gospel truth is expressly contradicted in the words of their own Bible. Where the unspecified "Protestants" got their doctrines Heigham did not say, nor did he mention the Thirty-Nine Articles or call into question any of the many Protestant authors subsequently invoked on all sides by the disputants in the controversy that erupted over Montagu's alleged answer to his little crib. The sheer simple-mindedness of the thing guaranteed it a long life in print, but it scarcely required an individual of Montagu's erudition and polemical skill to massacre Heigham's tract, and the blatant irrelevance of the massive and recondite *New Gagg* to its pretended subject was dramatically demonstrated by the failure of a single Catholic apologist to write a rejoinder.

Fellow Protestants were much quicker to respond. Montagu had used the occasion to demonstrate what he had good reason to suspect James wanted to have proved. By denying that most of Heigham's fifty-three erroneous propositions *were* necessary Anglican doctrine and by a controversial exposition of the remainder, he worked up an anti-Catholic stance that required neither an implacable conflict between the reformed churches and the Romish Antichrist nor a basic theological accord with the Calvinist churches of the Continent to justify the Protestantism of the Church of England. A counterattack came almost immediately, and, significantly, it was a collaborative effort stage-managed by John Pym on behalf of the various factions, Puritan and non-Puritan, who supported a Protestant foreign policy.[53] The arena for the opening stages of the combat was also well chosen: the Parliament of 1624, dedicated to forcing English intervention on behalf of the Netherlands and against Catholic Spain. On this occasion, however, the bulk of the MPs preferred to avoid so potent a controversy while it still remained in embryo, only to have Montagu, pressing his luck, use the complaint against him (unpublished until he called attention to it) as he had the Heigham tract. In the form of a justification against a charge that had brought him no harm, he quickly published *Appello Caesarem*, at once a full-fledged statement of his position and a bid for the protection and patronage of James I. In this new tract he enunciated an anti-Calvinist view of justification in more detail than in *A New Gagg*, but he did not so much argue for his theology as extend his defense of the proposition that it was as consistent with the Thirty-Nine Articles as the Calvinist views of the so-called orthodox, which he dismissed as "the problematicall opinions of Private Doctors, to be held or not held eyther way." By consequence, he was in a position to deny any close correspondence between the central doctrines of the Church of England and the creeds of the endangered Protestant churches of Europe, and he could be in equal proportion charitable toward Catholicism, holding Rome to be a true church badly misordered by the tyranny of the papacy. The exercise parallels in a remarkable degree the case for the Church of England a Bradshaw or Ames made in answer to Separatist criticisms. Where Puritan apologists defended their church as an "imperfect" but full member of the general communion of Reformed churches and non-Puritan Calvinists excused these "imperfections" as legitimate and desirable national variations within that communion, Montagu made his Church of England, in effect, what Rome would be if its serious but less than fatal errors were purged and its virtues perfected.[54] The political implications were immediately evident. "He inveigheth against our brethren of *France*, and the *Low Countries*, as not conformable to us in their discipline," an anonymous critic wrote. "But his hatred is more to their doctrine of faith, then of discipline. This is only to make a division, and to stirre up mens hatred against them, that in the end they and we may have our throats cut for our doctrine of faith."[55]

Appello Caesarem was entered on the Stationers' Register with considerable fanfare as early as 18 February 1625. Unfortunately for the calculations of its author, the caesar in question died the next month, and Montagu's opponents quickly renewed their assault against him with a vengeance. To his understandable despair, they pursued him through the next three parliaments and a full-scale pamphlet war in an attempt to capture the allegiance of the initially uncommitted new king, Charles I, and his favorite Buckingham, and after this proved impossible they turned their energies with equal vehemence to a campaign to drive from power the individuals taken to be behind Montagu's manifestos. Henry Burton, who liked to call himself a cashiered courtier, was the frankest in explaining what the fuss was all about. *Appello Caesarem* had been assigned to no less a stationer than the master of the company and licensed by no less an ecclesiastical personage than the distinguished controversialist and future bishop Francis White, gleefully obeying the orders of James I himself. Burton, whose considerable repertory of polemical techniques included brutal candor when it suited him, noted in his preface to the *Plea* he wrote in answer to Montagu's "appeal" that he was "spurred thereunto, more (I confesse) by Doctor *Whites Approbation*, then Maister *Mountagues Appeale*."[56]

Because there was admittedly so much more to the *Appello* than its author, when the battle was joined at last, the long line of poor Montagu's opponents stretched well beyond a congerie of Puritan polemicists to include two Calvinist bishops, a secretary of state, and almost every major opposition figure in the Commons. Montagu had given the traditionally conservative, Hispanophile faction of the court and council, often improperly labeled Catholic, the one thing it had always lacked, a sophisticated *Protestant* rationale for its position. The brazenness with which Arminianism was now suddenly advocated was also a signal that a powerful minority among the episcopal hierarchy had become sufficiently confident of its strength to risk coming into the open in the hope that old caesar or new could be won over by what it had to offer, for the first time sans apology or qualification. The various opponents of this group were obliged to respond by unity demonstrations that briefly submerged the specifically Puritan element in English politics in a much larger coalition organized around narrow, deceptively simple goals. John Pym and Sir Edwin Sandys jointly brought in an impeccably moderate, broad-based report for the committee on religion in 1625, and John Preston and Bishop Thomas Morton combined to defend Calvinism against Montagu and White at the York House debate of 1626. At the high point of the latter event, Viscount Saye and Sele and Secretary of State Sir John Coke (a hard-bitten Puritan oppositionist from the Lords and a bureaucrat who served as a government mouthpiece in the Commons) dramatically joined together to beseech Buckingham to assent to the proposition that the articles of the Synod of Dort, the symbol of the unity of the Calvinist churches, should be adopted by the Church of England. Significantly, this last appeal fell flat. In some versions of the York House debate Buckingham merely demurs at the crucial demand; in the one written by an Arminian he comes out saying, "No, no away with it."[57]

However natural the alliance may have seemed to Puritan politicians and clerics already eagerly seeking friends, however formidable the allies, beyond either the vagaries of court and ecclesiastical politics or the temperaments of two such unlike individuals as James and Charles Stuart, there were good reasons why so apparently puissant a combination would fail and Richard Montagu become successively bishop of Chichester and Norwich, Richard Neile archbishop of York, and William Laud primate of all England. There was more to this theological conflict than the obvious power play; there was the conflict in the respective theologies. The most unanswerable thing about the Arminian argument was that it did not need to be argued. The predestinarians had no such advantage. They and not their opponents required commitment rather than neutrality.[58]

In predestinarian doctrine Christ's atonement is effectual only for the elect. In the redaction of that theology that the Puritans in particular had developed, Christians strive for faith by attempting to comprehend this very proposition and its personal application to their individual cases. Only the elect, of course, are predestined to succeed, but for God's hidden will to be fulfilled his revealed will, the inescapable and eternal prior sentences of election and reprobation, must be relentlessly preached and its fullest meaning pursued year in and year out through the interconnecting web of means so painfully built up since the reign of Elizabeth. Arminianism in Montagu's formulation (by no means a typical one if the General Baptists, the Quakers, and Puritans of the John Goodwin stripe are kept in mind) rests on a wholly different spiritual economy. Men are born in sin, but Christ's atonement is universal in the sense that his righteousness is presumptively efficacious for all; the reprobate are merely those who have willfully rejected Christ or who, having once grasped salvation, lapse into their natural courses again and receive at the end the reward of their deliberate culpability. The trick, therefore, becomes getting the would-be believers to keep what, for all intents and purposes, they already have, or, at the worst, to accept what is, after all, universally available if only it is not explicitly refused. A preaching ministry is still desirable, but there is no need to hammer home the main points of predestinarian doctrine, which Montagu considered as much hidden mysteries as the roll call of the elect. Ritual, elaborate ceremonial, set prayer, the solemn and impressive administration of the sacraments, even the images of saints, though not efficacious in themselves, are all more pertinent to the task Christ has set his church than a feverish and futile pursuit from sermon to sermon, conventicle to conventicle, of God's "*Arcana Imperii*." Montagu shrewdly told his opponents: "For you and men of your *Companie*, are never at quiet with God's *Arcana Imperii*; can never let his eternall *Predestination* alone. The most ordinarie Theame of your . . . and their popular Preachings, is touching that *comfortable* Doctrine of *Election* and *Reprobation*. M. Mountagu rubbed somewhat upon this sore, thus: That *Men in Curiosity have presumed farre upon, and waded deepe into the hidden secrets of the Almighty*."[59]

In such a scheme of salvation catechisms and homilies can vie in importance with sermons, the content of which should, in any case, be kept to the simple fundamentals on which all sides agreed. The *Appello* accordingly is laced with declarations positively anticontroversial in stance. "Questions of obscurity and speculation [are] not fit for pulpits and popular eares," it announces flatly, and more than once Montagu boasts, "One thing I promise you for my part. I will not lightly talke of my opinion in Pulpits: will you say as much for your opinion? I thinke not."[60] It is an attractive line of argument and it is also, of course, thoroughly misleading. Montagu's closest match in polemical skill, Henry Burton, went to the heart of the matter when he wrote that the brute fact of election, God's revealed will, is

> the onely ordinary means to bring all his people elect to an effectuall participation and fruition of grace and glory by Jesus Christ. . . . No man in particular, though never so wicked, and so farre gone in sin, and sunke downe in rebellion, is (for ought he knoweth) excluded from salvation, if upon the word of grace preached he beleeve and repent . . . faith & repentance is required in every one that heares the word, that he may be saved, and not the elect themselves are exempted from this condition of beleeving.[61]

If the various proclamations and instructions against controversy had been evenhandedly enforced (and it was widely complained that they were not), the result was not neutral.[62] A group of London area ministers putting in what Laud in 1629 called an "intended petition about liberty of preaching predestination" correctly complained that because of the injunction against disputations preaching they could not by their lights "faithfully discharge our Embassage, in declaring the whole Councell of God."[63] Predestination had to be preached by its own logic, Arminianism did not.

Laud in his way understood this distinction well enough. Samuel Brooke, one of his more ardent supporters, took the tack "that their doctrine of Predestination is the roote of Puritanisme and Puritanisme the roote of all rebellions and disobedient intractableness in Parliaments etc. and all schisme and sauciness in the Countrey, nay in the church, itself." Therefore, logically enough in his way, Brooke proposed to settle the nation's political problems by a treatise against Calvinism. Laud in reply accepted the premise and faulted the conclusion on the grounds "that something about these controversies is unmasterable in this life." They were, that is, "Arcana Imperii," not fit for pulpits and common audiences or even in this instance a learned polemic—all very well *if* one first began with the premise that grace was so unqualifiedly offered that no strenuous intellectual efforts were needed in a well-regulated church to accept it.[64] Neile in much the same fashion allowed himself a self-proclaimed ignorance of the deep grounds of the controversy that no

Calvinist bishop could ever dared have claimed.[65] Silence, both men knew, was the language of Arminianism.

In effect, the Laudian syllogism ran: if Richard Montagu and Arminian doctrine, then John Cosin and high church ritual; if Montagu and Cosin, then William Laud and Richard Neile and a repressive episcopal policy. Laud and Neile proposed to reduce sermons in number and scope while amplifying edifying ceremonial. The authorized, reinvigorated Sunday service, in turn, in its totality would replace the amalgam of extraparochial activities that had been built around the doctrinal, exhortative sermon. Theirs would have been a deeply spiritual religious life but one without further divisive social implications or factional political entanglements. To secure these ends, the church would have to be restored to its pre-Reformation grandeur or, rather, what was romantically assumed to be its medieval standing, by the vigorous contestation of alienated revenues, privileges, and powers (a conflict with parish vestries, town corporations, and county benches that did as much or more harm to the crown as the anti-Puritan campaign).[66] And it would be necessary to identify and suppress opposition and to impose conformity through a more strenuous administration of existing rubrics, increased ceremonial, mostly involving the sacrament, and the administration of the perfect shibboleth, the reissued Book of Sports. The peace of the church, that is, was to be achieved by full-scale war.

Whatever the risks of such a strategy, James I entertained taking them in the last years of his reign, and his far less prudent son quickly and vigorously followed in his father's path upon his accession. In the dangerous decade of the 1620s government seemed to need, above all, a free hand—to make war or peace in a calculated manner, to secure with relative facility the sums and, when appropriate, the manpower necessary to carry out its diplomatic and military ventures. Public opinion was a liability under any circumstances, an incipient sedition at all times, but a public opinion informed and aroused by inflexible religious principles and inculcated through unauthorized channels was simply intolerable. To the extent that one believed (on however imperfect evidence) that men really were moved more by religion than anything else, even the sword, it became an apparently inevitable point of statecraft in the midst of the European maelstrom to adopt an anti-Puritan policy at home and to seek to institute a faith whose only collective manifestations would be controlled by a disciplined, elegant, and, above all, strictly bounded format. Puritan preachers might extol obedience to the higher powers with, on occasion, an unqualified assertiveness that would have embarrassed the champions of nonresistance Richard Sibthorpe and Roger Manwaring. They did not convince authority, and perhaps they should not have. At a spreading series of unauthorized exercises, ministers, magistrates, and the godly received detailed reports of the latest disasters, foreign and domestic, and attempted to fit current events into some sort of cosmic scheme that implicitly found the failings of church and state responsible. When the longtime minister of Stamford, Lincolnshire, John Vicars, came to the attention of the High Commission in 1631, he was charged with conventicling and organizing a select portion of his parish into a covenanted inner church with its own restricted sacrament—but also with giving a running political commentary on the way the hand of the Lord could be seen in local and national politics. (Buckingham's assassination was, understandably, his favorite theme.) Thomas Hooker, Henry Burton, and Hugh Peter were similar notorious examples of well-connected preachers who mixed politics with extraparochial activities in the guise of improving upon the times to encourage their followings to personal repentance.[67]

Even the more innocuous steps taken by the saintly John White of Dorchester betrayed the same semisectarian organization and penchant for topical commentary that were the fruits of Puritan practical divinity in a decade of crisis. White began to require that his parishioners, as a condition of taking the sacrament, subscribe to ten articles committing them to a course of individual and collective moral improvement that bore comparison with the Dedham Orders of four decades earlier. The context, however, was very different. The occasion of the rudimentary covenant at Dorchester was declared to be the "fierceness of the Lords indignacion powred out upon the Neighbour churches round about us and threatened unto us by the preparacions made against us," and the remedy was "to enquire what the Lord requires of us in particular for averting his wrath if not from the Church and state yet at least from our own heads." In light of White's patronage of the New England migration, the last clause may be taken as the most significant, a sign on the doorpost to indicate to the Angel of Death as he passed above that there were Israelites not Egyptians in the subscribing Dorchester households. But if the element of exclusive mutuality points forward to the Congregational churches of New England in the next decade, the Dorchester covenant is also a link between the Dedham orders and the jeremiad tradition of the 1670s, a confession of social and national wrongdoing and an undertaking of reformation. This public character of the whole arrangement is surely the aspect of White's covenant that most troubled Laud as he examined the document, and it was of White that he was obviously thinking when he took the occasion of the trial of the much more blatantly political Vicars to complain of similar covenanting in the West Country.[68] The patriarch of Dorchester was institutionalizing in his articles the private fast for public sins, the activity most congenial to Puritans of a pragmatical disposition eager to move public opinion as much as the Lord. It was Alexander Leighton, himself "a great *conventicle-keeper* (as they say)" and the most self-consciously political of all the radicals of the 1620s, who had declared of the private collective fast, "this will be like an earthquake to your enemies, it will sink them, it will swallow them up."[69] For the Puritans, the times called for organized attempts at repentance and reformation so unavoidably political in their implications, whether made explicit or not, that for the authorities, whether they confronted a Hooker, a Leighton, or a White, the very same times called just as urgently for Laud and a church without politics.

So although the campaign against Arminianism seemed the most promising coalition strategy for Puritans in need of allies, it was inherently self-defeating: the more it was pressed, the more it confirmed the Arminian plea to the crown that Puritanism (meaning any shade of Calvinism) was popular politics masquerading as orthodox religion. Arminians positively battened on parliamentary hostility—when the Commons was not in session. As that truth penetrated their ranks, Puritan politicians went sour on the court and increasingly emphasized their natural alliance with the defenders of the "liberties of the subject." By 1627 the godly leadership in the most actively Puritan centers of England was also the heart and soul of the resistance to the forced loan on the grounds that its creators labored "to suppresse Parliament that so great offenders might not be called in question, and so they might imposse what burthens they please uppon the people and never be called to account."[70] When the session of 1628 did try to call the offenders to account, Christopher Sherland, a Puritan MP and an ideologue of the final coalition, spelled out its rationale by asking, "Why is the faction of the Arminians so fostered" so he could give as the answer, "these have most flattered greatness in the late oppressions." Laud and his coterie also obligingly played the part assigned to them, elevating the royal prerogative at the expense of Parliament, because they were well aware that if a session went on long enough for the king and his people to come to happy union they would be the sacrificial lambs at the love feast.[71] Each side, that is, as the 1620s drew to a close, took the correct measure of the other, though both committed the error of putting too much weight on the allegedly inexorable force of ideas and too little on the happenstances of politics.

These new arrangements brought Puritan politicians successes of a kind. In 1628 Parliament passed (and Charles I as a futile goodwill gesture signed) the only Sabbath bill before the Civil War that came anywhere close to the severe limitations on Sunday activity proposed by Nicholas Bownd, and Puritan church reform legislation revived in the Commons in the sessions of 1626, 1628, and 1629, now pressed with a renewed boldness and able once more to attract a broad measure of support. A bill sharply limiting clerical subscription survived to a third reading in 1628, despite the complaint of the solicitor general that "this will open a gap to silenced ministers," and in the same session Ignatius Jordan, who had been repeatedly frustrated and humiliated in earlier parliaments, saw his bill for liberty of hearing sail through the Commons against token opposition.[72] As Pym, Earle, and Sir Nathaniel Rich took advantage of the growing desperation of the MPs, they secured a major share of the parliamentary leadership and ensured that the Puritan program became inseparable from the demand for limitations on the arbitrary power of the crown.[73] Neopopery in religion, speaker after speaker in the Commons declared in 1629, was the appropriate faith for those who advanced themselves by advocating unconstitutional taxation and who championed discretionary power because it allowed them to relieve Catholics of the disabilities of the penal laws, engage in the biased licensing of books to favor Arminians, and endorse without fear of impeachment subservience to Spain and neutrality or worse toward the drive to extirpate Protestantism in Europe.[74] The climax came on 2 March 1629, when Sir John Eliot in his very last speech named first Bishop Neile and then Lord Treasurer Sir Richard Weston as both equally the disturbers of church and state, and the Commons passed its famous three resolutions denouncing Arminianism and unconstitutional taxation. The Puritan and parliamentary causes had by dint of much clever and desperate politicking been made inseparable.

The next week there was no more parliamentary session and little likelihood of another ever being called. Within two months, John Winthrop was writing Margaret the letter that served her in place of a sermon. The Puritan movement in England had been undone at the last through its very assimilation into the fabric of English society and its consequent reliance on the ordinary means of agitation within the existing political system when politics had just turned extraordinary and the existing arrangements were being abrogated. The tactics had been so moderate, the course chosen so self-evidently just, the progress (within the Commons) so palpable that defeat was that much more final. A decade of Puritan agitation, begun in apprehension and pursued thereafter through successive routs and rallies, had abruptly ended in an overthrow so complete it could be taken as the English equivalent of the fall of La Rochelle, the last thunderclap in the mounting crescendo. The storm could no longer be prevented; one could only pray and endure or fly before it.

4

From Exodus to Revelation
The Move toward Sectarianism in
England and America, 1630–1650

In the chain of events beginning in 1617, if not earlier, the sailing of the Winthrop fleet of 1630 is still another link, an act as impassioned yet as inevitable as anything that happened on the floor of the Commons just over a year before. In no sense is it a terminus, much less a beginning. It would be convenient to think of Winthrop and his thousand-odd fellow passengers in this first wave of New England colonization as having actually escaped, as being in some sense exempted from the unhappy further development of the English Puritan movement in the next thirty years. But English migrants continued to move to America at a steady rate throughout the decade of the 1630s, and though immigration had all but ceased by 1642, New Englanders remained acutely aware of developments at home through correspondence, remigration, and their participation in the fierce pamphlet wars over "Independency." In the shaping of the most characteristically Puritan of New England institutions, the most significant English determinant is not the much discussed regional variations in the origins of the migrants but simply the time of their migration. The England of their immediate past shaped the demands they placed on their new society in their American present.[1]

Colonists who came with Winthrop in 1630 or who arrived in the next few years were fearful of impending judgment, but they had not actually experienced it. Their range of complaints was broad and, however much the toleration and promotion of Arminians may have foretold trouble, their strongest single indictment of the English church and state remained their ineffectiveness, just as it had in 1621. England may have been judged past saving after the effective suspension of Parliament in 1629, but for the first few years of the Migration the mother country remained apostate Israel and not corrupt Babylon. For these emigrants their nation's failure was the more culpable precisely because it was volitional, a shirking of a major task for which formidable resources had been available, and the style of Puritanism they transferred to the first New England towns in the early 1630s was not exactly the same as the more militant, more explicitly sectarian faith imported later in the same decade by exiles in flight from the full force of Laudian repression. The migrants who came to America from the mid-1630s onward narrowed the subject of their condemnation to the Church of England and saw there in its latest form the flowering of a corruption that must have been, judging from its effects, implanted at the very root. They were bitter, not frightened, disillusioned, not frustrated. Having seen all the work of the generations since the collapse of Elizabethan Presbyterianism repudiated in short order, they took Laud more or less at his own valuation, not as a wrong turning but as a fulfillment—and as the chastisement exactly suited to the decades-old sin of temporizing. This refugee mind-set had to be blended with the aspirations and experiences of the earlier migrants to produce the tentative, halting, and, as it turned out, highly unstable New England Way of the Cambridge Platform of 1648. The Puritan colonies could have suffered divisions as deep and irreparable as those that overtook the parent movement in Interregnum England. In America, however, the necessary adjustments were made, not smoothly, not lastingly, but with enough success to ensure that there was a Puritanism left intact to recover some of its initial balance when the word *Puritan* back in England had become mainly of historical interest.

The American achievement appears the more remarkable if it is contrasted with the simultaneous predicament of the English Puritans at their moment of apparent triumph. The Puritan leadership in the first years of the Long Parliament, more strategically placed than ever, had no way to deal with the changes wrought in their movement over the preceding two decades. Like their counterparts across the Atlantic, the English Puritans were the legatees of both the increased lay autonomy that accompanied the politicking of the 1620s and of the religious radicalism that had taken hold in the 1630s after the Personal Rule of Charles I deprived the newly aroused laity of a parliamentary focus for their enthusiasms and the Laudian regime had done its work in discrediting the tradition of compromise with the established church. Puritan MPs in the early 1640s nevertheless insisted upon acting as if nothing much had happened since the death of James I in 1625 until the pressure of forces wholly external to Parliament forced them to recognize that they were no longer the unchallenged masters of their own movement.

Contemporaries judged the obvious lack of direction in the Long Parliament over so major a question as the settlement of religion proof of the negative character of the Puritan movement, agreed, it was said, on delenda but not agenda until the need for Scottish aid decided the matter, and the same verdict is echoed by a good deal of recent historiography. Yet it is hardly likely that MPs of the theological sophistication of Sir Henry Vane, Francis Rous, or Nathaniel Fiennes (among others) had never given much thought to what constituted a visible church and where within it the keys of the kingdom were placed or that they thought these questions of secondary importance. The general goals were clear enough and had been for decades: a national church endowed with a preaching ministry adequate in numbers and quality, discipline that was both more uniform and more effective, greater, more systematic clerical participation in ordination and government, at least a modest role for the laity in questions of polity and church censures, and a degree of legal sanction for the collective religious life of the godly outside the ordinary parish services, provided such exercises did not spill over into outright heterodoxy or schism. The Laudian episcopacy had come to seem an insuperable bar to these goals, and therefore the Laudians certainly and the office of bishop quite possibly would have to be eliminated. (The trouble with the reformed episcopacy touted by moderate MPs was that Charles got to appoint the new bishops.) What happened next was the problem.

The apparent lack of an agenda was rather the lack of an institutional means for achieving generally agreed-upon ends, when and if episcopacy was abolished, or even if it were merely limited. No matter what the revisions, a new polity would have to accommodate somewhat contradictory imperatives and also be squared with the entrenched privileges of the governing classes in matters of patronage and tithes. And then, however imperfect and qualified the result, it would also still have to satisfy the new militancy of parts of the clergy and much of the godly, driven to extremism by the Laudian hegemony and further aroused by the scent of blood once their persecutors were called to account. The clergy could perhaps have been bought off, although successive generations might have demanded a higher and higher price. Those of the laity who strayed into definable heterodoxy might possibly have been managed by a judicious combination of repression and limited toleration, although the rise of the Quakers would eventually have put an end to the cleverest of half measures. But in any case, from the calling of the Long Parliament the insuperable bar to the creation of a new national polity in England was the mass of the godly, closer to full-blown sectarianism than ever because they had come to see themselves for the first time in generations less as the vanguard of national reformation than as the saving remnant.

The origins of this shift, it must be stressed, can be traced back to the decade preceding the American migration and not simply to an unexpected reaction to Laudian repression. The 1630s, and especially the years of fullest Laudian ascendancy, from 1633 to 1640, mark so dramatic a turning point in the history of the Puritan movement that they can be endowed with too much creative power. The Laudians would introduce a drastic change by repudiating Calvinist theology and attacking the previously respectable Puritan causes of Sabbatarianism and the provision of a preaching ministry, they would openly and rigidly enforce ritualism, and above all, they would launch a wide-ranging assault on the incumbent Puritan ministry, filling a variety of New England and Dutch pulpits with the victims of their purge. The disillusion created in the Puritan movement in these years was a mortal wound to the moderates in its ranks and served as a heroic catalyst for lay initiatives on both sides of the Atlantic. But *catalyst* is an apt metaphor: the elements in the reaction were already there. Throughout the 1620s the godly were reminded that their individual fates were part of a much larger drama. As only ten just men might have saved Sodom, so the prayers and tears, the unauthorized gatherings of the select minority, might move an angry God to withhold his wrath from the whole of England. It was no wonder if the individuals so denominated, called on to reform themselves, to make special entreaties for their nation, perhaps to vote for MPs worthy of the uncompromising ranks of the judges of Israel, should themselves begin to question the compromises already made by those who addressed the exhortations to them.[2] Thus a much quoted affirmation of conformity made by John Davenport in 1625 was issued *precisely because he was under attack on the subject* and not from any Separatist but from a militant member of his own side, Alexander Leighton. The latter was already notorious for a sinister combination of activities: the authorship of an incendiary pamphlet against episcopacy and in favor of a "holy war" against Spain; the composition of a second tract criticizing another leading London Puritan, Ezekiel Culverwell, for softening the doctrine of predestination in a popular work of practical divinity; and most alarmingly, the leadership of private fasts. Leighton had influence with the laity and, without being a Separatist himself, served as a convenient bridge to Separatism at a moment when the Fabian posture traditional since the 1590s was wearing thin. The danger was so obvious that John Yates took time out from his three-hundred-page diatribe against Montagu and the Arminians to devote two pages to savaging Leighton, "that furious and factious Separatist," and Davenport admitted that he was driven into a public reply to the man "or else my ministry will suffer by my silence, whilst it is undoubtedly received by some, that eyther out of ignorance in these particulars, we take things as they are imposed without examining them, or out of a corrupt mind, we dispense with ourselves in these things against our knowledge, for worldly expectacions."[3]

Leighton insisted that the Church of England was a true church but denounced every concession to episcopal authority: in his most famous work, *An Appeale to the Parliament, or Sions Plea against the Prelacy*, published at the height of the parliamentary crisis of 1629, he accused the Puritan clergy of communing with Antichrist if they so much as heeded a diocesan court's summons or laid down their ministry upon being officially silenced. His was a style of extremism that had begun by the end of the 1620s to exert a terrible fascination for a narrow but significant circle seeking the opportunity to stand at Armageddon. *Sions Plea* was issued in two small editions of no more than six hundred copies between them and had to be smuggled into England from Holland and circulated clandestinely, yet one copy ended up in the hands of Calvin Bruen, the Puritan bookseller and sheriff of Chester, another in the library of Sir Simonds D'Ewes, and three at the least crossed the Atlantic with their New England–bound owners. Where Leighton's "aut hoc o nihil," this or nothing, logic could lead was demonstrated very shortly by the Amsterdam Separatist John Canne, who coupled the book with William Ames's last work (itself containing a preface by Hooker accusing the English ministry of just the corruption and ignorance denied by Davenport) and claimed the two authors inadvertently established the case for Separatism. Canne's book in its turn was so much admired by Roger Williams that he invoked it to defend his own peculiar brand of Separatism against his favorite enemy and the leading New England apologist, John Cotton.[4]

At the parish level, too, there were already signs in the 1620s of a distaste for failing and failed compromises. If the godly were who they were repeatedly told they were—that discernible elect whose prayers and repentance could cancel out the carnal indifference of the reprobate majority—then it stood to reason that election carried the responsibility to avoid condoning sin by taking communion cheek by jowl with sinners. The special sacramental inner circles in Boston and Stamford, like the communion articles of Dorchester, amounted to attempts to indulge these separationist tendencies without the final step of including the unworthy entirely: in the former version the elect, however roughly selected, were not offended by a common rite with the majority of the parish; in the latter, at least a modest winnowing of communicants had been effected with the rejection of that dross so visibly reprobate they would not agree to the articles of reformation.[5] Beyond these limited steps, the ministry could do little more than warn its constituents off the subject as not proper to the laity. The demand for exclusivity in the sacrament picked up substantial clerical backing over time, but it seems to have begun with the laity and to have remained peculiarly their special property. Although Thomas Shepard did not see the evil of mixed communion until well into the 1630s, in 1626 or so Thomas Hooker was already lecturing his congregation that exclusion of the unworthy was the job of "those that have public authority in their hands" and that it was no sin for godly persons to share the sacrament with the wicked multitude when control of the matter rested with their superiors. "We confess the fault; let it lie where it is; we cannot reform it. We can only mourn for it, and that God will accept." Fourteen years later, writing from the vantage of New England, Richard Mather would flatly reject this same proposition that "the people of God may without sinne, live in the want of such Ordinances as Superiors provide not for them," but here he was, like most of the Puritan ministry, following and not leading. The Scottish commissioner Robert Baillie, too ignorant of the thickets of English ecclesiastical politics to realize his indiscretion, would candidly admit as much in 1645, when he observed that any plan for reformation of the English church had to include some fairly drastic device for purging the sacrament, "for upon this point," according to his informant in the English ministry, "depends their [the clergy's] standing, all the godly being resolved to separate from them, if there be not a power, and care, to keep the prophane from the Sacraments."[6]

Laud's role in this delicate situation had been to turn tendencies into rapid, irreversible movements and to make potentials actual. Most seriously of all, his policies at the height of his power divided the English Puritan ministry to an unprecedented extent and incriminated the more moderate wing in the eyes of the godly as mere collaborationists, who because they could not claim the excuse of ignorance must be adjudged corrupt. Even at the theoretical level, the traditional apologetic that had been serviceable in defending the clergy from the maturity of Cartwright to the maturity of Cotton suddenly became an empty formula. In the midst of an earlier Puritan debacle, in 1590, Cartwright could still tell his Separatist sister-in-law that his church remained true "untill such tyme as the Lord takinge away the ministry of the Word from her, and the administracion of the Sacraments hath as it wer by bill of divorcement disabled her."[7] Unfortunately, Laud was prepared to oblige the Separatists on both counts. A measurable portion of the ministry of the word *was* taken away and full-scale efforts were put in motion to get the rest to conform to obnoxious ceremonies and an enforced doctrinal blandness, not to mention the outright Arminian errors broadcast, it was regularly claimed, by the indulgence of those in authority. And though no one in the episcopacy except the bishop of Gloucester accepted the doctrine of transubstantiation, the godly were hardly likely to see the difference when the Lord's Supper was administered with elaborate ceremonial to a congregation kneeling before a railed-in table, renamed the altar and relocated to its pre-Reformation position. There were those who still reiterated the old argument (Robert Abbot and John Ball to name two), but under the circumstances, it took a peculiar degree of courage or faith or desperation to go on telling an angry laity that the Church of England still possessed the infallible marks of a true church.[8]

In any event, such a theoretical exercise was just that, theoretical, if the godly were not there to listen to it. By leveling their guns on the Puritan ministry, through enforced ceremonial and the requirement of reading the Book of Sports, the Laudians inadvertently assured that the members of the one group charged with moderating lay demands were either insurgent, hopelessly compromised, or in exile. Conformity or resistance, the result was the same: the laity were left to their own devices or to a ship bound for America.

The survival of the Puritan clergy had always been a history of negotiation and compromise, but the tractable majority of ministers found that the demands of the new regime sooner or later included one concession too many. "Know I am not more zealous of Ceremonies this day, then when you first called me to Groton," William Leigh wrote to his former patron John Winthrop in 1636. "I then wore the Surpliss, lesse frequentlie for your sake; now more frequentlie for my Ministeries sake." Neither Winthrop nor Leigh's diocesan, the implacable Mathew Wren, was much impressed, and the latter suspended Leigh for refusing to read the Book of Sports. More pliable ministers than Leigh simply caved in whole and adopted a dash or two of Laudianism, exchanging the ascetic pleasure of running with the hares for the fleshly delights of hunting with the hounds. Muriel Sedley Gurdon, the stalwart Puritan wife of a no less stalwart Puritan member of the Suffolk gentry, lamented in 1636 "that in so short a time so many of Gods faithfull ministers should be silenced: and that which is wors [worse]; many that seemed to be zeleous doe yield obedence to the inventions of men: it will be a hard matar to chous the good and lav [leave] the evill."[9]

It was not in the event so hard. The "unconscionable ministry," as Francis Rous was to call those who did Laud's bidding, paid the price in the form of lay disgust and, in many areas, of the growth of various forms of semiseparatism. The famous Broadmead Baptist church of Bristol had its origins in such circumstances, as nothing more than a group of "awakened soules and honest minded people," who had already been meeting together for private exercises for some time before the advent of Laud but who took to relying almost exclusively on these gatherings "when the Clergy began to be high" in the 1630s. By the time of the calling of the Long Parliament, they were too habituated to their independent existence to think of reembracing the old arrangements, even somewhat purified, and in the mid-1640s at the behest of various radical preachers they finally organized themselves as a separate and Separatist church.[10]

Courageous nonconformity was not necessarily any better. A minister who resisted Laud and lost his pulpit lost his flock too—or from time to time regained a portion of them under very different conditions. John Pym is reported to have remarked in the debate over the Root and Branch Petition that "ministers [were] driven out of England for not reading the booke of sports, and they are now separtists beyond [the] sea."[11] He might have added that not all of them had bothered to take ship. In the archdeaconry of Essex alone in 1636 Laud's informants came up with four recently silenced ministers leading conventicles, one of whom, the sometime London lecturer Edward Sparrowhawk, had taken to announcing that for want of a Jeremiah God had deserted England because of "our altars, and such superstitious adorations and bowing at names, and such new idolatrous mixtures of religion and the treading down of God's people."[12] In Ipswich after Mathew Wren's visitation in 1636 had deprived the town of half of its old-line Puritan ministers, the empty pulpits were filled on an occasional basis by unlicensed radicals who preached sermons "tending to the Disparagement of the State and Disquiet of the People." One of these supply preachers was good enough to underline with alarming explicitness the moral of the story: in the absence of a godly ministry, he announced, "it is the peoples duety to labore to maynetayne the gospell . . . with might and mayne and withall the power they have, yea they must fight for the gospell and purity of it."[13] At Norwich the story was the same: in the wake of an episcopal visitation, an increasingly restive and radical laity took to extensive conventicling, spurred on by their new-found independence in the absence of the old clerical leadership and by their distaste for the conforming ministry. Warning the city against "your new teachers" in 1637, Michael Metcalfe, about to depart for New England, advised the godly to "imitate the wise Bereans, and search the scripture whether [i.e., by which] you become such proficients as to try the doctrines of your preachers." At roughly the same time, the silenced preacher William

Bridge, from the safety of the new Congregational church at Rotterdam, went further still, practically ordering the city's conventiclers to set up their own churches: "What? You have no Elders, Pastors, What? You sit, stand, kneele at the command of that [prelatical] government." By the time that government was no longer able to bother them, the godly of Norwich were very sure of their own prerogative to judge a ministry many of whose members had already been weighed in their balances and found wanting. Passing through Norwich in January 1641, the Norfolk Royalist Thomas Knyvett reported to his wife that "heers like to be such a Purgation of Black-Coates, as, if the Parliament intertaines all the complaintes of the Brethren, I knowe not wher they will finde newe ones to put in. Conventicles every night in Norwich, as publickely knowne as the sermons in the day time, and they say much more frequented." Witnessing without comprehending the whirlwind harvest first sown in Wren's episcopate, Knyvett concluded that the "brethren" of the city had respect for only two preachers—"the rest all Praters."[14]

Magisterial Puritanism in 1640 had no real means for accommodating or even accurately acknowledging the existence of an assertive laity. Apart from enjoying the sweets of revenge in their judicial and administrative actions against Laud and selected Laudians, the Puritan leader in the Short Parliament and, until they were forced into other courses, the Long Parliament as well, spent their energies on a program that came straight from the good old days of 1610 and 1614. They trotted out the usual series of bills for the reformation of the clergy and the restraint of episcopal tyranny, making some alterations out of respect for the mood of the times.[15] Puritan MPs in the early 1640s enjoyed the luxury of operating in a Commons far angrier than its predecessors—it could hardly be otherwise after the archiepiscopates of Laud and Neile—and therefore far more willing to use ruthless means, but to familiar ends only. New agenda was tackled hesitantly and inconclusively unless and until events dictated otherwise. Even the Root and Branch Bill, when it came up, was attractive to MPs because it was confessedly an interim arrangement that replaced episcopal government with temporary, lay-dominated commissions. Final settlement of the issues of liturgy and ceremony was initially postponed by referring it to a proposed convention of learned divines (the origins of the Westminster Assembly); voluntary religion received no attention until the Rump, and not much then. Instead, it fell to the General Courts of Massachusetts and Connecticut to enact proposals similar to those that had lain dormant in the Winthrop papers since the age of James I by protecting "private meetings for edification in Religion amongst christians of all sorts of people so it be without just offence."[16]

The direct onslaught on the institution of episcopacy and on the Book of Common Prayer that finally gave the Long Parliament its Puritan character originated neither with magisterial Puritanism nor with one wing or another of the clergy. At the loftier heights of the Puritan movement in 1640 the most widely canvassed reform programs centered on collegiality. A godly ministry, purged of scandalous and popish members, would be "associated" in some way with its bishops, now reduced in power to the status of their "primitive originals," in ordination and the exercise of discipline. (Even this presbytery in episcopacy had been anticipated in the early parliaments of James I.)[17] The Scottish Presbyterian ministers in London did try to organize a more radical petition movement, but by the confession of their leading member they lost control of the agitation, if they ever had it in the first place: "the people's patience could no longer [keep] in." In any case, whatever the Scots did, they were merely shooting sparks at dry tinder. In May 1640 large outdoor prayer meetings in London had preceded an assault on Lambeth Palace and similar exercises had accompanied crowd violence at St. Paul's Cathedral in October and November of the same year. Again in November 1640 the antiepiscopal martyrs Burton and Prynne were welcomed home from prison by "an infinite confluence of the vulgar, having in their hats and hands rosemary and bayes." Finally, on 11 December, some hundreds, perhaps a thousand Londoners— "a world of honest citizens, in their best apparell, in a very modest way"— gave in to a leery Commons the Root and Branch Petition with fifteen thousand signatures attached, and a further battery of county petitions, all signed by an appropriately large number of hands, was to follow.[18]

Item by item, the petitions for the abolition of episcopacy revealed the new boldness of the godly. In the London version the liturgy was "for the most" Catholic in origin, excommunication "of right" did not belong to the church courts (the petition refrains from saying who *could* properly exercise discipline), and the bishops sinned by "the putting of ministers upon parishes, without the patron's and the people's consent," thereby implying that the flock had the right to approve its pastor. More ominously, the authors of the Root and Branch Petition were prepared to open their list of prelatical sins with a blast at the English ministry in general for toadying to the bishops. Before they got around to denouncing the episcopacy for silencing the uncompromising clergymen, they scored the "faint-heartedness of ministers to preach the truth of God, lest they should displease the prelates" and the "encouragement of ministers to despise the temporal magistracy, the nobles and gentry of the land; to abuse the subjects, and live contentiously with their neighbors, knowing that they, being the bishops' creatures, shall be supported."[19]

For opportunistic reasons, the bulk of the Puritan leadership in the Commons eventually came around to supporting a patched-together Root and Branch Bill, but it was a bitterly divisive measure that hardly survived a second reading and was ultimately dropped as a unity gesture in the face of the growing threat of a royal coup. Then the matter of polity devolved on the Westminster Assembly, which put forth a classic Presbyterian platform of discipline that satisfied so few people the Long Parliament immediately substituted a "lame Erastian presbytery" of its own that had even less appeal. The Rump Parliament in its brief lifetime from 1649 to 1653 came closest to a successful Puritan establishment through the simple device of avoiding any platform at all: individual churches were allowed to do as they pleased, subject to restrictions on the old ceremonialism, and national ecclesiastical institutions were restricted to committees of clergymen appointed for "trying" candidates for the ministry and "ejecting" wayward incumbents. And finally in 1660, whatever contributions Puritan ministers and politicians might have made to the Restoration settlement they forfeited by divisions in their own ranks that allowed the Laudian survivors to outmaneuver both them and the Anglican moderates.[20]

This sorry tale is so repetitious that its outcome may seem more inevitable than it actually was. An alternative history is, in fact, already written in the form of the contemporary progress of Puritan institutions in New England. The year the divisions in the English Puritan movement were admitted to be so permanent that only military violence could settle the dispute, 1648, also marked the comparative triumph of the Cambridge Platform in America. Granted the American document is a marvel of carefully worded imprecisions and deliberate elisions; at least it was there, composed and more or less adopted by the churches and governments of New England and without the benefit of a Colonel Thomas Pride to vet the membership of the decisive assemblies. The American Puritans muddled through to a happy inconclusiveness at a time when the English half of their movement pulsated with militance and a large share of the New England population had brought with them the very same corrosive zeal.

Some idea of the disruptive forces at work within the Puritan movement in the decade of the Great Migration can be gleaned from the spiritual education of the Newcastle coal merchant and mercer John Blakiston. He never left England, but he was at one with those who did, bankrolling a number of emigrants and writing of one group, whom he saw off in 1635, "What worthy Jewells are cabinet in those Ship[s] now agoeinge[.] I hear by New England men that God blesses the place exceedingly both with Spirituals and temporalls. It is in all the best mens opinion a place likeliest for the people of God to escape into whom he gives liberty to remove."[21] Despite these sentiments, Blakiston was not a born extremist: he hailed from an old and prominent County Durham family securely entrenched in the nearly hereditary episcopal oligarchy of the diocese (his father was a clerical pluralist of genuinely impressive proportions, and his sister married John Cosin), and he respected the learned and unimpeachably Calvinist bishop of Durham, Thomas Morton. But in the latter half of the 1630s Blakiston's personal affairs and the course of religion in Newcastle both took a turn for the worse, which he interpreted as a single, deserved judgment. He himself was cited before the Durham High Commission in 1636 for defaming the Arminian vicar of Newcastle, Yeldard Alvey, during a public slanging match in which, typically, theology served as the flashpoint for a broad range of local tensions. Blakiston did not like Alvey's preaching or Alvey and had avoided taking communion at his hands, but he did not get around to open abuse of the man until he came across him at a wedding reception explaining his doctrine to Susan Blakiston. He complained at once that his husbandly authority had been ignored, and it probably did not help matters that the obnoxious vicar seems to have had something of a reputation when it came to women. What really set him off, however, was Alvey's crack, "what, art thou comen to outface me, man? thou art but a priestes sonne more then [i.e., the same as] I am." His amour propre breached, the very armigerous Blakiston immediately shot back that he could name seven heresies in a single sermon by the parvenu Alvey and when pressed on that point offered to up the number to seventy.[22] In the ensuing litigation Blakiston should have been the one with the strings to pull, and he did actually solicit Morton's intervention, only to have Alvey get around the bishop by calling in the aid of a fellow upstart, Archbishop Laud. Blakiston was fined and excommunicated and Morton effectively nullified as a power in Newcastle affairs as long as the Arminians held their trump card of an appeal to Canterbury. Blakiston could only sit by, humiliated, and watch "superstition" (ceremonialism) grow "upp like the hemlock" in the city churches and be "troubled to see how willingly many imbrace these yokes." But he could discern the new lesson the Lord was teaching him in his adversity: "For myne owne part I purpose to follow the light I have which the Lord hath bestowed to discerne their wicked plotte and cursed aymes, and never put my necke under this miserable bondage [the ceremonies], I lament that I have stooped and yielded in former more tollerable services so much as I have done, I finde the Lord is asquareinge of my heart and furnishinge of my spirt to doe him some service in an active or passive way." As it turned out, the way was active. As MP for Newcastle in the Long Parliament Blakiston was a war party man, an early republican, and, in 1649, a signatory to the death warrant of Charles I.[23]

The "worthy Jewells" en route to New England took with them similar sentiments. These later migrants arrived convinced, like Blakiston, that the reward for temporizing, their own and that of previous generations, was the ascendancy of Laud. Michael Metcalfe in his farewell to the godly of Norwich had told them that the desolation of their ministry was their punishment for "siding with the times, and yielding too much through slavish fear"; Charles Chauncy to the end of his long life considered his thirty-four years of service in New England inadequate expiation for his two submissions to the High Commission; and William Hooke, Davenport's colleague in the New Haven pulpit, included himself and his entire congregation in a single blanket indictment in 1640 for their Laodicean lukewarmness before their emigration: "Thy sinnes, O man, have begotten many sins there; there is many a formalist, and many a conformitant the more for thee, as indeed I feare there is for mee."[24] One hears in these words the American expression of an English mood, now less concerned with staving off national judgment than with individual perseverance in the coming fires of persecution. By the mid-1630s English Puritan martyrs in training were savoring in manuscript a classic cautionary tale of the wages of apostasy, *A Relation of the Fearfull Estate of Francis Spira*, an account of a sixteenth-century Italian Protestant who renounced his profession when put to the test by the authorities, only to die immediately of a guilty conscience. When the work finally appeared in print in 1638, they snapped up four editions of it in just the next two years. In 1640 a new communicant in Thomas Shepard's Cambridge church could tell his audience (many of them relatively recent arrivals) that in the case of his own pilgrimage he had come to fear "that I was another Francis Spira and so was afraid to pray," sure that the collection of attested and aspirant saints would catch the reference.[25] Confronted with the Laudian regime, the English godly could feel themselves hardening in the fire and the American refugees take their Atlantic crossing as proof they were already hardened. In a way, the growing exclusivity of both groups was a repudiation of the Puritan commitment to the English nation and through England to the Christian world; in another sense, the trend represented a simple extension of the Puritan genius for placing the turmoil and excitement of each individual's spiritual struggle within the larger framework of the great conflicts of the day. Only now, as the 1630s progressed, Rome ceased to be solely an external enemy or a fifth column.

The consequent changes that came over the English Puritans, the "squaring" of their hearts in the decade between the Winthrop fleet and the Long Parliament, had their American counterparts in the demand for rigorous definition and for an appropriately altered polity both civil and ecclesiastical. Migrants crossed the Atlantic, not the Lethe: in explaining the rapid and remarkable alterations in the New England Way in its first decade, recourse must repeatedly be had to the question of where the migrants stood in relation to the English church they had left behind, and this matter, in turn, depends entirely on the particular state it was in when various groups left.

Curious and inconvenient as the progress of New England institutions seems in the entire period up to 1660, the tortuous result was a masterpiece of ecclesiastical statesmanship when compared to the Interregnum. In part, this was because the American Puritans faced a simpler problem. They had no tithes, though clerical maintenance was still subject to dispute. They were equally without lay patronage, though calling a minister was not necessarily made less contentious by assigning it to a multitude of hands. In general, they had no need to mount a frontal assault on an old order before they took to building the new. There was, however, one large disadvantage offsetting the relative lack of complexity in the American situation: the godly, merely one element in an elaborate English equation, were the bulk of the New England population. Their demands had to receive priority, their internal tensions were immediately of urgent colonywide interest. The most serious of these imbroglios, the crisis over Antinomianism in the Bay Colony from 1636 to 1638, took its origins from a very traditional English Puritan form of voluntary exercise, Anne Hutchinson's conferences to apply the general principles of recently heard sermons to the particular conditions of the participants in their various stages of spiritual progress. Governor Winthrop might complain to Mrs. Hutchinson that "the occasions which hath come of late hath come from none but such as have frequented your meetings so that now they are flown off from magistrates and ministers," but she could reply that she was hardly the originator of such exercises, which were "in practice before I came therefore I was not the first."[26] The long-standing and highly articulated devices for inciting a vital, operative knowledge of doctrine could become vehicles for criticism and insurrection in the supercharged atmosphere of the 1630s.

Quite apart from the Antinomian crisis, a variety of controversies in the early years of the Puritan colonies demonstrated that it was no longer easy to reconcile familiar establishmentarian goals with lay autonomy in a period when boatload after boatload brought ashore the refugees from Laud's church. Yet as Mrs. Hutchinson's unhappy fate, isolated and then exiled, testified, the trick could be accomplished, and if the credit can be assigned to any one group, it is to the New England clergy. Their central position in New England culture allowed, indeed required them to reconcile their movement's conflicting demands. They were the ones who would preside over exclusivist churches built around the privileges of self-professed saints and yet also create an effective, comprehensive establishment able by a multitude of means to nourish the fragile growth of the mustard seed of grace in a mass of weak Christians.

The ministry profited in particular from its transplantation to America in a socially mature state. Few of the New England laity could have chosen a minister before their immigration; none of the magistracy had previously possessed anything like the same authority or responsibility. Members of the clerical profession mostly stepped ashore already well initiated in clerical snuggery, in the clubbing together that flourished through full-fledged exercises in the province of York and through the meetings accompanying combination lectureships throughout England. The liberty to continue these gatherings was written into colonial law just as definitely as the rights to private exercises guaranteed to the laity, and the clergy made good and frequent use of their "consociations."[27] To diverse and scattered lay initiatives arising in different towns at different times the clergy could respond with well-prepared, impressively uniform declarations, and they alone as a body were in a position to learn from the experience of a crisis in one church how to squelch trouble before it started in others.

Out of some residual Turnerianism we are always tempted to regard the sheer rawness and rough material equality of colonial society as necessarily subversive of traditional authority: mitered bishop needs mailed seignior to keep the keeling peasant from turning into a yeoman individualist. In actuality, the Puritan ministry in American gained in stature from what we see as the "disruptions" of traditional forms of control. The American magistracy was never the rival source of power that the English squirearchy and aristocracy had been, the hierarchy and its courts run by lay civilians had vanished completely, and the general run of the colonists, dispersed and disorganized, were initially deprived of most of the familiar grievances against clerical authority out of which a concerted lay movement could have been fashioned. The ministry alone retained and improved upon its English institutional strengths. Theirs was anything but an uncontested victory, but the odds were with them from the start and lengthened in their favor as the seventeenth century progressed. This same corporate identity and its attendant perquisites did eventually make the New England clergy targets for the anticlerical sentiment that increasingly possessed the Puritan movement on both sides of the Atlantic. But in the years of settlement their long training in dealing with the godly of England served the New England ministry well when it came time to moderate and channel the demands of the colonial laity. At the time of the Migration the ministers and laity inclined to flee a wicked England were already speaking the same language, if with different inflections, and had been doing so for decades.

The result of their negotiations, the New England Way, was neither uniquely American nor a simple English transplant but a further and continuing development in America of an ongoing and long-running English process of adjustments. Theory and practice in American Congregationalism took their origin from the prominent place that had regularly been accorded the godly in radical Puritan apologetics. The early Jacobean controversialists for whom polity still mattered, the Bradshaws and Jacobs, had replied to the newly plausible Separatist critique of the English establishment by singling out the numbers of incontrovertible saints as proof that the stuff of particular true churches could be found dispersed throughout the land. To the Separatist rejoinder that saints without a covenant were no more a true church than bricks and lumber unassembled were a building, they parried by pointing to the voluntary nature of the religious life of the godly, arguing that the willing assembly of a body of saints in a parish amounted to an implicit covenant. (It did not alter their case, they added, that in the days of popery the bulk of the population was involuntarily conjoined to this gathered core and that an elaborate hierarchy was then grafted on top of these distended churches; however disordered and disguised, the gems remained gems amid the ashes in which statute and canons had buried them.)[28] The next generation, the Cottons and Thomas Hookers, built on this standard apology by invoking what was by then the formidable numbers of the godly "to justifye the congregations in which they are called," that is, converted. A false church would hardly have received such a harvest of souls, "for god is not wont to blesse the bedd of an adulteresse with greater increase then the bed of the married wives."[29]

These words occur in a letter Cotton wrote in England in 1630 to reprove Francis Higginson in New England for Separatist deviations in the newly founded church of Salem, but the same argument can be found in a sermon of Thomas Hooker's written before his exile from England in 1631. That other leading theorist of the New England Way, Richard Mather, thought so much of Cotton's reasoning that somehow, up in Lancashire, he secured a copy of the letter to Salem some eight months after it was written.[30] All three men were familiar with the classic statements of "nonseparating Congregationalism" before they arrived in America, and such intimate knowledge of these works is itself a sign of an early commitment to Congregational polity: the books in question were very hard to acquire, and only a disciple would have been likely to have gone to the trouble to obtain copies and then to have preserved them for the Atlantic crossing in order to be able years later to quote the relevant section in a defense of the New England Way. Nor is the evidence of the American apologies written in the 1640s particularly surprising: two decades earlier, in the 1620s, Cotton and Hooker had virtually dramatized the writings of Bradshaw, Ames, et al. by forming explicitly the covenanted inner circles held to exist implicitly at the center of English parishes. Mather had not gone so far, but he had not needed to because his cure, a Lancashire "chapelry," was already a voluntary gathering of a congregation so saintly they earned for their neighborhood of Toxteth the nickname "the Holy Land."[31]

Cotton set down in his letter of 1630 a definition of a true church that would undoubtedly have been acceptable to Hooker and Mather and, very probably, to many other Puritan ministers looking toward America: "a flocke of saints called by god into the fellowship of Christ meeting together in one place to call upo[n] the name of the Lord and to edifye themselves: in communicating spirituall gifts and partaking in the ordinances of the Lord."[32] The running engagement with the Separatists and a (not unrelated) watch on the godly had by 1630 produced a cast of mind among the more radical Puritan ministry that virtually dictated that the churches of New England, as they were founded one by one in the course of the next few decades, would conform to a pattern that would be called Congregational. These churches were not spontaneous American improvisations but took their form from a line of thinking about polity that stretched from the Elizabethans through the Jacobean theorists to the apologists for the New England Way. Neither, however, were the American churches merely the realized products of English treatises of polity employed as how-to manuals, for these treatises had been attempts to legitimate and by legitimating to control the direction of contemporary English developments. Quite simply, the earliest New England ecclesiastical foundations were the only way according to both theory and practice (at about 1630) that professing Christians could have been organized in a church way—provided, of course, that one made the fundamental assumption that such organizations alone constituted units of the visible church.

When asked for his instructions for New England at the very end of 1629, William Ames had no advice to give, being ignorant, as he said, "of special difficulties; and supposing the general care of safetie, libertie, unitie, with puritie, to bee in all your mindes and desires."[33] He could, that is, count on the New Englanders to do the right thing in general. And so they did at Boston, Roxbury, and Watertown, among other places, over the next twelve months by covenanting together, electing a minister, and subsequently exercising the power of discipline at the congregational level. Whatever alterations would later be made in New England to this fundamental understanding of the nature and function of a church, they would be within the limits of polity as it was conceived of on the eve of Migration. (One New England church, Windsor, was even gathered just before its members' departure from England.)[34] But as subsequent events were to show, these limits were very flexible, just as the working out of details was various and subject to interpretation. If it had not been so, New England would have had its own version of the ecclesiastical chaos of the Interregnum.

William Ames died in 1634 and therefore did not see the unfolding of New England Congregationalism. If he had, it probably would have shocked him, unless he had become, as he had wanted, a part of the process, caught up in changes as rapid as they were subtle so that American participants understood them simply as the perfection of the common notions of a true church when most English observers found the New England experiments straightforward apostasy. In an odd twist of fate, men who had originally cited chapter and verse from anti-Separatist writers ended up within ten years sounding very like their erstwhile opponents. John Cotton in 1640 was more dour on the Church of England than ever the abused Francis Higginson had been; John Winthrop, longtime defender of the needs of weak Christians, found himself in 1643 positively gloating over a due form of government in church and state that required "no smale Company left out of Church fellowship, and Civill Offices, and freedome [to vote] hitherto."[35] By the early 1640s English Puritans took it as a commonplace that the Laudian regime had forced numbers of the godly in their despair either to New England or into Separatism and also, on occasion, into both.

Much of the intellectual energy of early New England went into denying this accusation, which nonetheless contained an uncomfortable element of truth. Separatists maintained as their defining tenet that the Church of England was too corrupted by its Romish "dross" to be a true church, and on this point the New Englanders did maintain a proper charity toward the

English churches as their official stance (although its application in detail invariably undercut the general proposition). But Separatism also, as a result of its first principle, involved indifference or hostility to the basic Puritan goal of using the combined resources of church and state to Christianize and civilize the English people. A few Separatists did come to advocate religious liberty, but most simply gave the question a cold shoulder by taking no interest in the state and assuming that the church existed only for the tiny minority of the demonstrably elect. As a relatively late statement of this position put it, "it is a sequestration, and not a reformation that will heale us, helpe us, and give us a right Church estate to joyne unto."[36] Except for Plymouth Colony, the New Englanders were of another mind and never quite rejected reformation in favor of sequestration. But over time they concentrated more and more of their efforts on defining the rights and privileges of certified saints and especially on the exact degree of rigor that would be needed in the certification. New England Puritanism in the 1630s was moving in tandem with its English counterpart, primarily because of steady immigration, and also, to a small degree, because of some reverse influence as the insurgent godly of the mother country received the heady news of what might be done in the lands where the saints ruled. The alterations in America in the 1630s were an overt register of more submerged tidal flows at home, as the politicians in the Long Parliament were to discover.

Perhaps the most dramatic contrast between the original, broadly based Puritanism of the early migration and its more militant, more sectarian successor can be found in Connecticut, where by an odd set of circumstances the leadership in the river towns ended up largely free from the influence of the later migrants and the dominant group in the New Haven Colony was unalloyed with any elements from among the first settlers. Though claiming a settlement date of 1636, two of the three river towns that originally composed Connecticut had begun much earlier as gathered congregations, Hartford at Newtown (later Cambridge) in the Bay in 1633, Windsor earlier still, in 1630. Both John Warham of the Windsor church and Thomas Hooker of Hartford had left England early in the 1630s, and the former had defended mixed communion during his early days in the Bay, while the latter rejected the more rigorous tests for church membership introduced in some Massachusetts churches between 1634 and 1636. In Connecticut their churches adopted relatively generous tests of visible sainthood, and both men were advocates of a liberal standard for baptism. The colony itself, unlike the Bay and New Haven, never required church membership as a condition for voting and holding office.[37] By contrast, the last of the Puritan colonies was also the strictest. The gathering of the New Haven church under John Davenport's leadership in 1639 had taken well over a year because of the thoroughness with which the would-be pillars had scrutinized evidence of the work of saving grace in each other's souls, and this rigor was not relaxed in subsequent admissions. Only a saint so carefully certified, however, could participate in political affairs, and for good measure the New Haven Colony enjoyed the distinction of being the only Puritan polity in America to adopt whole into its laws John Cotton's biblically derived *Moses his Judicials.* Before the union with Connecticut in 1664, there was no wavering from these standards, not even to the limited degree granted by the Bay Colony's franchise laws, and under Davenport's leadership the churches of the colony vigorously resisted the Halfway Covenant of 1662.[38]

Ironically, Davenport had originally been the most moderate of the English ministers who eventually became major figures in New England. Thomas Shepard vacillated over conformity, John Cotton abstained but equivocated, and Richard Mather apparently conformed in part until 1630 and then gave over all the ceremonies.[39] But John Davenport was an unabashed and unapologetic conformist as late as 1631, and in 1632 he went out of his way to denounce as schismatic the Southwark church that had originally been gathered by the pioneering Congregationalist Henry Jacob. Davenport spelled out his early philosophy in his reply to Leighton, written about 1625, when he called on all parties to undertake a common battle, through the enhancement of the preaching ministry, "against those who oppose us in Fundamentalls." In the church of Archbishop Abbot the ceremonies could be dismissed as superficial ornaments on a basically sound structure. The real danger came instead from the Catholic menace, incipient Arminianism of the Montagu stripe, and the old enemies of vice and irreligion. "Who can, without sorrowe, and fear observe how Atheisme, Libertinisme, papisme, and Arminianisme, both at home, and abroad have stolne in, and taken possession of the house, whilest we are at strife about the hangings and paintings of it?"[40] Davenport was a perfect instance of Jacobean Puritanism at its most respectable, content to pour its energies into preaching campaigns and Sabbatarianism until the Laudians repudiated both and incorporated ceremonialism and Arminianism into the very fabric of the episcopacy. Men in that position had a longer way to fall than the Richard Mathers and Thomas Hookers, and they landed harder and meaner. The same disillusionment that made a radical of John Blakiston in England turned John Davenport into the unbending patriarch of the New Haven Colony.

In the Bay Colony the process was more subtle because the new immigrants regularly interacted with the old over the course of the decade of the 1630s. Yet there was a discernible drift toward purity—toward a definition of the church that gives first thought to the calling of the saints and deduces the terms of the Puritan mission from their needs and privileges. As the enthusiasm for the pure church rose in New England, the failings of the English churches seemed progressively more serious. New Englanders continued to find saving graces in at least some English parishes, but increasingly old and new Puritans adopted a de facto Separatism in their concept of the parochial system. By the time Ezekiel Rogers and his Yorkshire company arrived in the Bay in 1638 they encountered no opposition when they made their announcement that the "many corruptions" of the Church of England had forced them out of its communion even before they emigrated. "Hereupon they bewailed before the Lord their sinful partaking so long in these corruptions, and entered a covenant together, to walk together in all the ordinances, etc."[41] The Yorkshire group may have been one step ahead of the previous settlers of the Bay Colony, but by 1638 it was one step only. Less than two years later, John Cotton was discovering the Church of England in the thirteenth chapter of the book of Revelation, in the beast risen from the sea, and informing his hearers that if they were unwise enough to return to the mother country and "be once incorporated into any of their Parishes," then "you will finde the body of the Church rent from you, or you will be rent from the body, if you shall walk roundly and sincerely in the ways of God."[42]

Cotton's corollary to this proposition, offered with relentless logic in the same set of sermons on Revelation, finished the job of breaking with 1630. A new parliament, "as nowe we have speech of it" (the Short Parliament, presumably), would not help matters because there were simply too many of the unregenerate in the kingdom to make a true reformation possible along the lines the Bay Colony had pioneered. "If the Lord give free passage of a Parliament, you will find it a very difficult thing, to have the State ruled by Apostolical judgment, to reject all devices of men, to shut out the greatest part of a kingdom from the Lords Table."[43] With almost prophetic power— and with no consideration for the main aspirations of the leaders of his movement a mere decade earlier—Cotton thus pronounced the epitaph on the hopes the Puritans had pinned on Parliament in the 1620s. John Winthrop need never have left England in frustration over the failure of reform because it was now revealed that he never should have stayed to attempt it. The sins of England were no longer the incomplete nature of its reformation and the popish pretensions of a part of its clergy but the foolhardy attempt to achieve a national reformation in the first place, which could have no other end than it did. New England was no longer a refuge and a hiding place; it was the logical and necessary next step for those the Lord had taught to grow in grace when he sent the appropriate chastisement of the Laudian regime.

This dramatic turnabout was not absolutely predictable in the first years of the Bay Colony. In 1631 the General Court, such as it was, had restricted the franchise to church members, though almost certainly as a means of keeping the few really wicked from the reins of power rather than as a way of placing the right to vote exclusively in the hands of the few really deserving. At the time only a handful of churches had actually been founded and no very restrictive tests for admission had been laid down, nor had communion with the Church of England been formally rejected. The Boston church in particular began its existence on a very cautious note, affirming explicitly that its new pastor, John Wilson, enjoyed this ministerial status both by virtue of his episcopal ordination in England and his election to a pulpit in America: "We used imposition of hands, but with this protestation by all, that it was only a sign of election and confirmation, not of any intent that Mr. Wilson should renounce his ministry he received in England."[44]

These earlier churches began by late 1634 or early 1635 to suffer the consequences of their informal beginnings. The growing disillusionment imported into America year in and year out with each new lot of migrants could be seen in a series of schisms and near schisms as well as in the measures necessary to prevent further trouble. Local conflicts and personal animosities determined the particular form of these disputes, but whether at Salem or Lynn or a few years later at Scituate (in Plymouth Colony) the terms of the divisions were more or less the same. Some portion of the membership as the champions of purity called into question the casual manner in which the church had been founded and run, "withal making question, whether they were a church or not."[45] Most of the more famous ecclesiastical institutions of the Bay Colony derive in one way or another from efforts to damp the potentially explosive element in the population produced by the heavy immigration of the mid-1630s, efforts that were on the whole successful in marked contrast to the disintegration of Puritan unity in England in the same period.

The most direct and immediate response was the covenant renewal, a device initiated to prevent divisions in the 1630s and not an invention of the revivalist 1670s. The new covenants were expanded, tightly defined documents that supplied any elements in congregational polity that might have been lacking without acknowledging that the earlier church foundations were void *ab initio*. The Boston church, as well, on the occasion of the

"distractions" at Lynn and Salem took the further precaution in 1636 of
indulging the Separatist penchant for purification rituals by including a portion of the renewal ceremony in which the members "acknowledged such
failings as had fallen out, etc." A similar expiatory ritual, not strictly Separatist but very close to it, would be used at the gathering of the church of
Concord in 1637 to absolve the New England ministry of ever having upheld
an unlawful calling by accepting episcopal ordination. The intellectual formula was, in fact, very similar to the covenant renewal. The earlier practice
was not totally denied: the ordained ministry had been true ministers in
England despite their sinful ordinations because they had received a call,
explicit or implicit, from the people to whom they ministered. But the crime
of coupling this legitimate call with a usurped, episcopal one was acknowledged and repented of, and the privilege of the saints, their unique and
precious right to constitute a church, was emphatically affirmed when the
clergy denied being ministers except at the call of a gathered, covenanted,
and certifiably gracious society. (The conclusion was the opposite of the
claim made at John Wilson's ordination in 1630, again in just so many
words.) This arrangement did not explicitly repudiate past commitments, yet
it satisfied any purist less extreme than a follower of Roger Williams—the
question of the ministerial call indeed was moved on this occasion "by one
sent from the church of Salem."[46] To purists who *were* as extreme as Williams a more summary answer could be given: exile to Rhode Island. But
most of the time the Separatists were not repressed; they were assimilated.

Even the level-headed John Winthrop showed the effects of the new rigor-
ism in his changing perceptions of the schism at Lynn in 1635 and 1636. At
the time he had been primarily interested in getting the business settled, with
an acknowledgment of the importance of church ordinances rightly ordered,
certainly, but especially as quietly and amicably as possible. He accepted with
relief an early and familiar compromise (later repudiated) that found Lynn a
true church on the basis of "consent and practice." (That is, however incomplete the outward gathering of the church, the members had now been doing
the right things long enough to provide their polity with a retroactive baptism by desire.) Two years later, in 1638, after the Lynn church had been
regathered under careful outside supervision and "with much ado," he compared the new arrangement with similar disorders at Weymouth and attributed Lynn's subsequent success to its repentance for its original laxity: "They
did not begin according to the rule of the gospel, which when Lynn had
found and humbled themselves for it, and began again upon a new foundation, they went on with a blessing." Evidently, the atmosphere in the Bay

Colony was becoming very rarefied if it could make the likes of Winthrop a little pixilated. He was still the same born politician trying to find a middle ground that accommodated all but the extremes in the colony, but as the boundaries of his field of operations shifted leftward, so did the middle point.[47]

Responding to these repeated contentions, actual and potential, the General Court on 3 March 1636 required the majority of the colony's magistrates and ministers to be present at the gathering of any new churches.[48] Although the law has a repressive air to it, its original purpose was mainly prudential: the "sad breaches which other churches have had" demonstrated that if these mixed councils of civil and ecclesiastical officers were not present at the start of any new church, they would sooner or later be called in anyway to deal with the claim of some aggrieved faction that errors in the foundation invalidated the entire edifice.[49] Nevertheless, indirectly the crisis of the mid-1630s did force a greater degree of uniformity on the churches of the Bay, for the significance of these statutory councils lies in their function as devices for determining and adjusting common goals. As at Concord in 1637, in each instance the ministry in full regalia told the new church—and each other— what the New England Way was all about and where it was headed.

The earliest authorized council, at the first attempt to gather the Dorchester church in 1636, had profound consequences for the religious life of the Bay Colony and New Haven. On this occasion the resident clergy taught their newly learned lessons in exactness to a newcomer, Richard Mather, when they rejected his would-be pillars on the grounds that their conversions were spurious and for the most part merely "legal" (resting on faith in their own abilities rather than a sense of their total dependence on free and unmerited saving grace). Thomas Shepard, who had organized the first public demonstration of the members' saving faith at the gathering of his own Cambridge church two months earlier, took the lead in halting the Dorchester proceedings under the new statute because, as he told Mather, "we come not here to find [i.e., discover] gracious hearts, but to see them too. 'Tis not faith, but a visible faith, that must make a visible church, and be the foundation of visible communion."[50]

The Dorchester episode always seems a little puzzling, partly because Mather, who devoted most of his intellectual life to questions of polity, should have been the last man in New England to gather a church carelessly, partly because the development cannot be readily explained as a qualified accommodation with the growing Separatist spirit. The classic Separatists of Amsterdam and Leiden did not require conversion narratives as part of the procedure for admission to church fellowship; if anything, changing the focus of the admissions test from external conduct to internal grace had anti-Separatist implications eventually put to good use.[51] The affinity of the requirement promulgated at Dorchester is probably with the Antinomian controversy in the church of Boston, which erupted later in the same year and which also centered on discerning between a legal and a truly gracious conversion. Antinomianism in America needs to be understood primarily as a hyper-Puritanism rather than an alternative faith with deep roots in English sectarianism. A growing hostility to legalism had appeared in covenant theology early in the seventeenth century, and the open defense of Arminianism after 1624 had produced exaggerated counterstatements from all sections of the Puritan movement.[52] There was irony but no great contradiction in Anne Hutchinson finding in her eventual nemesis Thomas Shepard the least objectionable of the body of the New England clergy, whom she accused of a covert reliance on the covenant of works, for Shepard was a product of very much the same English circumstances as the Hutchinsonians and just as sure as they that many an apparent saint was an unknowing legalist. ("He makes them all afraid that they are all hypocrites," an older colleague said of his preaching.)[53] Shepard had introduced the test of the conversion narrative at Cambridge and presided over the rejection of the Dorchester church the same year, and in both instances, no less than at Mrs. Hutchinson's Boston, we are dealing with a pervasive reaction to the Laudian attack on the long-standing predestinarian tradition of the mother church and to the feebleness with which most English contemporaries resisted these new (or newly revealed) episcopal corruptions. "Though the light be hindered with us with the Foggs and Mists of Pelagian and other heresyes," an English Puritan declared, "there [in New England] it breakes forth and shines."[54] The New England clergy might have been responding "Amen" when they faulted poor Richard Mather's pillars because "they expected to believe by some power of their own, and not only and wholly from Christ." In the face of the dwindling size of the minority who were still ready to do their duty by opposing the episcopacy, and because of the increasing exaltation of the few who had actually migrated for truth's sake, it became necessary, for reasons of principle and prudence alike, to demonstrate as publicly as possible the *visible* sanctity of the genuine remnant as they arrived and built their churches in America. Even as Mrs. Hutchinson was just beginning to object to the overly charitable standards used in awarding sainthood in New England, she was already being answered. "By this means, I believe and hope, that the communion of saints will be set at a higher price," Shepard told the unfortunate Mather, significantly, at the very moment when he was also about to assume the lead in blunting the Antinomian threat in the colony.[55]

Undeniably, the test for saving grace had its experiential roots in the elaborate manuals for self-examination that had always made up much of the literary corpus of English Puritans.[56] But the laity gave the clergy's directions an unusual twist when they exposed their introspective soul-searchings to each other in the course of their private exercises. By about 1633, godly London apprentices meeting to "repeat" sermons and apply them to their particular conditions were carrying matters one step further than the minister would have prescribed by "communicating to each other what experience we had received from the Lord." The participants in the private meetings that Mrs. Hutchinson joined in Boston about the same time were similarly engaged. (She rose to prominence in them because she excelled, in the manner of her spiritual mentor John Cotton and her brother-in-law John Wheelwright, in dissecting the personal experiences delivered by would-be saints to show them that they were still unconsciously relying on a covenant of works.)[57] The quality of a believer's conversion, therefore, was already being examined collectively and, in effect, publicly in both England and America before it became a distinguishing requirement of admission to Congregational churches.

This subsequent institutionalization of the test, however, and the insistence that a church cannot be right without some version of it, must be understood as a manifestation of the spirit of embittered extremism characterizing the refugee politics of those Puritans who chose exile after Laud came to power at Canterbury. The driving force was the collapse of the carefully limited world of the old nonconformity and the sense of freedom that came with release from the never-ending necessity of compromise. The expatriate church that gathered at Arnhem in the Netherlands under the ministry of Thomas Goodwin and Philip Nye instituted the same test at about the same time without the benefit of any American influence, and its ministers and congregation alike would become prominent members of the Independent cause in England upon their return home in the 1640s.[58] Indeed, the Arnhem group had almost ended up in New England in the first place: before they had settled in the Netherlands as their place of exile, Nye was already serving (in 1635 and 1636) as the agent for a proposed home at Saybrook for these "gentlemen," as the Puritan ultras were prudently termed.[59] In their different ways, Arnhem, Dorchester, and the Antinomian crisis centered in a single impulse.[60]

In this context there was nothing anomalous in Richard Mather being the first New England minister whose church was found wanting in vital matter. Throughout his career Mather was the foil of John Davenport, and the two men were appropriately ranged on opposite sides of the Halfway Covenant at the very end of their lives. In the wilds of the diocese of Chester, Puritan clergymen like Mather had enjoyed a unique degree of freedom until Neile's first visitation of the northern province. He had never been forced to face the issues of mixed communion or of the legitimacy of a national church organized on parochial lines. Until he was abruptly deprived of his English calling in 1634, he had ministered to the "chapelry" of Toxteth Park, a voluntary, gathered body. The situation was not unusual in the sprawling, undersupervised diocese. Just across the Mersey from Mather's Toxteth Park lay Samuel Eaton's parish of West Kirby, which, according to its minister, "consisted of the choycest Christians of many Parishes, who met constantly together upon the Lords day, and enjoyed the Word, and Seales of the Covenant, and maintained a Pastor to dispense the same unto them, and never, or very rarely repaired to such Parishes where their habitations were." Samuel Clarke the martyrologist was another veteran of the area, and he gives an even more detailed description of the religious life of the godly in that part of the diocese of Chester. His appointment to his cure was by way of being "importuned" by "some Godly christians," his maintenance "came by voluntary contribution out of all those Christian Purses," his flock was drawn from miles around without distinction of parishes, and he regularly supplemented his public service with private exercises at fasts held at homes all over the area. "Love, by frequent Society, was nourished and increased; so that all the Professors, though living ten or twelve miles asunder, were as intimate and familiar, as if they had been all of one houshold."[61]

Clarke's career was entirely English, but for Mather and Eaton this common experience in the most unusual of circumstances was definitive for their years spent in America, endowing them uniquely with a positive alternative to the growing indifference in New England to the traditional nurturing functions of church, state, and society in general. For both men during their English ministries their saints had already been visible without any special scrutiny and, unlike the majority of the emigrant clergy, their decision to remove did not implicitly entail a wholesale repudiation of previous concessions to ritual, hierarchy, and parochial communion. Mather, in fact, recorded his reasons for leaving: he was simply looking for work and for a refuge that merited God's protection. (Like Winthrop in 1630 he fled the wrath of God, not the face of Antichrist.) But doing what came naturally at Dorchester, he promptly ran afoul of those of his colleagues who had been reborn in the 1630s and who were making up for the time he himself had never lost by a thoroughgoing reversal of their earlier caution. Eaton similarly collided with John Davenport over another central issue of the new sectarianism, the church member franchise, and returned to Cheshire, where, back in his own milieu, his still unchanged commitments made him once again a disruptive radical. Mather, who was better at acclimating himself to differing environments, stayed on in New England and managed to get an acceptably exclusive church formed a little later in 1636, but he remained one of the earliest and, without deviating into any form of Presbyterianism, certainly the most consistent advocate of a broader definition of church membership.[62]

It seems a left-handed compliment to the New England Way that Richard Mather, the man with the most generous concept of the church's agenda in America, should be its single most ingenuous Congregationalist. His more self-conscious colleagues concentrated their intellects and attentions for the most part on defining the ecclesiastical framework most appropriate to saints of tried and proven fidelity. If the concatenation of New England innovations is added up, the composite picture by 1638 is at odds with the clergy's repeated claim to revere particular English parishes as basically true churches. No new migrants were allowed to join a New England church on the basis of their former good standing in English parishes, and New Englanders returning home were enjoined from participating in mixed communion. (After Dorchester, as well, the effective standards for locating the residue of gracious souls in the mixture were raised considerably.) A true parliamentary reformation was deemed all but impossible, and the hierarchy was held (in Ezekiel Rogers's words) to be "wholly antichristian." To take ordination at episcopal hands was accordingly now adjudged a sin even when joined with a lawful popular call. Further, given the covenant renewals required to reform the earlier Massachusetts churches, even when the English parishes were able to get out from under the control of the bishops, as they did after 1640, they "could not be right without a renewed Covenant at least, and the refusers excluded."[63] It was all very well for New Englanders to attempt to find "implicit" truth in some English congregations (left unspecified) for the benefit of their old friends in the Puritan clergy now under increasing fire from the Separatists and the militant wing of the laity—a laity not very different from their fellows who had migrated to New England to find purity there. "Implicit" legitimacy was not worth much under the circumstances. "That much favor will be graunted us by the strictest of the separacion," a correspondent of Governor Winthrop's shot back in 1637 and suggested for good measure that the cause of the moderate Puritans was not being helped by letters from New England calling the members of the English churches (in no implicit terms) "doggs and swine, especially those of the profaner sort among us, nor questioning our ministry and calling to it."[64]

From about 1636 on the New England clergy began to receive detailed complaints from their sometime colleagues in England. When they responded with tact and circumlocution, they were met with rejoinders that were a notch less brotherly than the original criticisms. The further replies were less generous and more argumentative in their turn, and before long the entire correspondence ended up included in the polemical exchanges that erupted into print as part of the ever-proliferating pamphlet warfare of the Interregnum.[65] The whole business converted no one (or almost no one—John Owen and one or two others claimed to have come over to the Independents after reading John Cotton's apologies for Congregationalism). Yet in an important way English criticism did begin the gradual cooling down of the New England colonists' love affair with purity. In the 1640s the ministers, caught short by the rising volume of English Puritan attacks, took stock of themselves and halted their continuing indulgence of lay initiatives. Consequently, they found themselves in an off-again, on-again round of skirmishing with the laity that produced few casualties and no victors. But this round of drawn engagements did effectively stop further movement in a sectarian direction.

New England writers in the Presbyterian-Independent exchanges of the 1640s never seemed to understand precisely what it was their opponents were attacking—or, more likely, they chose not to understand. Charged with embracing Separatism, they responded by examining "rigid" Separatist writings of the Jacobean period and then congratulated themselves upon finding that New England Congregationalism differed in major ways from the polity of Henry Ainsworth and John Robinson. The English critics, however, were not worried about competition from Amsterdam and Leiden. For them the burden of the Laudian years had been the multiplication of impromptu, lay-dominated exercises and the concomitant growth in impatience with clerical leadership. At the same time and for the same reason, the moderates were similarly threatened by the increasing aggressiveness of very loosely organized clusters of Separatists in such places as the Kentish Weald and the city and suburbs of London and by the activities of groups such as the Broadmead conventiclers, who walked out on the few Bristol ministers they had been willing to hear when "many times a great deale of bitternesse came from them against the New England ministers, and those that went thither."[66] For all these groups the New England example was all too apposite in its condemnation of mixed communion, set prayer, and episcopal ordination and its endorsement of gathered churches. Reports from the New England colonies, thirteen Puritan ministers claimed in 1637, "have so taken with divers in many parts of this Kingdome that they have left our Assemblies because of a stinted Liturgie, and excommunicated themselves from the Lords Supper, because [of] such as are not debarred from it. And being turned aside themselves, they labour to ensnare others, to the griefe of the godly, the scandall of Religion, the wounding of their own soules ... and great advantage of them, that are wily to espy, and ready to make use of all advantages to prejudice the truth."[67] Whatever their natural inclinations, the New England clergy by example and, when they were put to it, by explicit statements were aligning themselves with the most radical critics of the English church. They left their former brethren with no shred of comfort, even on the most delicate and dangerous of all the issues involving the perquisites of the English clergy and their gentry protectors. New Englanders rejected lay patronage out of hand, and though they pursued an ambiguous course on compulsory maintenance of the clergy, they objected to tithes entirely. More awkward still, their official spokesmen, as early as 1636 or earlier, explicitly endorsed gathering true (that is, fully Congregational) churches in England separated from the parish assemblies and in flat defiance of the authorities, civil and ecclesiastical.[68] William Bridge's thunderings from Rotterdam calling on the Norwich conventiclers to set up their own churches had equally emphatic American echoes.

In the 1630s there was not much middle-of-the-road English Puritans could do about the Separatist threat besides issue irrelevant calls for forbearance and trot out the same familiar apologies for true but imperfect churches. Liberated at last in 1640 by the fall of Laud, they rushed to the Presbyterian cause as the last hope for retaining a national church with a comprehensive mission, only to find that the disappearance of the episcopal courts and the High Commission left their Separatist and neo-Separatist opponents stronger than ever. What was worse, the respectability lent to Congregationalism by the rather distant example of New England was now enormously increased by the return of the Holland exiles to become the Dissenting Brethren in the Westminster Assembly and by a sprinkling of former New Englanders and prestigious English converts to their form of polity (including Henry Burton and John Goodwin). Yet, maddeningly, there was nothing concrete to attack. Thomas Gataker in 1640 found himself grumbling about "a great noise in England" for the last three or four years in favor of "a New light and a New way," which, unlike bona fide Separatism, was never spelled out "yet further than by private letters and clancular manuscripts" originating from abroad.[69] The "dark lanthornes," however, still did not shine brightly after the calling of the Long Parliament and the Westminster Assembly: with the exception of a few of the Separatists and the ever intrepid Burton, the English Independents mostly held their hand, refusing to come up with a full statement of church polity or even, in the case of the Dissenting Brethren, to admit before 1644 that they so much as constituted a distinct party.

At this juncture, between 1642 and 1645, the correspondence begun with New England in the late 1630s suddenly and conveniently appeared in print. In his *Antapologia* of 1644 the notorious Thomas Edwards (of *Gangraena* fame) claimed that during the formal truce between the Dissenting Brethren and the Presbyterian majority in 1642 and 1643 the Independents simply got round the peace terms by bringing out account after account of New England polity.[70] Actually, both sides played the same trick: the defense of the parochial system in the 1630s against New England innovations appeared in print in the 1640s grafted on to the new Presbyterian campaign against Independency. Nothing loath to respond, the New England clergy promptly took up the next round in the dispute, and for the rest of the decade they were active and eager literary contributors to the anti-Presbyterian camp, even though that group included English allies who would have very quickly wound up in Rhode Island if they had ever set foot in Massachusetts or Connecticut.

As an issue, however, Presbyterianism changed the nature of the debate in New England no less than in old. The English criticism of the 1630s could be written off as misinformed (as it was on some points), and charges of apostasy were answered with the double reply of new light and new liberty. In America, free from episcopal interference, the New England clergy had grown in grace and realized to their sorrow that in some instances they had engaged in unlawful acts in England; further, many things not strictly unlawful in the English church were thoroughly inconvenient, and it was surely the New Englanders' moral duty to reform what was amiss now that they no longer had to tolerate these undesirable impositions from above as the price of continuing their ministry. In turn, the American apologists assumed that if the English ever had the like freedom they would at the least immediately do as the New Englanders did in the case of inconvenient practices. (They would, for example, reorganize their churches with explicit covenants.) Hope was even expressed that in time the English Puritans might very well find their way to the New England view of the lawful after the new light broke out on their side of the Atlantic. Instead, after 1640 New Englanders found themselves replying to full-blown doctrinal Presbyterianism—not even the semi-Erastian compromise that eventually emerged from the Long Parliament, which could easily be faulted for its obvious imperfections, but a wholly theoretical system of indisputably Reformed pedigree. Issues of congregational polity that had been handled piecemeal before and in their own terms now had to be faced systematically and defined against a plausible alternative system. Presbyterianism, therefore, became the burning question of the 1640s. Anti-Presbyterian conventions of the whole body of the New England clergy were held at Cambridge in 1643 and 1645, and the full-scale synod that held its sessions there from 1646 to 1648 was confessedly looking over its shoulder at England at regular intervals during the course of hammering out a platform of discipline. (Virtually all of its ten-page preface is an apology for gathered congregations and a rejoinder to Presbyterian charges of schism.)[71]

Most of the defense of Congregationalism was a theoretical exercise. A genuine Presbyterian sentiment in New England could be found only in a few towns, and when Robert Childe and the Massachusetts Remonstrants of 1646 sought broader support for an alteration in civil and ecclesiastical polity they had little success.[72] But the very need to go on the defensive affected the American clergy's conception of themselves and the churches to which they ministered. They became aware, to begin with, of the relatively extreme position they had gradually adopted in the 1630s. As early as 1642 Thomas Hooker affirmed the American ministry's isolation when he declined an invitation to the Westminster Assembly on the ground that he did not intend "to go 3,000 miles to agree with three men" (actually five).[73] As a result, it became necessary to build paper bridges to the Presbyterians while denying any direct debt to the Separatists.

The New Englanders and the Independents hit on the joint strategy of labeling their Congregationalism a "middle way" between the Brownists and the Presbyterians, an assertion historically untrue—Presbyterianism was not a live issue for the exiles in the 1630s—but polemically useful. The consequences, however, were far more profound for the American authors of this myth than for the English audience they were attempting to misdirect, though they did thoroughly bamboozle at least one naive Scot into making so complete a misstatement of New England polity that he became a sitting duck for a rebuttal from one of the Dissenting Brethren. In general, the New Englanders in statements intended for English readers persistently understated their differences with Presbyterianism. In his own journal, for example, Winthrop described a Cambridge synod of 1643 straightforwardly as having "concluded against some parts of the presbyterial way." The summary of the results sent to England was much more guarded and ambiguous. A New England congregation was described not as sharing the keys but as giving its "consent" to the eldership's verdicts on disciplinary cases; "fit matter for a Church" was not visible saints but anybody who did not "live in the commission of any known sin, or the neglect of any known dutie" and might very well include individuals who "are not alwayes able to make large and particular relations of the worke and doctrine of faith," and the clerical consociations of the Puritan colonies were described as far more regular in their meetings and far more official in function than these occasional gatherings actually were. (The gloss put in 1648 on the "liberty" guaranteeing these meetings reads simply, "No Presbyterial authority over Churches.")[74] But by replying to English criticism with a certain degree of inspired vagueness, the New England ministry was also rediscovering how flexible the boundaries of the ecclesiology that had been brought to America really were. The upshot was hardly a reversion to 1630, but to the extent that the clergy bent their efforts to distinguishing their polity from its alleged Separatist parent, they did become more reluctant to endorse anything that looked like an advance beyond the situation achieved by the end of the 1630s. In particular, they reaffirmed the sacerdotal and distinct quality of their office through the Cambridge Platform's gingerly endorsement of ordination by the laying on of the hands of the clerical eldership rather than those of the laity. And when they came to detailed definition of that amorphous and traditional formula of church government as an unspecified blend of clerical aristocracy and lay democracy, the clergy usually spelled out the particulars for the benefit of their own side. The Cambridge Platform of 1648 in small but significant ways takes back something of what the laity had gained in the last eighteen years, and in the course of defining terms it formulates them in a manner that precludes further lay encroachments. In this one area, the status and power of the clergy, the sectarian drift was actually reversed in the course of demonstrating how far the New England Way was from Separatist "popularity."[75]

For the most part the "democracy" did not put up much of a sustained opposition to the clerical resurgence. Nasty controversies over ministerial power broke out in a few churches, most notably at Hartford in the 1650s, but the brunt of the laity's concern was elsewhere. They were English refugees, not Scottish, and seventeenth-century saints, not democrats: the aspect of Presbyterianism they feared most was impurity, not inequality, a revival in a new form of a comprehensive national church. That specter was fought at every turn, whenever any possible change could be construed as defining a church in terms broader than a single gathered and covenanted society of saints. The demands for more liberal baptismal membership that originated with the clergy from 1645 on always ran head-on into lay resistance, and anything that hinted at interchurch organization was sure to provoke criticism from one segment or another of the laity. At Woburn in 1642 the congregation insisted on ordaining their minister themselves, fearing that the laying on of hands by ministers of other churches "might be an occasion of introducing a dependency of churches, etc. and so a presbytery." Wenham in 1644 was so afraid that impurity in other churches might infect its own that it virtually abandoned the Congregational principle of communion of the saints by insisting that individuals dismissed to it from other churches undergo an entirely new examination of their conversion experiences. The Cambridge Synod drew opposition on similar grounds in 1646 from "some of Boston, who came lately from England, where such a vast liberty was allowed, and sought for by all that went under the name of Independents." Among the deputies fear of Presbyterian inroads was so strong that the General Court twice had to adopt equivocal formulas to deal with the synod, first in calling for its assembly in 1646 (a recommendation only, though not one that implied any incompetence to require a synod), then in accepting the final results in 1651 ("approbation" only was awarded and that on the murky grounds "that for the substance thereof it is that wee have practised and doe believe").[76] Even so, fourteen deputies (out of forty) objected by name to this tepid endorsement, and four of them were to be found a good twenty years later heading the opposition to the Halfway Synod on the identical grounds that its proposals represented an unlawful intrusion on congregational autonomy.[77]

By 1650 the New England Way had achieved little more than a temporary state of stasis. The dramatic movement of the 1630s was stopped but not really reversed. The Cambridge Platform, the *summa* of the decade, indeed of the first thirty years of Puritanism in America, simply spelled out the stalemate article by article. Both its language and its politics demonstrate mainly that the ministry had become anxious over the distance they had traveled from so many of the men in England with whom they had once shared a common cause, and the laity had no intention of tolerating the least step in the direction of the schemes of polity and discipline now advocated by all but a relative handful of these same Englishmen. Neither a peace treaty nor even a truce, the Platform is really a map of the disposition of the contending forces as night fell on the first day of battle. On the whole, each side respected the other and was willing to allow the Platform to serve as the basis for negotiations when conflict resumed in earnest, in the 1660s, but further substantial changes in the New England Way were ruled out for the time. The area of greatest urgency, the redefinition of eligibility for baptism, was too controversial, however, even for discussion: the Platform simply skips the issue.[78] The ordeal of English Puritanism in the 1630s had spurred rapid and significant redefinition in New England; in the 1640s the fissures in the English movement gave the impetus for a series of alarums and excursions that canceled each other out by the time the Massachusetts General Court nerved itself in 1651 to approve the Cambridge Platform primarily on the grounds that it did not change anything.

The next ten years were more of the same. Presbyterianism largely faded away as an issue in the 1650s, to revive in the Connecticut River Valley in the 1660s, but only in a distinctly local form in response to distinctly local problems.[79] The improvisatory, neo-Erastian religious establishment of the Commonwealth and Protectorate periods came closer to resembling the New England Way than any previous or subsequent English arrangement, but that was little consolation in America for other, more sinister developments in the mother country. Under the prevailing conditions of de facto toleration, the sectarian fragmentation of the radical wing of the Puritan movement, which began as early as the 1620s, reached its apogee in the emergence of Seekers, Ranters, Muggletonians, Fifth Monarchists, every variety of Baptist, and, most enduringly, in the rise of the Quakers. The Puritan colonies had given only sporadic attention to the Baptists and the Gortonists in the early 1640s, but beginning in 1649 they registered their recognition that the "Opinionists" had come into their own in England by the remarkable alacrity with which they elaborated their own heresy statutes to take cognizance of species of error undreamed of in the simpler days just passed, when heresy and casual blasphemy were difficult to distinguish and principled heterodoxy rarely got beyond denying infant baptism.[80] Fear of the English contagion spoiled for a decade or more any hope of the New England colonies addressing their own major problem. This was not really defections to the Quakers, or even to the Baptists, but, rather, the loss of definition in the traditional Puritan mission that occurred at some indeterminable point in the 1630s when the main object of all practical divinity, the weak Christians, pretty well dropped out of colonial calculations, overwhelmed by the influx of masses of the spiritually stouthearted.

There is a kind of snapshot of the transition in the spiritual autobiography of Susanna Bell, a woman whose experience managed in a very brief time, probably a matter of months, to straddle the great divide of the first years of the Puritans in New England. Alone among conversion narratives,

Bell's includes one episode in which she failed to prove her spiritual credentials. When she applied for membership in the church of Roxbury sometime in 1636, she was faced with the interrogatory, "what promise the Lord had made home in power upon me," but could give no personal and immediate sense of the application of scriptural promises. She was advised "to wait a little longer" and immediately embarked on a round of listening to sermons at nearby churches. To this activity she joined bouts of self-contemplation so manifestly serious that John Eliot himself invited her to reapply. She demurred, however, while she sought for a fuller description of the requisite spiritual experience in an unnamed work of John Preston. After some two weeks of reading and rereading the relevant passages, she was sure that her own condition genuinely fit the one detailed by Preston and finally joined the Roxbury church as a visible saint. Susanna Bell's experience is routine enough except for that first unsuccessful attempt. She was evidently taken by surprise by the new requirements. She had already lived in Roxbury for a brief period, and her husband had joined the church before her application for admission. She had, therefore, no reason to expect that the spiritual ante would be upped so abruptly, as, of course, it was after the Dorchester episode of the same year, and so her motives for first trying to enter church fellowship were traditionally and inappropriately English. She had thought that "if I could but get into the fellowship of the people of God, that that would quiet my spirit and answer all my objections." A decade earlier it might have, but under the new circumstances this desire had suddenly become a presumption.[81]

There was nothing novel or un-Puritan in seeking a nurturing environment in which to enact an individual spiritual progress, and the English godly had routinely found it in both the institutions of the church and their own extraparochial exercises. In New England the church foundations reflected the same understanding until the influx of angry refugees changed the meaning of communion with the godly: it became less a form of spiritual strengthening than a certification of strength. In the case of Susanna Bell the shift did not really matter because so many of the elements of her conversion had already been supplied for her in England that she needed only to rearrange them with a little intensity (generated by her rejection) to finish the job. For the generations reared in New England the case was otherwise.

Weak Christians still figured in these new arrangements, but only if their weakness were of a special and convenient sort. The elaborate ceremonies of admission, and especially the public conversion narratives, were held to have a didactic and evangelical effect on the onlookers, stirring them up to imitate the gracious even as it reaffirmed the arduous nature of the route to graciousness. It might genuinely work as designed for individuals such as Susanna Bell, who could without much difficulty see the new members as themselves a few steps further down the road and enter imaginatively into what they heard because their own experience, largely gained in England, was analogous. But those who came on this drama late in the action, because they were very young at immigration or were born in America, could be little more than passive observers, unable, as Puritans of all people should have known, to make their formal commitment to doctrine into operative knowledge. Their failure was in no sense volitional, though it came to be labeled as such, but was the inevitable result of the lack of nurturing mechanisms that undergirded the spiritual lives of the founding generation before they had emigrated to form their communities of attested (and prepared) saints. Yet for decades those in authority in New England had little interest in rebuilding or replacing an English environment while their own attention continued to be riveted, as it had been from the mid-1630s, on preserving those self-regarding ecclesiastical bodies whose heroic creation was the defining experience of New England Puritanism. Because of this neglect, no less than because of the primitive material conditions of early America, the plenitude of means the first, English-bred migrants took for granted became for their descendants a paucity. Sooner or later someone was going to have to admit that the repair of this deficiency was the real mission of the Puritan movement in its American maturity.

5

Reconstruction and Conflict
The Halfway Covenant and
Declension Controversies, 1650–1680

American Puritans were spared an Interregnum of their own only in part. Their internal struggles in the thirty years after 1650 were both more diffuse in organization than those of their English counterparts of the Civil War era and more muted in intensity, but they were also more enduring, smoldering on like some moor fire inextinguishably lodged in the constituent peat just below the surface when more visible conflagrations had burned themselves out. Conflicts at once so protracted and so subtle are not as easily understood as the episodes centering on some one or another prominent heresiarch; few of the contestants allowed their positions to be defined with enough rigor and consistency to make the charges of schism and apostatizing stick, however frequently they were hurled on all sides. The most revealing vantage, therefore, from which to start any investigation of a murky period full of half-consummated alliances and unfinished arguments is that of a more ordinary dissident, who built his protest out of his English and American experiences without undergoing any single great revolution of conscience.

John Trumbull, it will be recalled, was the first-generation New Englander whose spiritual pilgrimage in England had coincided with his putting out to sea: on ship he found the leisure to read *The Plaine Mans Path-way to Heaven* and upon arrival in London the opportunity to enmesh himself in the densely woven plenitude of means offered by the great city.[1] He related these English experiences in his conversion narrative before the Cambridge church about 1637, but unlike any other of Thomas Shepard's tested and proven saints Trumbull a good thirty years later also left another firsthand testimony of his faith. One would expect from such a source an old man's conjuring of the next generation to live up to the heroic standards of the founders, but this record is something else. It consists of the liveliest and most spirited passages in the exchange between the Charlestown Baptists (whom Trumbull championed) and the New England ministers assigned to confute them at a conference in 1668. The man who thirsted after the word as expounded by Obadiah Sedgwick and bared his soul for Thomas Shepard now disputed biblical exegeses with Thomas Shepard, Jr., and told the clergyman plainly, when the latter was about to launch the major premise of his latest syllogism, "We can't be saved by answering your arguments. We must be saved by the scripture."[2]

Trumbull the archetypal weak Christian had through decades of practice become typical instead of the kind of Puritan layman more familiar to us from England in the same period, the self-willed saint who had learned his lessons so well that he was able to dismiss his teachers. One is reminded of the Quaker firebrand James Nayler, who, when converted with "many more" by George Fox, was a member of the Congregational church at Woodkirk, located in the heartland of the Wigglesworths and the Reyners and ministered to by a returned New Englander.[3] There was, indeed, some hint of more radical doctrines among the Charlestown Baptists whose part John Trumbull was taking. Thomas Osborne objected to "our allowing none but such as had *humane learning* to be in the ministry"; his wife, Sarah, had boldly defended the heterodox minister of Malden, was said to have denied that New England's congregations were true churches, and, most recently, was charged with having been "leavened with principles of *Anabaptisme,* and *Quakerisme.*"[4] Trumbull himself made his objections to the New England Way on much less extreme grounds, though events proved that his form of criticism was not the less explosive for his narrow concentration on a single key issue. He was not the apostate, he said, for "if that form of church order" that he had joined when he first came to America "had still been continued in: I had remained where I was for aught I know." He had been "as clear in my fancy for infant baptism as any other" for over twenty years, until the attempt to extend the ordinance to the children of individuals who were not in full communion had abruptly altered his own judgment and that, he made clear in no uncertain terms, of many others. "I told some of you," he said to Salem's minister John Higginson, a leading proponent of the Halfway Covenant, "that you were about at the synod to make an Anabaptiste."[5]

Trumbull gave vent in exaggerated form to a more pervasive lay sentiment. If the Halfway Synod of 1662 did not actually create many outright opponents of all infant baptisms, it did, for many of the laity, transform such

Baptists as there were from sectaries of a suspiciously foreign provenance professing a bottomless error into good Christians who had gone a little far down the right road at a time when so many of the clergy were trying to force the Puritan colonies down the wrong one. The whole episode nicely encapsulates most of the dominant themes of New England history in the second half of the seventeenth century: the ministry's attempt to reexpand the limits of the visible church to accommodate the second generation of American Puritans, the sectarian counterthrust carried by the Quakers and the Baptists, the related questions of toleration and clerical authority. Only one main strand of the ensuing controversies went unmentioned at the conference, the relationship of the colonies to Restoration England, but the participants are not likely to have forgotten about the matter: the first royal commissioners to visit New England had arrived only four years earlier, bringing demands for fundamental revisions in both the civil and ecclesiastical governments of the Puritan colonies, including the toleration of dissenters. Baptists, and to a degree Quakers, found themselves in the curious position of enjoying their greatest sympathy among the advocates of a hard-line policy against English encroachments, while the parties willing to seek an accommodation were also the vociferous advocates of wholesome severities against the dissenting groups that the royal government was attempting to protect. None of these three issues (church membership, toleration, English interference) was ever separable from the others, and their complex intertwining enormously complicated the reconstruction of the Puritan mission in America after 1650. The solutions reached at the end of the century commanded widespread allegiance among a fragmented public largely because the controversies of the period had first become thoroughly muddled together and had then, rather suddenly in the 1680s, reduced themselves to a single overriding imperative: the survival of the New England Israel in the face of the destruction of its political autonomy. Until this moment of enforced unity, the dominant note would be what contemporaries called "contention."

There remains one other item of some relevance to be noted before John Trumbull can be allowed to finish his work of delivering a prologue to the tangled narrative of the restructuring of New England ecclesiology. No one, not even Trumbull, mentioned the matter, and in this omission there lies hidden a cautionary tale for historians of the Puritan movement. By 1668 many churches and even some of the magistrates had lost interest in persecuting church members who scrupled over infant baptism and refused to present their newborn children for the sacrament. The debate at Charlestown, therefore, centered on the lawfulness of the protagonists withdrawing from the town's church over this issue and on their forming a new fellowship while still under the censure of excommunication. The charge, that is, read schism and not heresy.[6] Trumbull, however, could not be faulted on these grounds because he had not formally joined the Baptist communion—free spirit that he was, he never did—and, more significantly, because he could not be censured by the Charlestown church. He had moved to the port town from Cambridge years before to return to his old trade of the sea, he attended religious services there, paid his rate to support its minister, and all the while never sought dismission to its church.[7]

Trumbull was by no means unusual in retaining his old church membership long after he lived and worshiped somewhere else. Some New Englanders waited a period of years, often a long one, and then finally sought dismission, some were never dismissed at all, but many, possibly most of the New Englanders who moved during their adult years, were for long periods in communion with the "wrong" church. Almost any extant church record with a sufficiently long run will yield a few of the names of these individuals, who were by the standards of Congregational ecclesiology resident aliens, discernible only in the instances when they baptized their children by communion of churches or finally joined their local church at last by dismission from a fellowship left behind years before.[8] Boston, the town to which immigration from the surrounding area began earliest, had even by 1649 forty-six families who baptized their children at its church without choosing to transfer their membership, but this number is nothing like a measure of absenteeism: individuals who had no unbaptized children or who were married to a member of the Boston church would leave no trace in its records of their membership elsewhere.[9] If anything, the New England church records speak most pertinently to this question by their ominous silence. There are nowhere near enough instances of dismission to cover the very large number of New Englanders who moved at least once in their lifetimes.[10]

The absentees must have been impervious to church discipline. (Such few examples of censure by remote control as do exist indicate why these clumsy experiments were rarely attempted.)[11] Their invisible presence mocks our own attempts to establish the percentage of church members in any given town's population.[12] (So dubious an undertaking rests, anyway, on still more doubtful premises, not least the equation of commitment with membership.) Their preference for long-range fellowship rebukes our notion of what the primitives of the past should have wanted, putatively a "tightly knit" local community in which memberships in immediately tangible civil and sacred societies were as nearly congruent as possible. (Only toward the end of the seventeenth century would the churches begin to conceive of their mission as directed to their locality rather than to an original guild of saints, wherever its members had subsequently scattered.)[13] But their perverse indifference to the rules that seventeenth-century congregational theory and twentieth-century social science alike would impose on them is most significant as a reminder that the Puritan laity always retained at the last a measure of autonomy as to the terms on which to pursue their individual pilgrimages. When, from the middle of the seventeenth century onward, the New England clergy campaigned to make the church and its ordinances—baptism, the covenants, the Lord's Supper—the matrix of lay religious life, they were neither trying to recover lost ground nor retreating from the advanced positions of the 1630s to the safety of a more traditional brand of ecclesiology, though they sometimes claimed to be doing one or the other and we doltishly swallow these misrepresentations whole. Rather, the clergy hoped to achieve a situation that had never existed before, either in England or America. They proposed somehow to contain and direct the religious life of a collection of "spiritual vagabonds" (to vary John Robinson's description) through well-defined ecclesiastical and cultural institutions, mostly under their own control, and at the same time, without forfeiting the loyalty of the majority of the godly, to comprehend in these same constructions the American-bred believers, who grew up under radically different conditions than the John Trumbulls. Instead of counting every instance of lay resistance as proof of the declining power of the clergy, we should be marveling that, with much struggle, they eventually had a degree of success. John Trumbull, after all, was in 1668 what he had always been: a dedicated believer piecing together his spiritual experiences from disparate sources (tracts, sermons, other saints) according to a pattern he chose to evolve as he went along. At his death in 1687, aged eighty, he was still in Charlestown, up until the last moment a member (presumably in good standing) of the church of Christ gathered at Cambridge, absent but present for roughly forty years.[14]

This extraordinary challenge would be met in time by an appropriate response. As eras of conflict often are, the thirty-year period from the mid-1650s to the mid-1680s proved to be highly creative, though often in forms unintended by the creators. But before the imminence of English intervention brought an abrupt halt to decades of controversy, the ministry had despaired of the "Morellianism," "Separatism," and "Apostasy" of the laity, the laity had resisted clerically inspired initiatives as "Presbyterian," if not "Prelatical," and the magistrates had divided more or less evenly in the conflict according to their personal prejudices. The divisions in this most disunited period in the history of the Puritan movement in America turned on a single question, posed by the Bay Colony General Court for the synod of 1662 simply as "who are the subjects of baptisme?" But this question, of great emotional power in itself, attained its full divisive force because in the context in which it was asked it embodied in irreconcilable form the tensions between competing imperatives that had always defined the nature and course of the Puritan movement on both sides of the Atlantic. In America at midcentury the enduring Puritan dilemma had for the time being resolved itself into the problem of shaping a church and society capable of enlisting the formidable spiritual energies of the John Trumbulls yet also responsive to the quite different needs of their children.

Ideally, reformation and separation should have been compatible in New England. Freed of their English encumbrances, ministry and magistracy could provide the nurturing environment for the many that justified restricting church membership to the proven few. However fenced about the communion table might be, the due form of government, civil and ecclesiastical, would be able to train up new converts among the children of the first settlers in sufficient numbers to fulfill the promise of Genesis 17:7, wherein God establishes his covenant with Abraham "and thy seed after thee in their generations."

We have it on what seems the best of authority, the nearly unanimous testimony of contemporaries, that things did not work out that way. "We that have lived to bury the most of the good old generation of professors doe by experience see that our youth cannot fill the roums of their farthers, and yet are such as are to be incouraged and received in the Lord."[15] John Eliot's gentle comment of 1667 had a score of harsher echoes to the same effect, that the children of church members were morally delinquent and spiritually bankrupt, either indifferent to their baptismal vows or too enervated to act upon them. Ever the prisoners of the clergy, we have followed their original reports closely in our histories while slightly revising the nomenclature to suit our own tastes: worldliness and formalism we transliterate as secularism and individualism. Alternatively, the alleged inanition of the second generation in America can be seen as the product of a more rarefied sensibility, in effect, the Georgians succeeding Victorians and Edwardians. More sensitive than their parents to nuance and ambiguity in the pilgrim's progress, the children are held to have that much less capacity for acting decisively. Either way, the break between English migrant and American-born colonist is held to be as wide as the Atlantic.

There have been as yet no scales devised for calibrating either sincerity or sophistication so that historical inquiry, aside from merely echoing contemporary moral judgments, has to concentrate on the knowable "externals" of the second generation, even if some aspects of their particular plight can be reconstructed only in fragmentary form. And the first point to note about the young is who they were and how large a fraction of the New England population they were becoming. For some reason (and it was not an inevitable choice) the American Puritans held that spiritual and moral responsibility began at approximately age sixteen. Up to seven years (a more familiar figure) the child of a church member was an infant incapable of reason, from seven to sixteen a "youth" capable of progressively greater autonomy, but only at sixteen responsible enough to be held accountable for breaches of most of the capital laws and to undertake the most fundamental duties assigned to adults in colonial society: for women, to dispose of themselves in marriage, for men, to be obligated for military service, for both sexes, to be accounted independent members of the workforce. And so, apparently by analogy, at sixteen children of the church, hitherto members in right of their parents, could also be called upon to complete their proper adult roles by personally enrolling in the church's covenant.[16] Until 1642 or so, this odd choice for the beginning of adulthood would not have made much difference because the bulk of the adult population, however defined, had migrated to America in their mature years and their conversions were already complete or nearly so. These were the individuals for whom the tests for saving grace were part of the natural order. For them the relation of their individual adventures to their fellow saints became the most vital part of their religious life, "a means of engaging of our affections, mutually beholding Christ in such."[17] Recalling the early days of the Dorchester church, Captain Roger Clap dwelled on the didactic, self-renewing value of these ceremonies, as each of the new converts under examination taught those just behind them the final steps of the common journey:

> Many were Converted, and others established in Believing: many joined unto the several Churches where they lived, confessing their Faith publickly, and shewing before all the Assembly their Experiences of the Workings of God's Spirit in their Hearts, to bring them to *Christ*: which many Hearers found very much Good by, to help them to try their own Hearts and to consider how it was with them; whether any work of God's Spirit were wrought in their own Hearts or no? Oh the many Tears that have been shed in *Dorchester* Meeting-House at such times, both by those that have declared God's Work on their Souls, and also by those that heard them.[18]

After 1642 large-scale migration ceased, and the continued rapid growth in the New England population is generally attributed to natural increase. A high birth rate and a benign death rate resulted in an increase in the proportion of adults over fifty, but at the same time the New England population in aggregate actually grew younger—that is, the median age fell because of the radical growth in the younger and youngest age groups. At some point in the seventeenth century, probably not determinable with absolute precision, the age distribution reached the remarkable state that held up until the Revolution: the median age for the entire population stood at sixteen, perhaps as many as one-quarter of all those over sixteen were under twenty-one, and perhaps another quarter were between twenty-one and thirty. When John Eliot remarked that "the care and wise management of the lambs of the flock, is one third part of the charge of the ministry, and in some respects the difficultyst," he was speaking literally, if not underestimating.[19]

The so-called reforming legislation passed by the Bay Colony in 1675 and imitated by Connecticut in 1676 reveals a little too precisely for comfort, even now, the quality of life in a society with such a large contingent of late adolescents and young adults. Of the Bay Colony's thirteen statutes intended to remedy the "provoking evils" that had brought down upon the Puritan colonies the judgment of King Philip's War, four single out the young as the main delinquents and by implication they figure prominently in a fifth because, with slaves and servants, they are the "inferiours" given to "absenting themselves out of the families whereunto they belong in the night, and meeting with corrupt company without leave, and against the mind and to the great griefe of theire superiours." (This is the activity better known as "unseasonable night walking.") In addition, they wore their hair too long, and in the case of the young women let their locks fall in an immodest manner; they were the cause of "much disorder and rudenes" in the meetinghouse; and "oft times" they walked or rode about together "upon pretence of going to lecture, but it appears to be meerely to drincke and revell in ordinarys and tavernes." One suspects they were also the main target of the law against "bravery" in apparel, and they may possibly have been the object of the statutes against tavern haunting and idleness.[20] Magistrate no less than minister looked out on a sea of young faces, unconverted, uncontrolled, and adjudged unworthy of the foundations that had been laid by a godlier generation.

Pouring vituperation on the young was a favorite Puritan habit without much regard to time and circumstances, and a sinful youth was also a staple of the church confessions and spiritual autobiographies. The issue is not so much the extent of the degeneracy of the younger generation of New Englanders—they had their advocates, even in the Bay in the 1670s—as the fact of their presence en masse in a culture that had been shaped entirely to the demands of a mature, refugee population. Sixteen years of age represented nothing more than an approximation of the earliest point at which an individual could claim a conversion experience and not be immediately suspect.[21] Claims for conversion at a significantly younger age usually involved relations of deathbed acts of piety, where it was no longer possible to cross-examine the testimony. Even at sixteen, or twenty-one for that matter, admissions were unusual in most churches except in the case of an outright prodigy such as Cotton Mather, sixteen years, six months, and nineteen days old when he joined his father's North Church in 1679. Religious experience was ordinarily a long-drawn-out process culminating in a degree of assurance only when full psychological autonomy was attained in general. John Winthrop was thirty before he reached this stage, and the mean and median ages for joining a church in New England were usually in this range or higher, from roughly the mid-twenties to the mid-thirties, with the later ages predominant.[22] The first generation of New England ministers had prepared for themselves and their successors a situation in which a very large portion of their audience was nominally eligible but practically incapable of the most significant ordinance of their churches, the conversion narrative and the acceptance of the believer into the fellowship of the saints.

But the clergy had done worse than this. Their ladder to heaven was long, yet it lacked rungs. When the immigrant generation offered their confessions in rapid-fire succession in the first two decades of settlement, they were enacting the climax of a mostly English experience. They had been brought up in a plenitude of means celebrated by the sternnest of Puritan critics of contemporary English society, and their relations were accounts of miracles already wrought. These narratives inevitably set an impossibly high standard for those who were in the early stages of spiritual growth or who had yet to begin the process under, to put it mildly, much less favorable material circumstances. Roger Clap as much as admitted that these performances intimidated him and entreated the younger generation not to be as easily browbeaten. John Warham, the original minister of the Dorchester congregation, subsequently complained that "som christians," failing to realize that "the rule of membership is san[c]tity, not eminency," refused to join the churches "for want of evidans when others may see that in them that themselves cannot, but thinkes by false rulles thay have no right [to]."[23]

By midcentury there were no other "rules" in New England beyond the duplication of these much-advertised experiences without most of the advantages that had produced them. Printed matter was in short supply, sermon gadding was hindered by poor transportation, private meetings were an extramural privilege of the saints, and the numbers of conversion narratives had diminished sharply after the bulk of those eligible to give them were taken up into the church in the rush of the early decades of settlement.[24] Communion services could hardly have been much of an inducement to stir up nonmembers because they were rarely held, as infrequently as five times a year, and, in the case of a church lacking an ordained minister, not for years at a time. When they did take place, the visible saints demonstrated that they had been more interested in keeping the sacrament undefiled than in risking it themselves—"the people do Throng so fast out of Doors before a sacrament," Cotton Mather admitted.[25] Pure discipline, much vaunted, also did the young little good because no one was sure it applied to children of the church once they reached the age of sixteen, and so, like the baptism of their children once they married and began a family, it was left in abeyance. Urian Oakes had been back in New England less than two years when in 1673 he repeated a variation on a currently popular adage that Puritan children were treated like young hogs sent out to fend for themselves as soon as they were weaned: "We own them so far as to baptize them: But then Fare ye well Children, we have nothing more to do with you."[26]

Contemporaries understood the problem, after their fashion. Despite our own fascination with their lists of sins of commission, they spent most of their time excoriating failures of will and purpose. Family duties, they claimed, were neglected or performed perfunctorily, sermons were taken in without preparation or meditation, above all an enveloping spiritual malaise prevented the sparks of the gospel from taking fire. "Doth not a careless, remiss, flat, dry, cold, dead frame of spirit, grow in upon us secretly, strongly, prodigiously?"[27] Eliminate the hyperbole and professional censoriousness in which these lamentations are drenched, and a valid observation can be found in the residue. By the standards that had first propelled Winthrop and his company out of England and across the Atlantic, the spiritual life of New England after 1650 was becoming undernourished, underorganized, and whether the professed object was lamb, sheep, or goat, misoriented. Part of the problem was the scarcity of means, the lack of so many of the ways (apart from the sermon) by which English Puritans had gained imaginative possession of doctrinal abstractions; the rest of it derived from the radical readjustment of American Puritanism in the 1630s and 1640s, which had been essential to its survival at the time but had become increasingly inappropriate. Since no one was willing to say as much, the matter had to be talked out in terms of a massive, inexplicable declension that rested on an intangible change in mood from vitality to sloth, and the burden of this betrayal was then assigned to "the rising generation," thereby converted from victims into criminals.

On the whole, the New England leadership possessed the intelligence and, by the last third of the century, a little of the resources to do something more than moan. In 1669, when they were bitterly divided on most other issues, the Massachusetts magistrates found the unity to issue a proclamation, self-consciously lifted from the Savoy Platform of the English Independents, that pointedly reminded the clergy of its pastoral and didactic obligations to nonmembers. (John Eliot promptly commented on their recommendation, "we have allmost lost our rising generation for want of it.")[28] Connecticut made some gestures in the same direction in 1676 and more forcefully in 1680, as well as in the latter instance proposing a weekly Wednesday combination lectureship in each of its counties.[29] By falling back on English devices both colonies were acknowledging for the first time on American soil the fundamental Puritan axiom that separation did not automatically beget reformation and that, consequently, links would have to be established between the pure churches and the larger society if weak Christians were ever to find the means to grow strong. To admit, by the most implicit of implications, that there *were* weak Christians out there, and not just so many reprobates without the courage of their lack of convictions, was something of a triumph under the circumstances: when Samuel Willard came to say in 1680 that "it is not in the nature of fallen man, spontaneously to own and acknowledge God," he was merely repeating a proposition his Elizabethan forebears would have found self-evident, but in the New England of his day the commonplace had been rediscovered through a long and painful process.[30]

Unfortunately, weak Christians came in two different forms. There were the indisputable nonmembers (a minority in most towns) and the disputable kind that Willard was talking about—individuals sixteen or older who had been baptized because of their parents' church membership but who had not themselves qualified for admission to communion. It was easy to be charitable in a general way to the former group, who could not be accused of treating with contempt the baptismal obligations that had never been bestowed on them, but children of the church over sixteen were potential storm centers every time they misbehaved or had a child of their own. As adults, their membership had to be personal and not in right of their parents, but they had not proven themselves to be the "matter" of a true church in the manner of adults by presenting acceptable accounts of the workings of saving grace. Yet if they were not subject to discipline and could not request baptism for their children, it was hard to see how they remained church members in any meaningful sense, even though few New Englanders were willing to claim that their original membership could be abrogated without an overt cause.

Attempts to resolve this recurring predicament went back as far as the Cambridge Platform of 1648 and for a few churches earlier still. Pretty much the same solution in outline was put forward on each of these occasions, and each time it aroused enough hostility to make further agitation of the point imprudent. Unless they demonstrated their own sanctity in the usual manner, the adult children of church members were rarely subject to discipline and were almost never granted baptism for their own offspring, but no church officially voided their membership. This ballet of inconclusive alarums and excursions had been repeated in enough individual churches to make the risks involved unavoidably obvious when in 1656 both Connecticut and the Bay chose to seek a collective and final decision on church membership—at a cost they must have known would be considerable.

Strictly speaking, three decades of bitter divisions originated in a vague resolution of the session of the Connecticut General Court convened on 15 May 1656. That body, in a paroxysm of discretion, appointed the colony's governor and three other magistrates a committee to confer with the clergy "about those things that are presented to this Courte as grevances to severall persons amongst us." The four men also had the power to draw up with the clergy "an abstract from the heads of those things, to be presented to the General Courtes of the several united Collonyes," and this authorization they quickly employed, passing on to the other colonial legislatures twenty-one queries in all, a number that may represent an attempt to dilute the controversy by fragmenting it. New Haven's General Court, typically with undisguised indignation, rejected the very idea that there was anything to discuss about the status of children of the church who did not proceed to the sacrament once they came of age. New Plymouth, no less typically, found itself incapable of doing anything. But the largest and most powerful colony, Massachusetts, judged the moment appropriate to become the dog wagged by Connecticut's tail: the General Court responded favorably in October 1656 with a call for an intercolonial assembly of the clergy to meet in Boston in the following June and there determine the matter once and for all. At the appointed time, four Connecticut ministers joined more than three times that number from the Bay to formulate the details of what became known as the Halfway Covenant.[31]

The assembly of 1657 was about as definitive as anyone in New England could have hoped or feared. It answered the twenty-one queries at length, holding that children of church members originally joined in the church covenant by means of their parents' engagement but were nonetheless members of the church *in their own right*. Thus their turning sixteen in no way changed their situation. They remained subject to church discipline as before, and when they had children of their own they had the right and duty to have them baptized, provided they then personally "owned" the church covenant by publicly reaffirming as morally responsible adults the document's continued binding power. They could not, however, take the Lord's Supper or vote in church affairs until they satisfied the certifiably visible saints that they were of their number by a confession that according to the judgment of rational charity could be considered a valid account of the work of saving grace. This specification of partial privileges earned the formula the nickname of a Halfway Covenant, but its proponents insisted that the children's church *membership* was as full and entire as their parents', however incomplete their degree of *communion*.[32]

Over the next four years attempts to implement the assembly's proposals came up against familiar lay intransigence, but this time the Bay Colony decided to see the matter through and in December 1661 called for a full-fledged synod, an authoritative body of lay and clerical delegates representing all the orthodox churches of New England. (In the end, however, Connecticut backed away from what it had begun in 1656, or had been precipitated into beginning by Massachusetts, and all the representatives came from the latter colony.)[33] Credit for the Halfway Covenant usually goes to the synod of 1662, not the assembly of 1657, because of its larger size and the more formal and theoretical character of its resolutions. But for all its greater prestige, the synod merely formulated an apology in defense of the institutional arrangements spelled out five years earlier. The call for an assembly in 1656 properly represents the moment at which those in authority, lay and clerical, summoned up the resolution to address in a concerted way the case of the children of the founding generation.

A small point, perhaps, yet it is significant on several grounds. So early an origin to a dispute still potent at the end of the century indicates the extent to which the long-term reconstruction of the New England churches was a continuation of the original Puritan quest rather than a New World innovation: all of the seventeen clergymen at the assembly were English-born; all but two were English-educated and had come to America as adults. Although many of them died within a single decade of their work and most were gone within two, the conflict they engendered went on at full tilt among their successors for close to thirty years. The authorship of the controversial measure and the subsequent longevity of the controversy suggest that a better and more complex explanation is needed for the history of the Halfway Covenant than the mere repetition of a partisan argument of the period: that the proposed reform represented a decline from the "first principles of New England" that gained ground slowly as the advocates of those principles died off and were replaced by a more tame generation, neither purely English nor purely American and therefore more willing to rest content with cultural hybrids than either their full-blooded predecessors or successors. New England was not old enough in the mid-1650s to have "first" principles, except those of the Puritan movement generally from its inception in the 1570s. Within the range of the possibles thus delineated, the Halfway Covenant was an acceptable and rather cautious step devised by the very same people who had led in the formulation of the New England Way in the first two decades of colonial settlement. Their proposals did not go so far as to return the standards of church membership to where they had been in the early 1630s and, on any meaningful scale of comparison, lacked the boldness of the experiments in baptismal and eucharistic theology that were to be advocated by the Stoddardeans or the Mathers in the last two decades of the seventeenth century.

Taken by itself, the Halfway Covenant was a modest, incomplete, and essentially conservative measure and was ultimately recognized as such in Connecticut, where the ensuing conflict was more overt and less entangled with other issues than in the Bay: after a series of church schisms over the issue all of the Congregationalists of the colony, quickly enough on the whole, rallied around this form of extended church membership as the best means to preserve traditional New England polity from one version or another of Presbyterian innovations.[34] Some amount of heartburning and breast-beating was de rigueur in New England, which never once witnessed an uncontested synod. So extraordinary a contest over so limited and necessary an adjustment points to a more interesting situation than the usual, and the key to these divisions is to be found in the timing. The controversy began in the immediate shadow of the Interregnum and took most of its points of reference ("Morellian," "Separatist," "Presbyterian," "Prelatical") from the internecine conflicts that were then destroying the Puritan movement in England. The parallel contest raged on for so much longer in America (or rather in Massachusetts Bay) because the imposition of royal power that brought a forlorn unity to the English disputants after 1660 was delayed some twenty-six years on the other side of the Atlantic. As much or more than ever, in the second half of the seventeenth century the most decisive force in the course of the history of the colonies was the mother country.

An assertion of the centrality of England to the development of Puritan America would hardly have come as much of a surprise to New Englanders of the 1650s, on the face of it one of the least promising decades of the century because of the almost gravitational force of events taking shape back home. Younger talent in the colonies acknowledged the obvious, that the main event was being played out elsewhere, and retraversed the Atlantic as quickly as opportunities allowed.[35] Those left behind rendered a different tribute to the inescapable English presence by their frantic efforts to seal the colonies off from the contagion of Interregnum sectarianism. As early as 1652 the magistrates of the Bay Colony, the entrepôt for things English destined for America, were complaining of the spread of "erroneous books brought over into these parts," and in the same and the following year when the new North Church in Boston, unable to retain a young minister from the English bound herd, gave a call to a candidate without a university education, the General Court forbade him to accept, "considering the humour of the times in England, inclining to discourage learning." In 1653 the Court attempted to add lay preaching as well to the prohibited list by proposing (unsuccessfully) to restrict this well-established activity through a rigorous licensing system, and in 1654 it charged the overseers of Harvard College and the selectmen of the towns to be especially careful about the lives and opinions of those responsible for the instruction of the young.[36]

Up until the crucial year of 1656 the Bay Colony was mostly flailing away at English shadows, while the other Puritan colonies mimed this same contest with the winds by passing slightly less severe versions of the Massachusetts heresy laws. There was certainly a startling variety of "opinionists" in New England in the 1650s—there had always been colorful and vociferous dissenters from the earliest days of settlement, whether home-grown or receiving their inspiration from contacts with their English counterparts. Few, however, had ever lasted for long outside Rhode Island and the sections of New Plymouth too remote for that colony's feeble government to take effective action against them. Then, in May 1656, as Connecticut was appointing its committee to deal with the carefully unspecified "grevances," the Bay called a fast "in behalf of our native countrie, in referenc to the abounding of errors, especially those of the Raunters and Quakers." In July, about the time the twenty-one queries would have arrived in Boston, the first of the wave of Quaker missionaries also came to town, and in October, as Massachusetts responded enthusiastically to Connecticut by calling for the ministerial convention, the General Courts of both colonies were passing the first of their series of anti-Quaker statutes. (Connecticut's law threw in "Ranters, Adamites, or such like notorious heretiques," suggesting a somewhat more abstract concept of the enemy than was the case in the Bay.)[37] These measures had little effect, and more ferocious ones that followed only served as an invitation for Friends based in England or Rhode Island to come to the orthodox colonies to bear their witness against the antichristian pharisaism there maintained by law. Alone among the dissenters who had challenged the Puritan colonies, the Quakers would not rest content with a testimony of their faith, followed by a fine, imprisonment, or a whipping and then deportation. No matter how severe the punishment, extending to the death penalty in four instances over the next five years, new missionaries kept coming, until the authorities' will to use the gallows and the cart's-tail collapsed under the twin pressure of widespread public repugnance against brutality and the obvious futility of these bloody exercises.[38] Nor were the Quakers, missionary or proselyte, content to withdraw and worship their particular truths in private, if not in secret. They could never be conveniently overlooked and officially forgotten because they attacked both the Puritan churches and the civil authorities openly and theatrically, marching through the town of Boston on one occasion, "crying, 'Repent, etc.,'" running naked in the streets of Salem on another, and in a third instance disrupting the services in the Old South Church so effectively that Samuel Sewall described the event as "the greatest and most amazing uproar that I ever saw."[39] For the first time since 1638 the leadership of the Puritan colonies was neither locked in combat with some unnameable inner corruption nor sparring with opinions rarely broached within their borders, even by implication. There was someone very tangible and very radical to be afraid of.

In the event, the Quakers made their converts in New England mainly in the familiar places on the geographical periphery of orthodoxy, where the mechanisms for inculcating the Puritan message were absent or unusually impaired: in Rhode Island, in Kittery in Maine, on Long Island, far out on Cape Cod in Plymouth Colony, and in pockets of endlessly festering, ever-combustible Salem. But this mediocre showing was in no way foreseeable at the time, either in terms of contemporary English experience or of the opportunities apparently available for proselytizing in America. In their early days the Quakers did away at one stroke with the elaborately achieved compromises and awkwardly balanced tensions that made up the stuff of Puritan religious life, eliminating all those nagging, disputed conflicts over baptism, the sacrament, the authority of the ministry, and the rights of the laity as so many dead questions about extinct institutions. Radical ecclesiology was joined to an equally bold political critique of entrenched privilege in church, state, and society (at a time when other protest movements had failed or gone stale) and worked up into an appeal that was so evidently honest and vital that the Quakers became a mass movement in England in the same few years when they made only limited headway in New England.[40] The remarkable disparity is worth some comment.

It would be tempting to attribute the relative failure of the New England Quakers to a colonial society already so responsive and equitable that their message simply found no response among a mostly contented people. There were, however, exploited and mistreated people in New England too, perhaps not in such numbers as in England but there all the same, and the English Quakers had also shown that they were capable of articulating the grievances and frustrations of numerous individuals higher up the social scale.[41] Clerical pretension in particular, no matter how much it was justified in New England by educational attainments and a congregational call, was liable to be resented simply because it was there. John Farnum, an original pillar of the Boston North Church, in the course of bolting his old society for the all-lay company of the Charlestown Baptists, paused long enough to declare "that there was never an elder in the country that would have any one reed the Scriptures beside themselves," demanded the reinstitution of lay prophesying, and finished up by telling his poor pastor to his face, "don't use the name of Christ to me; I am not one that can stoop and bow to every one." The only person in Boston to say as much in the year 1666, Farnum can hardly have been the only individual in Massachusetts to think that the ministry was just another clever interest group, as the explosion of anticlerical sentiment in the General Court just three years later was to demonstrate in detail. Farnum himself looks as if he ought to have ended up with the Quakers, and in his case, after a very tortuous journey, he did, announcing in 1709 "that he did consider them to be the only people of god now in the world."[42]

The New England ministry was equally vulnerable in the traditionally delicate area of maintenance. Tithes had provided the English Quakers with one of their best talking points: a parish where the inhabitants had made trouble over tithes in the 1640s was likely to see Friends in the 1650s rejecting all hireling priests. Archaic and irrational, tithes had little to do with the services rendered (if any) in return, and they were difficult to collect as well, thereby making ministers and lay impropriators visibly obnoxious when they sought to obtain their legal due.[43] By contrast, New Englanders at least had a sense that they were paying a man of proven qualifications in exchange for a bona fide exercise of his professed specialization. By English standards the arrangement was manifestly fair, but by English or American standards it was no less manifestly expensive. As clerical incomes in that era went, the New England ministry's stipends were very respectable indeed, ranging on average from sixty to ninety pounds per annum, in addition to (in most instances) the provision of a house and substantial amounts of land. This level of maintenance would have put its recipient well up in the hierarchy of clerical incomes in England and did make him stand out in his particular locale in America.[44] On the valuation list of 1657 John Allen was the second wealthiest man in Dedham, one of only six individuals worth over two hundred pounds, and he owned the largest house in town. Richard Mather of Dorchester in the same year enjoyed one hundred pounds for his services, and his son Eleazer brought in another ten pounds to the household for occasionally supplying his father's place; together they cost more than every other public charge in Dorchester combined.[45]

From time to time in the history of Christianity the laity and the occasional renegade clergyman develop a certain zeal for improving the work of the ministry by reducing its members to apostolic poverty. The successors of the apostles in seventeenth-century New England had little use for this recurrent enthusiasm. A town that could not pledge at least sixty pounds per annum or make up the deficiency with large grants of land went without a permanent minister, as did the tiny Massachusetts town of Hull, too small to come up with more than forty pounds from its foundation until 1670, when it settled its pulpit for the next half-century on the singularly unambitious Zechariah Whitman, straight out of Harvard and fortunately possessed of private means.[46] Puritan New England boasted no real-life equivalent of Trollope's Mr. Crawley, saving souls and teaching school while enduring the desperately shabby gentility of a perpetual curacy at Hogglestock, Barsetshire. Josiah Crawley is a fictional creation, not to mention a madman and a saint. Visible (and sane) saints in New England with a university degree and gentlemanly aspirations did otherwise under the same circumstances: they abandoned either America or their clerical vocation.

This contradiction, if it is such, is inherent in the very basis of a profession at once a sacred calling and a way of earning a living. But the New

England clergy caught in these crosswinds found their particular situations especially complicated by Congregational theory and the economic realities of colonial New England. Despite their embarrassing prominence on the tax lists and the records of town rates, they had by their own pronouncements and symbols reduced the distance between clerical and lay saint, and they had always stressed the voluntary and loving bond between shepherd and flock that alone would make the relationship viable. And yet they had to press their demands for maintenance, legally guaranteed only in the most general terms, year after year on towns where the nonmembers always had every reason to wonder if they were getting value for money and the whole congregation sooner or later found it inconvenient in some years to pay up the full amounts agreed upon at first settlement.[47] No minister in New England was foolish enough to sue for his arrears in the seventeenth century, as English incumbents were in the habit of doing without any thought of the cost to their vocations. But the clergy did complain publicly about their salaries often enough to provide a very real opening for the Quakers and for other sectarian groups with parallel solutions to the contradictions of establishment. Completely voluntary maintenance, much touted by the Baptists and the actual practice of all of the Boston churches, made matters worse: the minister who had to go begging from month to month was more visible in his importunities than his colleagues on a fixed stipend, and rumor always had it that he was not so poor as he let on. "It has been thot," grumped Increase Mather in his last will and testament, "that I have Bags by me, which is a great Mistake: I have not Twenty Pounds in Silver or in Bills."[48]

All this may seem a petty business compared to rival eschatologies, but it was in part on this mundane stuff that the mass support of the English Quakers was built. The same resentment was there in New England, and in such a superheated religious environment the American Quakers should have been able to organize both the John Farnums and the disgruntled nonmembers into a common fellowship that repudiated all distinctions of persons beyond the willingness to heed the inner light. They did not do so in large part because in good Christian fashion the Puritan establishment in New England blunted the Quaker thrust through its own failings and weaknesses. That mass of the spiritually indecisive who were the despair of the ministry were so much damp powder when exposed to the Quaker spark. People who lacked the courage to claim a conversion experience or take the sacrament when they were entitled to it were not very likely to find themselves suddenly in possession of an inner light. "Contention," on the other hand, was useful in reining in the spiritually advanced: when the quarreling was built around the questions of who should be baptized and where in the church the power of the keys was located, the issues in contest were strictly delimited. Anyone who had become passionately engaged within these limits for any length of time, no matter how much he might resent the claims of the clergy, was naturally going to find a faith that abolished baptism, governance, and the church itself strikingly irrelevant. The elaborate hierarchy of "meetings" that the Quakers evolved after the Restoration must have seemed appalling to New Englanders, who were agitated over the actions of occasional councils and synods. One can hardly see, for example, a partisan of First Church, Boston, in 1669, angry over what he took to be the "presbyterian" tyranny of the clergy in interfering with his congregation's dealings with its dissenting faction, fleeing for solace to a group that assigned the last word in disciplinary cases to the yearly meeting in London. Quaker apologists enjoyed repeating the litany of New England self-reproach to prove the inadequacy of the Puritan churches; their own missionary efforts, it turned out, foundered on precisely the same reefs of "worldliness," "formalism," and "spiritual pride."

Irony was not ordinarily a strong suit among the ministers of New England. In the late 1650s and early 1660s they perceived mainly the obvious weaknesses of their position—the potential for anticlerical sentiment, the volatility of the practiced saints, the apparent imperviousness of the young to their ministrations, the broad agenda available for possible confrontations. The Quakers, a unique and remarkable phenomenon, became for them only the latest and most extravagant instance of the endemic lay insurgence that had corroded the unity and energy of their English contemporaries and was likely to do the same in America. Certainly the signs of the schisms to come seemed to be all around them. When Connecticut made its appeal to Massachusetts in 1656, the oldest church in the colony, Hartford, was tearing itself asunder with the greatest possible publicity in a dispute over the claims to all but absolute authority advanced by its pastor Samuel Stone. The controversy presently spread to Wethersfield, splitting the church there along similar lines, and for good measure drew in the Massachusetts ministry, who sent a delegation to mediate the Hartford dispute in April 1657, just months before the meeting of the assembly at Boston to promulgate the Halfway Covenant.[49] The more jaundiced or timorous clergy saw every issue regardless of substance as grounded on a single crux: the intention of the visible saints to strip the minister of the powers of his office, dilute the distinctiveness of his vocation, and restrict his evangelical obligations so they could claim the exclusive right to his services and reduce him to the executor of their decisions. The Quakers seemed merely to be taking this species of lay hubris to its logical conclusion by dividing the clerical calling equally among each of the brethren. John Norton, the only minister bold enough to take on the Massachusetts General Court's commission to defend the execution of two Quaker missionaries in 1659 in the face of widespread opposition, made the damaging admission that this latest embodiment of ancient errors would likely find adherents among attested professors and not just the "hungry and irregenerate multitude." The unconvincing apology that followed read more like a threnody, concluding on its very last page with foreboding vision that the "*light upon an Hill*" that was New England "should at last go out in the *snuff of Morrellianism*."[50]

The eponymous term that takes its original from Jean Morély, a French critic of Calvin's ecclesiology, refers by itself to nothing more than the proposition that each individual church should be run democratically.[51] Norton employed it for the Quakers, rather than the more obvious *Familism* or *Antinomianism*, because he was more frightened of the self-intoxicated few than the slothful and licentious many traditionally held to be ready converts to any easy way to heaven. *Separatism* became another synonym for incipient Quakerism for much the same reason.[52] Separatists did practice a more or less Morellian polity in their congregations, and they were held to be so puffed up with pride over their own spiritual attainments that they schismatically withdrew from any churches less than perfect and rent even their own fellowships at the least hint of impurity. The model for the future gone wrong, a New England of Quakers and neo-Quakers, was not really Münster or even Rome but Hartford and Wethersfield on the grand scale. Thus Norton and his fellow pessimist John Higginson of Salem chose the early 1660s to revive the anti-Separatist casuistry of the 1620s on the curious grounds that it spoke directly to New England's current peril. "In matters of Religion," pronounced Norton, "let it be known that we are for Reformation, and not for Separation," and Higginson revealed that in coming to New England "we made no separation, but a locall secession only into this wilderness."[53]

These charitable judgments on the English mother church come from the election sermons of 1661 and 1663 respectively. An act of Parliament in 1660 had ejected more than seven hundred Puritan ministers from their livings; the more notorious Uniformity Acts of 1662 had finished the job, bringing that number close to two thousand. The ejected clergymen, for the first time under such circumstances, took a portion of their congregations with them and set up new churches of their own, ending the historical commitment of the Puritan movement in England to the cause of establishment. As Richard Baxter told John Eliot in 1668, regardless of their formal predilections on polity, the Dissenting churches were perforce "ordered just like the Congregationall way, or rather as the old Separatists, in many places."[54] Norton and Higginson were driven to their perverse ecumenicism because, between the Interregnum and Connecticut, they preferred a kinship with the Church of England, even in its Restoration form, to admitting the least affinity with the dark forces of Morellianism under however plausible a guise. Norton's election sermon in particular contains what must surely be the single most authoritarian assertion of that literature of paeans to authority. Having denounced the reigning passion for "liberty" and exalted the binding power of councils (meaning the ministerial assembly of 1657), he concluded: "Israel must stand to this; if it be in matters Religion, there is the Priest; if in matters Civil, there is the Magistrate, and he that stands not, or submits not to the Sentence of these, *let him be cut off from Israel*; so requisite a thing is Order.[55]

When Norton died suddenly in 1663, it was said his heart had been broken by the abuse heaped upon him as an alleged lackey of the Restoration government. Higginson lasted a good deal longer, but twice, in 1672 and again in 1680, he almost lost a sizable part of his congregation, and his appeals to fellow ministers and to the Massachusetts General Court failed to produce the support he expected.[56] As their unhappy fates suggest, neither man was especially typical of an increasingly divided Puritan leadership. Their very ingenuousness in confessing their fears singled them out for criticism, but their extremism has the virtue of revealing explicitly some of the concerns prodding better-balanced individuals to support the causes of which they were the too frank heralds. The Halfway Covenant was an intelligent response along traditional Puritan lines to a real and growing evangelical problem. The decision to have it out on an issue long known to be controversial, to press ahead with it in 1662 in the teeth of the predictable opposition that had been encountered since 1657, is another matter, attributable in part to the horrific possibility that without such gestures to the rising generation New England was doomed to Separatism, Morellianism, and finally sheer chaos. Baptism for the grandchildren of the saints was (for the time being) a less immediate problem because in 1657 or 1662 large numbers of the children of the founding generation were still too young to be parents themselves. Migrants who came with their parents as adolescents were old enough to be caught up in the whirlwind of church foundings and to have become full members themselves in the 1640s or early 1650s. Individuals who were very young at migration or who were born in America in the earlier part of the 1630s were less fortunate, and they can be found in some instances in the later 1660s at such places as Roxbury and Charlestown employing the Halfway Covenant to baptize their own young children. But when Norton's First Church voted in 1657 to recognize baptized adults over sixteen within the church's watch, the first person to be disciplined was an errant unmarried twenty-one-year-old. In January 1661, when Norton induced the church to require the adult children to own the covenant, "which had been this long, for the most part neglected," the subjects of the ceremony were "youth, maids, men, and women (though not many was grown up to married estate)." The case of Chelmsford was much the same: in 1657 seventeen-year-old Nathaniel Shipley became the first child of the church to be disciplined under the new arrangements, and in 1658 sixteen-year-old Moses Fiske, the son of the pastor, became the first person to own the covenant as a way of affirming his personal membership and his acknowledgment of the church's watch over him before he set off for Harvard.[57] Through these two measures, the extension of discipline and the ceremony of owning the covenant, a large segment of the population, previously left in some undefined limbo, became acknowledged church members once again, the brand of orthodoxy placed on them before they were stolen away by some opinionist or another.

Discipline was probably no more effective in redeeming adolescents and young adults than it was with more mature delinquents. What mattered was the visible act of inclusion of the young offenders in the church's ongoing struggle and the vicarious participation of the mass of individuals of the same age in the drama of their censure and reformation. If anything, the 1657 rules on halfway membership actually aggravated the problems of disciplining nonresidents by creating an additional class of individuals, children over sixteen who moved with their parents but who remained absentee members of their original churches unless they requested dismission. "The father is in Covenant with one Church, the mother with another, the child was Baptized in a third and lives in a fourth," Solomon Stoddard complained in 1700, after four decades of confusion had done their work.[58] But amid the crossed wires of interchurch communications so deliberately created, adult children would remain members of *some* church somewhere, even (as might well be the case) if their parents' new homes were holdouts against the Halfway Covenant. Owning the covenant served a similar purpose because it allowed individuals too timorous to join the saints by claiming a conversion experience to have their moment to pledge allegiance, either when they presented their children for baptism or in the mass ownings on ceremonial occasions originated by Boston and imitated at a later date elsewhere. No children of church members in New England were going to be allowed to slide into spiritual neutrality or drift casually toward heterodoxy. They would at least first have to think of the prior commitments that they had made as knowing adults and that they would be explicitly repudiating.

As the Halfway Covenant threw up a wall around the lambs of the church, it also served as a pointed rebuke to the incipient Morellianism of the full-fledged sheep. In a single stroke the minister was definitively freed from any obligation to be the creature of the members in full communion, reduced by definition to just one of his several constituencies, and the collective nature of the New England Way was reaffirmed by two formidable exercises in conciliar power. Once they found the resolve to start this long-delayed process going, the clergy decided they might as well make the most of their newfound boldness and insist to the Massachusetts General Court that the agenda of the synod of 1662 include an endorsement of the "conscociation of churches." The opposition minority in the midst of this anti-Separatist binge was dismissed as "Adhaerents to Brownisticall notions, and what not," and John Norton (or perhaps one of his patrons) noted with satisfaction that though the "primitive arrangements" of the Puritan churches in America could be criticized "as too much favouring the way of the Separation," "an Expedient" had now been "found out for the holding communion with other Orthodox churches."[59] New England was declared in solemn council, after much debate and prayerful deliberation, to be the best of what there was, not a new heaven and a new earth, and thus spared all the liabilities recent English experience had shown to be entailed in the more singular designation.

So many different tensions were already bound up in the promulgation of the Halfway Covenant that the ensuing controversy found almost at once elective affinities with almost every other question agitating the Puritan colonies. Unremarkably, enthusiasts for extending church membership usually favored severity in dealing with the Quakers and refused to believe that the relatively small differences between orthodoxy and the Baptists justified their toleration. The younger Thomas Shepard discoursing "of Reformation, especially the disorderly Meetings of Quakers and Anabaptists: thought if all did agree, i.e. Magistrates and Ministers, the former might easily be suprest, and that then, The Magistrates would see reason to Handle the latter." In virtually the next breath he then expressed his wish "that all the children in the country were baptised, that religion without it [would] come to nothing."

Imprisoning Baptists and whipping Quakers were just part of what he else-where called "an *holy*, and *brotherly* Reformation," to which a comprehensionist polity was a necessary and loving corollary.[60]

Whips hurt, and seventeenth-century jails were not very comfortable either. (On occasion, short stays amounted to sentences for life.) Nonetheless, the call for persecution came to mean more to the persecutors than to the victims, who as time passed were mercifully spared the full share of abuse they were initially forced to endure. The absolute limit on persecution had been established by the early Quaker missionaries. After their sufferings and martyrdom there was too much public opposition, and eventually too much danger of provoking the English government, for anyone of any opinion to stand in danger of more than intermittent harassment—provided they manifested just enough courage to imply that they would if necessary suffer the same unacceptable degree of brutality in order to maintain their opinions. In effect, the Quakers endured and died to make New England safe for the Baptists. William Hubbard, who favored toleration on principle, dourly remarked in his history of New England that it already existed for the Baptists in practice because they "would not forbear, unless the laws had been sharpened to a greater degree of severity than the authority of the place were willing to execute on that account."[61]

By the time Hubbard wrote, sometime in the early 1680s, Baptists and even Quakers enjoyed more security in Boston than they did in Bristol or London. One may therefore wonder what Increase Mather was doing in 1682 still exhorting the magistrates to persecution in the same terms he had used for a decade, when his own North Church was shortly to delay restoring to communion none other than a penitent John Farnum until first inquiring of the Baptists with whom he had sojourned for some seventeen years, "whether they had any matter of scandal to object against" him.[62] Mather's failure to record this transaction in the church records may indicate his sense of unease at the way the Baptist fellowship had become de facto another Boston church, but he continued to demand that the magistrate use his sword when it was manifestly irrelevant to the case in point because his call retained its power to evoke a vision of an American Israel in which society and congregations were one long after everyone, including Mather, knew it would be necessary to write in exceptions now and again. It was not so much that there should be no Baptists—though Mather would have preferred that there not be too many—as that the Baptists represented to him and to those of like mind the same threat their English forebears had seen in the Separatists. The Baptists were what the churches of New England might become if the competing energies within the Puritan movement were not kept in tandem: impermeable, self-regarding bands of the spiritually elect who employed a minister as a town meeting did its clerk.

The Halfway Covenant also seeped into politics in ways that were less clear-cut than in the divisions over toleration but more dangerous in the end. Confrontation with the Restoration government began at the very start of the 1660s, and in ensuing decades English pressure became more intense, the scope of royal demands ever more sweeping, until they ended in an attempt at the wholesale takeover of the New England colonies. Connecticut and New Plymouth quickly found themselves obliged to take a tractable line with England, though it never did them much good. Possessing greater resources, the Bay Colony had more capacity to resist and more to lose from English intervention. Its leadership promptly split over the question of English demands along lines that were more consistent than not with the existing divisions over the extension of baptism. In the 1660s, especially, clergy and lay leaders who had been frightened by the political and religious chaos of the English republic, like their "Presbyterian" counterparts at home, regarded the restored monarchy as, whatever its faults, a bulwark against anarchy and the more extreme forms of heterodoxy. "It is not a Gospel-spirit to be against Kings," said John Norton in 1661, and then moved on to his fulmination against "liberty." John Higginson in 1663 went further, and in between his endorsement of the Halfway Covenant and "frequent use of *Councils* amongst us," he pointedly reminded the General Court that it was "a subordinate Government." It would not do for such a body to take too unyielding a line with its English superior—"standing upon extream right, may prove extream wrong."[63]

At issue was whether to negotiate at all, and if so what was negotiable, two propositions that permitted a wide variety of answers. Individuals willing to do a little business on one occasion sometimes turned into irreconcilables at a later date when the full extent of royal demands became apparent. And there were some people who never fit the obvious categories at any time in their careers.[64] Generally speaking, advocates of an accommodationist policy in the Bay Colony pretty regularly stood behind the Halfway Covenant, but the converse does not always hold. In the most clearly defined test case, the secession of the dissident faction from Boston's First Church to found Old South in 1669 and institute the Halfway Covenant, all of the partisans of First Church in the magistracy were also reliable opponents of concessions to England. So, unfortunately, were three Old South sympathizers. One of them, Thomas Danforth, who would succeed to the leadership of the hard-line faction upon the death of John Leverett, roundly denounced the narrow conception of church membership as the root evil of the day, "a practical rendering [of] the church covenant to be an empty, useless and mere titular matter."[65] His position on the Halfway Covenant made as much sense for an advocate of resistance to England as the opposite and more common correlation: in the midst of the final conflict there was no sense in summarily tendering dishonorable discharges to the bulk of the new recruits.

Opponents of the Halfway Covenant tended toward a greater degree of predictability on concurrent issues because their position was mostly reactive, their implicit dissatisfaction with extended church membership hardening into organized hostility only after some of the advocates of baptismal reform spelled out its potential implications: clericalism, monarchism, a national church and a centralized hierarchy, and in general a whole congeries of Anglicized horrors that John Oxenbridge was to describe in 1671 as a campaign "to backslide and to fashion your selves to the flaunting mode of *England* in worship or walking."[66] Already in 1656 New Haven, in a response almost certainly written by John Davenport, dismissed the suggestion for reconsideration of baptismal practice as the work of sinister individuals scheming to "obteyne great alterations, both in civill goverment and in church discipline" by advancing the proposition that membership in an English parish would qualify an immigrant for full communion in New England "without holding forth any worke of faith, etc."[67] For Davenport, the Restoration in England meant the triumph of tyranny and imperialism no less than of prelacy. In the midst of his critique of the result of the synod of 1662 he took time off to relay to the regicide William Goffe, in hiding in nearby Milford, accounts he received from England of ejections under the Act of Uniformity, along with rumors of "Exceeding great Taxes layd upon the People," a report that all the municipal charters had been nullified and that the Commons was willing to give the king "power of ordering, and disposing, mens person[a]l estates," and finally the dire warning that "there was a Gen[era]ll Govern[ou]r and a Majo[u]r Gen[era]ll chosen for this Countrie to seize upon the Melitia for the King: and a Bishop and a Suffracan, for Ecclesiasticall Goverm[en]t." By 1665, after New Haven had been forced to merge with the less rigorously governed Connecticut, Davenport was in an ecstasy of despair. He wrote William Goodwin, protector of Goffe and Edward Whalley at Hadley, Massachusetts, and, earlier, an opponent of Samuel Stone at Hartford, that God was bringing about "even the greatest changes that have beene since the 1st coming of Christ. The witnesses that are now killed," that is, the executed regicides, "shall arise shortly. Rome shall be ere long ruined." So would England, already punished by the plague and the reverses of the Dutch war, and "New England allsoe hath cause to tremble, whose day is coming, if speedy repentance, and reformation prevent not, for our backesliding, and changing our waies, from the ancient pathes to comply with Old England, in theire corruptions."[68]

Davenport's extravagant fears were no more without logic than Norton's and Higginson's; indeed, much of his conviction came simply from paying attention to the two high priests of clerical conservatism. Given the news from England, it was a strange moment to be finding virtue in monarchy and colonial subordination or to be rediscovering the fundamental soundness of the Church of England and (as Davenport saw it) to recreate its promiscuous inclusiveness in the last bastions of true religion and godly government. Even this last charge was not wholly fantastic. Higginson, apologist for monarchy and advocate of frequent ministerial councils, also proposed in 1663 "one *Catechisme*, one *confession of Faith*, and one *Covenant*" for all of the churches of the Puritan colonies, and he shortly afterward provided his version of what this one covenant might look like. In 1665, the year of Davenport's apocalyptic vision, he got his Salem church to agree to the baptism of children of halfway members, and he also induced them to allow all candidates for *full* communion to submit solely to his personal examination of their qualifications followed by their public subscription to a confession of faith and a church covenant that made no mention of works of saving grace. These two documents he put into print immediately for the edification of the rest of New England, and almost twenty years later, in 1683, he could still be found agitating for the universal adoption of some similar pair of very general statements.[69]

Events at the synod of 1662 confirmed the same anxieties that the Halfway Covenant was merely the signal for a wholesale assault on the autonomy and initiative of the individual churches. "There was scarsce any of the Congregationall principles," Eleazer Mather reported to Davenport, "but they were layen at by some or other of the Assembly."[70] The clergy had answered their own question, "whither, according to the word of God, there ought to be a conscociation of churches," with a resounding "yes" but otherwise, out of caution or conviction, they did not in the end make much of the matter in their result. Instead, they reserved their main onslaught against "schismatical" opinions "tending to a sinful separation" for the seventh of the seven propositions on baptism, which enjoined all the churches to recognize as valid the standing of individuals admitted into halfway membership in other churches. A dissenting church that did not adopt the Halfway Covenant was still obliged to baptize children under it by communion of churches and, if halfway members were lawfully dismissed into its keeping from elsewhere, to take them into their fellowship. These dissenting churches must sooner or later silt up with halfway members through the ordinary process of migration or, in resisting this proposition, be "justly accounted Schismatical."[71] No previous synod had issued such an anathema for rejection of its conclusions or provided such an insidious method for enforcing them. The single question of baptism, partly by its own formidable weight, mostly by deliberate initiative, had broadened rapidly into contention over every main node of Congregationalism and could serve as a focus for controversies over politics that were at best indirectly related to the points officially in dispute.

As the ramifications of the Halfway Covenant became clear in congregations such as Boston and Salem that had consented to the portion of the 1657 document covering discipline and had indicated a certain initial willingness to consider infant baptism, an insurgent party formed to undertake what it considered a life-and-death defense of the purity of New England's institutions against English corruptions. At the First Church of Boston this counter-revolution triumphed when a majority of the church voted to call John Davenport to its vacant pulpit and precipitated a secession by the substantial minority still in favor of extended baptism. The subsequent treatment of the church by successive ecclesiastical councils in 1668 and 1669 spelled out for opponents of the Halfway Covenant all over the Bay Colony the fundamental significance of their struggle: a single, unified campaign to preserve church and state in New England from both the power of Restoration England and the insidious temptation of its example. If "you will forget," John Oxenbridge told the Massachusetts General Court, "your errand of Planting this Wilderness, and if you have a minde to turn your Churches into Parishes, and your Ministers into Priests and Prelates, I cannot think the Lord will ever endure it."[72]

First Church, Boston, was the merchants' and magistrates' church par excellence. Its membership in 1668 included Governor Richard Bellingham, magistrates John Leverett and Edward Tyng, and Thomas Clarke, a frequent choice for speaker of the House of Deputies, who would join the magistracy in 1672. Three of these men had made their fortunes in trade; all four opposed the Halfway Covenant and accommodation with England and favored toleration of the Baptists. These three motifs were mutually reinforcing, but so were their opposites: the offer of the pastorate to Davenport forced out of the church a body of individuals no more or less mercantile than those who stayed but who were identified with the Halfway Covenant, persecution (with some honorable exceptions), and the attitude toward England that has come to be called, after the terminology of a royal official, moderation. First Church's attempt to discipline its thrice-obnoxious dissenters came to nothing when they twice successfully appealed to councils from neighboring churches for license to found a religious society of their own, and attempts to invoke the secular powers were no more effective. The three First Church magistrates, joined by three others of a similar inclination from outside Boston, attempted by one means or another to delay the new church but were outvoted by the remaining members of the magistracy, and in December 1669 Old South Church was founded, complete with the Halfway Covenant from its inception.[73]

Throughout its losing battle, First Church had taken and publicized a very high view of congregational autonomy and denounced the intervention of the two councils in a local disciplinary dispute (as its partisans saw matters) as undisguised Presbyterianism. A few of the members became so embittered that they were ready to declare that simply "to grant a Councill tends to overthrow the Congregationall way."[74] This heightened enthusiasm for congregational independence, and not, as opponents charged, a covert yearning after the same form of heterodoxy, brought the First Church stalwarts to a more sympathetic attitude toward the Baptists, who were seen as at least erring in the right direction compared to the deviations of the so-called orthodox who could not tell a gathered church from an English parish. The Baptists' position on polity was held to be nearer the truth than the prelatical pretensions of those who would tyrannize over both them *and* First Church, and their example, lonely as it was, was seen as testifying eloquently to an endangered truth. An English Congregational divine praised the Baptists to a prominent member of First Church as "a means to preserve your churches from apostasy, and provoke them to their primitive purity," and most members of First Church agreed. Their new minister, John Davenport, quondam patriarch of a colony notorious for its severities, in the midst of denouncing deviations from the pristine ways of the founders somehow worked into the election sermon of 1669 a plea for toleration (not previously known as a leading virtue of the generation he claimed to represent), "lest other Rulers be encouraged by your Example, to measure to us again, with what measure we mete unto others, they accounting [us], as we do them." On Davenport's death in 1670, First Church called John Oxenbridge, who promptly became a staunch friend of the Baptists (who had moved from Charlestown to Boston), as did the longer-lived James Allen, First Church's teacher.[75] By November 1670 the alignment over toleration had become nearly perfect: all six magistrates who signed a warrant to imprison the leaders of the Boston Baptists had endorsed Old South the previous year; four or, more likely, five of the six magistrates willing to sign a release order were First Church partisans.[76]

The dispute over the founding of Old South had firmed up the alignments that had been taking place throughout the 1660s and prepared the way for the bitter, controverted politics of the ensuing decade. Polity, baptism, toleration, accommodation, the role of the clergy, had each as points of dispute sufficient linkages between them, once the stimulus was given by the Davenport affair, to provide the basis for hard-core parties expressing in irreconcilable positions the anxieties that had begotten the original struggle over the reconstruction of the churches of New England. Norton and Davenport were both gone, but their respective apprehensions set the terms of discourse in the 1670s.

Out of this contested decade would come one of American Puritanism's major cultural contributions, the identification of New England with apostate Israel and the rituals of self-denunciation and renewal associated with it. These devices that we subsume under the single label "the jeremiad" were not, as is sometimes thought, in their origin a healing gesture, an unconscious act of artistry by which a wounded society secretes a creative pearl around otherwise inexpressible contradictions.[77] The jeremiad did have a broad resonance, but it was still the ideology and program of one group of contestants, recognized as such by their adversaries and fiercely resisted, most of the time with success, until the very end of the 1670s. Urian Oakes delivering the election sermon of 1673 did not see himself as the celebrant of a mass consensual rite but as the inadvertent referee of a free-for-all, and he warned that if the contest continued New Englanders must look for a royal governor and a bishop to reign over them.[78] No one listened to that argument for some ten years, until Oakes seemed to be proved something of a prophet and the logic of his party for the first time became the common property of Puritan America.

The opening gambit, in 1670, immediately recalled the multiple origins of the controversy. Quite possibly by prearrangement, the town of Hadley submitted to the House of Deputies a petition drawn up by its minister, John Russell, asking for an inquiry into the reasons the hand of the Lord lay heavy on New England. The ensuing answer was written by Peter Tilton, deputy from Hadley and deacon of its church, and located the source of the Lord's displeasure in "innovation threatening the ruin of our foundations, and the extirpation of those old principles of the congregational way laid by so many of the Lord's worthies who are now at rest." Asked for particulars by the upper house, the deputies obliged by charging the ministers and magistrates who approved of the founding of the Old South Church with "irregularities and breach of order and law."[79] The upper house nonconcurred, and in round three the deputies finally broke the rules of political debate in New England for the first time since the abortive impeachment of Governor Winthrop some twenty-five years earlier. They attacked individual magistrates for political decisions by a stipulation that a joint committee proposed by the upper house be required to look into "perticular evills of persons standing in a publick capassitie, in Cases wherein they may be concerned or rather concerne themselves unnecessarilye, which may occasion publick calamitye." Removal of the offending individuals was only implied, but John Oxenbridge, the deputies' choice to preach the next election sermon, drew the implication in full on the appointed day. He cited two of the Body of Liberties allegedly infringed by the malefactors and called on the freemen to purge the magistracy in order that "none may take their places for an Inheritance to use it as they list." The Bay Colony in 1670 had reached a level of openly acknowledged political impasse not seen in almost three decades.[80]

The First Church schism, the proximate cause, is better understood as the flashpoint for much more durable antagonisms, civil and ecclesiastical. The town of Hadley, which presented the petition that opened the crisis, had been founded in 1659 by settlers from Wethersfield and Hartford who were little short of religious refugees: they were, like Peter Tilton and William Goodwin, the losers in the fight at Hartford against Samuel Stone, champion of extended baptism and the most extreme forms of ministerial authority, or they were adherents of John Russell, who must have enjoyed the confidence of *all* of his church, since they moved with him in a body from Wethersfield to Hadley, leaving the Connecticut town's insurgent nonmembers behind. In either political or religious terms the new town of Hadley was consistently radical for the rest of the century. As early as 1662 Russell and Tilton attempted to secure the services of Increase Mather as an assistant minister just after he had first become prominent for his opposition to the majority in the synod of 1662. Russell would subsequently denounce the synod as the harbinger of the unqualified open communion practiced by his neighbor Solomon Stoddard at Northampton, and he displayed his political sympathies by hiding the regicides Whalley and Goffe in his own house for the remainder of their lives. Tilton simultaneously served as their business agent and was so unremittingly anti-English in his politics that he was elected to the Bay Colony magistracy from 1681 until the imposition of royal government in 1686.[81] Russell and Tilton stood for positions locked in place quite early and hardened by events, until to them the fate of New England seemed to rest on punishing the clergy for their supposed backsliding and purging the magistracy of everyone who by supporting Old South indicated presumed sympathy with the growing, essentially English "corruptions" in the Bay Colony.

The events of 1670 should by rights have initiated a period of unnegotiable conflict. Almost as if to make that issue inevitable, the majority of the magistrates who had been attacked in May banded together in November to arrest the leaders of the Boston Baptist Church, the symbol of the sectarian values they attributed to their political opponents. (The timing of the event is so perfect, the coincidence in positions so exact, as to suggest an element of calculation in the step, possibly an act of defiance, possibly an attempt to cloak the accused "innovators" with the mantle of orthodoxy.) In the event, what should have been the ultimate confrontation blew up in its architects' faces, as the electorate chose to rebuke first one camp and then the other, the only means available to them for avoiding the final conflict the prominent spokesmen on both sides seemed so eager to bring on.

The leading spirits among the deputies had come up in 1670 with logically impeccable strategy and coupled it with an idiotic set of tactics. Their extreme stand and their indiscriminate indictment of everyone who supported the gathering of Old South promptly cost them much of their popular support in the next election, in the spring of 1671. The leadership of the anticlerical party held its own fairly well, but a large portion of the following took a beating, so that when the group's appointed spokesman John Oxenbridge issued his fiery call for a new magistracy he was addressing the wrong audience, one that included no less than six members of Old South serving as nonresident deputies from country towns and an overall majority eager to quash the charges made by their predecessors.[82] On no very substantial evidence this electoral victory has been credited to a behind-the-scenes campaign by the clergy. Presumably, there was some degree of coordination by somebody in an election in which so many absentees gained office and so many small towns took the trouble to send deputies for the first time in years. But Tilton and his allies mostly undid themselves. The scope of their indictment broke all the natural alliances that had been formed by including among the Achans two advocates of toleration and two of the most uncompromisingly anti-English members of the magistrates.[83] All four were highly popular, and the magistrates as a whole naturally coalesced in self-protection, without distinction according to their actions in 1669, when the prerogatives of their office were challenged by the deputies and the chief clerical spokesman for the lower house, Oxenbridge, advocated their rotation in office to "make men more modest and mindful in their place." These men would need no prompting from the clergy to seek a more moderate lower house in 1671 and probably very little additional aid in securing one.

In the new house a petition from the clergy seeking vindication was sympathetically received and speedily agreed to.[84] But this vote to declare the resolutions of the previous year's session "accounted uselesse" in no way represented an endorsement of the Halfway Covenant. As a body, the clergy had pressed their proposals on baptism with discretion. Certain individual clergymen were vulnerable, and this vulnerability was afterward exploited by their opponents, but the recoil against "that antiministerial spirit that too much runs through the country" was sufficiently strong in 1671 to win the ministry a gesture of appreciation—and no more. John Richards, one of the new Boston men serving as absentee delegates, began a prominent political career in 1671 by supporting repudiation of the reports of the previous house, but he was still the man who held up almost single-handedly the adoption of the Halfway Covenant by his own North Church for almost another two decades. Most of the towns whose church member electorates sent proclergy deputies to Boston in 1671 were still hesitating over extended baptism at the very end of the decade.[85] The most extraordinary thing about this episode is not the defeat of anticlerical sentiment and antimagisterial protest when they were presented in their most destructive and disruptive form but the strength and persistence of the militants once they were aroused: of fifty deputies in 1671, a full third formally dissented from their house's vindication of the ministry, and that group included five men subsequently elected to the magistracy.[86] Battle had only just been joined.

First Church and its sympathizers took their revenge almost immediately, at Newbury and at Salem. John Hull, who had helped lead the secession to found Old South, was complaining by 1672 of "many too much abetting one Edmund Woodman and his party" in opposition to Thomas Parker, the longtime minister of Newbury. Hull specified the "many" as "above five magistrates" (that is, the four survivors of 1669 who had opposed the Old South, plus the newly elected Thomas Clarke), "above twenty deputies" (seventeen had dissented from the vindication of the clergy the previous year), "and two ministers; viz., Mr. James Allin and Mr. John Oxenbridge." Two years later Hull was bemoaning a breakaway group from John Higginson's Salem Church who had "proceeded so far that they had seven messengers from Boston Old [First] Church" to found a schismatic church of their own.[87]

Parker and Higginson were obnoxious to the First Church party on nearly identical grounds. Parker was the only avowed Presbyterian in the Bay Colony, at best a persistent nuisance, at worst an embarrassment abroad, notoriously royalist in his politics, autocratic in his theory and practice of church governance, and inclusionist in his views of membership. (Woodman had complained "that he would set up a prelacy, and have more power than the pope.")[88] Higginson resented the charges that he too was a Presbyterian who had "taken away the liberties of the Church," but it is easy to see why his critics considered him (unfairly) another Parker in aspiration, if not in dogma. In addition to his politics, his enthusiasm for persecution, and his praise of councils and uniformity of doctrinal statement, he had gone beyond the Halfway Covenant to relax the standards for full communion at Salem and, for all intents and purposes, to take control personally of determining the candidates' fitness. If Higginson had had his way at Salem, admission to full membership in this Congregational church (and, therefore, to the right to vote in the Bay Colony) would have been practically identical to the same procedure at avowedly Presbyterian Newbury. Minister and ruling elder would pass on the applicants' credentials in private and then, without reference to a conversion experience, propound them to the church for admission on the understanding that lack of substantial objection meant consent. Oxenbridge may have had Higginson in mind in particular when he warned in his election sermon of 1671, "if ye admit of a carnal party into the priviledges due here to visible Saints, they will be likely to eat out the heart of liberty and religion."[89]

In form and in eventual outcome the disputes ran parallel courses. At Newbury the aging and ailing Parker attempted to perpetuate his views by bringing in his cousin John Woodbridge as co-minister in the face of the hostility of about half of his church. At Salem, the town and (despite the apparent unanimity in their records) a good part of the church opposed the Halfway Covenant and the discontinuation of the conversion narratives. They attempted, in a move the mirror image of Newbury's, to impose on Higginson as his co-minister the more tractable Francis Nicholet, and when that effort failed, to set up a church of their own with Nicholet as sole pastor.[90] Arbitration committees sent by the General Court had an appearance of neutrality but were really weighted against the two incumbent ministers, and, after admonishing the respective insurgent parties for disrespect to the clergy and lack of Christian charity, they indirectly granted them the better part of what they demanded. In the case of Newbury, Woodbridge was obliged to give up the attempt to join his cousin in the pulpit and the minister's party was warned against further appeals to the Essex country court, its favorite weapon for harassing the dissidents gathered around Edmund Woodman. At Salem the mediators pointedly ignored Higginson's calls for an inquiry into his rival's orthodoxy and recommended Nicholet's reinstatement as co-minister until such time as an amicable separation could take place to found a new church under his pastorate.[91] He chose, instead, to leave for England, preferring favorable letters of reference to the risk of another imbroglio, whereupon the promoters of his cause attempted to secede all over again in 1680 and once more obtained the approval of the General Court in the face of new objections from Higginson.[92]

Neither dispute can be explained primarily in local terms or adduced exclusively as undifferentiated instances of the continuous tensions within Congregational polity. As Woodman recalled in the case of Newbury, the church "have spent twenty-five years and more in uncomfortable and unprofitable contention and divission," and the same could be said of Salem. The interesting question, even for contemporaries, was why "now of late the cry hereof hath bin more loud in the eares of the Churches then in former times," and the answer is better sought in Boston than locally. Woodman, the prime mover among Newbury's dissidents, was one of the four deputies to present the anticlerical reports of 1670, William Hathorne, éminence grise of the Nicholet affair at Salem, was one of the six magistrates to object to the founding of Old South.[93] The rival parties in each town formed, up to a point, around well-worn lines of division, familial and social, within their little societies, but the dissidents acted when they did and as they did because their parochial squabbles had become enmeshed in the larger complex of issues that centered on the Halfway Covenant, and this linkage assured them help from powerful outsiders of similar persuasion. Nicholet at Salem boasted that "he acted by the advise of the best in the Country, mentioning the Governor [John Leverett] and Major [William] Hawthorn," while his supporters rallied around "the good old way" that "their Fathers lived and dyed in before them, which they intended to set up in their meeting house."[94] Woodman at Newbury played a similar role and enjoyed an overlapping set of allies: when he was found guilty by the Essex County Court of slandering the Presbyterian Parker, Hathorne and Samuel Symonds (another magistrate on the same side in the First Church schism) dissented from the sentence, and Daniel Denison and Simon Bradstreet (the leading supporters among the magistrates of Old South, persecution, and accommodation) immediately took the extraordinary step of protesting the dissent. Hathorne and Symonds were convinced of what Denison and Bradstreet denied, that the defamation case and the dispute at Newbury were part of the epic struggle of New England. "We perceive," they wrote in their dissent, that the Woodman party "doe stand for the congregational way of church government and discipline to be exercised amongst them (which is the way the churches here doe professe to the whole world to be the way and only way according to the gospel of Christ,) and that it is and hath been for a long time a very great burthen and grievance to them, that they have not freedom in that respect."[95] The Halfway Covenant did not even have to be at issue—it was not at Newbury—for the party divisions to run along familiar lines. As far back as 1653 the men who would be leaders of the Newbury Congregationalists twenty years later can be found enlisting in the successful campaign to force the General Court to repeal the law against lay preaching, and Parker's future supporters had been accommodationists in the 1660s in the first contest over submission to English demands. The subsequent careers of the main figures on both sides of the Newbury dispute are equally predictable: Parker's protégé John Woodbridge, sacked from the ministry, entered politics as a moderate favoring compromise with England; Edmund Woodman ultimately joined the Baptists, and his two closest allies in the anti-Parker camp became heroes of the resistance to the Andros regime.[96] Salem has a parallel story to tell. Hathorne, like his longtime political partner Henry Bartholomew, had dissented from the General Court's endorsement of the Cambridge Platform and later in the 1650s from its censure of the magistrate William Pynchon for heterodoxy. Their Ipswich ally Symonds had rendered a judgment in 1657 that would have, if upheld, virtually abolished compulsory support for religion in the Bay Colony. Bartholomew alone of the three lived on into the period of the Dominion, and he made his final political statement by moving to Boston and joining First Church.[97] Rooted in local circumstances as these disputes in Newbury and Salem may have been, they were still simultaneously instances of a far more fundamental and continuing tension. In America after 1660 the contrasting pulls of the Puritan movement, the drive for establishment and the assertion of the rights of the demonstrably elect, had come to be expressed as an opposition between those who feared that the New England colonies would dissolve into the sectarianism and anarchy of the Interregnum and those who saw them succumbing to the corruptions of the Restoration.

Throughout the 1670s the two sides remained evenly matched and prone to intermittent skirmishing. First Church's adherents gained a slight edge from 1672 on, when John Leverett became governor, Samuel Symonds deputy governor, and Thomas Clarke regained the speakership of the deputies before passing it on to the equally partisan Richard Waldron upon his own election to the magistracy in the same year. The group marked their ascendancy by publishing John Oxenbridge's election sermon of 1671 at public expense in 1673, and their influence can be felt throughout the decade. Their dislike of Leonard Hoar for failing to secure proper dismission both before joining Old South and then again after leaving it to accept the presidency of Harvard played a part in the ruin of his short-lived tenure at the college.[98] Their antagonism to anything that looked like clerical interference in politics delayed a new synod for the Bay until 1679. Even after the demise of the leaders of the party and the submergence of most of the organizing issues, distant echoes of the original conflict were still to be heard in such an unlikely place as the notorious church of Salem Village, where each of the four ill-fated ministers of the parish took an opposite view of the Halfway Covenant and inherited the enmity of his predecessor's supporters.[99] And under the New Charter of 1692 Elisha Cooke, son of one of the seventeen dissenting deputies of 1671, son-in-law of John Leverett, and a First Church member himself, would lead the party still hostile to the English government. Into the third decade of the eighteenth century the byzantine civil and ecclesiastical politics of the Bay Colony still swirled around some of the same issues as fifty years before and around the same names: Leverett, Cooke—and Mather.

Self-inflicted wounds were so regular a feature of the Puritan movement that they were no more likely to be fatal in the 1670s than in any other decade, although the healing physician at this particular juncture was an unlikely candidate for the role. Increase Mather did not reach his fortieth year until 1679 and must have made more enemies than friends in 1675 by announcing that he had switched from outspoken opposition to the Halfway Covenant to equally emphatic support. Such turnabouts were almost the rule with him. He had petitioned for liberty for Dissenters while still in England and then favored repression upon his return to New England but would finally discover toleration with no less sincerity after the Revolution of 1689. Throughout the 1670s his diary similarly reveals him to have been an accommodationist, urging the clergy to take a leading part in defining the terms of a possible compromise, but in 1683 he would seize the leadership of the party endorsing a last-ditch defense of the Old Charter, and in 1692 he became the architect and advocate for the new charter that turned the Bay into a royal colony. Even by New England standards he was quick to see the hand of God in his affairs, generally pointing him in the direction of great deeds, and he "experienced signal Answers of prayer" at regular intervals.

But it turned out that he was right to believe in his destiny, and his changes of opinion make an appealing contrast with the rigidities of his contemporaries. Having taken most of the sides on the key questions of his day, he was uniquely well equipped to formulate a vision that became in the 1680s and early 1690s the common refuge for almost all the contestants as the internal struggles of New England were abruptly halted by the interposition of imperial power.[100]

Increase Mather invented nothing; he organized and arranged. The various traditions he refashioned and elaborated into a unified whole we now label the jeremiad with unintentional appropriateness, since the book of Jeremiah was a party document in a divided and contested Hebrew society for a long time before it became part of the revealed wisdom of Western civilization. The name, however, has been bestowed because the central element in the American Puritan configuration was the analogy between New England and latter-day Israel in the prophetic period before the Exile—in covenant with Lord still as his chosen people, but decaying in spirit and liable to ever more severe chastisements. Puritans had used the metaphor before, in England, and the overall resemblance between its earlier invocation in the 1620s and its American application turns out to be striking.[101] There is, however, no evidence of conscious borrowing or direct descent. If Mather or his frequent collaborator Samuel Willard of Old South had known of English precedents, they certainly would have employed them to counter charges of "innovation." Instead, they seemed to have done their recreating unwittingly, a parallel stimulus producing a parallel response drawn from a common cultural inheritance.

The various ideas the new Jeremiahs fused together into the great cultural rite of Puritan America had been there for the asking since 1630. John Cotton had already expounded on the special relevance of Jeremiah 2:21 for later generations of colonists in the sermon that saw off the founding fathers: "Yet I had planted thee a noble vine, Wholly a right seed: How then art thou turned into the degenerate plant Of a strong vine unto me?"[102] Subsequent development of the theme in New England is obscured because the annual and occasional public sermons likely to record its history were not routinely put into print until the crop of the 1660s, and the earlier efforts do not survive in manuscript. The theme of declension seemed particularly pertinent to second-generation New Englanders, it has been suggested, because of their sense of having failed in their mission to influence England or because in the more geared-up economy of the later seventeenth century the tensions be-

tween "worldliness" and "spirituality" always inherent in Puritan doctrines
of work and wealth became unbearable without ritual expiation. There is no
way to validate either claim, but for what they are worth public breast-
beatings over a collapse of zeal or a whoring after material possessions can
be found in the New England of the 1640s, if not earlier. In 1680 Increase
Mather took great pride in quoting an unpublished sermon of his older
brother, in which from the very same Boston pulpit Samuel Mather announced in 1650, "It is too plain to be denied, that there is a dying spirit in
New England to the wayes of God." A conviction of decay was a New
Englander's birthright.[103]

There is nothing remarkable, then, in the earliest published election sermons, those of the 1660s, discovering, as their unpublished predecessors
likely did, that God was punishing New England for its growing list of
"abominations" and would punish it more severely still if there was not a
speedy repentance. But most of these exercises in prophecy, by Norton, Higginson, or Jonathan Mitchell, and, more surprisingly, those of a few years
later by Samuel Danforth and Connecticut's James Fitch, lack most of the
other elements associated with the jeremiad. They do not make much of the
pristine virtues of the founders and the special relationship with God to
which they had pledged themselves and their descendants, and (with the
exception of Fitch's effort) they fail to dwell on the internal nature of the
current corruption. They do carry on at a little length about provoking evils
but do not give a long and systematic particularization of various sins that
are then held to be external manifestations of spiritual inanition. Nor, perhaps most significant, do these sermons offer a program for reform coupled
with an urgent warning of impending and total destruction.[104] The prize for
the earliest extant election sermon to present anything like a comprehensive
and sustained jeremiad must go to a very different preacher, the most cynical,
disloyal, worldly, and justifiably infamous graduate Harvard managed to
produce in the seventeenth century, with the possible exception of Sir George
Downing.

In *New-Englands True Interest; Not to Lie*, preached in 1668 but not
published until 1670, the climactic year of the deputies' resolutions against
the clergy, William Stoughton worked up the various pieces of the jeremiad
into a single unified literary form. There was still much work left for Increase
Mather to do in the 1670s, but at least Stoughton had given him the sermonic centerpiece for his own subsequent cultural masterpiece. The crucial
assertion from which all else follows is the reassignment of Israel's Old Testament status to the Puritan colonies now that England no longer fit the role:

"The Lords promises, and expectations of great things, have singled out *New-England,* and all sorts of ranks of men amongst us, above any Nation or people in the world." The trouble with a relationship this special was that those who enjoyed it were forever being put to the test—"this hath been and is a time and season of eminent trial to us." And (Stoughton's major achievement) the standards by which they were judged and invariably found deficient were fixed and unalterable because of the heroic, even unparalleled stature of the men who had first set them. "God sifted a whole nation that he might send choice Grain over into this Wilderness." What *they* created their unworthy progeny had only to maintain, a secondary undertaking they were still managing to botch. "There can be *no other foundation laid then those which have been laid.* . . . It is a fixed unalterable thing: It is not now to be Found by any *New Light.*"[105] Stoughton may have founded New England filiopietism, if that habit of mind is capable of being invented whole and by a single man; certainly, he was the first person to go on record with the use of the absurd concept of "our Fathers," contrasted with "the *Present Genera-tion.*" (In 1668 many of the most prominent members of his audience—Leverett, Symonds, Thomas Danforth, among others—had come to New England in the 1630s as teenagers and belonged to neither group.)

New-Englands True Interest; Not to Lie is a consummate piece of hypoc-risy. The preacher who flayed the spiritual weaknesses of his own generation, those born in the 1630s, had not yet at age thirty-seven found the courage to submit an account of his own conversion to a group of attested visible saints. And the man who exhorted his hearers to eminent reformation on the grounds that "there can be no *neutralizing* therefore in this day" was about to abandon the ministry for a political career in which he became New England's leading neuter, a prominent member of every succeeding govern-ment, whether under the Old Charter, the Dudley interim administration, the Andros regime, the revolutionary government, or the New Charter. The ser-mon was worthy of the man: it enjoyed two editions in a year of bitter political contests (one would love to know who paid for the publication) and launched its author directly into his opportunistic career as a magistrate the following spring.[106] And well it might. Stoughton combined an oratorical extravagance perfectly suited to the passions of 1670 with a characteristic and total lack of explicit commitment. He took no position on the Halfway Covenant or relations with England and said only a little about toleration, appealing to all sides by his furious denunciation of an unnamed and unspeci-fiable Them. Twenty-two years after his sermon was published, Stoughton would make his only real mark on history when as chief judge of the witchcraft court in 1692 he grew intransigent for the first time in his life and almost alone insisted on the validity of the spectral evidence that hanged nineteen people. This, his most famous moment, is anticipated in his sermon, otherwise a model of rhetorical bad faith. The spiritually weak are "*imposed upon by deceitful* workers" until in the end, "being *given up by God, they* fall *quite off, Men gather them,* they are joyned in with the Instruments of Satan and turn *underminers*, at least if not *open Persecutors.*" As he spoke, there were already many, "*The Brood of Antichrist,* that are *Travailing with Mischief*," but these inveterate enemies of New England were hard to identify because they were outwardly pious individuals who had secretly fallen into the especially strong temptations by which the Lord chose to try his peculiar people. "Men think they will go but thus far or so far in treacherous false wayes, and remain hid all the while under some fur cloak, but they shall proceed until they be known."[107] Increase Mather often preached a religion of conflict too, but his enemies of the moment, though unnamed, were scarcely difficult to identify; already in a sermon preached in 1668 Stoughton was exposing a genuinely invisible world.

Election preachers fell into the habit in the 1670s of citing their predecessors as a way of emphasizing the continuum on which their individual effort took its place, and *New-Englands True Interest; Not to Lie* probably gets the most references. Stoughton had perfected a pattern, or perhaps had just put into print a perfect model of it, but in one special area his own distinctive personality had its contribution to make, and this is his marvelously facile set of ineffables. His pervasive social decay is spread gossamer thin, unavoidable and insubstantial at once, and therefore irrefutable. "The *first Generation* which was in this Land, had much of the power of Godliness," said Increase Mather in working the same vein in 1676, "but the present *Generation* hath the form, and as to the *body* of *the Generation,* but little of the power of *Religion.*"[108] The failings in question were matters of attitude and emotional intensity; the measure to be applied, the supposed spiritual temperature of a past generation. Mather, however, was bold enough to claim that moral standards in New England were also demonstrably in decline. The assertion became an important part of his overall program and a point of contention with his opponents, who must have been grateful for something tangible at last to grapple with. But Mather's closest allies, Fitch in Connecticut and Willard at the Old South, followed Stoughton and avoided giving the opposition this opening. They blithely announced that no one could judge New England degenerate who was not already in on the secret. Fitch, in the sermon of 1676 that inaugurated a wave of covenant renewing in New England's churches, admitted that "concerning that absolute Apostasie, it is not seen in many in *New-England*, nor usually seen in any" but outright heretics. Rather, one could see a "comparative and gradual Apostasie," a matter of "how far *New-England* is declined from being *New-England*." Willard had much the same to say six years later in the Massachusetts election sermon of 1682, when he admitted that "by the very confession of unprejudiced strangers, here is more of sobriety and honest conversation, then almost in any place they have occasion to be conversant in." New Englanders could know they had fallen into a state requiring immediate repentance mainly because in the election sermons the minister regularly told them so—"It hath not been the voice only of one or two, but such things have been told us from year to year."[109]

Indeed, they had, and, most impressively, without regard for partisan allegiance. Stoughton's effort had proven, as it must have been composed to prove, that the claims for declension fit nicely into the armories of both camps. Oxenbridge and Allen could on this one item join with Mather and Willard. The children were not the saints their parents were, all agreed, and the Halfway Covenant proved it. Increase Mather felt no embarrassment in bringing out his brother Eleazer's *A Serious Exhortation to the Present and Succeeding Generation in New England* in 1669, when he shared its criticisms of the "faithlessness" of those who sought extended baptism and in republishing it in 1678, when he had reversed himself on that key point, as a prelude to his own *Pray for the Rising Generation.*[110] Eleazer was still held to be correct in his diagnosis; his younger brother had, however, come to see that the weak formalists for whom the Halfway Covenant was fashioned were so enfeebled that nothing less would serve their needs. Oakes, the self-appointed "neutral" observer of New England society, put the matter with exemplary candor: "All sides are agreed that things are in a declining posture, that there is a great degeneracy, that things look with another Face, that there is a defection and declension: though all are not resolved wherein it doth consist, some charging it one way, some another, as their judgement or Affection, or party and Interest leads them; yet they all center in this, that there is a backsliding and declension among us[.]"[111]

Increase Mather's genius lay in the uses to which he put this universal and unrebuttable presumption of degeneracy and also in the way he could broadcast and publicize his creations. He had the advantage of a satellite pulpit in his father's old church of Dorchester, where he could preview and echo the experiments made in Boston; he enjoyed unprecedented influence with the printers and booksellers of Boston and Cambridge in the decades when the production of the colonial presses was finally about to move into high gear; and alone among the ministers of New England's metropolis he cultivated an extensive correspondence in the provinces with fellow clergymen of an intellectual bent who were frustrated by their inability to do more than, as one of them put it, talk to trees and Indians. The strength and extent of these contacts were revealed in 1675–76 and again in the early 1680s in the number of individuals otherwise of very local eminence who got their names into print by flooding him with details for, respectively, his history of King Philip's War and his collection of New England's "remarkables," *Illustrious Providences*. James Fitch of Norwich, who promulgated in Connecticut Mather's pet device, the covenant renewal, received favorable mention in both works, as well as a write-up in Cotton Mather's *Magnalia*, and owed to Increase's patronage the publication (with adulatory prefaces) of three of his five titles.[112] (This is not a large total but high for a Connecticut minister before the establishment of a printing press in that colony.) Another Connecticut favorite, Nathaniel Collins of Middletown, was in possession of a printed copy of a 1674 sermon within eleven weeks of the day Increase Mather first preached it, and he was almost as fast in his turn in 1679 when he "expressed in a Great assembly" (presumably the Connecticut General Court) a call for his colony to endorse the Result Mather had written for the Massachusetts Reforming Synod of that year: "Your hearing the mind of God, declared by the *Synod*, will be a signal Testimony of an humbled People." (Collins published nothing; the quotation comes from Mather, in receipt of the manuscript sermon, who used the puff in 1680 to show the broad support his proposals enjoyed.)[113] Certain historians are sometimes held to suffer from a confusion between "the New England mind" and the enormous bibliography of the Mathers, father and son, but when it comes to the output of press and pulpit in the late 1670s and 1680s, the father had the wit and political talent to effect, however briefly, this very conjunction.

Mather was able to cultivate his formidable clerical following because to all those willing to come within his orbit he purveyed a coherent package of arguments coupled with an appealing plan of action. Perhaps borrowing some of his hyperbole and sense of crisis from the Davenport faction, to which he had belonged in the 1660s, he chose (in contrast to Stoughton) to describe the degeneracy of the "present generation" in reassuringly distinct and specific terms. There was nothing secret or insidious in the carriage of Mather's Israelites, nor was an undefined segment a hidden party of traitors. New Englanders of his day were all potential or actual apostates and outright reprobates, visible in their brazen iniquity to any competent witness without the necessity of a spiritual x-ray. "Yea, the present Generation as to the body of it, is an unconverted Generation." Put to the temptation of suffering persecution for their faith, "it is to be feared, that the greatest part of this Generation would comply, and disown that cause which their Fathers suffered for." Among those who heard him utter these gloomy prophecies, many had "never prayed in their lives, or never in earnest." He was accordingly less than clear on what his audience was doing in the North Church on various fast days between 1677 and 1680, listening to him abuse them for their failings, but he was sure that, all evidence to the contrary, they really wanted to be somewhere else indulging in the sins of the flesh. Church members were to be seen "spending many pretious hours, nay (which is lamentable to be spoken) dayes" in taverns. Equally, the "debauched and profane" behavior of young New Englanders journeying abroad revealed what they would all do at home if left to their own devices. "How would madded and inraged profaneness know no bounds?"[114]

With particular ingenuity Mather inverted Davenport's claim that children of church members who did not proceed to communion were *felones-de-se*, spiritual suicides who had excommunicated themselves by defaulting on their baptismal vows. He repeated the accusation in extravagant terms but turned it into an indictment of an errant generation the more culpable (and therefore liable to temporal judgments) because they *were* still in the original church covenant pledged in their baptisms. Speaking with the voice of Davenport, he endorsed the Halfway Covenant by issuing a tirade against its beneficiaries, and, with still more craft, he converted Davenport's implicit mass excommunication of individuals guilty of sloth into the as yet unrealized threat of a wholesale casting off of apostate Israel. Where Davenport was ultimately conservative and pessimistic, Mather indulged the same satisfying vehemence and repugnance to the times so as to conclude with an urgent but essentially hopeful exhortation: "Let us every one in our several places, and capacityes endeavour that the present and succeeding Generations in New-England, may not forsake the Lord God of their Fathers, and so endanger their being cast off for-ever."[115]

Mather also followed Davenport in predicting that the punishment awaiting this degeneracy was more than a corrective chastisement, though he would not follow his long-dead mentor into the bloodcurdling comforts of chiliasm until, like him, he too saw his vaunted power slipping away in a society no longer worthy of such a prophet. Early in 1674, in *The Day of Trouble is Near*, he announced on no particular evidence that "it is a very solemn Providence, that the Lord should seem at this day to be *numbering many of the Rising Generation for the Sword*; as if the Lord should say, I will bring a Sword to avenge the quarrel of a *neglected Covenant*." The audience was quickly assured, however—"Destruction shall not as yet be." Like his friend Fitch, Mather was thinking of the Dutch recapture of New York and of a further extension of the European wars to America.[116] King Philip's War the next year accidentally turned him into an instant prophet, a mantle he was quick to claim, but otherwise the awful conflict with the Indians of 1675–76 was a distinct disappointment, over too quickly and not universally convincing as a judgment on an unreformed people. Led by Mather, the Massachusetts ministry actually showed a remarkable reluctance to let the war go: they pointed to the continuing conflict in Maine as a sign that the end might still be nigh, resisted without success the proclamation of a day of thanksgiving to celebrate the victory they were in no hurry to accept, and fell back on the war in the Result of 1679 as still their main talking point in the apodictic assertion "that God hath a Controversy with his New-England People is undeniable, the Lord having written his displeasure in dismal Characters against us."[117] What was being attempted was a piece of exorcism. Adopting the imprecatory posture of a Thomas Hooker or a John Winthrop about 1630, as well as the attendant sense of crisis and even the covenant renewal, the clergy who followed Mather hoped to undo much of the Separatist tendency that had become manifest in American Puritanism in the intervening decades and to restore its dynamic equilibrium to a balance more approximate to that of the period they echoed.

This strategy required a level of specification that carried obvious risks. People might not believe the taverns were full of church members so many hours of every day, or alternatively, a catastrophe might not happen on schedule and one would be forced to instance a perfectly ordinary drought or a localized disaster like the Boston fire of 1679. Mather was willing to take the gamble because his claims of palpable iniquities provoking imminent debacles gave him, uniquely, a design by which to rebalance the disparate elements of public commitment and private piety that went into Puritanism. Along the way to his new synthesis he could shore up the authority of the ministry and extend the reach of the church, not to mention attaining at less than forty years of age a central role in New England religious life unequaled by any member of his father's generation. But he could succeed only if he could recruit both magistrates and laity into the themes of the jeremiad through the twin measures of moral legislation and covenant renewal.

The whole program was necessarily controversial and controverted. Mather's opponents, led by Governor John Leverett, were perfectly well aware of the implications of the proposals he was pressing on them—extended church membership, religious repression, a marked expansion in the role of the clergy as arbiters of New England culture and expert advisers on all serious matters of state. They resisted the details of Mather's plan and rejected the premise, the claim for a declension so rapid and complete as to justify an urgent reform campaign. And for some time they held their own very successfully. Eventually, all that took place between 1675 and 1686 would come to seem the "natural" reactions of Puritan society to threats from the Indians and the English. This act of mystification has succeeded, however, only because late in the day Mather and his party did get to define what the nature of that society was, and then they proceeded to cover up the struggle by which they attained their power. Thus the series of "reform" laws that the General Court passed in November of 1675 for the suppression of vice and Quakers and for the religious education of the rising generation comes across in Mather's *Brief History* of King Philip's War as an unexceptional response to an indisputable stimulus. In our turn, we say much the same thing when we speak of Puritan "fanaticism" leading the General Court to persecute Quakers, catechize children, and restrict the licensing of taverns as a direct means to placate an angry God and an indirect one to combat hostile Indians. Our values are different, but our version of causality is the very one Mather would have us accept unthinkingly. His diary, however, tells a very different story: "Alas that Reformation should stick at the head!" The magistrates, dominated by Leverett and other First Church members and sympathizers, initially rejected the bills the deputies sent up, and their subsequent acceptance of a revised version failed to satisfy Mather, who complained that the Court "broke up in discontent," an outcome he found "lamentable" and "to the scandal of religion." He would declare victory anyway in the *Brief History*, but in his personal war still in progress he was very much aware that he was in no position to ask for more in the way of new moral legislation, and in March 1676 he changed the burden of his complaint against his opponents in the magistracy, announcing that "our defect is not so much in respect of the want of good Laws, as in the non-execution of those Laws that are good." William Hubbard, Mather's only heavyweight antagonist among the clergy at the time, immediately parried with the declaration in the election sermon in May 1676 (he was the magistrate's choice for the honor) that "the making of more Lawes then need or can be executed, may weaken the authority of them that are in force, and necessary to be attended."[118] And there matters rested.

The winter and spring of King Philip's War (1675–76) went badly for

Mather in general. His favorite sins, the only ones he thought worth dwelling on, were bravery in apparel and drunkenness. The choice may seem odd, but he could hardly have asked the General Court to pass a blanket statute against worldliness. In the long catalog of provoking evils those two stood out as the only enumerated transgressions even nominally susceptible to remedial legislation or more effective enforcement of existing laws. Mather made the most of alcohol and gold braid, and his critics faithfully gave him battle on these grounds. In January 1676, after a sermon in which Mather claimed "that strangers said, that they had seen more drunkenness in New England in halfe a year than in England in all thir lives," the sixty-year-old Leverett publicly informed the thirty-six-year-old minister that "they that said so lyed. And that there was more drunkennes in New England many years agoe than there is now, yea at the first beginning of this Colony." Then Stoughton, now a magistrate and ever one to back the current winner, twisted the knife by adding "pleasantly, that I must preach a Recantation sermon," a not very veiled allusion to Mather's recent announcement of his conversion to the Halfway Covenant. Seventeen years later, Mather would repay that remark with interest, when he swept away the single enthusiasm of Stoughton's life, the witchcraft trials. For the time being he could do no more than complain to his diary of the large number of taverns that Leverett, experienced soldier that he was, had licensed in wartime Boston.[119]

Things went no better at first among Mather's purported friends. A mere week after his exchange with Leverett, he read several of the reform laws to a meeting of his North Church, "particularly those laws which respect excess in apparel, and Townedwellers being at Taverns, and solemnly exhorted the church to attend the things there mentioned." Then he turned to the very first of the new laws, calling on the ministry to pay greater attention to the children of the church, and asked the members for the names of their children of adult years "that I might send for them, and inquire into thir spirituale estates etc." This proposal looked suspiciously as if it would lead to a mass ceremony of owning the covenant, and opposition was immediate, if circumspect. Directly after the meeting, when the bulk of the members had left, two of Mather's leading supporters, Thomas Lake and John Richards, took him to task for his exhortation on clothing and taverns. Lake announced, with Richards "seconding him," that "when ministers did lay a solemn charge upon people, it might take in the ignorant, but no rational man would regard what was said the more for that."[120] Lake was killed in King Philip's War a few weeks later and left no record of his views on the Halfway Covenant, but Richards, as has been mentioned, was its leading opponent in the North Church. The point at issue was once again, as in the confrontation with the magistrates a week earlier, the state of the colony's morals, but immediately conjoined, as in the earlier humiliation, were the issues of church membership and clerical interference.

It all seems on the quaint side, a series of salvos in code exchanged back and forth at great speed among the members of an inbred society gorged on symbols. No great hermeneutic skill, however, is needed to recover the stakes in these word games, as long as it is remembered that the vulnerability of Mather's logic, no less than its attraction, lay in the way each part implied the other. Deny the need to enforce the laws and you denied the crisis, the wrath of Jehovah, the apostasy of New England that allegedly provoked it, the extension of church membership that was implicitly required in any ceremony of repentance, the whole sense of urgency by which the clergy was wrapping itself in the mantle of Jeremiah in order to assert its preeminence in Puritan society. William Hubbard knew exactly what he was doing when in his single election sermon in the course of a long life he attributed the reverses in King Philip's War solely "to nothing more then to contempt of our enemies," congratulated New England on the "many hopeful buds springing up amongst the rising Generation," and paraded a set of commonplaces about "order" with the intent of telling the more ambitious clergy and their lay adherents to leave the business of government to the governors.[121] He was, over and over again, hitting Mather where it hurt, and very probably enjoying it.

Covenant renewing had more immediate potential for the implementation of Mather's scheme. Leverett, ably assisted by Hubbard, could and did frustrate his efforts here too in the Bay, where before the governor's death only Dorchester had undertaken the ceremony. New England churches, however, claimed a unity that extended beyond the legal boundaries of the colonies, and there were allies in both Connecticut and Plymouth willing to oblige the minister of Boston. The revival of covenant renewals in the Puritan colonies is often attributed to James Fitch at Norwich, Connecticut, but Increase Mather was the true source. Fitch did conduct the first ceremony in the form championed by Mather, on the colonywide fast day of 22 March 1676.[122] But Mather himself almost two months earlier, on 28 January, the day after his contretemps with Leverett over the history of drinking, wrote in his diary that the "Magistrates have no Heart to doe what they might in order to Reformation. especially the Governor. Nor will they call upon the churches to renew thir covenant with God." On 13 March 1676, as Fitch issued a manifesto informing the Connecticut General Court of his intention to hold his ceremony, Mather spent the morning writing a letter "about Renewing Covenant." Subsequently, it was to Mather at Boston, not Fitch at Norwich, that a curious Connecticut minister would turn for "your instructions concerning Renewal of Covenant."[123] Governor Leverett was well aware of the hand behind the renewals outside his jurisdiction. When the Plymouth General Court used a day of humiliation in June 1676 to recommend that the colony's churches renew their covenants, he went out of his way, with Hubbard's endorsement and over Mather's repeated protests, to make sure that the Bay kept a public thanksgiving that month.[124] He wanted the Indian war officially and finally over, the debt to the Lord discharged, before Mather could make use of the public fasts the conflict occasioned in profusion as a means of imposing his program on the colony.

Covenant renewing in itself was nothing new. In the 1630s several New England churches had renewed their covenants as a way of reorganizing their polity along stricter congregational principles without denying the validity of the original gatherings, and in 1656 the church of Chelmsford had done much the same thing when the majority of its members moved to the new town from Wenham and accepted mass dismissions from neighboring churches at the same time.[125] Mather's version of the renewal drew on this tradition in outward form, but for purposes much closer to those of John White's Dorchester articles of the 1620s. White had required of his congregation as the terms of admission to the Lord's Supper subscription to a series of articles pledging reformation after they confessed to having "relapsed into Lukewarmness" and to growing in "carnall security, and deadnes of hart," not to mention "pride and self love," worldliness, and contention—the usual symptoms, running rampant among Puritans in the decade *before* New England had been founded, let alone had the time to degenerate. As Samuel Willard was to say accurately some fifty years later when the Old South went through the identical motions, "Degeneracy, Apostacy, and Covenant breaking" were "the hereditary disease of the visible Church."[126]

The parallel, however, went much further and deeper. White's articles, no less than New England's renewals, were a response to political and military crisis. The Dorchester communicants cheerfully took the blame for "the fierceness of the Lords indignacion" against the Protestants of the Continent "and threatened unto us by the preparacions made against us," and they pledged to conduct their reformation according to a careful scheme of religious duties and mutual watchfulness and by systematic instruction and discipline of their children. Public calamity and personal transgression were linked in a ceremony, centered on the sacrament, that required a reinvigorated and more systematic pursuit of the plenitude of means and that bound the undertakers "to endeavour the furthering of the Gospell at home, and abroad." (The diffuseness of this call to action was unavoidable in the politics of the time.) The New England renewal of a much later date was similarly, as the earliest of those in the Bay calls itself, a "Covenant for Reformation" along lines equivalent to White's at almost every point: those involved in the ceremonies acknowledged their guilt for the latest disasters and specified their various forms of apostasy and covenant breaking under the traditional headings and then pledged a new beginning built around a more systematic religious life and special attention to the children of the church. After 1679 it was not even necessary to find local examples of the pervasive degeneracy because the renewing church could just read off the Result of the Reforming Synod. There were also four printed versions of covenants of reformation in circulation in the early 1680s for imitation by additional churches as they fell into line, so that by the time Cotton Mather came to write the *Magnalia* he had only to give Old South's text as "the *form* which, with little variation, was most used."[127] Covenant renewals attained the distinction of becoming the single most homogeneous ordinance in a religious system built on congregational autonomy.

White's articles demonstrate how deeply ingrained in the logic of Puritanism the covenant renewal was and how likely it was to be resorted to in one form or another when the skies grew ominous, whether in Dorset or Massachusetts. But this original Dorchester document was still an improvised affair, put together by a man clearly on the defensive. The work of Fitch, Willard, John Cotton of Plymouth, and, above all, Increase Mather was much more carefully crafted: its brilliance was displayed particularly in the ways it could resolve so many of the Puritan colonies' outstanding difficulties and still serve as the weapon of a particular party and as a vehicle of clerical aggrandizement.

White has used his articles as a means of separating out and organizing the godly minority, or what would pass for it, from the body of the mixed multitude. Mather and his allies had exactly the opposite task, to reaffiliate large segments of the New England population. In his sermon inaugurating the Dorchester renewal of 1677, Mather asked rhetorically of the baptized noncommunicants, "Are not thousands of the Children of the Church guilty of breaking the Covenant, in that they remember not their *Baptismal Vow*" and accused them of "the dreadfull and amazing guilt of *Sacramental Perjury*." But there was yet hope if they could renew their covenant with the rest of the church, a neat elision that took for granted the fact of their membership and gave them a way to affirm it through a common ceremony with visible saints and minor children.[128] To renew the covenant, therefore, was to accept the first and less controversial part of the Halfway Covenant, the acknowledgment that adult children of the church remained members even if they did not proceed to the sacrament. Dorchester took the next step at its renewal ceremony by adopting the second part as well, finally acceding to the baptism of children of the church a good two decades after Increase's father Richard Mather first brought the issue before it. Norwich under Fitch had done exactly the same thing at its pioneering renewal the previous year, and time would show that the logic of linking the Halfway Covenant to this new ceremony was all but irresistible once covenant renewals became widespread and frequent.[129]

Covenant renewing gave the children of the church what they most needed: an alternative to the conversion narrative by which they could make a dramatic and visible statement of commitment. Even in the case of those churches that had previously adopted owning the covenant for children of members, the beneficiaries had remained perceptively second-class, birthright saints until the renewal ceremonies gave them the opportunity to become active moral agents called on to make an intelligent and meaningful choice as demonstrably valid as the visible saints who took the same covenant. Samuel Willard told Mather's North Church in 1680 on the occasion of their renewal: "Good and evil, God and the world have been set before you, if you have chosen God, you approve him as he is propounded; you have considered what it is that he requires of you, and you do approve of it, and consent to it, and what it is he promiseth, and it is well pleasing to you."[130]

For the first time in decades the personal and public dimensions of Puritan soteriology could be reintegrated. The renewal normally took place on a day of humiliation, another reinvigorated tradition. Collective fasting had been one of the defining ordinances of English Puritanism, a moment when searchers after faith could locate their own pilgrimages in the struggles of church and nation, but the institution was underdeveloped in America until after 1660. Then, for no obvious reason, and certainly not because of increased occasions, public days, especially days of humiliation, multiplied rapidly, perhaps as a concomitant to a spreading acceptance of the jeremiads communicated by the election sermons.[131] One should be cautious about attributing any New England development to a "felt need"—generally, somebody in particular did something in particular, usually at the expense of somebody else—but for whatever reason the fasts were already back in force. Mather actually had to dwell in his history of King Philip's War on the number of times disasters befell New England on days of humiliation as a means of insisting that the fast by itself was not enough to satisfy an angry God.[132] It was nonetheless the ideal setting for the renewal. Inward resolution, progress in the means, and moral reformation could all be fused through the ceremony, at once a stage on the individual path to salvation, a means for the restoration of wayward Israel, and a rite for averting divine judgment. The covenant renewal, Willard told Mather's church, was the banner under which they fought. "When Satan or any of his Instruments at any time seek to draw you aside, and perswade you to joyne with them in any vain and sinful deed," their resource would be to "call this day to remembrance, and say, shall I do this thing, who have covenanted with God against it?" It did not matter, Mather added, that those who took the covenant might still sometimes falter in the struggle. "That's no good Objection." As in taking communion, God would honor the sincerity of the resolution with which the covenant was made without regard to the likelihood that it would always be kept. Covenants, as a result, could and should be renewed regularly, at least annually.[133] Effectively, the renewal would replace the conversion narrative so dear to an earlier generation as the locus of the Puritan experience in America, the occasion on which the disparate strands of spiritual life came together and were given a common statement and direction.

No such results, however, could be achieved while the magistracy of the Bay remained under the domination of Leverett and his allies. Mather had coyly observed in 1676 that it would be desirable if the General Court would "recommend" covenant renewing to all the churches of the colony. "Otherwise it will meet with insuperable obstructions in some places." The circumstances under which he made this suggestion were a good measure of his immediate chances of having anyone accept it: his own unofficial version of an election sermon, delivered in his own bailiwick of the North Church because the magistrates had chosen his archrival Hubbard as the election preacher.[134] Next year, 1677, he got the chance by courtesy of the deputies to trot out his favorite themes before the General Court on an official basis, but his reception from "some" (one can guess whom) was so hostile he put off publication of the sermon until more suitable times two years later.[135] In the greatest indignity of all, one project he plumped for in the election sermon, an official history of New England to point up the lessons of the heroic generation for their unworthy successors, went by default to Hubbard, who chose in his *General History* to write a dull, patternless narrative in which the founders of the colonies held no privileged positions.[136]

At last in 1679 fortune favored Mather. Governor Leverett and Deputy

Governor Symonds both died and Salem's Hathorne retired from the magistracy. Thomas Clarke was already dead, leaving only Tyng among Mather's hardened opponents to linger on for one more year in the Bay Colony's upper house. And for lack of a figure of stature the governorship fell to the only surviving member of the original magistrates of the 1630s, Simon Bradstreet, who was temporarily in sympathy with Mather on most points. The Boston minister's sense of the dramatic would begin to fail him after 1700, with disastrous results, but for most of the seventeenth century he must have had the best timing in New England, and on this occasion he immediately took advantage of the situation in the showiest possible way. Leverett died on 16 March 1679. On 29 April Mather and Samuel Willard together took the freeman's oath before the Suffolk County Court, a visible symbol of the clergy's role in the politics of the colony.[137] On 28 May the General Court received a petition signed by a representative sampling of the colony's ministers but in Mather's handwriting calling for a synod "that there bee a more full enquiry made into the Causes and State of Gods Controversy with us."[138]

Considered by itself, the work of the Reforming Synod of 1679–80 must be the most exiguous in the history of Congregationalism. To avoid the least show of disunity, the synod propounded no original statement of polity or doctrine and deliberately took refuge in ambiguities on any point liable to dispute. The Cambridge Platform of 1648 was accepted as the fundamental draft of the New England Way "for the substance," but not clause by clause. The second session of the synod also adopted verbatim the Savoy Conference's mildly revised version of the Westminster Confession, but, in its only two additional changes, put in an article on church membership so generous it accommodated Solomon Stoddard and a statement on the magistrates' power in matters of religion (one of the avowed purposes in holding the meeting) so charitably worded it could have been written by the Baptists. On matters of moral reformation, Mather's masterpiece, *The Necessity of Reformation*, ended up ticking off the familiar catalog of sins and then calling for a more vigorous prosecution of laws already on the books.[139] The substance of the meeting was minimal, the gesture of enormous importance.

Under the heading, "What is to be done that so these Evils may be Reformed," the synod in the longest single article by far of its Result expounds on the theme, "Solemn and explicit Renewal of the Covenant is a Scripture Expedient for Reformation." Two further articles explain the terms to be used in the renewal, warning against a mere repetition of the original founding document of the church. The covenant of reformation should avoid contention and be broadly acceptable to all members of the particular church, but "it is needful that the sins of the Times should be engaged against, and Reformation thereof (in the name and by the help of Christ) promised before the Lord."[140] By banning controversy, the synod—really, Increase Mather, author of the call and the Result, as well as moderator of the second session—committed New England to what had been a highly controversial position only three years earlier. In convening the synod, the General Court accepted the crucial proposition, heretofore resisted, that a spiritual crisis of life-and-death proportions had gripped New England and demanded concerted effort to avert further disaster. First Church, though sans Leverett, saw the moral before the tale was ever told and answered the original call by the declaration that "wee doe not see light for the Calling of a Synod att this time," but then—sign of the new order—bowed to the inevitable and resolved to send delegates anyway in order to have a say in the outcome.[141]

Cotton Mather called the spate of covenant renewals that followed in 1680 (in North Church and Old South Church in Boston, at Salem and at Haverhill, and probably elsewhere) "the most notable Effect" of the Result of 1679. When the General Court in its wishy-washy manner judged it "meete to commend the same to the serious consideration of all the churches and people in this jurisdiction" and ordered the document printed at public expense, Increase Mather had at last his endorsement, however oblique, from the "civil Authority." The two ceremonies in Boston, along with successive renewals in the same churches, were a very effective form of publicity because so many nonresidents routinely passed through the economic center of New England and "there was usually a vast Confluence of People on these Occasions."[142] It was all going very well—if only Mather's synod could have found a way of overcoming the unmovable object that had necessitated the work of the assembly of 1657 and the synod of 1662 and then frustrated the implementation of their proposals. The scrupulosity and hesitancy of the laity were not going to evaporate merely from reading another set of clerically authored propositions.

People who were reluctant to seek full church membership or, if they were full members, to take communion, were doubly nonplussed by so tremendous an engagement as the covenant renewal. A God as angry as the clergy would have him had best not be provoked still further by annual declarations impossible to fulfill in all particulars. Two full years after their personal triumphs at the synod, Mather's coworker Samuel Willard was bemoaning (in the election sermon of 1682) the "damps and demurs" that were "cast on the work by the many that hold back." They all gave the same excuse, "viz. Lest it should encrease the guilt of the Churches through neglect of performance."[143] First Church, Boston, had played the only card left to it back in 1679 when it questioned the need for a synod, but it was a trump: the logic of the jeremiad, irresistible once in motion, would take hold only if the laity first found a motivation strong enough to overcome their deep-rooted hesitancy. John White had the international Protestant crisis and the tumult of English politics with which to call his Dorchester following into battle according to his plan; Increase Mather was making do with the continued fighting in Maine and the Boston fire of 1679.

The God of the Mathers had not done with New England yet, though he chose to move in ways too mysterious even for them to understand him. Mather had prophesied that the ultimate fate for a New England that failed to heed the Lord was to be "destroyed" in some physical sense and to be "cast off" spiritually in the manner of its biblical analogue Israel. Actually, he was mixing his biblical precedents. In the usual exegesis the Jews lost their status as a people chosen by God when they defaulted on their original engagement to believe that the messiah would come by denying Christ when he did come; thereupon, the designation *Israel* devolved upon all of the faithful regardless of nationality. The Israel of the prophetic period, which bore the main brunt of the New England analogy, was punished for its covenant breaking by the destruction of the Temple and the Babylonian captivity. It was "destroyed" but *not* "cast off." It remained Israel still, and the task of its prophets became one of comfort and explanation in place of their earlier mission to exhort to reformation. They must render the Exile intelligible by showing how a people without a polity or homeland or material religious symbols retained their special identity as the chosen, and they must offer hope by declaring how Israel would be again in some way what it had once been. New Englanders had no exact equivalent of the Temple, but they did possess charters that guaranteed their political autonomy and enabled them to protect and further the religion that was the basis of their distinctive identity, the New England Way. From 1680 onward it became apparent that these charters were in real danger of revocation and that the hour of temptation that Mather had been casting about for desperately in the 1670s was now about to have an all too literal fulfillment. There was a meaning to be distilled from this latest instance of imminent overthrow, one with more resonance and power than anything that had been imposed on the reverses of King Philip's War. It was to be found in Jeremiah, even more in Isaiah, and it was to be on this basis that the clergy of New England, Increase Mather in the van, were to complete their work.

6

Israel's Fate
The Definition of Establishment in
Puritan America, 1681–1700

Like his fellow Bostonian Samuel Sewall, Increase Mather double-dated the entries in his diary for the months when the Julian and Gregorian years did not correspond but really thought of New Year's Day as the first of January. Sewall reserved the opening month of the Gregorian year for the dramatic gestures he was so fond of, in one famous instance waking up the town of Boston with trumpets early on the morning of 1 January 1701 to welcome in the eighteenth century. (Appropriately, he would rest from his labors on New Year's Day in 1730.) Mather used the beginning of January more conventionally, to take stock of the past and speculate on the future. For January 1681 his diary opens with the simple entry, "This year begins awfully."[1]

He was referring to various prodigies and apparitions that seemed to betoken evils to come and that were the more ominous for following so soon after a giant "blazing star" at the end of the previous year. The very air of New England must have seemed thick with portents in the early months of 1681. Mather judged the moment propitious to organize his most ambitious project, the miscellaneous collection of signal occurrences, natural and supernatural, that was finally completed in late 1683 and published in 1684 as *An Essay for the Recording of Illustrious Providences*. It is easily the best-known item in a bibliography stretching to a good hundred entries published over almost six decades. Earlier generations of scholars saw a direct link between the long section of the book defending the reality of witchcraft and the Salem Village tragedy of 1692; more recent investigations take the book as representative of an essentially premodern collective mentality that still looked out in fear and reverence on a material world ruled by one form or another of invisible spirit. Actually, *Illustrious Providences* is a more parochial docu-

sand Ministers of God were Silenced at once as to their publick Testimony." His advice to New England on the impending calamity was for once concise: to "make sure of an Interest in Christ" and to remember that God had saved Israel from the pharaoh of Egypt and the king of Babylon.[9]

Making sense of this crisis was not nearly as easy as in the case of King Philip's War. That event was a sharp, discrete chastisement for colonial apostasy and debauchery. Relief came (in Mather's exegesis of the event, if not in Hubbard's or Governor Leverett's) when repentance was pledged in earnest by covenant renewal and the acceptance by the ministry of the Bay and the General Court of the Result of 1679. Further reverses of a similar nature were to be expected when reformation faltered, and they would call for rehearsal of the same measures. Diplomatic maneuvers and legal proceedings did not fit this scheme: they lacked the teleological and dramatic potential of the defeat at Bloody Brook or the Lancaster massacre. However unfortunate the final results were likely to be, the course of events and even its climax, the revocation of the charters, were in the first instance painless and intangible, not to mention hard to follow, full of wrong turnings, and, worst of all, protracted. From the first intimations of what was to come, in early 1681, to the arrival of the resident Nero in the person of Governor Sir Edmund Andros at the end of 1686, was a period of almost six years, and there was not a really theatrical moment in the entire course of it, except for the ceremonial transfer of power in early 1686 to an interim council under the renegade Joseph Dudley, and even this body represented only a caretaker tyranny. The most that could be done with this unpromising raw material was to grow vivid in describing the simultaneous miseries being inflicted on the Protestants in Hungary and in France or to seize on Colonel Percy Kirke's butchering of good Protestant rebels in the West Country in 1685 as a deliverance— it kept him, after all, from butchering better Protestants still in New England, to which he had initially been assigned as the first royal governor.

A William Hubbard, to be sure, had no need to invest the imminent fall of the charters with any special significance. He could just announce that Christians generally needed strong doses of adversity as an antidote to the temptations of prosperity, though in his characteristically individual fashion he ascribed the present lapses to a change in New England's carrying trade from transporting necessities to corrupting luxuries—"all the produce in a manner of the whole Countrey is converted to maintain a commerce of superfluous vanities," especially sack and West Indian sugar.[10] Mather's ally Samuel Willard, a cooler customer than his colleague from the North End, similarly invoked a cyclical notion of the fortunes of the Lord's people, though he laced his exhortation to the traditional Christian virtues of fortitude and resignation with a certain grim confidence in the ultimate outcome of times of trial: "Be quiet, let God alone, he will do his own work, and that to purpose; Tarry a little and you shall see these Bravos weltering in their own gore, and the arrows of the Almighty drunk with their blood."[11] Mather was not by temperament given to tarrying, and he was in no position to let the Lord alone. He needed something more than timeless generalities to explain the meaning of New England history as it now seemed to run from its fated foundations to the absurd denouement of a quo warranto writ brought against the Bay charter in 1683. He had to show that the Puritan colonies were not just northerly New Yorks or Virginias.

In *Illustrious Providences* he did not show it. He had no real signs of his own to guide him, so he settled for his desperately piled together heap of instances tending, more often than not, to prove that God works in man's affairs, somehow or other. But by 1684 he had felt his way to firm ground in *The Doctrine of Divine Providence Opened and Applyed*, a kind of introduction to *Illustrious Providences* that provided the interpretive commentary it so obviously lacked. He had discovered in the jeremiad tradition the unexpected corollary that afflictions were a guarantor against total destruction. The Lord had put in much too much time on New England to throw the whole thing away. "The great and wonderful things which God has done for his New-England People," molding them by alternate chastisements and deliverances, ensured that so purposive a work would have to continue, if only to be a fit object of further discipline when the occasion arose: "And shall we think that God has done these great and marvellous things, that so all his work might be destroyed again within one Generation? . . . The Lord may afflict us because of our Backslidings which are many, but he will not destroy us."[12]

The timing once again was exquisite. This declaration of optimism appeared in a sermon collection bearing a preface written on 28 October 1684. On 23 June of that year Chancery had finally vacated the Massachusetts charter. Word of the decision was read out before the General Court on 11 September and acted upon in an inconclusive manner on 16 October, when the Bay Colony's legislature—if such it remained—instructed its London counsel to do something, anything, to get the charter back, though "wee know not what could be done more, nor cannot direct for future."[13] The General Court would linger on, absorbed in a progressively more acrimonious debate over its expiring legality, for another nineteen months, and Connecticut and Plymouth would escape for a little longer, but only the clergy of the colonies, whose authority did not rest on any charters, were in a position to know what do more and to direct for the future. In the long contest among the constituent elements of the Puritan movement, the balance of power was about to be altered decisively in favor of the ministry.

Jeremiah and Isaiah, already much employed in controversial fashion in the 1660s and 1670s, could be used to provide a universally acceptable meaning for the 1680s. The reason the lights were going out was obvious enough: "Alas that this people hath layn no more low before God, let the Prophets of the Lord and all the Lord's people mourn, and their souls weep for the Pride of *New-England*, as he *Jer.* 13.17." So said William Adams in the Massachusetts election sermon of 1685, which he had every reason to believe to be the last in that series ever to be preached under the authority of the charter. (Appropriately, that honor actually fell to an effort by the author of *The Day of Doom*.) But it was visibly late in the day in New England, and Adams's main theme was his exegesis of the final chapter of Isaiah, in which God declares that he needs no temple, and the restoration of Zion after the Exile is foretold. Notwithstanding "the *removal* of the Glory and of his Kingdom" from the nation of Israel because of "their particular sins, and their Obstinacy in them," the Lord "promises *to preserve a remnant* in this calamity, whom he would follow with signal favours where ever they should be cast, and reserve to better times."[14] If the word *remnant* seemed a little alarming, the next month Increase Mather applied the promises of Isaiah broadcast out of verse 14, chapter 32 (the assurance of the preservation of Judah after the destruction of the ten tribes by the Assyrians): "Doctrine The Church of God shall stand and abide for ever. Probable that New England Church shall doe soe." On 28 January 1686, when the arrival of a royal governor was expected momentarily, it was Cotton Mather's turn, preaching on Isaiah 33:17, "Thine eyes shall see the King in his beauty: They shall behold the Land that is very far off." Samuel Sewall immediately praised "the excellency and seasonableness of the subject."[15] In his go at the subject Increase Mather had not said that the *governments* of the colonies would abide forever. The churches were the Israel that would survive the equivalent of the fall of Jerusalem, the destruction of the Temple, and the Exile. The analogy was potent because it had very real and practical points of reference in the self-governing ecclesiastical societies of each town, provided they could extend their reach to include in one gradation of affiliation or another virtually the entire population. This was not a vision of the churches of the catacombs or of the conventicles, select bands preserving the light in a land of darkness. That would do for Marian or Caroline England perhaps, but no one in the

Puritan colonies assumed that the greater share of the population was primarily an irreligious multitude only too eager to follow timeserving and turncoat clergy. Nor was the biblical analogy preferred in America in any way indebted to contemporary Dissenting writers, who used a collective metaphor for the individual struggle against worldly trials and sinful inclinations and so usually favored periods of Israelite history before the establishment of the Hebrew kingdom, especially the Egyptian bondage and the forty years of wandering in the wilderness.[16] The Puritan colonies had been established too long and with (dare it be admitted) too much success for their inhabitants to refer to themselves only in terms of the travails of the church militant everywhere without geographic specification. The New England Way, rather, was obliged to become the New England identity; a common religious profession and a distinctive code of conduct would have to form the basis of, in effect, an ethnic collectivity. The visible organization of this people without a polity would be the only one left to them, their churches. If the personal rule of Charles I had cast the Puritan movement in its most sectarian mold, the Andros regime completed the reverse movement in favor of comprehension.

At the moment of truth, in the mid-1680s, individual churches were less in need of liberalized standards of admission than of some rationalization of the various forms of membership that had accreted haphazardly around the two sacraments and the administration of discipline. Since lack of coordination remained a hallmark of New England Congregationalism, even when exposed to the same acute stimulus, responses were typically varied. Salem and Dorchester, two churches that had been unusually innovative in the previous decades, again revealed most clearly the direction in which inchoate movements elsewhere also tended.

Salem's case is made the more interesting by the lack of significant protest in a church that as recently as 1680 had verged on schism. In November 1684 John Higginson, twice previously the target of dissenters who resented his deviations from "pure" Congregationalism, was able to obtain unanimous consent to his latest changes after giving potential opponents the opportunity to "express their scruples, fears and doubts." He received carte blanche to invite into a degree of membership in the church anyone not openly scandalous or ignorant and to clean up the various forms of anomalous status that time and chance had created. The Halfway Covenant was offered to four classes of individuals, of whom the largest was undoubtedly "the children of such Christians as live amongst us, though not members of this or any other Particular church." The other three groups, however, are not without historical significance: children of members of the Salem church whose parents had died before presenting them for baptism, adult children of the church who had not been baptized because of their parents' scruples over infant baptism, and their children as well, and the nonresidents once more, "the children of other churches who live amongst us and they have children also." Two and a half years later, in May 1687, Higginson put the finishing touches on this reorientation of the church membership by proposing to invite "divers of the Children of other Churches being amongst us desiring to be admitted to the Lords Supper" into full communion on the same generous terms already available to children of Salem's own church. The vote in favor was "nemine contradicente."[17] Church membership at Salem had ceased to be either the exclusive property of the fraternity of saints, however scattered over the landscape since their original pledge of fellowship, or a simple heritable right transmitted through the loins of the elect over the generations. It had become the ordinary way the people of the town affirmed their allegiance to New England in the location in which they resided. This organization was in no sense a parish system: membership was still voluntary and still a little arduous so that it had to be taken up in steps, and not every believer rose to first-class sainthood. But membership at whatever stage was a universally available form of volitional commitment, the only such form in a royal colony lacking any other meaningful exercise of citizenship.

At Dorchester the direct influence of the crisis of the charters on ecclesiology was even more overt. Throughout the early 1680s the church treated itself to two or three fasts a year "in respect of the troubles and sad estate of the protestant interest in other parts of the world and in our native country, and the great fears concerning our selves." In mid-1685 the defenses began to be put in order—a monthly lecture under the new minister was voted in March, the Result of the Reforming Synod was read out in April for the purpose of explaining "the provoking sines that we stood guilty off and to be Humbled for" (a curious banner to rally around but what they had). In May the church went back further still into the past and revived the magistrates' order of 1669 "to excit the Elders and minester to take Care of their flocks" (meaning the entire population) by house-to-house pastoral visits and religious instruction for all residents. Dorchester organized catechizing sessions for all children aged eight to sixteen, as well as sexually separate meetings for religious instruction for the sixteen- to twenty-four-year-olds.[18] Every person in Dorchester would know the cause for which all must endure.

Once the Andros regime took hold, the Dorchester church became a shadow government, paralleling the public days called by the Dominion with fasts of its own (never thanksgivings) that were appointed for good jere-miadic reasons echoing the language of the proclamations of the Old Charter magistrates. The next logical step, the extension and reorganization of disci-pline, waited until 1688, but when the time came Dorchester made the bold-est moves of any New England church. On 9 September the children of the church that "weer grown up and had not submitted to the Government of Christ in the Church" were called to do so, probably as in 1677 by taking hold of the covenant of reformation, and adults who had submitted but had since moved received a blanket dismission to the churches of their present residences, "nemine contradicente." On the same day the tie to the nonresi-dent members in full communion was cut at last, and they too were dismissed en masse to whatever churches they happened to live near. "The Church would have noe more to do with them or others recommended except in Case they fall into Scandall." (It was not possible, even here, to exorcise uncondi-tionally those invisible bonds of the original fellowship pledged no one was sure how many years before.) Admission to halfway membership of individu-als who had no blood ties to existing members did not come until the 1690s, but the die was cast in the last days of the Old Charter and under the Dominion, when the church became for a time the only institutional reposi-tory for the cultural identity of a people somehow led into Babylonian captiv-ity without being forced into physical exile.[19]

Elsewhere in New England the adaptations were less dramatic. A number of churches agreed to make qualification for full communion a less painful process by allowing written conversion narratives or, abandoning the fiction that oral narrations stirred up nonmembers to emulation, by restricting the witnesses to the ceremony to the relatively small number already full mem-bers themselves. Covenant renewals must have increased measurably if Sam-uel Willard, never given to Matheresque hyperbole, was able to say in 1694, just twelve years after he had made the opposite observation, that "many also, if not the most of our *Churches* have with Solemnity revived their *Covenant* Obligations to God." A rush of people into halfway membership in a number of churches in the years 1685 to 1688 similarly indicates a new popular willingness to take a qualified risk, venturing the hazard of a moder-ately angry god in order to declare solidarity against a potentially heathen magistrate.[20] The bulk of the population of New England became in the 1680s, without distinction as to genealogy, the people of God, for whom succor and exhortation were more relevant than imprecation. Speaking of the sin against the Holy Ghost (incorrigibly refusing Christ), Increase Mather in the fall of 1685 was "perswaded there is not one soul in this Congregation this day, that ever was guilty of it." It was the same congregation to which just a few years earlier he had announced that some of them had never prayed in their lives and that many of them who were not spending days at a time in Boston taverns secretly wished that they were. Now his message read, *The Greatest Sinners Exhorted and Encouraged to Come to Christ and that Now without Delaying.*[21]

As direct rule from England became more likely, leading ministers in the Bay began to take precautions against the awful time when the churches might not be permitted to continue openly. "And wither we may live to see the doors of Gods house shut up, and publick Worship interdicted, is with Him alone to determine," wrote Samuel Willard in the first year that the possibility was relevant, 1686. God's people elsewhere had experienced sore temptations to deny their faith, and (nice pun) "we dwell in a world where they may be expected, nor have we any *charter* that gives us special immunity from meeting the like."[22] Recourse was to be had where Puritans had been forced to find it before, though never previously in America: first in the printed word, which could speak when the preacher was silenced, and then in visible and distinguishing orthopraxy, which could bear witness to the truth in mundane deeds when words said in public were at the disposal of the wrong people.[23] The heathen magistrate could divest the Sabbath of its rightful legal protection, he could profane it himself, but he could not make the godly follow him if they fully understood the meaning and importance of this weekly renewal of the covenant with Abraham. If worst came to worst, the laity would be left with more than consolation; they would have the guides to enable them to carry on independently until the Lord saw fit, most likely sooner rather than later, to restore his people to their rightful liberties.

Heavenly Merchandize, the work in which Willard had uttered his dire prophecy, was also one of the survival manuals. Willard provided a detailed account of how the truth may be known when either persecution or too much toleration makes discerning it difficult: follow neither authority, popularity, esotericism, or undiluted rationalism, but rely on the obvious sense of Scripture. An extended discussion of exegetics follows, directed to a lay audience.[24] *A Brief Discourse on Justification*, his other major work of 1686, is designed to present a statement of that central doctrine that is short, cheap, and accessible, "considering that the smalness of the Book might invite some to read it, that would not allow themselves time to peruse larger tracts on the Subject; or to be at the expense to purchase them." The tract remarks almost in passing (as Willard was wont to do) that the wicked may give the righteous "a great deal of outward molestation; they may pervert Justice, and *condemn* you as wicked persons, they may *rifle* your houses, imprison your persons, take away your lives, and remove you from off the face of the earth, yea and make you the scorn of men, and expose your names to slanders and obliquie." Christians had passed through all this before, and the cause for which they suffered had never been extirpated and never would be.[25]

Increase Mather's contribution to the projected guerrilla warfare was a republication of an English dissenting manual, *Self-Employment in Secret*, in late 1684, and then in 1686 a simple guide to Christology, his exhortation to the greatest sinners, and his *Arrow* against mixed dancing. ("'Twas not a time for New England to dance," as Joshua Moodey remarked.) Later in 1686, after royal government had taken hold, the Mathers fooled the censor (no longer *their* censor) by using the abandoned college press at Cambridge to issue anonymously *A Brief Discourse Concerning the Unlawfulnesse of Common Prayer*. Finally, in the fall of the year Increase varied this trick by writing a *Testimony* against a long list of vices no longer forbidden by law (health drinking, gambling, observing Christmas, giving gifts at New Year's, cockfighting, keeping saint's days, and following the old Christian calendar in general) and then sending it to London for publication in 1687, with a Boston reprint of the "English" tract following in 1688.[26]

There is an obvious exuberance in this resort to underground techniques by members of the former establishment. But the grimness of the vision, serious measures for a deadly serious situation, gave it its true force. The grip of this clerically inspired interpretation of imperial politics is revealed vividly in the other cause célèbre of 1686, the execution of one James Morgan at Boston for a murder committed during a drunken brawl, precisely because the entire episode was on the surface nonpolitical. Sermons preached at Morgan by both Mathers and First Church's Joshua Moodey, along with a final colloquy between the condemned man and Cotton en route to the gallows and up the scaffold steps, provided a cycle of printed works, immediately popular and frequently reprinted. Morgan by his own confession and through reiterated clerical commentary is made to stand for the reigning vices of New England: intemperance, neglect of the means, Sabbath breaking. A few moments before his execution, asked to name "which of all your sins you are now most sorry for—which lies most heavy," he omits his victim altogether and instead replies dolefully and dutifully, "On sabbath days I us'd to lie at home, or be ill employ'd elsewhere, when I should have been at church." As he is representative sinner, so he becomes representative penitent, and, after much cross-examination, is left with the hope of salvation through unfeigned reliance on Christ's righteousness, his last words being "O Lord—I come, I come, I come."[27]

No doubt a part of the attraction of this event lay (and lies) in its lurid interest. The lesson was, however, intended to be, in Cotton Mather's words, "applyed unto *All men* in general, and unto a *Condemned Malefactor* in particular." Morgan's life is in pared-down form the story of all redeemed and redeemable sinners in the apparently successful travail of one such, exemplary in both his guilt and expiation. But "all men" were not the audience for the event or the clerical moralizing on it; only those living in New England were. Given the vices confessed by Morgan and the climactic year in which this well-arranged, well-publicized ceremony was staged, it was also the story of New England, faced with deserved cultural extinction for the guilt enumerated by jeremiad after jeremiad but offered salvation nonetheless in return for genuine repentance. This was quintessential Puritanism, the fusion of a personal salvation with both the ordo salutis and immediate, epochal political struggle. At last, in the white heat of 1686 there was no way of denying the logic of the argument of the jeremiad; indeed, apart from outright apostasy, it was the only argument that had any logic left in it.

Earlier in his career Increase Mather had predicted that "if that wall of Government, which hath hitherto been such a mercy to this people" should be taken away, "there are three Evils, that would quickly follow; *viz. Superstition, Prophaneness,* and *Persecution.*"[28] By the time Governor Andros finally arrived, the Puritan colonies had thrown up emergency ramparts and herded most of the population behind them. Andros trampled on local sensibilities with an unplanned, purposeless vigor in an orgy of tactlessness no subsequent royal governor in his right senses would dare to imitate—violating the Puritan Sabbath with gusto, forcing deponents in legal cases to take their oaths on the Bible, "confiscating" Old South Church for a period of hours every Sunday to hold Common Prayer services before he turned it back to its protesting congregation for the rest of the day. He received in turn, however, neither substantial resistance nor significant cooperation. New Englanders under the Dominion were as far removed as could be from the inhabitants of East Anglia in the days of Wren and Laud, driven in polarized directions toward acquiescence or riot, submission or emigration.

By 1686 American Puritans possessed in the clergy an alternative leadership and, no less important, a meaningful theology and a persuasive theodicy already worked out for them in the divisive decades of the 1660s and 1670s. That heroic past originally invoked for partisan reasons to upbraid the present inhabitants by comparing them to their mythologized forebears now served the very different purpose of assuring the posterity that the great work of their ancestors was too solidly built to be toppled by a royal governor. Degenerate or not, the present generation was incorporated into the common, divinely secured errand of its parents and grandparents. Early in 1686, as the news circulated in Boston of the sighting of the frigate *Rose*, bearing official notification of the voiding of the charter, Samuel Sewall was circulating the first American reprint of the sermon in which John Cotton in 1630 had seen off the Winthrop fleet with an explication of 2 Samuel 7:10: "Moreover I will appoint a place for my people Israel, and will plant them, that they may dwell in a place of their own, and move no more; neither shall the children of wickedness afflict them any more, as beforetime."[29] John Higginson, who had come to America before Winthrop, fleshed out the contemporary significance of the Migration in a sermon of his own a few months after Sewall brought out the reprint. Seeing potential martyrs where covert Morellians had once stood, Higginson found it appropriate that the mission of New England should include a bout of persecution to give the descendants of the founders their own turn to display an exemplary testimony for the benefit of a benighted world: "Our Fathers came into this Wilderness merely and purely upon this account, *viz.* for their Testimony to Christ and his Gospel, and against Humane Inventions and additions in the Worship of God." Half a century of peace had been allotted New Englanders to perfect the truths of the gospel, and now that it could reasonably be assumed that the task was finished, "the witnessing work is now devolved upon us and committed unto us." The Laudian regime had fathered New England, the parallel persecution of the fall of the charters confirmed its meaning as "engaged by the special Providence of God, in this duty of bearing witness unto Christ and against Antichrist, and that more than any people in the world that we know of."[30] In America, as in England, but with different consequences, the Good Old Cause received its most compelling formulation at the very point when officially it was defunct.

The most profound effect of the hurried reshuffling of familiar themes in the 1680s was the detachment of church and culture from any presumption of direct and regular intervention by the state except perhaps of a hostile nature. Such permanence as Puritanism attained in the eighteenth century rested on this uncoupling and the alternative modes of thought and action that were developed in consequence. But in the brief era of the Dominion, from 1686 to 1689, and in the three succeeding years, when the Puritan colonies lacked any civil government of indisputable legitimacy, the most immediate effect of what might be called Exilic thinking was almost the opposite of the eighteenth-century settlement. By default, an unusual measure of political responsibility suddenly devolved on the clergy and on the man who used the 1680s to gain paramountcy among his fellow clergymen, Increase Mather. There was, of course, a little more to Increase Mather's new centrality besides his mastery of theodicy. He enjoyed his popular standing, short-lived as it was, because he was also a proven patriot. When push came to shove in the last years of the Old Charter, he dramatically chose the right side, making it the winning side by his addition of strength, growing stronger himself by assuming its leadership. He gave his endorsement at the crucial moment to the last-ditch resisters of the coming royal government, the men whose political cohesion rested in large part on their earlier opposition to the Halfway Covenant and anything that smacked of clerical power. It may, perhaps, have seemed a little anomalous to have presided over the expansion in the definition of the New England churches while switching sides from (in contemporary parlance) the "Presbyterians" to the "Morellians," but the inapposite combination of ecclesiastical and political loyalties made for a genuine coalition.

Politics in the early 1680s amounted to a new game with old players. In 1680 the government of Charles II had ordered that the Bay Colony obey the terms of its charter and elect a full complement of eighteen men to the office of assistant, hoping that the extra eight magistrates would all be individuals "serviceable" to his majesty's interests in the colony. In fact, the new men elected over the next three years left the upper house evenly divided between conciliationists and old-fashioned hard-liners, with the result that in 1683, when the crown ordered Massachusetts to surrender the charter for "remodeling" or face its certain voiding in the courts, the upper house was deadlocked and the deputies were solidly opposed to surrender.[31] The initiative then fell to the clergy, who on the whole had little idea of how to use their heightened political role. As a body the ministry of the Bay were never the remorseless guardians of a threatened "theocracy" as they are sometimes pictured. Though mostly conciliationists up to a point, they had also committed themselves to oppose "any thing that may have the least tendency towards yielding up or weakening this government as by patent established." But when Governor Bradstreet actually asked their advice in this crisis they gave a completely equivocal reply to his queries concerning the morality of surrender.[32]

It was a moment of equilibrium, almost of stasis, the ideal setting for one of Increase Mather's ventures in self-appointment, and he seized the opportunity with considerable panache. Late in 1683 he turned on Bradstreet and the conciliationists, throwing in his lot with what was fast becoming the party of

Leverett *redivivus*. It was all carefully prepared, from private lobbying to public performance. First he gathered together in coherent form the arguments against surrender currently in circulation, then added some more of his own devising, and finally communicated the results to some of the *résistant* magistrates, "who so well approved of them as to disperse copyes thereof, that they came into many hands, and were a meanes to keep the Countrey from complying with that proposal." An invitation followed from the Boston deputies (to a man First Church stalwarts with impeccable sectarian pedigrees) for a grand appearance before the town meeting on 23 January 1684, at which Mather, rising to the occasion, brilliantly united secular and religious, moral and prudential arguments in favor of holding out to the bitter end: surrender would be self-defeating, a violation of the trust handed down from the founding to the present generation, apostasy of the highest order, and (a new theme) an act unworthy of those who proudly claimed the rights of Englishmen.[33] Mather undoubtedly took his stand on principle, but as usual he had prepared his ground carefully beforehand, chosen the forum for the decisive gesture deliberately, and so timed matters that he was inevitably swimming with the tide.

In the next election, in May 1684, the results were unprecedented. Under Mather's leadership the "Morellians" accomplished what they had so dismally failed to do in 1671 at Oxenbridge's behest. Three of the magistrates who had signed Bradstreet's letter to England promising to work for surrender failed of reelection and the remainder took a tumble in their vote totals, while five hard-liners marched in to fill the vacancies created by the death or defeat of incumbents, radically altering the balance of power in the upper house.[34] "The prudent man is no changling," complained Mather's old nemesis William Hubbard. "There is nothing more directly tends to confusion in Church or State, than for persons of principal place in either, to shift their station."[35] It was a good shot at the man who now had added a political turnabout to his earlier reversal on the Halfway Covenant, but the target was way out of range. The two succeeding elections only ratified the trend, as another two of the moderates gave way to men committed to holding out until the last moment.[36] When that moment came at last in 1686, the General Court, packed with deputies from towns sending their full delegations for the first time in years and boasting a solid majority of patriot magistrates, knew exactly where to look for their second Nehemiah.

The single most startling feature of this abrupt shift in Bay Colony politics is the continuing importance of the ancient but still fundamental cleavage in American Puritanism originally exposed by the controversy over the Halfway Covenant. Of the new patriot magistrates elected in the last years of the Old Charter, four had signed the deputies' dissent of 1671 against repealing the anticlerical blast of the previous year, and another three were the sons and political heirs of signers.[37] On the other side, among the purged assistants, two had been supporters of Higginson in the disputes at Salem and a third was John Woodbridge himself, the occasion of the Newberry church controversy. "He must need be very dull of understanding," wrote William Hubbard about 1684, "who doth not observe how in our Constitution, Difference in church matters are like to have no small influence upon our Civil Affairs; especially when it is ready to come to siding and making of parties." The text to which these words serve as an introduction identifies the parties in question as, respectively, those individuals, clerical and lay, stigmatized as Presbyterian and the group called by them in turn Morellians and Brownists.[38]

Chief beneficiary of this unprecedented mobility in Bay Colony politics was the Morellian citadel, Boston's First Church. Without being actively hostile to the expansion of church membership taking place all around it, First Church had remained aloof from the trend. It had come to terms with the crisis of the charters principally by initiating a reconciliation with the schismatic Old South in 1682.[39] This conciliatory gesture laid the basis for a potent political alliance of Boston South Enders in years to come, but the church itself remained a gathered community of proven and tested visible saints. Such uncompromising purity attracted militants from other churches who moved to Boston and served the members in good stead in politics at a time when any compromise was discredited as submission to both tyranny and popery.[40] From its nadir at the death of Governor Leverett in 1679 the church roared back into dominance in the mid-1680s, election after election. By 1686 no less than seven of the eighteen magistrates were from the town of Boston and a full five of them were First Church zealots. All three of Boston's deputies that year were also members of the church, and one of them was elected speaker by a defiant house on 13 May 1686 as the *Rose* finally hove into view off Boston Bay. In the next election of town selectmen, the only form of representative government permitted under the Dominion, Boston chose five First Church men (three of them members of the final General Court), giving them an absolute majority in local government.[41] However generously the body of Israel might be defined in its Exile under the Dominion, First Church members were Israelites indeed; a vote for them was an affirmation of New England's enduring values and a witness that the values did most certainly endure.

The fortunes of what subsequently came to be known throughout the provincial period as the "popular party" in Massachusetts were laid here in the very last years of the Old Charter. At a time when prudent men of all parties feared that hostility to England would verge over into outright disorder and hoped to reach a consensus on keeping the peace until a royal governor arrived, Samuel Nowell and Elisha Cooke in particular were notorious fire-eaters and the First Church gang as a whole cultivated an electoral following on the basis of their diehard stance.[42] Their popularity was such that the deputies elected one of their number speaker of the house on almost every occasion from 1683 on and in 1685 tried to throw the entire power of the magistracy in their hands by proposing that laws might pass in the upper house when voted for by the "greater number of the Magistrates present" rather than an absolute majority.[43] (Ordinarily, Boston's magistrates, overwhelmingly First Church in allegiance, would be much more likely to be present at a meeting of the magistrates than assistants from more distant towns.)

Men who came to the fore by flaunting their irreconcilability made unusual allies for the supreme tactician Increase Mather, but in the decade of the 1680s demonstrations of inflexibility were just another tactic in his considerable repertoire. On 19 November 1685 at the Boston weekly lecture he can be found taking as his text Numbers 25:11, in which the Lord averts his wrath from Israel because of the zeal of Phineas, and applying it to mean "that if the Government of New England were zealous might yet save this People." Then the congregation sang the second part of the seventy-ninth Psalm: "Let not the Heathen Prevail."[44] Asking whether Mather really thought there was much chance of saving the charter government is beside the point. He was keeping in with his new allies, who made support for the charter a symbol of their allegiance to a Puritan New England even as the document was in its last days. On 9 May 1686 Boston elected a First Church militant, Penn Townsend, as its deputy in the place of still another First Church man, Isaac Addington, promoted to the magistracy for the hours left to that office, when everyone in town must have known that the action had no practical value, whatever its power as a witness: Edward Randolph, the collector of customs, had already been through Boston that very morning bearing the royal commission for a new, assemblyless government, and two of the most pliable magistrates had been sent to inform the rest. On the Sunday following, it was still no compromise with the inevitable. Samuel Willard at the Old South, ever the realist, "prayed not for the Governour or Government, as formerly, but spake so as implied it to be changed or changing." The minister in the pulpit at First Church doggedly "prayed for Governour and Deputy Governour."[45]

The trouble with such an alliance from Increase Mather's point of view was not the terms themselves—he had played the purist before—but that they were by definition not open to renegotiation at some later date. In 1686, however, this awkward contingency could hardly be envisioned. What *was* apparent in the devastated political landscape of New England was the residual authority left with the clergy now that all popular civil government was in abeyance and the prominence of one masterful clergyman as the leader and spokesman of all his kind. The most useful and important native ally the royal government had recruited, Joseph Dudley, who had more political sense than the whole of English officialdom in America combined, recognized the way things had come to be arranged when, at the very moment he inaugurated his brief interim government in place of the Old Charter, he also ostentatiously courted Increase Mather. He assured the North End minister that "for the things of my soul I have these many years hung upon your lips, and ever shall; and in civil things am desirous you may know with all plainness my reasons of procedure, and that they may be satisfactory to you."[46] Dudley did not mean any of it; Mather must have known as much, and Dudley probably sensed Mather's skepticism. They went through the courting dance anyway, even to the point of the governing council over which Dudley presided legalizing and making permanent Mather's presidency of Harvard, because the royalist adventurer knew, as his successor, Edmund Andros, did not, that he had too few bayonets even to sit on. Sensibly, Dudley chose to negotiate with the man who had become the recognized spokesman of the real tribal heads of the native population.

Privately, Mather was "wayting and praying for an earthquake, which shall issue in the downfall of the Lords enemies and the exaltation of Christs Kingdome and Interest." It was to come in 1689, but in the meanwhile, in 1687, he got up addresses, first from the ministers of the Bay, then from the churches as a whole, thanking James II for his Declaration of Indulgence allowing liberty of worship to Nonconformists. Next, late in the same year, after consultation with "sundry good and wise men" he got himself commissioned by the churches to present this vote of thanks to the monarch in person in England—and in the name of "the Dissenters of New England" to work for security of land titles, confirmation of Harvard's legal standing, restoration of the colonial assembly, and, under the heading of the aforementioned liberty of conscience, an end to those symbolic but obnoxious gestures by which Andros had so efficiently and pointlessly confirmed the Puritans' worst fears.[47] When James II fled England in 1688, Mather took on the responsibility of trying to secure the restoration of the Bay Colony charter from the new government of William III, and this undertaking marked both the height of his power and the origins of his subsequent undoing.

Mather was not the first minister to serve the Bay Colony as an agent in England while still ordained over a New England church. He was, however, the first clergyman whose religious vocation was central to the nature and success of his mission. A secular element of sorts was added to his agency in 1690, when the restored General Court appointed him its official representative, but the old Massachusetts legislature had no legal standing, and Mather was in England primarily to speak in the name of the congregations of New England. He was able to accomplish anything at all mainly because of this prior commission from the Bay Colony churches and his own skill at exploiting it, not because of a dubious delegation from a pretended legislature vulnerable at any moment to the charge of treason.

In all probability, Mather did not much relish calling himself or his countrymen Dissenters and Nonconformists, but the political capital to be made from assuming this uncomfortable stance was considerable. As an important New England minister and the president of the colonies' college—he learned to flaunt that title, which he had not originally thought much of, only in England, where it looked formidable—he enjoyed considerable standing among English Nonconformists. Both James II and William III were, for different reasons, on such precarious ground that they were obliged to give the Dissenting interest a prominent place in their political calculations, a circumstance Mather traded on heavily and the only really strong card he held. He did not get the Old Charter restored in the end, though he tried hard, but he did secure a new one in 1691 restoring an elected lower house to the Bay Colony. He was also able to nominate the first royal governor and name all twenty-eight members of his council.[48] No single man in New England had exercised so much influence since the death of the elder John Winthrop, and no clergyman ever had. On the slender basis of his clerical fame and his Harvard presidency Mather could and did claim to be the only universally accepted leader of the only acknowledged polity in New England, the concert of congregations he had gotten to commission him in 1686. The Puritan colonies had come closest to being the "church-state" still beloved of the textbooks (and as a hybrid roughly on the same logical order as the Snark or the Chimera) in this single period from 1686 to 1692, when they could hardly have been anything else. There would nonetheless be a price to pay for this too complete realization of the theocratic ideal, and well before the bill came due to Increase Mather twenty lives would be lost to the witchcraft epidemic and the Bay Colony's ministry would have made an irreparable shipwreck of a good conscience. When the Bay Colony ministry resumed their role as the leading interpreters of the Puritan movement, it would be as chastened men who had learned to their cost (and to the cost of several hundred others) just how dangerous it could be to possess in any degree the imperium that Mather had projected for them in the 1670s and that he had obtained with unforeseen consequences in the era of the Dominion.

While Increase Mather in England was seeking restitution of the Old Charter, all went well as long as he failed to accomplish anything practical. In time, however, Mather's fundamental tractability resurfaced. Realizing that the colonial policy of William and Mary was mostly that of James II tempered by a little caution, he worked out the best deal he could. The New Charter, which came into effect in 1692, added New Plymouth to the Bay Colony and confirmed its jurisdiction over Maine, replaced the church member franchise with a generous property requirement, and mandated religious liberty. Connecticut and Rhode Island were allowed to resume their original elected governments, but Massachusetts was saddled with a royal governor and a much expanded executive also appointed by the crown and was obliged for the future to submit its statutes to the King in Council for final approval. Mather's charter did restore to the colony an elected lower house, now called the House of Representatives, and he was also able to secure a unique arrangement by which the upper house, the Council, was elected annually by the newly elected representatives and the outgoing board of councillors voting jointly, although these choices too were subject to the royal governor's veto. The larger half of the new Israel was now just another royal colony, enjoying a few extra privileges in recognition of its half-century of virtual independence but otherwise unremarkable in its explicitly subordinate polity.

Mather had the talent to infuse even this unpromising situation with the spirit of New England's historic mission. The Puritan colonies remained distinctive because of their ancestry, their primitive achievements, their current degeneracy, and their ecclesiastical order, all the more important now because Congregationalism at least had the advantage of being unusual. The heroic first generation had fled to America to create the only churches in Christendom genuinely ordered in all particulars according to biblical precepts. "Other Plantations were built upon a Worldly Interest but *New-England* was founded on an Interest purely Religious, and this not so much in respect of the Faith of [the] Gospel (in which we agree with all other Reformed Churches in *Europe*) as of the Order of it." The present generation was "much degenerated from what once we were," and everyone agreed "that there are far more ill men amongst us, than there were Forty years ago." (This calculation made the execrated 1660s the benchmark from which to measure the current decline.) Nevertheless, there were still left "some Thousands of them who fear God," and the church order, though threatened by exponents of new doctrines, still remained in the form that the builders of the Temple propounded.[49] Under these circumstances, the New Charter preserved and protected the essence of the original mission through the degree of home rule it guaranteed. It required toleration of all Protestants, but in matters of faith abstractly considered New Englanders were just a branch of the Reformed churches and had no business molesting the worship of adherents of other branches. The General Court should, indeed must, give positive encouragement by law to Massachusetts' own distinctive church order—it was the reason they were all there in the first place in this scheme—and this, as Increase Mather read his handiwork, the New Charter of 1692 most certainly permitted. As in England, there would be an establishment and a licensed dissent, though the roles of Congregationalists and Anglicans (among others) would be reversed.[50]

On the whole, Mather's plausible apology for an anomalous situation took hold.[51] But it failed utterly to satisfy his latest set of allies, the men who had used their uncompromising refusal to accept the revocation of the Old Charter as the basis of their political identity. Elisha Cooke, First Church's leading politician and a fellow agent in England, would have nothing to do with the document Mather reluctantly accepted, and he came home to head the party dedicated to opposing royal government and seeking a formal restoration of at least a part of the Bay Colony's original autonomy. At times variously labeled the "popular" and the "country" party, both misleading descriptions, Cooke and his followers were originally a direct continuation in personnel and spirit of the militants of the 1680s. They were probably no more hopeful of getting the Old Charter back in 1695 or 1700 than they had been of salvaging it in 1685. The Old Charter was a standard for them in both senses of the word, a symbol to rally around and a basis of judgment. Cooke and his faction were announcing that they were skeptical of the value of the imperial connection and well aware of its cost and that they had every intention of getting the best of the royal governor, by popular politics or fiscal coercion as the case required. The leadership of this country party was located solidly in the South End of Boston, among the members of First

Church, still, as late as the 1720s, "reckoned the most narrow in their Principles, and to approach nearest the *Brownists*."[52] Tensions over the Halfway Covenant had receded in the wake of a general acceptance of the necessity of enlarging church membership in one way or another and because the issue no longer served as the focus for so many other conflicts. Toleration for Quakers and Baptists was a closed question after the Glorious Revolution, and the dissenters' subsequent campaigns for exemptions from ecclesiastical rates created new issues and different alliances.[53] But the members of the county party were true to their origins in their special hostility to Anglicanism and in their suspicion of pretensions to power among clergymen of their own persuasion. As the lineal and spiritual descendants of deputies who denounced the clergy in 1670 for innovation and of magistrates who held out to the last in 1686, it was only appropriate that they be employed in the 1690s in denouncing government according to a document championed by New England's leading clergymen, Increase and Cotton Mather, that surrendered the Bay Colony's autonomy.[54]

In 1692 Increase Mather was the most important political figure in Massachusetts. He must have realized that a clergyman could not hold this position for very long after the resumption of electoral politics, but for the moment he alone bore the responsibility for getting the New Charter government to work. Failure was not worth thinking about, although he could not help but think of it: a return of royal government along the old lines. "New England would have bin in the same case with New York, Virginia, and the other plantations."[55] New York was the most sinister example and the best known because it had formed part of the Dominion briefly and shared with New England in its overthrow. The new royal governor under William and Mary had immediately aligned himself with the faction opposing the revolution of 1689 and at their behest arranged for the trial and execution of the leading revolutionaries. Massachusetts *had* to have a quiet settlement to its own revolution.

Unfortunately, the problems facing Mather were daunting—and mostly of his own making. He had to thread his way through popular dissatisfaction with the loss of total independence, on one side, and, on the other, the suspicions of the English government about colonial loyalty, which former adherents of the Dominion were sure to encourage. He must walk, that is, between Elisha Cooke and Joseph Dudley, and he must do this after having repudiated successively both of the major groupings in Massachusetts politics. Somehow Mather would have to wind the machine up, see that it could run by itself in the face of opposition from two different camps, and then, as befitted his calling, retire to the sidelines of the North Church and Harvard, from which joint vantage points he could still on not infrequent occasions continue to lead the clergy in issuing gloomy pronouncements on spiritual and moral issues, broadly defined.

Mather's solution for New England was an apolitical politics. As the Bay Colony's agent in London, he was invited as a conciliatory gesture to nominate the first governor and lieutenant governor and the first members of the new council. The governorship fell to Sir William Phips, a local man popular in both the Bay Colony and London, who had no ecclesiastical or political past to speak of nor any government experience: he had made his name diving for sunken treasure and had not been much interested in New England religious life until he came in contact with Cotton Mather and joined North Church in 1690. (Phips was accused of being Mather's puppet; matters would have gone better with Massachusetts if he had been.) Something still had to be done, however, for that large class of people who did have a past to embarrass them, and here Mather proceeded with particular delicacy. William Stoughton had been, next to Joseph Dudley, the Bay Colony magistrate most deeply implicated in the revocation of the Old Charter, and he had shared in a degree of Dudley's unpopularity, despite having deserted his long-time partner at the last moment in 1689 to become one of the revolutionaries. His political stock had recovered some by 1691, when he was elected to the restored upper house, and Mather, acting on the recommendation of his son Cotton, proceeded to nominate him as the new lieutenant governor as a significant overture to the Dominionists.[56] A similar degree of nice judgment and evenhandedness dictated Mather's choice of councillors. He divided half of the council seats representing the Bay neatly between equal numbers of men drawn from the more conciliatory elements of both pre-1689 groupings and then balanced this set of familiar figures with nine neutrals, new men who had become prominent in politics only since 1689.[57] Anyone from the Lords of Trade and Plantations looking over the list would see at least a few names described in the past as well-affected and they would not find anyone who had distinguished himself by the vigor of his opposition to the demands of the crown, most obviously former Deputy Governor Thomas Danforth, who had confessed "how great an object I am of their hatred." First Church, however, was virtually unrepresented.[58]

Mather probably hoped that this nominated coalition would set Massachusetts politics on an entirely new foundation. As he had arranged it, the Council, if it retained its unity, could be self-perpetuating because twenty-eight votes cast in a bloc by the incumbents would all but assure their reelection. He made it plain the first time he came to deliver an extended commentary on his handiwork that he intended his handpicked magistracy to continue in perpetuity, even if that required him to claim on no very obvious constitutional grounds that the royal governor had the right to retain his old council if he were dissatisfied with the lower house's choice for the new.[59] If he had had his way (and he did not), government would have become a rather neutral business of aging provincial senators and minor backcountry representatives without partisan organization, elections would have been an annual bore, and the Bay Colony would have been secure from dissension and the threat of imperial intervention—incidentally leaving the clergy and its acknowledged leader with a measure of the political authority they and he had gained in the previous decade. If it was a vision that involved a degree of self-aggrandizement—all of Increase Mather's schemes did—it was founded on a keen sense of the realities and dangers of the Puritan colonies' precarious situations.

The terrible end of Leisler's Rebellion in New York foreshadowed eloquently what might happen in Massachusetts if Mather did not somehow prevent a recurrence of factionalism and short-circuit popular protests against the new government. Yet he was confronted almost from the moment of his return with another crisis, this one over witchcraft at Salem Village. This situation also demanded careful management and got it. But in the course of a year of cautious, ultimately successful maneuvering more people lost their lives in Massachusetts than had in New York and to a judicial proceeding at Salem more infamous than that perpetrated against the Leislerites just the previous year.

As he recalled it, Increase Mather arrived home in Boston on 14 May 1692 to discover "the Countrey in a sad condition by reason of witchcrafts and possessed persons." He found a widespread notion that "the devill could not Represent Innocent persons as afflicting others," and, therefore, sworn testimony by the alleged victim of a witch that she saw the "spectre" of some named individual afflicting her (the deponents were all girls) automatically condemned that unfortunate person. "I doubt [fear]," wrote Mather in his autobiography, "that Innocent blood was shed by mistakes of that nature." Mather accordingly published *Cases of Conscience Concerning Evil Spirits* refuting this lethal notion, "by which (it is sayed) many were enlightened, Juries convinced, and the shedding of more Innocent blood prevented."[60] Admirably succinct, this account conceals an important elision in its apparently straightforward chronology. Mather arrived in May; *Cases of Con-*

science was put into circulation in October and into print in November. In the meanwhile, between 2 June 1692 and 22 September, nineteen people were tried, convicted, and hanged, and on 19 September one man was pressed to death for refusing to plead. If Increase Mather had the power to stop these murders, why did he take so long to use it?

The autobiography is correct on one central point: the witchcraft crisis was in full swing when Mather arrived home in the company of Sir William Phips. The epidemic had mushroomed very rapidly from the first cases of affliction in Salem Village in early March 1692 until 25 May, when Phips, in the absence of a judicial system created by statute, authorized a special court of oyer and terminer to deal with the more than one hundred persons in jail on the charge of having made a compact with the devil. At the head of this notorious tribunal stood the new lieutenant governor, William Stoughton, for once in his life immovably attached to a fixed conviction, that spectral evidence was irrefutable. On this basis he led eight other justices, some more willingly than others, on his grisly crusade until in late October pressure from the House of Representatives and the ministry, perhaps coordinated, convinced Phips to suspend the special court. At that time "there were at least fifty persons in prison in great misery by reason of the extream cold and their poverty," awaiting trial. They and perhaps a hundred others also under suspicion were released between November 1692 and May 1693 according to the ordinary process of law dispensed by the recently established statutory courts. There was no single, grand ending to the business: some of the accused were not indicted by the grand jury, some were found innocent in trials presided over by judges who "were convinced and acknowledged that their former proceedings were too violent and not grounded upon a right foundation," a few were convicted but pardoned by Phips, and the remainder just went their way unmolested.[61]

There are similar complications, unmentioned in Mather's autobiography, in the question of the methods employed to secure automatic convictions before the judges finally agreed that forms of spectral evidence would not have "the same stress laid upon them as before." Pressed on the issue of the devil assuming the form of an innocent person, Stoughton, though not yielding materially, would reply that such evidence merely began the judicial inquiry. In the course of their trials the convicted "witches" had also been found guilty by "humane testimony." Their look had cast their victims into torment and their touch had then cured them, they had been named in the depositions of confessed witches as accomplices, or they had been observed in acts of preternatural strength or diabolical clairvoyance by witnesses who had given their testimony under oath. The claim was that the prosecution routinely overproved its case, an apology that conveniently ignored the prior prejudice created against the accused by the initial assumption of the universal validity of accusations based on spectral evidence.

These minor points in a major horror are worth emphasizing because they lead back to a central concern for both Increase and Cotton Mather and for the rest of the ministry that in 1692 willy-nilly deferred to their leadership—the integrity of the judges. Under Stoughton's leadership the court routinely used spectral evidence to imprison numbers of people in a potentially lethal jail, and then, convinced of guilt in advance, they gathered the other evidence that would ensure conviction. They also led the jury, uncritically accepted adverse testimony, and browbeat the more easily intimidated defendants into confession through "rude and barbarous methods," a combination of suggestions, overt threats, and the hint (or perhaps more than that) of physical duress—"buzzings and chuckings of the hand," as Thomas Brattle called it. "And let me tell you," Samuel Willard wrote of the confessions, "there are other ways of undue force and fright, besides, Racks, Strappadoes and such like things as Spanish Inquisitors use."[62]

Whatever one's faith in the reality of witchcraft in general, these particular trials were manifestly unfair in their procedure and blatantly absurd in their results. No matter what their previous reputations, individuals accused by the afflicted girls and examined were invariably indicted and if brought to trial always convicted. A handful of young women were being allowed to ruin anyone and everyone simply by seeing their specters, a feat of sustained illogic that was apparent to contemporaries not under Stoughton's immediate influence. Brattle described the ministry as a whole as "very much dissatisfied," noted that two leading political figures, Thomas Danforth and Nathaniel Saltonstall, refused to sit on the court, and claimed that "some of the Boston justices were resolved rather to throw up their commissions than be active in disturbing the liberty of their majesties' subjects, merely on the accusations of these afflicted, possessed children."[63]

Increase and Cotton Mather, the spokesmen on each crucial occasion for the much dissatisfied ministry, regularly objected to Stoughton's pet notion that spectral evidence was infallible from May 1692 onward. But they made their strictures only in the most abstract terms and never criticized the manner of the court's proceedings. Cotton in the *Return* of the Cambridge Association (a monthly gathering of ministers in the Boston area) urged on 15 June 1692 "a very critical and Exquisite Caution" in the use of this evidence, lest "there be a Door opened for a long Train of miserable Consequences," yet he still called for "speedy and vigorous Prosecution" and commended "our Honourable Rulers" for their zeal.[64] In September he agreed to write *Wonders of the Invisible World*, the book that destroyed his posthumous reputation by a defense of the trials little short of frenetic. Nor was Increase any better. In *Cases of Conscience* he declared "that to take away the life of any one, merely because a *Spectre* or Devil, in a Bewitched or Possessed person does accuse them, will bring the Guilt of Innocent Blood on the Land, where such a thing shall be done," and added that in New England "I trust that as it has not, it never will be so."[65] Even the repeated assertions, from Cotton in May to Increase in October, that the devil could take the shape of an innocent person in order to afflict his victim could in themselves do nothing to alter the course of the trials because they were always hedged around with the qualification (in Increase's version of 1 August 1692) that "such things are rare and extraordinary especially when such Matters come before Judicatures."[66] If spectral evidence was probable but not conclusive indication of guilt, it could still arguably serve as a basis for examination of an accused witch and from that point would follow the concocted "humane testimony" that made indictment and conviction a foregone conclusion and execution certain unless the accused confessed and added new "humane testimony" to the cases against others. No trial results were going to be changed merely by calling for caution in the use of this one form of evidence, even if it did constitute the core of the subsequent and inevitable conviction.

Some indication of the limitations Increase Mather placed on himself in *Cases of Conscience*, the most emphatic statement of opposition he or his son produced, can be gained from comparing the work to other critiques of the trials that were written at about the same time. Increase took the position that the nineteen executed witches had been rightly convicted but that statements made at their trials and the nature of certain accusations against others imprisoned or accused revealed principles of evidence that could ultimately lead to injustice in future proceedings. Spectral evidence was not conclusive by itself; use of the effects of the sight and touch of the accused witches on the afflicted girls resembled popish exorcism too closely to be admitted in evidence; and the accusations made against others by confessing witches were not to be credited because of the admitted bad character of the witnesses. Testimony from two witnesses of preternatural powers he blandly accepted as valid, and he added that in the one trial he had witnessed, that of the Reverend George Burroughs, where testimony of this sort had figured prominently, the proceedings has been fair and the verdict just.[67] As opposed to the later statement in his autobiography, in *Cases of Conscience* no innocent blood has been shed, although there is some danger of a miscarriage of justice in the future.

Three other individuals addressed the same set of questions. Robert Pike wrote a long letter to one of the judges of the Salem tribunal on 9 August 1692; Samuel Willard put out the anonymous and clandestinely printed *Some Miscellany Observations Respecting Witchcraft* at an unknown date; and Thomas Brattle, a leading Boston merchant and amateur scientist, composed an epistolary pamphlet that may or may not have circulated in manuscript and that claims to have been written on 8 October 1692.[68] The arguments of all three efforts overlap with Mather's at most points, indicating the extent of the consensus against Stoughton's bloody circus. But Pike dismissed the entire testimony of the afflicted girls on the grounds that they were either outright liars or under diabolical influence.[69] Brattle and Willard were not addressing one of the judges, and they went further in attacking the court, arguing that the confessions were extracted under duress and that the guilt of the accused had been prejudged. Brattle also condemned the testimony about spectral tormentors out of hand as so incoherent and inherently incredible that the judges themselves did not believe this evidence when it touched one of their friends or relatives. Willard followed Pike in rejecting all testimony from the afflicted on the grounds that the past life of some of them and the present irrational behavior of the whole lot rendered them incompetent witnesses. Brattle would not admit evidence of preternatural powers because it was impertinent to the matter of the indictment (afflicting some named person), Willard would accept the firsthand testimony of two witnesses to the *same* act, but he attacked the practice of combining evidence about different magical acts into a cumulative case so vigorously that his witch-hunter character declares, "If this Rule be always followed, it will be hard to punish Wickedness."[70] By the lights of any of the three men *no one* executed in 1692 could have been convicted, and if that were the case, it would be hard to deny that at least some of them had been innocent. The boundaries of the possible in 1692 were considerably wider than either of the Mathers was willing to allow.

Yet it was the Mathers who enjoyed the prestige and the habit of leadership, Increase in his own right, Cotton as his deputy during the four years his father was in England. Willard was bolder than either Increase or Cotton in word and deed alike, but he was probably one of the ministers assenting to Cotton's *Return*, and he was certainly present at the Cambridge Association meeting of 1 August 1692 that adopted Increase's overqualified resolution on spectral evidence. He also wrote the preface for *Cases of Conscience* and was one of the fourteen ministers listed as endorsing the text. He knew better, and one suspects that some of the other clergymen trapped in the endorsement with him also did. Still, they all gave precedence to the Mathers in their public and collective voice. And both of the Mathers tacked.

Increase Mather was never a weak man, and neither was Cotton, for all the times he has been made to play a neurotic Richard II to his father's hearty Bolingbroke. But there were other players in their game besides themselves, and all knew the stakes were high. The members of the special court of oyer and terminer so vulnerable to the ridicule of Brattle and Willard were the appointees of Phips, its leader was the indispensable Stoughton, visible symbol to the Dominion collaborators that all was—and would be—forgiven. The membership by accident or design mirrored exactly Increase's projected coalition. And to their own great and good fortune First Church members were excluded, as they had been from the Council. Immune to political pressures because none of their leaders were implicated in Stoughton's doings, they were free to take the moral high ground and dissociate themselves from the trials.[71] Threading their way between Cooke's malcontents and unreconstructed Tories, the Mathers were in no position to bring into total disrepute the first major act of their new government, carried on by the very combination of men they had designed to give a fresh start to politics. They dared not, in Cotton's words, run the risk by their criticisms of having the judges "brought unto the Bar before the Rashest *Mobile*." The rest of the ministry understood the predicament well enough to follow the lead of the men who had demonstrated that they had the greatest skill in dealing with it. On 30 May 1692, just sixteen days before their issuance of Cotton's schizoid *Return*, the Cambridge Association, in its first meeting since the return of Increase, "did only discourse of affairs in England."[72] Exquisite caution was needed as much by the clergy who advocated it as the judges on whom it was urged.

The fledgling New Charter government was also in danger of being discredited by popular disorder. We have been left a picture, largely out of Cotton's biography of Increase, in which "the Spirit of the Country ran Violently upon Acquitting all the *Accused*" only *after* the publication of *Cases of Conscience*.[73] What evidence there is on the subject suggests the opposite relationship. In his wild polemic against the Mathers, *More Wonders of the Invisible World*, Robert Calef has Cotton on horseback quelling a riotous crowd intent on saving George Burroughs and four other condemned witches from the gallows. The story is apparently a fanciful invention by a skilled polemicist, that is, one who knew how to create credible fabrications.[74] Widespread discontent there certainly was, and violence was always possible in such circumstances. As early as 25 June 1692 William Milborne, the preacher of the Baptist church in Boston, was jailed for "very high reflections upon the administration of public justice" in Massachusetts. Phips, returning to Boston at the end of September, found "many persons in a strange ferment of dissatisfaction which was increased by some hott Spiritts that blew up the flame."[75] For that matter, Cotton, when not making a hero of Increase, made a martyr of himself by claiming he had been reviled by "the people thro the country" because he published his defense of the trials to uphold the personal integrity of the judges against "most other People, whom I generally saw enchanted into a raging, railing, scandalous and unreasonable Disposition, as the Distress increased upon us."[76] The choice of words does not suggest any great sulking about in corners or taverns but a passion, if not a panic, on the edge of explosion.

The parallels with Leisler's Rebellion were apparent. William Milborne, the Baptist preacher, was the brother of Jacob Milborne, Leisler's lieutenant, who had been executed along with his chief. Thomas Newton, the prosecutor at Salem, had previously performed exactly the same function against the Leislerites, and Joseph Dudley, back in Roxbury during much of 1692, had as the chief justice of the province of New York presided over the trials. These were not mere coincidences, for Dudley and Milborne in their different ways represented the threats to the new government coming from those who thought it insufficiently under English control and looked to Dudley to replace Phips and from those who held that any royal government was a betrayal of the freedom regained in 1689. When Thomas Brattle prefaced his own attack on the witchcraft tribunal by denying he had anything to do with those "men of a factious spirit" who were "never more in their element than when they are declaiming against men in public place, and contriving methods that tend to the disturbance of the common peace," he was probably referring to followers of Milborne rather than of Elisha Cooke, but the distinction tended to blur. Milborne had been very visible in the uprising that overthrew Andros, and his Baptist church was familiarly associated with First Church, whose members were critical of both the trials and the charter.[77]

In this volatile situation the Mathers had too much of what they had gained for New England tied up in the reputation of Stoughton and his associates. They could not afford an open breach with these new allies and so moved by degrees only, while the rest of the ministry followed their lead. Time-honored tactics of private insinuation and limited but symbolic public demonstration were trotted out once more to damp down the impending confrontation between an obdurate, reckless court and an increasingly desperate population. Cotton Mather cautioned John Richards, the only judge from the North Church, against excessive reliance on spectral evidence even though "there are wise and good men, that maybe ready to stile him that shall advance this Caution, A Witch Advocate."[78] Increase Mather rated off in no uncertain terms a prominent Bostonian who had taken his "afflicted" child to Salem to ask the victims there for the names of the witches responsible, "asking him whether there was not a God in Boston, that he should go to the devil in Salem for advice."[79] The commitment of John Alden, a prominent Boston sea captain, on spectral evidence alone became the occasion for something approaching a clerical protest meeting attended by representatives of all three of Boston's churches. Samuel Willard's hostility to the court in particular became so well known that in his dialogue he has the witch-hunting S make the well-known observation that his fellow disputant B makes an admirable advocate for witches and then gives his persona the sardonic riposte, "This is not the first time."[80]

None of these familiar devices worked this time around, no matter how energetically pursued. As long as it was given privately, the ministerial advice was ignored, while petitions in favor of individual defendants went unheeded and the public gestures were overlooked or provoked visions of afflicting specters taking the shape of ministers and magistrates critical of the trials. Judicious measures could in no way allay the growing fear that no one was safe for the good and sufficient reason that no one was, unless related to a judge by blood or marriage. A petition to the General Court, possibly the one got up by Milborne, begs that body "to order by your votes that no more credence be given" to spectral evidence or "a woeful chain of consequences will undoubtedly follow besides the uncertainties of the exemption of any person from the like accusation in the said Province."[81] Unless Stoughton could be persuaded into a moderate course of hangings, the new government was likely doomed anyway, regardless of how prudently the designated keepers of the public conscience behaved.

Stoughton and his henchmen chose not to be persuaded. Instead, they attempted to counter the assertion that the devil could assume the shape of an innocent person with evidence from the best of authorities. John Hathorne, who had become the most rigid of Stoughton's supporters, along with several other judges (left unnamed) secured the confessions of a group of Andover "witches," including an admission by one of them that they had "carried the shape" of the minister of the town, Francis Dane, about with them "to make persons believe that Mr. Dean afflicted." Immediately upon this declaration the confessing witch, Mary Osgood, is asked, "What hindered you from accomplishing what you intended?'" Back comes the pat answer: "The Lord would not suffer it so to be that the devil should afflict in an innocent person's shape."[82]

Increase Mather had run out of room to maneuver. On 3 October 1692 he presented the full text of *Cases of Conscience* to the Cambridge Association, which adopted it unanimously, condemning the uncritical use of spectral evidence for the third time since June. The authority of this ex cathedra statement, argued at length and signed by a body of fourteen ministers, was sufficient to stop the trials while it remained in manuscript, especially when the force of its argument was coupled with the obvious self-interest of the majority of the population. Phips acted to stay further indictments as early as 12 October. On the twenty-sixth a resolution for a fast squeezed through the House of Representatives, expressing dismay at "the most Astonishinge Augmentation and Increase of the Number of Persons Accused, by the Afflicted" and was interpreted as a call to halt the sittings of the court of oyer and terminer. Samuel Sewall missed the point entirely when he complained that the small majority in favor of the resolution included a number of representatives personally interested in the outcome because accusations had been leveled against them personally or against their relatives.[83] Given half a chance, the sense of self-preservation was going to assert itself, and even in manuscript *Cases of Conscience* was more than half a chance.

A public break with the witchcraft judges, however, could not be avoided. Having been forced into a dogfight, Mather showed that he had a talent for it. He went up to Salem jail sometime in mid-October and secured the recantation of the confessed witches from Andover, including Mary Osgood, on the nineteenth. *Cases of Conscience* was then given a false date, 1693, to circumvent a proclamation by Phips against publishing materials about the trials and put into print by early November of 1692.[84] Carrying Mather's title of "president of Harvard College at Cambridge" on the front page, the attestation of so many ministers, and a preface by Willard, the work had the character of a manifesto: any further trials along the old lines would openly flout the received wisdom of the most prestigious men in the colony. The court of oyer and terminer would probably have fallen without the work being printed, but its publication surely was decisive in ensuring that future trials before the Superior Court (and these continued until May 1693) were carried on in a way that made convictions impossible. In addition, the spate of retractions Mather had initiated at Andover went a long way toward exposing the methods by which the original confessions were secured, bringing the conduct of the court of oyer and terminer as a whole into question. In a mass recantation document the Andover confessors blamed "the hard measures" their examiners used with them for their self-incrimination, admitted that they "said any thing and every thing which they desired, and most of what we said, was only but, in effect, a consenting to what they said," and revealed that they had been threatened with execution when they subsequently attempted to take back their confessions.[85]

All in all, the Mathers had handled a very dangerous crisis with a sure touch. The executions had been brought to an end and the trials left to fizzle out in a string of anticlimaxes without any very specific repudiation of the Salem tribunal. Opposition between the ministry and the judged had been kept to the necessary minimum. Cotton was on record in a sustained defense of the executions, now that they were over, and Increase had rallied his fellow ministers around a statement that destroyed the evidentiary basis of future proceedings without taking issue with previous ones. Increase's electoral disaster in 1693 was still to come, but he had already avoided far worse, for himself and for Massachusetts. The only sore point was twenty dead, a hundred or more at one time or another made to endure the rigors of imprisonment, and at least another hundred brought into peril and ill fame for no good reason.

These figures can be written off, with an appealing hard-edged realism, as no worse than the hardships wrought on various New England towns throughout King William's War. If anything, the witchcraft judges made less havoc in Andover in 1692 than the Indians were to do in 1698. But the New England ministry, unfortunately for them, had no grounding in realpolitik. This most recent experience of participation in colonial politics as leading players left a very bad taste, witnessed by their repeated calls for compensation for the families of the victims of the judicial murders.[86] King William's War was not in the first instance their responsibility; the Salem trials were. "That the Resolutions of such Cases as these is proper for the Servants of Christ in the Ministry cannot be denied," Willard wrote in his foreword to *Cases of Conscience*.[87] But they had done their work badly, palpably so, following Increase Mather's lead in his desperate attempt to avoid rocking the fragile craft he had constructed for Massachusetts. Conscience had been subordinated to a worldly consideration more relevant to politicians because the ministry had been led since the mid-1680s into a more nakedly political role than anything they had been accustomed to.

Between them the two Mathers had not even allowed the clergy to finish clean in 1692. *Cases of Conscience* makes its argument forcefully, and the text proper contains only one brief assertion that no one convicted of witchcraft to date had suffered solely on account of spectral evidence. Perhaps the tract did not go to the heart of the matter in the most direct way. Still, it challenged the validity of most of the Salem court's procedures and coming when it did, with its phalanx of ministerial endorsements, it could claim pride of place in preventing further executions, and this, at least, was consolation for the months of half-measures before its appearance. If only the Mathers had let matters rest there.

While *Cases of Conscience* was in press, the fourteen endorsements already on it, Increase decided he had to do more to prove that he was no enemy of the judges. He added an extended "postscript" praising their wisdom, no less than their humanity for having "out of tenderness declined the doing of some things, which in their own Judgements they were satisfied about," and he insisted in emphatic terms that because "that which is called *Spectral Evidence*" had not been decisive in previous trials, no harm had been done as yet and his sole concern was "to prevent it for the future." To add force to this vindication of twenty murders he threw in his concurrence with Cotton's *Wonders of the Invisible World* and singled out the Burroughs trial as one he knew personally to be just. Nothing in this postscript implies that it is excepted from the same endorsement as the text.[88]

Cotton Mather claimed to have given way to "a most charming Instance of *Prudence* and *Patience*" on the part of the judges when he wrote his defense of the trials they had conducted by principles he repudiated.[89] Thanks to Increase, the ablest ministers in New England, Hubbard, Michael Wigglesworth, Willard, the great Charles Morton, and John Wise among them, were now partakers in his son's unfortunate susceptibility. They found themselves committed in public to a position (that no innocent lives had been lost) all of them were willing to repudiate by 1696 and that others besides Willard must have rejected even then as empirically dubious and logically tenuous in the extreme. (Hubbard and Wise in particular had signed petitions in favor of condemned persons.) Small wonder that Willard put *Some Miscellany Observations* into print the same year as *Cases of Conscience* or that Michael Wigglesworth was still telling Increase Mather as late as 1704, "I fear (amongst our many other provocations) that God hath a Controversy with us about what was done in the time of the Witchcraft. I fear that innocent blood hath been shed; and that many have had their hands defiled therewith."[90]

Sixteen Ninety-Two marked the high point on Increase Mather's curve. Not that he or Cotton suddenly and unequivocally fell from influence. Taken together, their bibliographies for the 1690s add up to an incredible one-third of the production of the Massachusetts printing presses in that decade, and one or the other of them was before the General Court preaching the election sermon five times in the first ten years of the New Charter. But they were still the heroic figures of the Dominion years and the subsequent Interregnum, the embodiment of New England beleaguered and then restored, only to those whose knowledge of public life was intermittent or gleaned at very considerable distances from Boston. Politicians who knew better, and that included most everybody serious about the game of politics, were already taking aim in 1692 from one side or another, and after Salem neither Mather could claim to be the undisputed spokesman for the clergy. The way down may not have been steep, but from Salem on it was unbroken.

An abrupt reverse followed almost immediately on the collapse of the witchcraft trials, in the first elections for the new upper house, in May 1693. In the election sermon he delivered before the General Court Increase Mather, presuming on his ability to lead Phips, threatened the House of Representatives with a mass veto of their choices if they elected "*Malcontents*," who will "do what in them is to make others to be Disaffected to the Government." The representatives and the old councillors responded by electing a total of ten new men out of twenty-eight, a turnover not to be seen again until the impasse over the land bank in 1740. These replacements mostly had a familiar look to them, especially a bloc of old hard-liners from First Church, back en masse at the expense of Mather's neutrals to form the nucleus of the country party.[91] Mather's projected new politics had gone flat at its first airing.

Ironically, the bond among First Church members forged in their years of hostility to the predominant clerical faction and their magistrate allies provided under the changed conditions of the New Charter the strongest basis of reconciliation between the uncompromising opponents of accommodation and their few politically wayward brethren and between the church as a whole and the rival Old South. Mather's promotion of neutrals and new faces, many drawn from his own North Church, was meant to accomplish a similar task, but all it did in the end was solidify an alliance of the South End, so that even a few of his own choices for the Council from Old South ended up joining Elisha Cooke and the First Church intransigents.[92] They formed a powerful group in undisguised antipathy to him, and for the first time they possessed a clerical spokesman of their own with formidable intellectual powers and equal political skill.

First and last, the most unkind cuts of all were assigned to Mather's onetime political partner, Samuel Willard. He was the minister most bitterly humiliated by his politic acquiescence in the Mathers' tactics and to him belongs the honor, in the election sermon of 1694, of issuing the first formal call for repentance over Salem and compensation for its victims: "Yea such may be the influence of the Male-administration of Rulers, though done without malice, and in an heat of misguided *zeal* for the People of GOD . . . that the Guilt may ly long upon a Land, and break out in Terrible Judgments a great while after, and not be expiated till the sin be openly Confessed, and the Atonement sought unto."[93]

The context of the passage is significant, for *The Character of a Good Ruler* is also a rebuttal of *The Great Blessing of Primitive Counsellours*, Increase Mather's ill-fated effort at dictating the choice of councillors in the previous election sermon. In place of any clerically inspired political program, Willard in a much shorter piece, exhorted in an old-fashioned way to virtue, wisdom, and moderation and to leaving the business of government to the civil rulers thus endowed. He had seen in detail what happened to the clergy when they tried their hand at politics.

It was appropriate and inevitable, therefore, that Willard would also give the death blow to Increase Mather's political career. In 1700 the country party convinced Phips's successor as royal governor, the earl of Bellomont, of "Mr. Mather's Selfishnesse and pedantick pride" as president of Harvard in an attempt to pack the corporation.[94] The next year the leading First Church operators on the Council, Elisha Cooke and the ambidextrous Nathaniel Byfield, forced Mather out of the college entirely by an ingenious stipulation that dismissed the North Church minister for nonresidence and allowed the equally absent Willard to succeed him as vice-president and acting head.[95] Mather implied in his autobiography that Willard's willingness to take his place at Harvard was an unanticipated betrayal, but in fact the two had quarreled over the governance of the college in 1697 so violently that Mather told him "He will never come to his House more till he give him satisfaction."[96] Cotton Mather similarly got no help from Willard in 1700 in answering Robert Calef's vicious and unremitting libel, *More Wonders of the Invisible World*, which goes out of its way to invoke Willard's name in blaming the witchcraft trials on the Mathers.

Cool as ever, Willard also made no response to Calef's overtures for support, but he did find a way to say a little more indirectly on the subject of witchcraft and the accompanying clerical debacle. The death of Stoughton in 1701 occasioned Increase Mather to liken the former chief justice of the court of oyer and terminer to a second Moses and to take him as a type of

Increase Mather, a selfless figure whose love for New England was proven by his contributions to Harvard and his agency in England, much criticized by ignorant folk who knew nothing of the difficulties under which he had labored.[97] Willard approached the character of the man who had put such a strain on his conscience back in 1692 very differently, considering his awkward situation as the Boston minister next in rotation to preach the Thursday lecture when Stoughton died. He managed somehow to come up with a funeral sermon on the theme that the death of a reforming magistrate in his prime is a judgment on a professing people for their iniquities. (Stoughton at his death was seventy-one and had been inactive in his last years.) More interesting still, he prefaced the argument with the observation that good magistrates might yet have infirmities that so break out in the course of their government as to provoke God to continue them in their destructive courses in punishment for the sins of their people.[98] And Willard was not finished. The following September the Council called a fast, instancing Stoughton's death as a prime cause. On this occasion Willard was in the catbird seat, having ousted Increase Mather at Harvard a few days earlier, and he evidently found the temptation to settle old scores once and for all too great to resist. He preached a very genial sermon, more appropriate to a thanksgiving, in which he noted the cyclical nature of the church's prosperity but looked forward to a gradual onset of the millennium that would bring *"abundance of peace, tranquility, and prosperity upon the Church."* The late lieutenant governor never got so much as an indirect allusion, but there *were* topical references to the Mathers: a few blistering shots at those who try to pin down the date of the fulfillment of Revelation with specious exactitude (Cotton) and at "Prognosticators" given to foretelling the future by private inspiration (Increase).[99]

By succeeding to the headship of Harvard, Willard had taken the place of Increase Mather as the symbolic leader of the New England clergy. This is what the nonresident presidency of the college amounted to (it certainly had never involved much control over the running of the place), and this was exactly the way Mather had used the post once he discovered its value in England among the Dissenting interest. It was also the reason he held on to it so desperately after having shown no great interest in taking it, and it is why Cooke and Byfield, no fools when it came to the point of the knife in politics, bent all their efforts to taking it from him. The change, however, had a significance beyond political intrigue and the arcana of a clerical debate conducted mostly in parentheses. Since 1694, at the latest, Willard had come to fill the role originally occupied by William Hubbard among the clergy and still held among the laity by Samuel Sewall, that of the crusty conservative of such recognizable probity that all sides trusted him. He might comment on public affairs from time to time, but he would be irreproachably independent and in a partisan sense nonpolitical. As a representative figure Willard did not stand for a repudiation of the formulas of the 1680s—their meaning had been driven home ineradicably by the years under the Dominion. But he had learned the lesson of Salem, itself in some ways a painful, concentrated repetition of earlier experience. New England was a culture rather than a set of charters; Puritanism was a movement, with multiple potentials and directions simultaneously, not a single set of propositions tricked out by a clergyman with a "talent for quick compositions"; and the recognized mediators of culture and movement alike had by virtue of that charge to stand at some distance from the politics of their colonies. If the clergy could take this last step—and after Salem there must have been few ministers willing to take any other—then in a period of reduced official support they could exercise far greater influence. Lay challenges to their position and to their claims to include the whole of New England society within their mission had pretty much subsided with the Dominion; resentment persisted but was sporadic and diffuse, lacking the unifying set of causes or means of political expression that had enlivened the 1670s. The magistracy, once a rival source of power capable of wielding the more formidable of the two swords, the one with corporeal punishments, lost still more ground after 1689 with the effective impairment of local autonomy. The Bay Colony upper house, in particular, in the days of the Old Charter the forum for the most powerful men in New England, was in time to become a body in which "the most likely way to secure a seat for many years is to be of no importance."[100] Events had favored the clergy alone. Provided they could adapt the most recent formulations of Puritan imperatives to the realities of colonial dependence, they were in a position to become a corporate, state-sponsored intelligentsia, in effect, the Puritan colonies' vatic civil service.

In taking stock of American Puritanism at the end of the seventeenth century it is salutary to separate the cultural history of New England from the progressively bitter intellectual travail of the Mathers. Increase was a sinking ship after 1692 and pretty much underwater after 1701; poor Cotton was pulled down in his father's wake without ever quite getting to float on his own bottom. They remained important in the eighteenth century and influential at times. Cotton's friendship was invaluable to the growing proportion of ministers in the New England hinterland located away from the densely populated region near Boston who nonetheless aspired to see their names in print, and he had just enough of his family's political sense to cultivate an interest in Connecticut to use to his advantage in Massachusetts.[101] Despite his undiminished penchant for controversy and his genius for waging his contests under disadvantages that Increase would never have accepted, his following and that of his father revived considerably in their later years.[102] Yet only Increase was ever in a real sense a representative figure, and he gained that status by contesting for it in the 1670s and lost it the same way by the end of the 1690s. After that in their different ways father and son would take refuge in a chiliasm more explicit than most other clergy would allow, doubt if New England had a special role reserved for it, and cease to see saving knowledge as a traditional fusion of rational understanding and emotional apprehension.[103]

With or without their help, American Puritanism required a definition of purpose and forms of institutionalization that accommodated the inescapable alteration in its circumstances as the seventeenth century came to an end. Massachusetts was a royal colony, and Connecticut, although it recovered its charter, was perfectly aware of the limitations it now functioned under as imperial administration achieved a degree of permanence and expertise. Moreover, existing degrees of self-government could not be taken for granted. A bill was introduced in the Lords in 1701 providing for the "reunion" of all the colonies with the crown, failed to get anywhere, and was reintroduced with similar results the next year. Further efforts in 1706 and 1715 were no more successful, but contemporaries had no way to predict that the New England colonial charters would endure until the Revolution.[104] They were made aware of the hostility of the Board of Trade to American "independence" and they could hardly have forgotten the last reunion, the years of the Dominion. All plans in the early eighteenth century had to be provisional. When the Mathers on the one side and South Enders Samuel Sewall and Isaac Addington on the other gave their advice to the founders of Yale in 1701, it was to create a college in no way dependent on the Connecticut government for its existence and having as little formal organization as possible, for fear that a foundation of more visible proportions, a second Harvard, would be too tempting a prize for a second Andros.[105] In theory, Connecticut was a different case from Massachusetts. Its election preacher in 1697, Gurdon Saltonstall, could just echo John Winthrop as of 1630 by announcing that "God hath designed the Civil Government of his People, to concenter with Ecclesiastical Administrations." In fact, practical individuals like Saltonstall (he laid down the ministry of New London to become governor of the colony) had always to imagine an imminent situation in which the two spheres did not "concenter" any more than they did in Massachusetts and take the appropriate precautions. When an appeal to the Privy Council in 1728 overturned the colony's intestacy law, another clergyman with political ambitions, Elisha Williams, at the time president of Yale, afterward speaker of the lower house of the Connecticut assembly, complained, "Will they not Say our Ecclesiastical Establishment is a Nullity? Our College Charter a Nullity?" He feared that "we Shall in a Little Time be in no better Circumstances than our Dissenting Brethren in England."[106]

Connecticut intellectuals were not going to think the problem through themselves; they would take over and adapt what Massachusetts came up with. The smaller of the Puritan colonies remained to a large degree dependent on the northeast corner of Massachusetts for its intellectual life, no less than for its commerce. The two points are not unrelated: Connecticut lacked a center of its own—it was certainly not Hartford—and the flow of intellect and intellectuals was not through some either but along the existing ligaments of trade, either with New York, which had little cerebral to offer, or with Boston, which had plenty. All of the Mathers had always known as much and had, from Richard to Cotton, used Connecticut as a back door to the Bay. But their willingness to weave a web in Connecticut by keeping up a large correspondence with ministers starved for news and ideas and by entertaining visitors when they came in from the provinces merely exploited systematically the pervasive fact that the cultural and economic hub of all New England was to be found in that same small area where they had been set to play out their personal dramas.

The challenge was fundamentally the same for all of Puritan America. The people of New England were to continue to think of themselves as the people of God. The conception was to be vivified in some way, made tangible in the imagination. And yet all must have registered somewhere in their minds the reality that they were colonists. Cotton Mather was probably the first to tackle the paradox in the 1690s, and he chose to make a virtue of the necessity. New Englanders were the most English Americans: they had shared with the mother country a common revolution against tyranny and popery and were now joined with her in conflict with the French and Indians, a holy war for Protestantism and liberty against Antichrist. This formulation, however, did little more than make the colonies "a poor *Leanto*" in relation to the English "*Great House*," and in actual fact it could compensate repeated New England losses for the sake of the cause only with faraway European victories.[107] A joint crusade would make more sense in the mid-eighteenth century, when the partners were more evenly matched and the triumphs more equally distributed. In the late 1690s and early 1700s the partnership was a distinct liability on the American side. The most convincing line of attack lay elsewhere in facing up to the hardships that were the most visible tokens of the imperial connection and varying the jeremiad tradition to suit slightly different circumstances.

In the 1670s the preacher turned prophet to apostasizing New England had been obliged to prove his case by compiling empirical evidence that the covenant had been broken and by finding recent disasters to demonstrate a pattern of punishment. If his thesis was accepted on these grounds, he could threaten worse to come unless there was reformation and renewal, a return to the original virtues of the founding generation that set the standards by which the current declension was to be measured. The crisis of the charters had broadened the reach of the church covenants and made them, through the ceremony of renewal, the instrument for public affirmation of the national covenant: the terms of both covenants were extended to the population at large as New Englanders rather than as unworthy children and grandchildren of worthy ancestors. In the face of the Andros regime the importance of the national covenant and of the special status of New England lay in the guarantee that Israel in America still existed as a holy people, despite the absence of civil polity, and could look forward one day to a restoration of its liberties. None of these themes disappeared after 1689, and the Exilic identity of New England in particular remained crucial. But it was no longer necessary to go in search of disasters when the imperial wars and the colonial economy obliged so nicely, only to interpret them now that they were taken for granted. These reversals gave significance to New England, proved it was not just Virginia or New York but Israel. Why else would God punish its people with such severity except as a "Retaliation," in Samuel Willard's words, for covenant terms still extant and binding?

The miseries of the moment, now that they were bitterly real and not impending, became a sort of comfort. They warranted New England against some wholesale overthrow and even against too drastic a succession of poor harvests, Indian raids, or losses at sea. God "doth not come to *kill* them, but to *cure* them, if it may be." As "a wise *Physitian*" he administers his potions in ascending degrees of strength, waiting for the working of each "a competent time, not looking that it will work, as soon as it is down."[108] Reformation was still the object of this regime, but the bill of divorcement threatened by Increase Mather in the 1670s (up to a point pronounced by him in the 1700s) was an unlikely possibility. God had promised to save New England,

Samuel Torrey preached in his third and last election sermon, in 1695, "not by might, nor by power, but by his Spirit, and that in a way of Sovereign Grace." There was no way to earn this collective salvation, any more than the individual variety could be merited. After all the efforts at reformation by statute, covenant renewal, and public fasts, "until (we may fear) that we have wearyed our God, as well as ourselves by our gross Formalities," all that was left to New England was gratitude to an all-merciful, all-powerful God who chose to save the corrupt two tribes of Judah as a token of his enduring promise when he delivered the comparatively less evil ten tribes to the Assyrians.[109]

This was the theodicy of the Dominion period reworked a little in more promising times to render irrevocable the analogy between the population of New England taken as a whole and the Israel of the prophetic and Exilic periods.[110] The conception, however, had still to be made operative knowledge, a live metaphor and not an empty phrase lacking recurring and multiple referents. Frequent days of humiliation would help, whether colonywide or held by individual churches. On these occasions the congregation could hear the message expounded in detail and see it given point by the latest misfortune or military preparation. But if the clerical exegesis of public events was to acquire genuine imaginative force, then the spiritual progress of the individual auditors needed to be woven into this unfolding pattern of routs and rallies. Each believer had to be both pilgrim and Israelite; at frequent intervals the spiritual progress of the individual and the ongoing struggle of the chosen people must intersect.

Much of the problem lay in specifying the Israelites. In a series of jerky steps between 1657 and 1687 the question at issue had been shifted away from a contest over some putative original purity to the far more interesting project (familiar enough in Elizabethan and Jacobean phases of the Puritan movement) of creating the means to enlist the bulk of the population in a common struggle. The churches had already in various ways broadened their membership in the face of the Dominion as a way of replacing the failing civil polities. The most significant assignment of the clergy after 1689 was their attempt to systematize this effort: they had to provide a generous definition of the church but also to ensure that membership, however comprehensive, continued to be divided into a series of ascending grades or there would be no individual pilgrimages to undertake. The Cambridge Association in 1704 capped a long series of varied adaptations in ecclesiology (including extensions of the Halfway Covenant and redefinition of baptism as a universal right of professing Christians) by urging the entire New England clergy to resume house-to-house visitation. The object of this policy was to "bring on their people, as far as they can, publicly and solemnly to recognize the covenant of God, and come unto such a degree of the church state as they shall be made willing to take their station in." That portion of the population unwilling to respond would be conscripted into the enterprise, like it or not, by the extension of "admonition" even to them. At one time, within the living memory of an aging Increase Mather or Samuel Willard, the American Puritans could not agree whether the baptized children of visible saints were the proper subject of church censures once they reached the age of sixteen; in 1704 this former privilege of the visible saints and their immediate minor offspring was conceived of as a basic right of the English population of the New England colonies.[111]

Maintaining the "degree of the church state" was a vital point. Though the distinctions had been abandoned in some parts of Connecticut and western Massachusetts, most New Englanders still needed ranks within the church militant, classes of certified sainthood short of full communion. These gradations fit the natural order of things anyway because some people were not going to take that last risk no matter what blandishments were offered or chastisements threatened. And the ascending ladder of sainthood provided a spiritual adventure, not always completed, by which the creative forces of the individual could be drawn along orthodox channels. The Cambridge Association exhorted the clergy not to "leave off" until all the people of their areas "shall be qualified for and persuaded to communion with the church in all special ordinances." There was to be a universal voluntarism, universal to the extent that everyone was recognized as a fit subject for the ministrations of the church and would be pestered to begin the march to full communion, voluntary in that the stage individuals reached rested entirely on their own efforts. This struggle, in turn, once extended to the whole population could be paralleled with the adventures of Israel compassed about by enemies. The imperial wars provided external adversaries aplenty, the path to salvation the matching internal conflict, and the congruence of churches and people the regular points of contact between the two fields of battle. No one need feel alienated, impotent, or tempted into some alternative faith when personally charged with the power of drawing down punishment on all New England by individual misconduct and bringing on blessings by individual reformation. There was always a vital role to play: "If we are in a *Private Capacity*, and cannot actively influence the Publick so as to mend it, Yet may we not mend one? . . . Who of us is there that dares to appear, and own that we have done nothing to the continuance of these Judgments?"[112]

In England before the Great Migration the godly were both the vanguard of the hero nation and the saving remnant amid the mixed multitude comprising the majority of the English people. Such ambivalence no longer seemed necessary in the early decades of settlement in America when it was assumed that most adults were or would be visible saints. The early eighteenth-century version in America twisted both conventions together. The godly were all of Puritan New England, but not all New Englanders were equally visible in their godliness. The duality was recognized by law in both Massachusetts and Connecticut in the distinction made between the congregation and the church. The church (those in full communion) chose the minister, the congregation (all those taxed for his support) approved the choice. A concession to necessity because it was hard to get people to pay up otherwise, these prosaic statutes embodied a nagging tension between establishment and sect brought, for a time, to fruitful issue. The church was the vehicle by which the mission of New England became the responsibility of all its inhabitants and affiliation within it was effectively a birthright of the whole population. But at its core the church was also still a gathered and selective society.

Some people in both colonies objected to this clever arrangement on the grounds that they were Baptists, Quakers, or Anglicans made to run a Puritan race. Once establishment itself had been effectively constituted, it was comparatively easy to deal with such protests by defining them as anomalies rather than heresies, exceptions to the rule permitted to exist under prescribed circumstances. It was also, apart from intellectual considerations, much easier that way because dissenters—for so they could now be called—could make trouble by civil disobedience and appeals to the Board of Trade. Government simply granted a variance when the appropriate conditions were met. Everyone was prima facie a Congregationalist; this was the very meaning of New England. Individuals could elect to exempt themselves from the official mission if they certified to a county court that they regularly attended a dissenting church of a denomination specified in the relevant statutes (passed in the late 1720s and early 1730s). Then they could go their own way, no longer players in the great game, provided their numbers remained small, their behavior quiescent, and their religious organizations reasonably similar to the legally sanctioned churches. Less complaisant varieties of dissent, which grew in size and militance as a result of the Great Awakening, were in for a battering as a reward for their efforts over the course of a full fifty years until the Standing Order, as it came to be called, could be made to see the virtue of extending the aura of the new Israel to a plurality of Protestant denominations.[113] For most of the eighteenth century dissent under license was another device to attest to the "natural" and ordinary equivalence between New Englanders, the people of God, and the Congregational Way.

The church, whether gathered or extended, remained in eighteenth-century New England, as much as in the England of Elizabeth, the keystone in the Puritan arch—and only that. Puritanism was in its origins also a social movement calling for a coercive reorganization of society to give daily point to the weekly sermon and a cultural phenomenon offering participation in the great concerns of the day to large classes of people previously held to be inert. Neither theme was absent from America at the end of the seventeenth century. Loss of complete autonomy did mean that the emphasis had to be shifted some, away from the good ruler and on to, first, the preservation by the judicial system of that distinctive moral code that is still the first thing brought to mind by the word *puritan* and, second, the propagation of what the nineteenth century called a "mental culture," a broadly accessible, frequently reiterated and reinterpreted sense of the meaning of it all.

By English standards the enforcement of the criminal law in the Puritan colonies after 1689 was familiar but a little quaint. Assizes and quarter sessions in seventeenth-century England had depended on the cooperation of the great mass of the propertied, smallholder as well as the more substantial sort, and the justice they administered had gained its broad support by the inescapably Protestant character of both the dooms meted out and the acts of mercy liberally dispensed: penitent sinners guilty of impetuous crimes got off relatively lightly, reprobates whose acts suggested premeditation and whose life histories indicated professional criminality went to the gallows. By the eighteenth century, however, communal participation and judicial moralism were in retreat before the intertwined forces of legal professionalism and centralized administration.[114] In the very same period New Englanders of ordinary social standing continued to staff county courts that spent a remarkable amount of time on Sabbath breaking, moral offenses, and enforcement of the laws requiring compulsory education.

One could if one wished simply dismiss the New England practice as an archaism likely to occur in a provincial society, where distance from the metropolitan power can be measured in years no less than in miles. But such a judgment would miss the way in which English institutions were invested in New England with special significance by virtue of their function within an explicitly Puritan design. In the case of the judicial system in the colonies, simply carrying on in an old-fashioned English way assured that the functions of discipline, once assigned mainly to ecclesiastical polities, would as intended eventually ensnare the broadest possible spectrum of New England society in a collective educative rite. The members of the community involved in the judicial process were witnesses in the older sense of the term, meaning to bear witness, an affirmation of the common faith that would endow doctrinal abstractions with immediate and mundane reference.

County courts in New England had been growing in their importance for the entire course of the last thirty years of the seventeenth century, but the degree of neutrality in matters of religion forced on the rest of colonial governance after 1686 assured them from that date forward of a unique prominence in carrying on the public mission of the Puritan movement.[115] In pursuit of godly discipline, the first General Court in Massachusetts elected under the New Charter, in the midst of the witchcraft epidemic, reenacted and extended the battery of laws barring cursing, drinking, defamation, sexual misconduct, and scoffing at the Bible (itemizing the protected contents, book by book), passed legislation for keeping the Sabbath, and required the towns to maintain ministers and schoolmasters. Enforcement was still a didactic exercise in the "use" of the gospel. Grand juries continued to be, as under the Old Charter, locally elected panels so large in size and so frequent in their sessions that every adult male of even modest reputation was likely to serve on them on several different occasions in the course of his lifetime. New legislation extended the term of service from half a year to a year, but a further provision that no one had to serve more than one year in three guaranteed a broad degree of participation, and it was still almost certain that most jurors on any given panel were going to be repeaters.[116] Criminal law, unlike civil litigation, was still comprehensible and so still an affair of lay practitioners rendering justice in an inherently dramatic setting rather than of technicians spinning out an inevitably unsatisfactory settlement according to abstruse rules several removes from fundamental questions of morality. New Englanders were more likely to be litigants than defendants, but service on the grand jury was the closest most of the men would ever get to wielding the magisterial fasces, though the analogy would just as properly be to congregational participation in church discipline. The grave ruling elder, often missing in the churches themselves, was there in the form of the judge giving the charge. (Samuel Sewall began one of his with Adam's fall.)[117] The minister had a good chance of being present in propria persona, ready with an apposite sermon.

It did not much matter under the circumstances that towns presented for failing to maintain a schoolmaster found ways to go on avoiding that expense or that there were surely more Sabbath breakers in Suffolk County than the relatively small number presented to the inferior court in the entire decade of the 1690s. "Social control" was not what contemporaries were after, nor were they as fascinated with the regulation of morals according to the sense of the local community as we claim they were. The regulations in question were not made by the locals but at the behest of a political and clerical elite, sometimes, as in the case of the law on the prohibited degrees of marriage, in direct contradiction to the prevailing moral consensus. *Reproof* better fits what contemporaries saw in the enforcement of the law—a collective testimony against sin in which the act of administering discipline was more important for the actors than for the punishment inflicted on the hapless object who happened to get caught. The courts, and especially the grand juries, were the most readily available civil forums available to the majority for enacting and affirming their Puritanism. When the Coercive Acts attempted to take this ordinance away from the people of Massachusetts, they saw to it that the fact was noticed in the Declaration of Independence.

If the godly magistrate had receded some, and the laity were holding their own under this latest dispensation, the clergy, who would never bring themselves to admit it, were the group that gained most from the readjustment of the place of Puritanism within colonial society. Their first role was still parsed in the singular, as the individual minister of a particular church. Their collective presence, however, was more pervasive and less subject to dispute by the early eighteenth century. Attention to changes in their function has usually focused on formal organization: the failure of the centralized bodies proposed in Massachusetts by the clergy in 1705, the adoption with some changes of the same plans in Connecticut as part of the Saybrook Platform in 1708. Connecticut may have become a little more hierocratic than Massachusetts as a result of its consociations and associations established by law, but these bodies are a secondary matter, neither very innovative nor wholly effective.[118] They probably made their only important contribution to increasing the standing of the ministry through the practice of the ministerial associations in both colonies of licensing young college graduates to preach while they were seeking a pulpit. The license did little to maintain orthodoxy, considering some of the people who received one, but it did create officially an order of Puritan levites, lesser clerics, and thereby, without repudiating the proposition that no man was a minister until ordained over a congregation, added an element of institutionalization to the corporate character of the clergy.[119] Apart from this one device, the most significant change was much less formal and therefore less provocative and more deadly: the metamorphosis of the New England clergy as a body into a recognizable clerisy.

To begin with, the ministers wrote most of what there was to read in New

England in a period, roughly from the last quarter of the seventeenth century onward, when the local presses finally began to turn out titles with sufficient frequency to fulfill the tasks Puritans classically assigned to reading. Most of this material amounted to different ways to say the familiar, but that was precisely what an inbred audience found exciting.[120]

What the ministry wrote, however, was less important to their growing concentration of moral authority within the Puritan movement than the simple fact that they wrote anything at all. Before 1680 only a few New England authors had been able to get into print, and they were either located near Boston or clients of Increase Mather. Young men entering the ministry in the last decades of the seventeenth century were more ambitious to see a piece of the material they routinely committed to paper achieve publication and found more opportunities to fulfill that ambition, and those who entered on their ministry in the first quarter of the eighteenth century were as likely to publish as not, usually more than once.[121] It is a situation we can imagine only with difficulty: a society in which most people could read yet in which in any town other than Boston there was only one person by profession who might reasonably be expected to contribute to the sum total of reading material. The rise of American Grub Streets would one day cheapen the value of mastery of the printed word, but until the Revolution created a second agenda and the advent of new technology bred up a race of hacks, only the New England ministry enjoyed as a class the prestige that a literate society bestowed on the vocation of author.

An increase in the number of towns and in their size and wealth, as well as in the quantity of graduates Harvard and Yale annually pumped into society, similarly aided in creating a clerical stranglehold on learning because by the early eighteenth century the village schoolmaster was typically a recent graduate waiting for a call to the pulpit or a failed minister who continued on as a teacher and generally did a little supply preaching on the side.[122] Every form of education but the most basic was identified with the clergy and the end of higher education normally taken to be a clerical career. Merchants' sons might go to Harvard and become merchants themselves or lawyers and officeholders, but the average farmer fortunate enough to have a bright son with academic inclinations would get him some Latin tuition with a nearby minister or schoolteacher and hope to send him to college on the assumption that the young man would enter the ministry on graduation.[123]

Like them or not, the clergy were assumed to be, without real question, the ordinary source of noetic culture in New England. As the Great Awakening would demonstrate, the only effective way to break their monopoly was to repudiate intellection in general. Before that cataclysmic turn of events, so complete a triumph could be disputed only in indirect ways.

There were too many original and intelligent minds in New England to be contained in every instance within the standardized molds. Two controversies in particular in which the Mathers became embroiled between 1700 and 1708 have been taken to represent the end of "intellectual solidarity" in American Puritanism, a judgment that puts more weight on the centrality of the protagonists than they can bear, at least after 1700. Both forms of dissidence, rather, indicate just how successful the reorganization of Puritanism had been and how hard it was by the early eighteenth century to formulate alternatives.

Solomon Stoddard, the longtime minister of Northampton, is usually taken as the most thoroughgoing critic of the New England establishment within its own ranks and is sometimes presented as the patriarch of a new, frontier order in church and state organized along the Connecticut River Valley. Stoddard combined innovative ecclesiology with a personality so forceful his name has been attached to positions he did not originate and that formed only one part of a critique of American Puritanism too radical in its entirety to find widespread acceptance. Stoddardeanism has come to mean eliminating the conversion narrative as a requirement for full communion. In this sense (and no other) many churches in Connecticut and a few in Massachusetts were Stoddardean and, among others, Samuel Willard at the end of his life and Benjamin Wadsworth (minister of First Church from 1696 until 1725, when he became president of Harvard) can be numbered in Stoddard's camp. The two Boston men typify a growing feeling that tests for saving grace were humiliating and put worthy individuals off from full communion without being in any way conclusive. Willard could not see much difference between the external signs of grace in those who had made their relations and in those too timorous to attempt the feat, and he concluded somewhat testily that to censure anyone as a hypocrite who conformed adequately to the outward forms of religion "is to usurp Gods Prerogative in judging the heart."[124]

Stoddard agreed that "Grace is many times under Hatches and invisible," but he went much further than this straightforward caution against making elaborate spiritual calibrations where none could be given.[125] He swept away at one time or another the church covenant and most of the voluntaristic elements in Puritan ecclesiology. He had no great patience with weak Christians who had to be nursed along the path to full membership in steps appropriate to their slow maturity in grace. Real saints knew when they had been saved, and the confidence generated by the vivid experience of receiving grace would sustain them far better than any subsequent certification from other alleged saints. "The Prodigal knew well enough the time of his return to his Fathers house: The Children of Israel knew the time of their passing over Jordan."[126] Anxious pilgrims should not flit from preacher to preacher or inch along the ordinances, but join the church where they lived and faithfully attend all its ordinances including the sacrament; this full-fledged commitment alone would lead to that unmistakable moment of conversion if they were predestined to have it.[127]

Particular churches Stoddard held to be the fundamental units of a national church, as the individual synagogues had been the congregational gatherings of the national church of the Jews in the Old Testament. They were not bands of proven saints tightly welded together by a pledge of mutuality but simply the appropriate unit of worship for professing Christians. "If a Christian live in a Town, where there is a Church, he is immediately bound to joyn with that Church; and that Church is bound to him to govern him, and give him Christian Priviledges." Following this simple rule would end all the nonsense caused by nonresidence, itself the ill effect of the unscriptural church covenant.[128] The rights of the fraternity accordingly went the way of the needs of the weak Christians. Beyond their initial right to elect their minister, church members were soldiers in an army waiting on the officer's orders. Each minister was to rule his own roost, and all particular churches were to be organized in a hierarchical fashion under regional and national governing bodies with substantial powers of intervention in the affairs of each congregation.[129]

Stoddard's pronouncements all have a refreshing boldness and power to them that has made their author of perennial interest. As a contemporary remarked, he was "another guess man" (another sort of man) than Cotton Mather, and those tired of the involuted arguments, fluctuating moods, and endless introspection of the Boston minister are liable to turn toward Northampton with relief. Stoddard, however, spoke so little to the traditional concerns of the Puritan movement and to the spiritual needs of so much of the population that he found comparatively few takers for his visions outside of some of the churches of Hampshire County immediately under his personal spell. In Connecticut, where Stoddardeanism antedated Stoddard, the majority of the churches founded after 1700 were nonetheless Congregational. Changes in formal organization, in any case, were not likely by themselves to overcome lay reticence. Stoddard never got the whole of his own congregation to proceed to the Lord's Supper, and the record in Connecticut was much the same. In Windham, for example, where admission to the sacrament required only a "serious Belief" in the Scriptures and a "desire to have your Dependance upon" Christ, the church was still in 1747 employing the Half-way Covenant for the same purposes that Cotton Mather, hardly a Stoddar-dean, had advanced for its use in Boston's North Church in 1690, as a resting place for those worthy souls suffering from "the Fear of coming Unworthily" until such time (if ever) as "they shall have received more Light." Through-out Connecticut "Stoddardean" churches enrolled no higher a percentage of their town's population than churches following the more traditional and exclusive standards for membership.[130]

Stoddardeanism seems in many ways a parallel revolt with "liberal reli-gion," but the similarities are deceptive. For all his originality, Stoddard came up with a brilliant variation on the common theme. Old Testament Israel for him was neither a type for the body of believers everywhere nor a simple metaphor for the people of New England but a model, to be followed literally and in no way discontinued by the Jews' denial of Christ. "Every Christian Nation is a Church," and the same covenant God made with the church of the Jews is made with these successor nations, through their churches and not their government.[131] This was to take to drastic extremes the very same trend toward replacing the faltering state with an ethnic and cultural identity for the people of New England that had dominated most American Puritan thinking since the Dominion. Stoddard's position on the matter of admission to church membership, along with his denial that particular churches were formed by covenant, allowed the Mathers to associate him with similar forms of "laxity" advocated by a group of young clergymen and their wealthy lay backers who founded or supported the fourth Boston church, at Brattle Street. The two controversies overlapped, fragments of one finding their way into polemics generated by the other, but the resemblance is deceptive. At its root Brattle Street was a deeper, more total repudiation of American Puritan-ism than anything coming out of Northampton.

Brattle Street is a term like Bloomsbury in denoting a group of individuals bound by personal ties and a very rough congruence of attitude rather than a place of residence. The analogy continues in that the group included some of the most socially prominent individuals in the Boston area and some of its ablest intellectuals: Thomas Brattle (in his early forties the old man of the group), William Brattle and John Leverett, who as tutors had virtually run Harvard in the 1690s, Simon Bradstreet (grandson of the governor and min-ister of Charlestown), and the church's first minister, Benjamin Colman. All professed what is now, with necessary vagueness, described as "liberal religion," or as they would have put it, a large and catholic spirit. The group saw as its defining genius an up-to-date, nondogmatic receptiveness to new ideas and a basic sympathy for the inquiring intellect associated with the natural sciences. Labeled Arminian on occasion, their theology was reasonably orthodox Calvinism, and their innovations, such as they were, were to be found more in moral philosophy and psychology. Their heterodox reputation arose from their openly expressed admiration for the Latitudinarian movement in England because of its professed broad-mindedness, enthusiasm for science, and hostility to doctrinal polemic.[132]

The Brattle Street Church was organized along suitably good-natured lines, if one allows for its irenic principles having been announced in a pugnacious *Manifesto* of 1699. There was no covenant, no ruling elders, no specific disciplinary procedures. A church was pretty much any group of people who thought they were, its uniting bonds nothing more than the "mutual promise and engagement" that gradually arose among the members as "the law of nature dictates to us." The minister at his discretion could baptize any child presented by a morally responsible adult, and he would along equally tolerant lines admit to the sacrament; the congregation was not much interested in either question. Brattle Street was so deliberately underorganized that John Higginson of Salem, who might be thought of as concurring in enlarged membership and ministerial discretion, twice sarcastically suggested the leading figures reread John Cotton's *Spiritual Milk for Babes.* In that simplest of catechisms they might at least find out what a church was supposed to look like.[133]

The Mathers carried on the struggle with Stoddard without much help. In the case of Brattle Street, William Hubbard, Higginson, James Allen, ultimately the entire First Church, joined in on their side despite the diversity of their previous allegiances.[134] They knew the real challenge when they saw it, not an alteration in the New England Way but a rejection of the idea of New England. Combining youthful verve with adolescent cuteness, the Brattle Street apologists wrote off the notion that the first planters had come to America to institute "some little Rites, Modes or Circumstances of Church Discipline." It could not be that "their great design" should lie "in so small matters."[135] Brattle Street solved the fate of Israel with a shrug of the shoulders and an interest in other matters, frankly acknowledging their provinciality in their preference for participating in the modish intellectual concerns of the mother country.

Nonchalance is, on the face of it, an unlikely driving force for the composition of a manifesto and a polemic or two. Brattle Street was a rebellion, heartfelt and in its way bitter. When so much of the intellectual energy and imaginative life of New England was locked up in pursuit of a handful of time-honored themes, one of the very few ways out was to find some wider concerns, more timeless or more contemporary or both, that would show up the dominant obsessions as parochial and obsolete. Latitudinarianism worked for Brattle Street; later generations would try High Church Anglicanism and its appeal to patristic authority and an unbroken episcopal succession, or, at a later date still, Catholicism (suitably de-Celticized) and German romanticism. The affront given to the powers that be might be memorable, but the gesture is a secession, not the basis of an opposition movement. Brattle Street took as its organizing principle the axiom that the prevailing dialogue was not worth talking about, and once the manifesto and its defense were away, its members did very little talking except to each other. Boston's ancient landmark, Ezekiel Cheever of the Latin School, complained of the champions of the new principles because "they do not write against the Books put out for the Old" and thereby deprived the public of its chance for an intelligent choice. But Thomas Brattle, who called Increase Mather "the Reverend Scribbler" did not propose to trouble the public with the same failing himself. William Brattle and Simon Bradstreet were more silent still, and Leverett must be the only man to have been president of Harvard who never published a line. Benjamin Colman alone has a bibliography, a huge one, but he restricted his writings until late in his long life to uncontroversial practical divinity, eloquently expressed.[136] Attractive as this group is, their existence is an unwitting tribute to the awesome solidity of the dominant culture.

The state the Puritan movement had arrived at in America by the beginning of the eighteenth century was as ill-proportioned and incongruous as ever. New England Puritanism looked like nothing so much as huge fragments from the previous English experience piled together in no special way. Perhaps the most prominent features were Jacobean: the plenitude of means, wholesome laws, learned and well-provided preaching, even a confessional foreign policy. The combination of toleration and establishment recalls Cromwellian England and some of the proposals of the Independents. Nonconformity after the Restoration was represented by the frequent reprinting of devotional manuals by dissenting authors, intended as supplements (and sometimes substitutes) for a fugitive ministry and frequently disrupted ecclesiastical organizations. Earlier than any of these in origin, and more fundamental to Puritanism, were the organizing motifs of a covenanted nation and of a church as a gathered group of saints. The combination no longer made sense in England of the same period, but the Elizabethans would have understood this paradoxical union very well.

Almost every constituent element of the Puritan movement had been rearranged; nothing significant had been entirely forgotten. The proclamation celebrating (there is no other word for it) the Deerfield Massacre in 1704 recalls "the Errand of our Fathers into Wilderness (which was to Plant pure Churches, that should maintain the *Evangelical Faith* and *Worship*)" and recommends to the citizenry "the Expedients offered for a REFORMATION" by the Reforming Synod of 1679. The very same year the clergy of Massachusetts in their annual convention were scoring off once more "such as have submitted unto the *Government of* CHRIST in any of His churches" and then escaped discipline by worshiping at a different church without transferring their membership.[137] As in the beginning, so in the end, the same themes endure: national mission, collective reformation, and self-propelled, sometimes vagabond saints.

By the early eighteenth century it had all become so natural and familiar that the coda of the Puritan movement in New England could be given to any number of clergymen speaking on almost any occasion of a vaguely public nature. Still, a layman, Samuel Sewall, put it most succinctly, in his last major public appearance, this time on the day after New Year's, 2 January 1723. It was not a very promising moment. The royal governor, Samuel Shute, had fled the colony in despair the previous morning to take back to England as bad a report as he could and put the charter into jeopardy again. Lieutenant Governor William Dummer, a local man, took his oath as head of the province in the absence of Shute and made an inaugural to "the Deputies," as Sewall called them in an anachronism dating back forty years. Then it was the turn of the Council and of its senior councillor.

Sewall was not quite seventy-one, the last man left alive in New England who had served as a magistrate before the Dominion. Samuel Willard had died sixteen years earlier; Increase Mather had only months to live. Cotton Mather at fifty-nine was dogged by misfortunes and a sense of his own unpopularity; his health was about to break, and he would last only five years longer. So it was up to Sewall to explain the purpose of his new trust to the acting governor: "You have this for your Encouragement, that the People you Have to do with, are a part of the Israel of GOD, and you may expect to have of the Prudence and Patience of Moses communicated to you for your Conduct. It is evident that our Almighty Saviour Counselled the First Planters to remove hither, and Settle here; and they dutifully followed his Advice; and therefore He will never leave nor forsake them, nor Theirs."[138]

A little to Sewall's embarrassment, and much to his delight, Dummer and the entire Council "would stand up all the while, and they express'd a handsom Acceptance of what I had said. *Laus Deo.*" And *exeunt omnes.*

Envoi
The Long Argument and Its Ending

Cotton Mather, in common with Machiavelli and Milton, wrote his best-known work in response to an abrupt reversal in his personal fortunes and those of his cause. Conceived in the shadow of Salem Village and begun two months after Increase Mather's electoral disaster in 1693, *Magnalia Christi Americana* appeared in print in 1702 just after the final disgrace of the elder Mather's ouster from Harvard. In part *Magnalia* makes good an old obligation no longer in need of fulfillment by organizing the story of New England around jeremiadic themes, the effort Increase had failed at in *Illustrious Providences*. In part, the work is also a running commentary on the bitter, losing battle the Mathers waged in the 1690s and a plea for Increase's lost hope of a new and judicious politics freed from the long-standing divisions of the Old Charter period: in the long series of biographies that are the most frequently consulted item in Cotton's compendium the essence of leadership is regularly discovered in nonpartisan moderation, the section on the "troubles" of the churches is taken up with instances of "zealotry," and even the catastrophe at Salem Village is explained as a loss of balance, "a going too far in this affair."[1] The work was hardly a tract for the times in which it finally appeared, dominated by the fierce rivalries between political camps headed by Elisha Cooke and Joseph Dudley, and, appropriately, the longest single section in *Magnalia* is a reprint of Cotton's pointless hagiography of Sir William Phips, long dead by 1702 and by the universal verdict of everyone but the Mathers a dismal failure removed from the royal governorship in well-earned disgrace.

Cotton was no better at his business when he freed himself from Increase's cause long enough to tackle the most pressing cultural concern of his day, the identity of American Puritanism within the emergent English empire. For most of *Magnalia* the foundation of New England is the proper and providential climax of the Reformation, but in the introductory sections, and at times in the core of the huge book, the epic tone is betrayed by a strenuous cosmopolitanism: Cotton insists on these occasions, almost in the manner of Brattle Street, that the entire Migration was caused by "the mistake of a few powerful brethren" in demanding conformity on secondary matters.[2] New Englanders were just good Protestants who presumably would not be where they were if judicious counsel had prevailed at home. Unsure of whether he was Vergil or Irenaeus, Cotton never made a sustained effort to come up with a meaningful statement in the one area in which he might have regained something of Increase's tarnished authority.

Yet we still recur to the book and debate just what its vision really is. (There are numerous options.) *Magnalia*'s bulk and detail, in which New England history just happens without any real human action or interaction, are a fitting symbol of the clergy's attainment of supremacy within the Puritan movement and of their ingenious camouflaging of their ascent to power. After a truncated prologue (the only underdone section of the book), Puritanism in this received version finds its definition in the decades of the founding of America, is attacked in the mid- and late seventeenth century by diffuse and disembodied forces, of which inanition is the strongest, and is jerked back into life from time to time by various reforming movements. Cotton did not live to see the Great Awakening, but the subsequent interpretation of that event could be deduced without difficulty from the factitious logic underlying every page of his disordered epic. *Magnalia* is a representative statement of American Puritanism at maturity: evasive and contradictory but entirely successful in disguising the actual achievements of its subjects.

In the discussion now concluded, an attempt has been made to reverse this clerical legerdemain by restoring to the American Puritans the previous history their authorized interpreters implicitly denied; one might almost say, the object has been to restore to American Puritanism the process of history itself. The "argument" of the title and of this envoi does not refer primarily to the disputes that ran through the course of the Puritan movement— though there were plenty of them—but to its continuing narrative, as when Claudius in act three of *Hamlet* nervously inquires of the play within the play, "Have you heard the argument? Is there no offense in't?" The argument here, in Claudius's sense of plot, has deliberately been a long one, covering 130 years of the Puritan movement, and it is this length that accounts for many points at which issue has been taken with the prevailing interpretations on the subject. After the first sixty years of Puritanism have been put back into the American story, change has become adaptation, internal conflict an essential and generally healthy state, a certain diversity of aims and practices an ordinary and unalarming characteristic of a movement complex in its constituencies and ramshackle in its organization. In particular, when placed squarely in the middle of Puritan history, the early decades of American settlement lose their privileged position as the authentic formulation of New England ideals and become merely the setting for another epicycle in a continuing process. Accordingly, commercial development later in the seventeenth century, no longer the serpent in this decommissioned Eden, can be seen as the English Puritans originally saw it, as the only practical material basis for underwriting their ambitious programs. John Field or John Udall would be hard to imagine in a permanent ministry, but if they could have settled down in any place or time with a modicum of comfort, it would certainly have been Boston in the early eighteenth century, the largest city and the greatest port in British America.

The world of the Mathers and Sewalls did not mechanically replicate the condition of England midway through Elizabeth's reign. On the contrary, the changing fortunes and tactics of the Puritan movement over the intervening decades were written all over the face of the establishment that had been created in early eighteenth-century America. But the rough-hewn alliance of clergy, gentry, and ordinary laity that cohered in Elizabeth's day had enough points of congruence among its disparate parts to survive in England until the Civil War and to continue in existence, protean and vital, for a century and more in its American setting. The Great Migration is a turning point of sorts, but only of sorts. The role of the clergy within the movement increased, the gentry was substituted for by a magistracy somewhat diminished in importance compared to the English original, and the godly, no longer united by their separation from the multitude, became an increasingly variegated group in their respective degrees of confidence in their own sainthood. New arrangements had been contrived, though always out of inherited materials, and the inevitable resistance was in one way or another accommodated, overcome, or, in a number of instances, ultimately tolerated as a pardonable deviation within the larger unity of New England. But at each point in the movement's history the same central Puritan vision endured: the magistracy guaranteed the social conditions under which the laity, part volunteers and part conscripts, pursued their individual destinies in a collective context interpreted and mediated by the clergy. New England's distinguishing culture a hundred years after the Winthrop fleet was in its broadest outlines of one piece with its Elizabethan beginnings.

We can scarcely now comprehend the liberating power that made so demanding an undertaking the common program of such anomalous combinations of social groupings for so long a time. Limited as possibilities remained in the English speaking world of the early modern era, for the first time substantial numbers of unremarkable people discovered that the insular and cyclical routines dominating their lives could be fractured, their place taken by movement and direction. As an imaginative scheme Puritanism was unique in possessing a plot line and a significant role for the individual caught up in it. Liturgies said for the living, obits and perpetual masses offered to shorten the travail of the dead, put the action of the piece into hands of someone other than their nominal subject. Magic was mostly a series of ad hoc attempts to restore the status quo after some unfortunate contingency, and the people resorting to fortune tellers as much as admitted that the future was something that happened to them. Even when a collective effort, as in the case of the communally produced mystery plays, religious ritual amounted to a normative or descriptive representation of a fixed state, a tableau vivant and not a sustained narrative.[3] Predestination alone gave each and all their own fate, one they were charged to work out for themselves, in fear and trembling to be sure but also in discovery and purposive struggle. Puritans took matters further by linking these individual destinies together in the unfolding fortunes of the English nation and the grand mission of English Protestantism. After 1660 the range of Puritan allegiances narrowed to New England, and for the sake of convenience the work of the current generation was represented, absurdly, as regaining the original purity of the founders, but the underlying formula remained the same as ever and as potent. Despite a sharp increase in the ferocity with which the continuing contest for the definition of New England was waged, ultimately the laity elected to settle for the ministry's terms, grudgingly and with their eyes open, because they still found in the latest formulation of the Puritan movement, New England as apostate and Exilic Israel, the same sense of volition and engagement that had always enlisted their loyalties.

Because of this popular commitment, and only because of it, coercion, an integral part of the design, worked tolerably well when and where applied. Or, rather, it worked in New England, where the population was more unified and higher levels of authority hostile to Puritanism could be appealed to only with difficulty. It was not a very happy situation for the recalcitrant by choice or by nature—the much censured, much fined, much forgiven church members addicted to alcohol, the unrepentantly eccentric of various hues, the poor of the port towns. But force could never be uninterruptedly brutal or intrusive without waiving the widespread tacit consent that made its occasional use possible. Towns could be pestered into getting a schoolmaster sooner or later, Baptists in the counties that made up the Old Plymouth Colony and Rogerenes scattered about Connecticut could be harassed pretty regularly, but sumptuary legislation rotted unenforced on the statute books and four Quaker hangings were too many. Only once did these limits fail for a time, when too much mutual forbearance in 1692 killed twenty people.

However creaky these arrangements may seem, they survived for over a century, adapting to new circumstances in the end. By all rights the Puritan movement should have held together in America for generations beyond the heyday of the Mathers until it gradually lost meaningful definition in the successive cultural upheavals of the nineteenth century and blended in with the new landscape. In fact, by 1800 or so there was no longer a movement in any sense in which the same term can be applied continuously to the discernible Protestant opposition in pre–Civil War England and the dominant culture of New England for most of the colonial period. Having kept the Puritan movement together into the eighteenth century, one is tempted now to commit a familiar mistake by making the prevailing characteristics of this last period definitive and claiming any subsequent alterations as decline and fall. But change was never in itself fatal. The symptoms of morbidity, rather, are to be located in the loss of the facility to accommodate the latest set of changes to the continuing imperatives. And this loss of adaptive power was not brought about, much as Puritans would have liked it so, by any internal decay, but by the pressure of external events. The Great Awakening, the great religious revival of the 1740s, did what it is often represented as doing, fatally rupture the Puritan movement. It must be understood, however, that the victim was subsequently a long time dying.

In 1640 the calling of the Long Parliament, hailed by the English Puritans as the answer to their prayers, turned out to mark the end of their unity and identity. In much the same way a hundred years later the arrival of the English preacher George Whitefield on his first tour of New England in the fall of 1740 was welcomed enthusiastically as the occasion for a long-awaited renewal. Clergymen of all shades of opinion had earlier endorsed Jonathan Edwards's narrative of "surprising conversions" at Northampton, and Whitefield's itinerancy was now seen as a wonderful opportunity to put the living force of the Holy Spirit back into religious life throughout all of New England. Yet within two to three years the clergy, and in their train the secular leadership of the colonies, had divided bitterly over what Whitefield and his assorted imitators were doing to the population. Clerical factionalism was nothing new, but never before had the divisions become permanent, running so deep that they precluded shifts in alliances as circumstances altered. By 1750 the split over the Awakening *was* the dominant circumstance of New England, and each side denied the fundamental legitimacy of the position held by the other. Nor was this merely a split at the top. About one in five of the churches in Massachusetts and one in three in Connecticut suffered outright schisms over the Awakening, mostly in the form of enthusiasts for the revival either seceding to form Strict Congregational churches, evangelical in piety and Morellian in polity, or going over to the new Separate Baptists, who unlike their cautious predecessors were militant in their opposition to any form of establishment. Splits were most likely to occur in churches in eastern Connecticut and in the region of Massachusetts that had been Plymouth Colony, areas where the establishment was least clearly defined and sectarian activity traditionally strongest, but well organized, historically durable churches in Boston, Salem, New London, New Haven, Hartford, and elsewhere fell to pieces too.[4] By any measure of comparison with past imbroglios, the challenge of the new evangelicism was blithely accepted and then miserably failed.

Such a thorough and sudden wreck suggests a need for explanations couched in terms of "structural" causes. The differential responses to the Awakening, it is assumed, can be explained only by recourse to the distinctive social characteristics of the revival's ardent supporters. It has been suggested that they were successful individuals using the dramatic self-accusation and wholesale regeneration of the evangelical conversion experience as a salve to guilt incurred by participating in economic expansion. Alternatively, the Awakening has been presented as a safety valve for the frustrations created by declining economic opportunity, or as recourse for those afflicted by the anomie overtaking the mobile elements of the population in an era of geographic expansion, or as emotional compensation for the bewilderment among the stable sections of the population as the migrants came falling in on them.[5] In studies of the Awakening on the ground, the Boston separate church ministered to by the sometime itinerant and ultrarevivalist Andrew Croswell is seen as a lower-class protest against the sacrifices inflicted by the growth of the commercial economy; the widespread acceptance of revivalism by the established churches in Gloucester and Marblehead is taken as incorporating the two towns' marginal and vulnerable groups into a newly formed unity in the face of the disrupting effects of the commercialization of the economy; and the formation of a Strict Congregational church in the Ipswich parish of Chebacco is described as a benign development that had little effect on an economy and society that did not change much at any time in the eighteenth century.[6] The Awakening was diverse in its effects and is consequently liable to equally divergent interpretations. The obvious danger is not so much of overgeneralization from limited instances as of merging together apposite cases from disparate occasions, touched up with shreds of theology and patches of social science theory, to produce a single frankensteinian construct endowed with superhuman powers.

It would not be to the point in this discussion to start adding to the list of interchangeable spare parts from which explanations of the Awakening can be fitted together. It is more pertinent here to evaluate the Awakening in light of the preceding history of the Puritan movement, to which it unexpectedly turned out to be the denouement. And on this question someone who has followed the Puritans over various terrains and through any number of adventures is immediately struck by what he, at least, coming up on the 1740s from this perspective, perceives as an anomaly. A common thread, really an unexamined assumption, runs through most of the accounts of the Awakening, however opposite they may be in other respects, and that is the axiom that we are dealing with some form of pathology. Behind the emotionalism of the revival and the bitter cleavages it produced must lie some social disruption that could not be addressed by existing religious patterns. And if this is so, then these existing institutions and the culture they embodied must have been in some sense inexpressive, empty, dead, at most the bland faith of the untroubled, whoever these fortunate and presumably well-endowed individuals may have been.

When applied to American historiography, allegedly secular social science often turns out to be so much de-moralized moralizing. Behind the assumption about the low state of religion in New England on the eve of the Awakening we can trace, at one remove, a remarkable instance of the persistence of a nineteenth-century phenomenon: the dominance German scholarship gained over the high culture of American religion. Church historians trained in Germany or by expatriate German scholars, in awe of the prestige of German Protestant theology, insisted on forcing the history of English-speaking Calvinism into a Germanic mold and loaded the New England establishments with the failings the romantic sensibility attributed to the German churches before the rise of Pietism, which in turn is seen as the equivalent of the Great Awakening. Colonial New Englanders were admittedly fond of accusing themselves of degeneracy, which they thought of primarily as a failure to infuse the outward forms of religion with a genuine inner commitment. This single self-criticism, repeated so often it became a patriotic rhetoric, marks the only point of contact with the faults Pietist critics found in the institutionalized Lutherism of the same period. It would take a stretch of the imagination to judge eighteenth-century Congregationalism, even in the Connecticut of the Saybrook Platform, as hierarchical, ritualist, coldly credal, or narrowly legalistic, and, therefore, desperately in need of a fervently preached, broadly accessible religion of the heart.

A number of imaginations, unfortunately, have been so stretched, and the consequence has been to put the Awakening into the wrong setting. As a result, the widespread opposition it created becomes incomprehensible except as either a defense of entrenched privilege or a curious first-ditch stand by men who would in some instances several decades later become pioneers of American Unitarianism. The New Lights, the supporters of the Awakening, must similarly be seen as doing little more than breathing new life into old forms, even though, as the name suggests, they only rarely claimed to be reinvigorating traditional rites—that exercise, after all, was the burden of the jeremiad, the primary religious rite of the old order. Unqualified enthusiasm for the Awakening was based on the reverse impulse, on an abrupt rejection of the main tenets of Puritan practical divinity and of all that had been created over a century of effort to put them into effect in America. Whitefield, to be sure, when prompted by his New England promoters, claimed he would restore the "rising Generation" ("settled on their Lees," his hosts told him) to the original principles of the founders, but he spoke as a poorly informed and credulous tourist, just as he obligingly repeated what had been intimated to him about the poor moral character of the Church of England in the Puritan colonies and its gloomy missionary prospects.[7] A native son such as Jonathan Edwards knew better than to credit the customary restorationist rhetoric and praised the course of the Awakening in New England precisely because it was visibly a new order of the ages and perhaps the last revolution in human affairs before the millennium.

To appreciate the challenge of the Awakening, one has to forget the Pietist analogies, ignore the American Revolution in the offing for a moment, and recall exactly what was under attack. No one in New England on the eve of Whitefield's tour in 1740 had so far forgotten Puritan practical divinity as to think that the road to heaven was a contiguous set of syllogisms arranged in ascending order of complexity or a code of social decorum so well mannered it could hardly do other than compel a gentlemanly God to dispense salvation to its successful practitioners. Saving knowledge was still "operative knowledge," neither merely "notional" nor "speculative," nor reducible to a set of moral precepts. It could be conceived as working in the first instance on the will in order to vitalize the intellect, or, alternatively, as informing the intellect in order to command the will rightly. But either way, saving knowledge consisted in wholehearted belief in the justice of God's decrees, trust in his promises, and love of him for his willingness to extend mercy to the undeserving. Attaining such a commitment took an extended training, a sentimental no less than a substantive education, through the plenitude of means—the network of ecclesiastical ordinances, private duties, and social institutions that gradually endowed earnest believers with a vital apprehension of abstract propositions and schooled their imaginations to interpret the events of their lives, public and private, in the terms of the orthodox scheme. The guide through this long process was the Word, and the guide through the Word was the sermon. Sermons were not, as is sometimes supposed, to be larded with esoteric learning to overawe a groundling audience—not even Cotton Mather indulged himself that way in his pulpit oratory. They were intended to "smell of the lamp" or be composed of "*well beaten oil*" only in the specific sense of being the product of study and reflection, and they were to be written in a carefully prepared, prayerful mood. The preacher was regularly advised to fit his sermons to his congregation's capacity and to "let them come *Flaming* out of your hand with Excitations to some *Devotion* and *Affection* of Godliness, into the *Hearts* of those whom they are addres'd unto."[8] Well before Whitefield it was well understood in New England that "it is the Mind that convinces the Mind; and the Heart, that perswades the Heart. If we are burning and flaming in our own Breasts, there is the greater likelihood of inkindling holy Affections, in the Hearts of others."[9] But the sermon's primary function, however forcefully phrased, was didactic, a running commentary on an extended journey that stretched from the earliest stirrings of grace to the last moments of the assured saint.

Knowing what is coming, we can distort the content of Puritan soteriology by seeing it as *necessarily* predictive of Enlightenment naturalism or environmentalism. Charles Chauncy, the foremost opponent of the Awakening and in time a prophet of universalism, may seem to be deviating toward outright rationalism, at least supernatural rationalism, as early as 1732 when he writes, "if we would become truly religious, we must *take heed to our way*, i.e. We must not live at random; without care or caution: but must advise with our reason and conscience; make a pause before we act, and not enter upon any course heedlessly; without tho't or consideration." Events would eventually oblige Chauncy to make so strong a reading of his own words that he became what his adversaries suspected of him all along, but he would have preferred his original comfortable ambivalence. Of and in itself his proposition is consistent with Orthodox Protestant intellectualism and contains nothing that could not have been preached in Boston sixty years earlier, that had not actually been preached in terms very similar as an essential element of predestinarianism. Inherently obdurate and perverse, went the orthodox argument, fallen human nature could come to saving knowledge not in the wake of sudden impulses but only by gradual degrees, through discipline and reflective experience, the essence of the "means" through which God's hidden will was fulfilled for the elect. Or as Chauncy put it in 1732, "I deny not but the holy Spirit may convert persons without means: but instances of this kind are very uncommon, if there be any such at all."[10]

Jonathan Edwards, dissatisfied with this familiar synthesis of piety and intellect, saw in operative knowledge a philosophical confusion that led to inadvertent Pelagianism, grace reduced to little more than a habit acquired by long practice in imitating the gracious. He had a point, though his own form of determinism got him into as many difficulties as the doctrines he criticized for allowing too much to human ability.[11] This critique in any case had little influence on the course of the Awakening, except in the immediate circle of his followers. The twenty-five-year-old Whitefield, cocksure and anything but knowledgeable, set the actual terms of the debate over the New England Way by applying his ready-made stricture, suitable for any Christian polity in need of his services: "Many, nay most that preach, I fear, do not experimentally know Christ." Nothing besides the sermon was worth serious attention, and New England's preachers could be written off as failures *ipse dixit* because in the pulpit they were guides and interpreters (presumably to a land they knew only at second hand) when they should have been exhorters. Happily, Whitefield was there to supply personally and by his example what was lacking, indeed all that was needed: extemporary, theatrical preaching, "affectionate" to the point of being abusive in its detailed, imagistic evocation of the flames of hell awaiting the multitude whose religion until then was only of the head because they had learned it of a ministry similarly disabled. This single-minded assault on the hearers by a gracious preacher would reproduce in them the same intense, tightly focused conversion experience he himself had undergone a few years earlier and at a stroke take the place of the spread-out Puritan pilgrimage, with its dry periods and "freshenings" measured out over the course of a lifetime. "N.B.," wrote Ebenezer Parkman, the minister of frontier Westborough, on first meeting Whitefield, "The Account which he gave of the Time and Manner of the powerful working of the Spirit of God upon him." And for the afternoon of the same day, 24 September 1740, Parkman wrote, "He preach'd in the College Yard again. . . . It was to incredible multitudes, and with wondrous power."[12]

It did work. Thousands came to see Whitefield on his itinerancy, and numbers of them had the requisite experience in response to his brilliant delivery of a form of evangelical preaching they had never heard before. Other itinerants followed in Whitefield's path, with similar effect. A few of them abandoned the sermon form entirely, alternately exhorting, praying, and singing as the spirit moved them, and multitudes were converted in this manner. Some of the settled clergy took up the new evangelical style, placing their emphasis for the first time on inducing an acute sense of desperation in the unconverted, on the theory that a deep enough feeling of conviction would almost automatically spill over into conversion. It worked for them too, for almost anyone, clerical or lay, who took a try at revivalism and had a little skill at building up a menace. It *had* to work, if one considers even for a moment the audience at which this new style of preaching was directed. Whitefield at the end of his 1740 tour wrote of New England that "on many Accounts it certainly exceeds all other provinces in America, and, for the establishment of religion, perhaps all other parts of the world."[13] He was probably intending to please his hosts, on this count at least, but he did see that the people struck to the heart had been in some way prepared by the elaborately textured institutional fabric of Puritan religious life.

New Englanders took to Whitefield's message because it was already *their* message, the message they had been born and bred to hear, newly condensed in content and tricked out in images unusual in sermons but all too real to a people whose much reprinted classic was *The Day of Doom* (sixth edition, Boston, 1715; seventh edition, Boston, 1751). Friend or foe of Whitefield, the New England clergy had done his advance work. Israel Loring, the minister of Sudbury, became so adamant an Old Light (an opposer of the Awakening) that he eventually got into serious trouble with a substantial part of his congregation. He was also the author of *Serious Thoughts on the Miseries of Hell*, published in 1732. In his election sermon of 1737 he advised his clerical brethren to, "in the most clear and affecting Manner we can, represent to Sinners the dreadful Miseries of Hell, that they are exposed unto, and are in daily Danger of," and he also repeated the standard line that contemporary New Englanders were an unworthy generation of formalists "not animated with spiritual Frames, which are the soul" of worship. Three years before Whitefield's tour, Loring (who would be of another mind when he found out what the "most clear and affecting manner" really was) took heart "from what God has wrought in some Parts of this Land," meaning Edwards's revival at Northampton, and asked for prayers that God would extend this favor "that the whole Land may partake of the like blessed Effusions of the Holy Spirit."[14] No evangelicals themselves in Whitefield's sense, Loring and his cohorts, the evangelical ministry of New England (as *they* understood the term), had for generations been weaving for their congregations an imaginative universe in which Whitefield's narrow-gauge terrorism could hardly do otherwise than make convincing, bone-chilling sense.

The situation was not without its piquant aspect. By concentrating so exclusively on the moment of conversion and by attributing the experience solely to the power of the new preaching, the New Lights largely ignored the cultural and ecclesiastical institutions that had made their miracle possible. Or they went out of their way to repudiate them. In the journal of his second trip, in 1744, Whitefield (now twenty-nine) has the aging John Rogers of Kittery, scion of several generations of clergymen and progenitor of more, confess that in his more than thirty years in the ministry "he was not acquainted with real religion, till I was last in New England."[15] The remark, if accurately recorded, is a tribute to the degree to which New Lights were so taken with the strangeness of their mass successes that they were willing to regard the work of the Puritan ministry since 1660 as so many essays in pharisaism. For those who rode the wave, the Awakening was an intoxicating experience. Behind their fascination with the epidemic of conversions that justified this radical new departure, however, lies an interesting and suggestive confusion.

Actually, all sorts and ages of people responded to the new evangelical preaching, but only the "unconverted" could make the dramatic gesture, conversion, that drew most of the attention. Church members, the already converted, could and did come to hear revival preachers, weep for their sins, and manifest a more serious and sustained concern for the things of religion. All the New Lights say as much—but in passing only. This behavior was too tame, too possible under ordinary conditions, to be of much interest in comparison with the sudden rush of newly converted individuals into the churches. Edwards's *surprising* conversions, a great and unexpected outpouring of grace rather than simply a quickening of the already gracious, was held up as the distinguishing sign that a unique moment in salvation history was at hand. The work of God in the course of the Awakening, as New Lights conceived of it, "has been chiefly amongst those that are young; and comparatively but few other have been made partakers of it."[16] Matters could hardly have been otherwise if the revival was defined in New Light terms, as the mass conversion of an unlikely group, because the population at risk for the signal experience was, just as in the seventeenth century, disproportionately young. Under the traditional dispensation many of these unexpected youthful converts would have joined the churches anyway at the usual glacial pace, in small batches scattered over a period of decades as they performed the unremarkable feat of growing older. Whitefield and his imitators may have also reached young people who would never otherwise have made it all the way to full communion, or they may have merely pushed the usual pilgrims into running their races at the trot so that they all ended up at the finish line together and well ahead of schedule. There is no way of telling. But the New Lights indisputably concentrated their attention (and thus they have managed to rivet ours) on just one part of the general phenomenon of the Awakening. In turn, when the great bursts of new admissions ceased in the New England churches after 1743, the Awakening was (and is) held to have "ebbed," though New Englanders were not necessarily jaded or emotionally exhausted. In 1744 Whitefield drew just as large crowds as four years earlier and they were just as enthusiastic. This alleged "drought" resulted from nothing more than the simple fact that all the vulnerable individuals in the pool of possible converts had been reached in the first three years of the Awakening and that further "revivals" (in the sense of mass conversions) would have to wait until the ranks of the young and unconverted were replenished by the ordinary course of nature.[17]

Unfortunately, the most strenuous New Lights were wholly taken up with the *un*natural aspect of the Awakening. A renewed sense of dedication among middle-aged church members did not render the work an unprecedented outpouring of the Holy Spirit; hordes of adolescents and young adults abruptly under conviction, repentant, and applying for church membership were the genuine evidence of divine power at work, promising great things for New England and Christendom. Deborah Prince, the gifted and tragically short-lived daughter of the Awakening's chief publicist, summed up the hopes of her side with engaging candor in 1743: "It is the opinion of many eminent divines, that it is the dawning of that glorious day, when the whole earth shall be filled with the knowledge of the Lord as the waters cover the sea. It seems as if the Lord was hastily calling in his elect. Sometimes a new face of things spreads over a whole town in a week or two's time. Sometimes there has been an hundred struck with convictions together in one sermon."[18]

While this epochal prospect lasted, it could, for those caught up in it, justify relegating the whole of the Puritan achievement in practical divinity to the dustbin of Arminianism. It could make minor-league itinerants such as Samuel Buell or the younger John Rogers for a brief moment commanders with Whitefield at the approaching Armageddon. And, perhaps most important, the vision restored New England to center stage in the drama of Christian history. New England, if it were awakened, could be what Whitefield

had explicitly invited the colonies to become, the place where the new reformation "certainly will prevail more than in other places." Fulsome tributes by
New Lights to the recovery of interest in seventeenth-century New England
authors points to the persistence of a barely submerged inferiority complex,
as nagging as a toothache. The popularity of English authors such as Tillotson, Berkeley, even Doddridge and Watts, let alone Pope and Addison, were
so many reminders of the obvious, the provinciality of New England, a more
or less prosperous corner of a great empire.[19] But when Isaac Watts in 1744
could circulate in Scotland a reprint of a Boston manifesto in favor of the
Awakening by the thousands and probably by the tens of thousands, the
transatlantic connection was visibly weighted for the first time toward the
American side. Through the Awakening New Englanders could resume the
status of exemplar nation for Whitefield's reformation, while its guiding
spirit triumphed where Cromwell had failed and converted the Church of
England to the ideal New England would exemplify.[20]

All at once New Light clergy had been offered freedom from the suspicion of insignificance and visible proof that the long, mundane course of
godliness could be abruptly transcended when the grace of God was being so
generously poured out. Their sense of release goes a long way toward explaining the New Lights' recklessness and aggression in their dealings with
the critics of the Awakening. Edwards at the height of the revival, in 1742, in
offering considerations for advancing the great work, did what no other New
England controversialist had ever previously dared to do. Carefully and calmly he accused Old Lights of sinning against the Holy Ghost:

> I am persuaded that those who have openly opposed this work, or have
> from time to time spoken lightly of it, cannot be excused in the sight of
> God, without openly confessing their fault therein; especially if they be
> ministers. . . . For 'tis Christ that they have spoken against in speaking
> lightly of, and prejudicing others against this work; yea, worse than that,
> 'tis the Holy Ghost. And though they have done it ignorantly and in un-
> belief, yet when they find out who it is they have opposed, undoubtedly
> God will hold them bound publicly to confess it.[21]

This much appeared in a work by the New Lights' most distinguished intellectual, sporting a preface from the equally renowned William Cooper of
fashionable Brattle Street and written at a moment when the revivalists were
still flush with success. Old Lights were not to be allowed the modest distinction John Winthrop had courteously awarded Roger Williams, the status of
misguided saints whose works bore evil fruit without prejudicing their own
acknowledged election. If they persisted in opposing the Awakening, Ed-

wards could not see how they could be numbered among the elect. Neutrals, the "many that are silent and unactive, especially ministers," were subject to the curse of Meroz; outright opponents of the revival were put on notice that "it is in vain for any of us to expect any other, than to be greatly affected by it in our spiritual state and circumstances, respecting the favor of God, one way or the other."[22]

Edwards's immoderation is more symptomatic than causal. Conflict with the most conveniently situated enemies was virtually the sole outlet available for the energies and hopes let loose by the wave of conversions. In traditional practical divinity spiritual progress was ordinarily a continuum: the means used to capture the imaginative powers were mostly the same ones expected to nourish grace, as weak Christians matured in spiritual strength, and also to provide the agenda for assured saints. After having ignored or repudiated as Arminian these familiar devices in favor of the revivalist sermon and the contagion of mass conversions, the New Light spokesmen had nothing much to offer their herds of new converts except further news from the front of revivals elsewhere. Edwards himself in dealing with his surprising converts at Northampton, once he had them, came up only with a covenant renewal amplified by a set of articles pledging reformation of particular sins held to be especially prevalent in the town.[23] Such an expanded covenant of reformation had first been proposed by Cotton Mather back in 1690 and hardly spoke to the needs of the new church members: they had been converted by sermons concentrating on grace, not morality, and, having been rather abruptly called out of the world, they had no special interest in an inclusivist covenant ceremony designed to affirm New England's collective identity and bind together through the individual churches the whole population of the new Israel. Practical divinity was a blind spot in Edwards and in Edwardseans generally until the end of the century, when the work of Timothy Dwight and Lyman Beecher would finally develop devotional techniques and strategies of cultural envelopment appropriate to the new theology.[24] In the meantime, circuits so heavily charged went into overload.

New converts needed something to do appropriate to the kind of conversion they had experienced. They found it in many places by questioning the credentials of older church members, who, educated along the traditional lines, generally lacked the same dramatic experience, or by demanding that the various forms of partial membership short of full communion be discontinued, or by insisting on the return of restrictive membership open only to those who, like themselves, could give an acceptable narrative of their spiritual regeneration. And they turned on the clergy opposed to the Awakening or deemed insufficiently enthusiastic and, therefore, presumptively unconverted. Edwards for his part counseled meekness and forbearance to "those ministers that have been judged and injuriously dealt with," good if abstract advice that he unfortunately coupled with the suggestion that the lay critics might, after all, have something in their questioning of the spiritual states of their pastors. "We han't yet seen the end of things; nor do we know who will be most vindicated and honored of God in the issue."[25]

There had been many previous occasions when the godly had been critical of their ministers and few periods, if any, when relations were entirely amicable. In the Awakening, however, these tensions appeared in a particularly deadly guise. In the most extreme form of attack, the target would be denounced by a lay exhorter or itinerant preacher or by their local disciples as unconverted and consequently incapable of converting others. In its more moderate form the charge would be an idle and unprofitable ministry unable to bring the complainants to grace because of the minister's personal insufficiencies and lack of application. Both accusations were, like spectral evidence, irrefutable: a clergyman could no more prove the certainty of his election than anyone else, and the matter of unfruitfulness was self-evident if the complaint was made at all. The apologetics kept in reserve for such occasions had very little application in these instances. It had always been held that the power of the word of God, and not some charismatic gift of the individual preacher, worked conversion through the sermon, but the theoretical possibility of a gifted reprobate saving many people by his brilliant impostures was a textbook exercise, more fit for a Harvard disputation than an actual church controversy. Most people believed that an unconverted minister would botch the job most or all of the time because he did not truly understand the message he preached, even if he got the formal content right. Similarly, it was a truism that different ministers had different talents, a situation well suited to the different spiritual needs of the varieties of human character. Earnest believers unable to profit from the minister of their church should blame themselves for the failure and then in all humility remove to a ministry better fitted to their peculiarities. When a large part of a congregation—it did not have to be a majority—was in the mood to cry out against unprofitable preaching, the case was very different. Then, it could be argued, it made more sense for the one to go than the many.

Ministers under attack defended themselves, sometimes with gentleness and conciliation, sometimes with viciousness and cunning, but unless their supporters were numerous and their critics few, they had little chance of getting through the conflict with their ministry intact. If hostilities were allowed to reach the breaking point, a portion of the congregation would secede and form a Strict Congregationalist church or go over to the Separate

Baptists, and with them, when clerical incomes were already fragile, would go a sufficient portion of the minister's financial support to put him on starvation wages. He could turn to the law for his contractual maintenance, and sometimes did, but the litigation would ruin his standing in his community and was unlikely to restore his income, whatever injury it inflicted on his opponents. Cotton Mather had remarked in 1725 that ministers who went to court over "Synecdochical Pay" (substitution of the part for the whole) "would find the *Remedy* worse than the *Disease*, and by using the *Law*, wound the future Success of the *Gospel*."[26] His caution was even more valid two decades later, in the face of organized opposition. A prudent Old Light such as Theophilus Pickering, who was under siege from a separatist minority in his Ipswich parish when he died in 1747, was found by his heirs to have been the creditor to his flock (most of whom had stayed with him) for a full £1,100 in unpaid maintenance. He had never dared worsen his precarious situation by pressing for his arrears.[27] Alternatively, at the best, before matters reached a separation, a council of neighboring ministers would be called, the accused incumbent would generally be vindicated, and the congregation exhorted to peace and harmony. The dissidents would then persist, and another council might convene, and another, until the unavoidable verdict came down that whoever was at fault, there was no way for the gospel to continue to take root in the divided church without a new ministry acceptable to both sides. Ezra Carpenter, who succeeded the phlegmatic Zechariah Whitman at Hull in 1725, served with satisfaction on a grossly inadequate stipend for eighteen years, despite the lack of his predecessor's private means, only to fall victim to a separatist movement inspired by itinerants. He survived three conciliar investigations over a period of as many years and then gave up his impossible situation and resigned in 1746. After that he eked out a living by supply preaching in backwater and frontier towns for nine years, accepting aid from a special clerical dole administered by the Massachusetts provincial convention of ministers, and finally found another pulpit in 1755 in a New Hampshire town so uninviting (its adjoining neighbor had been burned by the Indians a few years earlier) that it could not afford any qualms about a clergyman cashiered from another church.[28] Old Light defensiveness and vehemence become easier to understand if the penalties of generosity and irenicism are considered: resignation of a ministry that had been deemed valuable before the arrival of Whitefield and thereafter a life of dependence or penury, certainly of limited usefulness. When the rumor went around that Whitefield had boasted of a corps of evangelical Scots ready to come to New England and take over the bulk of its pulpits, there were uncomfortably many good reasons to take the silly report seriously.

Once the breaches were opened, they stayed that way and widened. Whitefield, with plenty of native assistance, had finally unleashed the sectarian impulses within the Puritan movement in America and turned them against a portion of the establishment. Old Lights liked to compare lay critics to the Antinomians of the 1630s, but the Quaker challenge of the 1640s and 1660s would seem a better analogy, pertinent even in its roll call of separatist martyrs in Connecticut who were jailed for itinerancy or nonpayment of ministerial rates. In the Strict Congregational churches John Norton would have found everything he feared from Morellians in 1659: subordination of the minister to the fellowship, defiance of authority in the name of a higher law accessible to the spiritually enlightened, the narrowest possible definition of a church, congregational autonomy so strict as to verge on anarchy.[29] After all the near misses of the previous century New England Puritanism had finally succumbed to its own centripetal forces. Part of the credit for this intriguing achievement must be awarded to the revivalists, who struck the New England establishment at its most exposed points. A century earlier the Baptists had made too few waves, the Quakers too many. The revivalists were armed with an alternative familiar in its assumptions and logic and disruptive only in its corollaries. But pride of place in any inquiry into the Puritan collapse goes to the nature of the establishment itself. To a degree, this was a matter of clerical vulnerability; to a larger degree the clergy suffered from an excess of strengths.

The most obvious weakness in the clerical position was still the contrast between their lofty vocation and their mundane need to earn a living. Inflation in the first half of the eighteenth century, brought on by emissions of paper money during frequent intervals of warfare, seriously eroded ministerial salaries, ensuring that the issue of clerical maintenance would be the regular subject of complaint, both by individual ministers and by their various assemblies.[30] As the number of disputes between ministers and churches rose, doubling in the first half of the century, doctrinal issues came to rival long-standing financial ones, and the two became hopelessly entangled: a town unhappy with what it was hearing from the pulpit was liable to stint the preacher's salary, and a town in controversy with its minister over how many ounces of silver equaled how much paper money, old or middle tenor, or similar financial arcana was tempted to improve its side of the argument by scrutinizing his sermon for doctrinal eccentricities. Gilbert Tennent's famous blast against carnal men in the ministry "whose chief Desire, like their great Grandfather [Judas], is to finger the Pence, and carry the Bag," struck home in New England, not because the clergy had grown rich but for the opposite reason, because their reduced circumstances made maintenance a more frequent and irritating issue.[31] One may also speculate—only a bevy of local studies could confirm the point—that the auxiliary enterprises many clergymen were obliged to undertake, as farmers, storekeepers, doctors, lawyers, even brewers and blacksmiths, further compromised their traditional standing. Direct participation in the economy of a New England town may help to humanize the clergy in the eyes of posterity, but at the time it sucked the participant into the maelstrom of minor causes célèbres and never ending feuds that were the stuff of rural social intercourse. The ministry complained, and loudly, about their secular involvements because they understood implicitly what we are forever triumphantly rediscovering in our local studies—all the ways in which religious controversy easily became the perfect medium for expressing and perpetuating simmering social tensions—and they could count the cost of their growing inability to remain aloof from the daily neighborhood warfare.[32]

Perhaps the most remarkable instance of the way great causes turned on mundane contingencies is one of the most celebrated—the trials and triumphs of the Separatist layman Nathan Cole of Kensington Society in Farmington, Connecticut. In his autobiography Cole describes Whitefield's visit to his neighborhood in 1741, his own subsequent spiritual turmoil, ending in assurance of conversion, and in 1747 his separation from the established church and his consequent refusal "to pay rates to the hireling Ministers." Twice Cole was threatened with prosecution for his failure to pay the ministerial rate, and the accounts of these confrontations are among the best-written set pieces in Cole's narration, beautifully contrived in their apparent artlessness. On both occasions Cole parries Scripture with Scripture, confounds various formidable "Esquires," as well as the Princeton-educated minister of the parish, and successfully appeals to the fundamental sense of justice of the ordinary members of the society, who uphold the humble saint against the old order of Moses and Aaron. For Cole his two victories were the triumph of the Spirit over the great ones of this world. For us his adventures are more likely to be taken as a presage of another kind of spirit, that of '76, and our delight in this embattled farmer can only increase on learning that Samuel Clarke, the minister whose demands he foiled, ended his career both bankrupt through unwise speculation and under suspicion of Tory sympathies.[33]

Whether a saint or a Yankee egalitarian, however, Cole acted out his drama in the setting of a rural parish in western Connecticut, amid its commonplace crises. Samuel Clarke, only a short while after his failure to confute Cole had "killed the minister stone dead," declared to Kensington Church that "I doe not desire the money of those who do not desire my labors" and added that he did not wish anyone "tyed to me by the mere force of civil law." There *was* a clash of principles of a sort because Clarke still believed in the "wise and good civil regulations" concerning establishment for those willing to accept them, but he and Cole were hardly polar opposites. Most years Kensington society abated Cole's rate without any controversy, but twice local financial exigencies gave him a chance to play the disciple before the heathen magistrate. Cole's first period of persecution coincided with the setting off of New Britain society from Kensington after fifteen years of agitation and the simultaneous resort of the truncated parish to Princeton and Clarke, a well-heeled bachelor, after three Yale men in succession had turned down its overtures because of its depleted revenues. Cole's family still attended the established church, though he did not, and his neighbors, worried about their own rates, still insisted he pay for them even as his pleas moved them to grant him a personal exemption. The second time around, in the mid-1760s, a second division of the still oversized parish was being mooted (over the objections of Clarke, who had decided to marry at last), and a bare majority of the faction-ridden society had also voted to undertake repairs of the old meetinghouse and construction of a new one. Under the circumstances Cole's continued conscientious objection to ecclesiastical rates seemed like an expensive luxury until his adamancy in maintaining his position once again convinced the society to reaffirm his right to exemption.

Recovering this level of detail does not trivialize the importance of Cole's stand or the stand of other Separatists, who experienced much harder treatment in the same cause of voluntary maintenance. But once parish boundaries and hard-pressed clerical families, as well as quarrelsome neighbors and generations-old enmities, are restored to the fabric of New England society in the mid-eighteenth century we can begin to sense how enormous a problem the Awakening was for the New England ministry and why so many of them regarded the Separatists as incendiaries in a powder magazine. These literally parochial episodes were the standard stuff of parish histories; the peculiar contribution of the Awakening was to elevate them to the level of fundamental principle. But this had always been the genius of the Puritan movement— to invest transcendent, numinous meaning in happenstance and particularity. The Awakening merely turned this motor force against the establishment that had presumed to claim the exclusive right to direct its course.

After due allowance is made for the social and economic roots of anticlericalism, it must be said that the decisive force in the downfall of the clergy was their own disunity. They could hardly respond effectively to a challenge when a minority of them openly sided with the challengers and the majority was split into two camps, Old Light and New, more interested in doing in each other than in beating back lay initiatives. It is a moral appropriate to the tag end of a Puritan tale, however, that the divisions among the clergy were to a great degree the result of the means by which they had earlier assured their own standing and influence. By the beginning of the eighteenth century the clergy had become almost too proficient in their technique, and then in the next four decades they had flourished untroubled by the pervasive, organized opposition of earlier years. In the Awakening they carried on as before, oblivious to the way old sources of power unthinkingly deployed could become the very agents to vitiate their adaptive capacity. In particular, to confirm their moral force they had regularly smoothed over their genuine differences through ambiguity and indirection; when at last their divisions came to be spoken of, at a moment of intense excitement, they were inevitably taken as more complete and profound than they were. And they had cultivated their mastery of the printed words with such success that they ensured that their infighting would receive banner headlines and widespread publicity when they did come around to turning their artillery on each other.

In the early 1740s, at the height of the controversy over the Awakening, when one would assume that the masks were finally down, the clergy had still not given up the art of pussyfooting. Without supporting extratextual evidence it would be impossible to tell the two sides apart from their official pronouncements; it would scarcely even be possible to determine the game they were playing. A long *Testimony* against the "excesses" of the revival (itinerancy, lay exhorters, schism, Antinomianism) maneuvered through the annual convention of the Massachusetts ministry in May 1743 by questionable means, was subsequently criticized by New Light opponents solely for omissions and for the tactics used to get it adopted. The New Lights in a countermove organized a mass declaration of support for the Awakening at the other great clerical conclave, the Harvard commencement, in July 1743, and included the same catalog of abuses, but this time prefaced by an "attestation" of "our full Perswasion, either from what we have seen our selves, or received upon credible Testimony, That there has been a *happy and remarkable Revival of Religion in many Parts of this Land, thro' an uncommon divine Influence*." This introductory statement, at least, may seem to place the *Testimony and Advice* firmly in the New Light camp, but the manifesto remains almost identical in form to the resolutions of the General Consociation of the Connecticut churches that preface a *condemnation* of the Awakening (leading to the passage of repressive legislation) with the declaration that "it appears that there has for Some time past been a great and remarkable Work of God caried on in this Land and in this Government."[34] When the bulk of the clergy contented themselves with an exchange of documents separable only in their nuances, the full statement of the issues in dispute was going to be left to the likes of Andrew Croswell, bold enough to pronounce half the ministry of the colonies unconverted and to particularize on occasion, and his activities would be read by Old Lights as doing the New Lights' dirty work while they cheerfully distanced themselves from him in a flurry of generalities.[35]

New Light suspicions about Old Light motives were no less profound, nor were they lacking a grain of substance. In the course of the debate in May 1743 over the antirevival resolutions at the annual ministerial convention, Joseph Sewall (son of Samuel, pastor of the Old South, and a staunch New Light) had executed a byzantine but significant ploy by demanding that the manifesto's catalog of errors include a list of Arminian temptations to balance the condemnation of Antinomian tendencies. He was turned down, and his missing resolution accordingly appeared in the New Light *Testimony and Advice* instead. Edwards similarly shows a preoccupation with covert forms of Arminianism in the same defenses of the revival in which he looks with a certain indulgence on misguided but well-meant and possibly helpful lay criticisms of an unconverted ministry. Arminianism was a crucial sticking point in Old Light–New Light diplomacy (in the brief period when negotiations were still nominally possible), and yet the organizers of the Old Light *Testimony* were fundamentally correct in replying to Joseph Sewall that "we had no Evidence given of the prevailing of these Errors at this Day, in any Parts of the Land."[36] In all there had been exactly three cases, all between 1733 and 1738, when clergymen had been charged with Arminian tenets, and in each instance a feud between the accused and the local notables had been at the bottom of the proceedings.[37] Nevertheless, contemporaries sensed a fault line in 1740 among the ministry, and though they could never prove or even define the distinction, they could put the finger on it very exactly when they had to. The case of Samuel Osborn demonstrates this much with an eerie prophetic force.

Of the three cases in which a minister had been accused of Arminianism, Osborn's was the latest and the best established.[38] He lost his pulpit at Eastham on Cape Cod in 1738 after a local council of eight ministers found the charges proven. This "Antinomian Council," as he subsequently termed it, is of no great interest in itself: only one of its members was of any prominence in the Awakening (Peter Thatcher, who preached himself to death in his enthusiasm), most were probably Old Lights, and all were basically obscure characters, a fairly accurate representation of the undistinguished, un-exceptionable clerical community of the Cape.[39] Osborn, however, assem-bled a much more significant group of eleven ministers to endorse his innocence in 1740, a few months before Whitefield's tour began. Charles Chauncy and Ebenezer Gay, fated to become the fathers of universalism and Unitarianism in America, led the list, which included no fewer than seven future subscribers to Chauncy's *Seasonable Thoughts* of 1743, the classic manifesto of Old Light hostility to the Awakening.[40] As of June 1740, neither Chauncy nor Gay had enunciated any of the theological positions with which they were later identified, and, of course, none of the eleven could have known what was coming in just a few months' time. Osborn, a mostly self-taught Irish immigrant expelled from a minor Cape Cod pulpit, somehow knew where to go when he wanted the backing of men who would take his doctrinal deviations in a more relaxed and generous spirit than a Jonathan Edwards or a Joseph Sewall. And if he knew it, so did Edwards and Sewall. Rather than embracing a distinguishable heterodoxy, a portion of the clergy by 1740 had grown indifferent to the supposed centrality of orthodoxy—a principle, or lack of it, that would be systematized in the heat of the coming decades as the right of private judgment. To their opponents such a deliber-ately comfortable relationship with doctrinal ambiguity was bad in itself and suggested a covert enthusiasm for the deviations the "liberals" were willing to tolerate.[41] This sense that there was a soft center to some people's Calvin-ism was a slender basis on which to build a civil war, but its very indefinabil-ity, the need to flush out the hidden infection before it grew rotten, exacer-bated the nastiness of the clerical duel once the presence of Whitefield in New England induced the two sides to cross swords.

When battle was finally joined, it was carried on with a speed and pub-licity unimaginable in the controversies of the previous century. In a decade when Boston could boast four newspapers, there was just so much more print available to play with. Newspaper articles could guarantee almost a daily exchange of invectives; pamphlets could beget rebuttals and rebuttals rejoinders with astounding fecundity. And Boston's single economic achieve-ment in an otherwise stagnant period, its developing mastery of the com-merce of the region, ensured that every grievance put into print would indeed be heard all over New England.[42] Obscure brouhahas in places like the Scotland precinct of Windham, Connecticut, or Samuel Osborn's second par-ish of Eastham that, had they happened earlier, would have left a trace only in some antiquarian history, could now appear in the pamphlet exchanges in the 1740s in loving detail to intensify the local conflict and generalize the issues in dispute for the benefit of interested parties elsewhere in New England. With such means at their disposal, the contestants descended to the fine points, augmenting the differences by raising procedural questions that amounted to charges of dishonesty. The May 1743 ministers' convention was rigged by unqualified voters, announced Joshua Gee. If a fair and open contest was what they wanted, responded John Hancock, why were they organizing their postcommencement meeting to endorse the revival without disclosing the time and place?[43] Names at last could be named, lists of partisans drawn up and proclaimed in print, with places of residence carefully attached to avoid confusion among namesakes. Little more than the leadership is known in the disputes over the Halfway Covenant or the Old Charter, and some individuals somehow seem to figure prominently on both sides, but in the case of the Awakening the New Light ministry is mustered neatly in the more than a hundred signatories to the *Testimony and Advice* of 1743 (a group of potential waverers is identified by the reservations they attached to their endorsement), and the Old Light contingent displays itself in the equally long list of subscribers to Chauncy's *Seasonable Thoughts* of the same year.

In the decades of the 1670s and 1680s Increase Mather had built up his influence and provided a mechanism for unifying the ministry of the Puritan colonies through his extensive correspondence in the course of collecting materials for his two "histories," the *Relation* of King Philip's War and *Illustrious Providences*. Mather's equivalents during the Awakening were Charles Chauncy and Thomas Prince, the one collecting horror stories about broken parishes and wildly eccentric itinerants for his *Seasonable Thoughts*, the other soliciting stories of grace triumphant in one locale after another for his magazine the *Christian History* to validate the Awakening by accounts of its joyous reception. That clumsy but ingenious machine put together in the last decades of the seventeenth century and the beginning of the eighteenth to articulate a Protestant culture for New England was destroying itself.

Taking stock of the effects of the Awakening as of, say, 1760, it would just barely be possible to argue that in the end this controversy too was assimilated for the most part into a Puritan movement that was much the worse for wear but still mostly intact. Separatist movements had pretty much passed their peak by that date. Few new Strict Congregationalist churches were to be formed, and the older ones almost all sooner or later dissolved, were incorporated into the existing establishment as new parishes, or were converted to the Separate Baptist movement. The latter grouping presented a formidable challenge because of its preference for militant tactics and principled advocacy of the separation of church and state, but as late as 1800 its total numbers were still relatively small.[44] Evangelical techniques would gradually find acceptance among a large share of the New England ministry, most of whom remained pretty reliable characters and not given to questioning a fellow clergyman's conversion openly. And the single largest party by far among the clergy at any time in the second half of the eighteenth century could be termed "Old Calvinists," conservative ministers seeking to hold on to familiar theological compromises without giving up too much either to the elaborations of Edwardseanism that became known as the New Divinity or to the various and varied forms of rationalist speculation that would eventually cohere in Unitarianism.[45]

This line of argument is of value as a reminder that Puritanism had some vitality left even as it was coming apart. But the divisions and bitterness created by the Awakening persisted; in parts of Connecticut and western Massachusetts they had hardened into political factions, and everywhere in New England the new unwillingness to find common ground, however slippery, meant the end of coherent leadership for what had always been a diverse movement liable to fracture under the best of conditions. The lines of mistrust and hostility showed no signs of fading away. We may take the Separate Baptists, if we so please, as the authentic voice of the Awakening, but among the Congregational majority, New Lights where they had the power were quite as zealous to eliminate Old Lights as the latter had been to suppress the evangelicals when the means had been in their hands.[46] Nor can Old Calvinism be considered a real force for moderation and continuity; it was little more than the American equivalent of the "high-and-dry" church of nineteenth-century Anglicanism, a catchall group of individuals with little to unite them besides a dislike of the present and a fear of the future. People who have to defend an ambiguous tradition against well-considered and well-organized criticism coming at them from two opposite directions are in no position to make any very creative repose beyond lamentations and exhortations to moderation.[47] Nor were Old Calvinists an entity in the same way as the Edwardseans and the liberals. The term denotes a spectrum of opinions, and most of the individuals covered by it who were blessed with any intellectuality at all were closer personally and in theology to one or the other of the rival camps than they were to each other. The great schisms of the first third of the nineteenth century, marked by the Second Great Awakening and the Unitarian controversy, were already foredoomed by the last third of the eighteenth.

We may speculate, of course, on what might have been if evangelicism had come more gently to New England and been naturalized in familiar fashion, changing the equilibrium between establishment and sectarianism once again but leaving the Puritan leadership with the will to accommodate the different tendencies within the movement. The future would still have been uncertain in the extreme. Puritanism was the creature of a very spare environment. Its proponents always assumed that order and discipline, multiple reinforcements and regular practice, were the only ways of husbanding such precious resources as their civilization provided in the early modern era: taken together, arranged in the right series, and employed over an extended period, these limited means might overcome human nature for that fraction of the population selected to be so blessed. Civility was not godliness, but it was a necessary prior condition to it, and civility was itself a difficult and time-consuming creation. What such a mentality would have made of the lush possibilities of the nineteenth century, with its mass elementary education, steam-powered cylinder printing presses, and far-flung lecture circuits, is anybody's guess. The people who might have faced up to that challenge were not there to attempt it: they were feeling their way toward rationalism or refining and augmenting Edwards's great work, or, disgusted with "such a Spirit of Dogmatism and Bigotry in Clergy and Laity" (John Adams), they were in other lines of work.[48]

This development would not be an occasion for mourning, were it not for the primitive Aristotelianism of most contemporary historians, who are as positive as the Philosopher that it is nobler to write tragedy than comedy. If not quite "the emancipation of New England," the hundred years after 1760 were indisputably a period of brilliant innovation and of the extension of New England influence outside of its home territory. New Englanders had two enormous advantages derived from their Puritan past when they came to compete in a wider arena. They went into the contest possessing disciplined intellectual skills and organizational talent, inculcated in their densely built-up homeland, where they were to be acquired cheap so that they might be sold in parts less well endowed at high rates. And in an intensely Protestant country they had inherited what was still the most highly articulated and comprehensive vision. The various humanitarian and reform campaigns that originated in Connecticut in the first three decades of the nineteenth century or the widely imitated public school system developed in Massachusetts in the next three would have happened in the rest of the country anyway, had there been no New England, at some time and in some form. Material needs and a great variety of intellectual enthusiasms would have seen to that. New England gave the lead in both areas and gave them its distinctive stamp, that integral combination of voluntarism and coercion that went back at least as far as the Dedham Orders of 1585, because of the early date of its native efforts and the coherence of its schemes by which cultural innovations were married to irreproachably Protestant ends. New Englanders used the same language as the rest of the country with, in effect, a more complete grammar inherited from a Puritan past.

Horace Holyoke, the fictional narrator of Harriet Beecher Stowe's *Oldtown Folks,* parodies the ritual celebrations of these triumphs of New Englanders abroad (such as they were) when he declares grandiloquently that his native region "has been to these United States what the Dorian hive was to Greece." To ponder New England's early history is no less than to study "the seed-bed of this great American Republic, and of all that is likely to come of it." One can imagine a young reader of these words, say an intelligent Boston girl in midadolescence, a little uncertain of how to take Stowe's ambivalent satire, who survives into her vigorous seventies, only to open her monthly copy of *Harper's* in 1932 and discover from Bernard De Voto that New England was the sole "finished part" of America, a living museum piece set apart from the eternally inchoate drama of American life. The debate is an old one, and it rests, early and late, on the false (really falsified) premise that New England's cultural history begins with the landfalls of the *Mayflower* and the *Arbella.* In the authorized version (clerical, fictional, or academic), initial commitment to a compact, definable synthesis of imperatives called Puritanism gives way to a state of confusion, dissension, and inanition, succeeded in the mid-eighteenth century by an era of revitalization movements that eventually liberate the intellectual energies of New England's inhabitants for their destined role in the antebellum era as prophets of evangelicism, enterprise, and social and literary criticism. In the subsequent dispute over the region's priority in American history, what one takes the role of New England to be depends entirely on what one takes (or wants) America to be, not on any notion of the story already in progress when New England was founded. There is no sense that the pioneers of American Puritanism might have already been in the midst of their argument (in both senses of the term) when they stepped ashore.

One is tempted to say that neither Holyoke nor De Voto knew what he was talking about, but Holyoke did not know in a more interesting way. His creator was a clergyman's daughter, a theologian's wife, and the sister of a veritable clerical tribe. She knew from inside the order's bag of tricks, including their favorite: to define some supposed quiddity as aboriginal Puritanism, place their invention in peril from dissension and corruption, and then come to the rescue of it and (in later versions) America at appropriate intervals. The joke is on them in a way because the tactic has the inadvertent effect of making its creators out to be much less talented and intriguing people than they really were. In another sense, though, the joke is on us, for ever taking it seriously.

It does not much matter what the question is—the alleged social basis of Puritanism, the explanatory value of the term for the various aspects of New England's colonial history, the role of New England in national history, the dating and extent of the secularization of American life. By reducing the Puritan movement to a fixed set of characteristics and then tracking the fate of this or that item, or set of items, we can extend or foreshorten the history of Puritanism for whatever polemical purpose we choose, killing it off by 1700 or resuscitating its influence for an account of contemporary policy, foreign and domestic. The exercise may be chronologically arranged, but it will always be in essence ahistorical because it will be based on a denial of the multiple constituencies and varied responses that collectively and continuously make up the Puritan movement from English coherence to American fragmentation. In a history more ironic than that, we are left with a last irony. The most faithful adherents of a clerical mythologizing long since abandoned by its creators and never wholly convincing to its intended victims seems to be on too many occasions the practicing historians of colonial America.

From the inception of this study the Puritan movement has been endowed with an argument indeterminate in its beginnings, ambiguous at its climaxes, and short of finality in its ending. Books, however, conclude decisively—with a last page—even if their subjects are less conveniently bounded. Now, at the finish of this narrative, there remains after all the caveats the inevitable need to take away some generality from the mass of particulars, or at least to inquire if there is one. It may still be asked if any centripetal force other than the accidents of history or the inertia of habit held together a diverse collection of groups advancing a contrariety of agendas. What answer there is, it has been repeatedly suggested, will not be found in any one cultural preference, however widely shared among members of the Puritan movement, or in all of them together. Rather, the place to begin is with the Puritans' insistence that whatever the range of alternatives their culture had to offer (and this would change with time and circumstance), somehow the most suitable pieces of contemporary reality had to be selectively assembled in a way that provided immediate and multiple points of references—for the believer as lonely pilgrim, as political and social animal, and as an organic member of the churches militant and triumphant. Or, to put the proposition a little more directly, from the *Admonition to the Parliament* through Samuel Sewall's last grand gesture the closest thing to a unifying theme for the Puritans in England and America is their passion for creating imaginative context.

Appendix
Editions and Pressruns before the Civil War

Estimates in chapter 2 of the respective circulations of religious and popular titles were made on the basis of restrictions on pressruns promulgated in 1587 and revised in 1635. As a means of providing work for apprentice and journeymen printers, the Court of the Stationers' Company on 4 December 1587 limited the number of copies printed per edition of each work (for most kinds of books) to 1,250 to 1,500; that limit reached, the type used to print the piece would be broken up and any further demand for copies satisfied by a new edition reset from scratch. As a further precaution, the order required that, regardless of pressrun, "no formes of letters be kept standinge to the prejudice of Woorkemen at any tyme." Complaints about violation of this order were numerous, however, and on 16 November 1635, as a result of an arbitrated settlement, a new order upped the limit for most books to 2,000 per edition and authorized the master and wardens of the company to permit 3,000 if, upon application, they found sufficient cause.[1] So, to estimate circulation of a title it would seem necessary only to multiply the number of editions printed up through 1635 by 1,500, the number printed between 1636 and 1640 by 2,000 or 3,000, and add up the two figures. This operation has been performed in chapter 2, using 2,000 copies for the later editions to stay on the conservative side.

Unfortunately, the only item in the entire calculation not subject to argument is the math. The number of editions of frequently reprinted titles is difficult to ascertain accurately because the title pages of the latest known editions of many works make claims that cannot be verified exclusively from surviving copies, and it has been suggested that printers and booksellers deliberately inflated the number of editions of their works to exaggerate their popularity. Certainly, there is evidence that the publishers or printers of some titles were either careless in the extreme when it came to the edition number or downright cynical. To take a relatively extreme example from the second half of the seventeenth century, *The Dreadful Character of a Drunkard* by the pseudonymous John Hart (probably several different authors accidentally or deliberately conflated under a single pen name) survives today in only eight known editions issued between 1663 and 1686. Nevertheless, the first of these claims to be the tenth edition, but a later edition of 1669 calls itself number seven, a later one still of 1679 claims to be the sixth, and then the next known edition, issued three years later in 1689, grandly proclaims itself to be the thirtieth. A still greater degree of uncertainty surrounds the number of copies per edition, which in the case of works printed only once (most titles) probably never went any higher on average than about half of the regulatory limit.

The problem of the number of editions is the easier of the two to resolve. Allowing for a certain amount of nonsense on some title pages, the gap between number of editions claimed and number now extant is best explained by the low survival rate of small, unbound, frequently used titles—and by incomplete reporting of those copies that do survive. The damaged condition of the extant copies of Arthur Dent's titles has already been remarked on, and it is also instructive to compare the entries in the first edition of the *Short Title Catalogue* with those in the second for his most successful book, *The Plaine Mans Path-Way to Heaven*. STC in 1926 lists an edition in 1640 claiming to be the twenty-fifth but actually inventories only twelve distinct editions in all; in 1986 ten of the missing thirteen editions have turned up, and there is no reason to assume the three still unaccounted for are anything other than lost or uninventoried. For that matter, as far as misstatements go, the title pages often err by way of understatement. There are, for example, four known editions of *The Practise of Pietie* in the year 1636 alone; three claim to be the thirty-sixth edition, the fourth evades the issue by modestly giving no number at all. And publishers of pirated editions were not obligated to keep an accurate count by definition, though a Dutch edition of Bayly's work issued (or so it claims) the year before the three "thirty-sixth" editions overcomes its dubious origins by referring to itself merely as "the last edition."

Estimating pressruns of individual editions is a more vexed problem because the scattered evidence on the subject can hardly be compared with the massive information on editions critically examined and systematically laid out in the *STC*. When, as in the case of some of the romances and tales, a relative handful of editions are scattered over a century or more, it is legitimate to object that the publisher in each case was not necessarily going to take the risk of paying for a full quota of copies. Extending the courtesy of using the same multiplier for both editions of the tale of Bevis of Hampton (fourteen extant in all, but ranging in date from 1500 to 1639) and roughly the same number of editions of the exposition of the Ten Commandments by Dod and Cleaver probably serves to obscure the contrast between the modest if sustained demand for the one and the demonstrated enthusiasm for the other. When edition followed edition, as in the case of Dod and Cleaver's title (published first in 1603, it enjoyed fifteen editions by 1622 and twenty by 1635), the printer and publisher would have been foolish not to push the regulatory maximum to the limit, and they may have felt emboldened to go beyond it. Michael Sparke, a professional maverick among the booksellers in the Stationers' Company, estimated that one devotional manual of his own authorship, *Crumms of Comfort*, had gone through over forty editions by 1652 and sold sixty thousand copies, both figures consistent with the work's publishing history and the traditional edition multipliers.[2] And Sparke provides evidence in another case of the persisting temptation to circumvent the featherbedding rules or to flout them entirely.

In 1631 Sparke and the Oxford University printer William Turner were involved in a joint venture that brought both men before the High Commission for publishing unlicensed books. (The works may also have been pirated.) Most of the adventures that landed Sparke before the commissioners with alarming frequency were political in nature, but this time the offending titles were reprints of three popular religious tracts and of an abridgment of a husbandry manual. Of these four books, Sparke had Turner print only fifteen hundred of two, but he exceeded the existing limits set by the Stationers' Company for London printers by arranging for two thousand copies of Dent's *Sermon of Repentance* and for three thousand of a collection of five sermons by John Preston.[3] The resort to Oxford was occasioned by Sparke's running quarrel with the leading members of the Stationer's Company; more respectable stationers preferred to break the rules at home in London. In their agreement of 1635 permitting an increase in the limits on copies per edition the apprentices and journeymen complained that the old regulations had been routinely ignored by the master printers, who maintained standing type to run off new editions when needed and indulged in "extraordinary numbers of some Bookes printed at one Impression."[4] Nor did the new agreement do much to alter the established habits of old sinners, since the journeyman could be found petitioning for redress once again fifteen months later, begging Archbishop Laud in 1637 to get the master printers to live up to the terms.[5]

One group, however, was even less scrupulous than the London master printers and booksellers: the Dutch pirates, subject to no limits, save such minimal inconvenience as the English ambassador could cause them. Mathew Symmons, who was to become a leading printer for the Independents during the Civil War, testified in 1638, after his return from the Netherlands, that "John Johnson [i.e., Jan Janszon] of Amsterdam printeth practice of pieties by tenn-thousand at a time[.] his vent is most by marchantes."[6] Symmons was not likely to have been exaggerating: there were at least five separate Dutch editions of *The Practise of Pietie* in the mid-1630s.

There is a large amount of guesswork, not all of it necessarily inspired, in the estimates for total copies of various titles given in chapter 2 of this book. But the numbers of editions are probably about accurate, possibly a little low, and the figures used for copies per edition are probably distinct underestimates. In reality, religious titles were almost certainly even more widely available than has been suggested, perhaps dramatically so.

Notes

Abbreviations

AAS *Proc.*	*Proceedings* of the American Antiquarian Society
"Baxter-Eliot"	"Some Unpublished Correspondence of the Rev. Richard Baxter and the Rev. John Eliot, 'The Apostle to the American Indians,' 1656–1682," ed. F. J. Powicke, *Bulletin of the John Rylands Library* 15 (1931): 138–76.
Biog. Dict. Brit. Rad.	Richard L. Greaves and Robert Zaller, eds., *Biographical Dictionary of British Radicals in the Seventeenth Century* (Brighton, Sussex, 1982–84).
Boston 1st Ch. Recs.	Richard D. Pierce, ed., *Records of the First Church in Boston, 1630–1868*, Colonial Society of Massachusetts, *Publications*, 39–41 (Boston, 1961).
Commons Debates, 1621	Wallace Notestein et al., eds., *Commons Debates, 1621* (New Haven, 1935).
Commons Debates, 1628	Richard Johnson et al., eds., *Commons Debates, 1628* (New Haven, 1977–83).
Commons Debates, 1629	Wallace Notestein and Francis Relf, eds., *Commons Debates for 1629* (Minneapolis, 1921).
Conn. Recs.	J. Hammond Trumbull and Charles J. Hoadly, eds., *The Public Records of the Colony of Connecticut* (Hartford, Conn., 1859–90).
Cotton Mather Diary	*The Diary of Cotton Mather, 1681–1708*, ed. Worthington C. Ford, Massachusetts Historical Society, *Collections*, 7th ser., 7–8 (Boston, 1911–12).
CSM *Publ.*	*Publications* of the Colonial Society of Massachusetts
Hutchinson, *Original Papers*	Thomas Hutchinson, ed., *A Collection of Original Papers Relative to the History of the Colony of Massachusetts-Bay*, Prince Society, *Publications*, 2–3 (Albany, 1865).
I. Mather Diary	*Diary by Increase Mather, March, 1675–December, 1676, Together with Extracts from Another Diary by Him, 1674–1687*, ed. Samuel A. Green (Cambridge, Mass., 1900).
JBS	*Journal of British Studies*
J. Eccl. H.	*Journal of Ecclesiastical History*
Mass. Recs.	Nathaniel B. Shurtleff, ed., *Records of the Governor and Company of the Massachusetts Bay in New England* (Boston, 1853–54).
MHS *Coll.*	*Collections* of the Massachusetts Historical Society

MHS *Proc.*   *Proceedings* of the Massachusetts Historical Society
NEHGR   *New England Historical and Genealogical Register*
NEQ   *New England Quarterly*
P&P   *Past and Present*
Proc. in Parl. 1610   Elizabeth Read Foster, ed., *Proceedings in Parliament, 1610* (New Haven, 1966).
Proc. in Parl. 1614   Maija Jansson, ed., *Proceedings in Parliament, 1614 (House of Commons)*, American Philosophical Society, *Memoirs*, 172 (Philadelphia, 1988).
Proc. in Parl. 1625   Maija Jansson and William B. Bidwell, eds., *Proceedings in Parliament, 1625* (New Haven, 1987).
SCH   *Studies in Church History*
Sewall Diary   *The Diary of Samuel Sewall, 1674–1729*, ed. M. Halsey Thomas (New York, 1973).
Sibley's Harvard Graduates   John Langdon Sibley and Clifford Shipton, *Biographical Sketches of Graduates of Harvard University, in Cambridge, Massachusetts* (Cambridge, Mass., and Boston, 1873–1978).
STC, 1475–1640   *A Short-Title Catalogue of Books Printed in England, Scotland, & Ireland and of English Books Printed Abroad, 1475–1640*, 2d ed. (London, 1976–86).
Winthrop History   John Winthrop, *The History of New England from 1630 to 1649*, ed. James Savage (Hartford, Conn., 1853).
Winthrop Papers   Allyn B. Forbes et al., eds., *Winthrop Papers, 1498–1649* (Boston, 1929–47).
WMQ   *William and Mary Quarterly*

Introduction

1. W. H. Frere and C. E. Douglas, eds., *Puritan Manifestoes: A Study of the Origin of the Puritan Revolt* (London, 1954), 9.

2. Patrick Collinson, *The Elizabethan Puritan Movement* (Berkeley, 1967), 120–21; Glynn Parry, "William Harrison and the Two Churches in Elizabethan Puritan Thinking," *J. Eccl. H.* 36 (1985): 370–93.

3. Collinson, *Elizabethan Puritan Movement*, 291–302; Robert Paul, *The Assembly of the Lord: Politics and Religion in the Westminster Assembly and the "Grand Debate"* (Edinburgh, 1985); Dewey D. Wallace, Jr., *Puritans and Predestination: Grace in English Protestant Theology, 1525–1695* (Chapel Hill, 1982), chap. 4; Ellen More, "John Goodwin and the Origins of the New Arminianism," *JBS* 22 (1982), 50–70; David D. Hall, *The Faithful Shepherd: A History of the New England Ministry in the Seventeenth Century* (Chapel Hill, 1972), 93–120 (and see below, chap. 4); Williston Walker, ed., *The Creeds and Platforms of Congregationalism* (1893; rpt. Boston: Pilgrim Press, 1960), 345–53, 499–514.

4. That this situation *was* the defining ambivalence of the Puritan movement is, of course, a major contribution of the work of Patrick Collinson, in particular, *Elizabethan Puritan Movement*, 21–28, 372–82; "The Godly: Aspects of Popular Protestantism," in *Godly People: Essays on English Protestantism and Puritanism* (London, 1983), 1–17, and *The Religion of Protestants: The Church in English Society, 1559–1625* (Oxford, 1982), chaps. 4–6. My debt to Collinson's work is so general throughout this and the next two chapters (and so obvious) as to require only occasional acknowledgments.

5. For example, Thomas Hooker's letter to John Cotton from Rotterdam, ca. April 1633, in *Thomas Hooker, Writings in England and Holland, 1626–1633,* ed. George H. Williams (Cambridge, Mass., 1975), 297. For other instances, see below, chap. 2.

6. On the initial lack of any very strong association between Puritans and Sabbatarianism see Collinson, "The Beginnings of English Sabbatarianism," in *Godly People,* 429–33; Kenneth L. Parker, "Thomas Rogers and the English Sabbath: The Case for a Reappraisal," *Church History* 53 (1984): 335–47; John H. Primus, "The Dedham Sabbath Debate: More Light on English Sabbatarianism," *Sixteenth Century Journal* 18 (1986): 87–102. Evidence on royal proclamations for public fasts is incomplete, but there were clearly officially sponsored days of fasting in 1611, 1613, 1625, 1626, 1628, and 1629. See *STC, 1475–1640,* nos. 8833, 8889, 8915, 16538–40. Both Sabbatarianism and fasting are discussed in greater detail in chapter 2 below.

7. Joan Simon, *Education and Society in Tudor England,* rev. ed. (Cambridge, Eng., 1966), chap. 1; Claire Cross, *Church and People, 1450–1660: The Triumph of the Laity in the English Church* (Hassocks, Eng., 1976), chaps. 1–2; Margaret Aston, "Lollardry and Literacy," in *Lollards and Reformers, Images and Literacy in Late Medieval Religion* (London, 1984), 193–218; Jo Ann Hoeppner Moran, *The Growth of English Schooling, 1340–1548: Learning, Literacy, and Laicization in Pre-Reformation York Diocese* (Princeton, 1985).

8. John F. Davis, *Heresy and Reformation in the South-East of England, 1520–1559,* Royal Historical Society Studies in History Series, 34 (London, 1983), esp. chap. 6.

9. Lay involvement in late medieval religion in England is stressed in John Bossy, *Christianity in the West, 1400–1700* (Oxford, 1985), esp. 26–34; Miri Rubin, "Corpus Christi Fraternities and Late Medieval Religion," in *Voluntary Religion,* eds. W. J. Sheils and Diana Wood, *SCH* 23 (1986): 97–109.

10. Moran, *Growth of English Schooling,* chap. 6, esp. 134–35. The imbalance in the distribution of secular priests is not caused by a buildup of chantry priests over a period of many generations: fully 80 percent of those saying mass for the dead were *not* attached to some permanent endowment. Equally, the relatively small proportion of the seculars who were parish clergy was not compensated for by the regulars serving in parochial cures. Sixty-three percent of the benefices in Yorkshire were, indeed, appropriated to religious houses, but the Cistercian and Benedictine monks could have served only parishes in very close proximity to their monasteries because of the two orders' vows of stability and community. Among the canons regular, whose raison d'être was supposed to be staffing parochial cures, the Austin canons were too poor and disorderly to do much of anything, putting the main burden on the Premonstratensians. This order had, indeed, a large number of benefices in its gift but scarcely a majority. Moreover, fully one-third of all the livings in the county, whoever the patron, had no vicar at all but only a stipendiary curate, presumably not a member of the regular clergy even if the benefice were impropriated to a monastic house. One cannot avoid the obvious conclusions that even where the laity shaped the clerical establishment to their liking through the exercise of their financial power, late medieval religion in England was mostly centered on *posthumous* spiritual travail and that the living generations were spectators or at most secondary celebrants at the principal religious rites they organized and paid for. See A. Hamilton Thompson, *The English Clergy and Their Organization in the Late Middle Ages* (Oxford, 1947), 115–27; David Knowles, *The Religious Orders in England, III: The Tudor Age* (Cambridge, 1959), 50, 465. See also Margaret Bowker, *The Secular Clergy in the Diocese of Lincoln, 1495–1520* (Cambridge, Eng., 1968), 67, 100–101, 135–36; Diarmaid MacCulloch, *Suffolk and the Tudors: Politics and Religion in an English County, 1500–1600* (Oxford, 1986), 135, 139–43.

11. For the question of the faith of the "multitude" see Collinson, *Religion of Protes-*

tants, 195–230; Margaret Spufford, "Can We Count the 'Godly' and the 'Conformable' in the Seventeenth Century," *J. Eccl. H.* 36 (1985): 428–38; Eamon Duffy, "The Godly and the Multitude in Stuart England," *Seventeenth Century* 1 (1986–87), 31–55.

12. Quoted in Davis, *Heresy and Reformation*, 102–3.

13. Quoted in Edmund S. Morgan, *The Puritan Family: Religion and Domestic Relations in Seventeenth-Century New England*, 2d ed. rev. (New York, 1966), 5.

14. For attempts to identify a definitive (and defining) religious experience for English and American Puritans respectively see Peter Lake, "Puritan Identities," *J. Eccl. H.* 35 (1984): 112–23; Lake, "William Bradshaw, Antichrist and the Community of the Godly," *J. Eccl. H.* 36 (1985): 570–89; Charles Lloyd Cohen, *God's Caress: The Psychology of Puritan Religious Experience* (New York, 1986). It will be evident from the assertion above and the more extended discussions of this subject in chapter 2 and the Envoi that I am skeptical about this general undertaking.

15. Thomas Fuller, *The History of the Worthies of England*, ed. P. Austin Nuttall (London, 1840), 3:189, 220; R. C. Richardson, *Puritanism in North-West England: A Regional Study of the Diocese of Chester to 1642* (Manchester, 1972), 16–17, 133–76; Increase Mather, *The Life and Death of Mr. Richard Mather*, Dorchester Antiquarian and Historical Society, *Collections*, 3 (1670; rpt. Boston, 1850), 45.

16. Mark H. Curtis, "The Trials of a Puritan in Jacobean Lancashire," in *The Dissenting Tradition: Essays for Leland H. Carlson*, eds. C. Robert Cole and Michael E. Moody (Athens, Ohio, 1915), 78–99; Richard Parkinson, ed., *The Life of Adam Martindale*, Chetham Society, *Remains*, 4 (Manchester, 1845), 12, 12n.–13n.; Richardson, *Puritanism in North-West England*, 167–69; J. A. Newton, "Puritanism in the Diocese of York (excluding Nottinghamshire), 1603–1640" (Ph.D. dissertation, University of London, 1955), 293–304; John Bossy, *The English Catholic Community, 1560–1850* (New York, 1976), 88–89.

17. In addition to the cases from Yorkshire and Lancashire see the American instances of religious disputes as a means of organizing other kinds of tensions discussed below in chapter 5 and the Envoi, as well as MacCulloch, *Suffolk and the Tudors*, 199–212, 326–27; Anthony T. Fletcher, *A County Community in Peace and War: Sussex, 1600–1660* (London, 1975), 177–20; Fletcher, "Factionalism in Town and Countryside: The Significance of Puritanism and Arminianism," in *The Church in Town and Countryside*, ed. Derek Baker, *SCH* 16 (1979): 297–300; Patrick Collinson, *The Birthpangs of Protestant England: Religious and Cultural Change in the Sixteenth and Seventeenth Centuries* (London, 1988), 136–54.

18. Samuel Rawson Gardiner, ed., *Reports of Cases in the Courts of Star Chamber and High Commission*, Camden Society, *Publications*, 39 (Westminster, 1886), 149–53; George Selement and Bruce C. Woolley, eds., *Thomas Shepard's "Confessions,"* CSM *Publ.* 58 (1981): 73–74. See also William Hunt, *The Puritan Moment: The Coming of Revolution in an English County* (Cambridge, Mass., 1983), 146–55; David Underdown, *Revel, Riot and Rebellion: Popular Politics and Culture in England, 1603–1660* (Oxford, 1985), 54–63, 89.

19. *An Entire Commentary upon the Whole Epistle of St. Paul to the Ephesians . . .* , Nichol's Series of Commentaries, 11 (1618; rpt. Edinburgh, 1866), 323.

20. Selement and Woolley, eds., *Thomas Shepard's "Confessions,"* 173.

21. Parkinson, ed., *Life of Adam Martindale*, 46–47.

22. *Winthrop Papers*, 1:304; Selement and Woolley, eds., *Thomas Shepard's "Confessions,"* 193–94.

23. Patrick Collinson, "The English Conventicle," in *Voluntary Religion*, eds. Sheils and Wood, *SCH* 23 (1986): 228–34.

24. The comment is Arthur Hildersham's in Additional MSS, 4275, fol. 289, British Library. See also Richard Bernard, *The Isle of Man: Or, the Legal Proceeding in Man-Shire against Sinne*, 11th ed. (London, 1640), 16–17.

25. J. Horsfall Turner, ed., *The Rev. Oliver Heywood, B.A., 1630–1702* (Brighouse, 1881–85), 1:98.

26. *The Autobiography of Joseph Lister, of Bradford in Yorkshire*, ed. Thomas Wright (London, 1842), 8–9. For other instances see Brian Manning, "Religion and Politics: The Godly People," *Politics, Religion and the English Civil War*, ed. Manning (London, 1973), 91–95; Roger Hayden, ed., *The Records of a Church of Christ in Bristol, 1640–1687*, Bristol Record Society, *Publications*, 27 (Gateshead, Eng., 1974), 84, 86. In parts of Essex, however, where Puritans were relatively numerous, *they* led the rioting. See Hunt, *Puritan Moment*, 297–310.

27. William Bradford, *History of Plymouth Plantation* (Boston, 1912), 1:17–18; John Robinson, *A Manumission to a Manuduction . . .* ([Amsterdam], 1615), 20.

28. "Baxter-Eliot," 169.

29. Selement and Woolley, eds., *Thomas Shepard's "Confessions,"* 106–9. For the later stages of his pilgrimage, see below chapter 5.

30. See Alan Everitt, "Nonconformity in County Parishes," in *Land, Church and People: Essays Presented to Professor H. P. R. Finberg*, ed. Joan Thirsk (Reading, Eng., 1970), 188–97; Everitt, *Change in the Provinces: The Seventeenth Century*, Leicester University Department of English Occasional Papers, 1 ([Leicester], 1969), 22; Michael Walzer, *The Revolution of the Saints: A Study in the Origins of Radical Politics* (Cambridge, Mass., 1965), chaps. 5–6, esp. 183–93; Peter Clark, *English Provincial Society from the Reformation to the Revolution: Religion, Politics and Society in Kent, 1500–1640* (Hassocks, Sussex, 1977), chap. 5, esp. 173–84; Keith Wrightson and David Levine, *Poverty and Piety in an English Village: Terling, 1575–1700* (New York, 1970); Christopher Hill, "Parliament and People in Seventeenth-Century England," *P&P* 92 (Aug. 1981): 118–22. The latest and most ambitious discussion of the "ecology" of Puritanism, Underdown, *Revel, Riot and Rebellion*, chaps. 3–4, combines all three lines of argument. For amendatory or outright critical comments see Margaret Spufford, *Contrasting Communities: English Villagers in the Sixteenth and Seventeenth Centuries* (Cambridge, 1974), chap. 12, esp. 313–14; MacCulloch, *Suffolk and the Tudors*, 38–40, 176–80, 286–87; Collinson, *Religion of Protestants*, 153–77, 216–30, 239–41; Duffy, "The Godly and the Multitude in Stuart England," *Seventeenth Century* 1 (1986–87): 31–55; Martin Ingram, "Religion, Communities and Moral Discipline in Late Sixteenth- and Early Seventeenth-Century England: Case Studies," in *Religion and Society in Early Modern Europe, 1500–1800*, ed. Kaspar V. Greyerz (London, 1984), 177–93; Ingram, *Church Courts, Sex and Marriage in England, 1570–1640* (Cambridge, Eng., 1987), 98–106, 112–24; Margaret Spufford, "Puritanism and Social Control," in *Order and Disorder in Early Modern England*, eds. Anthony Fletcher and John Stevenson (Cambridge, Eng., 1985), 41–57; John Morill, "The Ecology of Allegiance in the English Revolution," *JBS* 26 (1987): 451–67, with a reply by David Underdown, 468–79.

31. Cf. Richard L. Bushman, *From Puritan to Yankee: Character and the Social Order in Connecticut, 1690–1765* (Cambridge, Mass., 1967); Philip J. Greven, *Four Generations: Population, Land, and Family in Colonial Andover* (Ithaca, N.Y., 1970); Kenneth A. Lockridge, *A New England Town: The First Hundred Years: Dedham, Massachusetts, 1636–1736* (New York, 1970). The remarkable contrariety between English and American accounts of the social sources of Puritanism can be traced in part to the Americans lumping communal and manorial controls, on one hand, in with patriarchalism (however defined), on the other, under the heading "traditional" (as opposed to

modern), whereas English historiography assumes a fundamental cultural distinction between manorial and household-oriented farming. For the boldest statement, deliberately paradoxical, that early American society was "traditional" (in these terms) see Philip J. Greven, "Historical Demography and Colonial America," *WMQ*, 3d ser., 24 (1967): 438–54. For a later discussion along similar lines, see Gerald F. Moran and Maris A. Vinovskis, "The Puritan Family and Religion: A Critical Reappraisal," *WMQ*, 3d ser., 39 (1982): 31–38.

32. Ronald A. Marchant, *The Puritans and the Church Courts in the Diocese of York, 1560–1642* (London, 1960), esp. chap. 6; Newton, "Puritanism in the Diocese of York," 19–66, 110–57; Claire Cross, "Parochial Structure and the Dissemination of Protestantism in Sixteenth-Century England: A Tale of Two Cities," in *Church in Town and Countryside*, ed. Baker, *SCH* 16 (1979): 269–78.

33. One might repeat here for the spread of Puritanism among the laity the observation of a distinguished historian of the English Reformation about the early growth of Protestantism: "The circulation of people and the flow of ideas were little impeded by geographical barriers, or by poor roads, least of all by poverty, which in fact so often becomes not a clog but a spur to movement and readaptation" (A. G. Dickens, *Lollards and Protestants in the Diocese of York, 1509–1558* [London, 1959], 246).

34. *A Narration of the Life of Mr. Henry Burton* (London, 1643), 1; Michael McGiffert, ed., *God's Plot: The Paradoxes of Puritan Piety, Being the Autobiography and Journal of Thomas Shepard* (Amherst, Mass., 1972), 36–37, 46–47.

35. Stephen Foster, *Notes from the Caroline Underground: Alexander Leighton, the Puritan Triumvirate, and the Laudian Reaction to Nonconformity*, Studies in British History and Culture, 6 (Hamden, Conn., 1978), 47, 90 n. 47; Richardson, *Puritanism in North-West England*, 182–83; Peter Clark, "Thomas Scott and the Growth of Urban Opposition to the Early Stuart Regime," *Historical Journal* 21 (1978): 1–26.

36. Hayden, ed., *Records of a Church of Christ in Bristol*, 83; Roger Howell, Jr., *Newcastle-upon-Tyne and the Puritan Revolution* (Oxford, 1967), 102–3; Paul Seaver, *Wallington's World: A Puritan Artisan in Seventeenth-Century London* (Stanford, 1985), 96–101; Kenneth W. Shipps, "The Puritan Emigration to New England: A New Source on Motivation," *NEHGR* 135 (1981): 83–97; Ann Hughes, *Politics, Society and Civil War in Warwickshire, 1620–1660* (Cambridge, Eng., 1987), 71–79.

37. Simon Bradstreet to Increase Mather, 20 Apr. 1681, MHS, *Coll.*, 4th ser., 8 (Boston, 1868), 477. For further discussion of Mather's correspondence see below, chap. 6.

38. Governor William Leete to the Committee for Trade and Foreign Plantations, 15 July 1680, *Conn. Recs.*, 3:297–99; Jackson Turner Main, *Society and Economy in Colonial Connecticut* (Princeton, 1985), 75–77, 104–5.

39. D. C. Coleman, *The British Paper Industry, 1495–1860: A Study in Industrial Growth* (Oxford, 1958), 12–23; Carl Bridenbaugh, *Cities in the Wilderness: The First Century of Urban Life in America* (New York, 1938), 32–34; Bernard Bailyn, *The New England Merchants in the Seventeenth Century* (Cambridge, Mass., 1955), 95–98.

40. On the importance of market towns and national connections to the Puritan movement see Richardson, *Puritanism in North-West England*, 11–14; Spufford, *Contrasting Communities*, 232n. Contemporaries expressed similar verdicts: Richard Baxter, *Reliquiae Baxterianae: Or, Mr. Richard Baxter's Narrative . . .* (London, 1691), 88–90; John Corbet, *An Historical Relation of the Military Government of Gloucester*, in *Bibliotheca Gloucestrensis*, ed. John Washbourn (1645; rpt. Gloucester, 1825), 10, 14. See also Christopher Hill's classic essay, "Puritans and 'the Dark Corners of the Land,'" in *Change and Continuity in Seventeenth-Century England* (Cambridge, Mass., 1975), 3–47, and for the most recent statement, Collinson, *Birthpangs of Protestant England*, chap. 2.

41. See F. J. Levy, "How Information Spread among the Gentry, 1550–1640," *JBS* 21 (1982): 11–34; Richard Cust, "News and Politics in Early Seventeenth-Century England," *P&P* 112 (Aug. 1986): 60–90.

42. Oliver Heywood, *Oliver Heywood's Life of John Angier of Denton*, ed. Ernest Axon, Chetham Society, *Remains*, 97 (Manchester, Eng., 1937), 68–69; *Thomas Hooker*, eds. Williams et al., 47–48, 49; Samuel Rawson Gardiner, *History of England from the Accession of James I to the Outbreak of the Civil War, 1603–1642* (London, 1884–86), 4:33.

43. Samuel Collins to Dr. Arthur Duck, 20 May 1629, SP16/142, 239r., Public Record Office; "Letter of the Rev. Thomas Welde, 1633," CMS *Publ.* 33 (1912): 130–31; "Baxter-Eliot," 159–60.

44. Peter Clark, "The Alehouse and the Alternative Society," in *Puritans and Revolutionaries: Essays in Seventeenth-Century History Presented to Christopher Hill*, ed. Donald Pennington and Keith Thomas (Oxford, 1978), 47–72; Clark, *The English Alehouse: A Social History, 1200–1830* (London, 1983), 158–60.

45. See, for example, the "kinde of agreement" suggested by four leading Elizabethan radicals to their bishop in 1571 "To the end that we mighte have occasion rather to goe forward to perfection then backewarde" (Albert Peel, ed., *The Seconde Parte of a Register: Being a Calendar of Manuscripts under That Title Intended for Publication by the Puritans in 1593, and Now in Dr. Williams's Library* [London, 1915], 1:82). For a later version of the same line, William Bradshaw, *The Unreasonablenesse of the Separation* (Dort, 1614), sig. Gr.

46. *Thomas Hooker*, ed. Williams et al., 330–31; Selement and Woolley, eds., *Thomas Shepard's "Confessions,"* 164; A. G. Matthews, *Calamy Revised: Being a Revision of Edmund Calamy's "Account" of the Ministers and Others Ejected and Silenced, 1660–2* (Oxford, 1934), xii–xiii.

47. William Haller, *The Rise of Puritanism: Or, the Way to the New Jerusalem as Set Forth in Pulpit and Press from Thomas Cartwright to John Lilburne and John Milton, 1570–1643* (New York, 1938), chap. 2; Patrick Collinson, "Lectures by Combination: Structures and Characteristics of Church Life in 17th-Century England," in *Godly People*, 467–98; Collinson, *The Religion of Protestants*, chap. 3; Rosemary O'Day, *The English Clergy: The Emergence and Consolidation of a Profession, 1558–1642* (Leicester, 1979), chap. 12.

48. William Bradshaw, *English Puritanisme Containening* [sic] *the Maine Opinions of the Rigidest Sort of Those That Are Called Puritans . . .* (N.p., 1605), 17.

49. McGiffert, ed., *God's Plot*, 54–56; W. H. D. Longstaffe, ed., *The Acts of the High Commission Court within the Diocese of Durham*, Surtees Society, *Publications*, 34 (Durham, 1858), 8–9, 111. See also Selement and Woolley, eds., *Thomas Shepard's "Confessions,"* 33, 50. (The "Mr. Glover" mentioned in these works is Cornelius, not Jose as the editors have it.)

50. *The Works of John Robinson, Pastor of the Pilgrim Fathers*, ed. R. Ashton (London, 1851), 3:375.

51. Selement and Woolley, eds., *Thomas Shepard's "Confessions,"* 83. See also Collinson, *Religion of Protestants*, 257–60.

52. Gardiner, ed., *Reports of Cases in the Courts of Star Chamber and High Commission*, 149; *Winthrop Papers*, 3:375.

53. For detailed comments on the disorderly nature of public worship from impeccably Puritan sources, see the remarks of Nathaniel Bownd quoted and summarized in chapter 1 below and Arthur Hildersham, *Lectures upon the Fourth of John* (London, 1629), 126–30. (Hildersham complained that "many of them that have most knowledge, and are forwardest professours offend this way.") For overcrowding and blocked vision

see John Cotton to Bishop John Williams, 31 Jan. 1624 [i.e., 1625], in Champlin Burrage, *The Early English Dissenters in the Light of Recent Research (1550–1641)* (Cambridge, Eng., 1912), 2:263; John Davenport to William Laud, 15 Jan. 1630 [i.e., 1631], in *Letters of John Davenport, Puritan Divine*, ed. Isabel Calder (New Haven, 1937), 35; and the articles objected against the church wardens of Rowley, C.P.H.2106, Borthwick Institute, York, England. For attempts at reform, see Sir Nathaniel Brent's orders of 20 Aug. 1634 concerning Cotton's Boston church, in Mark Spurrell, *"The Puritan Town of Boston" and Other Papers*, History of Boston Series, 5 (Boston, Lincs., 1972), 24–26; Marchant, *Puritans and the Church Courts*, 59–68.

54. These activities will be discussed in greater detail below in chapter 2. See also Foster, *Notes from the Caroline Underground*, 3–11; Collinson, *Religion of Protestants*, 249–82. The point to be emphasized is that of and in itself "conventicling," when organized around the preaching of the established ministry, was *not* inherently Separatist but just the reverse.

55. John Cotton, *An Exposition upon the Thirteenth Chapter of the Revelation* (London, 1655), 221.

56. The words are those of a Mr. Saxton of Batley parish, Yorkshire (perhaps Peter Saxton, afterward briefly minister of Scituate, Massachusetts), quoted in Newton, "Puritans in the Diocese of York," 383. On the richness of Yorkshire extraparochial activities generally see ibid., 383–91, 396–99.

57. Dudley Fenner, *The Artes of Logike and Rhethorike, Planelie Set Forth in the English Tounge, Easie to Be Learned and Practised* ([Middelburg], 1584). The conjunction of the treatise on family government with the Ramist translations was deliberate. Fenner was at pains to emphasize that he intended the work that "some of every sort" might "gleane, though by theyr cunning" logicians and rhetoricians "had purchased these artes, as corne fieldes proper to themselves," and warned those who would keep logic and rhetoric learned monopolies, "let them not still keepe in this corner to make it rare and excessively deere, least the people *curse them*" (ibid., sig A2v).

58. Quoted in Newton, "Puritanism in the Diocese of York," 384.

59. See Collinson, *Religion of Protestants*, 232–39.

60. *The Danger of Desertion* in *Thomas Hooker*, ed. Williams et al., 246, 252. See below, chapter 3.

61. David Grayson Allen, *In English Ways: The Movement of Societies and the Transferral of English Local Law and Custom to Massachusetts Bay in the Seventeenth Century* (Chapel Hill, 1981), chap. 2.

62. K. J. Allison, *The East Riding of Yorkshire Landscape* (London, 1976), chap. 6, esp. 115–22.

63. Ezekiel Rogers's will in George F. Dow, ed., *The Probate Records of Essex County*, 1 (Salem, 1916), 332; Cotton Mather, *Magnalia Christi Americana: Or the Ecclesiastical History of New England*, ed. Thomas Robbins (Hartford, 1853), 1:409; Kenneth W. Shipps, "Lay Patronage of East Anglican Puritan Clerics in Pre-Revolutionary England" (Ph.D. dissertation, Yale University, 1971), 107–15; *Biog. Dict. Brit. Rad.*, "Barrington, Sir Francis." For Rogers's firm way with members of the Barrington family other than Sir Francis see note 65 below and his letters to Lady Joan Barrington in *Barrington Family Letters, 1628–1632*, ed. Arthur Searle, Royal Historical Society, Camden, 4th ser., 28 (London, 1983), 128–30, 167, 198–99, 225–26.

64. Mather, *Magnalia*, 409; Dow, ed., *Probate Records of Essex County*, 1:332; Newton, "Puritanism in the Diocese of York," 235–36.

65. Marchant, *Puritans and the Church Courts*, 96–102; Dow, ed., *Probate Records of Essex County*, 1:332; Newton, "Puritanism in the Diocese of York," 268; *Winthrop History*, 1:335.

66. See *Biog. Dict. Brit. Rad.* and *The Dictionary of National Biography*, s.v., "Constable, Sir William."

67. Moran, *Growth of English Schooling*, 159–60.

68. *Calendar of State Papers, Domestic Series, Elizabeth I, 1598–1601*, 548–73; *Calendar of the Manuscripts of the Marquis of Salisbury*, Historical Manuscripts Commission, *Ninth Report*, 17 (London, 1938), 49, 86, 126, 133, 594.

69. *Commons Debates, 1628*, 4:128; *Commons Debates, 1629*, 240.

70. Arthur Perceval Newton, *The Colonizing Activities of the English Puritans* (New Haven, 1914), chap. 7; J. T. Cliffe, *The Yorkshire Gentry from the Reformation to the Civil War* (London, 1969), 306–8; *Winthrop Papers*, 3: 211–12, 226–27.

71. Cliffe, *Yorkshire Gentry*, 123, 351; Hugh Aveling, *Post-Reformation Catholicism in East Yorkshire, 1558–1790*, East Yorkshire Local Historical Society Series, 11 (N.p., 1960), 35–36, 44–46, 53, 55, 61.

72. Shipps, "Puritan Emigration to New England," *NEHGR* 135 (1981): 88; George W. Johnson, ed., *The Fairfax Correspondence* (London, 1848), 296–300, 302–3; Amos Everitt Jewett and Emily Mabel Adams Jewett, *Rowley Massachusetts: "Mr. Ezechi Rogers Plantation," 1639–1850* (Rowley, Mass., 1946), 33–34.

Chapter 1

1. The Dedham orders are printed in Roland Greene Usher, ed., *The Presbyterian Movement in the Reign of Queen Elizabeth, as Illustrated in the Minute Book of the Dedham Classis, 1582–1589*, Royal Historical Society, *Publications*, 3d ser., 8 (London, 1905), 99–101. All subsequent quotations from the orders are from these pages.

2. Nicholas Bownd, *The Doctrine of the Sabbath . . .* (London, 1595), 132, 268. See also Robert Cawdry, *A Treasurie or Storehouse of Similies*, 2d ed. (London, 1609), 209–10.

3. The covenant of Dedham in New England is reprinted and discussed in Lockridge, *New England Town*, 6–9.

4. For Kilby see W. J. Sheils, *The Puritans in the Diocese of Peterborough, 1558–1610*, Northamptonshire Record Society, *Publications*, 30 (Northampton, 1979), 56, 120–22; for Northampton, W. Ryland et al., eds., *The Victoria History of the County of Northamptonshire*, 2 (Westminster, 1906), 44–45. There were similar institutions in Wiltshire; see note 5 below.

5. Usher, ed., *Presbyterian Movement*, 47, 71. For the ready availability of the courts and the ambiguities of the law for vexatious prosecutions (and as a consequence, for an alternative tradition of informal but highly sophisticated devices of extralegal mediation), see M. J. Ingram, "Communities and Courts: Law and Disorder in Early-Seventeenth-Century Wiltshire," in *Crime in England, 1550–1800*, ed. J. S. Cockburn (London, 1977), 110–34, esp. 121–22, 125–27.

6. Usher, ed., *Presbyterian Movement*, 30, 47, 50, 53, 54, 56, 61, 67.

7. George Gifford, *A Brief Discourse of Certaine Points of the Religion, Which Is among the Common Sort of Christians . . .* (London, 1581), f. 84 [*recte* 83]r. Gifford was the minister of Maldon in Essex and the leading member of the Braintree classis; his classic *Brief Discourse* is better known under its running title of *The Countrie Divinitie.*

8. Ibid., ff. 5r–5v, 7r, 17v, 29r.

9. *The Lamentable Complaint of the Commonalitie* in *A Parte of a Register . . .* [Middleburg, 1593?], 212–13.

10. *The Unlawfull Practises of Prelates* in ibid., 287, 288.

11. Rosemary O'Day, *The English Clergy: The Emergence and Consolidation of a Profession, 1558–1642* (Leicester, 1979), chap. 10; Christopher Hill, *Economic Problems*

ered," *P&P*, 101 (Nov. 1983): 36–37; White, "A Rejoinder," *P&P*, 115 (May 1987), 221–22. Lake's *Anglicans and Puritans? Presbyterian and English Conformist Thought from Whitgift to Hooker* (London, 1988) appeared too late to be considered in this book.

59. Collinson, *Elizabethan Puritan Movement*, 432–67; Nicholas Tyacke, *Anti-Calvinists: The Rise of English Arminianism, c. 1590–1640* (Oxford, 1987), 13–15.

60. *Biog. Dict. British Rad.*, 1:89; Collinson, *Elizabethan Puritan Movement*, 452, 454, 456, 462–63.

61. Henry Jacob, *A Christian and Modest Offer of a Most Indifferent Conference . . .* (N.p., 1606), 29–30, 35.

62. Bradshaw, *English Puritanisme*, unpaged preface, "The Indifferent Reader." This is a point on which even Collinson nods, but see Stephen Brachlow, "The Elizabethan Roots of Henry Jacob's Churchmanship: Refocusing the Historiographic Lens," *J. Eccl. H.* 36 (1985): 228–54, for Bradshaw's meaning in particular and also for the continuity of the concept of polity among Elizabethan and Jacobean radicals. Brachlow's *The Communion of the Saints: Radical Puritan and Separatist Ecclesiology, 1570–1625* (Oxford, 1988) appeared too late to be taken into consideration here.

63. Mark Curtis, "William Jones: Puritan Printer and Propagandist," *Library*, 5th ser., 19 (1964): 38–66.

64. Stephen A. Bondos-Greene, "The End of an Era: Cambridge Puritanism and the Christ's College Election of 1609," *Historical Journal.*, 25 (1982): 197–208. For the particulars see Historical Manuscripts Commission, *Calender of the Manuscripts of the Marquis of Salisbury*, 31 (London, 1970), 139, 143.

65. Keith Sprunger, *The Learned Doctor William Ames: Dutch Backgrounds of English and American Puritanism* (Urbana, Ill., 1972), 29–30, 32–34, 233–36; Perry Miller, *Orthodoxy in Massachusetts, 1630–1650: A Genetic Study* (1933; rpt. New York, 1970), 107–26, 155–56.

66. Bradshaw, *English Puritanisme*, 6.

67. Henry Jacob, *The Divine Beginning and Institution of Christ's True Visible or Ministeriall Church* (Leyden, 1610), sigs. A3r–v. See also Jacob, *Reasons Taken Out of Gods Word. . . .* ([Middelburg], 1604), 28, 69–70; Jacob, *An Attestation of Many Learned, Godly, and Famous Divines. . . .* ([Middelburg], 1613), 280–81; Bradshaw, *English Puritanisme*, 24–32; Paul Baynes, *The Diocesans Tryall. . . .* 2d ed. ([London], 1641), 83–89.

68. Bradshaw, *English Puritanisme*, 5–9.

69. *Seconde Parte of a Register*, 1:86; Thomas Cartwright to Anne Stubbes, 30 Aug. 1590, in *Cartwrightiana*, ed. Albert Peel and Leland H. Carlson (London, 1951), 67–68. See also Lake, *Moderate Puritans and the Elizabethan Church*, 77–92.

70. Henry Jacob, *A Defence of the Churches and Ministery of Englande* (Middelburg, 1599), 86–87; [Arthur Hildersham and Francis Johnson], *A Treatise of the Ministery of the Church of England* (N.p., 1595), 116–21.

71. Jacob, *An Attestation*, 17. Jacobean Congregationalist apologetics have been much analyzed. (See Miller, *Orthodoxy in Massachusetts*, chap. 4, esp. 84–94, for summary and exegesis.) The rather neglected point I wish to stress here is that by comparing the mature polemics of the first two decades of the seventeenth century with the much slighter efforts of Elizabeth's reign, one can see the extent to which the Jacobean controversialists were indebted to the attacks of the Separatists for the range and sophistication of their later discussions of polity and especially for their new-found preoccupation with the matter and form of a pure church.

72. Murray Tolmie, *The Triumph of the Saints: The Separate Churches of London, 1616–1649* (Cambridge, Eng., 1977), 10–19; John Bellamie, *A Justification of the City Remonstrance and Its Vindication* (London, 1646), 22–23.

73. Tolmie, *Triumph of the Saints*, 19–27; Burrage, *Early English Dissenters*, 2:298–99; Geoffrey F. Nuttall, *Visible Saints: The Congregational Way, 1640–1660* (Oxford, 1957), 10–11, 34; Foster, *Notes from the Caroline Underground*, 22–23, 53; Henry Jacie to John Winthrop, Jr., ca. Feb. 1635, *Winthrop Papers*, 3:188–89. (Jacie subsequently became the third minister of the Jacob church, succeeding John Lothrop, who immigrated to New England.)

74. See the discussion of the Jacobean theorists and the origins of New England Congregationalism in chapter 4 below.

Chapter 2

1. *Seconde Parte of a Register*, 2:202–8 (quotation at 204); Sheils, *Puritans in the Diocese of Peterborough*, 64.

2. Robert Cawdry, *A Shorte and Fruitefull Treatise, of the Profite and Necessitie of Catechising* (London, 1580), sig. A7r; Cawdry, *A Treasurie or Storehouse of Similies*, sig. **2v; DeWitt T. Starnes and Gertrude E. Noyes, *The English Dictionary from Cawdrey to Johnson, 1604–1755* (Chapel Hill, 1946), 13–19. The universal failure to identify Cawdry the radical cleric with Cawdry the lexicographer has obscured the relationship between the *Treasurie* and the *Table Alphabeticall* and consequently the specifically Puritan origins of the latter work.

3. Sheils, *Puritans in the Diocese of Peterborough*, 38, 64; Strype, *Historical Collections of the Life of John Aylmer*, 87–97; P. W. Hasler, ed., *The History of Parliament: The House of Commons, 1558–1603* (London, 1981), 3:98–100.

4. Cawdry, *A Treasurie*, 220–21.

5. Ibid., 570. Cawdry does, however, offer a full page worth (612–13) of biblical precedents under the heading "private men and women, may greatly further the church."

6. Goodwin et al., *An Apologeticall Narration*, 22–23.

7. Edward Cardwell, ed., *Documentary Annals of the Reformed Church of England*, 2d ed. (Oxford, 1844), 2:202.

8. Sprunger, *The Learned Dr. William Ames*, 144–48 (quotation at 146); William Perkins, *An Exposition of the Symbole or Creed of the Apostles*, in *The Workes of . . . William Perkins*, 1 (London, 1626), 123–27, esp. 124; Perkins, *A Declaration of the True Manner of Knowing Christ Crucified*, ibid., 1, 626. For the distinction between the voluntarist and intellectualist schools (Ames and Perkins, respectively) see Norman Fiering, *Moral Philosophy at Seventeenth-Century Harvard: A Discipline in Transition* (Chapel Hill, 1981), 110–37. For other interpretations see R. T. Kendall, *Calvin and English Calvinism to 1649* (Oxford, 1979); Morgan, *Godly Learning*, esp. 301–10. I am inclined to think the former work overstates the intellectualism/voluntarism dichotomy and the latter largely ignores it, making voluntarism (as in Kendall) a truer reflection of Puritan faith than its rival and all but equating "will" with "emotion" rather than with the animating power of reason. See also the discussion of the same question in the Great Awakening in the Envoi.

9. Perkins, *An Exposition*, in *Workes*, 1:123–24.

10. Ibid., 127.

11. James Blanton Wharey and Roger Sharrock, eds., *The Pilgrim's Progress from This World to That Which Is to Come* (Oxford, 1960), 123–24, 162–63. I realize that lumping a Restoration Dissenter (and a Baptist to boot) with an *Elizabethan* Puritan invites objection, but on this point Bunyan is merely dramatizing in vivid form a common set piece: the interrogation of Ignorance (ibid., 144–49) reveals a character identical in

his fatal errors (and in the way he puts them) to Gifford's *Atheos* and Perkins's "many a one" who relies entirely on "the common talke of the world."

12. *A Christian and Plaine Treatise of the Manner and Order of Predestination* . . . , in *Workes*, 2 (London, 1631), 629. "This temporary felicity" refers to the natural reason and sense of morality that God bestows even upon pagan societies.

13. Perkins, *An Exposition*, in *Workes*, 1:123.

14. Ibid., 127.

15. Richard Greenham, *The Workes, Collected in One Volume*, 4th ed. (London, 1604), 40. See also ibid., 6, 324 (margin), 329. See also Hildersham, *Lectures upon the Fourth of John*, 309, 311–12.

16. *Winthrop Papers*, 1:156–59; Perkins, *An Exposition*, in *Workes*, 1:125–26.

17. Winthrop's 1637 "Christian Experience" is analyzed at length in Cohen, *God's Caress*, chap. 8, esp. 254–70. I am not sure, however, that I would describe the document as the record of a "reconversion" brought on by an initial paralysis in the face of Winthrop's isolation within the Boston church during the Antinomian crisis. The piece reads very like the conversion narratives Thomas Shepard had instituted in the Cambridge church eleven months earlier, which had become mandatory for new churches after the failure of the first attempt to found a church at Dorchester (see below, chap. 4). Winthrop had not been required to make such a confession when he helped found the Boston church in 1630, and he probably would not have found a very friendly hearing for his experiencia if he had delivered it to that body in 1637, but he may very well have circulated his account where a friendly reception was assured, since the only known copy is to be found in the notebook of Henry Dunster, a member of the Cambridge church. In any event, under the circumstances, Winthrop's relation fulfilled much the same function as the newly instituted conversion narratives—it proved to its author (and to anyone to whom he showed it) that his faith was not "legal," as the Hutchinsonians would have it, but operative. I have discussed what I take to be the relationship between these narratives and the Antinomian crisis in "New England and the Challenge of Heresy, 1630 to 1660: The Puritan Crisis in Transatlantic Perspective," *WMQ*, 3d ser., 38 (1981): 654–60.

18. Perkins, *Oeconomie: Or, Houshold-Government*, in *Workes*, 3 (London, 1631), 690. See also Robert Cleaver and John Dod, *A Godly Forme of Houshold Government* . . . (London, 1630), sig. Gr.

19. Sprunger, *The Learned Doctor William Ames*, 144. See also John C. Adams, "Alexander Richardson's Philosophy of Art and the Sources of the Puritan Social Ethic," *Journal of the History of Ideas* 50 (1989): 227–47.

20. Sprunger, *The Learned Doctor William Ames*, 189–93.

21. Lake, *Moderate Puritans and the Elizabethan Church*, 280–85; see also chap. 3 below.

22. On the rather too exact fit between population dynamics and improvements in agricultural productivity see E. A. Wrigley and R. S. Schofield, *The Population History of England, 1541–1871: A Reconstruction* (London, 1981), chap. 3; Keith Wrightson, *English Society, 1580–1680* (New Brunswick, N.J., 1982), chap. 5. For the mercurial course of trade see Barry Supple, *Commercial Crisis and Change in England, 1600–1642: A Study in the Instability of a Mercantile Economy* (Cambridge, Eng., 1959). On literacy, Cressy, *Literacy and the Social Order*, chap. 7, charts the uneven and less-than-inevitable progress against illiteracy. And for the ministry and its finances see the discussion above in chapter 1.

23. Cleaver and Dod, *A Godly Forme of Houshold Government*, sigs. X5r–X6v.

24. Cf. Arthur Ferguson, *The Articulate Citizen and the English Renaissance* (Durham, N.C., 1965); Simon, *Education and Society in Tudor England*, chaps. 2–4; G. R. Elton, *The Tudor Revolution in Government: Administrative Changes in the Reign of Hen-*

ry VIII (Cambridge, Eng., 1953); Elton, *Reform and Renewal: Thomas Cromwell and the Common Weal* (Cambridge, Eng., 1973); Joan Thirsk, *Economic Policy and Projects: The Development of a Consumer Society in Early Modern England* (Oxford, 1978). For links instead of parallels see Margo Todd, *Christian Humanism and the Puritan Social Order* (Cambridge, Eng., 1987).

25. See John Winthrop's comment on "this wanton heart of ours," *Winthrop Papers*, 1:207; John Dod and Robert Cleaver, *A Plaine and Familiar Exposition of the Ten Commandments* (London, 1615), 150–51, 154, 155; Stephen Foster, *Their Solitary Way: The Puritan Social Ethic in the First Century of Settlement in New England* (New Haven, 1971), 108–14.

26. Hugh F. Kearney, *Scholars and Gentlemen: Universities and Society in Pre-Industrial Britain, 1500–1700* (London, 1970), 61–62, 68; Louis B. Wright, *Middle-Class Culture in Elizabethan England* (Chapel Hill, 1935), 249–50. Thomas Adams, "the Shakespeare of the Puritans," is another case in point: he ended up in 1644 as a sequestered royalist. See A. G. Matthews, ed., *Walker Revised: Being a Revision of Walker's Suffering of the Clergy* (Oxford, 1948), 42.

27. *Dictionary of National Biography*, s.v. "Sutton, Christopher"; Christopher Sutton, *Disce Vivere: Learne to Live* (London, 1634), unpaged preface "to the Christian Reader," 335–45 (quotation at 340); Sutton, *Disce Mori: Learne to Die* (London, 1634), unpaged preface "to the Godly Reader."

28. Selement and Woolley, eds., *Thomas Shepard's "Confessions,"* 108. (The editors are mistaken, ibid., 108n., about the works Trumbull is referring to.) Trumbull was precisely the individual Sutton did *not* wish to write for. He offers no scheme for making one's calling and election sure, and he avows his purpose in *Disce Vivere* (unpaged preface to "the Christian Reader") as using the life of Christ as an example to make his "side" (as he regularly calls it) to be "as ready as our adversaries themselves" to "repaire devotion and piety," giving the lie to their claims for a special status. The work subsequently recommended itself to the Oxford Movement, and a nineteenth-century reissue bears a preface from John Henry Newman himself.

29. Wilbur Samuel Howell, *Logic and Rhetoric in England, 1500–1700* (Princeton, 1956), chap. 4; R. J. W. Evans, *The Wechsel Presses: Humanism and Calvinism in Central Europe, 1572–1627*, *P&P* Supplement 2 (Oxford, 1975), 43–52.

30. For contemporary verdicts (besides those of Fenner and the Wottons) on the general accessibility and "progressive" nature of Ramism see William Kempe, *The Education of Children in Learning* (London, 1588), sigs. F2r–v; Abraham Fraunce, *The Lawiers Logike* (London, 1588), unpaged preface to "the Learned Lawyers of England." More recent assessments on the same lines are Frank Pierepont Graves, *Peter Ramus and the Educational Reformation of the Sixteenth Century* (New York, 1912), 114–19; Peter Sharratt, "The Present State of Studies on Ramus," *Studi Francesi* 47–48 (May–Dec. 1972): 207; Anthony Grafton and Lisa Jardine, *From Humanism to the Humanities: Education and the Liberal Arts in Fifteenth- and Sixteenth-Century Europe* (London, 1987), chap. 7. The latter work, however, simplifies some in restricting the enthusiasm for Ramism to a need on the part of an ambitious haute bourgeois to acquire the technical skills that would gain them entrance to the royal bureaucracy (see esp. 184–96.) Advocates of Ramism had many audiences in mind: John Eliot translated the logic and rhetoric into Algonquian to accompany his Indian Bible.

31. M. [Thomas] Blundeville, *The Arte of Logik*, 2d ed. (London, 1617), sig. *3v; Howell, *Logic and Rhetoric in England*, 285–91.

32. Margo Todd, "Humanists, Puritans, and the Spiritualized Household," *Church History* 49 (1980): 18–34; Margaret Aston, "Devotional Literacy," in Aston, *Lollards and Reformers*, 128–29, 128n.; Collinson, *Birthpangs of Protestant England*, chap. 3.

33. The quoted phrase comes from Josias Nichols, *An Order of Household Instruction. . . .* (London, 1596), sig. A8v. See also Dod and Cleaver, *A Godly Forme of Household Government*, sigs. [T6v–T7r], and the sources cited in notes 44–46 below.

34. See the discussion in the Introduction and esp. Collinson, "Beginnings of English Sabbatarianism," in *Godly People*, 429–43.

35. Thomas Shepard, *Theses Sabbaticae: Or, The Doctrine of the Sabbath* (London, 1649), "The Preface to the Reader," sig. A4r.

36. *Winthrop Papers*, 1:185, 187, 198.

37. Richard Greenham, *A Treatise of the Sabbath*, in *Workes*, 184–85.

38. Bownd, *Doctrine of the Sabbath*, 195–223, esp. 207–8, 212.

39. John Fessington in Selement and Woolley, eds., *Thomas Shepard's "Confessions,"* 176–77; *Theses Sabbaticae*, 48 (4th pag.). See the similar comments of Richard Mathew and William Tompson (both Lancashiremen, hailing from the region where the Sabbath was most in contest), *An Heart-Melting Exhortation Together with a Cordiall Consolation* (London, 1650), 24–25.

40. In addition to the secondary sources cited above in the Introduction, see also J. A. Sharpe, *Crime in Seventeenth-Century England: A County Study* (Cambridge, Eng., 1983), 163–81, 196–98 (the latter detailing a judicial offensive against popular recreation and idleness as late as the 1670s); Todd, *Christian Humanism and the Puritan Social Order*, 192–95. A broad spectrum of opinion supported the campaigns to discipline the poor and stamp out traditional recreations. Nor can they really be called *particularly* Puritan in the sense that they occupied a special status in their professed agenda. Rather, as Collinson observes (*Religion of Protestants*, 220–30), the Puritan complaint literature was primarily directed against newer, more expensive vices (theater going, excess in apparel, indoor dances) and concentrated especially on wayward youth.

41. Bownd, *Doctrine of the Sabbath*, 94–95, 114, 139, 143–44.

42. Ibid., 136–37; John Angier, *An Helpe to Better Hearts, for Better Times* in Axon, ed., *Oliver Heywood's Life of John Angier*, 138–51.

43. Greenham, *A Treatise of the Sabbath*, in *Workes*, 186.

44. Fenner, "The Order of Householde," *The Artes of Logike and Rhethorike*, sig. A4r.

45. See Charles E. Hambrick-Stowe, *The Practice of Piety: Puritan Devotional Disciplines in Seventeenth-Century New England* (Chapel Hill, 1982), chap. 5, esp. 143–50. Despite the book's subtitle, most of the material summarized in the section cited is English.

46. The work went through nine editions between 1598 and 1630. *STC, 1475–1640*, at 5382, questions the traditional assignment of the authorship and suggests Robert Cawdry as one possible candidate. I have kept Dod and Cleaver for the sake of convenience and because they definitely were the ones to "augment" later editions with blatant plagiarisms from similar titles.

47. Cleaver and Dod, *A Godly Forme of Houshold Government*, sigs. A3r–A4v ("The Epistle Dedicatorie").

48. Ibid., sig. Dr.

49. Richard Rogers, *Seven Treatises . . .* , 5th ed. (London, 1630), 380.

50. William Perkins, *A Warning against the Idolatry of the Last Times*, in *Workes*, 1:709–10.

51. Bownd, *Doctrine of the Sabbath*, 202. See also Richard Greenham, *A Short Form of Catechisms* in *Workes*, 234.

52. Nichols, *An Order of Household Instruction*, sigs. G7r–G8v. See in general, Collinson, *Religion of Protestants*, 232–36.

53. Nichols, *An Order of Household Instruction*, sig. G7r; Cleaver and Dod, *A Godly Forme of Houshold Government*, sigs. [X5r–X6v].

54. *Winthrop Papers*, 1:199–200.

55. Rogers, *Seven Treatises*, 380, 388. See also Sir Simonds D'Ewes's routinized use of *The Practice of Piety* during his college days (Ralph Marsden, ed., *College Life in the Time of James the First* . . . [London, 1851], 77).

56. The survival rate of small, popular books is notoriously low. For example, the revised *STC, 1475–1640*, could still find no copies at all of the first, sixth, tenth, sixteenth, twenty-second, twenty-fourth, twenty-ninth, and thirty-fourth editions of *The Practice of Piety*, and the second, eleventh, and sixteenth editions of *The Plaine Mans Path-way* each exist in a single, incomplete copy. In general, the *STC* inventory of extant copies for titles such as these is much smaller than for the average entry.

57. Selement and Woolley, eds., *Thomas Shepard's "Confessions,"* 115.

58. "To the Christian Reader," in Jeremiah Burroughes, *The Excellency of a Gracious Spirit* (London, 1638), sig. [B7v].

59. *Winthrop Papers*, 2:330 and n.

60. By contrast, although Perkins's *A Treatise of the Vocations or Callings of Men* has attracted substantial scholarly attention as a sort of Elizabethan precursor of Benjamin Franklin's *The Way to Wealth*, as an independent work it appeared exactly once and is normally read in the folio edition of Perkins's *Workes*.

61. The circulation figures are obtained by multiplying all editions of a given work appearing through 1635 by 1,500 and all subsequent editions through 1640 by 2,000. This method is somewhat controversial, and I will discuss its rationale and the objection that it overestimates pressruns in the Appendix. It can, in fact, be argued that the figures given here are distinct underestimates.

62. Francis R. Johnson, "Notes on English Retail Book Prices, 1550–1640," *Library*, 5th ser., 5 (1950): 83–112, esp. 93. In addition to this article, book prices have been taken from the 1616 inventory of the York bookseller John Foster in Robert Davies, *A Memoir of the York Press* (Westminster, 1868), 342–71; the prices listed by D'Ewes for his purchases, Andrew G. Watson, *The Library of Sir Simonds D'Ewes* (London, 1966); the 1644 inventory of John Audley, bookseller of Hull, C. W. Chilton, "The Inventory of a Provincial Bookseller's Stock of 1644," *Library*, 6th ser., 1 (1979): 126–43; and the 1648 inventory of Robert Booth, stationer of Warrington, Lancashire, W. Harry Rylands, "Booksellers and Stationers in Warrington, 1639 to 1657, with a Full List of the Contents of a Stationer's Shop There in 1647," *Transactions of the Historical Society of Lancashire and Cheshire*, 37 (Liverpool, 1888), 67–115. The cause of this relative stability in turn was probably, at least in large part, the lack of substantial fluctuations in the cost of paper. See James E. Thorold Rogers, *A History of Agriculture and Prices in England, from the Year after the Oxford Parliament (1259) to the Commencement of the Continental War (1793)*, 5 (Oxford, 1887), 606–7.

63. For wage rates see Joan Thirsk, ed., *The Agrarian History of England and Wales, 1500–1640*, 4:864; E. H. Phelps Brown and Sheila V. Hopkins, "Seven Centuries of Building Wages," *Economica*, n.s., 23 (1955): 200, 205. These figures, however, can be deceptive: the wage rate may or may not include meals, thereby raising or lowering disposable income, and the amount recorded is the amount *paid* by the employer, not the sum *received* by the laborer; in many instances the money passed through an intermediary who provided the work force and made individual deals with its members so that they actually earned less than their employers' account books reveal. See Donald Woodward, "Wage Rates and Living Standards in Pre-Industrial England," *P&P* 91 (May 1981): 28–46. To take some unambiguous instances from a single East Riding farm in 1641: sheep washers received 3d. per 20 sheep plus noon refreshment and averaged 120 to 130 sheep a day; sheep clippers got 4d. per 20, plus both lunch and dinner, and averaged 60 to 90 sheep a day; sheep greasers 1d. per greasing, but no food, and averaged 6 to 8 sheep a day; mowers received no meat and were paid 10d. a day or 1s. if they worked indepen-

dently; men reapers of "the best sorte" 8*d.* a day, women reapers similarly qualified, 6*d.* a day, and no food in either instance; and haymakers were paid only 4*d.* a day "and are to meate themselves" (*The Farming and Memorandum Books of Henry Best of Elmswell, 1642,* ed. Donald Woodward, British Academy Records of Social and Economic History, n.s., 8 [London, 1984], 20, 22–23, 31, 34, 37, 45, 72).

64. John Bunyan, *Grace Abounding to the Chief of Sinners,* ed. Roger Sharrock (Oxford, 1962), 8.

65. Arthur Dent, *The Plaine Mans Path-Way to Heaven* . . . (London, 1601), 2, 3.

66. A "sticht" octavo edition of the Dent sermon is listed on the 1616 Foster inventory (Davies, *Memoir of the York Press,* 363) at 2*d.* I have assumed this to be a trade price and made the retail figure 3*d.,* taking the commodity prices for 1620 from Thirsk, ed., *Agrarian History of England and Wales,* 4:821, 827, 833, 845. Trumbull's encounter with the "book of repentance" is in Selement and Woolley, eds., *Thomas Shepard's "Confessions,"* 107.

67. The prices are from Johnson, "Notes on English Retail Book Prices," 108, 110. For the poverty of vicars (as opposed to rectors) see Hill, *Economic Problems of the Church,* 108–13, and the discussion of clerical incomes in chapter 5 below.

68. The disastrous publication history of *A Guide to Godlynesse* may be extracted from *STC, 1475–1640,* nos. 7143–44.

69. John Fessenden in Selement and Woolley, eds., *Thomas Shepard's "Confessions,"* 176.

70. Greenham, *Workes,* 43; Cawdry, *A Shorte and Fruitfull Treatise,* sigs. [A6v]–[A7r].

71. See below, chap. 4, nn. 28, 29.

72. Winthrop, *History,* 1:335.

73. See Kendall, *Calvin and English Calvinism to 1649,* 1–13; Lake, *Moderate Puritans and the Elizabethan Church,* 116–68. There is, however, an unfortunate tendency, derived from Kendall but influencing Lake and others, to oppose practical divinity to doctrinal predestinarian preaching rather than to see it as contemporaries did as doctrine "practiced," that is, given full, vital meaning. Kendall's primary exhibit (apart from the Arminian patriarch Lancelot Andrewes) is the Elizabethan preacher Henry Smith (*Calvin and English Calvinism,* 80n.), credited with rejecting the possibility of any personal sense of election and with leaving as an open question "whether predestination, election, &c., are to be preached unto laymen." Smith was accordingly read out of the Puritan ranks entirely by Peter White, here a close adherent of Kendall.

In the first place, Smith's Puritanism is well attested to. He not only got in trouble for nonconformity, in *The Lost Sheep Found,* a sermon preached to an errant layman named Robert Dickons, whose errors included unstinting praise of the Church of England, Smith says in so many words, "I would all the wisdom of Elias could move England to learn of her sister Geneva; then should we have more religion and less ceremonies" (*The Works of Henry Smith,* Nichol's Series of Standard Divines, 39–40 [Edinburgh, 1866–67]), 2:311). Additionally, Smith's position is rather spectacularly misrepresented. The "Questions Gathered Out of his Own Confession, by Henry Smith, Which are yet unanswered," which include the query on preaching to the laity, are *not,* as Kendall would have it, Smith's doubts but additional interrogatories to be put to the eccentric Dickons (the antecedent of "his" in the document's title) because Smith was not satisfied of his subject's full repentance. He had been commissioned to retrieve Dickons from heterodoxy and had had only partial success (ibid., 2:318). The views attributed to Smith on an unerring sense of election cannot easily be checked because they are miscited, but they are not significant in any event: the phrases quoted by Kendall do not of themselves add up to a denial of the possibility of assurance, nor would they be wholly unacceptable to various evangelical predestinarians, certifiably Puritan or otherwise, active a good four or five decades after Smith's death in 1591.

74. Heywood, *Oliver Heywood's Life of John Angier*, ed. Axon, 56–57.

75. For the triumphant pattern Puritanism could impose on mundane life histories see Collinson, " 'A Magazine of Religious Patterns': An Erasmian Topic Transposed in English Protestantism," in *Godly People*, 499–525; Peter Lake, "Feminine Piety and Personal Potency: The 'Emancipation' of Mrs. Jane Ratcliffe," *Seventeenth Century* 2 (1987): 143–65.

76. See, for example, Rogers, *Seven Treatises*, 385.

77. Selement and Woolley, eds., *Thomas Shepard's "Confessions,"* 184–85.

78. *Winthrop Papers*, 3:12–13. The editor suggests that this document is a reply to Roger Williams.

79. John Cotton, *The Keys of the Kingdom of Heaven* (1644), in *John Cotton on the Churches of New England*, ed. Larzer Ziff (Cambridge, Mass., 1968), 100–101.

80. Edmund S. Morgan, *Visible Saints: The History of a Puritan Idea* (New York, 1963), 72–73, 90–92.

81. Greenham, *Workes*, 212. See also Baxter, *Reliquae Baxterianae*, 88 (1st pag.).

82. Hall, ed., "Cotton's Letter to Skelton," *WMQ*, 3d ser., 22 (1965): 484; John Cotton, *The Way of Congregational Churches Cleared . . .* (London, 1648), 20; "Baxter-Eliot," 159–60.

83. Greenham, *Workes*, 227–28.

84. Bownd, *Doctrine of the Sabbath*, 94, 224 (margin); Mather, *Magnalia*, 1:345.

85. Nicholas Bownd, *The Holy Exercise of Fasting . . .* ([London], 1604), 225–29; Additional MSS, 4275, fol. 289, British Library.

86. See Foster, *Notes from the Caroline Underground*, 17–18, 50.

87. Spufford, *Contrasting Communities*, 231–32.

88. Corbet, *An Historical Relation of the Military Government of Gloucester*, in *Bibliotheca Gloucestrensis*, ed. Washbourn, 10.

89. Stuart Barton Babbage, *Puritanism and Richard Bancroft*, (London, 1962), chap. 6, esp. 217–19. A recent study, noting four to five instances of ministers in Babbage's study who were actually deprived for scandal, not conformity, has suggested that even eighty to ninety casualties may be too high. See K. C. Fincham, "Ramifications of the Hampton Court Conference in the Dioceses, 1603–1609," *J. Eccl. H.* 36 (1985): 212n., 226n.

90. *Biog. Dict. Brit. Rad.*, 1:14–15, 51, 86–87, 2:137; Samuel Clarke, *A General Martyrologie . . .*, 2d ed. (London, 1660), 89, 90 (*recte* 29, 30, 2d pag.), 114–15, 118, 125 (*recte* 54–57, 58, 65, 2d pag.).

91. Ogbu B. Kalu, "Bishops and Puritans in Early Jacobean England: A Perspective on Methodology," *Church History* 45 (1976): 489 (Table 11). In turn, two of the five beneficed ministers Babbage does list lost their livings for nonresidence, not nonconformity.

92. Babbage, *Puritanism and Richard Bancroft*, 110–11; Kalu, "Bishops and Puritans," *Church History* 45 (1976): 477.

93. Marchant, *Puritans and the Church Courts*, 137–66, esp. 147–49.

94. Babbage, *Puritanism and Richard Bancroft*, 126–27, 127n., 206–11; Sheils, *Puritans in the Diocese of Peterborough*, 80–81; Hughes, *Politics, Society, and Civil War in Warwickshire*, 65. Two of the three ministers in Peterborough diocese who make the Babbage list actually were restored to their livings. In Warwickshire, William Meacocke of Hasley shows up only because he was deprived during Bancroft's metropolitan visitation; the records of the diocese of Worcester itself yield no information on the subject. Overall, Babbage has detailed records for only five of the fifteen dioceses he discusses.

95. *Biog. Dict. Brit. Rad.*, 3:9–10. Again, Parker may have been deprived in a metropolitan visitation.

96. Curtis, "Trials of a Puritan in Jacobean Lancashire," in *The Dissenting Tradition*, ed. Cole and Moody, 78–99; Curtis, "William Jones," *Library*, 5th ser., 19 (1964): 59.

97. *Dictionary of National Biography, s.v.*, "Fenn, Humphrey"; Collinson, *Elizabethan Puritan Movement*, 462–64.

98. Peter Clark, "Josiah Nicholls and Religious Radicalism, 1553–1639," *J. Eccl. H.* 28 (1977): 133–50. I think Clark underestimates the radicalism of the tract Nichols had a hand in composing, Thomas Whetenhall, *A Discourse of the Abuses Now in Question in the Churches of Christ* . . . ([The Netherlands?], 1606). The substance is unremarkable but not tame (see pp. 76–77, for example, where a visible church is identified with an individual parish), and the work first appeared as part of the propaganda campaign against Bancroft. A subsequent reprinting in 1617 was a product of the so-called Brewer-Brewster Press, a clandestine printing operation run by the exiled Separatists of Leiden.

99. Samuel Rawson Gardiner, ed., *Debates in the House of Commons in 1625*, Camden Society *Publications*, n.s., 6 (Westminster, 1873), 21, 21n., 26–27, 28–29; *Journals of the House of Lords* (London, 1767–), 3:480. Charles I was obliging where his father had been adamant because he was trying to coax subsidies out of the Commons for his war efforts. Thus Sir Henry Marten's remark (ibid., 121) that the royal answer "is worth a great deale of mony." (The corresponding citations in the new edition are *Proc. in Parl., 1625*, 157, 247–48, 262, 265, 462.)

100. Babbage, *Puritanism and Richard Bancroft*, 158–59; Paul Seaver, *The Puritan Lectureships: The Politics of Religious Dissent, 1560–1662* (Stanford, 1970), 176–78. Babbage, however, is in error in claiming that Culverwell subsequently conformed.

101. John Sprint, *Cassander Anglicanas: Shewing the Necessity of Conformitie to the Present Ceremonies of our Church, in Case of Deprivation*, 2d ed. (London, 1618), 40, 65.

102. Seaver, *Puritan Lectureships*, 224; *The Letters of John Chamberlain*, ed. Norman E. Maclure, American Philosophical Society, *Memoirs*, 12 (Philadelphia, 1939), 1:264; Marchant, *Puritans and the Church Courts*, 149, 155, 299, 311–12.

103. The details of his career are taken from Babbage, *Puritanism and Richard Bancroft*, 183–86, and *Biog. Dict. Brit. Rad.*, 2:89–90.

104. Benjamin Brook, *The Lives of the Puritans* (London, 1813), 3:383n.–384n.; Babbage, *Puritanism and Richard Bancroft*, 185. See Foster, *Notes from the Caroline Underground*, 7–8.

105. He did, however, encourage Henry Jacob to found the semiseparatist Southwark church (Burrage, *Early English Dissenters*, 1:313, 2:293).

106. Babbage, *Puritanism and Richard Bancroft*, 212–13; Sheils, *Puritans in the Diocese of Peterborough*, 86–87; Jeremy Collier, *An Ecclesiastical History of Great Britain*, ed. Thomas Lathbury (London, 1852), 9:371–72; *Calender of State Papers Domestic, James I, 1611–1618*, 254; J. T. Cliffe, *The Puritan Gentry: The Great Puritan Families of Early Stuart England* (London, 1984), 182–83; Samuel Clarke, *A General Martyrologie*, 3d ed. (London, 1677), 171 (2d pag.).

107. Fuller, *Worthies*, ed. Nuttall, 1:278.

108. Sheils, *Puritans in the Diocese of Peterborough*, 86; Shipps, "Lay Patronage of East Anglian Clerics," 110–15, 369; Babbage, *Puritanism and Richard Bancroft*, 205.

Chapter 3

1. *Winthrop Papers*, 1:168; Joseph Foster, ed., *The Register of Admissions to Gray's Inn, 1521–1889* (London, 1889), 132–33; Wilfrid R. Prest, *The Inns of Court under Elizabeth I and the Early Stuarts* (Totowa, N.J., 1972), 38, 206–9.

2. *Winthrop Papers*, 1:324–26, 336–37, 340–41, 371–74; Richard Cust, *The Forced Loan and English Politics, 1626–1628* (Oxford, 1987), 232–33.

3. *Winthrop Papers*, 2:74–75, 91, 92, 96.

4. Ibid., 2:91–92. (The biblical references are to Gen. 19:17–22, 1 Kings 17:8–24.)

5. Ibid., 122.

6. *Barrington Family Letters*, ed. Searle, 60–61. (I have silently rendered "thal-mighty" as "the almighty.")

7. *Winthrop Papers*, 2:121.

8. "Articles Objected by His Majesties Commissioners for causes Ecclesiastical against Charles Chauncey . . . ," MHS *Proc.*, 1st ser., 13 (Boston, 1873–75), 340; *Thomas Hooker*, ed. Williams et al., 246.

9. *Winthrop Papers*, 2:91, 124, 139. For economic conditions in general see below, note 10, and for the two riots at Malden, see John Walter, "Grain Riots and Popular Attitudes to the Law: Malden and the Crisis of 1629," in *An Ungovernable People: The English and Their Law in the Seventeenth and Eighteenth Centuries*, ed. John Brewer and John Styles (New Brunswick, N.J., 1980), 47–84; Hunt, *Puritan Moment*, 239–44.

10. W. G. Hoskins in his classic study of the fortunes of wheat production, "Harvest Fluctuations and English Economic History, 1620–1759," *Agricultural History Review* 16 (1968): 19–20, argues that the 1620s were on the whole prosperous after the disaster of 1622 and that the 1630s were mixed: there were few really good years, but only 1630 and 1637 were very bad, and the period 1637–46 was quite prosperous. An alternative analysis by C. J. Harrison employing data worked up by P. Bowden for the prices of all grains suggests a flatter curve for the 1622–34 period, in which good harvests in wheat were offset by indifferent harvests in barley and oats and vice versa. In this version, only 1627 stands out as a bumper year and 1630 as a bad one, while the rest of the harvests were merely average ("Grain Price Analysis and Harvest Qualities, 1465–1634," ibid., 19 [1971]: 135–55, esp. 154–55.) Textiles had an equally complex and hard to characterize history. The old draperies, after a period of recovery from 1600 to 1614, went into a long-term decline for the next quarter-century or more, although there was a brief bout of prosperity in 1624–25. New draperies, which were centered in East Anglia, enjoyed considerable expansion over the same period but were severely disrupted during the war years and just after (1625 into the early 1630s) and then again in 1636–37 (Barry Supple, *Commercial Crisis and Change in England, 1600–1642: A Study in the Instability of a Mercantile Economy* [Cambridge, Eng., 1959], 102–12, 122–24, 152–62). Winthrop wrote his dire prophecies in the worst year of all for the cloth trade, 1629, though even he would have been able to remember some relatively recent good times and have reasonable basis for expecting a degree of recovery. Similarly, if the disorders in Essex particularly impressed themselves on his thinking, it was precisely because they had been (and would remain) anything but common. See J. A. Sharpe, *Crime in Seventeenth-Century England: A County Study* (Cambridge, Eng., 1983), 77–79.

11. *Winthrop Papers*, 2:129–30, 138, 145–49.

12. Ibid., 114–15. For the constraints imposed on letter writers, even in their ordinary correspondence, see Cust, *The Forced Loan and English Politics*, 12.

13. *Winthrop Papers*, 2:124, 283. See Edmund S. Morgan, "John Winthrop's 'Model of Christian Charity' in a Wider Context," *Huntington Library Quarterly* 50 (1987): 145–51.

14. *Commons Debates, 1621,* 3:448–49.

15. *Commons Debates, 1628,* 6:53. The quotation comes from a draft reply to the Commons remonstrance of 14 June 1628.

16. *Winthrop Papers,* 2:121–22.

17. In the Parliament of 1621, in the course of a single debate, it was hard to distinguish the pessimism of the militant Puritan oppositionist Sir Nathaniel Rich from the equally gloomy diagnosis of the leading civilian and apologist for the Church of England Barnabe Gooch, although of Gooch it was unkindly suggested that in opposing church reform he "speaks for his penny." And in the Parliament of 1625, Sir Francis Seymour, a prickly political independent but a future royalist, denounced the demoralizing effects of official corruption with a desperate bluntness that rivaled Winthrop's on the same subject four years later (*Commons Debates, 1621,* 3:351, 361, 433; Gardiner, ed., *Debates in the House of Commons in 1625,* 111. Cf. *Proc. in Parl., 1625,* 450.)

18. *Winthrop Papers,* 1:296–97, 304; *Journals of the House of Commons,* 1 (London, 1742), 864, 885, 887, 889, 921; *Commons Debates, 1628,* 3:432–43. The editors of the *Winthrop Papers* assign the draft bills in question to 1624, but so definite a date is subject to argument. The collection includes proposed legislation for church reform of a sort common enough in early Jacobean parliaments but unlikely to come up after 1621, and the proposal for the relief of ministers suspended in Bancroft's purge (1:305) follows the wording of the Commons petition to the king in 1610 verbatim. (The matter became moot after 1625.) See *Proc. in Parl., 1610,* 2:256.

19. Joan R. Kent, "Attitudes of Members of the House of Commons to the Regulation of 'Personal Conduct' in Late Elizabethan and Early Stuart England," *Bulletin of the Institute for Historical Research* 46 (1973): 41–71, esp. 63–71; Keith Thomas, "The Puritans and Adultery: The Act of 1650 Reconsidered," in *Puritans and Revolutionaries,* ed. Pennington and Thomas, 272–75.

20. Kent, "Attitudes of Members of the House of Commons," *Bulletin of the Institute for Historical Research* 46 (1973): 69–71 (however, 3 Car. I, c. 2 is misdated under 1626 instead of 1628); *Commons Debates, 1621,* 4:76.

21. See *Commons Debates, 1621,* 4:33; Historical Manuscripts Commission, *The Manuscripts of the House of Lords,* n.s., 11 (London, 1962), 96–97.

22. Historical Manuscripts Commission, *Manuscripts of the House of Lords,* n.s., 11:101–2, 104–5, 108–9, 111–12, 127; *Proc. in Parl., 1610,* 1:125n., 2:405–10; *Journals of the House of Commons,* 1:245, 247, 248, 292, 293, 305, 348, 350, 372, 403, 421, 445. John Morrill, "The Attack on the Church of England in the Long Parliament, 1640–42," in *History, Society, and the Churches: Essays in Honour of Owen Chadwick,* ed. Derek Beales and Geoffrey Best (Cambridge, Eng., 1985), 105–24, argues for an unprecedented procedural boldness and substantive radicalism in the years in question, but the latter point is sustained by restricting the comparison to the parliaments of the 1620s. If the bills that passed the Commons between 1604 and 1610 are recalled, then the work of the Long Parliament before the irreparable breach with Charles I seems less remarkable.

23. *Biog. Dict. Brit. Rad.,* 1:306–7; Hasler, ed., *House of Commons,* 1:648–49.

24. *Biog. Dict. Brit. Rad.,* 3:29; Wallace Notestein, *The House of Commons, 1604–1610* (New Haven, 1971), 452; *Proc. in Parl., 1614 (House of Commons),* 37; Robert Zaller, *The Parliament of 1621: A Study in Constitutional Conflict* (Berkeley, 1971), 136–37; Robert E. Ruigh, *The Parliament of 1624: Politics and Foreign Policy* (Cambridge, Mass., 1971), 160, 223.

25. *Biog. Dict. Brit. Rad.,* 1:254–55; Mary F. Keeler, *The Long Parliament, 1640–1641: A Biographical Study of Its Members,* American Philosophical Society, *Memoirs,* 36 (Philadelphia, 1954), 165–66; *Commons Debates, 1621,* 5:353, 376 (bills against

nonresidency and scandalous ministers); Esther Cope and Wilson H. Coates, eds., *Proceedings of the Short Parliament of 1640*, Royal Historical Society, Camden, 4th ser., 19 (London, 1977), 157n, 174, 180–81; Judith D. Maltby, ed., *The Short Parliament (1640) Diary of Sir Thomas Aston*, Royal Historical Society, Camden 4th ser., 35 (London, 1988), 103.

26. *Proc. in Parl., 1614*, 75, 88–89, 91, 92, 483–508.

27. Ibid., 215–18; Thomas L. Moir, *The Addled Parliament of 1614* (Oxford, 1958), 109–10.

28. *Proc. in Parl., 1614*, 217, 221.

29. Ibid., 228, 231, 296, 303; *Commons Debates, 1621*, 2:150, 5:16, 502; Esther S. Cope, *The Life of a Public Man: Edward, 1st Baron Montagu of Broughton, 1562–1644*, American Philosphical Society, *Memoirs*, 142 (Philadelphia, 1981), 65, 82–87.

30. Conrad Russell, *Parliaments and English Politics, 1621–1629* (Oxford, 1979), 26–32. This argument, however, important as it is as a corrective, divorces the politics of the 1620s from those of the earlier parliaments of James I and makes too much of the Puritan MPs, such as Sir Robert Harley and Sir Henry Mildmay, who had close ties to Buckingham.

31. *Commons Debates, 1621*, 3:432–43. Of the MPs who followed Perrot's lead, the most significant was the notoriously anticlerical Sir Jerome Horsey, unfortunately best remembered for his intrigues and alleged defalcations during his service as a Muscovy Company adventurer decades earlier, in 1572–87. Horsey's Elizabethan career is more interesting for his religious and political affiliations and their extension after 1603. His earlier patrons were Walsingham, Leicester, and a relation, Sir Edward Horsey, who had been a Marian exile. Bossiney, which he represented in 1601, was part of the patronage of the Earl of Bedford. Horsey also boasted that as sheriff of Buckinghamshire he helped organize "the preaching of the Gospel through the whole county by most worthy, learned, godly and holy divines," and in the Parliament of 1621 he recalled the story of an MP who died the very day after voting in opposition to the Sabbath bill of 1593 (Hasler, ed., *House of Commons*, 2:340, 3:209).

32. *Commons Debates, 1621*, 4:76, 6:362.

33. Ibid., 3:260–62, 6:471–76, 7:606–8, 609n. Lambe would subsequently betray his old patron, Bishop John Williams, for tolerating conventicles and thereby gain the favor of Laud. With Laud's backing, in turn, he would replace the independent Sir Henry Marten as chief civilian for the province of Canterbury (Brian P. Levack, *The Civil Lawyers in England, 1603–1641: A Political Study* [Oxford, 1973], 177–78, 246–47).

34. *Commons Debates, 1621*, 4:63. Cf. Pym's very similar indictment of Richard Montagu, in Gardiner, ed., *Debates in the House of Commons in 1625*, 179.

35. S. L. Adams, "Foreign Policy and the Parliaments of 1621 and 1624," in *Faction and Parliament: Essays on Early Stuart History*, ed. Kevin Sharpe (Oxford, 1978), 139–71; Adams, "Spain or the Netherlands? The Dilemmas of Early Stuart Foreign Policy," in *Before the English Civil War: Essays on Early Stuart Politics and Government*, ed. Howard Tomlinson (London, 1983), 90–93, 97–99; Russell, *Parliaments and English Politics*, 145–48; James Fulton Maclear, "Puritan Relations with Buckingham," *Huntington Library Quarterly* 21 (1957–58): 111–32. See also Thomas Cogswell, *The Blessed Revolution: English Politics and the Coming of War, 1621–1624* (Cambridge, Eng., 1989), a work that appeared too late to be more than noted at appropriate places. In considering the tangled alliances of the 1620s and their oblique relationship to choices made in the Civil War, it is worth remembering that Puritans account for many of the troubling cases of future parliamentarians who were numbered among Buckingham's supporters during the attempts to impeach him. If Sir Robert Harley, Sir Henry Mildmay, and Laurence Whitaker, Buckingham's Puritan clients, are eliminated from the list of his supporters, the

remainder begin to appear a good deal less anomalous in their composition: virtually all of those who survived into the Civil War became royalists except for the future earl of Manchester, the totally nonprincipled placeman Sir John Hippisley, and the two most enigmatic and unpredictable politicians of the era, the earl of Holland and the elder Sir Henry Vane (Russell, *Parliaments and English Politics*, 434).

36. Harley, Mildmay, and Whitaker can be found speaking seriatim against Arminianism very early in the Parliament of 1628 (on 26 February), in what must have been a preconcerted demonstration, presumably to warn their patron and the government, and by the debates of 6 June almost all of Buckingham's Puritan supporters were in full cry against arbitrary government (*Commons Debates, 1628*, 2:93; Russell, *Parliaments and English Politics*, 381). Russell, ibid. and 230n., raises a question as to whether the "Mr. Whitaker" of 1628 debates was Laurence or William, but only the former was a member of this parliament.

37. Francis Rous, *Testis Veritatis: The Doctrine of King James . . .* (London, 1626), 105.

38. Thomas Hooker, *The Church's Deliverance*, in *Thomas Hooker*, ed. Williams et al., 85.

39. William Prynne, *The Church of Englands Old Antithesis to New Arminianisme* (London, 1629), "To the Christian Reader," sigs. [C4r–C4v].

40. *Commons Debates, 1628*, 4:238, 260. Tyacke, *Anti-Calvinists*, chap. 6, esp. 157–58.

41. For evidence of James's deep-rooted hostility toward Puritans as early as the Hampton Court conference, see Frederick Shriver, "Hampton Court Re-visited: James I and the Puritans," *J. Eccl. H.* 33 (1982): 60–61, 65–69.

42. James I to the earl of Somerset, ca. 1615, in *Letters of King James VI and I*, ed. G. P. V. Akrigg (Berkeley, 1984), 339.

43. *Proc. in Parl., 1610*, 2:103. See also the king's letter to Parliament of 14 Dec. 1621 about the claims of the Scottish "Puritans" to "plenipotency," *Commons Debates, 1621*, 5:416; John Rushworth, *Historical Collections of Private Passages of State . . .* (London, 1659–1701), 1:48.

44. David Laing, ed., *Original Letters Relating to the Ecclesiastical Affairs of Scotland . . .* , Bannatyne Club, *Publications*, 97 (Edinburgh, 1851–52), 2:663.

45. James Tait, "The Declaration of Sports for Lancashire (1617)," *English Historical Review* 32 (1917): 565 (I have silently corrected "preacherr").; *Commons Debates, 1621*, 4:53.

46. Moir, *Addled Parliament*, chap. 9.

47. Tyacke, *Anti-Calvinists*, 106–24, 126–27; Andrew Foster, "A Biography of Archbishop Richard Neile" (D.Phil. dissertation, Oxford University, 1978), 210–20.

48. Kenneth Fincham and Peter Lake, "The Ecclesiastical Policy of King James I," *JBS* 24 (1985): 198–206. I would dissent from this article in one particular: however significant the crisis on the Continent in firming up James I's resolve, his final anti-Puritan tilt had already begun before 1618 and represented the realization of a pervasive animus of long standing. When he issued his proclamation of 24 May 1618 requiring that the Book of Sports be read out by the clergy throughout the whole of England, James could not possibly have known of the revolt of Bohemia, which had begun the previous day.

49. Foster, *Notes from the Caroline Underground*, 20–21; Walter Wilson Greg, ed., *A Companion to Arber* (Oxford, 1967), 226–29; Jerry H. Bryant, "John Reynolds of Exeter and His Canon: A Footnote," *Library*, 5th ser., 18 (1963): 299–303. For a Paul's Cross sermon against the Spanish Match see *The Diary of Sir Simonds D'Ewes (1622–1624)*, ed. Elizabeth Bourcier (Paris, [1974]), 94–95, and for a political funeral sermon on the same subject, ibid., 98–99. (Both events occurred in September 1622.) See also Cogswell, *Blessed Revolution*, 20–32, 281–301.

50. Cardwell, *Documentary Annals of the Reformed Church of England*, 2:201–2. One obvious mistranscription in the fourth article has been altered by the correct reading in J. P. Kenyon, *The Stuart Constitution, 1603–1688: Documents and Commentary* (Cambridge, Eng., 1966), 146.

51. Peter Heylyn, *Cyprianus Anglicus: Or, The History of the Life and Death, of . . . William [Laud] . . .* (London, 1668), 95–97, 199–201; *The Works of William Laud*, ed. W. Scott and J. Bliss (Oxford, 1847–60), 5:pt. 2, 517–18; Kenyon, ed., *The Stuart Constitution*, 159. Archbishop Abbot in his letter explaining the 1622 *Directions* to preachers had "interpreted" the second injunction, "that those preachers be most encouraged and approved of, who spend the afternoon's excersise in the examining of children in their Catechism, and in the expounding of the several points and heads of the Catechism" as an invitation to *increase* the number of sermons "by renewing upon every Sunday in the afternoon, in all parish churches throughout the Kingdom, that primitive and most profitable exposition of the Catechism." (Cardwell, *Documentary Annals*, 2:201–2, 205). Laud in 1629 and 1633 precluded any possible reading of "exposition" as "preaching," but this interpretation is surely closer to James's intention and is anticipated by the restriction on the length of Sunday afternoon sermons in 1617. See Tait, "Declaration of Sports for Lancashire," *English Historical Review*, 32 (1917): 565.

52. Richard Montagu, *A Gagg for the New Gospell? No: A New Gagg for an Old Goose* (London, 1624), "To the Reader," unpaged. For Montagu's relationship to James I, see Sheila Lambert, "Richard Montagu, Arminianism and Censorship," *P&P* 124 (Aug. 1989): 42–50.

53. Shipps, "Lay Patronage of East Anglian Puritan Clerics," 46–48, 348–50; Tyacke, *Anti-Calvinists*, 147–50; Adams, "Foreign Policy and the Parliaments of 1621 and 1624," in *Faction and Parliament*, ed. Sharpe, 142–48.

54. *Appello Caesarem: A Just Appeale from Two Unjust Informers* (London, 1625), sigs. av–a2r, 88, 140–61; Cf. Miller, *Orthodoxy in Massachusetts*, chap. 4; George Carleton (bishop of Chichester), *An Examination of Those Things Wherin the Author of the Late Appeale Holdeth the Doctrines of the Pelagians and Arminians to Be the Doctrines of the Church of England*, rev. ed. (London, 1626), 121, 217–18; Jonathan M. Atkins, "Calvinist Bishops, Church Unity, and the Rise of Arminianism," *Albion* 18 (1986): 411–27.

55. *A Brief Censure upon an Appeale to Caesar* (N.p., n.d.), 36 (*STC, 1475–1640*, no. 18032). See Sir Miles Fleetwood's similar lament on 12 Feb. 1629, *Commons Debates, 1629*, 194.

56. Edward Arber, ed., *A Transcript of the Registers of the Company of Stationers of London, 1554–1640 A.D.*, 4 (London, 1877), 136; Montagu, *Appello Caesarem*, "The Epistle Dedicatory," sig. 93v; Henry Burton, *A Plea to an Appeale Traversed Dialogue Wise* (London, 1626), "To the Reader," sig. [a4]v.

57. Gardiner, ed., *Debates in the House of Commons in 1625*, 18 (cf. *Proc. in Parl., 1625*, 260); Tyacke, *Anti-Calvinists*, 168–71, 176–77; *The Works . . . John Cosin . . .*, ed. J. Sansom (Oxford, 1843–55), 2:38, 63.

58. Since Kendall's *Calvin and English Calvinism* there have been various attempts to distinguish between "evangelical" and "credal" Calvinists and to identify a continuing "Whitgiftian" tradition in the Church of England. Adherents of this latter position, it is held, though often formally endorsing predestinarian theology, were skeptical of the need for dogmatic, doctrinal preaching and hostile to anything potentially divisive from press or pulpit. See, for example, Peter White, "The Rise of Arminianism Reconsidered," *P&P* 101 (Nov. 1983): 34–54, esp. 37, 37n.; Peter Lake, "Calvinism and the English Church, 1570–1635," *P&P* 114 (Feb. 1987): 32–76, esp. 56–59. I have already taken issue with Kendall's separation of doctrinal and practical divinity, above, chapter 2, note 73. In addition, whatever the positions taken up in anti-Puritan polemics in Elizabeth's reign, they

were inapposite fifty years later: the theologian picked out by Lake as the carrier of the Whitgiftian ethos in the 1620s and 1630s was by any definition an evangelical Calvinist (Peter G. Lake, "Serving God and the Times: the Calvinist Conformity of Robert Sanderson," *JBS* 27 [1988], 81–116).

59. Montagu, *Appello Caesarem*, 39.

60. Ibid., 76–78, 142. See also Lake, "Calvinism and the English Church," *P&P* 114 (Feb. 1987): 72–75.

61. Henry Burton, *The Seven Vials or a Briefe and Plaine Exposition upon the 15: and 16: Chapters of the Revelation* . . . (London, 1628), 124–25. See also John Yates, *Ibis ad Caesarem . . . in Answer to Mr. Montagues Appeale* . . . (London, 1626), 33 (1st pagination).

62. For complaints that the bans on controversy were enforced one-sidedly see *Commons Debates, 1629*, 58–59, 99; Lake, "Calvinism and the English Church," *P&P* 124 (Feb. 1987): 63–66; Tyacke, *Anti-Calvinists*, 48–50, 77–78, 85–86, 182–83. But cf. Lambert, "Richard Montagu, Arminianism and Censorship," *P&P* 124 (Aug. 1989): 58–68.

63. William Prynne, *Canterburies Doome: Or the First Part of a Compleat History of the . . . Tryall . . . of William Laud* (London, 1646), 164–65. The original (from which Laud's endorsement is taken) is miscalendared in *Calender of State Papers Domestic, Charles I, 1638–1639*, 279–80.

64. Brooke to Laud, 15 Dec. 1630, SP 16/177, 13r, Public Record Office; *Works of William Laud*, ed. Scott and Bliss, 6:292. This attitude, regularly reiterated by Laud, put him in the same camp as the Arminians regardless of the exact degree to which their respective theologies coincided, as he himself realized very well when he lobbied Buckingham for Montagu's protection as early as 1625 (see Tyacke, *Anti-Calvinists*, 266–70).

65. Foster, "Biography of Archbishop Richard Neile," 202–8; Tyacke, *Anti-Calvinists*, 111–13.

66. Hill, *Economic Problems of the Church*, 318–31.

67. For Vicars see Gardiner, ed., *Cases in the Courts of Star Chamber and High Commission*, 202–3; Clive Holmes, *Seventeenth-Century Lincolnshire*, History of Lincolnshire, 7 (Lincoln, 1980), 62–63; for Hooker see chapter 2 above, and for Burton and Peter, Foster, *Notes from the Caroline Underground*, 17–18, 85 n. 14, 49–50.

68. Francis Rose-Troup, *John White, the Patriarch of Dorchester (Dorset) and the Founder of Massachusetts, 1575–1648* (London, 1930), 418–20; Gardiner, ed., *Cases in the Courts of Star Chamber and High Commission*, 236.

69. Foster, *Notes from the Caroline Underground*, 16–18.

70. Cust, *The Forced Loan and English Politics*, 170–75, 298–99 (quotation at 173).

71. Ibid., 78–80; *Commons Debates, 1628*, 4:116; Foster, *Notes from the Caroline Underground*, 34–36.

72. 3 Car. I, c. 2, *Statutes of the Realm*, 5 (London, 1819), 25, apparently incorporating stricter provisions eliminated from the first Sabbath law of 1625 (see Sir Robert Harley's comments, *Commons Debates, 1628*, 2:383); *Journal of the House of Commons*, 1:838, 898–99; *Commons Debates, 1628*, 3:459, 432–43, 513–22.

73. Russell, *Parliaments and English Politics*, 379–82; Christopher Thompson, "The Divided Leadership of the House of Commons in 1629," in *Faction and Parliament*, ed. Sharpe, 245–84.

74. E.g., *Commons Debates, 1629*, 12–14 (Francis Rous), 47–52 (almost every speaker in the debates of 7 Feb. 1629), 241–42, 259–61 (Sir John Eliot). See also Russell, *Parliaments and English Politics*, 404–8.

Chapter 4

1. This and succeeding passages are not meant as contributions to the perennial debate, greatly reinvigorated in this age of computers, over the relative primacy of religious and economic discontents in the motivation of the New England immigrants. (The latest statements on the points in dispute may be found in Virginia DeJohn Anderson, "Migrants and Motives: Religion and the Settlement of New England, 1630–1640," *NEQ* 58 [1985]:339–83; David Cressy, *Coming Over: Migration and Communication between England and New England in the Seventeenth Century* [Cambridge, Eng., 1987], chap. 3.) This controversy is only marginally relevant to the case being made here: Puritans who would not have migrated except for other causes do not lose their Puritanism on that account, and the argument of this chapter is that there was a shift in emphasis in the specifically religious grievances that later migrants possessed, whatever other English developments may have also made them miserable. There is no need to plumb the exact depths of their various grievances for purposes of comparison.

The economics/religion debate takes on some relevance for the present discussion only in the case of the claim that *exclusively* economic motives must be presumed for the majority of the migrants in the absence of detailed evidence about their individual conditions at the time of emigration and in light of our knowledge of the generally depressed circumstances of England in the 1630s. One could, on the face of it, make just the opposite claim on the basis of the same nonevidence, but any detailed knowledge of the history of England and the New England colonies would suggest *some* element of Puritan commitment in the body of the migrants, regardless of its animating force in their migration. In the first place, though (it must be stressed) only a minimal measure, the substantial proportions becoming church members in the first two decades in almost every town where it has been possible to take a measure hardly suggests widespread apathy or anti-Puritan sentiment (see Stephen Foster, "The Puritan Social Ethic in the First Century of Settlement in New England" [Ph.D. dissertation, Yale University, 1966], Appendix; Foster, *Their Solitary Way*, 173–76; Gerald F. Moran, "The Puritan Saint: Religious Experience, Church Membership, and Piety in Connecticut, 1636–1776" [Ph.D. dissertation, Rutgers University, 1973], 104–29; and the discussion in chapter 5 below). In the second place, as chapter 1 has stressed, few English people in contact with Puritans were likely to be neutral on the subject: they were either in sympathy with the Puritan movement, amenable in a general way to its aims, or in some degree hostile. And, if anything, widely publicized attacks on New England's religious eccentricities increased in the later 1630s (for evidence see T. H. Breen and Stephen Foster, "Moving to the New World: the Character of Early Massachusetts Immigration," *WMQ*, 3d ser., 30 [1973]: 206–7; Hughes, *Politics, Society and Civil War in Warwickshire*, 77; and the comments of the Broadmead conventiclers instanced later in this chapter). English emigrants bound for New England would have had a sense of what they were letting themselves in for and what they wanted to get out of the protean religious establishment when they arrived. In this sense, the Migration can legitimately be called a product of the history of the English Puritan movement, among other things.

2. See the instances in Collinson, "The English Conventicle," *SCH* 23 (1986): 248–54; Derek Hirst, *The Representative of the People? Voters and Voting in England under the Early Stuarts* (Cambridge, Eng., 1975), 151–52; Hunt, *Puritan Movement*, 209–12; Holmes, *Seventeenth-Century Lincolnshire*, 107–8; Cust, *The Forced Loan and English Politics*, 264–74, 293–306, 311–12.

3. *Letters of John Davenport*, ed. Calder, 23–26; Foster, *Notes from the Caroline Underground*, 9–10, 18, 21; Yates, *Ibis ad Caesarem*, 38–40 (3d pag.).

4. Foster, *Notes from the Caroline Underground*, 25–28, 33, 90 n.47, 91 n.54; John Canne, *A Necessitie of Separation from the Church of England, Prooved by the Nonconformists Principles* (Amsterdam, 1634); Roger Williams, *Mr. Cottons Letter Lately Printed, Examined and Answered* (1644), ed. Reuben Aldridge Guild, Narragansett Club, *Publications*, 1st ser., 1 (Providence, 1866), 381.

5. Collinson, *Religion of Protestants*, 269–73.

6. McGiffert, ed., *God's Plot*, 55; *Thomas Hooker*, ed. Williams et al., 110–11; Richard Mather, *Church Government and Church Covenant Discussed* (London, 1643), 35 (1st pag.); *Letters and Journals of Robert Baillie*, ed. Laing, 1:307.

7. Peel and Carlson, eds., *Cartwrightiana*, 64–65.

8. For the dilemma of some moderates (not really Puritans but certainly good Calvinists), see Margot Todd, " 'An Act of Discretion': Evangelical Conformity and the Puritan Dons," *Albion* 18 (1986): 581–99.

9. *Winthrop Papers*, 3:243, 311, 353, 380, 391.

10. Cope and Coates, eds., *Proceedings of the Short Parliament*, 147; Hayden, ed., *Records of a Church of Christ in Bristol*, 83–91. For other instances of increased boldness in lay conventicling under Laud see the situation in Colchester described in Norman C. P. Tyack, "The Humbler Puritans of East Anglia and the New England Movement: Evidence from the Court Records of the 1630s," *NEHGR* 138 (1984): 91–92, and the evidence summarized in Stephen Foster, "English Puritanism and the Progress of New England Institutions, 1630–1660," in *Saints and Revolutionaries: Essays on Early American History*, ed. David D. Hall et al. (New York, 1984), 24–25, 25n.

11. John Bruce, ed., *Verney Papers: Notes of Proceedings in the Long Parliament, Temp. Charles I*, Camden Society, *Publications*, 1st ser., 31 (London, 1845), 123.

12. *Calender State Papers Domestic, Charles I, 1636–37*, 513, 514, 545.

13. Ships, "Lay Patronage of East Anglian Puritan Clerics in Pre-Revolutionary England," 259–65 (quotation at 261). For a parallel situation at Great Yarmouth, see ibid., 233, 241.

14. Ibid., 297–98; *NEHGR* 16 (1862): 279–84; *The Knyvett Letters, 1620–1644*, ed. Bertram Schofield, Norfolk Record Society, *Publications*, 20 (London, 1949), 98–99. A case before the northern High Commission from Kneesall, Nottinghamshire, in 1634 similarly suggests that even a strongly Puritan minister could lose ground to more militant types, lay and clerical: William Clough, the vicar of the parish, accused John Garnon of being "a frequenter of private meetings and conventicles" whose members had "taken upon them or some of them to expound the holie scriptures and make prayers of their owne" and who had "mainteyned abetted and countenanced" Luke Bacon, an unbeneficed minister of more radical propensities than Clough (H.C.C.P. 1634, Garnon *c.* Clough, Borthwick Institute, York). See also Marchant, *Puritans and the Church Courts*, 187, 295.

15. Cope and Coates, eds., *Proceedings of the Short Parliament*, 141–42, 145–48, 150–52, 181; Anthony Fletcher, *The Outbreak of the English Civil War* (London, 1981), 91–134. And see the discussion in chapter 3 above, esp. note 22.

16. William A. Shaw, *A History of the English Church during the Civil Wars and under the Commonwealth, 1640–1660* (London, 1900), 1:92–102; Fletcher, *Outbreak of the English Civil War*, 102–5; Blair Worden, *The Rump Parliament, 1648–1653* (Cambridge, Eng., 1974), 119–38; *The Book of the General Lawes and Libertyes Concerning the Inhabitants of the Massachusetts* (Cambridge, Mass., 1648), 19; *Conn. Recs.*, 1:311–12. (The New England statutes in question protect private meetings for religious purposes; that is, they license conventicling as long as the gathering is not in effect a schismatic church.)

17. Michael Mendle, *Dangerous Positions: Mixed Government, the Estates of the Realm, and the Making of the Answer to the XIX Propositions* (University, Ala., 1985),

141–47; Historical Manuscripts Commission, *Manuscripts of the House of Lords*, n.s., 11: 98–99; *The Journal of Sir Simonds D'Ewes from the Beginning of the Long Parliament to the Opening of the Trial of the Earl of Stratford*, ed. Wallace Notestein (New Haven, 1923), 458–59, 465–70, 471–73.

18. *Letters and Journals of Robert Baillie*, ed. Laing, 1:280; Valerie Pearl, *London and the Outbreak of the Puritan Revolution: City Government and National Politics, 1625–1643* (London, 1961), 107–8; Burrage, *Early English Dissenters*, 1:313–15; Mendle, *Dangerous Positions*, 156; *The Diary of Henry Townshend of Elmley Lovett, 1640–1663*, ed. J. W. Willis-Bund, 1 (London, 1915), 10. For other mob actions in the same period see Fletcher, *Outbreak of the English Civil War*, 109–10; Sharpe, *Crime in Seventeenth-Century England*, 83–88; *Journal of Sir Simonds D'Ewes*, ed. Notestein, 282–83. On this point, a leading revisionist work and the classic statement it seeks to revise concur, agreeing that the initiative for the Root and Branch Petition came from outside of Parliament, which tackled the issue hesitantly and indecisively. Cf. Fletcher, *Outbreak of the English Civil War*, 94; Samuel R. Gardiner, *History of England from the Accession of James I to the Outbreak of the Civil War, 1603–1642*, 9 (London, 1884), 276–87.

19. Samuel Rawson Gardiner, ed., *The Constitutional Documents of the Puritan Revolution, 1625–1660*, 3d ed. (London, 1906), 138, 14–43.

20. Gardiner, *History of England*, 9:382, 388–95, 10 (London, 1884), 1, 37; J. T. Cliffe, *Puritans in Conflict: The Puritan Gentry during and after the Civil Wars* (London, 1988), 102–3, 126–34; Shaw, *A History of the English Church*, 2:284–86; Douglas R. Lacey, *Dissent and Parliamentary Politics in England, 1661–1689: A Study in the Perpetuation and Tempering of Parliamentarianism* (New Brunswick, N.J., 1969), chaps. 1, 3.

21. Blakiston to William Morton, 22 May 1635, SP16/540, pt. 4, f. 355, Public Record Office; *NEHGR* 38 (1884): 79.

22. Langstaffe, ed., *Acts of the High Commission Court within the Diocese of Durham*, Surtees Society, *Publications*, 34:155–67. (The wedding feast was held at the house of the man who had been the chief promoter of Cornelius Glover's itinerant mission to the area.) For Alvey's reputation see Selement and Wooley, eds., *Thomas Shepard's "Confessions,"* 76. (Alvey is the unnamed vicar with whom Jane Holmes, like Susan Blakiston, chose to discuss theology, though she "thought she did not live holily enough.") For his social standing, see Joseph Foster, ed., *Alumni Oxonienses, Early Series*, 1 (Oxford, 1891), 21, where he is listed in 1594 at Trinity as "cler. fil." and of Bedfordshire. Obviously, he is the son of Arthur Alvey of Huntingtonshire, who was rector of Knotting, Bedfordshire, in 1592 and had been at Trinity in 1577. The elder Alvey is described simply as "pleb." Blakiston's formidable pedigree can be found in Mervyn James, *Family, Lineage, and Civil Society: A Study of Society, Politics, and Mentality in the Durham Region, 1500–1640* (Oxford, 1974), 31, 116.

23. Blakiston to Morton, 2 Mar. 1638, SP16/540, f. 29, Public Record Office; Howell, *Newcastle-upon-Tyne and the Puritan Revolution*, 126–29; *Biog. Dict. Brit. Rad.*, 1:72–73.

24. *NEHGR* 16 (1862): 283; Mather, *Magnalia*, 1:466; William Hooke, *New Englands Teares for Old Englands Feares* (London, 1641), reprinted in Samuel H. Emery, *The Ministry of Taunton, with Incidental Notices of Other Professions* (Boston, 1853), 1:94–95.

25. Seaver, *Wallington's World*, 202; Selement and Woolley, eds., *Thomas Shepard's "Confessions,"* 168. The author of the tract, Nathaniel Bacon, was a political and religious dissident of long standing who became successively a recruiter MP, a Rumper, and an officeholder under the Protectorate (see *Biog. Dict. Brit. Rad.*, 1:32–33). For the origin and popularity of the Spira story, see David D. Hall, *Worlds of Wonder, Days of Judgment: Popular Religious Belief in Early New England* (New York, 1989), 132–33, a work that appeared too recently to be more than noted at a few appropriate points.

26. David D. Hall, ed., *The Antinomian Controversy, 1636–1638: A Documentary History* (Middletown, Conn., 1968), 314, 316.

27. Robert F. Scholz, "Clerical Consociation in Massachusetts Bay: Reassessing the New England Way and Its Origins," *WMQ*, 3d ser., 29 (1972): 391–414.

28. See above, chapter 1 at notes 70–71.

29. Hall, ed., "John Cotton's Letter to Samuel Skelton," *WMQ*, 3d ser., 22 (1965): 482.

30. Ibid., 485; Thomas Hooker, *The Christians Two Chief Lessons . . .* (London, 1640), 203–4.

31. See chapter 2 above, note 82; Increase Mather, preface to Richard Mather, *An Answer to Two Questions* (Boston, 1712), ii; Richard Mather, *Church-Government and Church Covenant Discussed* (London, 1643), 10, 36–37, 54 (1st pag.); Miller, *Orthodoxy in Massachusetts, 1630–1650*, chap. 5 (and for Hooker in particular, 108–9); and for Mather at Toxteth, the discussion in this chapter, below.

32. Hall, ed., "Cotton's Letter to Skelton," *WMQ*, 3d ser., 22 (1965): 483.

33. *Winthrop Papers*, 2:180.

34. *Memoirs of Roger Clap* (1731), Dorchester Antiquarian and Historical Society, *Collections*, 1 (Boston, 1844), 39.

35. For Cotton see below, note 42; for Winthrop, *Winthrop Papers*, 4:409.

36. Robert Coachman [i.e., Cushman], *The Cry of a Stone* (London, 1642), 16–17. For this tract and its author, see Stephen Foster, "The Faith of a Separatist Layman: The Authorship, Context, and Significance of *The Cry of a Stone*," *WMQ*, 3d ser., 34 (1977): 375–403.

37. Morgan, *Visible Saints*, 106–8; Frank Shuffleton, *Thomas Hooker, 1586–1647* (Princeton, 1977), 168–70, 289–91; Baird Tipson, "Samuel Stone's 'Discourse' against Requiring Church Relations," *WMQ*, 3d ser., 46 (1989): 786–99; Robert Pope, *The Half-Way Covenant: Church Membership in Puritan New England* (Princeton, 1969), 22, 31.

38. Isabel M. Calder, *The New Haven Colony* (New Haven, 1934), chaps. 4–5; Pope, *Half-Way Covenant*, 264–65; Morgan, *Visible Saints*, 108–9; Gail Sussman Marcus, " 'Due Execution of the Generall Rules of Righteousness': Criminal Procedure in New Haven Town and Colony, 1638–1658," in *Saints and Revolutionaries*, ed. Hall et al., 99–137. See also the accounts of the New Haven towns of Milford and Guilford in, respectively, Gerald F. Moran, "Religious Renewal, Puritan Tribalism, and the Family in Seventeenth-Century Milford, Connecticut," *WMQ*, 3d ser., 36 (1979): 238–40; Paul Lucas, *Valley of Discord: Church and Society along the Connecticut River, 1630–1725* (Hanover, N.H., 1976), 32–34.

39. For Shepard, see McGiffert, ed., *God's Plot*, 48. For Cotton see his *The Way of the Congregational Churches Cleared*, 18–19, 34; Burrage, *Early English Dissenters*, 2:260–64. The evidence on Mather is contradictory. His son Increase in his *Life* of his father claims he never used the ceremonies. William Thompson, Richard Mather's closest friend and a fellow Lancashireman, however, recalled that both of them read the Book of Common Prayer "or some parte of it usually" and that they both "did use ceremonies" until the metropolitan visitation of Archbishop Samuel Harsnet, which Thompson misdates at 1635 but which took place in 1629–30. I interpret these statements to suggest partial conformity (a common arrangement in the diocese of Chester) before 1630. Cf. Increase Mather, *Richard Mather*, 49–51, 56; Ralph J. Coffman and Mary F. Rinelander, eds., "The Testament of Richard Mather and William Thompson: A New Historical and Genealogical Document of the Great Migration," *NEHGR* 140 (1986): 16; Richardson, *Puritanism in North-West England*, 22–40.

40. *Letters of John Davenport*, ed. Calder, 13–16, 19, 23–24, 33–38; Burrage, *Early English Dissenters*, 2:298.

41. *Winthrop History*, 1:335.

42. John Cotton, *An Exposition upon the Thirteenth Chapter of the Revelation* (London, 1655), 19–20. (The unpaginated preface indicates that these sermons were preached between January and April of 1640.)

43. Ibid., 259.

44. *Winthrop History*, 1:38–39. Winthrop was sensitive about charges of Separatism because of a dispute he had helped to arbitrate the previous year (while still in England) arising out of the organization of the church of Salem by covenant. See *Mass. Recs.*, 1:51; *Winthrop Papers*, 1:157.

45. *Winthrop History*, 1:187; Richard P. Gildrie, *Salem, Massachusetts, 1626–1683: A Covenant Community* (Charlottesville, Va., 1975), 31–38; Samuel Deane, *A History of Scituate, Massachusetts, from Its First Settlement to 1831* (Boston, 1831), 60–88.

46. *Winthrop History*, 1:216, 259–60; Gildrie, *Salem*, 51–55; Alonzo Lewis and James R. Newhall, *History of Lynn, Essex County, Massachusetts* (Boston, 1865), 165–67. At Scituate, however, the liberal admissions party used a covenant renewal in 1642 to assert its separate and prior existence as a church in answer to the claims of the purist faction (Deane, *History of Scituate*, 60–61).

47. *Winthrop History*, 1:187, 243–44, 346.

48. *Mass. Recs.*, 1:168.

49. The origins and purpose of the law appear clearly in its preamble, in the original order of the Court a year earlier (on the occasion of the Lynn dispute) for devising a means to ensure against further trouble, and in a draft version of the final act that explains the logic behind it in greater detail. The quotation, in turn, comes from Thomas Shepard's letter of 2 April 1636 to Richard Mather justifying the first use of the newly enacted procedures. Cf. Ibid., 142; *Winthrop Papers*, 3:231; John A. Albro, *The Life of Thomas Shepard* (Boston, 1847), 216.

50. *Winthrop History*, 1:218–19; Albro, *Shepard*, 214.

51. See John Cotton, *A Sermon Preached by the Reverend Mr. John Cotton, Deliver'd at Salem, 1636* (1713), in *John Cotton on the Churches of New England*, ed. Ziff, 57–58.

52. Michael McGiffert, "Grace and Works: The Rise and Division of Covenant Divinity in Elizabethan Puritanism," *Harvard Theological Review* 75 (1982): 463–502; McGiffert, "From Moses to Adam: The Making of the Covenant of Works," *Sixteenth Century Journal* 19 (1988): 131–55; Wallace, *Puritans and Predestination*, 100–104, 113–20; Philip F. Gura, *A Glimpse of Sion's Glory: Puritan Radicalism in New England, 1620–1660* (Middletown, Conn., 1984), 168–80.

53. Hall, ed., *Antinomian Controversy*, 413; McGiffert, ed., *God's Plot*, 18, 28.

54. Richard Walker, preaching at St. Leonard's Eastcheap in 1640, SP16/164, 83r–v, Public Record Office.

55. *Winthrop History*, 1:219; Albro, *Shepard*, 217.

56. Morgan, *Visible Saints*, 67–73.

57. William Kiffin, *Remarkable Passages in the Life of William Kiffin . . .* , ed. William Orme (London, 1823), 11–12; Hall, ed., *Antinomian Controversy*, 262, 314, 411–13.

58. *The Works of Thomas Goodwin, D.D.*, ed. John C. Miller (Edinburgh, 1861–65), 11:536. There is evidence of similar practices in use at the church of the English exiles in Rotterdam in 1637 in W. H. D. Longstaffe, ed., *Memoirs of the Life of Mr. Ambrose Barnes*, Surtees Society, *Publications*, 50 (Durham, 1866), 131. For the Arnhem group see Burrage, *Early English Dissenters*, 2:291; Cliffe, *Yorkshire Gentry*, 306–8.

59. *Winthrop Papers*, 3:211, 212, 226–27. The "gentlemen" included Sir William Constable, Sir Matthew Boynton, Sir Richard Saltonstall, and the future president of the Protectorate Council of State, Henry Lawrence. They had, in fact, covenanted together as a church well before they emigrated. See Thomas Edwards, *Antapologia: or, A Full Answer to the Apologetical Narration . . .* (London, 1644), 22–23, 35.

60. I have sketched out what I take to be the relationship between English developments, the conversion narratives, and the Antinomian crisis in "New England and the Challenge of Heresy," *WMQ*, 3d ser., 38 (1981): 654–58. The Hutchinsonian cause embraced individuals with a wide range of radical opinions, English-bred or home grown (see Gura, *A Glimpse of Sion's Glory*, chap. 9, esp. 253–73). I would suggest, however, that their relatively large following, as well as its evanescent nature, came from their claim to be Puritanism further purified from decades of clerical casuistry at a moment in the progress of the movement when the various compromises that had made up its history all seemed fatal concessions. As the more heterodox elements among the Hutchinsonians asserted themselves, most of the followers fell away at one stage or another and were reassimilated into Bay Colony religious life, albeit some of them and their descendants continued to stand for the more sectarian wing of the Puritan movement in America (see below, chapter 5).

61. Richardson, *Puritanism in North-West England*, 16–22, 97–99; Samuel Eaton and Timothy Taylor, *A Defense of Sundry Positions, and Scriptures, Alleged to Justifie the Congregationall-Way* (London, 1645), 2; Samuel Clarke, *The Lives of Sundry Eminent Persons in This Later Age* (London, 1683), 4–5.

62. Increase Mather, *Richard Mather*, 57–68; Pope, *Half-Way Covenant*, 17–23, 33–35, 134–35; Mather, *Magnalia*, 1:585–86; Matthews, *Calamy Revised*, 178; J. S. Morrill, *Cheshire, 1630–1660: County Government and Society during the English Revolution* (Oxford, 1974), 35–37, 53, 164–65. But cf. Bruce Steiner, "Dissension at Quinnipiac: The Authorship and Setting of *A Discourse about Civil Government in a New Plantation whose Design is Religion*," *NEQ* 54 (1981): 14–32; Foster, "English Puritanism and New England Institutions," in *Saints and Revolutionaries*, ed. Hall et al, 22n.

63. *Winthrop History*, 1:335; Walker, ed., *Creeds and Platforms of Congregationalism*, 138. See also E. Brooks Holifield, *The Covenant Sealed: The Development of Puritan Sacramental Theology in Old and New England, 1570–1720* (New Haven, 1974), 163–64.

64. *Winthrop Papers*, 3:398–99.

65. *Winthrop History*, 1:331; Walker, ed., *Creeds and Platforms of Congregationalism*, 138.

66. Clark, *English Provincial Society*, 370–71; R. J. Acheson, "Sion's Saint: John Turner of Sutton Valence," *Archaeologia Cantiana* 99 (1983): 183–97; Murray Tolmie, *The Triumph of the Saints: The Separate Churches of London, 1616–1649* (New York, 1977); Hayden, ed., *Records of a Church of Christ in Bristol*, 84–85. See also Foster, "Richard Neile," 254; John Ball, *A Friendly Triall of the Grounds Tending to Separation* (London, 1640), preface, sig. Bv.

67. Simeon Ashe and William Rathband, eds., *A Letter from Many Ministers in Old England . . . Written Anno. Dom. 1637* (London, 1643), sig. Azv. The original manuscript of the letter (which has the full list of signatories) is in the Prince Collection, Cotton Papers, pt. 2, no. 9, Boston Public Library.

68. See the Cambridge Platform in Walker, ed., *Creeds and Platforms of Congregationalism*, 215, 221; B. Richard Burg, ed., "A Letter of Richard Mather to a Cleric in Old England," *WMQ*, 3d ser., 29 (1972): 89, 94; Mather, *Church-Government and Church Covenant Discussed*, 34–36, 77 (1st pag.); John Cotton, *The Doctrine of the Church to Which Are Committed the Keyes of the Kingdom of Heaven*, 2d ed. rev. (London, 1643), 13.

69. Anonymous preface to William Bradshaw, *The Unreasonableness of the Separation*, 2d ed. rev. ([Amsterdam?], 1640), unpaginated.

70. Edwards, *Antapologia*, 220, 240–43.

71. *Winthrop History*, 2:165, 304–5; *Mass. Recs.*, 2:154; Walker, ed., *Creeds and Platforms of Congregationalism*, 195–202.

72. Robert Emmet Wall, Jr., *Massachusetts Bay: The Crucial Decade, 1640–1650* (New Haven, 1972), 202–3.

73. *Winthrop History*, 2:92. See also *Winthrop Papers*, 4:418.

74. *Winthrop History*, 2:165; *M.S. to A.S. with a Plea for a Libertie of Conscience, in a Church Way* . . . (London, 1644), 8–9; *Lawes and Libertyes*, 19 (margin).

75. David D. Hall, *The Faithful Shepherd: A History of the New England Ministry in the Seventeenth Century* (Chapel Hill, 1972), 102–16.

76. Ibid., 207–18; *Winthrop History*, 109–10, 329–30, 338–39; *Mass. Recs.*, 2:155–56, 3:240, 4:57–58; *Creeds and Platforms of Congregationalism*, ed. Walker, 164–74, 186–88. For Wenham see below, chap. 5, n.17.

77. *Mass. Recs.*, 3:240 (margin). The four are William Hathorne, Henry Bartholomew, Thomas Clarke, and John Leverett.

78. Pope, *Half-Way Covenant*, 17–19.

79. Ibid., chaps. 3–4.

80. See *Mass. Recs.*, 2:176–79, 4:78, 277–78. The first of these laws is a diffuse, carelessly worded omnibus "blasphemy" statute of 1646 that lists a few heterodox opinions but spends most of its unwarranted length on scoffing and irreligion; the second is a concise, tightly drawn heresy statute of 1652; and the last is an anti-Quaker enactment of 1656 that targets its intended victims with no little skill. See also chapter 5 below, and Foster, "English Puritanism and New England Institutions," in *Saints and Revolutionaries*, ed. Hall et al., 31–35.

81. Susanna Bell, *The Legacy of a Dying Mother to Her Mourning Children*, in *The Complete Works of Thomas Brooks*, ed. A. B. Grosart, 4 (Edinburgh, 1867), 453–55; *Roxbury Land and Church Records, Sixth Report of the Record Commissioners of Boston* (Boston, 1881), 80, 81.

Chapter 5

1. See chapter 1, above.

2. William G. McLoughlin and Martha Whiting Davidson, eds., "The Baptist Debate of April 14–15, 1668," MHS *Proc.* 76 (1965): 131.

3. Marchant, *Puritans and the Church Courts*, 108, 264; Matthews, *Calamy Revised*, 340; John L. Nickalls, ed., *The Journal of George Fox* (Cambridge, Eng., 1952), 73, 100–101.

4. James Frothingham Hunnewell, ed., *Records of the First Church in Charlestown, Massachusetts, 1632–1789* (Boston, 1880), Appendix, ii, iv.

5. McLoughlin and Davidson, eds., "The Baptist Debate," MHS *Proc.* 76 (1965): 117–18.

6. In the case of the leader of the Charlestown Baptists, Thomas Goold, the church had proceeded to admonition on his refusal to baptize his child but waited a full seven years, until he actually formed a separate church, before excommunicating him (Nathan E. Wood, *The History of the First Baptist Church of Boston (1665–1899)* [Philadelphia, 1899]), 42–51. Other churches went further and implicitly or explicitly agreed to tolerate members who conscientiously refused to baptize their children provided they did not withdraw from the church or try to press their views on others. For instances, see the evidence from Salem cited below, chapter 6, note 7; the case of John Farnham of Boston's North Church, cited below, note 42; and the case of Henry Shrimpton of Boston's First Church, *Boston 1st Ch. Recs.*, 1:335; Wood, *History of the First Baptist Church of Boston*, 70.

7. James Savage, *A Genealogical Dictionary of the First Settlers of New England*

(Boston, 1860–62), 4:336. Trumbull was warned in 1667, along with two of the founders of the Baptist Church, for not contributing to the support of the ministry and for not attending public worship at Charlestown (Wood, *History of the First Baptist Church of Boston*, 70–71).

8. For instances see Pope, *Half-Way Covenant*, 141–42; and attempts to deal with the problem at Dorchester and Salem, *Records of the First Church at Dorchester in New England, 1636–1734* (Boston, 1891), 39, and chapter 6 below, note 19. And see also the much more persistent (and successful) efforts made by the younger John Cotton to get absentees from his Plymouth Church to seek dismission to their new homes, although he did include absentees from *other* churches living in Plymouth in his church's covenant renewal of 1676 (*Plymouth Church Records, 1620–1859*, CSM *Publ.* 22 [1920]: 143, 151–52, 138, 163, 165, 175, 181). Even Pope, who is well aware of the dangers absenteeism poses to any inference about church membership, falls into error at least once by suggesting that the baptism of the children of Captain James Pendleton at Stonington, Connecticut, in 1675 and 1679 indicates a departure from that church's hostility to the Halfway Covenant (*Half-Way Covenant*, 118–19). Pendleton was born in England, lived in Sudbury and Watertown, became a founding member of the church of Portsmouth, New Hampshire, in 1671, but then moved to Stonington in 1673 or 1674 (baptizing his two children by communion of churches), and finally got around to joining the town's church (presumably by dismission) in 1680. Immediately after that he moved just across the colony border to Westerly, Rhode Island (Everett Hull Pendleton, *Brian Pendleton and His Descendants, 1599–1610* [N.p., 1910], 30–38).

9. Darrett B. Rutman, *Winthrop's Boston: Portrait of a Puritan Town, 1630–1649* (Chapel Hill, 1965), 195.

10. On internal migration see Breen and Foster, "Moving to the New World," *WMQ*, 3d ser., 30 (1973): 209–13; Virginia DeJohn Anderson, "To Pass Beyond the Seas: The Great Migration and the Settlement of New England, 1630–1670" (Ph.D. dissertation, Harvard University, 1984), chap. 3. (My thanks to Professor Anderson for letting me read a revised version of this chapter.)

11. See, for example, the two proceedings in Hunnewell, ed., *Records of the First Church in Charlestown*, ix, x, which resemble the complicated legal fiction used to break an entail more than they do ordinary disciplinary cases. For Trumbull's immunity from discipline by the Cambridge church, see below, note 14.

12. One notes with a certain degree of apprehension Moran's conclusion ("Puritan Saint," 117–19) that the fall in the proportion of the population of Connecticut towns who were church members can be attributed primarily to the "church's inability to admit settlers who continued to enter the community after it had become established, and its inability to replace the members it lost through death and emigration with recent arrivals."

13. See chapter 6, below.

14. The Cambridge church records are not extant before the pastorate of William Brattle, which began only in 1696. But if Trumbull *had* been under censure, this fact would surely have been mentioned, both in the debates of 1668 and in subsequent anti-Baptist polemics. Creating a fellowship out of persons under church censure was the main legal basis for prosecution of the Baptists and the main charge leveled against them by Congregational apologists.

15. "Baxter-Eliot," 165.

16. Cf. the conclusions of the ministerial assembly of 1657, Walker, ed., *Creeds and Platforms of Congregationalism*, 293–94; *Lawes and Libertyes*, 6, 9, 12; W. H. Whitmore, ed., *The Colonial Laws of Massachusetts, Reprinted from the Edition of 1660, with the Supplements to 1672* (Boston, 1889), 177. There is an instance of such analogous thinking in 1657 in Chelmsford, where the church defended the age of fifteen as the

proper one for personal responsibility for the covenant by pointing to the age of responsibility in the 1653 statute against Sabbath-breaking (*The Notebook of the Reverend John
Fiske, 1644–1675*, ed. Robert C. Pope, CSM *Publ.* 46 [1974], 117).

17. The 1644 statement of the Wenham (later Chelmsford) church, which was so
fond of the personal, orally delivered narratives that it required them from women candidates and new members admitted by dismission from other churches (*Notebook of the
Reverend John Fiske*, ed. Pope, 3–4).

18. *Memoirs of Roger Clap*, 21.

19. Robert Paul Thomas and Terry I. Anderson, "White Population and Extensive
Growth of the New England Economy in the Seventeenth Century," *Journal of Economic
History* 33 (1973): 634–67; Main, *Society and Economy in Colonial Connecticut*, 8–10,
table 1.1; "Baxter-Eliot," 165.

20. *Mass. Recs.*, 5:59–63. The association between youth and taverns is made explicit
in the "collections" of the Connecticut ministers in 1676 in response to the Bay Colony
legislation (*The Wyllys Papers*, Connecticut Historical Society, *Collections*, 21 [Hartford,
1924], 236–37). And see Clark, *English Alehouse*, 147–48; Ross W. Beales, "In Search of
the Historical Child: Miniature Adulthood and Youth in Colonial New England," *American Quarterly* 27 (1975): 395–97.

21. Beales, "In Search of the Historical Child," *American Quarterly* 27 (1975): 388–
91.

22. Pope, *Half-Way Covenant*, 279–86; Moran, "Puritan Saint," 150–54.

23. *Memoirs of Roger Clap*, 22, 24–27; Moran, "Puritan Saint," 105–6.

24. Pope, *Half-Way Covenant*, chap. 8; Moran, "The Puritan Saint," chap. 4; Stephen
Foster, "The Godly in Transit: English Popular Protestantism and the Creation of a Puritan Establishment in America," in *Seventeenth-Century New England*, ed. David D. Hall
and David G. Allen, CSM *Publ.* 63 (1984), 214, 220–27.

25. Cotton Mather, *A Companion for Communicants* (Boston, 1690), 67. The instance of only five communion days a year comes from Cambridge under Thomas Shepard (Joshua Coffin, *A Sketch of the History of Newbury, Newburyport and West Newbury, from 1635 to 1845* [Boston, 1845], 107). Evidence for anxiety over communion is
presented in Hall, *Worlds of Wonder, Days of Judgment*, 156–62. Without denying this
diffidence, however, it might be noted as well that congregations generally did not put the
same value on the sacrament as their ministers did.

26. Urian Oakes, *New England Pleaded With* (Cambridge, Mass., 1673), 58.

27. Samuel Danforth, *A Brief Recognition of New Englands Errand into the Wilderness . . .* (Cambridge, Mass., 1671), 13.

28. Walker, ed., *The Creeds and Platforms of Congregationalism*, 405; *To the Elders
and Ministers of Every Town within the Jurisdiction of the Massachusetts in New-England* (Cambridge, Mass., 1668 [1669]), broadside; "Baxter-Eliot," 453.

29. *Conn. Recs.*, 2:260–83; 3:64–65.

30. Samuel Willard, *Covenant Keeping and the Way to Blessedness* (Boston, 1682),
112–13. The sermon was preached to Old South just before its covenant renewal of 29
June 1680 and emphasizes (114–16) the church's duty to see "that all means be used" to
help its children come to full communion.

31. Walker, ed., *Creeds and Platforms of Congregationalism*, 257–61; *Conn. Recs.*,
1:281; Charles J. Hoadly, ed., *Record of the Colony or Jurisdiction of New Haven*, 2
(Hartford, 1858), 196–97; *Mass. Recs.*, 4:pt. 1, 280.

32. Walker, ed., *Creeds and Platforms of Congregationalism*, 291–300.

33. Ibid., 262–64; Pope, *Half-Way Covenant*, 31–38.

34. Pope, *Half-Way Covenant*, chaps. 3–4.

35. Hall, *Faithful Shepherd*, 185–86.

36. Govr. and Assistants to Sir Henry Vane, 20 Oct. 1652, MHS *Coll.*, 3d ser., 1 (Boston, 1825), 36; *Mass. Recs.*, 4:pt. 1, 113–14, 122, 151, 177, 183, 191, 328.

37. *Mass. Recs.*, 4:pt. 1, 276, 277–78; *Conn. Recs.*, 1:283–84.

38. Patria U. Bonomi, *Under the Cope of Heaven: Religion, Society, and Politics in Colonial America* (New York, 1986), 26–29; Jonathan M. Chu, *Neighbors, Friends, or Madmen: The Puritan Adjustment to Quakerism in Seventeenth-Century Massachusetts* (Westport, Conn., 1985), chaps. 5–7. The abatement in the worst of the severities inflicted on the Quakers is usually attributed to fear of English intervention, but, as John Gorham Palfrey pointed out, the erosion of the will to persecute began well before the government of Charles II made any sympathetic noises on behalf of toleration in the colonies (*History of New England during the Stuart Dynasty* [Boston, 1882–85], 2:472–83).

39. *Sewall Diary*, 1:18, 44; Gildrie, *Salem*, 133–37.

40. Barry Reay, *The Quakers and the English Revolution* (London, 1985), chap. 2.

41. Ibid., 20–26.

42. Chandler Robbins, *A History of the Second Church, or Old North, in Boston* (Boston, 1852), 292–93; Wood, *History of the First Baptist Church of Boston*, 188–89.

43. Barry Reay, "Quaker Opposition to Tithes, 1652–1660," *P&P* 86 (Feb. 1980): 98–120; Margaret James, "The Political Importance of the Tithes Controversy in the English Revolution, 1640–60," *History*, n.s., 26 (1941–42): 1–18.

44. For Massachusetts examples see the Suffolk County survey of 1657, MHS *Colls.*, 3d ser., 1:49–51; *Town Records of Salem*, 1 (Salem, 1868), 97, 203–4, 210, 228, and the further instances cited in note 45 below. For Connecticut, see *Conn. Recs.*, 3:300; Main, *Society and Economy in Colonial Connecticut*, 266–68. English comparisons are taken from O'Day, *English Clergy*, chap. 13, esp. 175–76; Stieg, *Laud's Laboratory*, 73, 124–28.

45. *Dorchester Town Records*, Record Commissioners of Boston, 4th Report (Boston, 1880), 87–89; Don Gleason Hill, ed., *The Early Records of the Town of Dedham*, 3 (Dedham, Mass., 1892), 153–54. The important point is the *relative* prosperity of the clergy. Ezekiel Rogers was notoriously hard up after his move to America and enjoyed an annual salary of £60, at the lower end of the acceptable range. Nonetheless, his estate at his death in 1661 still exceeded that of all but one of the eleven men who served as deputies for Rowley under the Old Charter and whose inventories are extant. The average value of estates probated in Rowley before 1686 (excluding those of these eleven men) was £283, about one-fifth of Rogers's. See Benjamin P. Mighill and George B. Blodgette, eds., *The Early Records of the Town of Rowley, Massachusetts, 1639–1672* (Rowley, Mass., 1894), 79; Dow, ed., *Probate Records of Essex County, Massachusetts*, 1:334–35; Robert Emmet Wall, "The Membership of the Massachusetts General Court, 1634–1686" (Ph.D. dissertation, Yale University, 1965), 112–13.

46. MHS *Coll.*, 3d ser., 1:51; *Sibley's Harvard Graduates*, 2:251–52. Whitman was the first and last man in the colonial period to finish out his clerical career in Hull. (For his unhappy successor, Ezra Carpenter, see the Envoi.) He was also unusual (for a minister who lived relatively close to Boston and who survived well into the eighteenth century) in never publishing anything.

47. For comments to this effect, see the diary of John Hull, American Antiquarian Society, *Transactions*, 3 (Boston, 1857), 212; the result of the synod of 1679, in Walker, ed., *Creeds and Platforms of Congregationalism*, 434; Samuel Willard to Increase Mather, 10 July 1688, MHS *Coll.*, 4th ser., 8:571.

48. Robbins, *History of the Second Church*, 213.

49. George L. Walker, *History of the First Church in Hartford, 1633–1883* (Hartford, Conn., 1884), 146–75.

50. John Norton, *The Heart of New England Rent at the Blasphemies of the Present Generation* (Cambridge, Mass., 1659), 26–27, 56–57.

51. Robert M. Kingdon, *Geneva and the Consolidation of the French Protestant Movement, 1569–1572*, Travaux d'Humanisme et Renaissance, 92 (Geneva, 1967), 37–148.

52. See the terms of opprobrium in the Bay Colony election sermon of 1667: Jonathan Mitchell, *Nehemiah on the Wall in Troublesome Times* (Cambridge, Mass., 1671), 27–29; and in Thomas Shepard, Jr.'s, preface to Samuel Danforth, *A Briefe Recognition of New-Englands Errand into the Wilderness* (Cambridge, Mass., 1671), sig. A2v.

53. John Norton, *Sion the Outcast Healed of Her Wounds*, in *Three Choice and Profitable Sermons* . . . (Cambridge, Mass., 1664), 12; John Higginson, *The Cause of God and His People in New England* . . . (Cambridge, Mass., 1663), 11–12.

54. "Baxter-Eliot," 446.

55. Norton, *Sion the Outcast Healed of her Wounds*, 8.

56. For Norton's end, see Mather, *Magnalia*, 1:297; for Higginson's plight, see below.

57. *Boston 1st Ch. Recs.*, 1:56; Hull diary, American Antiquarian Society, *Transactions*, 3:198; *Notebook of John Fiske*, ed. Pope, 113–15, 120–21, 126–28, 130; Pope, *Half-Way Covenant*, 25–26, 35–39. I think, however, that Pope is in error in seeing the seventy-five children "presented" to the church of Chelmsford on 1 Feb. 1657 as participants in a mass baptism inaugurating the Halfway Covenant. Rather, all were the children of parents (listed with them) in full communion and, presumably, already baptized without controversy. The list of names amounts to a formal affirmation that the seventy-five were those individuals in Chelmsford *not* in full communion but still bona fide children of the church and under its watch, regardless of their ages.

58. Walker, ed., *Creeds and Platforms of Congregationalism*, 294, 298; Solomon Stoddard, *The Doctrine of Instituted Churches Explained and Proved from the Word of God* (London, 1700), 8.

59. *Mass. Recs.*, 4:pt. 2, 38; Walker, ed., *Creeds and Platforms of Congregationalism*, 264; Eleazer Mather to John Davenport, 6 July 1662, MHS *Colls.*, 4th ser., 8:192–93; *A Copy of the Letter Returned by the Ministers of New-England to Mr. John Dury about His Pacification*, in Norton, *Three Choice and Profitable Sermons*, sigs F4r, Gr.

60. *Sewall Diary*, 1:30.

61. William Hubbard, *A General History of New England*, ed. William Thaddeus Harris, 2d ed. (Boston, 1848), 591.

62. Robbins, *History of the Second Church*, 296.

63. Norton, *Sion the Outcast Healed of Her Wounds*, 11; Higginson, *The Cause of God and His People in New England*, 16, 20–22.

64. The "pure" pattern was: opponent of the Halfway Covenant, advocate of toleration for the Baptists and perhaps the Quakers, hard-line resister to compromise with the English government; advocate of the Halfway Covenant, enthusiast for persecution of the Baptists and Quakers, accommodationist in attitude toward the demands of the English government. Cf. two articles published simultaneously but rarely taken together: E. Brooks Holifield, "On Toleration in Massachusetts," *Church History* 38 (1969): 188–200; Richard C. Simmons, "The Founding of the Third Church in Boston," *WMQ*, 3d ser., 26 (1969): 241–52. There are numerous exceptions to this triple congruence, but only the engagingly sui generis William Hubbard comes anywhere close in his pronouncements to what is often (incorrectly) taken to be the most logical allignment: Halfway Covenant, toleration, accommodation.

65. Hamilton Andrews Hill, *History of the Old South Church (Third Church) in Boston, 1669–1884* (Boston, 1890), 1:98–99. The other two magistrates who supported Old South but took a hard line on England were Daniel Gookin and Richard Russell. Gookin favored persecution of the Baptists; Russell supported toleration for the most part.

66. John Oxenbridge, *New-England Freeman Warmed and Warned* (Cambridge, Mass., 1673), 19. The sermon was preached on 31 May 1671.

67. See above, note 31. See also a very similar response from Deacon John Wiswall of the Dorchester church on 27 September 1657, when he called Richard Mather's attempt to baptize the granddaughter of a church member "a Corruption Creepinge in as an harbenger to old england practice viz. to make all members" (*Records of the First Church of Dorchester*, 168).

68. *Letters of John Davenport*, ed. Calder, 198–201, 256–57.

69. Higginson, *The Cause of God and His People in New England*, 16; *A Direction for a Public Profession in the Church Assembly, after Private Examination by the Elders* [Cambridge, Mass., 1665]; Richard D. Pierce, ed., *The Records of the First Church in Salem, Massachusetts, 1629–1736* (Salem, Mass., 1974), 103–7; Higginson to Increase Mather, 5 Feb. 1684, MHS *Coll.*, 4th ser., 8:283–85.

70. Eleazer Mather to John Davenport, 4 July 1662, MHS *Coll.*, 4th ser., 8:192–93.

71. Walker, ed., *Creeds and Platforms of Congregationalism*, 335–37.

72. Oxenbridge, *New-England Freeman Warmed and Warned*, 19.

73. Pope, *Half-Way Covenant*, chap. 6, and see above, note 64.

74. Hill, *History of the Old South Church*, 1:52–53.

75. Isaac Backus, *A History of New England, with Particular Reference to the Denomination of Christians Called Baptists*, 2d ed., ed. David Weston (Newton, Mass., 1871), 1:312, 316–17; John Davenport, *A Sermon Preach'd at the Election of the Governour* . . . ([Cambridge, Mass.], 1670), 14–15, photostatic reprint in CSM *Publ.*, 10 (1907): 6ff.; Oxenbridge, *New-England Freeman Warmed and Warned*, 37–38; James Allen, *New-Englands Choicest Blessing* . . . (Boston, 1679), 19.

76. Backus, *History of New England*, 1:316–17. The six who signed the warrant were Simon Bradstreet, Daniel Denison, Thomas Danforth, Daniel Gookin, Simon Willard, and John Pynchon. Edward Drinker, the author of the letter giving this information, claims that a further six magistrates were willing to sign a release order but that Governor Richard Bellingham hesitated to join them. With six magistrates committed to persecution and Bellingham eliminated, only seven names remain from which to make up the six tolerationists: Samuel Symonds, William Hathorne, John Leverett, Edward Tyng, Eleazer Lusher, Deputy-Governor Francis Willoughby, and Richard Russell. The last two alone supported Old South so at least four of the six pro-Baptist magistrates had to be First Church partisans and enemies of the Halfway Covenant. I am inclined to think, however, that all five of the men in this category were willing to sign the release order and that Russell is the odd man out. He showed considerable sympathy for the Baptists while the Charlestown church was debating their censure, but after they seceded to form a church of their own he ordered their arrest, and later, in 1669, he had joined with the uncomplicated persecutors among the magistrates in publicly attacking the elders of First Church for their publication of a letter from another tolerationist "reflecting much upon this Government and their proceedings against some Anabaptists." Moreover, because of illness or ambivalence he was absent from Boston for most of the session of the General Court held just before the arrest of the Baptists in 1670. (ibid., 1: 292, 295, 297; Hill, *History of the Old South Church*, 1:145; *Mass. Recs.*, 4:pt. 2, 462). Hathorne, it is true, is now remembered only for his brutality toward the Salem Quakers, but that incident is an exception in a career consistently devoted to opposition to any act by clergy or General Court that abridged religious freedom or congregational autonomy: he was on record voting against the Court's endorsement of the Cambridge Platform, against the burning of William Pynchon's *Meritorious Price*, and against the censure of Maldon for its unauthorized call to the suspect Marmaduke Matthews, and he had even at first objected to legislation aimed at the Quakers. However obnoxious the Quakers of Salem became to him, he was hardly likely to have felt the same way about the Baptists of Boston and came, in time, for that matter, to abandon his severity toward the former group (Gildrie, *Salem*, 133–37, 149–50; Chu, *Neighbors, Friends, or Madmen*, 41–42).

77. The historiography of the jeremiad is reviewed critically in Theodore Dwight Bozeman, *To Live Ancient Lives: The Primitivist Dimension in Puritanism* (Chapel Hill, 1988), chap. 20, esp. 311–16, 335–43, a work published too recently to be more than noted here at appropriate points. My own discussion will differ from its predecessors in emphasizing what I take to be the political context the jeremiads addressed and, consequently, the partisan, controversial nature of the form at its first enunciation; the extent to which the sermonic literature in question was merely a part of a much larger "reform" movement and, therefore, intimately linked to programs for the extension of church membership, increased moral regulation, and the revival of the covenant renewal; and the way in which the identification of New England with Israel in the Prophetic and Exilic periods became the primary imaginative device of the American Puritans for recovering a public frame of reference for individual spiritual progress.

78. Oakes, *New-England Pleaded With*, 37–53.

79. Hill, *History of the Old South Church*, 1:95–100.

80. Ibid., 100–101; Oxenbridge, *New-England Freeman Warmed and Warned*, 26, 34. On the traditional immunity of the magistrates from removal for purely political grounds see Foster, *Their Solitary Way*, 87–92. (But Governor Bellingham is misidentified, 91, as a foe of toleration.)

81. See Walker, *History of the First Church in Hartford*, 146–75; *Sibley's Harvard Graduates*, 1:110–18; Wall, "Membership of the Massachusetts General Court," 685–86; Russell, Tilton, et al. to Sarah Mather, 13 Aug. 1662, MHS *Coll.*, 4th ser., 8:78–79; Russell to Increase Mather, 28 March 1681, ibid., 83–84.

82. Pope, *Half-Way Covenant*, 174–79.

83. That is, Willoughby, Russell, Danforth, and Gookin.

84. *Mass. Recs.*, 4:pt. 2, 489–94.

85. Wall, "Membership of the Massachusetts General Court," 293–94; Cotton Mather to John Richards, 14 Dec. 1692, MHS *Coll.*, 4th ser., 8:397–401; Pope, *Half-Way Covenant*, chap. 7.

86. Hill, *History of the Old South Church*, 1:111. The five are Thomas Clarke, Peter Tilton, Humphrey Davy, Daniel Fisher, and Oliver Purchas. Moreover, Richard Waldron and John Waite both subsequently served as speaker of the deputies and would certainly have been elected to the magistracy (the invariable fate of the speaker in this period) had not the former been prevented by the detachment of New Hampshire from the Bay Colony and the latter by blindness. Edward Johnson, Edward Hutchinson, and Richard Cooke were also likely candidates for the magistracy, but they died in 1672, 1675, and 1673 respectively. All three fathered sons who did make it to the upper house under the Old Charter and who carried on their fathers' politics: William Johnson, Elisha Hutchinson, and the leader of the Popular Party himself, Elisha Cooke, Sr.

87. Hull diary, American Antiquarian Society, *Transactions*, 3:234, 239.

88. Coffin, *Sketch of the History of Newbury*, 74; Walker, ed., *Creeds and Platforms of Congregationalism*, 137–39, 266–67.

89. "John Higginson's Apology," MHS *Coll.*, 4th ser., 8:276; Pope, *Half-Way Covenant*, 144–47; Oxenbridge, *New-England Freeman Warmed and Warned*, 26; see also above, note 69.

90. Hall, *Faithful Shepherd*, 212–14; Richard P. Gildrie, "Contention in Salem: The Higginson-Nicholet Controversy, 1672–1676"; *Essex Institute Historical Collections* 113 (1977): 116–39.

91. *Mass. Recs.*, 4:pt. 2, 522; MHS *Coll.*, 4th ser., 8:274–75; 5:34, 67–68; Pierce, ed., *Salem Church Records*, 134–36.

92. Sidney Perley, *The History of Salem, Massachusetts*, 3 (Salem, Mass., 1928), 153–54; Christine Alice Young, *From "Good Order" to Glorious Revolution: Salem, Massachusetts, 1628–1689* (Ann Arbor, 1980), 130–38. Samuel Eaborne and Thomas Roots,

the fomenters of the Nicholet affair, are signatories on the petition for a new meeting-house in 1680, but this time, no longer in the shadows, William Hathorne's name leads the list.

93. George F. Dow, ed., *Records and Files of the Quarterly Courts of Essex County, Massachusetts*, 4 (Salem, 1914), 363; Hill, *History of the Old South Church*, 1:79, 97.

94. MHS *Coll.*, 4th ser., 8:269–70, 272. In addition to Oxenbridge and Allen, First Church sent as its representatives to an abortive council intended to set up a breakaway church under Nicholet, Edward Hutchinson and Anthony Stoddard, two of the dissenting seventeen deputies of 1671. The only magistrates present were Leverett and Hathorne (*Boston 1st Ch. Recs.*, 1:72; Lewis and Newhall, *History of Lynn*, 261).

95. Coffin, *Sketch of the History of Newbury*, 75–76; Dow, ed., *Records and Files of the Quarterly Courts of Essex County*, 4:122.

96. James Pike, *The New Puritan* (New York, 1879), 39–42; Robert Lord Goodman, "Newbury, Massachusetts, 1635–1685: The Social Foundations of Harmony and Con-flict" (Ph.D. dissertation, Michigan State University, 1974), 166–68, 201–2; Coffin, *Sketch of the History of Newbury*, 135; Wall, "Membership of the Massachusetts General Court," 470–71, 478–80.

97. *Mass. Recs.*, 2:240, Wall, "Membership of the Massachusetts General Court," 446–47, 503; Hutchinson, *Original Papers*, 2:4–6; *Boston 1st Ch. Recs.*, 1:83. Bartholo-mew also signed the 1671 deputies' dissent and, like Hathorne, had gone on record in opposition to the General Court's interdiction of Marmaduke Matthew's ministry at Maldon.

98. The main account of the Hoar controversy is Samuel Eliot Morison, *Harvard College in the Seventeenth Century* (Cambridge, Mass., 1936), 2:401–8. Hoar's affilia-tion with Old South did not of and in itself ruin his credit with First Church magistrates, including Governor Leverett. The fatal actions for them were Hoar's failure to secure dis-mission from John Collins's Congregational church in London, his subsequent acceptance of a ministerial call from Old South and his abrupt abandonment of the post (over the church's protest) when the Harvard presidency came open, and his prevarication over the matter when he was challenged about it. The whole business all too closely resembled the schismatic origins of Old South and First Church's simultaneous imbroglio over John Davenport's falsified dismission from his New Haven pulpit, for which Leverett never for-gave him. For Hoar's difficulties with Old South see Thomas Danforth to John Winthrop, Jr., 1 Aug. 1672, MHS *Proc.*, 1st ser., 13 (1873–75): 235. Governor Leverett's anger over the whole affair is indicated in his letter to John Collins, 24 Aug. 1674, and Collins's let-ter to Leverett, 19 March 1675, Hutchinson, *Original Papers*, 2:196, 205.

99. I am not suggesting that the Halfway Covenant caused the witchcraft episode in Salem Village, only that a continuing controversy over extended baptism and church membership helped organize and exacerbate the local tensions that erupted in 1692. Salem Village was an ecclesiastical jurisdiction created out of the church of Salem when the parent polity was in a state of crisis over these issues, and the new church ran through ministerial candidates at an extraordinary rate. Each of the four men, moreover, who tried out for the Salem Village pulpit before 1692 had opposite views on the crucial ques-tions from his predecessor and successor. James Bayley was clearly a proponent of ex-tended baptism, because he grew up in Newbury and was a member of its church, the most overtly Presbyterian polity in Massachusetts, and left Salem Village after a short, stormy career, for the pulpit of Killingworth, the most overtly Presbyterian polity in Con-necticut. His supporters were not reconciled to his loss and promptly ruined the tenure of the next man up, the unfortunate George Burroughs (*Sibley's Harvard Graduates*, 2:291–92, 295, 324–25). Burroughs could not have been in sympathy with any attempt to ex-tend baptismal rights. A child of the church of Roxbury, which had long used the Half-

way Covenant, he did not avail himself of his privilege to baptize his own child until the day he was himself admitted in full communion (*Roxbury Land and Church Records*, 87, 91, 132). After the failure of Burroughs's attempt to settle in Salem Village, he was succeeded by an English immigrant, Deodat Lawson. Lawson is the shadowiest figure of the four, but he evidently did accept the Halfway Covenant: he had joined Old South upon his arrival in Boston, and in 1682, while preaching in Plymouth Colony, he wrote an elegy on the death of Thomas Savage, founding member of Old South and its political leader in its confrontation with First Church (Savage, *Genealogical Dictionary of New England*, 3:63; American Antiquarian Society *Proc.*, 93 [1983]: 205–8). Lawson's successor, Samuel Parris, was another English immigrant to Boston, but he had chosen to join First Church. He explained his views on baptism at some length to the Salem Village Church: they would have precluded any use of the Halfway Covenant (*Boston 1st Ch. Recs.*, 1:68; Paul Boyer and Stephen Nissenbaum, eds., *Salem-Village Witchcraft: A Documentary Record of Local Conflict in Colonial New England* [Belmont, Calif., 1972], 270–71).

100. Michael G. Hall, *The Last American Puritan: The Life of Increase Mather, 1639–1723* (Middletown, Conn., 1988), a full-scale reinterpretation of its title subject, appeared too late to be more than noted at a few points in this study.

101. On the English history of the sermonic form see Michael McGiffert, "God's Controversy with Jacobean England," *American Historical Review* 88 (1983): 1151–74; Bozeman, *To Live Ancient Lives*, 290–98.

102. John Cotton, *Gods Promise to His Plantation . . .* (London, 1630), 19. See also Thomas Shepard, *Wine for Gospel Wantons; or, Cautions against Spiritual Drunkeness* (Cambridge, Mass., 1668), a sermon preached in 1645.

103. Increase Mather, *Returning unto God the Great Concernment of a Covenant People* (Boston, 1680), 9. See also Foster, *Their Solitary Way*, 123 and n., and for Elizabethan and Jacobean precedents, Collinson, *Birthpangs of Protestantism*, 18–26.

104. The most recent surveys of this sermon literature are Bozeman, *To Live Ancient Lives*, chap. 10, and Harry S. Stout, *The New England Soul: Preaching and Religious Culture in Colonial New England* (New York, 1986), 70–74. Both authors see considerably more continuity than I do between the sermons of the 1660s and early 1670s, on the one side, and those of the next periods on the other.

105. William Stoughton, *New-Englands True Interest; Not to Lie* (Cambridge, Mass., 1670), 17, 19, 25–29.

106. The sermon was not published at public expense but by an unnamed "person of worth." Although brought out in a year of deep political divisions and much longer than its predecessors, it is, compared to most election sermons, singularly apolitical, an ironic circumstance in light of its author's rapid elevation to the magistracy—a full six months before he managed to join the Dorchester church (*Records of the First Church at Dorchester*, 24).

107. Stoughton, *New-Englands True Interest*, 31, 34, 39–40.

108. Increase Mather, *An Earnest Exhortation to the Inhabitants of New England . . .* (Boston, 1676), 9.

109. James Fitch, *An Explanation of the Solemn Advice Recommended by the Council of Connecticut Colony . . .* (Boston, 1683), 5–6; Samuel Willard, *The Only Sure Way to Prevent Threatened Calamity*, in *The Child's Portion . . .* (Boston, 1684), 179, 181.

110. See Eleazer Mather's comments in *A Serious Exhortation . . .* 2d ed. (Boston, 1678), 19, 22, 26–27. Increase published his about-face on the Halfway Covenant in 1675 but dated his actual change in convictions to early 1671 (Pope, *Half-Way Covenant*, 182–83).

111. Oakes, *New-England Pleaded With*, 23–24.

112. Thomas James Holmes, *Increase Mather: A Bibliography of His Works* (Cleve-

land, 1931), 2:585; Increase Mather, *A Brief History of the War with the Indians in New-England* (London, 1676), 45; Mather, *Magnalia*, 2:334; Fitch to Increase Mather, 23 May 1679, 16 Apr. 1683, MHS *Colls.*, 4th ser., 8:473–74.

113. According to its title page, Increase Mather's *The Day of Trouble Is Near* (Cambridge, Mass., 1674) consists of two sermons preached on 11 February 1674. The Library of Congress copy (examined in the Early American Imprints microcard series) bears the name "Nath: Collins" written in ink at the top of its title page and at the bottom, "Received the 30th of the second month 1674" (30 Apr. 1674). Increase quotes Collins's sermon in *Returning unto God*, 11. Cotton Mather's 1685 *Elegy* on Collins is one of the earliest entries in his enormous bibliography, and he also gave the Connecticut minister a good write-up in *Magnalia*, 2:141, though, of course, too late to do him any good. For other instances of Connecticut clients of Increase see his correspondence with Simon Bradstreet of New London, MHS *Colls.*, 4th ser., 8:477–81, and the instance of Samuel Hooker of Farmington, cited below, note 123.

114. Increase Mather, *A Discourse Concerning the Danger of Apostasy*, in *A Call from Heaven to the Present and Succeeding Generations . . .* (Boston, 1679), 64–65, 67–68; *A Call to the Rising Generation*, ibid., 29; *Returning unto God the Great Concernment of a Covenant People*, preface, sigs. A2v–A3v.

115. Mather, *A Discourse Concerning the Danger of Apostasy*, in *A Call from Heaven*, 55.

116. Mather, *The Day of Trouble Is Near*, 24, 27. There are several references (e.g., 25–26) to the Third Anglo-Dutch war and to the Dutch recapture of New York. See *Mass. Recs.*, 4:pt. 2, 572–74; Palfrey, *History of New England*, 3:119–26.

117. *Roxbury Land and Church Records*, 193–94; Walker, ed., *Creeds and Platforms of Congregationalism*, 426–27.

118. Mather, *Brief History of the War with the Indians*, 17–18; *I. Mather Diary*, 44; Mather, *An Ernest Exhortation*, 12; William Hubbard, *The Happiness of a People in the Wisdome of Their Rulers Directing and in the Obedience of Their Brethren Attending unto What Israel Ought to Do* (Boston, 1676), 44.

119. *I. Mather Diary*, 23–24. Taverns were not just a source of diversion in grim times; the numerous licenses served as a form of welfare for widows and for families ruined by the war.

120. Ibid., 24–25.

121. Hubbard, *The Happiness of a People*, 46–47, 52–53. (This sermon also rejects further moral legislation and calls, 32–42, for toleration of the Baptists.) David D. Hall pointed out to me more than twenty years ago that a political stance was implied in Hubbard's flaunted apolitical irenicism; I did not understand his point then, but I acknowledge his priority now. See also Anne Kusener Nelsen, "King Philip's War and the Hubbard-Mather Rivalry," *WMQ*, 3d ser., 27 (1970): 615–29, a neglected article that is in error on some details but gets the gist of the conflict (and the point that there *was* a conflict) quite accurately.

122. Pope, *Half-Way Covenant*, 242.

123. *I. Mather Diary*, 24, 27; *Conn Recs.*, 2:417; Samuel Hooker to Increase Mather, 5 June 1677, MHS *Coll.*, 4th ser., 8:338. (The Hooker inquiry is the more interesting for his also being a correspondent of Fitch's; he still sent to Boston for his information.)

124. *Roxbury Land and Church Records*, 193–94.

125. See the discussion chapter 4, above, and *Notebook of the Reverend John Fiske*, ed. Pope, 106.

126. Rose-Troup, *John White*, 418–21; Willard, *Covenant Keeping the Way to Blessedness*, 84–85.

127. Cf. the document from Dorchester in England with *Records of the First Church at Dorchester*, 18–20; Fitch, *Explanation of the Solemn Advice*, 69–72; *A Copy of the*

Church Covenants Which Have Been Used in the Church of Salem . . . (Boston, 1680), 4–8; Mather, *Magnalia*, 2:332–33. (This last is a verbatim transcription of Old South's *The Church Renewed Covenant, June 29, 1680* [Boston, 1680].)

128. Increase Mather, *Renewal of Covenant the Great Duty Incumbent on Decaying or Distressed Churches* (Boston, 1677), 14, 19.

129. Pope, *Half-Way Covenant*, 120–21, 188–89, 245–46.

130. Samuel Willard, *The Duty of a People That Have Renewed Their Covenant with God* (Boston, 1680), 5–6.

131. See Foster, "The Godly in Transit," in *Seventeenth-Century New England*, ed. Hall and Allen, 215–19.

132. Mather, *Brief History of the War with the Indians*, 3, 7–8, 16–17, 20. In contrast to the inefficacy of mere fast days, the implementation of Mather's two pet devices, moral legislation and mass covenant renewals (in Plymouth Colony), *was* followed by signal victories (ibid., 39, 42, 44). And see also his *Renewal of Covenant*, 17–18, 18 margin.

133. Willard, *Duty of a People*, 10–11; Increase Mather, *Returning unto God*, 18–19.

134. Mather, *An Earnest Exhortation*, 12. As if to emphasize the contest with Hubbard, the work was mostly issued tacked on to *A Brief History*, which was also in a contest with Hubbard's own account of King Philip's War. See Holmes, *Increase Mather*, 1:225; Nelsen, "King Philip's War and the Hubbard-Mather Rivalry," *WMQ*, 3d ser., 27 (1970): 628–29.

135. Mather, *Discourse Concerning the Danger of Apostasy*, in *A Call from Heaven*, 35–36; Holmes, *Increase Mather*, 1:96–97. Mather must have been deliberately courting trouble to suggest (*Discourse*, 81) that the rash of fires threatening Boston was retribution for the heat of the contentions over the founding of Old South. There were three First Church members among the assembled magistrates and two strong supporters of their failed attempt to block the establishment of Boston's third church; there were no Old South magistrates at all, although Thomas Savage did hold the speakership of the House of Deputies.

136. On the marked underdevelopment of Hubbard's providentialism see Kenneth B. Murdock, "William Hubbard and the Providential Interpretation of History," AAS *Proc.* 52 (1942): 15–37.

137. *Records of the Suffolk County Court, 1671–1680.* CSM Coll. 30 (1933): 1015.

138. Walker, ed., *Creeds and Platforms of Congregationalism*, 414–15.

139. Ibid., 280n., 389n., 393n.–394n., 418–19, 425, 433, 434–35.

140. Ibid., 435–37.

141. *Boston 1st Church Recs.*, 1:75–76.

142. Cotton Mather, *Parentator, Memoirs of . . . Dr. Increase Mather* (Boston, 1724), 85–86; *Mass. Recs.*, 5:244. For the evidence of a Haverhill covenant renewal, see John Brown, *Solemn Covenanting with God . . .* (Boston, 1727), 14.

143. Willard, *The Only Sure Way to Prevent Threatened Calamity*, in *The Child's Portion*, 190.

Chapter 6

1. *I. Mather Diary*, 52.

2. Mather, *A Discourse Concerning the Danger of Apostasy*, in *A Call from Heaven*, 70–72.

3. *Mass. Recs.*, 5:378.

4. On the change in conception see John Higginson to Increase Mather, 17 Aug. 1683, MHS *Coll.*, 4th ser., 8:285–87. The preface to *Illustrious Providences* bears the date 1 Jan. 1684, but the back matter advertises the *Doctrine of Divine Providence* as

forthcoming, even though this work contains material not preached until August and September 1684. The delay between preface and publication was probably used for some of Mather's stop-press insertions.

5. Samuel Wakeman, *Sound Repentance the Right Way to Escape Deserved Ruine* (Boston, 1685), 31. Bishop wrote the preface to the work and usually served as the intermediary in the Wakeman-Mather correspondence. For Increase's patronage of both men see MHS *Coll.*, 4th ser., 8:307, 309, 585–86. Mather's cultivation of James Fitch of Norwich and Simon Bradstreet of New London has already been noted; both men sent him material for *Illustrious Providences*, as did Bishop.

6. Holmes, *Increase Mather*, 1:232–38.

7. The meeting of the ministers of the Bay to which Mather announced his project on 12 March 1681 was called to coincide with the session of the General Court engaged in drafting a reply to the king's letter. Increase Mather, *An Essay for the Recording of Illustrious Providences* (Boston, 1684), preface, sig. [A7r]; *Mass. Recs.*, 5:312–13.

8. *I. Mather Diary*, 24, 42, 51.

9. Increase Mather, *The Latter Sign Discoursed of*, in *Kometographia* (Boston, 1683), 13–14, 27, 31. (The sermon was preached on 31 August 1682.) Cf. *Heavens Alarm to the World*, 2d imp. (Boston, 1682), 36, 37–38, which deals with the comet of 1680. "Nefandous" means unspeakable or atrocious.

10. William Hubbard, *The Benefit of a Well-Ordered Conversation* . . . (Boston, 1684), 73, 76–93, 97–98.

11. Samuel Willard, *All Plots against God and His People Detected and Defeated*, in *The Child's Portion* (Boston, 1684), 222–23.

12. Samuel Willard, *The Doctrine of Divine Providence Opened and Applyed* (Boston, 1684), 56–59.

13. *Mass. Recs.*, 5:458.

14. William Adams, *God's Eye on the Contrite* . . . (Boston, 1685), 1, 19.

15. *Sewall Diary*, 1:66, 94–95. See also ibid., 80, 116, 122, 129.

16. N. H. Keeble, *The Literary Culture of Nonconformity in Later Seventeenth-Century England* (Athens, Ga., 1987), 264–65, 273–82.

17. *Salem Church Records*, 161–62, 165; Pope, *Half-Way Covenant*, 141–42.

18. *Dorchester Church Records*, 91, 93.

19. Ibid., 95–98; Ross W. Beales, Jr., "The Half-Way Covenant and Religious Scrupulosity: The First Church of Dorchester as a Test Case," *WMQ*, 3d ser., 31 (1974): 471–79.

20. Hunnewell, ed. *Records of the First Church in Charlestown*, 43, ix; *Roxbury Land and Church Records*, 96–99; *Plymouth Church Records*, 163, 165, 168; *Sewall Diary*, 1:73–75; Pope, *Half-Way Covenant*, 209, 222, 274–76; Samuel Willard, *Reformation the Great Duty of an Afflicted People* (Boston, 1694); "To the Reader," sig [Av]. See also Stout, *The New England Soul*, 175–79.

21. Increase Mather, *The Greatest Sinners Exhorted and Encouraged to Come to Christ and That Now without Delaying* (Boston, 1686), 31.

22. Samuel Willard, *Heavenly Merchandize* . . . (Boston, 1686), 140, 149. (Emphasis added.)

23. Keeble, *The Literary Culture of Nonconformity*, 78–92; Stout, *New England Soul*, 94. I cannot, however, find any support for the claim that publication of the works in question was "commissioned" by "the Cambridge Press's board of censors," whatever that entity may be, or by anybody else.

24. Willard, *Heavenly Merchandize*, 111–12.

25. Samuel Willard, *A Brief Discourse on Justification* (Boston, 1686), preface, sig. A3v, 162.

26. *Sewall Diary*, 1:83; Holmes, *Increase Mather*, 1:20–26, 46–63, 2:566–75.

27. Holmes, *Increase Mather*, 2:479–87; Thomas J. Holmes, *Cotton Mather, A Bibliography of his Works* (Cambridge, Mass., 1940), 1:109–13; Mather, *Magnalia*, 2:409–13; David Levin, *Cotton Mather: The Young Life of the Lord's Rembrancer, 1663–1703* (Cambridge, Mass., 1978), 119–27.

28. Increase Mather, *A Sermon Wherein Is Showed That the Church of God Is Sometimes a Subject of Great Persecution* (Boston, 1682), 19.

29. *Sewall Diary*, 1:109.

30. John Higginson, *Our Dying Saviour's Legacy of Peace to His Disciples in a Troublesome World . . .* (Boston, 1686), 147–48.

31. Palfrey, *History of New England*, 3:379–85. On 7 December 1683 Governor Bradstreet and seven assistants wrote Secretary of State Sir Leoline Jenkins that the majority of the magistracy approved total submission to the crown's demands (*Calender State Papers, Colonial Series, 1681–1685* [London, 1898], 563). This claim has often been repeated since, but it is deceptive at best: when Bradstreet secured his "majority" two hard-line magistrates (Samuel Nowell and Peter Tilton) were absent from the General Court's session and two seats in the upper house had been left vacant by the death of their incumbents (John Hull, Daniel Fisher), neither of whom would likely have voted for so sweeping a surrender.

32. [Increase Mather], "Arguments against Relinquishing the Charter," MHS *Coll.*, 3d ser., 1:78; Hill, *History of the Old South Church*, 1:249–50. A similar attempt to formulate a broadly worded ministerial consensus in July 1685 ended in a failure to agree even on what had been agreed upon (*Sewall Diary*, 1:71–72; MHS *Proc.* 12 [1871–73]: 105–7).

33. "The Autobiography of Increase Mather," ed. Michael G. Hall, AAS *Proc.* 71 (1961), 307–8. The "Arguments" cited in note 32 are those Increase gave at the Boston town meeting. For proof of his authorship, see Mather, *Parentator*, 90–92.

34. My assertion to the contrary (*Their Solitary Way*, 92), unfortunately echoed elsewhere, is incorrect, pure and simple. The system used for voting for magistrates made wholesale turnovers difficult, but insofar as it was possible, Increase Mather effected it in the three elections between 1684 and 1686. In 1684 Bradstreet's vote total took a sharp tumble, Bartholomew Gedney, William Browne, and Joseph Dudley were voted out, and Elisha Cooke, Sr., William Johnson, John Hathorne, Elisha Hutchinson, and Samuel Sewall were voted in. See William H. Whitmore, *The Massachusetts Civil List for the Colonial and Provincial Periods, 1630–1774* (Albany, 1870), 26; Thomas Hutchinson, *The History of the Colony and Province of Massachusetts-Bay*, ed. Lawrence Shaw Mayo (Cambridge, Mass., 1936), 1:289n.; Hall, *Last American Puritan*, 192. The reversal in Peter Bulkeley's popularity that cost him his seat in 1685 also began in 1684 (Wall, "Membership of the Massachusetts General Court," 603).

35. William Hubbard, *A Funeral Meditation*, in *The Benefit of a Well-Ordered Conversation*, 143–44.

36. In 1685 Peter Bulkeley and John Woodbridge failed of reelection, Joseph Dudley made a brief comeback (although he gained only the second lowest total of any man elected to the magistracy that year), and Oliver Purchas, who had signed the anticlerical dissent of 1671 as deputy from Lynn, was elected but declined to serve. In 1686 Dudley was kicked out of office again, and Isaac Addington and John Smith were elected.

37. See above, chapter 5, note 86.

38. The quotation comes from Hubbard's unpaged preface to Daniel Dennison's *Irenicon*, which takes up pages 177–218 of *The Benefit of a Well-Ordered Conversation* and uses the party labels regularly. (See esp. 179–82.)

39. Hill, *History of the Old South Church*, 1:243–46.

40. John Wiswall, who held up Dorchester's adoption of the Halfway Covenant for decades, Henry Bartholomew, the leading ally of William Hathorne at Salem, and Samuel Nowell of Cambridge, perhaps the most radical of the Bay Colony's preachers before he turned to politics and became a hard-line magistrate, all ended up with First Church. For Nowell see his *Abraham in Arms . . .* (Boston, 1678), 10; his letter of 26 Sept. 1676 to John Bull, MHS *Coll.*, 8:573; and T. H. Breen, *The Character of a Good Ruler: A History of Puritan Political Ideas, 1630–1730* (New Haven, 1970), 117–22.

41. The five magistrates were Humphrey Davy, Elisha Cooke, Sr., Elisha Hutchinson, Samuel Nowell, and Isaac Addington, all hard-liners. The three Boston deputies were Timothy Prout, John Saffin, and Penn Townsend; Saffin was elected speaker. There were nine selectmen in 1686, two from North church, two from Old South, and the First Church five: Cooke, Hutchinson, Prout, John Fairweather, and Henry Allin (Whitmore, *Massachusetts Civil List*, 26; *Mass. Recs.*, 5:514; *Sewall Diary*, 1:134).

42. An amicable meeting of accommodationist and moderate holdout magistrates took place at Bradstreet's house on 2 July 1685, along with four representative ministers; Increase Mather, John Allin, and all the First Church assistants were conspicuous by their absence (*Sewall Diary*, 1:68). On fear of popular disorder see ibid., 102, 108.

43. Ibid., 67.

44. Ibid., 85.

45. Ibid., 112–13. First Church's preacher was a visitor, Samuel Phillips, who had befriended the Newbury dissidents and was minister of Rowley, a town that was still holding out against the Halfway Covenant. Willard had had no use for Mather's theatrics at the Boston town meeting in 1684 and had made a point of telling him so in no uncertain terms (Hall, *Last American Puritan*, 191).

46. Hutchinson, *History of Massachusetts-Bay*, 1:299n.

47. "Autobiography of Increase Mather," AAS *Proc.* 81:319–20. For evidence that Mather himself took the initiative in organizing these documents and his own mission see Robbins, *History of the Second Church*, 50n., 51.

48. Hall, *Last American Puritan*, chap. 7. Mather had been fending off the Harvard presidency for ten years in 1685, when he finally agreed to take it on a pro tempore basis provided he could retain his Boston pulpit (Morison, *Harvard College in the Seventeenth Century*, 2:472–73). He did not identify himself by the title in any of his 1686 publications, contenting himself with "teacher of a church of Christ in Boston," but beginning with his first London tract, in 1687, virtually all of his works bear the designation and two identify him solely as Harvard's president. He handled his ouster from the college presidency in 1701 with considerable suavity: his next four titles have no identification apart from his name. The implication is that Increase Mather's authority did not rest on the offices he held.

49. Increase Mather, *The Surest Way to the Greatest Honour* (Boston, 1699), 37, 40–41.

50. Ibid., 15; Increase Mather, *The Great Blessing of Primitive Counsellors* (Boston, 1693), 22.

51. Perry Miller, *The New England Mind: From Colony to Province* (Beacon paperback ed., Boston, 1961), chap. 12; Stout, *New England Soul*, 118–22, 128–31.

52. Daniel Neal, *The History of New-England*, 2d ed. (London, 1747), 2:227. (The first edition in 1720 also contains this description.)

53. William G. McLoughlin, *New England Dissent, 1630–1833: The Baptists and the Separation of Church and State* (Cambridge, Mass., 1971), vol. 1, chaps. 6–8. Two First Church men, Nathaniel Byfield and Elisha Hutchinson, actually framed the Massachusetts apologies in reply to the protests of the Baptists from the old Plymouth Colony over compulsory ecclesiastical taxation (Ibid., 172–74, 182–83). It will be remembered,

however, that the Plymouth Baptists, unlike their Boston brethren, were more inclined to make their main tactic appeals to England.

54. This argument is at odds with the most recent and detailed appraisals of 1690s politics, which find little continuity between Old and New Charter periods. Cf. Richard R. Johnson, *Adjustment to Empire: The New England Colonies, 1675–1715* ([New Brunswick, N.J.], 1981), chap. 5; William Pencak, *War, Politics and Revolution in Provincial Massachusetts* (Boston, 1981), chap. 2.

55. "Autobiography of Increase Mather," ed. Hall, AAS *Proc.* 71 (1961): 341.

56. Hutchinson, *History of the Massachusetts-Bay*, 1:350n.; *Sewall Diary*, 1:278–79.

57. Waitstill Winthrop, Bartholomew Gedney, Simon Bradstreet, Nathaniel Saltonstall, and James Russell had all been for remodeling the Old Charter in 1683 and/or held office under the Dominion; John Richards, Samuel Sewall, Samuel Appleton, John Hathorne, Elisha Hutchinson, and Robert Pike were hard-liners in 1683, though Hathorne had subsequently accepted office under the Dominion. The rest of the councillors from the old Bay Colony had not made a name for themselves in Old Charter politics (Whitmore, *Massachusetts Civil List*, 30–31, 45).

58. Danforth to Increase Nowell, 22 Oct. 1688, Hutchinson, *Original Papers*, 2:310; Hall, *Last American Puritan*, 251. Mather's councillors included no fewer than eleven Bostonians, but only Elisha Hutchinson was a First Church member. A twelfth man, Stephen Mason, had been a member of the church but had been dismissed to a London congregation in 1687; perhaps his inclusion was meant to serve as a blank to be filled by a First Church man at the first election under the New Charter.

59. Mather, *The Great Blessing of Primitive Counsellours*, 19–20. New councillors were nominated by the old Council and the House of Representatives voting jointly and not just by the lower house alone. In the election of 1693 just twenty-eight votes could nominate an individual to the Council; if its members (or at least the bulk of them) voted together they could easily make up most or all of the tally an incumbent would need for reelection. Even should the Council split, if a decent majority voted for a man, he would probably pick up the rest of the votes needed to put him over.

60. "Autobiography of Increase Mather," ed. Hall, AAS *Proc.* 71 (1961): 344.

61. Sir William Phips to the earl of Nottingham, 21 Feb. 1693, in George Lincoln Burr, ed., *Narratives of the Witchcraft Cases, 1648–1706*, Original Narratives of Early American History, 16 (New York, 1914), 200.

62. "Mr. Brattle's Account of the Witchcraft, & c.," MHS *Coll.*, 1st ser., 5 (1798): 71–72, 72n.; Samuel Willard, *Some Miscellany Observations . . . Respecting Witchcrafts, in a Dialogue between S. & B.* (Boston, 1692; rpt. 1869), 12. For the question of Willard's authorship see below, note 68.

63. "Mr. Brattle's Account," MHS *Coll.*, 1st Ser., 5 (1798): 75.

64. *The Return of Several Ministers*, in Increase Mather, *Cases of Conscience Concerning Evil Spirits . . .* (Boston, 1693 [i.e., 1692]), postscript (unpaged).

65. Ibid., 34.

66. "Records of the Cambridge Association," MHS *Proc.* 17 (1880): 268. Cf. Cotton Mather to John Richards, 31 May 1692, MHS *Coll.*, 4th ser., 8:392–93.

67. Mather, *Cases of Conscience*, 65–66, postscript.

68. The odd form of the Brattle and Willard tracts, like the deliberate misdating of *Cases of Conscience*, can be attributed to Phips's panicky proclamation against publications about the trials because he saw "a likelyhood of kindling an inextinguishable flame if I should admitt any publique and open Contests" (Phips to William Blathwayt, 12 Oct. 1692, Burr, ed., *Narratives of the Witchcraft Cases*, 197). It is necessary to dispose of two persistent misconceptions concerning these tracts. First, the Brattle piece is most definitely not a private letter. It lacks a named recipient, is tightly organized and polemically effec-

tive, includes footnotes, and, in the original version (MHS *Coll.*, 1st ser., 5:79–80) even throws in a documentary appendix. Second, there is no good reason for the continuing hesitancy to assign *Some Miscellany Observations* to Willard merely because he never chose to acknowledge it as his own. The case for his authorship was made effectively by George H. Moore a hundred years ago and needs only to be summarized here. Robert Calef explicitly credited Willard with the piece in 1700, an attribution accepted by Cotton Mather in 1701 and never denied by Willard. Further, Willard's posthumously published *Compleat Body of Divinity* includes *Some Miscellany Observations* in its list of his publications and virtually repeats a passage from the pamphlet at the relevant point in its text. See Robert Calef, *More Wonders of the Invisible World* (London, 1700), 38; Obadiah Gill et al., *Some Few Remarks upon a Scandalous Book . . .* (Boston, 1701), 34–35; George H. Moore, "Notes on the Bibliography of Witchcraft in Massachusetts," AAS *Proc.* 5 (1889), 248n., 250.

69. Robert Pike to Jonathan Corwin, 9 Aug. 1692, in Pike, *New Puritan*, 156–58.

70. Willard, *Some Miscellany Observations*, 12–16, 22; "Mr. Brattle's Account," MHS *Coll.*, 1st ser., 5 (1798): 62–64, 66–68, 77.

71. Brattle mentions by name only one First Church member, Nathaniel Byfield, as objecting to the trials. But "some of the Boston justices" who "were resolved rather to throw up their commissions" than participate in the trial (see above, note 63) must refer to the Suffolk County justices of the peace, whose Boston contingent was dominated by First Church. Brattle cannot mean Boston members of either the Superior Court of Judicature or the Suffolk County Inferior Court, because neither body had yet been appointed, while the context of the passage and subsequent discussion make it plain that he is not referring to the four Boston judges on the witchcraft tribunal itself. See Whitmore, *Massachusetts Civil List*, 126.

72. Cotton Mather to John Cotton, 20 Oct. 1692, in Holmes, *Cotton Mather*, 2:551; "Records of the Cambridge Association," MHS *Proc.* 17 (1879–80): 267. My line of argument will parallel closely that in Perry Miller, *The New England Mind: From Colony to Province*, chap. 13, esp. 198–208, but will lay much heavier stress on the immediate political context of the Mathers' actions.

73. Mather, *Patentator*, 166.

74. See Levin, *Cotton Mather*, 215.

75. Burr, ed., *Narratives of the Witchcraft Cases*, 196, 196n.–197n.; Moore, "Notes on the Bibliography of Witchcraft in Massachusetts," AAS *Proc.* 5 (1889): 246–47.

76. *Cotton Mather Diary*, 1:151.

77. George H. Moore, "Notes on the History of Witchcraft in Massachusetts," AAS *Proc.* 2 (1882–83): 170–71; "Mr. Brattle's Account," MHS *Coll.*, 1st ser., 5:61; David Lovejoy, *The Glorious Revolution in America* (New York, 1972), 240, 302, 372; Johnson, *Adjustment to Empire*, 277–85.

78. Mather to Richards, 31 May 1692, MHS *Coll.*, 4th ser., 8:392–93.

79. "Mr. Brattle's Account," MHS *Coll.*, 1st ser., 5 (1798): 71.

80. *Sewall Diary*, 1:293; Willard, *Some Miscellany Observations*, 23; *Sibley's Harvard Graduates*, 1:376–77.

81. Moore, "Notes or the Bibliography of Witchcraft in Massachusetts," AAS *Proc.* 5 (1889): 246–47. For the claim that not even the judges believed all the accusations from spectral evidence see "Mr. Brattle's Account," MHS *Coll.*, 1st ser., 5 (1798): 69–70.

82. Hutchinson, *History of Massachusetts-Bay*, 2:25.

83. Moore, "Notes on the History of Witchcraft in Massachusetts," AAS *Proc.* 2 (1882–83): 172; *Sewall Diary*, 1:299.

84. Holmes, *Increase Mather*, 123, 130–31.

85. Hutchinson, *History of Massachusetts-Bay*, 2:31–32. Cf. the original retraction secured by Mather, in MHS *Coll.*, 2d ser., 3 (Boston, 1815), 221–25.

86. For Willard's call in 1694 (the first), see below, note 93; for Michael Wigglesworth in 1704, below, note 90; and for Cotton Mather in 1709, *Theopolis Americana: An Essay on the Golden Street of the Holy City* . . . (Boston, 1710), 29–30. The last such exercise of the clerical conscience on the witchcraft episode seems to have been in 1737, when Israel Loring in the election sermon of that year once again called for compensation for the victims, although George Burroughs's descendants were still petitioning to the same effect in 1749 (*Sibley's Harvard Graduates*, 2:333; 5:78).

87. Mather, *Cases of Conscience*, sig. A3v.

88. The postscript is unpaged. For evidence that it is a late addition to the work put in *after* the fourteen ministers signed the manuscript version, see Holmes, *Increase Mather*, 1:114–15, 125–27, 130–31.

89. *Cotton Mather Diary*, 1:151. See also ibid., 1:153–54.

90. Moore, "Notes on the History of Witchcraft in Massachusetts," AAS *Proc.* 2 (1882–83): 173–78; Moore, "Notes on the Bibliography of Witchcraft in Massachusetts," AAS *Proc.* 5 (1889): 263–65; Thomas Franklin Waters, *Ipswich in the Massachusetts Bay Colony*, 1 (Ipswich, Mass., 1905), 290–91, 293, 299; Michael Wigglesworth to Increase Mather, 22 July 1704, MHS *Colls.*, 4th ser., 8:646.

91. Increase Mather, *The Great Blessing of Primitive Counsellours*, 19. Only Elisha Hutchinson, among First Church members, had been a member of Mather's nominated Council of 1692. In 1693 Hutchinson was reelected along with Isaac Addington, John Saffin, and Elisha Cooke (although Phips used his veto on Cooke), and Thomas Danforth, the recognized leader of the hard-liners in the 1680s also regained a seat (*Sewall Diary*, 1:309).

92. G. B. Warden, *Boston, 1689–1776* (Boston, 1970), 37–48. The political careers of Nathaniel Byfield and Samuel Shrimpton, both of whom at various times supported royal government, will seem less anomalous if their First Church ties are remembered and the circumstances under which their allegiance was manifested: Byfield was the son of a leading English nonconformist clergyman and joined First Church in 1685, when the very act was deemed heroic, while Shrimpton, a child of the church, was the son of a man with marked Baptist leanings and had himself signed the pro-Baptist petition of 1668 (see Johnson, *Adjustment to Empire*, 357–60; Holifield, "On Toleration in Massachusetts," *Church History* 38 [1969]: 192 and n.). Whatever their political opportunism—and it was considerable—they enjoyed their greatest electoral successes in the years when the country party's power was at its height and finished their careers on the "right" side: Byfield was back in favor with the Cookes, father and son, after 1710; Shrimpton's funeral in 1698 looked like a country party caucus (Pencak, *War, Politics, and Revolution*, 64–65; *Sewall Diary*, 1:387).

93. Samuel Willard, *The Character of a Good Ruler* (Boston, 1694), 17–18.

94. Bellomont to Samuel Sewall, 14 Aug. 1700, NEHGR 19 (1865): 236. Bellomont would have put William Brattle and Ebenezer Pemberton on the Harvard corporation even though they were in the process of attacking Increase Mather in *The Order of the Gospel* by claiming, among other things, that he misused the Harvard presidency to make ex cathedra statements.

95. Morison, *Harvard College in the Seventeenth Century*, 533–35.

96. "Autobiography of Increase Mather," ed. Hall, AAS *Proc.* 71 (1961): 351; *Sewall Diary*, 1:383; Holmes, *Increase Mather*, 1:140–41.

97. Increase Mather, *The Excellency of a Public Spirit* (Boston, 1702), 33.

98. Samuel Willard, *Pragnosticks of Impending Calamities* (Boston, 1701), 12–15, 18.

99. Samuel Willard, *The Checkered State of the Gospel Church* (Boston, 1701), 36, 51–52, 55–56. Willard recurred to Salem witchcraft, which was evidently still on his conscience, less than two years before he died. In a lecture sermon preached on 8 January

1706 he reiterated his critique of the evidence accepted during the trials, which "hath taken away the Lives of the Innocent, and left a Publick Guilt & Blot behind it, which not Time, but only a Repentence will wipe off" (*A Compleat Body of Divinity . . .* [Boston, 1726], 727).

100. Hutchinson, *History of Massachusetts-Bay*, 2:7.

101. For Cotton Mather and Connecticut see *Cotton Mather Diary*, 2:135, 201–2, 467, 538, 553; Richard Warch, *School of the Prophets: Yale College, 1701–1740* (New Haven, 1973), 34–38. For the rise in ministerial publication, see George Selement, "Publication and the Puritan Minister," *WMQ*, 3d ser., 37 (1980): 219–41.

102. Miller, *The New England Mind: From Colony to Province*, 450–51.

103. Robert Middlekauff, *The Mathers: Three Generations of Puritan Intellectuals, 1596–1728* (New York, 1971), 173–74, 179–87, 305–49.

104. Johnson, *Adjustment to Empire*, 249–51.

105. Franklin B. Dexter, ed., *Documentary History of Yale University* (New Haven, 1916), 1–7. For similar worries at Harvard, see Morison, *Harvard College in the Seventeenth Century*, 2:526–27.

106. Gurdon Saltonstall, *A Sermon Preached before the General Assembly of Connecticut* (Boston, 1697), 53–54; Elisha Williams to Timothy Woodbridge, 27 July 1728, CSM *Publ.* 6 (1899–1900): 208.

107. Cotton Mather, *The Wonderful Works of God* (Boston, 1690), 42; Cotton Mather, *Things for a Distres'd People to Think Upon* (Boston, 1696), 69. See also Cotton Mather, *A Pillar of Gratitude* (Boston, 1700), 32–35.

108. Willard, *Reformation the Great Duty of an Afflicted People*, 43, 62.

109. Samuel Torrey, *Man's Extremity, God's Opportunity* (Boston, 1695), 26–57 (quotations at 26, 46).

110. See also Stout, *New England Soul*, 166–74.

111. "Records of the Cambridge Association," MHS *Proc.* 17 (1879–80): 281.

112. Willard, *Reformation the Great Duty of an Afflicted People*, 74. See also the 1693 resolution of the Cambridge Association that the ministry ensure that "all due means were used, for the bringing of more than there are and as many as may be, to submit unto our *Church Watch*" on the grounds that those outside church discipline "do from thence encourage themselves, in the *Liberty* which they take, to do the *things for which the wrath of God comes upon the Land*" ([Cotton Mather], *Thirty Important Cases Resolved with Evidence of Scripture and Reason* [Boston, 1699], 30).

113. The limited co-option of the Anglicans and the Baptists is laid out in Brace Steiner, "Anglican Officeholding in Pre-Revolutionary Connecticut: The Parameters of New England Community," *WMQ*, 3d ser., 31 (1974): 369–406; Edward M. Cook, Jr., *The Fathers of the Towns: Leadership and Community Structure in Eighteenth-Century New England* (Baltimore, 1976), 134–41. The legal advantages enjoyed by the Standing Order are described in McLoughlin, *New England Dissent*, chaps. 6, 13–15.

114. Cynthia B. Herrup, "Law and Morality in Seventeenth-Century England," *P&P* 106 (Feb. 1985): 102–23; Herrup, *The Common Peace: Participation and the Criminal Law in Seventeenth-Century England* (Cambridge, Eng., 1987), esp. 3–7, 93–130. By English standards, even in the seventeenth century, and emphatically so in the eighteenth, New England courts spent a great deal of time on moral offences. See the sources cited in note 116 below; Herrup, *Common Peace*, 99–129; Sharpe, *Crime in Seventeenth-Century England*, 49–70; Keith Wrightson, "Two Concepts of Order: Justices, Constables and Jurymen in Seventeenth-Century England," in *An Ungovernable People*, ed. Brewer and Styles, 302–3 (appendix); Ingram, *Church Courts, Sex and Marriage*, 372–74.

115. On the increasing importance of the county courts, see David Thomas Koenig, *Law and Society in Puritan Massachusetts: Essex County, 1629–1692* (Chapel Hill, 1979), 90–107; Allen, *In English Ways*, 226–27; Everett C. Goodwin, *The Magistrate*

Rediscovered: Connecticut, 1636–1818, Studies in American History and Culture, 24 (Ann Arbor, 1981), chap. 3, esp. 50–52.

116. Foster, "The Godly in Transit," in Seventeenth-Century New England, ed. Hall and Allen, 232–35; Acts and Resolves, Public and Private, of the Province of the Massachusetts Bay, 1 (Boston, 1869), 51–55, 56, 58, 62–63, 102–3, 191, 193–94, 470, 597, 679; Conn. Recs., 4:30, 5:324, 7:338; Goodwin, The Magistracy Rediscovered, 50–51, 144, nn. 137–38. On the extent of morals cases actually before the eighteenth-century county courts, see David Flaherty, "Crime and Social Control in Provincial Massachusetts," Historical Journal 24 (1981): 341n.; William E. Nelson, Dispute and Conflict Resolution in Plymouth County, Massachusetts, 1725–1825 (Chapel Hill, 1981), 23; Franklin P. Rice, ed., Records of the Court of General Sessions of the Peace for the County of Worcester, Massachusetts, Worcester Society of Antiquity, Collections, 5, no. 18 (Worcester, Mass., 1883), 35–40, 42, 51–53, 58, 61–62, and passim.

117. Sewall Diary, 2:1048. See also ibid., 713–14. By the same token, church discipline (in Connecticut at least) gradually came to resemble contemporary judicial proceedings. See Bruce H. Mann, Neighbors and Strangers: Law and Community in Early Connecticut (Chapel Hill, 1987), 143–55.

118. The dependence of the Connecticut Platform on the earlier Massachusetts Proposals is demonstrated in the item-by-item comparison in Walker, ed., Creeds and Platforms of Congregationalism, 503n.–506n. (It took Connecticut a very long time to escape the Bay Colony's intellectual hegemony.) On the weaknesses of the Saybrook Platform, see Lucas, Valley of Discord, 191–93, and for similar troubles encountered by the Hampshire Association, the most aggressive of the Massachusetts' clerical organizations, ibid., 193–95.

119. Walker, ed., Creeds and Platforms of Congregationalism, 505–6 (item 12). See ibid., 487 and n., for the origins of this licensing, which also took hold among the Massachusetts associations. The requirement that the Connecticut associations supply "bereaved churches" with candidates for their pulpits may seem formidable, but its force was very much reduced in practice. Most Connecticut ministers were not local men so that whether association or individual church did the searching, they were both dependent, just as before the Platform, on the traditional recourse of writing to the president of Harvard (and later the president of Yale) and the leading Boston ministers. See Main, Society and Economy in Colonial Connecticut, 319; J. William T. Youngs, Jr., God's Messengers: Religious Leadership in Colonial New England, 1700–1750 (Baltimore, 1976), 24–25.

120. Foster, "The Godly in Transit," in Seventeenth-Century New England, ed. Hall and Allen, 220–21, 227–31.

121. Selement, "Publication and the Puritan Minister," WMQ, 3d ser., 37 (1980): 219–41, esp. 222 (table).

122. Main, Society and Economy in Colonial Connecticut, 257–59; Warch, School of the Prophets, 270–71; Morison, Harvard College in the Seventeenth Century, 2:562–63; James Axtell, The School upon a Hill: Education and Society in Colonial New England (New Haven, 1974), 187–89, 212n.

123. Warch, School of the Prophets, 269–70; James W. Schmotter, "Ministerial Careers in Eighteenth-Century New England: The Social Context, 1700–1760," Journal of Social History 9 (1975): 249–67.

124. Samuel Willard, The Peril of the Times Displayed (Boston, 1700), 143–47; Holifield, Covenant Sealed, 219–20.

125. Solomon Stoddard, The Defects of Preachers Reproved . . . (New London, Conn., 1724), 17–18.

126. Ibid., 10–11.

127. Holifield, Covenant Sealed, 210–13.

128. Stoddard, The Doctrine of Instituted Churches, 8.

129. Paul Lucas, " 'An Appeal to the Learned': The Mind of Solomon Stoddard," *WMQ*, 3d ser., 30 (1973): 264–66.

130. Ibid., 278–83; Moran, "The Puritan Saint," 91–93, 131–32, 156; Ebenezer Devotion, *An Answer of the Pastor & Brethren of the Third Church in Windham . . .* (New London, Conn., 1747), 2–3.

131. Stoddard, *Doctrine of Instituted Churches*, 25–32 (quotation at 26); Holifield, *Covenant Sealed*, 216–17.

132. Fiering, *Moral Philosohy at Seventeenth-Century Harvard*, chaps. 5–6.

133. Samuel Kirkland Lothrop, *A History of the Church in Brattle Street, Boston* (Boston, 1851), 23–24, 33; John Higginson and William Hubbard, *A Testimony to the Order of the Gospel, in the Churches of New-England* (Boston, 1701), 8.

134. Holmes, *Increase Mather*, 2:393–94; *Boston 1st Ch. Rec.*, 1:99–100.

135. [Thomas Brattle et al.], *Gospel Order Revived* ([New York], 1700), unpaged Epistle Dedicatory. For the question of authorship, see Holmes, *Increase Mather*, 2:395.

136. Hill, *History of the Old South Church*, 1:336n; Isaiah Thomas, *The History of Printing in America*, 2d ed. rev., American Antiquarian Society *Transactions*, 5–6 (Albany, 1874), 1:418; Teresa Toulouse, *The Art of Prophesying: New England Sermons and the Shaping of Belief* (Athens, Ga., 1987), chap. 2.

137. Samuel Willard, *Israel's True Safety . . .* (Boston, 1704), sigs. F2r–F3v; Walker, *Creeds and Platforms of Congregationalism*, 484.

138. *Sewall Diary*, 2:1003–4.

Envoi

1. Mather, *Magnalia*, 2:477. The phrase is not Mather's but John Hales's. *Magnalia* deals with the Salem Village episode by extracting the relevant portion of Hales's *A Modest Enquiry into the Nature of Witchcraft* (published in its entirety and in its own right in 1702), and recommends the author (2:471) as "a writer who would not for a world be guilty of over-doing the truth in an history of this importance."

2. Mather, *Magnalia*, 1:26, 65. See also Kenneth Silverman, *The Life and Times of Cotton Mather* (New York, 1984), 160–66.

3. Mervyn James, "Ritual, Drama and Social Body in the Late Medieval English Town," in *Society, Politics and Culture: Studies in Early Modern England* (Cambridge, Eng., 1986), 16–47.

4. In Massachusetts there were about 211 churches in 1740, of which 38 (18 percent) suffered schisms by 1750 and a further 6 by 1760, for a total of 44 (21 percent). In Connecticut there were about 131 churches in 1740, of which 36 (27.5 percent) had split by 1750 and a further six by 1760, for a total of 42 (32 percent). The numbers are obtained from Edwin Scott Gaustad, *Historical Atlas of Religion in America*, 2d ed. rev. (New York, 1976), 175; C. C. Goen, *Revivalism and Separatism in New England, 1740–1800: Strict Congregationalists and Separate Baptists in the Great Awakening* (New Haven, 1962), 302–18 (table). (On the geographical preponderance of certain areas in the Separatist movement, see ibid., 186–88.) Gaustad gives the number of Congregational churches in 1750, but I have subtracted from his numbers Separatist churches founded in the previous ten years; this procedure, of course, would not eliminate new churches first established in the 1740s, but I do not think the degree of imprecision substantial in so rough a calculation. The number of disrupted churches, however, is a hard one: I have eliminated from the list in Goen all churches that were entirely new foundations (and a few other inappropriate instances) before adding up the remainder.

5. Bushman, *From Puritan to Yankee*, 188; John C. Miller, "Religion, Finance, and

Democracy in Massachusetts," *NEQ* 6 (1933): 29–58; John M. Bumsted, "Religion, Finance, and Democracy: The Town of Norton as a Case Study," *Journal of American History* 57 (1971): 830–37; Greven, *Four Generations*, 279; Moran, "Puritan Saint," 416–23.

6. Gary Nash, *The Urban Crucible: Social Change, Political Consciousness, and the Origins of the American Revolution* (Cambridge, Mass., 1979), 204–19; Christine Leigh Heyrman, *Commerce and Culture: The Maritime Communities of Colonial Massachusetts, 1690–1750* (New York, 1984), chaps. 5, 11; Christopher M. Jedry, *The World of John Cleaveland: Family and Community in Eighteenth-Century New England* (New York, 1979), chaps. 2–3, esp. 51–52. For still another account, see Peter Onuf, "New Lights in New London: A Group Portrait of the Separatists," *WMQ*, 3d ser., 37 (1980): 627–43.

7. George Whitefield, *A Continuation of the Reverend Mr. Whitefield's Journal from a Few Days after His Arrival at Savannah . . . to His Leaving Stanford, the Last Town in New England . . .* (Philadelphia, 1741), 124–25. I am using this edition in this one instance, rather than some more easily accessible version, because when Whitefield came to publish his journals in collected form in 1756 he toned down some of his observations about the Congregational clergy and excised the derisive remarks about New England Anglicans entirely, and all subsequent reprints of his journals, even the most recent, follow this authorized (and bowdlerized) version.

8. Cotton Mather, *Manuductio ad Ministerium: Directions for a Candidate of the Ministry*, Facsimile Text Society, 42 (1726; rpt. New York, 1938), 90–106 (quotations at 90, 105).

9. Israel Loring, *The Duty of an Apostatizing People* (Boston, 1737), 61–62. (Loring became an Old Light in the Awakening. See *Sibley's Harvard Graduates*, 5:79–80.)

10. Charles Chauncy, *Early Piety Recommended and Exemplified* (Boston, 1732), 20, 23; Fiering, *Moral Philosophy at Seventeenth-Century Harvard*, 137–38.

11. Fiering, *Moral Philosophy at Seventeenth-Century Harvard*, 138–44.

12. *George Whitefield's Journals* ([London], 1960), 482; Francis G. Wallet, ed., "The Diary of Ebenezer Parkman, 1739–1744," *AAS Proc.* 72 (1962): 132.

13. *George Whitefield's Journals*, 482.

14. Loring, *The Duty of an Apostatizing People*, 12, 45–46, 45n., 60; *Sibley's Harvard Graduates*, 5:79–80.

15. *George Whitefield's Journals*, 526. See also the confession of an unnamed "old minister" in 1740, ibid., 482.

16. Jonathan Edwards, *Some Thoughts Concerning the Present Revival of Religion in New England*, in *The Great Awakening*, ed. C. C. Goen, *The Works of Jonathan Edwards*, 4 (New Haven, 1972), 504. See also the similar comments of William Cooper, ibid., 219; Edwin Scott Gaustad, *The Great Awakening in New England* (New York, 1957), 104.

17. Richard Walsh, "The Great Awakening in the First Congregational Church of Woodbury, Connecticut," *WMQ*, 3d ser., 28 (1971): 543–62, esp. 547–53; Stephen R. Grossbart, "Seeking the Divine Favor: Conversion and Church Admission in Eastern Connecticut, 1711–1832," *WMQ*, 3d ser., 46 (1989): 696–740; Moran and Vinoskis, "Puritan Family and Religion," *WMQ*, 3d ser., 39 (1982): 45–46, 46n.

18. Hill, *History of the Old South Church*, 1:547–48.

19. See Norman Fiering, "The First American Enlightenment: Tillotson, Leverett, and Philosophical Anglicanism," *NEQ* 54 (1981): 307–44; Ian K. Steele, *The English Atlantic, 1675–1740: An Exploration of Communication and Community* (New York, 1986), 265–69.

20. Susan O'Brien, "A Transatlantic Community of Saints: the Great Awakening and the First Evangelical Network, 1735–1755," *American Historical Review* 91 (1986): 811–

32; Michael J. Crawford, "Origins of the Eighteenth-Century Evangelical Revival," *JBS* 26 (1987): 375–87. For the Watts reprint of the 1743 *Testimony and Advice*, see Diane Susan Durden, "Transatlantic Communications and Literature in the Religious Revivals, 1735–1745" (Ph.D. dissertation, University of Hull, 1978), 132–33. I am grateful to Michael J. Crawford for bringing the reprint to my attention and for providing me with a copy of the relevant portion of the dissertation.

21. Edwards, *Some Thoughts*, in *The Great Awakening*, ed. Goen, *Works*, 4:497.

22. Jonathan Edwards, *The Distinguishing Marks of a Work of the Spirit of God*, in *The Great Awakening*, ed. Goen, *Works*, 4:275–76.

23. Edwards, *Some Thoughts*, ibid., 515–30; Edwards to Thomas Prince, 12 Dec. 1743, ibid., 550–54.

24. William Breitenbach, "Unregenerate Doings: Selflessness and Selfishness in New Divinity Theology," *American Quarterly* 34 (1982): 479–502. See also Charles Roy Keller, *The Great Awakening in Connecticut* (New Haven, 1942), chaps. 4–7; Marie Caskey, *Chariot of Fire: Religion and the Beecher Family* (New Haven, 1978), 37–67.

25. Edwards, *Some Thoughts*, in *The Great Awakening*, ed. Goen, *Works*, 4:499.

26. Cotton Mather, *Repeated Admonitions: A Monitory Letter about the Maintainance of an Able and Faithful Ministry* (Boston, 1725), 2–3. This is a revised edition of a work first published in 1700. In this later version the phrase just quoted is followed by: "They generally and generously scorn the method." The statement hardly held true after 1740.

27. *Sibley's Harvard Graduates*, 6:331–36. For instances of the futility of legal action, see the unhappy careers of the John Rogerses, father and son, ibid., 5:292–95, 9:189–98.

28. Ibid., 6:373–75.

29. Goen, *Revivalism and Separatism in New England*, chap. 5.

30. Schmotter, "Ministerial Careers in Eighteenth-Century New England," *Journal of Social History* 9 (1975–76): 257–60; Stephan Botein, "Income and Ideology: Harvard-Trained Clergyman in the Eighteenth-Century," *Eighteenth-Century Studies* 13 (1979–80), 396–413. But cf. Main, *Society and Economy in Colonial Connecticut*, 208–70, 275–77, who finds that the ministry was still a financially attractive profession in the eighteenth century.

31. James W. Schmotter, "The Irony of Clerical Professionalism: New England's Congregational Ministry and the Great Awakening," *American Quarterly* 31 (1979): 158–60; Schmotter, "Ministerial Careers in Eighteenth-Century New England," *Journal of Social History* 9 (1975–76): 256–57; Gilbert Tennent, *The Danger of an Unconverted Ministry* . . . (Philadelphia, 1740), 14–15. On the circulation of this sermon, see Bonomi, *Under the Cope of Heaven*, 143–45, 150, 258 n. 32. There was at least one Boston imprint of the work, in 1742, and possibly a second edition in the same year.

32. See Botein, "Income and Ideology," *Eighteenth-Century Studies* 13 (1979–80): 405–6. One of the clearest instances in which outside interests compromised a minister who then also fell afoul of his congregation for alleged Arminian deviations is the case of the minister-physician Benjamin Doolittle of Northfield, Massachusetts: Franklin B. Dexter, *Biographical Sketches of the Graduates of Yale College*, 1 (New York, 1885), 151. A less certain case is that of Samuel Brown of Abington, Massachusetts, who gained an ambiguous reputation for legal shrewdness when he doubled as the town's attorney and who subsequently ran afoul of the town for doctrinal irregularities and alleged misrepresentation (*Sibley's Harvard Graduates*, 5:480–81; Aaron Hobart, *An Historical Sketch of Abington* [Boston, 1839], 40–43).

33. The sources for these two episodes are as follows: Michael J. Crawford, ed., "The Spiritual Travels of Nathan Cole," *WMQ*, 3d ser., 33 (1976): 108–9, 119–21; David N. Camp, *History of New Britain, with Sketches of Farmington and Berlin, Connecticut, 1640–1889* (New Britain, Conn., 1889), 101–15; James McLachlan, *Princetonians*,

1748–1768: A Biographical Dictionary (Princeton, 1976), 35–36 (the sketch of Samuel Clarke). All quotations from Cole are from these two sections of his autobiography; all those from Clarke are from his sketch.

34. *The Testimony of the Convention of Ministers May 25, 1743 against Several Errors and Disorders in the Land* (Boston, 1743), 6–7; *The Testimony and Advice of an Assembly of Pastors . . . at a Meeting in Boston, July 7, 1743* (Boston, 1743); Joshua Gee, *A Letter to the Reverend Mr. Nathaniel Eels* (Boston, 1743), 10–12; "Resolves of the General Consociation, Nov. 24, 1741," *The Law Papers*, Connecticut Historical Society, *Collections*, 11 (Hartford, 1907), 5–10; Gaustad, *Great Awakening in New England*, 63–66; Edmund S. Morgan, *The Gentle Puritan: A Life of Ezra Stiles, 1727–1795* (New Haven, 1962), 38–41. The July *Testimony and Advice* is so broadly worded, despite the partisan pamphlet war that preceded it, that Nathaniel Eels, moderator of the May Assembly, and the staunchly Old Light-Liberal Nathaniel Appleton both found it possible to endorse it.

35. For Croswell, see Leigh Eric Schmidt, " 'A Second and Glorious Reformation': The New Light Extremism of Andrew Croswell," *WMQ*, 3d ser., 43 (1986): 214–44. I do not wish to imply that Croswell was an unimportant lunatic but merely to insist (as Leigh makes plain and as he himself understood) that his was in no sense simply an incautious or hyperbolic statement of generally agreed-upon New Light views; Croswell's basic theology and soteriology, no less than the conclusions he drew from them, were as opposed to the tenets of Edwards, Joseph Bellamy, et al., as they were to those of the liberals.

36. Gee, *Letter to the Reverend Mr. Nathaniel Eels*, 10–12; Edwards, *A Faithful Narrative of the Surprising Work of God*, in *The Great Awakening*, ed. Goen, *Works*, 4:148; Edwards, *Some Thoughts*, 502–4; Benjamin Prescott, *A Letter to the Reverend Mr. Joshua Gee . . .* (Boston, 1743), 20. It says something about the depth of distrust on both sides, despite the oblique wording, that Gee's complaint that the May *Testimony* will give the multitude of new converts made during the Awakening reason "to entertain Prejudices against their own Pastors as well as other Ministers" (10), looks very like a threat—and is so interpreted by Prescott (15–16, 18).

37. The three cases are those of Samuel Osborn, Benjamin Kent, and Robert Breck. For Osborn, see the sources cited in note 38, below; for Kent, *Sibley's Harvard Graduates*, 8:221–23; for Breck, ibid., 663–73. Osborn had been in trouble with the leading minister at the Cape, Nathaniel Stone, for almost twenty years on nondoctrinal grounds before his heterodoxy finally brought him down; Kent had offended the most important man in Marlborough, Massachusetts, a Colonel Woods, who boasted "that he Would out Mr. Kent or Have him out in a year"; Breck received a call to Springfield, Massachusetts, independent of the River Gods, who as Hampshire County justices of the peace tried to lock up both him *and* his ordaining council (mostly easterners).

38. The Osborn case is described in detail in J. M. Bumsted, "A Caution to Erring Christians: Ecclesiastical Disorder on Cape Cod, 1717 to 1738," *WMQ*, 3d ser., 28 (1971): 413–38; Edward M. Griffin, *Old Brick: Charles Chauncy of Boston, 1705–1787* (Minneapolis, 1980), 48–50, 77–78.

39. Samuel Osborn, *The Case and Complaint of Samuel Osborn* (Boston, 1743), 30.

40. Ibid., 22–23. Apart from Chauncy and Gay, the council included the leading Old Light polemicists Samuel Mather and Benjamin Prescott, as well as Daniel Lewis, Peter Clark, Nathaniel Henchman, and John Gardner, all subscribers to *Seasonable Thoughts*. There were only three nonsubscribers: the moderates Joseph Door and John Chipman, and William Hobby, alone in this company a vigorous New Light when controversy over the revival finally erupted.

41. Conrad Wright, *The Beginnings of Unitarianism in America* (Boston, 1955); Miller, *The New England Mind: From Colony to Province*, 452–63.

42. Massachusetts enjoyed four newspapers (all published in Boston) continuously

throughout the 1740s, and another appeared briefly in the same decade. Connecticut, as ever, depended on its larger neighbor, even for its own news, until 1755, when it acquired a native newspaper for the first time, but could claim three to four papers published on a regular basis by the mid-1760s (Edward Connery Latham, comp., *Chronological Tables of American Newspapers, 1690–1820* [Barre, Mass., 1972], 4–7). For the extension of Boston's commercial hegemony over its region, see Steele, *English Atlantic*, 63–66.

43. Gee, *Letter to the Reverend Mr. Nathaniel Eels*, 16; John Hancock, *An Expostulatory and Pacifick Letter . . .* (Boston, 1743), 14.

44. Goen, *Revivalism and Separatism in New England*, 193–207; Cook, *Fathers of the Towns*, 120, 226.

45. The outstanding statements for continued clerical unity despite the Awakening are David Harlan, *The Clergy and the Great Awakening in New England*, Studies in American History and Culture, 15 (Ann Arbor, 1980); Stout, *New England Soul*, 212–32. This is an argument that needed making. The next few paragraphs, however, will take issue with its final conclusion while acknowledging its partial validity. In addition, some of the evidence adduced is subject to argument, and in particular Stout's claim (222–28) for "persistent orthodoxy in rationalist preaching." Of the eight ministers whose sermons are quoted in the course of the chapter subsection bearing this title, three (Henry Messinger, Samuel Checkley, and Ebenezer Parkman) are relatively unproblematic New Lights, and a fourth, Thaddeus Maccarty, though initially a fence straddler (he signed the pro-Awakening *Testimony and Advice* but also subscribed to *Seasonable Thoughts*), ultimately lost his pulpit in 1745 for his continued endorsement of Whitefield (*Sibley's Harvard Graduates*, 6:76, 199, 521–22, 10:380–82). Samuel Niles was an ultraconservative Old Light who could scarcely be said to have a rationalist bone in his body: he was so fervent a heresy hunter that John Adams, addressing "Ye liberal Christians," called him "your once formidable enemy" (ibid., 4:485–91, quotation at 489–90). Andrew Eliot and "Johnny" Barnard are unclassifiable. Eliot was notorious for never being able to make up his mind (a trait that cost him dearly in the Revolution) and for advancing both sides of disputed questions (ibid., 10:133–37; Bernard Bailyn, "Religion and the Revolution: Three Biographical Studies," *Perspectives in American History* 4 [Cambridge, Mass., 1970], 88–93). Barnard was an original member of the Brattle Street group, but, as that fact indicates, he was an aging man by the time of the Awakening, and his liberalism (to the extent that he retained any of it) was that of a much earlier generation whose doctrinal orthodoxy was never in question. We are left as a result solely with Nathaniel Appleton (William Brattle's successor at Cambridge) to represent rationalists still wedded to Calvinist orthodoxy in their preaching, and even he does not fit very well: the opinions quoted from him (*New England Soul*, 226) do not really establish the case, and his later exposition of predestination hardly seems "orthodox" in a sense that would have satisfied a conservative such as Samuel Niles (see his *How God Wills the Salvation of All Men* [Boston, 1753], 7, 10, 15). Appleton represents second-generation liberalism at midcentury, self-consciously undecided rather than haphazardly indecisive and, therefore, pretty much willing to waive most questions of doctrinal orthodoxy, as when he participated in the ordination of Jonathan Mayhew (Wright, *Beginnings of Unitarianism*, 66). That position, in its fundamental theological premise no less than its charitable conclusion, was hopelessly in conflict with anyone for whom the word orthodoxy had any significance.

46. Morgan, *Gentle Puritan*, 197–202. And for Joseph Bellamy's systematic elimination of opponents of the New Divinity in the jurisdiction of the Litchfield Association, see Franklin B. Dexter, ed., *The Literary Diaries of Ezra Stiles* (New York, 1901), 3:419.

47. For the Old Calvinist predicament, see William Breitenbach, "The Consistent Calvinism of the New Divinity Movement," *WMQ*, 3d ser., 41 (1984): 241–64.

48. L. H. Butterfield, ed., *Diary and Autobiography of John Adams* (Cambridge,

Mass., 1961), 3:262. For the occasion of this remark, the heresy trial of Lemuel Briant, see *Sibley's Harvard Graduates*, 10:345.

Appendix

1. Edwin Arber, ed., *A Transcript of the Registers of the Company of Stationers of London, 1554–1640 A.D.* (London, 1875–94), 2:43, 4:22.

2. *Biog. Dict. Brit. Rad.*, 3:190.

3. Falconer Madan, *Oxford Books: A Bibliography of Printed Works Relating to the University and City of Oxford or Printed or Published There*, 2 (Oxford, 1912), 521, 524; W. W. Greg, ed., *A Companion to Arber* (Oxford, 1912), 268–73.

4. Arber, ed., *Transcript of the Registers of the Company of Stationers*, 4:21.

5. Greg, ed., *Companion to Arber*, 326.

6. Foster, *Notes from the Caroline Underground*, 59, 104n. 5.

Index

New England is abbreviated as NE in the subheadings of the index.

Abbot, George: as archbishop of Canterbury, 43, 105, 106; resists Book of Sports, 116; on 1622 *Directions,* 343 (n. 51)

Abington, Mass., 372 (n. 32)

Adams, John: on NE clergy, 311; on Samuel Niles, 374 (n. 45)

Adams, Thomas, 333 (n. 26)

Adams, William: on NE as Exilic Israel, 236

Addington, Isaac, 247, 269, 363 (n. 36), 364 (n. 41), 367 (n. 91)

Admonition to the Parliament, An: significance of, 2–3, 314

Ainsworth, Henry, 166

Alden, John, 261

Allen, James, 217; favors toleration, 204; supports Newbury and Salem dissidents, 208, 358 (n. 94); criticizes Brattle Street Church, 282

Allen, John, 192

Allin, Henry, 364 (n. 41)

Alvey, Yeldard, 149, 347 (n. 22)

Ames, William: and redefinition of polity, 58–64; on practical divinity, 69, 74; voluntarism of, 69, 331 (n. 8); barred from pulpit, 100; invoked by Separatists, 142; on NE polity, 155

Amsterdam, 17, 18, 62, 161, 318

Andover, Mass.: witchcraft epidemic in, 261–63

Andros, Sir Edmund, 234, 248, 260; miscalculations of, 242

Anglicans, New England, 274, 283; Whitefield criticizes, 371 (n. 7)

Antinomianism, 25, 303, 332 (n. 17); English origins, 151, 162; nature of NE movement, 162–63, 350 (n. 60)

Apologeticall Narration, 68

Apostacy, fear of: in England, 150; in NE, 217, 242

Appleton, Nathaniel, 373 (n. 34); liberalism of, 374 (n. 45)

Appleton, Samuel, 365 (n. 57)

Arminianism, 70, 119, 138, 141, 157; and Parliament, 123, 130, 344 (n. 64); political significance of, 124, 131; and James I, 124–30; and Charles I, 130–31; theology of, 132–33; critique of Puritanism, 136; linked to prerogative, 136–37, and Antinomian controversy, 162; in Great Awakening, 295, 300, 307–8

Arnhem (Netherlands): congregational church at, 30

Ashby-de-la-Zouche (Leicestershire), 104

Axton, William, 54

Aylmer, John: as bishop of London, 52, 54, 55

Babbage, S. B., 99–101

Bacon, Luke, 346 (n. 14)

Bacon, Nathaniel, 347 (n. 25)

Baillie, Robert: on Puritan laity, 143

Bancroft, Richard, 42, 56, 67, 120; on Puritan pamphlets, 50; enforces canons of 1604, 99–106

Baptism. *See* Halfway Covenant; Youth, New England

Baptists:
—English, 100, 132, 145
—NE, 172, 191, 193, 211, 260, 274, 290, 303, 364 (n. 53); at Charlestown, 176; find advocates, 176–77; partial toleration of, 178, 199, 351 (n. 6); in crisis of 1670, 205, 207, 356 (n. 76); in Great Awakening, 301–2, 309–10

Barnard, John: religious liberalism of, 374 (n. 45)

Barrington, Sir Francis, 28, 108

Barrington, Lady Joanna, 110, 326 (n. 63)

Barrington, Sir Thomas, 29

Barrington family, 28, 105, 326 (n. 63)

Bartholomew, Henry, 211, 358 (n. 97), 364 (n. 40)

Batley (Yorkshire), 326 (n. 54). *See also* Woodkirk

Baxter, Richard: condemns sectarianism, 14; on Dissent, 196

Bayley, James, 358 (n. 99)

Bayly, Louis: *The Practice of Piety,* 87, 88, 91, 316, 318; sympathy for Puritans, 93

Baynes, Paul, 67; on unconverted, 12; and Separatism, 14; and redefinition of polity, 58–64; unofficial ministry, 100

Becon, Thomas, 89

Beecher, Lyman, 300

Bell, Susanna: spiritual experiences of, 172–74

Bellamy, Joseph, 374 (n. 46)

Bellingham, Richard, 203

Bellomont, first earl of (Richard Coote), 266, 367 (n. 94)

Beverley (Yorkshire), 16

Birdsall (Yorkshire), 16

Bishop, John, 232, 362 (n. 5)

Blakiston, John: and NE, 148–49; growing radicalism of, 149–50, 347 (n. 22); significance of, 150, 157

Blakiston, Susan, 149, 347 (n. 22)

Bocking (Essex), 8

Book of Common Prayer, 24, 26, 41, 65, 147

Book of Sports, 79, 81, 98, 116, 122; origin and purpose, 125–26, 342 (n. 48); reissued by Charles I, 126, 134; compromises clergy, 144, 145

Bossiney (Cornwall), 341 (n. 31)

Boston (Lincolnshire), 93, 326 (n. 53); conventicles at, 96, 142

Boston, Mass., 29, 73, 189, 194, 208, 220, 241, 261; links to rest of NE, 17–18, 270, 308; church founding, 159; covenant renewal, 159–60; Antinomian controversy, 162; absentee church membership, 178; Quakers at, 190; Baptists at, 191, 356 (n. 76); and Great Awakening, 192; clerical maintenance at, 193; and resistance to England, 245. *See also* Brattle Street; First Church; North Church; Old South Church

Bourchier, Thomas: fears retribution, 109–10

Bownd, Nicholas, 74, 137; on parochial worship, 34; on Sabbath, 80–81; on literacy, 85; on fasting, 97–98

Boxford (Suffolk), 36, 86

Boynton, Sir Matthew, 349 (n. 59)

Bradford, William: Separatism of, 14

Bradford (Yorkshire), 13

Bradshaw, William, 67, 101; on partial conformity, 43; and Cartwright, 58; *English Puritanism,* 59–61; later influence, 63–64; unofficial ministry, 100; lectureship with Hildersham, 104

Bradstreet, Simon (magistrate): opposes Newbury dissidents, 210; governor of Massachusetts, 228; favors surrender of charter, 244, 245, 363 (nn. 31, 34); supports persecution, 356 (n. 76); in New Charter Council, 365 (n. 57)

Bradstreet, Simon (minister, 1640–83), 17, 324 (n. 37), 360 (n. 113)

Bradstreet, Simon (minister, 1671–1741), 281, 283

Braintree (Essex), 327 (n. 7)

Brattle, Thomas, 366 (n. 71); criticizes witchcraft trials, 256, 258, 259, 260, 365 (n. 28); and Brattle Street Church, 281, 283

Brattle, William, 281, 283, 367 (n. 94)

Brattle Street, 287; defined, 281–82; organizes church, 282; significance of, 282–83

Breck, Robert, 373 (n. 37)

Briant, Lemuel, 375 (n. 48)

Bridge, William: encourages Separatism, 146, 167

Bristol (Gloucestershire): Broadmead church at, 145, 166, 345 (n. 1)

Bromford (Suffolk), 23

Brooke, Samuel, 133

Brown, Samuel: clashes with congregation, 372 (n. 32)

Browne, William, 363 (n. 34)

Bruen, Calvin, 17, 142

Buckingham, first duke of (George Villiers), 98, 344 (n. 64); efforts to impeach, 30; attracts Puritan support, 123, 341 (n. 35), 342 (n. 36); at York House debate, 131; assassination of, 135

Buell, Samuel, 298

Bulkley, Peter, 363 (nn. 34, 36)

Bunyan, John, 69–70, 91, 331 (n. 11)

Burghley, Baron (William Cecil), 52, 67

Burrage, Champlin, xiii

Burroughs, George: Increase Mather on, 257; executed, 259; and Halfway Covenant, 358 (n. 99); descendants of, 367 (n. 86)

Burton, Henry, 135; youth of, 16; at unauthorized fast, 98; attacks Montagu, 130–31, 133; becomes Independent, 167, 168

Byfield, Nathaniel, 266, 267, 364 (n. 53), 366 (n. 71); political career of, 367 (n. 92)

Calef, Robert: on execution of Burroughs, 259–60; *More Wonders of the Invisible World,* 266, 366 (n. 68)

Calvert, Sir George, 122

Cambridge, Mass., 15, 150, 179, 332 (n. 17); Hartford church gathered at, 156; Shepard gathers church at, 161; anti-Presbyterian synod at, 170–71; infrequent communions at, 353 (n. 25)

Cambridge Association: and witchcraft epidemic, 256, 259; and extension of church membership, 272–73, 368 (n. 112)

Cambridge Platform, 33, 139, 170, 186, 356 (n. 76); ambiguity of, 5, 148; opposition to, 171, 211; significance of, 171–72; at Reforming Synod, 228

Cambridge University, 57

Canne, John: Separatist apologetics of, 142

Canons (1604), 97; impact on Puritan ministry, 99–106

Canons Ashby (Northamptonshire), 105

Canterbury (Kent), 17

Carpenter, Ezra: loses pulpit in Great Awakening, 302

Cartwright, Thomas, 57, 58, 103; on conformity, 42; and church government, 43; attacks Separatists, 61; and definition of true church, 143

Cawdry, Robert, 101, 334 (n. 46); radicalism of, 65, 67, 331 (n. 5); as lexicographer, 65–66, 331 (n. 2); significance of, 66–67, 75; optimism of, 92–93

Cecil, Sir Robert (later earl of Salisbury), 30

Chapman, Edmund, 57

Charles I (king of England), 140; Personal Rule of, xiv, 139, 338 (n. 99); and ecclesiastical policy of James I, 126, 134; Anti-Arminians bid for support of, 130–31

Charles II (king of England), 233

Charlestown, Mass., 15, 179; Baptists at, 176–78, 191, 204, 356 (n. 76); and Halfway Covenant, 197

Chauncy, Charles (1589–1671): causes panic, 110; regrets submission, 150

Chauncy, Charles (1705–87): on operative knowledge, 294–95; *Seasonable Thoughts,* 308, 309; and Osborn case, 308, 373 (n. 40)

Checkley, Samuel, 374 (n. 45)

Cheever, Ezekiel: on Brattle Street, 283

Chelmsford (Essex), 19; conventicles at, 96

Chelmsford, Mass.: adopts Halfway Covenant, 197; covenant renewal at, 355 (n. 57)

Chester (Cheshire), 17, 142

Chester, diocese of: Puritans in, 164

Childe, Robert, 169

Chipman, John, 373 (n. 40)

Churches, gathered. *See* Covenants, church

Church of England: English Puritans' attitude toward, 2–3, 5–6, 21, 26, 67–68, 76–77, 93–94, 113, 138–39, 142, 144, 150–51; parochial worship in, 34, 143; ministry of, 39–40, 43, 75, 144–45; Parliament attempts reform of, 117, 121–22, 137, 146, 148; Arminianism and, 124, 129–30, 131; growing hostility toward, 145–47; NE Puritans' attitude toward, 155–56, 158–59, 160, 168; Restoration church and NE, 195–96; church courts of, 328 (n. 29)

"Civil Man," 38–39

Civil War, English: in modern historiography, xiv–xv, 340 (n. 22), 341 (n. 30)

Clap, Roger: on conversion narratives, 181, 183

Clark, Peter, 373 (n. 40)

Clarke, Samuel (martyrologist): on Dod, 105; on Cheshire Puritanism, 164

Clarke, Samuel (New England minister): conflict with Cole, 304–5

Clarke, Thomas, 203, 208, 211, 228, 357 (n. 86)

Classical movement. *See* Presbyterianism—Elizabethan

Cleaver, Robert: on education, 75–76; on family religion, 83–84; praises printing, 86; works of widely read, 91, 317; deprivation and death, 105

Clergy, Puritan:

—in England: as preachers, 21–23, 24–26; ambivalence toward conventicling, 23–24, 54, 97; as lecturers, 50, 54–55, 100; Jacobean optimism, 92–94; deprivations of in 1604, 97–101; attracted to Separatism and semiseparatism, 102–6; Parliament attempts to aid, 117, 137; challenge to Long Parliament, 140; threatened by lay initiatives, 142–43; dilemma of under Laud, 144–46; complain to NE clergy, 166–67; ejected at Restoration, 195–96, 233–34. *See also* Church of England; Conformity

—in NE: guilt over England, 150–51; advantages over England, 152–53; convergence with laity, 154–55; organization of, 161; respond to English criticism, 166–67, 168–70; growing caution, 170–72; at ministerial assembly (1657), 187–88; maintenance of, 192–93; and Quaker challenge, 194–95; in crisis of 1670, 207, 208; authority strengthened in 1680s, 236–37, 242–43; divided over surrender of Massachusetts charter, 244, 363 (n. 32); leadership in Dominion period, 249–50; embarrassed by role in witchcraft epidemic, 263–64; final formulation of role in NE, 268, 272–73; institutional changes, 277; sources of authority in eighteenth century, 277–79; dissident groups, 279–83; apologetics inadequate in Great Awakening, 301–2; compromised by problems of maintenance, 303–4, 305; internal divisions and mutual distrust, 306–9, 373 (n. 36); lasting effects of Great Awakening on, 310

Clifton, Richard, 100, 103

Clough, William, 346 (n. 14)

Coercion: role of in NE, 290. *See also* Baptists; Quakers; Toleration

Coke, Sir Edward, 121

Coke, Sir John, 131

Colchester (Essex): conventicling at, 17, 346 (n. 10)

Cole, Nathan: refuses to pay parish rates, 304; significance of, 305

Collins, Edward, 23

Collins, Nathaniel, 218, 360 (n. 113)

Collinson, Patrick, xiii, 320 (n. 4)

Colman, Benjamin: and Brattle Street, 281, 283

Colonies: general relationship to England, ix–x. *See also* New England

Concord, Mass.: church gathered at, 160, 161

Conder, Richard: and Book of Sports, 98

Conformity: controversies over, 20–21, 41–43, 99–106, 141, 144–45

Congregationalism. *See* Conversion narratives; Covenants, church; Polity, ecclesiastical

Connecticut: ties to Boston, 17–18; early churches in, 156; calls for synod, 186, 189, 194; Halfway Covenant in, 188; antiheresy laws, 190; conciliatory toward England, 200; merges with New Haven Colony, 201; ministers of indebted to Increase and Cotton Mather, 218, 232, 269; covenant renewals in, 223; resumes charter, 250; autonomy of threatened, 269–70; remains dependent on Massachusetts, 270, 368 (n. 118); Saybrook Platform in, 277, 369 (n. 19); Stoddardeanism in, 279, 280–81; church schisms in during Great Awakening, 291, 370 (n. 4); General Consociation of condemns revivalism, 306–7; political factions in, 310; church membership in, 352 (n. 12)

Constable, Sir William: career of, 29–30, 349 (n. 59); influence of in East Riding, 31; significance of, 31–32

Conventicles: in England, 13, 16–17, 19–20, 23–24, 54, 96–98, 103, 104, 135–36, 145, 146, 147, 163, 326 (n. 54), 346 (n. 10); in NE, 146, 151, 184, 346 (n. 15)

Conversion narratives: English origins, 96, 163; required by NE churches, 161; relationship to Antinomian controversy, 162–63, 332 (n. 17); in Netherlands, 163, 349 (n. 49); at Wenham, 171; at Roxbury, 172–73; importance of in early NE, 181, 184; role of partly filled by covenant renewals, 220; in 1680s, 239; later skepticism over, 279–80

Cooke, Elisha, Sr., 260, 286, 363 (n. 34), 364 (n. 41), 367 (n. 91); background of, 212, 247, 357 (n. 86); refuses to accept New Charter, 251, 252; ousts Increase Mather from Harvard, 266, 267

Cooke, Richard, 357 (n. 86)

Cooper, William, 297

Cope, Sir Anthony: role in Parliament, 118; valedictory, 120

Cope family, 108

Corbet, John: praises Puritan laity, 98–99

Cosin, John, 124, 129; patronized by Neile, 126; significance of, 134

Cottingham (Yorkshire), 27

Cotton, John (1585–1652), 166, 243, 282; on knowledge, 25; and Lewis Bayly, 93; praises English ministry, 93; defends role of laity in discipline, 95–96; and conventicling, 96; replies to Separatists, 142; early ecclesiology, 153–54; definition of true church, 154; rejects Church of England, 155, 158–59; and conformity, 157; *Moses his Judicials*, 157; and Anne Hutchinson, 163

Cotton, John (1640–99), 225, 352 (n. 8)

Cotton, Thomas, 17

Covenant, national. *See* Jeremiad

Covenant renewals: at settlement of NE, 159–60; revival of and resistance to, 223–24, 227; English precedents for revived version, 224–25; and extension of church membership, 225–26; potential for practical divinity, 226–27; encouraged by Reforming Synod, 228–29, 234; laity hesitate over, 229–30; more widespread in later 1680s, 239; in Great Awakening, 300

Covenants, church: in England, 96, 135–36, 142, 349 (n. 59); New Englanders insist English churches need, 167, 168

Coventry (Staffordshire), 65, 101

Croswell, Andrew, 291, 307, 373 (n. 35)

Culverwell, Ezekiel, 67; postdeprivation career of, 102; attacked by Leighton, 141

Curtis, Mark, 59

Dane, Francis, 261

Danforth, Samuel, 214

Danforth, Thomas, 215, 357 (n. 83); and Halfway Covenant, 200–201; left out

of New Charter Council, 253; refuses to serve at witchcraft trials, 256; favors persecution, 356 (n. 76); restored to Massachusetts upper house, 367 (n. 91)

Davenport, John, 65, 150, 205; defends conformity, 140–41; radical turn, 157; contrasted with Richard Mather, 164; response of to Restoration, 201–2; accepts First Church pastorate, 203, 358 (n. 98); calls for toleration of Baptists, 204; death of, 204; influences Increase Mather, 218–19

Davy, Humphrey, 357 (n. 86), 364 (n. 41)

Declension, myth of, xiii, 213–17, 312–13; partisan uses of in NE, 217, 219, 225; disputed, 220–21, 223, 224, 227; and covenant renewal, 224–25; endorsed by Reforming Synod, 228; loses controversial character, 235–43; part of later NE identity, 251, 271, 284; and interpretations of Great Awakening, 292–93. *See also* Jeremiad

Dedham (Essex): classis at, 23, 34, 36, 47, 51, 55, 57

Dedham, Mass.: town covenant, 36, 38; ministry of, 192

Dedham "orders" (1585), 135, 312; terms of, 33–37; significance of, 37–38

Deerfield Massacre (1704), 284

Defenestration of Prague (1618), 127

Dennison, Daniel: politics of, 210; favors persecution, 356 (n. 76)

Dent, Arthur, 90, 91; *The Plaine Mans Path-way to Heaven*, 14, 87, 90–91, 175, 316; *A Sermon on Repentance*, 91–92, 317

DeVoto, Bernard, 312

D'Ewes, Sir Simonds, 142

Dickens, A. G., 324 (n. 33)

Digges, Sir Dudley, 121

Discipline. *See* Church of England: church courts of; Polity, ecclesiastical; Reproof, concept of

Dissenting Brethren. *See* Independents

Dissenting interest, 249

Dod, John: on education, 75–76; on family religion, 83–84; praises printing, 86; works widely read, 91, 312; later career and significance of, 103, 105

Doolittle, Benjamin: charged with Arminianism, 372 (n. 32)

Door, Joseph, 373 (n. 40)

Dorchester (Dorsetshire): church covenant at, 135, 142; comparison with NE
covenant renewal, 224–25

Dorchester, Mass.: failure to gather church
at, 161–62, 163, 164, 165, 332 (n. 17);
conversion narratives at, 181, 183; clerical maintenance at, 192; Increase Mather
uses pulpit at, 217, 225–26; and Halfway Covenant, 226, 356 (n. 67); church
of during Dominion of NE, 238–39

Dort, Synod of, 131

Dove, Thomas: as bishop of Peterborough,
105

Downame, George, 76, 93; on distinctions
among Puritans, 47

Downame, John: works by, 92

Downing, Emmanuel, 109

Drinker, Edward, 356 (n. 76)

Dry Dayton (Cambridgeshire), 50

Dudley, Joseph, 234, 252, 286, 363 (nn. 34,
36); gestures to Increase Mather, 248;
party of important under New Charter,
253; influence of on witchcraft trials,
260

Dummer, William, 284

Dunster, Henry, 332 (n. 17); on conformity, 21

Dwight, Timothy, 300

Dyke, Jeremy, 89

Eaborne, Samuel, 357 (n. 92)

Earle, Sir Walter: successor to Fuller, 119;
Sabbath bill, 120; scandalous ministers
bill, 121–22; leadership of in 1628–29,
137

Eastham, Mass.: church trial at, 307–8

Eastwell (Kent), 101

Eaton, Samuel: English and American
careers of compared, 164–65

Eccles, Richard: reading of, 88

Education: clerical dominance of in NE,
278

Edwards, Jonathan, 310, 311; views of on
Great Awakening, 293; accuses Old
Lights of sinning against Holy Ghost,
299–300; theology of lacks practical
divinity, 300; defends anticlericalism,
301; and Arminianism, 307, 308

Edwards, Thomas, 168

Eels, Nathaniel, 373 (n. 34)

Eliot, Andrew: indecisive theology of, 374
(n. 45)

Eliot, Sir John (MP), 30, 111; in Parliament
of 1629, 137

Eliot, John (minister), 173, 196; on NE
youth, 180, 182, 185; translates Ramus,
333 (n. 30)

Ely, diocese of: deprivations in, 101

Essex, 16, 28, 323 (n. 26)

Essex, archdeaconry of: enforcement of
1604 canons in, 100; conventicles in, 145

Essex's Rising (1601), 30

Etherington, Anne: conversion experience
of, 95

Fairfield, Conn., 232

Fairweather, John, 364 (n. 41)

Faith: in Puritan practical divinity, 69–
74; in Calvinism and Arminianism
compared, 132–33

Family religion: importance of in practical
divinity, 78, 83–85, 95

Farmington, Conn.: maintenance dispute
in, 304–5

Farnum, John: a Baptist then a Quaker
convert, 191; returns to North Church,
199

Fast days/fasting: in England, 6, 321 (n. 6);
sectarian and political potential of, 97–
98, 136; and NE covenant renewals,
226–27, 361 (n. 132)

Fawsley (Northamptonshire), 105

Fenn, Humphrey: postdeprivation career
of, 101

Fenner, Dudley: translates Ramus, 25, 74,
78; on household religion, 83, 326 (n. 57)

Field, John, 2, 288; on discipline, 43; on
election of ministers, 44; defines church,
47; denounces Separatists, 61

Fiennes, Nathaniel, 140

Fifth Monarchists, 172

First Church (Boston, Mass.): adopts Halfway Covenant, 197; schism in and foundation of Old South, 200, 203–4, 361
(n. 135); members and partisans favor
toleration and resistance to England,
204–5; supports dissidents at Newbury
and Salem, 208, 358 (n. 94); regains
power in Massachusetts government,

211–212, 221; death and retirement of leading members of, 227–28; resists Reforming Synod, 229, 230; allies with Increase Mather, 245; reconciled with Old South, 246; regains dominance of Massachusetts magistracy, 246–47; resists surrender of charter, 247–48, 364 (nn. 40, 42); center of popular party, 251–52; and witchcraft trials, 259, 366 (n. 71); members of win heavily in election of 1693, 265; turns on Increase Mather, 265–66; criticizes Brattle Street Church, 282; and Hoar presidency at Harvard, 358 (n. 98)

Fisher, Daniel, 357 (n. 86), 363 (n. 31)

Fiske, Moses, 197

Fitch, James, 214, 220, 225; on declension, 217; client of Mathers, 218; and covenant renewal, 223–24

Fleetwood, Sir Miles, 343 (n. 55)

Fleetwood family, 108

Fletcher, John, 54

Forced loan (1626), 108; Puritans lead resistance to, 136

Foreign policy, English: controversies over in 1620s, 123, 127; and Arminianism, 130, 134, 137

Fossecut (Northamptonshire), 16

Fox, George, 176

Fuller, Nicholas, 108; in Parliament of 1610, 117, 120; leadership role, 118–19; in Parliament of 1614, 119–20

Fuller, Thomas: on Lancashire, 10; on Dod, 105

Gardiner, Samuel Rawson, xiii, 68, 69

Gardner, John, 373 (n. 40)

Garnon, John, 346 (n. 14)

Gataker, Thomas: criticizes Independents, 167–68

Gay, Ebenezer, 308, 373 (n. 40)

Gedney, Bartholomew, 363 (n. 34), 365 (n. 57)

Gee, Joshua, 309, 373 (n. 36)

Gentry, Puritan: importance of, 12, 20; prerogatives threatened, 53–55, 167; reconstituted in NE, 152. *See also* Magistracy, New England; Parliament, Puritans in

Gifford, George, 38, 327 (n. 7), 332 (n. 11)

Gilby, Anthony: criticizes ceremonies, 42; defines church government, 44

Gloucester (Gloucestershire), 99

Gloucester, Mass., 291

Gloucestershire, 98–99

Glover, Cornelius: a Puritan itinerant, 22–23, 325 (n. 49)

Goffe, William, 201, 206

Gooch, Barnabe, 340 (n. 17)

Good, Thomas, 54

Goodwin, John, 132, 167

Goodwin, Thomas, 30, 163

Goodwin, William, 201

Gookin, Daniel, 355 (n. 65), 356 (n. 76), 357 (n. 83)

Gortonists, 172

Gould, Thomas, 351 (n. 6)

Government, church. *See* Polity, ecclesiastical

Grand Remonstrance, 119

Great Awakening, 4, 274; interpretation of anticipated in *Magnalia*, 287; as terminus of Puritan movement, 290; social and economic basis, 291–93; as interruption in secular history, 293, 297, 298–99; sources of evangelical success in, 296–97; leads to church schisms and anticlericalism, 300–301; and collapse of clerical unity, 305–9

Great Migration, 108, 109, 114; economic conditions and origins of, 110–12, 339 (n. 9), 345 (n. 1)

Great Stanbridge (Essex), 102

Greenham, Richard, 44, 74; on assurance, 71–72; and Sabbatarianism, 80, 81, 82; pessimism of, 92–93; on Sabbath conferences, 96, 97

Greenhill, William, 23; on Puritan readership, 88

Groton (Suffolk), 86, 144

Gurdon, Muriel Sedley: on ministry, 144

Hadley, Mass.: hiding place of regicides, 201, 206; politics of, 205, 206

Hales, John, 370 (n. 1)

Halfway Covenant, 157, 171, 180, 194, 208, 209, 211, 212, 215, 222, 272, 309; controversy over aids Baptists, 176–77; formulated (1657), 187; terms, 188; as response to heresy, 196–98; at synod of

1662, 198, 202; political implications of, 198–203, 355 (n. 64), 356 (n. 76); in First Church schism, 203–4; in Salem Village, 212, 358 (n. 99); and declension, 217, 219; and covenant renewal, 226, and crisis of charters, 237–39; and Massachusetts politics in 1680s, 245–46

Halifax (Yorkshire), 6

Hall, David D., 360 (n. 121)

Hall, Joseph, 81, 93

Haller, William, xiii, 21

Halley's Comet, 233

Hampton Court Conference (1604), 4, 57–58, 104

Hancock, John (minister), 309

Harley, Sir Robert, 341 (n. 35), 342 (n. 36)

Harrington, Sir James, 67

Harrison, James, 105

Harsnet, Samuel, 348 (n. 39)

Hart, John [pseud.], 316

Hartford, Conn., 18; liberal church admissions policy at, 156; church schism at, 194, 195; and foundation of Hadley, 206; not cultural center of Connecticut, 270; and Great Awakening, 291

Harvard, John, 89

Harvard College, 21, 189, 192, 197, 248, 253, 279, 369 (n. 119); Hoar presidency, 212, 358 (n. 98); use of presidency by Increase Mather, 249, 267, 364 (n. 48); ouster of Mather, 266–67; headship of Willard, 267–68; role of in eighteenth-century clericalism, 278

Hasley (Warwickshire), 337 (n. 94)

Hastings, Sir Francis, 57

Hathorne, John, 363 (n. 34), 365 (n. 57); witchcraft judge, 261

Hathorne, William: opposes Old South, 210; favors Nicholet and Woodman, 210–11, 358 (nn. 92, 94); earlier career of, 211, 358 (n. 97); retires, 228; and Baptists, 356 (n. 76)

Haverhill, Mass.: covenant renewal at, 229

Heaton, Martin: as bishop of Ely, 101

Heddon (Northumberland): Shepard at, 22–23

Heigham, John, 129

Henchman, Nathaniel, 373 (n. 40)

Heylyn, Peter, 128

Heywood, Oliver, 13

Higginson, Francis, 154, 155

Higginson, John, 176, 214, 246; defends Church of England, 196–97; urges conciliation of England, 200; ecclesiology of, 202, 209; Salem ministry attacked, 208, 209, 210; reorganizes Salem church, 237–38; on fall of NE charters, 243; criticizes Brattle Street, 282

Hildersham, Arthur, 67, 323 (n. 24), 325 (n. 53); and Hampton Court Conference, 57; controversy with Separatists, 62; defends unauthorized fasts, 97–98; later career and significance of, 103–4

Hill, Christopher, xiii

Hippisley, Sir John, 342 (n. 35)

Hoar, Leonard: president of Harvard, 212, 358 (n. 98)

Hobby, William, 373 (n. 40)

Holland, first earl of (Henry Rich), 342 (n. 35)

Holmes, Jane, 347 (n. 22)

Holme upon Spalding Moor (Yorkshire), 27–31

Hooke, William: and guilt over England, 150

Hooker, Thomas, 75, 135; political commentaries of, 19, 97; on clerical conformity, 20–21; denounces England, 26–27, 110, 142; praises English ministry, 93; and conventicling, 96; hopes for reform, 123; cautions laity, 143; early ecclesiology, 153–54; favors liberal admissions policy, 156; on Westminster Assembly, 169

Horne, Josiah: deprivation and post-deprivation career of, 101

Horsey, Sir Jerome, 341 (n. 31)

Hubbard, William: on toleration, 199, 355 (n. 64); refutes Increase Mather, 221, 223, 361 (n. 134); writes alternative histories, 227, 232; on fall of NE charters, 234; criticizes militants, 245; on basis of Massachusetts politics, 246; and witchcraft epidemic, 264; criticizes Brattle Street, 282

Hulkes, George, 105

Hull, John, 208, 363 (n. 31)

Hull (Yorkshire), 16

Hull, Mass.: clerical maintenance at, 192;

in Great Awakening, 302
Humphries, John, 89
Huntingdon, third earl of (Henry Hastings), 104
Hutchinson, Anne, 55, 73, 152; defends conferences, 151; significance of for NE Puritanism, 162–63.
Hutchinson, Edward, 357 (n. 86), 358 (n. 94)
Hutchinson, Elisha, 357 (n. 86), 363 (n. 34), 364 (nn. 41, 53), 365 (nn. 57, 58), 367 (n. 91)
Hutton, Matthew: as archbishop of York, 100
Hypocrisy, 70–72

Ignorance, 69–70
Independents: claim Elizabethan Presbyterians as predecessors, 48; use NE in controversy, 166, 167, 168
Indians, New England, 1–2, 263, 302; and Ramist logic, 333 (n. 30). *See also* King Philip's War
Infant damnation, 69
Ipswich (Suffolk): Puritan radicals in, 145
Ipswich, Mass., 211; in Great Awakening, 291, 302

Jacie, Henry, 331 (n. 73)
Jacob, Henry, 101, 157; and Hampton Court Conference, 57, 58–59; role in redefining polity, 59–62; founds Southwark church, 63, 100, 338 (n. 105)
James I (king of England): issues *Directions* (1622), 68–69, 128; hostility to Puritans, 116–18, 119, 120, 342 (n. 48); attacks Sunday bill, 122; definition of a Puritan, 125; issues Book of Sports, 125–26, 342 (n. 48); final ecclesiastical policy of, 126; interest in Arminians, 126–27; and Thirty Years' War, 127; influence on Charles I, 134
James II (king of England), 248, 249
Janszon, Jan, 318
Jenkins, Sir Leoline, 363 (n. 31)
Jeremiad, 205; origin and early history, 213–14; Stoughton's formulation, 214–17; Increase Mather's version, 218–20,

235; adaptations in 1680s, 236–37; refinements in 1690s, 271; in historiography, 357 (n. 77), 359 (n. 104). *See also* Declension, myth of
Johnson, Edward, 357 (n. 86)
Johnson, Isaac, 89
Johnson, William, 357 (n. 86), 363 (n. 34)
Jordan, Ignatius: frustrated in Parliament of 1621, 121–22; successful in Parliament of 1628, 137

Kendall, R. T., 336 (n. 73), 343 (n. 58)
Kent, Benjamin, 373 (n. 37)
Kent: Separatism in, 166
Kilby (Northamptonshire), 36
Killingworth, Conn., 358 (n. 99)
King Philip's War, 182, 218, 221, 222, 226–27; use of by Massachusetts ministry, 220, 224, 232; and moral legislation, 221; conflict over interpretation of, 234
Kingston-upon-Thames (Surrey), 50
Kirke, Percy, 234
Kittery, Maine, 190, 297
Knappen, M. M., xiii
Kneesall (Nottinghamshire), 346 (n. 14)
Knightley family, 105, 108
Knowledge: operative, 69, 70, 73–74; historical, 69–70; in Great Awakening, 293–95
Knyvett, Thomas, 146

Laity, Puritan:
—in England: self-conception, 10; conflicts with Catholics, 10–11; hostility to of non-Puritans, 11–14; engagement in politics, 18–20, 97–99, 135–36, 144; increasing sophistication of, 95–97; Parliamentary bills in aid of, 115–16, 340 (n. 18); challenge of for Long Parliament, 140, 146; restive in 1620s, 141–43; insurgent under Laud, 144–46, 346 (n. 14); initiate Root and Branch Petition, 147; carry radicalism to NE, 150–52
—in NE: criticize England, 165–66; fear Presbyterianism, 170–71; absentee church membership of, 178–79, 197, 238, 239, 284, 352 (n. 8); anticlericalism

of, 191, 206, 208; prove indifferent to Quakers, 193–94; hesitate over covenant renewals, 229–30; and crisis of NE charters, 239–40; challenge of to clergy blunted, 268; role in eighteenth century, 272–75; respond to Great Awakening, 295–97, 300–303. *See also* Popular religion

Lake, Thomas, 222

Lambe, Sir John, 122, 341 (n. 33)

Lambeth Articles (1595), 57

Lancashire, 22; Puritan-Catholic conflicts in, 10–11; conventicling in, 13. *See also* Chester, diocese of

Laud, William, 42, 67, 118, 124, 149, 318, 341 (n. 33); silences Shepard, 22; impact of on Puritan movement, 94, 139, 141–46, 150–51, 163; denies national crisis, 113; relations with Neile and James I, 126, 128; and Arminian controversy, 133–34, 344 (n. 64); overall program of, 134; attacks John White, 135–36; fears Parliament, 136

Lawrence, Henry, 349 (n. 59)

Lawson, Deodat, 359 (n. 99)

Leeds (Yorkshire), 16

Leiden (Netherlands), 161

Leigh, William: defends conformity, 144

Leighton, Alexander, 17, 33, 127, 157; on fasts, 136; attacks moderates, 141; *Sions Plea*, 142

Leisler's Rebellion: as warning to NE, 254, 260

Leverett, John (1616–79), 201, 203, 211, 212, 229, 234, 245, 246; supports Nicholet at Salem, 210, 358 (n. 94); resists Increase Mather, 220–21, 222, 223; death of, 227, 228; and Baptists, 356 (n. 76); and Hoar presidency at Harvard, 358 (n. 98)

Leverett, John (1662–1724): and Brattle Street, 281, 283

Lewis, Daniel, 373 (n. 40)

Lewis, Robert, 42, 55

Liberalism, religious, in New England: inchoate nature of, 294–95, 307–8; in aftermath of Great Awakening, 374 (n. 45)

Lister, Joseph: describes Yorkshire Puritanism, 13

Literacy: Puritan attitudes toward, 26, 35, 70, 75–76, 84–85; extent of in England, 75, 85

Literature, Puritan, 65–66; uses and forms of, 86–90; circulation of, 90–92, 315–18; in NE, 184, 217–18; importance of during Dominion of NE, 240–41; clerical dominance of, 277–78; low survival rate of, 335 (n. 56)

Lollardry, 7, 8

London, 14, 16, 18, 62, 102; conventicles in, 103, 163; riots and antiepiscopal demonstrations in, 147; Separatists in, 166

Long Island, N.Y., 190

Loring, Israel: on evangelical preaching, 296; and witchcraft trials, 367 (n. 86)

Lothrop, John, 331

Lusher, Eleazer: and Baptists, 356 (n. 76)

Lynn, Mass.: church dispute in, 159–60

Maccarty, Thaddeus, 374 (n. 45)

Magistracy, New England: compared with English Puritan gentry, 152; and youth, 182; and unconverted, 185; in crisis of 1670, 206, 207–8; numbers of increased in Massachusetts, 244; high turnover in 1680s, 245; ineffectiveness of after 1689, 268

Maldon (Essex), 52, 327 (n. 7); food riots at, 111

Maldon, Mass., 356 (n. 76), 358 (n. 97)

Marblehead, Mass., 291

Marbury, Francis, 55

Marlborough, Mass., 373 (n. 37)

Marprelate tracts, 33, 61, 65, 105, 329 (n. 53); radicalism of, 55–57; divisive impact of, 57

Marten, Sir Henry, 338 (n. 99), 341 (n. 33)

Martindale, Adam, 12

Mason, Stephen, 365 (n. 58)

Massachusetts: initial caution at founding of churches in, 159; conflicts and compromises in churches of, 159–61; tightened church admissions standards in, 161–62; Antinomian controversy in, 162–63; de facto Separatism of churches in, 165–66; favors call for synod on children of church members, 186–87, 194;

anti-Quaker laws in, 189–90; divisions in over conciliation of England, 200–201; crisis over First Church schism, 205–8; further conflict in, 208–12; charter of threatened, 233; charter vacated in Chancery, 235; triumph of militant party in, 245–47; status of under New Charter, 250; church schisms in during Great Awakening, 291, 370 (n. 4); clerical conventions of issue rival manifestoes, 306; Great Awakening produces political factions in western sections, 310

Mather, Cotton, 28, 258, 265, 300, 366 (n. 68), 370 (n. 1); on lay scrupulosity, 184; use of Connecticut by, 218, 269, 270; on covenant renewal, 225; preaches survival of NE, 236; draws moral from execution of James Morgan, 242; and Phips, 253; recommends Stoughton, 253; ambivalent over witchcraft trials, 256–57, 259; fears for New Charter, 259–60; defends judges, 264; ridiculed by Willard, 267; fails to achieve father's status, 268–69; and Yale, 269; on colonial relationship, 270; controversies with Stoddard and Brattle Street, 279, 281, 282–83; last years of, 284; *Magnalia Christi Americana*, 286–87; on affectionate preaching, 294; on reluctance of clergy to litigate, 302

Mather, Eleazer, 192, 217

Mather, Increase, 271, 286, 309, 348 (n. 39), 364 (n. 48); income of, 193; and Boston Baptists, 199–200; and Halfway Covenant, 206, 212, 359 (n. 110); character and significance of, 212–13; and jeremiad, 213–14, 216; seeks leadership of NE clergy, 217–18, 232; formulates version of declension myth, 218–19, 242; advocates Halfway Covenant, 219; threatens NE with destruction, 219–20; blocked on moral legislation, 220–23; revives and reconstructs covenant renewals, 223–27; organizes Reforming Synod, 228–29; *Illustrious Providences*, 231–33, 235, 361 (n. 4); abandons conciliation, 233–34; creates successful theodicy, 235, 236, 239–40; prepares for Dominion, 241; allies with militants, 244–45, 247; initiates purge of Massachusetts magistrates, 245; courted by Dudley, 248; organizes mission to England, 248–49; at zenith of power, 249; secures New Charter, 249, 250; on continuing mission of NE, 250–51; fears for New Charter, 252, 254; plans new politics, 252–54, 365 (nn. 58, 59); offers own account of witchcraft epidemic, 254–55; anxious to preserve integrity of judges, 256, 257, 258, 261, 264; cautious tactics, 260–61; publishes *Cases of Conscience*, 262; exposes Andover prosecutions, 262–63; compromises clergy, 264; authority challenged, 264–65; fall from power and its significance, 266–68, 269; and Yale, 269; controversies with Stoddard and Brattle Street, 279, 281, 282–83; death of, 284

Mather, Richard: early years of, 10–11; rejects mixed communion, 143; early interest in polity, 153–54; and conformity, 157, 348 (n. 39); Dorchester church of faulted, 161–62; influence of English career on NE, 164; significance of, 165; income of, 192

Mather, Samuel (1626–71), 214

Mather, Samuel (1706–85), 373 (n. 40)

Matthew, Tobie: as archbishop of York, 28, 100

Matthews, Marmaduke, 356 (n. 76), 358 (n. 97)

Meacocke, William: deprived, 337 (n. 94)

Messinger, Henry, 374 (n. 45)

Metcalfe, Michael: warns Norwich, 145, 150

Middletown, Conn., 218

Milborne, Jacob, 260

Milborne, William: opposes witchcraft trials, 260, 261

Mildmay, Sir Henry, 341 (n. 35), 342 (n. 36)

Mildmay family, 108

Milford, Conn., 201

Miller, Perry, x–xii, 366 (n. 72)

Minor, Thomas, 1

Mitchell, Jonathan, 214

Montagu, Sir Edward: parliamentary career of, 120–21

Montagu, Richard, 124, 141, 344 (n. 64); patronized by Neile, 126; bids for support of James I, 127–28; *A New Gagg,*

128–29; attacked in Parliament of 1624, 129; *Appello Caesarem,* 129–30; attacked in later parliaments, 130–31; at York House debate, 131; and salvation, 132; and controversy, 132–33; significance of, 134

Moody, Joshua, 241

Moore, George H., 366 (n. 68)

Moore, Robert: on lay patronage, 40; on polity, 48

Moral legislation: in England, 116, 334 (n. 40); in NE, 182, 221, 222, 275–76

More, John, 1

Morellianism, 179, 291, 303; defined, 195; in NE controversy, 195–96; and Halfway Covenant controversy, 198; in NE politics, 244, 245–47

Morély, Jean, 195

Morgan, Edmund S., xii

Morgan, James: execution of and its significance, 241–42

Morton, Charles, 264

Morton, Thomas, 93; at York House debate, 131; as bishop of Durham, 149

Naunton, Sir Robert, 108

Naylor, James, 176

Neile, Richard, 67, 105, 124; silences Ezekiel Rogers, 28–29; suppresses lectureship of Bradshaw and Hildersham, 104; favored by James I and founds "Durham College," 126; and Arminian controversy, 132–33; linked to Weston, 137

Newbury, Mass., 358 (n. 99); church dispute at, 208–11; political implications of controversy, 246

Newcastle-upon-Tyne (Northumberland): Puritan laity in, 22, 95, 148–50

New Divinity, 310

New England: and English Puritan aspirations, 27; and changes in English Puritanism, 106–7, 138–39; as refuge for English godly, 109–10, 148–49; impact of English sectarianism in, 148, 155–56, 163; example of encourages English Separatists, 166–67; fear of English heresy in, 172, 189; conflict with Restoration England, 177, 200, 233, 235;

compared with apostate Israel, 213; compared with Exilic Israel, 236–39, 242–43, 271; distinctive identity after 1689, 250–51, 268; charters of uncertain in eighteenth century, 269–70; mission reconciled with colonial status, 270–72; further extension of church membership in, 272–75; in Sewall's valedictory, 284–85; assigned special role in Great Awakening, 298–99; communication in during eighteenth century, 308–9; position in nineteenth-century America, 311–12

New Haven, Conn., 65, 150; church gathered at, 157; and Great Awakening, 291

New Haven Colony: sectarian religious establishment of, 56–57; rejects call for synod on baptism, 186, 201

New Lights. *See* Great Awakening; Whitefield, George

New London, Conn.: contacts with Boston, 17–18; and Great Awakening, 291

New Plymouth. *See* Plymouth Colony

Newton, Thomas: prosecutor of Leisler and of Salem witches, 260

New York, N.Y.: and Connecticut, 270; Dutch recapture, 360 (n. 116)

New York, colony of. *See* Leisler's Rebellion

Nicholet, Francis, 209, 210, 358 (nn. 92, 94)

Nichols, Josias, 83; criticizes Marprelate tracts, 57; understates Puritan grievances, 57–58; and literacy, 85; praises printing, 86; postdeprivation career of, 101–2, 338 (n. 98)

Niles, Samuel: conservative Old Light, 374 (n. 45)

Nonresidency bills, 117, 120

Northampton (Northamptonshire), 36, 50

Northampton, Mass., 206, 229; Stoddardeanism in, 280–81; revival at, 290, 296

North Church (Boston, Mass.), 217, 227; inhibited by General Court, 189; divided over Baptists, 191, 199; resists Halfway Covenant, 208, 222–23; covenant renewals at, 229; members of oppose witchcraft trials, 256, 259; as New Charter councillors, 265

Northfield, Mass., 372 (n. 32)

Norton, John, 214, 303; defends execution of Quakers, 195; anti-Separatist casuistry, 195–96; significance of, 196; introduces Halfway Covenant in First Church, 197, 198; conciliationist, 200

Norwich (Norfolk), 150, 167; growing radicalism in, 145–46

Norwich, Conn., 18, 218, 223, 224; adopts Halfway Covenant, 226

Norwich, diocese of, 24; deprivations in, 105

Nottingham, archdeaconry of: Separatism in, 100

Nowell, Samuel, 247, 363 (n. 31), 364 (nn. 40, 41)

Nye, Philip, 30, 31, 163

Oakes, Urian: on neglect of youth, 184; on jeremiad, 205; on consensus over declension, 217

Oakley (Suffolk), 23

Old Calvinism: not a meaningful term, 310

Old Lights. *See* Great Awakening; Liberalism, religious, in New England

Old South Church (Boston, Mass.), 208, 210, 216, 247, 307, 358 (n. 98), 359 (n. 99), 361 (n. 135); founded, 200, 203; members favor persecution and conciliation of England, 204; in political crisis of 1670, 206, 207, 355 (n. 65); and Hoar affair, 212; covenant renewals at, 229; reconciled with First Church, 246; and South Side alliance, 246–47, 265–66

Orwell (Cambridgeshire), 101

Osborn, Samuel: case anticipates Old Light–New Light split, 307–8, 373 (n. 37)

Osborne, Sarah: joins Baptists, 176

Osborne, Thomas: joins Baptists, 176

Osgood, Mary: confesses to witchcraft, 262

Owen, John, 166

Oxenbridge, John, 217; opposes Halfway Covenant, 201, 203; favors toleration, 204; attacks Massachusetts magistracy, 206, 207; befriends Newbury and Salem

dissidents, 208, 358 (n. 94); attacks John Higginson, 209; election sermon published, 212

Oxford University, 317

Parker, Robert: role in redefining polity, 58–64; deprivation of, 103

Parker, Thomas: Presbyterianism of, 208–9; in Newbury church dispute, 209, 210, 211

Parkman, Ebenezer, 374 (n. 45); on Whitefield's preaching, 295

Parliament, Puritans in: during Elizabeth's reign, 49, 53, 55; hopes of in 1620s, 108–14, 123–24; Jacobean bills, 115–17, 340 (n. 22); limited influence, 117–18, 119–22; continuity of leadership group, 118–19; early oppositionist tendencies, 121, 341 (n. 35); cautious behavior in early 1620s, 122–23; coalition politics, 131; prominent in opposition in later 1620s, 136–37, 342 (n. 36); dilemma of during Long Parliament, 139–40, 146; reluctant radicalism of, 147–48

Parris, Samuel, 359 (n. 99)

Patronage, ecclesiastical, 39–40, 52–53, 140, 151; attacked by New Englanders, 167

Pemberton, Ebenezer, 367 (n. 94)

Pendleton, James, 352 (n. 8)

Perkins, William, 43–44, 83, 86, 88, 332 (n. 11); intellectualism of, 69–70, 331 (n. 8); on hypocrisy, 71, 72; on assurance, 72–73; on sex as metaphor, 74; and literacy, 85; appeal of works of, 87; circulation of works of, 89, 92, 335 (n. 60)

Perrot, Sir James: critical of English self-indulgence, 112–13; role in Parliament, 118–19, 121, 122, 341 (n. 31)

Peter, Hugh, 135; at unauthorized fast, 98

Peterborough, diocese of: deprivations in, 100, 337 (n. 94); conventicles in, 105; lectureships in, 105

Phillips, Samuel, 364 (n. 45)

Phips, Sir William, 266, 367 (n. 91); chosen to be governor by Increase Mather, 253; in witchcraft epidemic, 255, 259, 262; and election of 1693, 265; portrayed in

Magnalia, 286
Pickering, Theophilus: ministry of
    attacked, 302
Pietism, Lutheran, 292–93
Pike, Robert, 365 (n. 57); criticizes witch-
    craft trials, 258
Plymouth, Mass., 100; covenant renewal
    at, 225; deals with absentee church
    members, 352 (n. 8)
Plymouth Colony, 156, 186, 189, 190; cove-
    nant renewals in, 224; merged with
    Massachusetts Bay, 250
Polity, ecclesiastical: divisive role of in
    Puritan movement, 43–44, 48–51; Eliza-
    bethan concept of, 44–47; sixteenth-
    and seventeenth-century concepts com-
    pared, 47–48; Jacobean reformulation
    of, 58–64, 330 (n. 21); a contentious
    issue in Long Parliament, 140, 147–
    48; English origins of New England
    Way, 153–55; in Connecticut, 156–57;
    in Massachusetts, 157–66; in Interreg-
    num controversy, 166–68; in Saybrook
    Platform and Massachusetts propos-
    als, 277; in Stoddardeanism, 279–80;
    Brattle Street indifferent to, 282. *See
    also* Morellianism; Presbyterianism—
    seventeenth-century
Popular party: pre-Dominion origins of,
    247, 357 (n. 86); character of, 251–52;
    and Harvard presidency, 266–67
Popular religion, English: before Reforma-
    tion, 7–8, 289, 321 (n. 4); Puritans and,
    8, 146, 289. *See also* Laity, Puritan
Portsmouth, N.H., 352 (n. 8)
Practical divinity: defined, 68, 73–74;
    and weak Christians, 72; and English
    society, 75–76; and Ramism, 77–78; and
    family religion, 78, 83–85; and Sabba-
    tarianism, 78–82; and Puritan literature,
    85–92; effectiveness of, 93–94; sectar-
    ian potentials of, 94–99; threatened by
    Arminianism, 132, 134; political impli-
    cations of, 135–36; attenuated state of
    in early NE, 183–85; reinvigorated, 185,
    205, 226–27, 242; and colonial status of
    NE, 270, 271–72; indifference of New
    Lights to, 300
Preaching. *See* Sermons
Presbyterianism:

—Elizabethan: goals of, 41, 43–47, 325
    (n. 45); relation to later stages of Puritan
    movement, 47–48, 60–61, 66–68, 74,
    101–2, 118, 283–84; collapse of, 51–57;
    and Hampton Court Conference, 57–58
—seventeenth-century, 147, 148, 179; and
    example of NE, 166–67, 168; version of
    in Westminster Assembly, 168; influence
    of on NE affairs, 168–71; advocates of
    in NE, 169, 172, 209, 358 (n. 99); use of
    term in NE politics, 244, 246
Prescott, Benjamin, 373 (nn. 36, 40)
Preston, John, 87, 173, 317; at York House
    debate, 131
Prince, Deborah: on Great Awakening,
    298
Prince, Thomas: *Christian History,* 309
Prout, Timothy, 364 (n. 41)
Prynne, William, 33; despairs in 1629, 124
Purchas, Oliver, 357 (n. 86), 363 (n. 36)
Puritanism/Puritan movement: trans-
    atlantic approaches to, xii–xiv, 3, 287;
    distinctive characteristics of, xiii, 2–
    3, 4–5, 6, 8, 9, 33, 37–38, 68, 77–78,
    117–18, 119, 288, 313–14; establishment-
    sectarian tensions in, xiii, 5–6, 8–9,
    14–15, 18–20, 26–27, 50–51, 94, 106,
    150–51, 155–56, 179–80, 211, 220, 232,
    272, 283–84, 303, 305, 320 (n. 4); fluid
    character of, xiii, 287–88, 313; histori-
    ography of, xiv, 4, 15–16, 313, 323 (nn.
    30, 31); relationship to later American
    history, 3–4, 311–13; component groups
    of, 9, 26–27, 288, 289; social and geo-
    graphic basis of, 15–20, 75–76, 288, 323
    (nn. 30, 31), 324 (n. 33), 334 (n. 40); shifts
    in internal balance of power in NE, 151–
    53, 235–36, 242–43, 249–50, 268, 277.
    See also Clergy, Puritan; Gentry, Puri-
    tan; Laity, Puritan; Magistracy, New
    England
Pym, John: defends Earle, 119; and criti-
    cism of Puritans, 122; organizes attack
    on Arminians, 129, 131; leadership of in
    Parliament, 137; on Separatism, 145
Pynchon, John: favors persecution, 356
    (n. 76)

Quakers, 132, 140, 172, 176, 177, 252, 274, 290, 303, 351 (n. 80), 356 (n. 76); strengths of in England, 190–91, opportunities for in NE, 191–93; relative failure in NE, 193–94; effect on NE controversy, 194–95; partial toleration of, 199, 354 (n. 38)

Ramist logic and rhetoric, 25, 26; Puritan uses of, 27–28, 326 (n. 57), 333 (n. 30)
Ramus, Petrus, 25
Randolph, Edward, 247
Ranters, 172, 190
Reading. *See* Literacy; Literature, Puritan
Reason, natural, 332 (n. 12). *See also* Knowledge
Reforming Synod (1679), 218, 220, 225, 233, 234, 238; lack of theological content in proceedings, 228; endorses Increase Mather's program, 228–29; effects of, 229–30; invoked after Deerfield Massacre, 284
Reproof, concept of, 37, 84, 328 (n. 29); secularized, 276
Reynolds, John, 127
Rhode Island, 189; Quakers in, 190; resumes charter, 250
Rich, Sir Nathaniel, 340 (n. 17); leadership in Parliament, 137
Rich, Robert, Lord. *See* Warwick, first earl of
Richards, John, 208, 365 (n. 57); conflict with Increase Mather, 222–23; serves as witchcraft judge, 261
Robinson, John, 166, 179; decides on Separation, 14; criticizes nonseparating laity, 23; influences nonseparating clergy, 62–63; deprivation of, 100, 103
Rogerenes, 290
Rogers, Ezekiel: background and influence, 28, 326 (n. 63); silenced and loses living, 28–29; influence on Rowley, Mass., 29; significance of, 31–32; verdict on Church of England, 93, 158; on English hierarchy, 165; wealth of, 354 (n. 45)
Rogers, John (1692–1773): on Great Awakening, 297
Rogers, John (1719–82), 298
Rogers, Richard, 86; on reading, 84, 87;

circulation of works of, 92
Root and Branch Bill, 146, 148
Root and Branch Petition, 145; origins and content of, 147, 347 (n. 18)
Roots, Thomas, 357 (n. 92)
Rotterdam: Congregational church at, 146
Rous, Francis, 140, 144
Rowley (Yorkshire), 27–32, 354 (n. 45)
Roxbury, Mass., 260, 358 (n. 99); and conversion narratives, 173; and Halfway Covenant, 197
Royston (Hertfordshire), 98
Russell, James, 365 (n. 57)
Russell, John: attacks Halfway Covenant supporters, 205–7
Russell, Richard, 357 (n. 83); and Old South, 355 (n. 65); and Baptists, 356 (n. 76)
Ryce, Robert: denounces England, 112
Rye (Sussex), 23

Sabbatarianism/Sabbath, 6, 74, 77, 95; role in practical divinity, 78–79; importance of to John Winthrop, 79–80, 86; as organizing force, 80–81; partisan implications of, 81; and "spirit of capitalism," 81–82; sectarian potential of, 96–97; parliamentary legislation in favor of, 116, 119, 120, 136–37; in NE, 240, 241. *See also* Moral legislation
Sacrament of the Lord's Supper: conflicting clerical and lay attitudes toward, 142–43, 179, 184, 353 (n. 25). *See also* Halfway Covenant; Stoddard, Solomon
Saffin, John, 364 (n. 41), 367 (n. 91)
Salem, Mass., 203, 245, 261, 358 (n. 99); early Separatist tendencies in, 153–54; dispute over pure church in, 159–60; Quakers at, 190; controversy in over Higginson's ministry, 208–11; covenant renewal at, 229; extension of church membership in, 237–38; and Great Awakening, 291
Salem Village: Halfway Covenant controversy in, 212, 358 (n. 99); witchcraft epidemic at, 255
Salisbury, diocese of: deprivations in, 101
Saltonstall, Gurdon: on church and state in NE, 269–70

Saltonstall, Nathaniel, 256, 365 (n. 57)
Saltonstall, Sir Richard, 349 (n. 59)
Sands, Henry: and Dedham classis, 36, 54, 55, 79; and Winthrop family, 78–79, 86
Sandys, Sir Edwin, 131
Savage, Thomas, 359 (n. 99), 361 (n. 135)
Savoy Platform, 5; in NE, 185, 228
Saxton, Peter, 326 (n. 56)
Saybrook, Conn., 163
Saybrook Platform, 5, 293; effectiveness of, 277
Saye and Sele, first viscount (William Fiennes), 131
Scituate, Mass., 326 (n. 56); church dispute at, 159
Scotland: compared unfavorably to England, 68; influence on English politics, 125, 126, 147; and Great Awakening in NE, 299, 302
Scott, Thomas (MP), 17
Scott, Thomas (minister), 127
Scrooby (Nottinghamshire), 103
Sedgwick, Obadiah, 14, 176
Seekers, 172
Separatism, 56, 58, 59, 64, 93, 179, 196, 326 (n. 54), 338 (n. 98), 349 (n. 44); lay sources of, 13–14; influence on Jacobean ideas of polity, 61–63, 153, 154, 330 (n. 71); and Bancroft's purge, 100, 102–3; relationship to later radicals, 141–42; encouraged by developments under Laud, 143–44, 145, 146; influence on NE, 155–56, 158, 160, 161–62, 166–67; and Halfway Covenant controversy, 198. *See also* Morellianism
Sermons: functions and context, 22–23, 24–26; James I attempts to restrict content of, 127–28, 132–33, 343 (n. 51); on eve of Great Awakening, 294, 296–97; in New Light evangelicalism, 296, 300. *See also* Jeremiad
Sewall, Joseph: suspects Old Lights of Arminianism, 307, 308
Sewall, Samuel, 190, 231, 236, 276, 307, 363 (n. 34), 365 (n. 57); circulates Cotton reprint, 243; serves as witchcraft judge, 262; significance of, 268, 284; and Yale College, 269; valedictory speech, 284–85, 314
Seymour, Sir Francis, 340 (n. 17)

Shepard, Thomas (minister, 1605–49), 95, 150, 175, 176; youth of, 16; rejects itinerancy, 22–23; on Sabbatarianism, 79, 81; rejects mixed communion, 143; requires conversion narrative, 161, 332 (n. 17); and Antinomian controversy, 162–63
Shepard, Thomas (minister, 1635–77): and Charlestown Baptists, 176; and Halfway Covenant controversy, 198–99
Shephard, Edward: and unconverted, 12
Shepherd, Thomas (MP): attacks Sabbatarianism, 126
Sherland, Christopher: links Arminianism to prerogative, 136
Shipley, Nathaniel, 197
Shrimpton, Henry, 351
Shrimpton, Samuel: political career of, 367 (n. 92)
Shute, Samuel: flees Massachusetts, 284
Sibbes, Richard: works by, 88, 91, 92
Smith, Henry: works by, 88, 91; Puritanism of, 336 (n. 73)
Smith, John (magistrate), 363 (n. 36)
South Luffenham (Rutlandshire), 65
Southwark church, 100, 338 (n. 105); foundation and influence, 63; criticized by Davenport, 157
Southworth, Robert, 100, 103
Spanish Match, 128, 342 (n. 49)
Sparke, Michael, 317
Sparrowhawk, Edward, 145
Spencer, Richard, 104
Spira, Francis, 150, 347 (n. 25)
Springfield, Mass., 373 (n. 37)
Sprint, John: on Separatist tendencies, 102–3
Stamford (Lincolnshire), 135, 142
Stamford, Conn., 232
Stoddard, Anthony, 358 (n. 94)
Stoddard, Solomon, 206, 228, 282; on absentee church members, 197; on assurance, 279–80; ecclesiology of, 280; limits of influence, 280–81
Stone, Samuel, 201, 206
Stonington, Conn., 352 (n. 8)
Stoughton, William, 218, 256; antagonizes Increase Mather, 222; lieutenant governor under New Charter, 253; role in witchcraft trials, 255, 260–62; death, 266–67

—*New-Englands True Interest; Not to Lie* (classic jeremiad), 214–15; character and significance of author and sermon, 215–16, 359 (n. 106); influence of, 216–17
Stowe, Harriet Beecher, 312
Strict Congregationalists, 291, 301; described, 303; persecuted over clerical maintenance, 305; decline of, 309
Strowd, John, 54
Stubbs, John, 55
Sudbury, Mass., 296
Suffolk, 12
Surrey, 11
Sussex, 11
Sutton, Christopher: not a Puritan, 76–77, 333 (n. 28)
Symmons, Mathew, 318
Symonds, Samuel: politics of, 210, 211, 356 (n. 76); deputy governor of Massachusetts, 211; death, 228

Talaeus, Omar, 25
Tennet, Gilbert: on clerical maintenance, 303
Terling (Essex), 19
Thatcher, Peter, 307
Thirty Years' War, 19, 110–11, 127, 224
Thompson, William, 348 (n. 39)
Throckmorton, Job: possible author of Marprelate tracts, 329 (n. 53)
Tilton, Peter, 357 (n. 86), 363 (n. 31); leader of anti–Halfway Covenant forces, 205–7
Tithes, 54, 140, 151, 191; New Englanders attack, 167
Toleration: issue in Massachusetts Bay, 177, 198–200, 355 (n. 64), 356 (n. 76); loses divisive force, 252; accommodated to clerical program, 274–75
Torrey, Samuel: on NE's special relationship, 271–72
Townsend, Penn, 247, 364 (n. 41)
Toxteth Park (Lancashire), 10, 154, 164
Trumbull, John, 77, 91, 333 (n. 28), 352 (n. 7); attracted to Puritanism, 14–15; defends Charlestown Baptists, 175–76; significance of, 176–77; retains Cambridge church membership, 177–79, 352 (n. 14)

Turner, William, 317
Tyng, Edward, 203, 228; and Baptists, 356 (n. 76)

Udall, John, 33, 288; on centrality of polity, 44; on election of ministers, 45; gathers following, 50; criticizes episcopacy, 51
Unitarianism, 293, 310. *See also* Liberalism, religious, in New England
Usher, Roland G., xiii
Ussher, James, 76, 81, 93

Vane, Sir Henry (the elder), 342 (n. 35)
Vane, Sir Henry (the younger), 140
Vicars, John: holds conventicles at Stamford, 135

Wadsworth, Benjamin, 279
Wages: in seventeenth-century England, 335 (n. 63)
Waite, John, 357 (n. 86)
Wakeman, Samuel, 232
Waldron, Richard, 212, 357 (n. 86)
Wales, Samuel, 26
Ward, Samuel, 127
Ware (Hertfordshire), 110
Warham, John: favors inclusive church, 156; on lay timidity, 183
Warwick, first earl of (Robert Rich), 37
Warwick, second earl of (Robert Rich), 98
Warwickshire: deprivations in, 101, 337 (n. 94)
Watts, Isaac, 299
Weber, Max, 82
Weld, Thomas: encourages conventicles at Terling, 19
Wenham (Suffolk), 36
Wenham, Mass.: fear of Presbyterianism at, 171, 353 (n. 17). *See also* Chelmsford, Mass.
Wentworth, Sir Thomas (later earl of Strafford), 131
Westborough, Mass., 295
West Kirby (Cheshire), 104
Westminster Assembly, 8, 47, 48, 146, 148, 167, 169

Westminster Confession, 5; in NE, 228
Weston, Sir Richard (later earl of Portland): attacked by Eliot, 137
Wethersfield, Conn.: church schism at, 194, 195; and foundation of Hadley, 206
Weymouth, Mass.: church dispute at, 160
Whalley, Edward, 201, 206
Wheelwright, John, 163
Whitaker, Laurence, 341 (n. 35), 342 (n. 36)
White, Francis, 130–31
White, John: organizes church covenant, 135–36; anticipates NE covenant renewal, 224–25, 230
Whitefield, George, 290, 294, 302, 303, 304, 308; on significance of Great Awakening in NE, 293; criticizes traditional NE preaching, 295; evangelical success in NE, 295–97, 298
Whitgift, John: as archbishop of Canterbury, 42, 50
Whitman, Zechariah, 192, 302, 354 (n. 46)
Wickham Market (Suffolk), 105–6
Wigglesworth, Michael, 236; and witchcraft epidemic, 264; *Day of Doom,* 296
Wilcox, Thomas, 2; on discipline, 43; on election of ministers, 44; defines church, 47; denounces Separatists, 61
Will. *See* Knowledge: operative
Willard, Samuel, 185, 213, 225, 228; on declension, 217; and covenant renewal, 224, 226, 227, 229–30, 239; on fall of NE charters, 234–35, 240; preparations for royal government, 240–41; acknowledges Dominion, 247–48, 364 (n. 45); role in witchcraft epidemic, 256, 258–64, 366 (n. 68); quarrels with Increase Mather, 265–66, 267; calls for compensation of victims, 266, 367 (n. 99); on death of Stoughton, 266–67; significance of Harvard headship, 267–68; and theodicy of New Charter, 271; and Stoddardeanism, 279; death, 284
Willard, Simon: favors persecution, 356 (n. 76)
William III (king of England), 249
Williams, Elisha: on Connecticut's loss of autonomy, 270
Williams, John, 341 (n. 33)
Williams, Roger, 299, 337 (n. 78); and

English Separatists, 142
Willoughby, Francis, 356 (n. 76), 357 (n. 83)
Wilson, John, 159
Wiltshire, 327 (nn. 4, 5)
Windham, Conn.: a Stoddardean church at, 281; and Great Awakening, 308
Windsor, Conn.: church of gathered in England, 155; liberal admissions policy, 156
Winthrop, John, xiv, 76, 90, 102, 137, 138, 144, 164, 165, 296, 299, 349 (n. 44); conversion experience, 72–73, 332 (n. 17); method of reading, 86–87; and death of Thomasine Winthrop, 94; criticizes Puritan laity, 95; involvement in English politics, 108; despairs of England, 108–9, 111; reasons for migration, 111–14, 339 (n. 9); criticizes Anne Hutchinson's conferences, 151; sectarian turn, 155, 160–61; on Presbyterianism, 169
Winthrop, Margaret, 108, 111, 112, 137
Winthrop, Thomasine, 79, 94
Winthrop, Waitstill, 365 (n. 57)
Winwick (Lancashire), 10–11, 101
Wise, John: and witchcraft epidemic, 264
Wiswall, John, 356 (n. 67), 364 (n. 40)
Witchcraft epidemic (1692), 231, 250, 358 (n. 99); anticipated, 216; role of spectral evidence, 254, 255, 257, 258; evidence of coercion and intimidation, 256; arouses criticism, 258; mounting opposition to, 260, 261; trials ended, 262; role of clergy in, 263–64; Cotton Mather's retrospect of, 286
Woburn, Mass.: fear of Presbyterianism at, 171
Woodbridge, John, 209–10, 211, 246, 363 (n. 36)
Woodkirk (Yorkshire), 176
Woodman, Edmund: leads Newbury dissidents, 208–9; motives of, 210; joins Baptists, 211
Wotton, Anthony: translates Ramus, 78
Wotton, Samuel: translates Ramus, 78
Wren, Matthew: as bishop of Norwich, 29, 144, 145–46

Yale College, 269–70, 369 (n. 118); role in eighteenth-century clericalism, 278

Yates, John: attacks Leighton, 141
York, diocese of: popular religion in before the Reformation, 7
York, province of: enforcement of 1604 canons in, 100
York House debate (1626), 131
Yorkshire, 12, 14, 22, 27–31, 88, 93, 158; Puritan-Catholic conflicts, 11; anti-Puritan sentiment, 13; distribution of Puritanism in, 16; pre-Reformation clergy of, 321 (n. 10); tradition of extra-parochial meetings, 326 (n. 56)

Youth, New England: alleged spiritual deficiencies, 180, 184–85; definition of, 181, 353 (n. 16); as fraction of NE population, 181–82; and reforming legislation, 182, 353 (n. 20); disadvantaged, 182–84; and church membership, 185–86, 197–98; threatened by Increase Mather, 219; defended by Hubbard, 223; conversion experiences center of attention in Great Awakening, 297–98

DATE DUE

F 7 .F758 1991
Foster, Stephen, 1942-
The long argument

DATE	ISSUED TO
951017	ILL: 1031377
FEB 19 '96	Rachael Bailey